Children

Children

Robert V. Kail
Purdue University

Prentice
Hall

Upper Saddle River, New Jersey 07458

Library of Congress Cataloging-in-Publication Data

Kail, Robert V.
    Children / Robert V. Kail.
        p.   cm.
    Includes bibliographical references and index.
    ISBN 0-13-085763-7
    1. Child psychology.   2. Child development.   3. Infant psychology.
    4. Infants—Development.   5. Adolescent psychology.   6. Adolescence.   I. Title.
BF721 .K22   2002
305.231—dc21

2002016927

Sr. Acquisitions Editor: Jennifer Gilliland
Editorial Assistant: Nicole Girrbach
AVP/Director of Production and Manufacturing: Barbara Kittle
Sr. Managing Editor: Mary Rottino
Director of Development: Susanna Lesan
Development Editor: Elaine Silverstein
Editorial/Production Supervision: Victory Productions, Inc.
Manufacturing Manager: Nick Sklitsis
Prepress and Manufacturing Buyer: Tricia Kenny
Creative Design Director: Leslie Osher

Interior and Cover Design: Anne DeMarinis
Director, Image Resource Center: Melinda Reo
Image Specialist: Beth Boyd
Manager, Rights & Permissions: Kay Dellosa
Photo Researcher: Kathy Ringrose
Art Manager: Guy Ruggiero
Electronic Art Creation: Maria Piper
Director of Marketing: Beth Mejia
Marketing Manager: Jeff Hester

Acknowledgments for copyrighted material may
be found beginning on p. 545, which constitutes
an extension of this copyright page.

This book was set in 10.5/13 Minion by Victory Productions, Inc.
and was printed and bound by RR Donnelley & Sons Company–Willard.
The cover was printed by Phoenix Color Corp.

Printed in the United States of America
10   9   8   7   6   5   4   3   2

ISBN 0-13-085763-7

Pearson Education LTD., London
Pearson Education Australia PTY, Limited, Sydney
Pearson Education Singapore, Pte. Ltd.
Pearson Education North Asia Ltd, Hong Kong
Pearson Education Canada, Ltd., Toronto
Pearson Educación de Mexico, S.A. de C.V.
Pearson Education–Japan, Tokyo
Pearson Education Malaysia, Pte. Ltd.

to ■Chauncey

Brief Contents

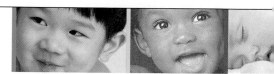

Contents

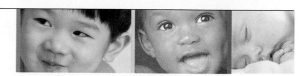

FOCUS ON RESEARCH

CULTURAL INFLUENCES

CHILD DEVELOPMENT AND FAMILY POLICY

MAKING CHILDREN'S LIVES BETTER

REAL CHILDREN

LOOKING AHEAD

Preface

When I first taught child development in 1975, I used a brand new textbook that provided students with an excellent overview of the field. In the 25 years since, researchers have made incredible progress in understanding children's development (and I'm proud to have been among those contributing). Unfortunately, authors have been overly enthusiastic about the emerging knowledge, and textbooks have grown ever larger as more and more complex findings are added. The book I used in 1975 described the field in a concise 471 pages in the original edition but in 652 pages in the fifth edition, which appeared in 1999. As this and other excellent texts grew, my students complained to me that, with so much information in the book, they had difficulty separating the wheat from the chaff (an appropriate metaphor since I was teaching in the Midwestern United States).

Greater length and complexity were only part of the problem. Most textbook authors avoid effective pedagogy like the plague. They (along with many instructors) seem to believe that students should learn on their own, without needing instructional aids. As a consequence, although child development texts still present a valuable overview of the field, they are not effective tools for student learning.

A few years ago, I decided that a new book was needed—one that would meet instructors' needs for a solid overview of the field and one that would emphasize effective pedagogy designed to enhance students' learning. *Children* is my effort to meet these goals. This book is traditional in its organization: I begin with theories and methods, move to biological bases of child development, then cover four major phases in children's lives—starting with infancy and ending with adolescence. Where this book begins to differ from the competition is length: it has about 20 percent fewer pages than most competing texts. To make the truly important child development work stand out for students, I have deliberately omitted some topics and described others relatively briefly.

But the focus on a student-friendly book is really evident in the way I've structured the entire book to help students learn about child development. One key aspect of the book is an emphasis on fundamental themes in child-development research. In Chapter 1, I describe four critical themes that pervade child-development research:

1. Early development is related to later development, but not perfectly.
2. Development is always jointly influenced by heredity and environment.
3. Children help determine their own development.
4. Development in different domains is connected.

Then, throughout the book I use these themes to provide a solid foundation for students to understand different theories and the many facts of child development. The themes appear in review questions throughout the chapters and are highlighted in an "In Perspective" feature that appears at the end of each major phase of development (e.g., the preschool years, adolescence). The themes provide students with familiar anchors to use as they learn about children.

I've also organized the chapters to make it easy for students to understand children and their development. Each chapter consists of two to five modules that provide a clear and well-defined organization to the chapter. Each module begins with a set of learning objectives and a vignette that introduces the topic to be covered. Within each module, all figures, tables, and photos are fully integrated, eliminating the need for students to search for a graphic. Similarly, boxlike feature material that is set off in other textbooks is fully integrated with the main text and identified by a distinctive icon, reflecting its importance in students' overall reading. Each module ends with several questions designed to help students check their understanding of the major ideas in the module.

The end of each chapter includes several additional study aids. "Critical Review" provides thought-provoking questions that require students to integrate the material they've just read. "See for Yourself" suggests activities that allow students to observe topics in child development firsthand. "For More Information About" includes books and Web sites where students can learn more about child development. "Key Terms" is a list of all of the important terms that appear in the chapter. The "Summary" is organized by module and the primary headings within each module; it reviews the entire chapter.

Each module includes at least one feature where selected issues are highlighted. The six different kinds of features are Cultural Influences, Focus on Research, Real Children, Making Children's Lives Better, Looking Ahead, and Child Development and Family Policy. The features are described in Module 1.1, but Focus on Research warrants extra attention here. Most textbooks describe research methods early on, then ignore them for the rest of the book. *Children* takes a different and unique approach. In Chapter 2, I portray child-development research as a dynamic process in which scientists make a series of decisions as they plan their work. In the process, they create a study that has both strengths and weaknesses. Each of the remaining chapters of the book contains a Focus on Research feature that illustrates this process by showing—in a question-and-answer format—the different decisions that investigators made in designing a particular study. I trace each of the steps and explain the decisions that were made. Then the results are shown—usually with an annotated figure so that students can learn how to interpret graphs—and the investigators' conclusions are described. Thus, the research methods that are introduced in Chapter 2 reappear in every chapter, in a setting that makes research come alive as a set of decisions that often involve compromises. (In my classes, I encourage students to think how the Focus on Research studies could be improved with different methods. At the same time, I ask them why the investigators might have resorted to the methods they did.)

I hope that the Focus on Research and other pedagogical elements will be effective in presenting complex topics to your students in an understandable and engaging way. Please let me know how well they work for you and your students. You can send comments directly to me at: rkail@sla.purdue.edu. I would love to hear from you.

Ancillaries

Children is accompanied by a superb set of ancillary teaching materials.

For Instructors:

Instructor's Resource Manual. This IRM contains a wealth of material for new and experienced instructors alike. Each chapter includes chapter organizers, learning objectives, a detailed lecture outline with suggestions, classroom demonstrations and learning activities, critical thinking questions and exercises, assigment ideas, journal exercises, suggested films and videos, and classroom handouts.

Test Item File. This text bank contains over 3,000 multiple choice, true/false, short answer, and essay questions that test for factual, applied, and conceptual knowledge.

Prentice Hall Test Manager and Custom Tests. One of the best-selling test-generating software programs on the market, Test Manager is available in Windows and Macintosh formats. Both formats contain a GradeBook, Online Network Testing, and many tools to help you edit and create tests. The program comes with full Technical Support and telephone "Request a Test" service.

Prentice Hall's Color Transparencies for Developmental Psychology. Designed in a large-type format for lecture settings, these full-color overhead transparencies add visual appeal to your lectures by augmenting the visuals in the text with a variety of new illustrations.

PowerPoint Slides and Online Graphics Archive. Each chapter's artwork has been digitized and is available for download into any presentation software. PowerPoint lectures for each chapter area are also available for download. These and other valuable teaching resources are located on our Prentice Hall Psychology Central site at www.prenhall.com/psychology. Contact your Prentice Hall representative for information on how to access this site.

Films for the Humanities and Sciences. A wealth of full-length videos from the extensive library of Films for the Humanities and Sciences, on a variety of topics in developmental psychology, are available to qualified adopters. Contact your Prentice Hall representative for a list of videos.

Media Support for Instructors and Students

www.prenhall.com/kail Companion Web site. This free online Study Guide allows students to review each chapter's material, take practice tests, and research topics for course projects.

ContentSelect **Research Database.** Prentice Hall and EBSCO, the world leader in online journal subscription management, have developed a customized research database for students of psychology. This database provides access to many popular periodicals and peer-reviewed psychology publications. For more information about *ContentSelect*, contact your Prentice Hall representative.

Online Course Management. For professors interested in using the Internet and online course management in their courses, Prentice Hall offers full customizable online courses in BlackBoard and Pearson's Course Compass powered by Black-Board. Contact your Prentice Hall representative or visit www.prenhall.com/demo for more information.

Developmental Psychology Observation/Demonstration CD-ROM by David Daniel. This interactive CD-ROM offers simulations and over 50 minutes of video footage of children demonstrating key concepts in developmental psychology. Each video begins with an introduction to the concept illustrated in the video, narratives to guide student viewing of the video, and questions to assess students' understanding of what they just watched. It is available to be packaged with *Children;* contact your Prentice Hall representative for more information and to request an examination copy.

For the Student:

Study Guide. This attractive, highly visual Study Guide written by Dea K. DeWolff (my wife) reinforces the key pedagogical features of the textbook by incorporating both illustrations and pedagogical elements from the text. Each chapter follows the same modular organization as the text. Each of the modules in every chapter of the Study Guide includes learning objectives, matching exercises to review key theories, definitions, terms and concepts, practice true/false questions, cumulative fill-in-the-blank chapter summaries, and multiple choice and essay questions.

Psychology on the Internet: Evaluating Online Resources. This supplement provides students with a hands-on introduction to the Internet and features numerous Web sites related to psychology with guidelines on how to evaluate online resources. This supplement is available free when packaged with the text.

Acknowledgments

Textbook authors do not produce books on their own. I want to thank the many reviewers who generously gave their time and effort to help sharpen my thinking about child development and shape the development of this text. Without their thoughtful comments, this book would be less complete, less accurate, and less interesting.

The reviewers:
Ann L. Adams, Community College of Southern Nevada
Rima Blair, College of Staten Island
Susan Bowers, Northern Illinois University
Tsu-Ming Chiang, Georgia College and State University
Lisa Daleo, Manhattanville College
Ruth Doyle, Casper College
Susan Elkins, Columbus State University
M. L. Fraser, San Jose State University
Wilma Holt, The University of Kansas
Kristine Jacquin, Mississippi State University
Jerry A. Martin, University of North Florida
Jessica Miller, Mesa State College
Colleen A. Moss, California State University, San Marcos
Judy Payne, Murray State University
Barbara Radigan, Community College of Allegheny County
Joseph D. Sclafani, The University of Tampa

I also owe a debt of thanks to many people who helped take this project from a first draft to a bound book. From the beginning, Jennifer Gilliland has supported this project enthusiastically. Elaine Silverstein did a superb job of critiquing my writing, making sure that topics were covered thoroughly and clearly. Leslie Osher and Anne DeMarinis designed a book that is both beautiful and functional. Ann Bearden skillfully orchestrated the many activities that were involved in actually producing the book. Kathy Ringrose found the marvelous photographs that appear throughout the book. To all these people, many thanks.

—*Robert V. Kail*

About the Author

Robert V. Kail is Professor of Psychological Sciences at Purdue University. His undergraduate degree is from Ohio Wesleyan University and he received his Ph.D. from the University of Michigan. Kail has served as Associate Editor of the journal *Child Development* and is currently Editor of the *Journal of Experimental Child Psychology*. He received the McCandless Young Scientist Award from the American Psychological Association and was named a fellow in the American Psychological Society. He was also named the Distinguished Sesquicentennial Alumnus in Psychology by Ohio Wesleyan University. His research interests are in the area of cognitive development and focus on the causes and consequences of developmental change in the speed of information processing. Kail has also written *The Development of Memory in Children,* and, with John C. Cavanaugh, *Human Development.* Away from the office, he enjoys flying his Cessna 172, playing soccer with his daughter, and working out.

The Science of
Child Development

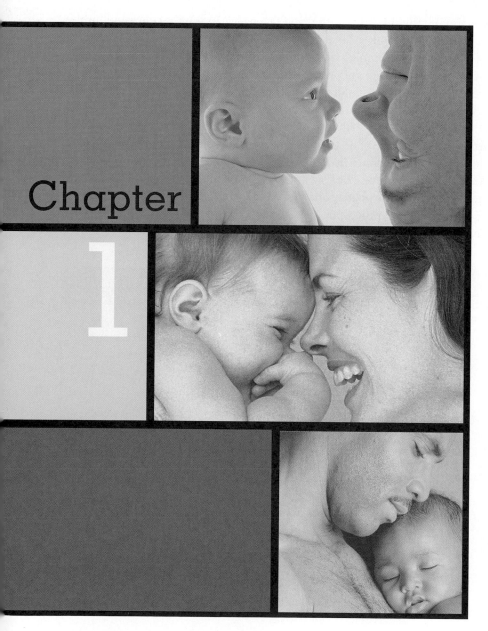

Chapter 1

eginning as a microscopic cell, every person takes a fascinating journey designed to lead to adulthood. Like any journey worth taking, this one is filled with remarkable events that make the trip both interesting and challenging. In this book, we'll trace this journey as we learn about the science of child development, a multidisciplinary study of all aspects of growth from conception to adulthood. As an adult, you've lived the years that are the heart of this book. I hope you enjoy reviewing your developmental journey from the perspective of child-development research. I expect that this perspective will lead you to new insights into the developmental forces that made you the person you are today.

Chapter 1 sets the stage for our study of child development. I begin, in Module 1.1, by giving you some tips on how to use this book. In Module 1.2, I explain theories that are central to child-development research. Finally, in Module 1.3, I describe themes that guide much research in child development.

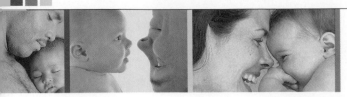

1.1

Using This Book

─Organization of Chapters

─How to Use These Features to
  Learn About Children

─Terminology

─A Final Word

Using This Book

In most textbooks, the material on the next few pages appears in a preface entitled "To the Student." But I'm afraid that most students never read this material, so I'm including it here at the beginning of Chapter 1. Please don't skip it now; read on to learn how to use this book. It will save you time in the long run.

In this book, we'll trace children's development from conception through adolescence. With this goal in mind, I've organized the book into the 16 chapters listed below. The first four chapters provide you with some necessary background on theories, methods, and biological bases of development. Then we'll look at each of the four major phases of children's lives: infancy, the preschool years, the elementary-school years, and adolescence. Looking at the list of chapters, you can see that three are devoted to each of these phases. The first covers physical growth, the second concerns children's cognitive processing (i.e., thinking), and the third concerns social and personality development.

Organization of the Book	
Chapter	**Title**
1	The Science of Child Development
2	Research in Child Development
3	Genetic Bases of Child Development
4	Prenatal Development and Birth
5	Physical Development in Infants and Toddlers
6	Cognition in Infants and Toddlers
7	Social Behavior and Personality in Infants and Toddlers
8	Physical Development in Preschool Children
9	Cognitive Development in Preschool Children
10	Social Behavior and Personality in Preschool Children
11	Physical Development in School-Age Children
12	Cognitive Development in School-Age Children
13	Social Behavior and Personality in School-Age Children
14	Physical Growth in Adolescents
15	Cognitive Development in Adolescents
16	Social and Personality Development in Adolescents

TABLE 1–1

Each of the chapters is organized similarly, in a way that should help you to understand the material within the chapter. This organization is explained in the next section.

Organization of Chapters

Each of the 16 chapters in the book includes two to five modules that are listed on the first page of the chapter. As you can see in the inset page below, each module begins with a set of learning objectives phrased as questions.

7.1

Emotions

⌐ Basic Emotions

⌐ Complex Emotions

⌐ Recognizing and Using
    Others' Emotions

⌐ Regulating Emotions

Learning Objectives

▪ **When do infants begin to express basic emotions?**

▪ **What are complex emotions and when do they develop?**

▪ **When do infants begin to understand other people's emotions? How do they use this information to guide their own behavior?**

▪ **When do infants and toddlers begin to regulate their own emotions?**

Nicole was ecstatic that she was finally going to see her 7-month-old nephew, Claude. She rushed into the house and, seeing Claude playing on the floor with blocks, swept him up in a big hug. After a brief, puzzled look, Claude burst into angry tears and began thrashing around, as if saying to Nicole, "Who are you? What do you want? Put me down! Now!" Nicole quickly handed Claude to his mother, who was surprised by her baby's outburst and even more surprised that he continued to sob while she rocked him.

Next is a brief vignette that introduces the topic to be covered in the module by describing an issue or problem faced by real people. In the margin is a mini-outline listing the major subheadings of the module—a kind of road map for reading. The learning objectives, vignette, and mini-outline tell you what to expect in the module.

Each module typically examines 3–4 major topics that are listed in the mini-outline. In addition, each module in Chapters 2–15 includes a special feature that expands or highlights a topic. There are six different kinds of features; you can recognize each one by its distinctive icon:

Focus on Research provides details on the design and methods used in a particular research study. Closely examining specific studies demystifies research and shows that scientific work is a series of logical steps conducted by real people.

Making Children's Lives Better shows how research and theory can be applied to improve children's development. These practical solutions to everyday problems show the relevance of research and theory to real life.

Cultural Influences shows how culture influences children and illustrates that developmental journeys are diverse. All children share the biological aspects of development, but their cultural contexts differ. This feature celebrates the developmental experiences of children from different backgrounds.

Real Children provides a case study that illustrates an issue in child development in the life of a real child. These authentic accounts make the study of child development come alive.

Looking Ahead presents a glimpse of development a few years down the road showing how some aspect of children's current level of development is related to their later development.

Child Development and Family Policy shows how results from research have been used to create social policy that is designed to improve the lives of children and their families.

The inset below shows another important element of each module: All illustrations and tables are integrated with the text.

Secure attachments and the different forms of insecure attachments are observed worldwide. As you can see in the graph, secure attachments are the most common throughout the world (van Ijzendoorn & Kroonenberg, 1988). This is fortunate because, as we'll see, a secure attachment provides a solid base for later social development.

Infants typically form the same type of attachment relationships with both parents (Fox, Kimmerly, & Schafer, 1991). An infant who is securely attached to its mother is usually securely attached to its father, too. In addition, siblings usually have the same type of attachment relationships with their parents (Rosen & Burke, 1999).

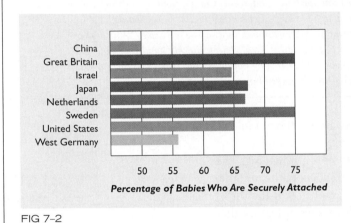

Percentage of Babies Who Are Securely Attached

FIG 7–2

Consequences of Quality of Attachment Erikson, Bowlby, and other theorists (Sroufe & Fleeson, 1986) believe that attachment, as the first social relationship, lays the foundation for all of an infant's later social relationships. In this view, infants who experience the trust and compassion of a secure attachment should develop into preschool children who interact confidently and successfully with their peers. In contrast, infants who do not experience a successful, satisfying first relationship should be more prone to problems in their social interactions as preschoolers.

Both of these predictions are supported by research, as the following findings demonstrate:

You won't need to turn pages searching for a picture or table that is described in the text; instead, pictures, tables, and words are linked to tell a unified story.

Two other elements are designed to help you focus on the main points of the text. First, whenever a key term is introduced in the text, it appears in **boldface italics** like these and the definition appears in **boldface**. This format should make key terms easier for you to find and learn. Second, about half the pages in the book include a sentence in large type that extends into the margin. This sentence summarizes a key point that is made in the surrounding text. When you see one of these sentences, take a moment to think about it—it is an important idea; reviewing these sentences later will help you prepare for exams.

Each module concludes with Check Your Learning questions to help you review the major ideas in the module.

Check Your Learning

1. Basic emotions include a subjective feeling, a physiological change, and
   _____.

2. During infancy, happiness is first linked to physical states and later to
   _____.

3. The first detectable form of fear is _____, which emerges at about 6 months.

4. Wariness of strangers is adaptive because it emerges at about the same time that
   _____.

5. Complex emotions, such as guilt and shame, emerge later than basic emotions because _____.

6. In social referencing, infants use a parent's facial expression _____.

7. Infants often control fear by looking away from a frightening event or by
   _____.

If you can answer the questions in Check Your Learning, you are on your way to mastering the material in the module. However, do not rely exclusively on Check Your Learning as you study for exams. The questions are designed to give you a quick spot-check of your understanding, not a comprehensive assessment of your knowledge of the entire module.

At the very end of each chapter are several additional study aids. Critical Review includes critical thinking questions that link important material within and between chapters as well as link the material in the chapter to important developmental themes (which I introduce in Module 1.3). See for Yourself suggests some simple activities for exploring issues in child development on your own. For More Information About ... includes books and World Wide Web sites where you can learn more about children and their development. Key Terms is a list of all of the important terms that appear in the chapter, along with the page where each term is defined. Finally, drawing the chapter to a close is a Summary—a review of the entire chapter, organized by module and the primary headings within the module.

> A sentence in the margin like this summarizes surrounding text. Use these sentences to help preview the text before you read.

How to Use These Features to Learn About Children

I strongly encourage you to take advantage of these learning and study aids as you read the book. In the next few paragraphs, I'm going to suggest how you should do this. Obviously, I can't know exactly how your course is organized, but my suggestions should work well with most courses, sometimes with a few changes.

Your instructor will probably assign about one chapter per week. Don't try to read an entire chapter in one sitting. Instead, on the first day, preview the chapter. Read the introduction and notice how the chapter fits into the whole book. Then page through the chapter, reading the learning objectives, vignettes, mini-outlines, and major headings. Also read the large sentences and the bold-faced sentences. Your goal is to get a general overview of the entire chapter—a sense of what it's all about.

Now you're ready to begin reading. Go to the first module and preview it again, reminding yourself of the topics covered. Then start to read. As you do, think about what you're reading. Every few paragraphs, stop briefly. Try to summarize, in your own words, the main ideas; ask yourself if the ideas describe your own childhood or others that you know; tell a roommate about something interesting in the material. In other words, read actively—get involved in what you're reading. Don't just stare glassy-eyed at the page!

Continue this pattern—reading, summarizing, thinking—until you finish the module. Then answer the questions in Check Your Learning to determine how well you've learned what you've read. If you've followed the read/summarize/think cycle as you worked your way through the module, you should be able to answer most of the questions.

The next time you sit down to read—preferably the next day—start by reviewing the second module, then tackle it with the read/summarize/think cycle. Repeat this procedure for all the modules.

After you've finished the last module, wait a day or two, then review each module, paying careful attention to the italicized sentences, the bold-faced terms, and the Check Your Learning questions. Also, use the study aids at the end of the chapter to help you integrate the ideas in the chapter.

With this approach, it should take several 30- to 45-minute study sessions to complete each chapter. Don't be tempted to blast through an entire chapter in a single session. Research consistently shows that you learn more effectively by having daily (or nearly daily) study sessions devoted both to reviewing familiar material and taking on a relatively small amount of new material.

Finally, *Children* has its own Web site:

www.prenhall.com/kail/

which includes much additional material that should be useful to you. In particular, as you begin to prepare for exams, the Web site has questions that you can use to see how well you've mastered the material in the book.

Terminology

Every field has its own terminology, and child development is no exception. I will be using several terms to refer to different periods of infancy, childhood, and adolescence. Although these terms are familiar, I will use each to refer to a specific range of ages:

newborn	birth to 1 month
infant	1 month to 1 year
toddler	1 to 2 years
preschooler	2 to 6 years
school-age child	6 to 12 years
adolescent	12 to 18 years
adult	18 years and older

Sometimes for the sake of variety I will use other terms that are less tied to specific ages, such as *babies, youngsters,* and *elementary-school children.* When I do, you will be able to tell from the context which groups are being described.

I will also use very specific terminology in describing research findings from different cultural and ethnic groups. The appropriate terms to describe different cultural, racial, and ethnic groups change over time. For example, the terms Negroes, colored people, Black Americans, and African Americans have all been used to describe Americans who trace their ancestry to tribal groups in Africa. In this book, I will use the term African American because it emphasizes a unique cultural heritage. Following this same line of reasoning, I will use the terms European American (instead of Caucasian or white), Native American (instead of Indian or American Indian), Asian American, and Hispanic American.

These labels are not perfect. Sometimes, they blur distinctions within ethnic groups. For example, the term European American ignores differences between individuals of northern or southern European ancestry; the term Asian American blurs variations among people whose heritage is, for example, Japanese, Chinese, or Korean. Whenever researchers identified the subgroups in their research sample, I will use the more specific terms in describing results. When you see the more general terms, remember that conclusions may not apply to all subgroups within the group.

A Final Word

I love teaching child development, and wrote this book to make child development come alive for my students at Purdue. Although I can't teach you directly, I hope this book sparks your interest in children and their development. Please let me know what you like and dislike about the book so that I can improve it in later editions. You can send e-mail to me at

> *rkail@sla.purdue.edu*

I'd love to hear from you.

The many topics described in the rest of this book all draw upon the same developmental theories, which are described in Module 1.2.

Theories of Child Development

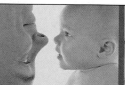

Learning Objectives

- What are the major tenets of the biological perspective?

- How do psychodynamic theories account for development?

- What is the focus of learning theories?

- How do cognitive-developmental theories explain changes in children's thinking?

- What are the main points of the contextual approach?

1.2

Theories of Child Development

- The Biological Perspective
- The Psychodynamic Perspective
- The Learning Perspective
- The Cognitive-Developmental Perspective
- The Contextual Perspective
- The Big Picture

Marcus has just graduated from high school, first in his class. For his proud mother, Betty, this is a time to reflect on Marcus's past and ponder his future. Marcus has always been a happy, easygoing child—a joy to rear. And he's always been interested in learning. Betty wonders why he is so perpetually good-natured and so curious. If she knew the secret, she laughed, she could write a best-selling book and be a guest on Oprah!

Betty is not the first person to ask these questions about children. In fact, such questions have occupied the minds of some of the greatest philosophers in history. Nearly 400 years ago, the English philosopher John Locke (1632–1704) claimed that the human infant is a tabula rasa, or "blank slate." Experience then molds the infant, child, adolescent, and adult into a unique individual. Locke's view was challenged by the French philosopher Jean-Jacques Rousseau (1712–1778), who believed that newborns were endowed with an innate sense of justice and morality that unfolds naturally as children grow.

By the middle of the nineteenth century, progress in science had merged with growing concerns about children's welfare to bring about the first scientific theories of child development. **In child development, a *theory* is an organized set of ideas that is designed to explain and make predictions about development.** For example, suppose friends of yours have a baby who cries often. You could imagine several explanations for her crying. Maybe the baby cries because she's hungry; maybe she cries to get her parents to hold her; maybe she cries because she's simply a cranky, unhappy baby. Each of these explanations is a very simple theory: It tries to explain why the baby cries so much. Of course, real developmental theories are much more complicated, but the purpose is the same—to explain behavior and development.

> Five major theoretical perspectives have guided most research on children and their development.

Theories lead to predictions that we can test in research; in the process, the theory is or is not supported. Think about the different explanations for the crying baby. Each one leads to unique predictions. If, for example, the baby is crying because she's hungry, we predict that feeding her more often should stop the crying. When results of research match the predictions, the theory gains support. When results differ from the predictions, the theory is incorrect and is revised.

Perhaps now you see why theories are essential for child-development research: They are the source of predictions for research, which often lead to changes in the theories. These revised theories then provide the basis for new predictions, which lead to new research, and the cycle continues.

Many theories have guided research and thinking about children's development for the past 100 years. Child-development scientists embraced these theories for a period, then abandoned them because they were disproved, generated relatively few testable predictions, or gave rise to improved theories. Nevertheless, understanding these theories is critical because they set the stage for modern theories of child development.

Some theories share assumptions and ideas about children and development, making it convenient to group them together to reveal their common perspective on child development. In the next few pages, I briefly sketch five major theoretical perspectives in child-development research: the biological, psychodynamic, learning, cognitive-developmental, and contextual. As you read about each perspective, think about how it differs from the others in its view of development.

The Biological Perspective

According to the biological perspective, intellectual and personality development, as well as physical and motor development, proceed according to a biological plan. One of the first biological theories, maturational theory, was proposed by Arnold Gesell (1880–1961), shown in the photo. **According to *maturational theory,* child development reflects a specific and prearranged scheme or plan within the body.** In Gesell's view, development is simply a natural unfolding of a biological plan; experience matters little. Like Jean-Jacques Rousseau 200 years before him, Gesell encouraged parents to let their children develop naturally. Without interference from adults, Gesell claimed, behaviors like speech, play, and reasoning would emerge spontaneously according to a predetermined developmental timetable.

Other biological theories give greater weight to experience. ***Ethological theory* views development from an evolutionary perspective. In this theory, many behaviors are adaptive—they have survival value.** For example, clinging, grasping, and crying are adaptive for infants because they elicit caregiving from adults. Ethological theorists assume that people inherit many of these adaptive behaviors.

So far, ethological theory seems like maturational theory, with a dash of evolution for taste. How does experience fit in? Ethologists believe that all animals are biologically programmed so that some kinds of learning occur only at certain ages. **A *critical period* is the time in development when a specific type of learning can take place; before or after the critical period, the same learning is difficult or even impossible.**

One of the best-known examples of a critical period comes from the work of Konrad Lorenz (1903–1989), a Nobel-prize-winning Austrian zoologist. Lorenz noticed that newly hatched chicks follow their mother about. He theorized that chicks are biologically programmed to follow the first moving object that they see after hatching. **Usually this was the mother, so following her was the first step in *imprinting,* creating an emotional bond with the mother.** Lorenz tested his theory by showing that if he removed the mother immediately after the chicks hatched and replaced it with another moving object, the chicks would follow that object and treat it as "mother." As the photo shows, this included Lorenz himself!

Lorenz also discovered that the chick had to see the moving object within about a day of hatching. Otherwise, the chick would not imprint on the moving object. In other words, the critical period for imprinting lasts about a day; when chicks experience the moving object outside of the critical period, imprinting does not take place. Even though the underlying mechanism is biological, experience is essential for triggering programmed, adaptive behaviors.

Ethological theory and maturational theory both highlight the biological bases of child development. Biological theorists remind us that children's genes, which are the product of a long evolutionary history, influence virtually every aspect of children's development. Consequently, a biological theorist would tell Betty, the mother of the high school graduate in the module-opening vignette, that her son's good nature and his outstanding academic record are both largely products of heredity.

The Psychodynamic Perspective

The psychodynamic perspective is the oldest scientific perspective on child development, tracing its roots to Sigmund Freud's (1856–1939) work in the late nineteenth and early twentieth centuries. Freud, shown in the photo, was a physician who specialized in diseases of the nervous system. Many of his patients were adults who suffered from ailments that seemed to have no obvious biological causes. As Freud listened to his patients describe their problems and their lives, he became convinced that early experiences establish patterns that endure throughout a person's life. **Using his patients' case histories, Freud created the first** *psychodynamic theory,* **which holds that development is largely determined by how well people resolve conflicts they face at different ages.**

Two aspects of Freud's theorizing have influenced child-development research: his theory of personality and his theory of psychosexual development.

Theory of Personality. In his theory of personality, Freud proposed that personality includes three primary components that emerge at distinct ages. **The** *id* **is a reservoir of primitive instincts and drives.** Present at birth, the id presses for immediate gratification of bodily needs and wants. A hungry baby crying illustrates the id in action. **The** *ego* **is the practical, rational component of personality.** The ego begins to emerge during the first year of life, as infants learn that they cannot always have what they want. The ego tries to resolve conflicts that occur when the instinctive desires of the id encounter the obstacles of the real world. The ego often tries to channel the id's impulsive demands into socially more acceptable channels. Suppose, for example, a child sees a peer playing with an attractive toy. The id would urge the child to grab the toy but the ego would encourage the child to play with the peer and, in the process, the attractive toy.

The third component of personality, the *superego,* **is the "moral agent" in the child's personality.** It emerges during the preschool years as children begin to internalize adult standards of right and wrong. If the peer in the previous example left the attractive toy unattended, the id might tell the child to grab the toy and run; the superego would remind the child that taking another's toy would be wrong.

Theory of Psychosexual Development. A second influential aspect of Freud's work was his account of psychosexual development. Freud believed that humans want to experience physical pleasure from birth. As children grow, the focus of the pleasure shifts to different parts of the body. The result is a sequence of developmental stages, with each stage characterized by sensitivity in a particular part of the body or erogenous zone. For example, from birth to the first birthday, infants are in the oral stage. As the name suggests, they seek pleasure orally, usually by sucking.

Freud believed that development proceeds best when children's needs at each stage are met but not exceeded. If children's needs are not met adequately, they are frustrated and reluctant to move to other, more mature forms of stimulation. For example, a baby whose needs for oral stimulation were not met may try to satisfy these needs as an adolescent or adult by smoking. If, instead, children find one source of stimulation too satisfying, they see little need to progress to more advanced stages. In Freud's view, parents have the difficult task of satisfying children's needs without indulging them.

Erikson's Psychosocial Theory. Freud's student, Erik Erikson (1902–1994), shown in the photo, believed that psychological and social aspects of development were more important than the biological and physical aspects that Freud emphasized. **In Erikson's *psychosocial theory*, development consists of a sequence of stages, each defined by a unique crisis or challenge.** The complete theory includes the eight stages shown in the table. The name of each stage reflects the challenge that individuals face at a particular age. For example, the challenge for young adults is to become involved in a loving relationship. Adults who establish this relationship experience intimacy; those who don't, experience isolation.

The Eight Stages of Psychosocial Development in Erikson's Theory

Psychosocial Stage	Age	Challenge
Basic trust versus mistrust	Birth to 1 year	To develop a sense that the world is safe, a "good place"
Autonomy versus shame and doubt	1 to 3 years	To realize that one is an independent person who can make decisions
Initiative versus guilt	3 to 6 years	To develop a willingness to try new things and to handle failure
Industry versus inferiority	6 years to adolescence	To learn basic skills and to work with others
Identity versus identity confusion	Adolescence	To develop a lasting, integrated sense of self
Intimacy versus isolation	Young adulthood	To commit to another in a loving relationship
Generativity versus stagnation	Middle adulthood	To contribute to younger people, through child rearing, child care, or other productive work
Integrity versus despair	Late life	To view one's life as satisfactory and worth living

TABLE 1–2

Erikson also argued that the earlier stages of psychosocial development provide the foundation for the later stages. For example, adolescents who do not meet the challenge of developing an identity will not establish truly intimate relationships; instead, they will become overly dependent on their partners as a source of identity.

Whether we call them conflicts, challenges, or crises, the psychodynamic perspective emphasizes that the trek to adulthood is difficult because the path is strewn with obstacles. Outcomes of development reflect the manner and ease with which children surmount life's barriers. When children overcome early obstacles easily, they are better able to handle the later ones. A psychodynamic theorist would tell Betty that her son's cheerful disposition and his academic record suggest that he handled life's early obstacles well, which is a good sign for his future development.

The Learning Perspective

Learning theorists endorse John Locke's view that the infant's mind is a blank slate on which experience writes. John Watson (1878–1958) was the first theorist to apply this approach to child development. Watson argued that learning determines what children will be. He assumed that with the correct techniques anything could be learned by almost anyone. In other words, in Watson's view, experience was just about all that mattered in determining the course of development.

Early Learning Theories. Watson did little research to support his claims, but B. F. Skinner (1904–1990), shown in the photo, filled this gap. **Skinner studied *operant conditioning*, in which the consequences of a behavior determine whether a behavior is repeated in the future.** Skinner showed that two kinds of consequences were especially influential. **A *reinforcement* is a consequence that increases the future likelihood of the behavior that it follows.** *Positive reinforcement* consists of giving a reward, like chocolate, gold stars, or paychecks, to increase the likelihood of repeating a previous behavior. The parents of the child whose room is shown in the photograph could use positive reinforcement to encourage her to clean her room. Every time she cleaned her room, they could reinforce her with praise, food, or money. *Negative reinforcement* consists of rewarding people by taking away unpleasant things. The same parents could use negative reinforcement by saying that whenever she cleaned her room, she wouldn't have to wash the dishes or fold laundry.

A *punishment* is a consequence that decreases the future likelihood of the behavior that it follows. Punishment suppresses a behavior by either adding something aversive or by withholding a pleasant event. When the child failed to clean her room, the parents could punish her by making her do extra chores (adding something aversive) or by not allowing her to watch television (withholding a pleasant event).

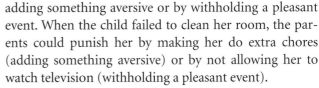

Skinner's research was done primarily with animals, but child-development researchers soon showed that the principles of operant conditioning could be extended readily to children's behavior (Baer & Wolf, 1968). Applied properly, reinforcement and punishment are indeed powerful influences on children. However, researchers discovered that children sometimes learn without reinforcement or punishment. **Children learn much simply by watching those around them, which is known as *imitation* or *observational learning*.** For example, imitation occurs when one toddler throws a toy after seeing a peer do so or when a school-age child offers to help an older adult carry groceries because she's seen her parents do the same.

Social Cognitive Theory. Perhaps imitation makes you think of "monkey-see, monkey-do," or simple mimicking. Early investigators had this view, too, but research quickly showed that this was wrong. Children do not always imitate what they see around them. Children are more likely to imitate if the person they see is popular, smart, or talented. They're also more likely to imitate when the behavior they see is rewarded than when it is punished. Findings like these imply that imitation is more complex than sheer mimicry. Children do not mechanically copy what they see and hear; instead, they look to others for information about appropriate behavior. When popular, smart peers are reinforced for behaving in a particular way, it makes sense to imitate them.

Albert Bandura (1925–) based his *social cognitive theory* on this more complex view of reward, punishment, and imitation. Bandura, shown in the top photo, calls his theory "cognitive" because he believes that children are actively trying to understand what goes on in their world; the theory is "social" because, along with reinforcement and punishment, what other people do is an important source of information about the world.

Bandura also argues that experience gives children a sense of *self-efficacy,* beliefs about their own abilities and talents. Self-efficacy beliefs help determine when children will imitate others. A child who sees herself as athletically untalented, for example, will not try to imitate Shaquille O'Neal dunking a basketball, despite the fact that he is obviously talented and popular. Thus, whether children imitate others depends on who the other person is, whether that person's behavior is rewarded, and the children's beliefs about their own talents.

Bandura's social cognitive theory is a far cry from Skinner's operant conditioning. The social cognitive child, who actively interprets events, has replaced the operant conditioning child, who responds mechanically to reinforcement and punishment. Nevertheless, Skinner, Bandura, and all learning theorists share the view that experience propels children along their developmental journeys. They would tell Betty that she can thank experience for making Marcus both happy and successful academically.

The Cognitive-Developmental Perspective

The cognitive-developmental perspective focuses on how children think and on how their thinking changes over time. Jean Piaget (1896–1980), shown in the bottom photo, proposed the best-known of these theories. Piaget believed that children naturally try to make sense of their world. Throughout infancy, childhood, and adolescence, youngsters want to understand the workings of both the physical and the social world. For example, infants want to know about objects: "What happens when I push this toy off the table?" And they want to know about people: "Who is this person who feeds and cares for me?"

Piaget argued that in their efforts to comprehend their world, children act like scientists in creating theories about the physical and social worlds. They try to weave all that they know about objects and people into a complete theory. Children's theories are tested daily by experience because their theories lead them to expect certain things to happen. As with real scientific theories, when the predicted events do occur, a child's belief in her theory grows stronger. When the predicted events do not occur, the child must revise her theory. For example, think about the baby in the photo on page 16 and her "theory" of objects like the rattle she is holding. Her theory of objects might include the idea that "If I let go, the rattle will fall to the floor." If the infant drops some other object—a plate or an article of clothing—she will find that it, too, falls to the floor and can make the theory more general: Objects that are dropped fall to the floor.

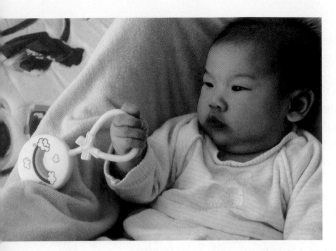

Piaget also believed that at a few critical points in development, children realize their theories have basic flaws. When this happens, they revise their theories radically. These changes are so fundamental that the revised theory is, in many respects, a brand-new theory. Piaget claimed that radical revisions occur three times in development: once at about age 2, a second time at about age 7, and a third time just before adolescence. These radical changes mean children go through four distinct stages in cognitive development. Each stage represents a fundamental change in how children understand and organize their environment, and each stage is characterized by more sophisticated types of reasoning. For example, the sensorimotor stage begins at birth and lasts until about age 2. As the name implies, sensorimotor thinking is closely linked to the infant's sensory and motor skills. This stage and the three later stages are shown in the table.

Piaget's Four Stages of Cognitive Development		
Stage	**Approximate Age**	**Characteristics**
Sensorimotor	Birth to 2 years	Infant's knowledge of the world is based on senses and motor skills. By the end of the period, infant uses mental representations.
Preoperational thought	2 to 6 years	Child learns how to use symbols such as words and numbers to represent aspects of the world, but relates to the world only through his or her perspective.
Concrete operational thought	7 to 11 years	Child understands and applies logical operations to experiences, provided they are focused on the here and now.
Formal operational thought	Adolescence and beyond	Adolescent or adult thinks abstractly, speculates on hypothetical situations, and reasons deductively about what may be possible.

TABLE 1-3

Not all cognitive-developmental theorists view development as a sequence of stages. Information-processing theorists, for example, draw heavily on how computers work to explain thinking and how it develops through childhood and adolescence. **Just as computers consist of both hardware (disk drives, random-access memory, and a central processing unit) and software (the programs we use),** *information-processing theory* **proposes that human cognition consists of mental hardware and mental software.** Mental hardware refers to cognitive structures, including different memories where information is stored. Mental software includes organized sets of cognitive processes that allow children to complete specific tasks, such as reading a sentence, playing a video game, or hitting a baseball.

How do information-processing psychologists explain developmental change in thinking? To answer this question, think about improvements in personal computers. Today's personal computers can accomplish much more than a computer that was built just a few years ago. Why? Because today's computer has better hardware (for example, more memory and a faster central processing unit) and because it has more sophisticated software that takes advantage of the better hardware. Like modern computers, older children and adolescents have better hardware and better software than younger children, who are more like last year's out-of-date model. For example, older children typically can solve math word problems better than younger children because they have greater memory capacity to store the facts in the problem and because their methods for performing arithmetic operations are more efficient.

For both Piaget and information-processing theorists, children's thinking becomes more sophisticated as children develop. However, Piaget's work is a single comprehensive theory, whereas information processing represents a general approach encompassing many different theories to describe specific components of cognitive development. Thus, the advantage of Piaget's work is that it is comprehensive—all the links between different facets of cognitive development are included in his theory. But the advantage of the information-processing approach is that specific components of cognition are described with great precision. In essence, Piaget emphasized the "whole" of cognitive development, whereas information processing emphasizes the "parts." Both the whole and the parts are important for complete understanding of cognitive development, so Piaget's theory and information processing complement each other.

> Piaget's theory of cognitive development provides a general orientation to cognitive development but information processing focuses on specific elements.

A second difference is that Piaget emphasized periodic, qualitative change in cognition: Children's thinking remains at one stage for years, then changes abruptly as thinking moves into the next, qualitatively different stage. In contrast, improved information processing typically produces a steady age-related increase in cognitive skill. Unlike Piaget's account, there are no abrupt or qualitative changes that create distinct cognitive stages. Instead, cognitive change is continual and gradual. Since both types of change play a role in development, here, too, Piaget's theory and information processing complement each other.

Neither approach would have much to say to Betty about Marcus's good nature. As for his academic success, Piaget would explain that all children naturally want to understand their worlds; Marcus is simply unusually skilled in this regard. An information-processing psychologist would point to superior hardware and superior software as the keys to his academic success.

The Contextual Perspective

Most developmentalists agree that the environment is an important force in development. Traditionally, however, most theories of child development have emphasized environmental forces that affect children directly. Examples of direct environmental influences would be a parent praising a child, an older sibling teasing a younger one, and a nursery school teacher discouraging girls from playing with trucks. These direct influences are important in children's lives, but in the contextual perspective they are one part of a much larger system, where each element of the system influences all other elements. This larger system includes one's parents and siblings as well as important individuals outside of the family, such as extended

family, friends, and teachers. The system also includes institutions that influence development, such as schools, television, the workplace, and a church or temple.

All these people and institutions fit together to form a person's *culture*—**the knowledge, attitudes, and behavior associated with a group of people.** Culture can refer to a particular country or people (e.g., French culture), to a specific point in time (e.g., popular culture of the 1990s), or to groups of individuals who maintain specific, identifiable cultural traditions, like this African American family that is celebrating Kwanzaa. A culture provides the context in which a child develops and thus is a source of many important influences on development throughout childhood and adolescence.

One of the first theorists to emphasize cultural context in children's development was Lev Vygotsky (1896–1934), shown in the middle photo. A Russian psychologist, Vygotsky focused on ways that adults convey to children the beliefs, customs, and skills of their culture. Vygotsky believed that, because a fundamental aim of all societies is to enable children to acquire essential cultural values and skills, every aspect of a child's development must be considered against this backdrop. For example, most parents in the United States want their children to work hard in school and be accepted in college, because this is the key to a good job. In the same way, parents in Efe (a developing nation in Africa) want their children to learn to hunt, build houses, and gather food because these skills are key to survival in their environment.

Vygotsky was the first proponent of the contextual view, but Urie Bronfenbrenner (1917–), shown in the bottom photo, is its best proponent today. Bronfenbrenner views the developing child embedded in a series of complex and interactive systems. As the diagram at the top of page 19 shows, Bronfenbrenner (1979, 1995; Bronfenbrenner & Morris, 1998) divides the environment into four levels: the microsystem, the mesosystem, the exosystem, and the macrosystem. **At any point in life, the** *microsystem* **consists of the people and objects in an individual's immediate environment.** These are the people closest to a child, such as parents or siblings. Some children have more than one microsystem; for example, a young child might have the microsystems of the family and of the day-care setting. As you can imagine, microsystems strongly influence development.

Microsystems themselves are connected to create the *mesosystem.* The mesosystem represents the fact that what happens in one microsystem is likely to influence others. Perhaps you've found that if you have a stressful day at work or school, you're grouchy at home. This indicates that your mesosystem is alive and well; your microsystems of home and work are interconnected emotionally for you.

The *exosystem* **refers to social settings that a person may not experience firsthand but that still influence development.** For example, a mother's work environment is part of her child's exosystem, because she may pay more attention to her child when her work is going well and less attention when she's under a great deal of work-related stress. Although the influence of the exosystem is at least secondhand, its effects on the developing child can be quite strong.

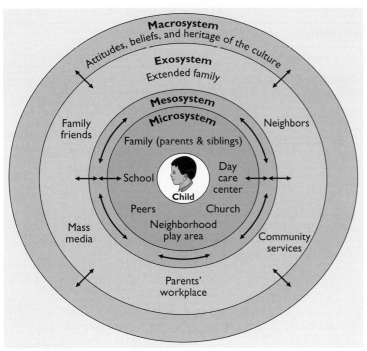

FIGURE 1–1

The broadest environmental context is the *macrosystem,* the subcultures and cultures in which the microsystem, mesosystem, and exosystem are embedded. A mother, her workplace, her child, and the child's school are part of a larger cultural setting, such as Asian Americans living in Southern California or Italian Americans living in large cities on the East Coast. Members of these cultural groups share a common identity, a common heritage, and common values. The macrosystem evolves over time; what is true about a particular culture today may or may not have been true in the past and may or may not be true in the future. Thus, each successive generation of children develops in a unique macrosystem.

Bronfenbrenner and other contextual theorists would agree with learning theorists in telling Betty that the environment has been pivotal in her son's amiable disposition and his academic achievements. However, the contextual theorist would insist that "environment" means much more than the reinforcements, punishments, and observations that are central to learning theory. The contextual theorist would emphasize the different levels of environmental influence on Marcus. Betty's ability to balance home and work so skillfully (which means that she is usually in a good mood herself) contributed positively to Marcus's development, as does Betty's membership in a cultural group that values doing well in school.

> In Bronfenbrenner's theory, the microsystem, the mesosystem, and the exosystem are different environmental systems embedded in the macrosystem—the broader cultural context.

The Big Picture

Comparing five major perspectives in these few pages is like trying to see all of the major sights of a large city in a day: It can be done, but it's demanding and, after a while, everything blurs together. Relax. The summary in Table 1–4 gives a capsule account of all five perspectives and their important theories.

◼◼◼◼ SUMMARY TABLE

Characteristics of Developmental Perspectives

Perspective	Key Assumptions	Specific Theories
Biological	Development is determined primarily by biological forces.	Maturational theory: emphasizes development as a natural unfolding of a biological plan.
		Ethological theory: emphasizes the adaptive nature of behavior and the importance of experience during critical periods of development.
Psychodynamic	Development is determined primarily by how a child resolves conflicts at different ages.	Freud's theory: emphasizes the conflict between primitive biological forces and societal standards for right and wrong.
		Erikson's theory: emphasizes the challenges posed by the formation of trust, autonomy, initiative, industry, and identity.
Learning	Development is determined primarily by a child's environment.	Skinner's operant conditioning: emphasizes the role of reinforcement and punishment.
		Bandura's social cognitive theory: emphasizes children's efforts to understand their world, using reinforcement, punishment, and others' behavior.
Cognitive-Developmental	Development reflects children's efforts to understand the world.	Piaget's theory: emphasizes the different stages of thinking that result from children's changing theories of the world.
		Information-processing theory: emphasizes changes in thinking that reflect changes in mental hardware and mental software.
Contextual	Development is influenced by immediate and more distant environments, which typically influence each other.	Vygotsky's theory: emphasizes the role of parents (and other adults) in conveying culture to the next generation.
		Bronfenbrenner's theory: emphasizes the influences of the microsystem, mesosystem, exosystem, and macrosystem.

TABLE 1–4

As I mentioned at the beginning of this module, many of these theories are no longer thought to be valid. Nevertheless, they have been invaluable in fostering research that led scientists to formulate modern theories. For example, today few child-development scientists believe that Piaget's theory provides the definitive account of changes in children's thinking. Yet this theory is the forerunner of a number of modern theories, including those of infants' understanding of objects (described in Module 6.1) and of preschoolers' theory of mind (Module 9.1). Similarly, Erikson's theory has been largely abandoned, yet it contributed to work on mother-infant attachment (Module 7.2) and formation of identity during adolescence (Module 16.1).

These examples reflect a common trend in theories of child development. Classic developmental theories were very broad; they attempted to account for (a) development across a broad age range, (b) a range of different phenomena, or (c) both. For the most part, this approach has given way to theories that account for much more restricted phenomena, usually across a narrower age range (e.g., understanding of objects in infancy, identity formation in adolescence). In general, this shift produces theories that are more precise, in the sense that they are more likely to produce specific, testable hypotheses. What's lost in the change, of course, is breadth: Modern theories are less likely to make connections between different phenomena.

> Classic developmental theories, which tended to be very broad, have given way to theories that are more precise but sometimes narrow.

Throughout this book, I describe modern theories that are derived from all five perspectives listed in Table 1-4. Why? Because no single perspective provides a truly complete explanation of all aspects of children's development. Theories from the cognitive-developmental perspective are useful for understanding how children's thinking changes as children grow older. Theories from the contextual and learning perspectives are particularly valuable in explaining how environmental forces such as parents, peers, schools, and culture influence children's development. By drawing upon all the perspectives, we'll be better able to understand the different forces that contribute to children's development. Just as you can better appreciate a beautiful painting by examining it from different viewpoints, child-development researchers often rely upon multiple perspectives to understand why children develop as they do. ■

Check Your Learning

1. The _____ perspective emphasizes the role of conflict in child development.

2. _____ proposes that children learn about the world through reinforcement, punishment, and imitation.

3. According to _____, development is linked to changes in mental hardware and mental software.

4. Vygotsky believed that a fundamental task for all cultures is _____.

5. The influence of multiple levels of the environment is central in _____ theory.

◨ **Connections** Freud and Piaget both proposed stage theories of children's development. Although the theories differed in emphasis—Freud was concerned with psychosexual growth and Piaget was concerned with cognitive growth—can you see similarities in their approach to development?

Answers: (1) psychodynamic, (2) Albert Bandura's social cognitive theory, (3) the information-processing approach, (4) to pass along beliefs, customs, and skills to children, (5) Bronfenbrenner's systems

Themes in Child-Development Research

1.3

Themes in Child-Development Research

— Early Development Is Related to Later Development but Not Perfectly

— Development Is Always Jointly Influenced by Heredity and Environment

— Children Help Determine Their Own Development

— Development in Different Domains Is Connected

Learning Objectives

■ **How well can developmental outcomes be predicted from early life?**

■ **How do heredity and environment influence development?**

■ **What role do children have in their own development?**

■ **Is development in different domains connected?**

> *Javier Suarez smiled broadly as he held his newborn grandson for the first time. So many thoughts rushed into his mind—what would Ricardo experience growing up? Would the poor neighborhood they live in prevent him from reaching his potential? Would the family genes for good health be passed on? How would Ricardo's life growing up as a Chicano in the United States be different from Javier's own experiences in Mexico?*

Like many grandparents, Javier wonders what the future holds for his grandson. And his questions actually reflect several fundamental themes in child development that are the focus of this module. These themes provide a foundation you can use to organize the many specific facts about child development that fill this book. Four themes will help you to unify your own understanding of child development. To help you do this, Check Your Learning questions at the end of each module always include a question about one of these themes. Also, every chapter ends with Critical Review questions that will help you link topics, themes, and theories across age ranges.

Here are the four unifying themes.

Early Development Is Related to Later Development but Not Perfectly

This theme has to do with the "predictability" of development. Do you believe that happy, cheerful 5-year-olds remain outgoing and friendly throughout their lives? If you do, this shows that you believe development is a continuous process: According to this view, once a child begins down a particular developmental pathway, he or she stays on that path throughout life. In other words, if Ricardo is friendly and smart as a 5-year-old he should be friendly and smart as a 15- and 25-year-old. The other view, that development is not continuous, is shown in the cartoon at the top of page 23. Sweet, cooperative Trixie has become a demanding, assertive child. According to this view, Ricardo might be friendly and smart as a 5-year-old but obnoxious and foolish at 15 and quiet but wise at 25! **Thus, the *continuity versus discontinuity issue* is really about the "connectedness" of development: Are early aspects of development consistently related to later aspects?**

In reality, neither of these views is accurate. Development is not perfectly predictable. A friendly, smart 5-year-old does not guarantee a friendly, smart 15- or 25-year-old, but the chances of a friendly, smart adult are greater than if the child were obnoxious and foolish. There are many ways to become a friendly and smart 15-year-old; being a friendly and smart 5-year-old is not a required step, but it is probably the most direct route!

Development Is Always Jointly Influenced by Heredity and Environment

Let me introduce this theme with a story about my sons. Ben, my first son, was a delightful baby and toddler. He awoke each morning with a smile on his face, eager to start another fun-filled day. When Ben was upset, which occurred infrequently, he was quickly consoled by being held or rocked. I presumed that his cheerful disposition must reflect fabulous parenting. Consequently, I was stunned when my second son, Matt, spent much of the first year of his life being fussy and cranky. He was easily irritated and hard to soothe. Why wasn't the all-star parenting that had been so effective with Ben working with Matt? The answer, of course, is that parenting wasn't the sole cause of Ben's happiness. I thought environmental influences accounted for his amiable disposition, but in fact, biological influences also played an important role.

This anecdote illustrates the *nature-nurture issue:* What roles do biology (nature) and environment (nurture) play in child development? If Ricardo is outgoing and friendly, is it due to his heredity or his experiences? Scientists once hoped to answer questions like this by identifying either heredity or environment as *the* cause. Their goal was to be able to say, for example, that intelligence was due to heredity or that personality was due to experience. Today, we know that virtually no aspects of child development are due exclusively to either heredity or environment. Instead, development is always shaped by both—nature and nurture interact. In fact, a major aim of child-development research is to understand how heredity and environment jointly determine children's development. Biology will be more influential in some areas and environment in others.

> Virtually all aspects of development are determined by the combined forces of heredity and environment.

Children Help Determine Their Own Development

Whenever I teach child development, I ask students their plans for when they have children. How will they rear them? What do they want them to grow up to be? It's interesting to hear students' responses. Many have big plans for their future children. It's just as interesting, though, to watch students who already have

children roll their eyes in a "You don't have a clue" way at what the others say. The parent-students in class admit that they, too, once had grand designs about child rearing. What they quickly learned, however, was that their children shaped the way in which they parented.

These two points of view illustrate the *active-passive child issue*: Are children simply at the mercy of the environment (passive child) or do children actively influence their own development through their own unique individual characteristics (active child)? The passive view corresponds to Locke's description of the child as a blank slate on which experience writes, whereas the active view corresponds to Rousseau's view of development as a natural unfolding that takes place within the child. Today, we know that experiences are indeed crucial but not always in the way Locke envisioned. Often, it's a child's interpretation of experiences that shapes his or her development. From birth, children like Ricardo are trying to make sense of their world, and in the process, they help shape their own destinies.

Also, a child's unique characteristics may cause him or her to have some experiences but not others. Think about the child in the photo, who is responding defiantly to her parent's discipline. Do you think this child's defiance will affect the way her parents discipline her in the future? You might predict that they will punish her more harshly the next time, showing the impact of her behavior on her parents' behavior.

Development in Different Domains Is Connected

Child-development researchers usually examine different domains or areas of development, such as physical growth, cognition, language, personality, and social relationships. One researcher might study how children learn to speak grammatically; another might explore children's reasoning about moral issues. Of course, you should not think of each aspect of development as an independent entity, one that is completely separate from the others. To the contrary, development in different domains is always intertwined. Cognitive and social development, for example, are not independent; advances in one area affect advances in the other. As Ricardo grows cognitively (e.g., he becomes an excellent student) this will influence his social development (e.g., he becomes friends with peers who share his zeal for school).

Having introduced the themes, let me present them together before we move on.

- *Continuity:* Early development is related to later development but not perfectly.
- *Nature and nurture:* Development is always jointly influenced by heredity and environment.
- *Active child:* Children help determine their own development.
- *Connections:* Development in different domains is connected.

Most child-development scientists would agree that these are important general themes in children's development. However, just as lumber, bricks, pipe, and wiring can be used to assemble an incredible assortment of homes, these themes show up in different ways in the major theories of child development.

Think, for example, about the nature-nurture issue. Of the five perspectives, the biological is at one extreme in emphasizing the impact of nature; at the other extreme are the learning and contextual perspectives, which emphasize nurture.

The perspectives also see different degrees of connectedness across different domains of development. Piaget's cognitive-developmental theory takes the hardest line: Because children strive to have a single integrated theory to explain the world, cognitive and social growth are closely interconnected. That is, because children interpret all aspects of their lives with the same unified view of the world, everything is linked. The learning perspective, in contrast, holds that degree of connectedness depends entirely on the nature of environmental influences. Similar environmental influences in different domains of children's lives produce many connections; dissimilar environmental influences would produce few connections.

Check Your Learning

1. The _____ issue concerns how early development relates to later development.

2. In determining the importance of nature and nurture, today scientists believe that _____.

3. The extent to which children help to shape their own development is central to the _____ issue.

Active Child: How might parents respond differently to a very active child compared to a very quiet child?

Answers: (1) continuity-discontinuity, (2) heredity and environment jointly influence most aspects of development, (3) active-passive child issue

Chapter Critical Review

1. Discuss the advantages and disadvantages of grand theories versus smaller-scale theories of development. Give an example of a research question for which each type of theory might be most useful.

2. Discuss the two psychodynamic theories presented in Module 1.2 in terms of the continuity-discontinuity theme.

3. Discuss the various learning theories presented in Module 1.2 in terms of the active-passive theme.

4. Compare and contrast Piaget's cognitive theory with information-processing theory. Explain how each theory would explain a specific activity, such as a 1-year-old who repeatedly drops a spoon over the side of a high chair.

For more review material, log on to http://www.prenhall.com/kail

See For Yourself

One good way to see how children influence their own development is to interview parents who have more than one child. Ask them if they used the same child-rearing methods with each child or if they used different techniques with each. If they used different techniques, find out why. You should see that, although parents try to be consistent in a general philosophy for rearing their children, many of the specific parenting techniques will vary from one child to the next, reflecting the children's influence on the parents. See for yourself!

For More Information About . . .

 the different theories described in Module 1.2, I recommend Patricia H. Miller's *Theories of Developmental Psychology* (W. H. Freeman, 1993) for its comprehensive account of each of the theoretical perspectives.

many of the theorists described in this chapter, visit the Web site of the Psychology Department of Muskingum College:

http://muskingum.edu/~psychology/history.htm

where you can find a biography, summary of the theory, and time line for Freud, Erikson, Skinner, Piaget, Vygotsky, and many other famous psychologists.

Key Terms

active-passive child issue 24
continuity-discontinuity issue 22
critical period 11
culture 18
ego 12
ethological theory 11
exosystem 18
id 12
imitation
  (observational learning) 14

imprinting 11
information-processing theory 16
macrosystem 19
maturational theory 11
mesosystem 18
microsystem 18
nature-nurture issue 23
operant conditioning 14
psychodynamic theory 12
psychosocial theory 13

punishment 14
reinforcement 14
self-efficacy 15
social cognitive theory 15
superego 12
theory 10

SUMMARY

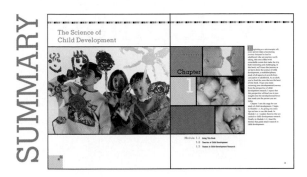

1.1 Using This Book

Organization of Chapters

Each chapter includes three or four modules that begin with learning objectives, a vignette, and a mini-outline. In the text, key terms and their definitions appear in boldface. Each module includes a special feature that examines a specific topic in depth. The module ends with questions that allow you to check your learning. Each chapter ends with several elements that should encourage you to think about the information in the chapter as well as a summary like the one you're reading now.

How to Use These Features to Learn About Children

Preview the entire chapter, then read one module daily. As you read, try to summarize the main ideas; ask yourself questions. When you've finished the chapter, review each module and use the study aids at the end of the chapter.

Terminology

I use specific terms to refer to people of different ages: newborn, infant, toddler, preschooler, school-age child, adolescent, and adult. Also, when describing different ethnic groups, I use terms that identify the unique cultural heritage of each: African American, Asian American, European American, Hispanic American, and Native American.

A Final Word

Enjoy the book! Let me know what you like and dislike!

1.2 Theories of Child Development

Theories are important because they provide the explanations for development and provide hypotheses for research. Traditionally, five broad theoretical perspectives have guided researchers.

The Biological Perspective

According to this perspective, biological factors are critical in shaping development. In maturational theory, child development reflects a natural unfolding of a pre-arranged biological plan. Ethological theory emphasizes that children's behavior is often adaptive—it has survival value.

The Psychodynamic Perspective

This perspective emphasizes the role of conflict or crises in development. Freud proposed a theory of personality that included the id, ego, and superego; he also proposed a theory of psychosexual development in which the focus of physical pleasure shifts to different parts of the body. Erikson proposed a life-span theory of psychosocial development, consisting of eight universal stages, each characterized by a particular struggle.

The Learning Perspective

Learning theory focuses on the development of observable behavior. Operant conditioning is based on the notions of reinforcement, punishment, and environmental control of behavior. Social learning theory proposes that people learn by observing others. Social cognitive theory emphasizes that children actively interpret the events they observe.

Cognitive-Developmental Theory

Cognitive-developmental theory focuses on thought processes. Piaget proposed a four-stage universal sequence based on the notion that, throughout development, people create their own theories to explain how the world works. According to information-processing theory, people deal with information as a computer does; development consists of increased efficiency in handling information.

The Contextual Perspective

Vygotsky emphasized the role of culture in children's development and Bronfenbrenner proposed that development occurs in the context of interconnected systems. These range from the microsystem (people and objects in the child's immediate environment) to the macrosystem (the cultures and subcultures in which all the other systems are embedded).

1.3 Themes in Child-Development Research

Four themes help unify the findings from child-development research that are presented throughout this book.

Early Development Is Related to Later Development but Not Perfectly

According to the view that development is continuous, children stay on the same pathway throughout development; according to the view that development is discontinuous, children can change paths at virtually any point in development. Research supports an intermediate view: Development is not completely rigid as in the continuous view, nor is it completely flexible as in the discontinuous view.

Development Is Always Jointly Influenced by Heredity and Environment

The nature-nurture issue involves the extent to which heredity and the environment influence children's development. Today scientists view heredity and environment as interactive forces that work together to chart the course of development.

Children Help Determine Their Own Development

Scientists once viewed children primarily as passive recipients of experience who are at the mercy of their environments. Today's view, however, is that children constantly interpret their experiences and, by their individual characteristics, often influence the experiences they have.

Development in Different Domains Is Connected

Although researchers usually study separate aspects of children's development, in reality development in different domains of children's lives is always connected. Cognitive development affects social development and vice-versa.

Research in Child Development

Chapter

2

When you think of research, what comes to mind? Maybe the chemicals and test tubes of a chemistry lab? Perhaps the telescope of an observatory? Or maybe the particle accelerator of high-energy physics? Test tubes, telescopes, and particle accelerators are indeed important tools for chemists, astronomers, and physicists. Like these other sciences, child-development research depends upon important tools, which I'll describe in this chapter. I begin, in Module 2.1, by explaining the techniques that researchers use to study children and their development. Then in Module 2.2, I show how child-development research can be used to create more informed public policies concerning children and their families.

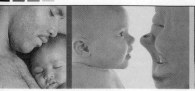

Doing Child-Development Research

2.1

■ How do scientists measure topics of interest in children's development?

■ What general research designs are used in child-development research? What designs are unique to child-development research?

■ What ethical procedures must researchers follow?

■ How do researchers communicate results to other scientists?

> *Leah and Joan are both mothers of 10-year-old boys. Their sons have many friends, but the basis for the friendships are not obvious to the mothers. Leah believes that "opposites attract"—children form friendships with peers who have complementary interests and abilities. Joan doubts this; her son seems to seek out other boys who are near clones of himself in their interests and abilities.*

Suppose that Leah and Joan know you're taking a course in child development, so they ask you to settle their argument. You know, from Module 1.2, that Leah and Joan each have simple theories about children's friendships. Leah's theory is that complementary children are more often friends, whereas Joan's theory is that similar children are more often friends. And you know that these theories should be tested with research. But how? In fact, child-development researchers must make several important decisions as they prepare to study a topic. They need to decide how to measure the topic of interest; they must design their study; they must be sure their proposed research respects the rights of the individuals participating; and, once the study is complete, they must communicate their results to other researchers.

Child-development researchers do not always stick to this sequence of steps. For example, often researchers consider the rights of research participants as they make each of the other decisions, perhaps rejecting a procedure because it violates the rights of research participants. Nevertheless, for simplicity, I will use this sequence as I describe the steps in doing developmental research.

Measurement in Child-Development Research

Research usually begins by deciding how to measure the topic or behavior of interest. For example, the first step toward answering Leah and Joan's question about friendships would be to decide how to measure friendships. Child-development researchers typically use one of three approaches: observing systematically, using tasks to sample behavior, and asking children for self reports.

Systematic Observation. As the name implies, *systematic observation* involves **watching children and carefully recording what they do or say.** Two forms of systematic observation are common. In *naturalistic observation,* **children are observed as they behave spontaneously in some real-life situation.** Of course, researchers can't keep track of everything that a child does. **Beforehand they must**

decide which *variables*—factors subject to change—to record. Researchers studying friendship might, for example, decide to observe children in a school lunchroom like the one in the photo at the right. They would record where each child sits and who talks to whom. Further, they might decide to observe children at the start of the first year in a middle school, because many children make new friends at this time.

In *structured observation*, the researcher creates a setting that is likely to elicit the behavior of interest. Structured observations are particularly useful for studying behaviors that are difficult to observe naturally. Some phenomena occur rarely, such as emergencies. An investigator using natural observations to study children's responses to emergencies wouldn't make much progress because, by definition, emergencies don't occur at predetermined times and locations. However, using structured observation, an investigator might stage an emergency, perhaps by having a nearby adult cry for help and observing children's responses.

Other behaviors are difficult for researchers to observe because they occur in private settings, not public ones. For example, much interaction between friends takes place at home, where it would be difficult for investigators to observe unobtrusively. However, children who are friends could be asked to come to the researcher's laboratory, which might be furnished with comfortable chairs and tables. They would be asked to perform some activity typical of friends, such as playing a game or deciding what movie to see. By observing friends' interactions in a setting like the one in the photo (perhaps through a one-way mirror), researchers could learn more about how friends interact.

Though structured observations allow researchers to observe behaviors that would otherwise be difficult to study, investigators must be careful that the settings they create do not disturb the behavior of interest. For instance, observing friends as they play a game in a mock family room has many artificial aspects to it: The friends are not in their own homes, they were told (in general terms) what to do, and they know they're being observed. Any or all of these factors may cause children to behave differently than they would in the real world. Researchers must be careful that their method does not distort the behavior they are observing.

Sampling Behavior with Tasks. When investigators can't observe a behavior directly, an alternative is to create tasks that are thought to sample the behavior of interest. For example, to measure memory, investigators sometimes use a digit span task: Children listen as a sequence of numbers is presented aloud. After the last digit is presented, children try to repeat the digits in order. To measure children's ability to recognize different emotions, investigators sometimes use the task shown in the diagram. The child has been asked to look at the photographs and point to the person who is happy.

FIG 2-1

Sampling behavior with tasks is popular with child-development researchers because it is so convenient. A major problem with this approach, however, is whether the task really samples the behavior of interest. For example, asking children to judge emotions from photographs may not be valid, because it underestimates what children do in real life. Can you think of reasons why this might be the case? I mention several reasons on page 41, just before Check Your Learning.

Self Reports. The last approach to measurement, using self reports, is actually a special case of using tasks to measure children's behavior. *Self reports* **are simply children's answers to questions about the topic of interest.** When questions are posed in written form, the report is a questionnaire; when questions are posed orally, the report is an interview. In either format, questions are created that probe different aspects of the topic of interest. For example, if you believe that children more often become friends when they have interests in common, then research participants might be told the following:

> *Tom and Dave just met each other at school. Tom likes to read, plays the clarinet in the school orchestra, and is not interested in sports; Dave likes to watch videos on MTV, plays video games, and is a star on the soccer team. Do you think Tom and Dave will become friends?*

Children would decide, perhaps using a rating scale, if the boys are likely to become friends.

Self reports are useful because they can lead directly to information on the topic of interest. They are also relatively convenient (particularly when they can be administered to groups of children or adolescents). However, self reports are not always valid measures of children's behavior, because children's answers are sometimes inaccurate. Why? When asked about past events, children may not remember them accurately. For example, an adolescent asked about childhood friends may not remember those friendships well. Also, children sometimes answer incorrectly due to response bias. That is, some responses may be more socially acceptable than others, and children are more likely to select those than socially unacceptable answers. For example, many children would be reluctant to admit that they have no friends at all. But, as long as investigators keep these weaknesses in mind, self reports are a valuable tool for child-development research.

The three approaches to measurement are summarized in the table:

> Child-development researchers use systematic observation, sampling behavior with tasks, and self reports to study children's development.

Ways of Measuring Behavior in Child-Development Research		
Method	**Strength**	**Weakness**
Systematic observation		
Naturalistic observation	Captures children's behavior in its natural setting	Difficult to use with behaviors that are rare or private
Structured observation	Can be used to study behaviors that are rare or private	May be invalid if the structured setting distorts the behavior
Sampling behavior with tasks	Convenient: can be used to study most behaviors	May be invalid if the task does not sample behavior as it occurs naturally
Self reports (questionnaires and interviews)	Convenient: can be used to study most behaviors	May be invalid because children answer incorrectly due to forgetting or bias

TABLE 2–1

After researchers choose a method of measurement, they must show that it is both reliable and valid. **A measure is *reliable* if the results are consistent over time.** A measure of friendship, for example, would be reliable to the extent that it yields the same results about friendship each time it is administered. All measures used in child-development research must be shown to be reliable, or they cannot be used. **A measure is *valid* if it really measures what researchers think it measures.** For example, a measure of friendship is only valid if it can be shown to actually measure friendship (and not, for example, popularity).

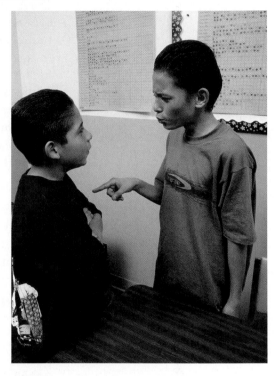

Validity is often established by showing that the measure in question is closely related to another measure known to be valid. We could show the validity of a questionnaire that claims to measure friendship by showing that scores on the questionnaire are related to peers' and parents' measures of friendship. Because it is possible to have a measure that is reliable but not valid (e.g., a ruler reliably measures length, but is not a valid measure of friendship), researchers must ensure that their measures are *both* reliable *and* valid.

Throughout this book, you'll come across many studies using these different methods. You'll also see that studies of the same topic or behavior often use different methods. That is because many topics can be studied in different ways. This is very desirable: Because the approaches to measurement have different strengths and weaknesses, finding the same results regardless of the approach leads to particularly strong conclusions. Suppose, for example, that a researcher using self reports claimed that arguments, like the one shown in the photo, are more common in boys' friendships than in girls' friendships. It would be reassuring that other investigators have found the same result from systematic observation and from sampling behavior with tasks.

Representative Sampling. Valid measures depend not only upon the method of measurement, but also upon the children who are tested. **Researchers are usually interested in broad groups of children called *populations*.** Examples of populations would be all American 7-year-olds or all African American adolescents. However, it would be extremely difficult for researchers to study every member of such large groups. **Virtually all studies include only a *sample* of children, which is a subset of the population.** Researchers must take care that their sample really is representative of the population of interest. An unrepresentative sample can lead to invalid research. For example, what would you think of a study of children's friendship if you learned that the sample consisted entirely of 8-year-olds who had no friends? You would, quite correctly, decide that this sample is not representative of the population of 8-year-olds, and you would therefore question its results.

As you read on, you'll discover that much of the research I describe was conducted with samples of middle-class European American youngsters. Are these samples representative of all children in the United States? Of children like those in the photo who grow up in developing countries? Sometimes, but not always. Be careful not to assume that findings from this group necessarily apply to people in other groups.

General Designs for Research

Having selected a way to measure the topic or behavior of interest, researchers must then put this measure into a research design. Child-development researchers usually use one of two designs: correlational or experimental studies.

Correlational Studies. In a *correlational study*, investigators look at relations between variables as they exist naturally in the world. In the simplest possible correlational study, a researcher measures two variables, then sees how they are related. Imagine a researcher who wants to test the idea that smarter children have more friends. To test this claim, the researcher would measure two variables for each child in the sample. One would be the number of friends that the child has; the other would be the child's intelligence.

The results of a correlational study are usually expressed as a *correlation coefficient*, abbreviated *r*, which stands for the direction and strength of a relation between two variables. Correlations can range from -1.0 to 0 to +1.0:

- When *r* equals 0, two variables are completely unrelated: Children's intelligence is unrelated to the number of friends they have.

- When *r* is greater than 0, scores are related positively: Children who are smart tend to have more friends than children who are not as smart. That is, more intelligence is associated with having more friends.

- When *r* is less than 0, scores are related, but inversely: Children who are smart tend to have fewer friends than children who are not as smart. That is, more intelligence is associated with having fewer friends.

In interpreting a correlation coefficient, you need to consider both the sign *and* the size of the correlation. The sign indicates the direction of the relation between variables: a positive sign means that larger values on one variable are associated with larger values on the second variable, whereas a negative sign means that larger values on one variable are associated with smaller values on a second variable.

The strength of a relation is measured by how much the correlation differs from 0, either positively or negatively. If the correlation between intelligence and number of friends were 0.9, this would indicate a very strong relation between these variables. Knowing a child's intelligence, you could accurately predict how many friends the child has. If, instead, the correlation were 0.3, this would indicate a relatively weak link between intelligence and number of friends. Although more intelligent children would have more friends on the average, there would be many exceptions to this rule. (Similarly, a correlation of -0.9 would indicate a strong negative relation between intelligence and number of friends, but a correlation of -0.3 would indicate a weak negative relation.)

The results of a correlational study tell whether variables are related, but this design doesn't address the question of cause and effect between the variables. In other words, suppose a researcher finds that the correlation between intelligence and number of friends is 0.7. This means that children who are smarter have more friends than those who are not as smart. How would you interpret this correlation? The top figure on page 35 shows that three interpretations are possible. Maybe being smart causes children to have more friends. Another interpretation is that having more friends causes children to be smarter. A third interpretation is that neither variable causes the other; instead, intelligence and number of friends are caused by a third variable that was not measured in the study. Perhaps parents who are warm and supportive tend to have children who are

Three Interpretations of a Correlation Coefficient

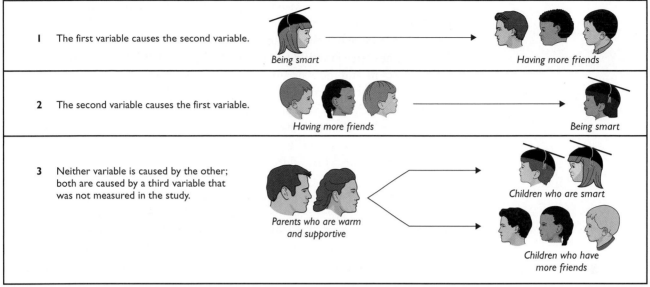

FIG 2-2

smart and who also have many friends. Any of these interpretations could be true. Cause and effect cannot be distinguished in a correlational study. When investigators want to track down causes, they must use a different design, an experimental study.

Experimental Studies. An *experiment* is a systematic way of manipulating the key factor(s) that an investigator thinks causes a particular behavior. The factor that is manipulated is called the *independent variable*; the behavior that is measured is called the *dependent variable.* In an experiment, the investigator begins with one or more treatments, circumstances, or events (independent variables) that are thought to affect a particular behavior. Children are then assigned randomly to different groups. Next, the dependent variable is measured in all groups. Because each child has an equal chance of being assigned to any group (the definition of random assignment), the groups should be the same except in the treatment they receive. Any differences between the groups can then be attributed to the differential treatment the children received in the experiment, rather than to other factors.

Suppose, for example, that an investigator believes children share more with friends than with children they do not know. The figure on the right shows how the investigator might test this hypothesis. Based on random assignment, some fifth-grade children would be asked to come to the investigator's laboratory with a good friend. Other fifth graders would come to the laboratory site without a friend and would be paired with a child unknown to them. The laboratory itself would be decorated to look like a family room in a house. The investigator creates a task in which one child is given an interesting toy to play with

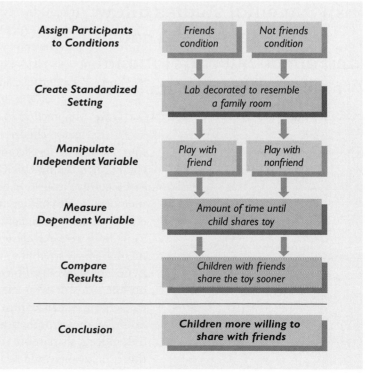

FIG 2-3

but the other child receives nothing. The experimenter explains the task to the children and then claims that she needs to leaves the room briefly. Actually, the experimenter goes to a room with a one-way mirror and observes whether the child with the toy offers to share it with the other child.

This same scenario would be used with all pairs of children. The room and toy would be the same and the experimenter would always be away for the same amount of time. The circumstances would be held as constant as possible for all children, except that some children participate with friends while others do not. If children who participated with friends give the toy more quickly or more readily to the other child, the investigator could say with confidence that children are more likely to share with their friends than with children they don't know. Conclusions about cause and effect are possible because there was a direct manipulation of an independent variable (participating with a friend or with an unknown child) under controlled conditions.

Child-development researchers usually conduct their experiments in laboratory-like settings to control all the variables that might influence the outcome of the research. A shortcoming of laboratory work is that the behavior of interest is not studied in its natural setting. Consequently, there is always the potential problem that the results may be invalid because they are artificial—specific to the laboratory setting and not representative of the behavior in the "real world."

To avoid this limitation, researchers sometimes rely upon a special type of experiment. **In a *field experiment*, the researcher manipulates independent variables in a natural setting so that the results are more likely to be representative of behavior in real-world settings.** To illustrate a field experiment, let's return to the hypothesis that children share more with friends. We might conduct the research in a classroom where students must complete a group assignment. In collaboration with teachers, children are placed in groups of three—in some groups, all three children are good friends; in others, the three children are acquaintances but not friends. When the assignment is complete, the teacher gives each group leader many stickers and tells the leader to distribute them to group members based on how much each child contributed. We predict that leaders will share more (i.e., distribute the stickers more evenly) when group members are friends than when they are not.

> Experimental studies allow conclusions about cause and effect, but correlational studies often are easier to conduct in natural settings.

Field experiments allow investigators to draw strong conclusions about cause and effect because they embed manipulation of an independent variable in a natural setting. However, field experiments are often impractical to conduct because of logistical problems. In most natural settings, children are supervised by adults (e.g., parents and teachers) who must be willing to become allies in the proposed research. Adults may not want to change their routines to fit a researcher's needs. In addition, researchers usually sacrifice some control in field experiments. In the example of distributing stickers to group members, some children no doubt actually worked harder than others, which means children's sharing will *not* be based simply on whether the other children are friends.

Both research designs used by developmentalists—correlational and experimental—have strengths and weaknesses. There is no one best method. Consequently, no single investigation can definitely answer a question, and researchers rarely rely on one study or even one method to reach conclusions. Instead, they prefer to find converging evidence from as many different kinds of studies as possible. Suppose, for example, our hypothetical laboratory and field experiments showed that children did, indeed, share more readily with their friends. One way to be more confident of this conclusion would be to do correlational research, perhaps by observing children during lunch and measuring how often they share food with different people.

Designs for Studying Development

Sometimes child-development research is directed at a single age group, such as fifth-grade children in the experiment on sharing between friends and nonfriends, memory in preschool-age children, or mother-infant relationships in 1-year-olds, like those shown in the photo. When this is the case, after deciding how to measure the behavior of interest and whether the study will be correlational or experimental, the investigator could skip directly to the last step and determine if the study is ethical. However, much research in child development concerns changes that occur as children develop over time. In these cases, investigators must make one further decision: Will they do a longitudinal study or a cross-sectional study?

Longitudinal Studies. In a *longitudinal study,* **the same individuals are observed or tested repeatedly at different points in their lives.** As the name implies, the longitudinal approach takes a lengthwise view of development and is the most direct way to watch growth occur. As the diagram shows, in a longitudinal study, children might be tested first at age 6 and then again at ages 9 and 12. The longitudinal approach is well suited to studying almost any aspect of development. More important, it is the only way to answer certain questions about the continuity or discontinuity of behavior: Will characteristics such as aggression, dependency, or mistrust observed in infancy or early childhood persist into adulthood? Will a traumatic event, such as being abandoned by one's parents, influence later social and intellectual development? How long will the beneficial effects of special academic training in the preschool years last? Such questions can be explored only by testing children early in development and then retesting them later.

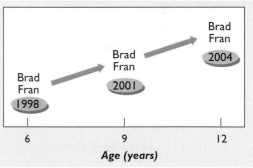

FIG 2–4

Usually the repeated testing of longitudinal studies extends over years, but not always. In a *microgenetic study,* **children are tested repeatedly over a span of days or weeks, typically with the aim of observing change directly as it occurs.** For example, researchers might test children every week, starting when they are 12 months old and continuing until 18 months. Microgenetic studies are particularly useful when investigators have hypotheses about a specific age when developmental change should occur.

The longitudinal approach, however, has disadvantages that frequently offset its strengths. When children are given the same test many times, they may become "test-wise." Improvement over time that is attributed to development may actually stem from practice with a particular test. Changing the test from one session to the next solves the practice problem but raises the question of how to compare responses to different tests. Another problem is the constancy of the sample over the course of research. It is difficult to maintain contact with children over time in a highly mobile society. And even among those who do not move away, some lose interest and choose not to continue. These "dropouts" are often significantly different from their more research-minded peers, and this fact alone may distort the outcome. For example, a group of children may seem to show intellectual growth between ages 4 and 7. What has actually happened, however, is that those who found earlier testing most difficult are the very ones who have quit the study, thereby raising the group average on the next round.

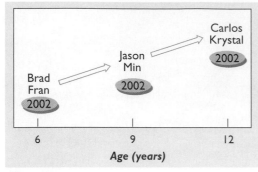

FIG 2–5

Because of these and other problems with the longitudinal method, child-development researchers often use cross-sectional studies instead.

Cross-sectional Studies. In a *cross-sectional study,* **developmental changes are identified by testing children of different ages at one point in their development.** In other words, as shown in the diagram, a researcher might chart the differences in some attribute between, for example, 6-, 9-, and 12-year-olds The cross-sectional approach avoids almost all the problems associated with repeated testing, including practice effects and sample loss. But cross-sectional research has its own weaknesses. Because children are tested at only one point in their development, we learn nothing about the continuity of development. Consequently, we cannot tell if an aggressive 4-year-old remains aggressive at age 10 because an individual child would be tested at age 4 or age 10, but not at both ages.

Cross-sectional studies are also affected by *cohort effects,* **meaning that differences between age groups (cohorts) may result as much from environmental events as from developmental processes.** In a simple cross-sectional study, we compare children from two age groups. If we find differences, we attribute them to the difference in age, but this needn't be the case. Why? The cross-sectional study assumes that when the older children were younger, they were like children in the younger age group. This isn't always true. Suppose, for example, that a researcher measures creativity in 8- and 14-year-olds. If the 8-year-olds are found to be more imaginative than the 14-year-olds, should we conclude that imagination declines between these ages? Not necessarily. Perhaps a new curriculum to nourish creativity was introduced in kindergarten and first grade, before the 8-year-olds entered these grades but after the older children had completed them. Because only the younger children experienced the curriculum, the difference between the two groups is difficult to interpret.

> Cross-sectional studies are more convenient but only longitudinal studies can answer questions about continuity of development.

Each of the two general research designs can be used with either of the two designs that are unique to studying development. When combined, four prototypic designs result: cross-sectional correlational studies, cross-sectional experimental studies, longitudinal correlational studies, and longitudinal experimental studies.

To illustrate the different possibilities, think back to our hypothetical laboratory experiment on children's sharing with friends and nonfriends (described on page 35). If we tested 7- and 11-year-olds with either friends or nonfriends, this would be a cross-sectional experimental study. If we tested 7-year-olds, then waited 4 years and tested them again, this would be a longitudinal experimental study. If, as suggested on page 36, we instead observed 7- and 11-year-olds' spontaneous sharing of food at lunch, this would be a cross-sectional correlational study. Finally, if we observed 7-year-olds' spontaneous sharing at lunch, then observed the same children four years later, this would be a longitudinal correlational study.

The different designs are summarized in Table 2–2. In this book, you'll read about studies using these various designs, although the two cross-sectional designs will show up more frequently than the two longitudinal designs. Why? For most developmentalists, the ease of cross-sectional studies compared to longitudinal studies more than compensates for the limitations of cross-sectional studies.

■■■■ SUMMARY TABLE

Designs Used in Child-Development Research

Type of Design	Definition	Strengths	Weaknesses
General Designs			
Correlational	Observe variables as they exist in the world and determine their relations	Behavior is measured as it occurs naturally	Cannot determine cause and effect
Experimental	Manipulate independent and dependent variables	Control of variables allows conclusions about cause and effect	Work is often laboratory-based, which can be artificial
Developmental Designs			
Longitudinal	One group of children is tested repeatedly as they develop	Only way to chart an individual's development and look at the continuity of behavior over time	Participants drop out and repeated testing can distort performance
Cross-sectional	Children of different ages are tested at the same time	Convenient, avoids problems associated with longitudinal studies	Cannot study continuity of behavior; cohort effects complicate interpretation of differences between groups

TABLE 2-2

Ethical Responsibilities

Having selected a way of measuring the behavior of interest and chosen appropriate general and developmental designs, one very important step remains. Researchers must determine whether their research is ethical, that it does not violate the rights of the children who participate in it. Professional organizations and government agencies have codes of conduct that specify the rights of research participants and procedures to protect those participants. The following guidelines are included in all those codes:

- *Minimize risks to research participants:* Use methods that have the least potential for harm or stress for research participants. During the research, monitor the procedures to be sure to avoid any unforeseen stress or harm.

- *Describe the research to potential participants so they can determine if they wish to participate*: Prospective research participants should be told all details of the research so they can make an informed decision about participating. Children are minors and are not legally capable of giving consent; consequently, as shown in the photo, researchers must describe the study to parents and ask them for permission for their children to participate.

- *Avoid deception; if participants must be deceived, provide a thorough explanation of the true nature of the research as soon as possible*: Providing complete information about a study in advance can sometimes bias or distort participants' responses. Consequently, investigators sometimes provide only partial information or even mislead participants about the true purpose of the study. As soon as it is feasible—typically just after the experiment—any false information must be corrected and the reasons for the deception must be provided.

- *Keep results anonymous or confidential*: Research results should be anonymous, which means that participants' data cannot be linked to their names. When anonymity is not possible, research results should be confidential, which means that only the investigator conducting the study knows the identities of the individuals.

Researchers must convince review boards consisting of scientists from many disciplines that they have carefully addressed each of these ethical points. Only then can they begin their study. If the review board objects to some aspects of the proposed study, the researcher must revise those aspects and present them anew for the review board's approval.

Communicating Research Results

When the study is complete and the data analyzed, researchers write a report of their work. This report describes, in great detail, what the researchers did and why, their results, and the meaning(s) behind their results. The researchers submit the report to one of several scientific journals that specialize in child-development research. Some of these are *Child Development, Developmental Psychology, Journal of Experimental Child Psychology, Infant Behavior and Development, Cognitive Development,* and *Social Development*. If the editor of the journal accepts the report, it appears in the journal, where other child-development researchers can learn of the results.

These reports of research are the basis for virtually all the information I present in this book. As you read, you'll see names in parentheses, followed by a date, like this: (Levine, 1983). This indicates the person who did the research and the year it was published. By looking in the References, which begin on page 517 and are organized alphabetically, you can find the title of the article and the journal where it was published.

Scientists communicate their results to other researchers by publishing them in scientific journals.

Maybe all these different steps in research seem tedious and involved to you. For a child-development researcher, however, much of the fun of doing research is planning a novel study that will provide useful information to other specialists. This is one of the most creative and challenging parts of child-development research.

The Focus on Research features that appear in the remaining chapters of this book are designed to convey both the creativity and the challenge of doing child-development research. Each feature focuses on a specific study. The table on page 41 lists all the studies that are described in the Focus on Research feature. Some are studies that have just recently been published; others are classics that defined a new area of investigation or provided definitive results in some area. In each Focus feature, we trace the decisions that researchers made as they planned their study. In the process, you'll see the ingenuity of researchers as they pursue questions of child development. You'll also see that any individual study has limitations. Only when converging evidence from many studies—each using a unique combination of measurement methods and designs—points to the same conclusion can we feel confident about research results.

Preview of "Focus on Research" Features	
Module	**Title**
3.1	Hereditary and Environmental Roots of Infants' Social Behavior
4.2	Impact of Prenatal Exposure to PCBs on Cognitive Functioning
5.4	Do Infants Integrate Sight and Sound When Others Speak?
6.1	What Do Infants Understand About Colliding Forces?
7.4	Temperament Influences Helping Others
8.2	Learning to Grip a Pen
9.1	Finding Toys in a Shrunken Room
10.4	Temperament, Parental Influence, and Self-Control
11.2	Why Participate in Organized Sports?
12.3	The Carolina Abecedarian Project
13.5	When Are Children in Self-Care at Risk?
14.2	How Parents Influence Adolescents' Sexual Behavior
15.1	Beliefs Can Interfere with Effective Reasoning
16.1	Identity in Children of Transracial Adoptions

TABLE 2-3

Responses to question on page 32 about using photographs to measure children's understanding of emotions: Children's understanding of emotions depicted in photographs may be less accurate than in real life because (1) in real life, facial features are usually moving—not still as in the photographs—and movement may be one of the clues that children naturally use to judge emotions; (2) in real life, facial expressions are often accompanied by sounds, and children use both sight and sound to understand emotion; and (3) in real life, children most often judge facial expressions of people they know (parents, siblings, peers, teachers), and knowing the "usual" appearance of a face may help children determine emotions accurately.

Check Your Learning

1. In _____, children are observed as they behave spontaneously in a real-life setting.

2. A problem with _____ is that children may give distorted answers due to response bias.

3. A _____ is a group of individuals considered representative of some larger population.

4. In a _____, investigators look at relations between variables as they exist naturally.

5. The _____ variable is measured in an experiment in order to evaluate the impact of the variable that was manipulated.

6. Problems of longitudinal studies include loss of research participants over time and _____.

7. Researchers must submit their plans for research to a review board that determines if the research _____.

8. Child-development scientists report the findings of their research by _____.

 **Connections:** Suppose that you wanted to determine the impact of divorce on children's academic achievement. What would be the merits of correlational versus experimental research on this topic? How would a longitudinal study differ from a cross-sectional study?

Answers: (1) naturalistic observation, (2) self-report, (3) sample, (4) correlational study, (5) dependent, (6) influence of repeated testing on children's performance, (7) preserves the rights of research participants, (8) publishing them in a scientific journal

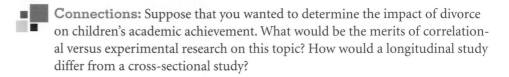

Child-Development Research and Family Policy

2.2

Child-Development Research and Family Policy

- Background
- Ways to Influence Social Policy
- An Emphasis on Policy Implications Improves Research

Learning Objectives

■ Why have child-development researchers recently become more involved in designing social policy?

■ How do child-development researchers influence family policy?

■ How has concern for family policy improved child-development research?

> Kendra loved her 12-month-old son Roosevelt, but she was eager to return to her job as a loan officer at a local bank. Kendra knew a woman in her neighborhood who had cared for some of her friends' children and they all thought she was wonderful. But down deep Kendra wished she knew more about whether this type of care was really best for Roosevelt. She also wished that this woman's day-care center had a "stamp of approval" from someone who knew how to evaluate these facilities.

The vignette about Kendra introduces the topics that form the title of this module: "Child-Development Research" and "Family Policy." Kendra wishes that child-development research could tell her more about the impact of day-care experiences on her son's development. **Family policy refers to laws and regulations that directly or indirectly affect families with children.** Kendra wishes that experts had used child-development research to create policies for child-care facilities and had certified that the neighbor's facility met those standards. In the rest of this module, we'll explore how research is used to foster children's development through sound family policies.

Background

Child-development researchers have long been interested in applying their work to improving children's lives. After all, when a researcher does an experiment and discovers that one set of conditions enhances children's growth but a second set does not, it would seem natural to use that knowledge to form standards and policies.

Links between child development and family policy have become much stronger in recent years. One reason for the stronger link is that families are changing in America (Zigler, 1998). The "traditional" family in which children are cared for by a stay-at-home mom and a working dad has given way to families with a single parent, families in which both parents are employed outside the home, and families with stepparents and half-siblings. Researchers and parents alike have been concerned about the potential impact of changing family arrangements. These changes in family life raise questions that trouble child-development professionals, parents, and policy-makers alike. For example, when parents divorce, who should receive custody of the children? When children like the baby in the photo spend most days at a child-care facility, what are the effects? Child-development researchers now work to provide data-based answers to questions like these.

Child-development researchers have also been prompted by evidence showing that many American youngsters—particularly those who are members of minority groups—face hurdles on the road to healthy development (Garfinkel, Hochschild, & McLanahan, 1996). Just as the Consumer Price Index or the Gross Domestic Product integrate several sources of data to serve as a barometer of the nation's economic health, the Index of Social Health for Children and Youth (ISHCY) integrates different kinds of evidence to assess the well-being of the nation's children (Miringoff & Miringoff, 1999; Miringoff, Miringoff, & Opdycke, 1996). Contributing to the ISHCY are variables such as infant mortality, child abuse, family poverty, teenage suicide, and teenage drug use. The graph, which depicts annual changes in the ISHCY, shows that America's children and youth faced ever-greater challenges at the end of the 20th century.

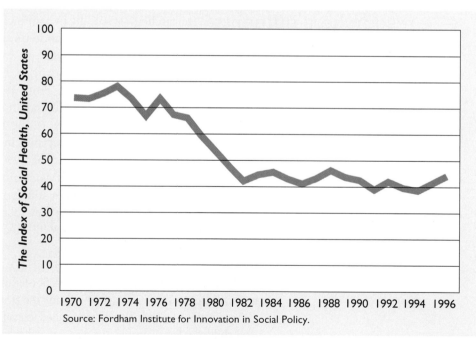

Source: Fordham Institute for Innovation in Social Policy.

FIG 2–6

Because of societal changes affecting American's children, many child-development researchers now participate actively in designing and implementing social policy concerning children and their families. In the next section, we'll look at the many different roles that child-development researchers play in formulating social policy.

Ways to Influence Social Policy

Child-development researchers contribute to sound family policy through a number of distinct pathways (White, 1996).

Build Understanding of Children and Their Development. When city officials decide how to solve traffic congestion during rush hour, they consult with transportation experts for background information and potential solutions. Similarly, when government officials need to address problems affecting children, child-development experts can provide useful information about children and their development. That is, sound policies should be based on accurate understanding of the key factors involved, not on stereotypes or assumptions about children and youth (Gilliam & Bales, 2001). For example, policy-making concerning adolescents is often unduly influenced by stereotypes of teenagers as irresponsible and defiant. In fact, as we'll see later in this book, most adolescents are neither, and to base policy for teens on these stereotypes can make for ineffective family policy. Thus, child-development researchers contribute to policy-making by ensuring that the general consideration of policy issues and options is based on factual knowledge derived from child-development research.

Serve as an Advocate for Children. Children are ill prepared to represent their own interests. They cannot vote and do not have the financial resources to hire lobbyists or prepare media campaigns. Often parents like to serve as advocates for their children, but individual parents usually lack the expertise and resources to represent children adequately. However, child-development researchers—typically in conjunction with a child advocacy group—can alert policymakers to children's needs and can argue for family policy that addresses those needs.

> Child-development researchers influence family policy by providing needed knowledge, acting as advocates for children, evaluating programs, and devising model programs.

One well-known advocacy group for children was Action for Children's Television (ACT). From 1968 until 1992, ACT worked to ensure quality television for children and to regulate the kinds of commercials aimed at children. With strong backing from ACT (and despite stiff opposition from the television industry), the U.S. Congress passed the Children's Television Act of 1990. This law required that the Federal Communications Commission, as it determines whether to renew a station's broadcast license, consider whether the station's programming meets children's needs. Child-development scientists were key players in ACT's efforts because their research demonstrated both the harmful effects of bad TV programs and the beneficial effects of good ones.

Evaluate Policies and Programs. Sometimes policies and programs affect families and children even though they are not the primary targets of the policy. In this case, child-development experts may be called to evaluate aspects of policy that affect families and children. For example, the aims of welfare reform have been to reduce the amount of money spent on welfare and to encourage people to be economically self-sufficient (i.e., to have more people support themselves through work rather than depending primarily on welfare payments). Consequently, most evaluations of welfare reform focus on changes in spending and employment. Yet changes in welfare programs may also affect families and children.

In evaluating the impact of policies on families and children, child-development researchers have two important tools. One is existing theory and research in child development, which can indicate how policy features are likely to affect families and children. For example, welfare reform includes mechanisms to encourage parents to pay child support. Research suggests that noncustodial parents, like the father in the photo, stay more involved with their children when they pay child support. Not surprisingly, their children benefit from this involvement. Thus, in this respect, welfare reform might benefit children.

A second important tool that child-development researchers can provide is a large catalog of methods to assess family functioning and child development. If, for example, policymakers are concerned that welfare reform may cause mothers to parent less effectively, a child-development researcher can offer a set of well-tested methods for measuring parental skill. Thus, by using existing findings to indicate the likely impact of policies and by providing proven methods to measure impact, child-development researchers can help judge how families and children are affected by policies.

Develop a Model Program. Elected officials usually like results, so one of the best ways to sway policymakers is to create an actual program that works. In other words, develop a program to combat "X" (where X could be teenage pregnancy, drug abuse, or infant mortality, for example), implement the program on a small scale, then show that it does indeed reduce "X." This tack is more complicated than some of the others I've mentioned because it requires obtaining resources to start the untested program as well as convincing families they should be "guinea pigs" in a program that may not work. Nevertheless, when this approach works, the outcome is powerful ammunition for influencing policymakers.

The School of the 21st Century (21C) illustrates this approach (Zigler & Gilman, 1996). Devised in the mid-1980s to meet the dual needs for improved child care and more successful schools, 21C includes year-round all-day care for preschool children as well as before-school, after-school, and vacation care for school-age children. The program also includes guidance for parents through home visits by parent educators like the one in the photo. Other components are a referral service that provides information about community services available to families and their children, health care, and training for child-care providers. Participation in the different program elements is voluntary; if, for example, a parent is home to care for a preschool child, that child is not forced to attend day care.

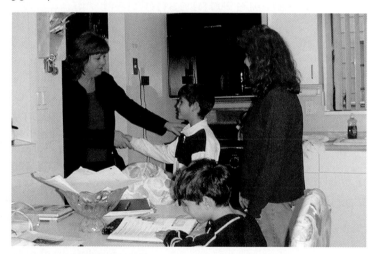

The 21C program was launched in 1988 in one city and has now spread to more than 500 schools across the United States. Research shows that children attending 21C schools learn more and have fewer behavioral problems; in addition, their parents are more involved in school and report less stress associated with arranging adequate child care (e.g., Finn-Stevenson, Desimone, & Chung, 1998). Based on this success, legislatures in Connecticut and Kentucky have made 21C the model for schools statewide. And 21C is a textbook example of first showing that a program effectively addresses a problem, then letting that success convince policymakers on a wider scale.

An Emphasis on Policy Implications Improves Research

Child-development research undoubtedly can lead to more informed policies toward children and their families. Less obvious is that the reverse is also true. When child-development scientists conduct their work with one eye focused on the public policy implications, the usual result is improved theory and research. One improvement is a greater emphasis on broader, more inclusive models of children and their development. When doing basic research, a common tactic is for scientists to simplify the problem, often by examining certain aspects of children's development but not others. One researcher might study how reading improves as children grow; a second researcher might look at how children benefit from having friends; a third might examine parents' influence on children's self-control. In contrast, when formulating programs for children, policymakers cannot use the basic researcher's "slice and dice" approach, because in real children these different elements—their reading skills, their friendships, their parents' influence—are all interconnected. Change in one element can often lead to change in another. Consequently, a focus on family policy forces researchers to take a much broader perspective on child development than they might otherwise.

> An emphasis on policy improves research by forcing scientists to take a broader perspective and to use more sophisticated research designs.

A concern for family policy has also improved the methods used by researchers. As I described in Module 2.1, the strongest claims about cause and effect come from experiments, in which participants are assigned randomly to various experimental conditions. Unfortunately, random assignment is often impossible in policy-oriented research, for pragmatic or ethical reasons. Obviously, we cannot randomly assign children to high-school-educated versus college-educated parents or to single- versus dual-parent families. Consequently, child-development researchers and statisticians have devised more powerful correlational methods that permit some statements about causality (West, Biesanz, & Pitts, 2000). **A *quasi-experimental design* includes multiple groups that are not formed by random assignment.** For example, researchers might want to compare children's reading level at the end of a school year in two schools, one using a traditional reading curriculum and another using an innovative curriculum. Because children were not assigned randomly to the two schools, this is a quasi-experiment. Children in the two schools might differ in reading or reading-related skills at the beginning of the year, prior to the onset of reading instruction. New methods allow researchers to account for such possible differences—using statistics to equate the groups of children at the beginning of the year—thereby making it easier to compare them at the end of the year and make conclusions about causality.

The message here should be clear. Closer links between child-development research and family produces better policy and better research. To emphasize this connection, many of the other chapters in this book have a feature called Child Development and Family Policy. These features, which are listed in Table 2-4 on page 47, provide a concrete example of the close ties between research and policy.

Preview of "Child Development and Family Policy" Features	
Module	**Title**
3.3	Screening for PKU
4.3	Back to Sleep
7.2	Determining Guidelines for Child Care for Infants and Toddlers
9.4	Providing Children with a Head Start for School
10.3	Assessing the Consequences of China's One-Child Policy
12.5	How Can Computers Promote Child Development?
13.2	Ending Segregated Schools
14.1	Preventing Osteoporosis
15.2	Promoting More Advanced Moral Reasoning
16.3	Preventing Violence

TABLE 2–4

Check Your Learning

1. Links between child-development research and family have become stronger because of changes in the family and because _____.

2. Child-development researchers contribute to policymaking by ensuring that discussion of issues is based on factual knowledge of children, by _____, by evaluating existing policies, and by developing model programs.

3. Concern for public policy has improved research by forcing researchers to take a broader perspective on children's development and through _____.

■ **Connections:** Suppose a child-development researcher was interested in the impact of nutrition on children's physical and cognitive development. Describe several different ways in which the researcher might help to form public policy concerning children's nutrition.

Answers: (1) measures of social health suggest that many children face numerous obstacles on the road to healthy development, (2) acting as advocates for children, (3) the development of more sophisticated research methods

Chapter Critical Review

1. Choose a topic in child development that interests you (some ideas are the effects of day care on infants and toddlers, or the relation between parenting style and a child's popularity with peers; the possibilities are endless). Working through the steps described in Module 2.1, design a research project that could be used to study the topic you have chosen.

2. Go to your library and find an issue of a child-developmental journal, such as *Child Development, Developmental Psychology*, or *Journal of Experimental Child Psychology*. Go through the issue and classify each study into one of the four principal categories (e.g., cross-sectional experimental, longitudinal correlational). What type of study is most common?

3. Explain in your own words why investigators can make judgments about causation when they use experimental research designs but not when they use correlational designs.

4. Find a newspaper report of child-development research. Determine what the investigators were trying to discover, and summarize their results. Do the results have public policy implications? If so, what impact are the investigators having on legislation or public policy?

For more review material, log on to www.prenhall.com/kail

See For Yourself

A good first step toward learning about child-development research is to read the reports of research that scientists publish in journals. Visit your library and locate some of the child-development journals mentioned on page 40. Look at the contents of an issue to get an idea of the many different topics that child-development researchers study. When you find an article on a topic that interests you, skim the contents and try to determine what design the investigator(s) used. See for yourself!

For More Information About . . .

 conducting research with children, I recommend Scott A. Miller's ***Developmental Research Methods,*** 2nd ed. (Prentice-Hall, 1998) for a clear description of all phases of doing developmental research, beginning with measurement and ending with a written report of the project.

 research in child development, visit the Web site of the Society for Research in Child Development (SRCD):
http://www.srcd.org

Key Terms

cohort effects 38	**field experiment** 36	**reliability** 33
correlation coefficient 34	**independent variable** 35	**sample** 33
correlational study 34	**longitudinal study** 37	**self reports** 32
cross-sectional study 38	**microgenetic study** 37	**structured observation** 31
dependent variable 35	**naturalistic observation** 30	**systematic observation** 30
experiment 35	**quasi-experimental design** 46	**validity** 33
family policy 42	**population** 33	**variable** 31

2.1 Doing Child-Development Research

Measurement in Child-Development Research

Research typically begins by determining how to measure the topic of interest. Systematic observation involves recording children's behavior as it takes place, either in a natural environment (naturalistic observation) or in a structured setting (structured observation). Researchers sometimes create tasks to obtain samples of children's behavior. In self reports, children answer questions posed by the experimenter. Researchers must also obtain a sample that is representative of some larger population.

General Designs for Research

In correlational studies, investigators examine relations between variables as they occur naturally. This relation is measured by a correlation coefficient, r, which can vary from -1 (strong negative relation) to 0 (no relation) to +1 (strong positive relation). Correlational studies cannot determine cause and effect, so researchers do experimental studies in which they manipulate an independent variable to determine the impact on a dependent variable. Experimental studies allow conclusions about cause and effect but the strict control of all possible variables often makes the situation artificial. Field studies involve manipulation of independent variables in a natural setting. The best approach is to use both experimental and correlational studies to provide converging evidence.

Designs for Studying Development

To study development, some researchers use a longitudinal design in which the same children are observed repeatedly as they grow. This approach provides evidence of actual patterns of individual growth but has shortcomings: repeated testing can affect performance and some children drop out of the project. The cross-sectional design involves testing children in different age groups. This design avoids the problems of the longitudinal design but provides no information about individual growth. Also, what appear to be differences due to age may be cohort effects. Because neither design is problem-free, the best approach is to use both to provide converging evidence.

Ethical Responsibilities

Planning research also involves selecting methods that preserve the rights of research participants. Experimenters must minimize the risks to potential research participants, describe the research so that potential participants can decide if they want to participate, avoid deception, and keep results anonymous or confidential.

Communicating Research Results

Once research data are collected and analyzed, investigators publish the results in scientific journals where they can be read and criticized by others. Such results form the foundation of scientific knowledge about child development.

2.2 Child-Development Research and Family Policy

Background

Child-development researchers have become increasingly interested in applying the results of their work to family policy because of many changes in the American family and because changes in infant mortality, child abuse, and other variables indicate that American children and youth face many challenges to healthy development.

Ways to Influence Social Policy

Child-development researchers help to shape family policy by providing useful knowledge about children and their development so that policies can be based on accurate information about children. They also contribute by serving as advocates for children, by evaluating the impact of programs on families and children, and by developing effective programs that can be implemented elsewhere.

An Emphasis on Policy Implications Improves Research

Focusing on public policy implications improves research because researchers must take a broader perspective on children's development than they would otherwise. Also, policy-related research has produced more sophisticated research methods, such as the quasi-experimental design.

Genetic Bases of
Child Development

Chapter 3

I wish I had a dollar for every time my parents or in-laws said about one of my children, "he (or she) comes by that naturally." Their comment was usually prompted because the child had just done something exactly as my wife or I did at the same age. By their remarks, grandparents are reminding us that some behavioral characteristics are inherited from parents just as physical characteristics like height and hair color are inherited.

In this chapter, we'll see how heredity influences children and their development. We'll start, in Module 3.1, by examining the basic mechanisms of heredity. In Module 3.2, we'll focus on disorders that some children inherit. Finally, in Module 3.3, we'll see how the environment is crucial in determining the way that heredity influences development.

Mechanisms of Heredity

3.1

Mechanisms of Heredity

├ The Biology of Heredity

├ Single Gene Inheritance

└ Behavioral Genetics

Learning Objectives

■ **What are chromosomes and genes?**

■ **What are dominant and recessive traits? How are they inherited?**

■ **How does heredity influence behavioral and psychological development?**

Leslie and Glenn have decided to try to have a baby. They are thrilled at the thought of starting their own family but also worried because Leslie's grandfather had sickle cell disease and died when he was just 20. Leslie is terrified that their baby could inherit the disease that killed her grandfather. Leslie and Glenn wish someone could reassure them that their baby would be okay.

How could we reassure Leslie and Glenn? For starters, we need to know more about sickle cell disease. Red blood cells like the ones in the left photo carry oxygen and carbon dioxide to and from the body.

When a person has sickle cell disease, the red blood cells look like those in the right photo—long and curved like a sickle: These stiff, misshapen cells cannot pass through small capillaries, so oxygen cannot reach all parts of the body. The trapped sickle cells also block the way of white blood cells that are the body's natural defense against bacteria. As a result, people with sickle cell disease—including Leslie's grandfather and many other African Americans, who are more prone to this painful disease than other groups—often die from infections before age 20.

Sickle cell disease is inherited and because Leslie's grandfather had the disorder, it apparently runs in her family. Would Leslie's baby inherit the disease? To answer this question, we need to examine the mechanisms of heredity.

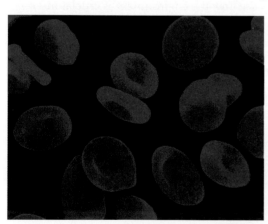
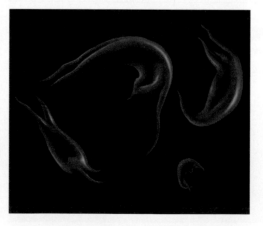

The Biology of Heredity

The teaspoon of semen released into the vagina during an ejaculation contains from 200 million to 500 million sperm. Only a few hundred of these actually complete the 6- or 7-inch journey to the fallopian tubes. If an egg is present, many sperm simultaneously begin to burrow their way through the cluster of nurturing cells that surround the egg. When a sperm like the one in the photo at the top of page 53 penetrates the cellular wall of the egg, chemical changes that occur immediately block out all other sperm. **Each egg and sperm cell contains 23 *chromosomes*, tiny**

structures in the nucleus that contain genetic material. When a sperm penetrates an egg, their chromosomes combine to produce 23 pairs of chromosomes. The development of a new human being is underway.

For most of history, the merger of sperm and egg took place only after sexual intercourse. No longer. In 1978, Louise Brown captured the world's attention as the first test-tube baby conceived in a laboratory dish instead of in her mother's body. Today, this reproductive technology is no longer experimental; it is a multi-billion-dollar business in the United States (Beck, 1994). Many new techniques are available to couples who cannot conceive a child through sexual intercourse. **The best-known, *in vitro fertilization,* involves mixing sperm and egg together in a laboratory dish and then placing several fertilized eggs in the mother's uterus.** The photo shows this laboratory version of conception, with the sperm in the dropper being placed in the dish containing the eggs. If the eggs are fertilized, in about 24 hours they are placed in the mother's uterus, with the hope that they will become implanted in the wall of her uterus.

The sperm and egg usually come from the prospective parents, but sometimes they are provided by donors. Occasionally the fertilized egg is placed in the uterus of a surrogate mother who carries the baby throughout pregnancy. Thus, a baby could have as many as five "parents": the man and woman who provide the sperm and egg; the surrogate mother who carries the baby; and the mother and father who rear the child.

New reproductive techniques offer hope for couples who have long wanted a child, but there are difficulties. Only about 20 percent of attempts at in vitro fertilization succeed. And when a woman becomes pregnant, she is more likely to have twins or triplets because multiple eggs are transferred to increase the odds that at least one fertilized egg will implant in the mother's uterus. These problems emphasize that, although technology has increased the alternatives for infertile couples, pregnancy on demand is still in the realm of science fiction.

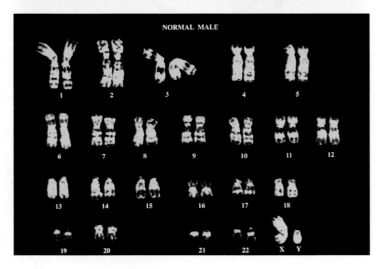

NORMAL MALE

Whatever the source of the egg and sperm, and wherever they meet, their merger is a momentous event: The resulting 23 pairs of chromosomes define a child's heredity—what he or she "will do naturally." For Leslie and Glenn, this moment also determines whether or not their child inherits sickle cell disease.

To understand how heredity influences child development, let's begin by taking a closer look at chromosomes. The photo shows all 46 chromosomes, organized in pairs ranging from the largest to the smallest. **The first 22 pairs of chromosomes are called *autosomes*; the chromosomes in each pair are about the same size.** In the 23rd pair, however, the chromosome labeled X is much larger than the chromosome labeled Y. **The 23rd pair determines the sex of the child and, hence, these two are**

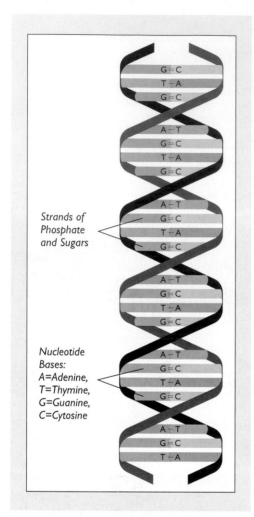

Strands of
Phosphate
and Sugars

Nucleotide
Bases:
A=Adenine,
T=Thymine,
G=Guanine,
C=Cytosine

FIG 3–1

known as the *sex chromosomes.* An egg always contains an X 23rd chromosome, but a sperm contains either an X or a Y. When an X-carrying sperm fertilizes the egg, the 23rd pair is XX and the result is a girl. When a Y-carrying sperm fertilizes the egg, the 23rd pair is XY and the result is a boy.

Each chromosome actually consists of one molecule of *deoxyribonucleic acid*—DNA for short. The DNA molecule resembles a spiral staircase. As you can see in the diagram, the rungs of the staircase carry the genetic code, which consists of pairs of nucleotide bases: Adenine is paired with thymine, and guanine is paired with cytosine. The order of the nucleotide pairs is the code that causes the cell to create specific amino acids, proteins, and enzymes—important biological building blocks. **Each group of nucleotide bases that provides a specific set of biochemical instructions is a *gene.*** For example, three consecutive thymine nucleotides is the instruction to create the amino acid phenylalanine.

Altogether, a child's 46 chromosomes include roughly 30,000–50,000 genes. Through biochemical instructions that are coded in DNA, genes regulate the development of all human characteristics and abilities. **The complete set of genes that makes up a person's heredity is known as the person's *genotype.*** Genetic instructions, in conjunction with environmental influences, produce a *phenotype,* an individual's physical, behavioral, and psychological features.

In the rest of this module, we'll see the different ways that instructions contained in genes produce different phenotypes.

Single Gene Inheritance

How do genetic instructions produce the misshapen red blood cells of sickle cell disease? **Genes come in different forms that are known as *alleles.*** In the case of red blood cells, for example, two alleles can be present on chromosome 11. One allele has instructions for normal red blood cells; another allele has instructions for sickle-shaped red blood cells. **The alleles in the pair of chromosomes are sometimes the same, which makes them *homozygous.* The alleles sometimes differ, which makes them *heterozygous.*** In Leslie's case, her baby could be homozygous, in which case it would have two alleles for normal cells or two alleles for sickle-shaped cells. Leslie's baby might also be heterozygous, which means that it would have one allele for normal cells and one for sickle-shaped cells.

How does a genotype produce a phenotype? The answer is simple if a person is homozygous. When both alleles are the same and therefore have chemical instructions for the same phenotype, that phenotype results. If Leslie's baby had alleles for normal red blood cells on both of the chromosomes in its 11th pair, the baby would be almost guaranteed to have normal cells. If, instead, the baby had two alleles for sickle-shaped cells, her baby would almost certainly suffer from the disease.

When a person is heterozygous, the process is more complex. **Often one allele is *dominant,* which means that its chemical instructions are followed whereas instructions of the other, the *recessive* allele, are ignored.** In the case of sickle cell disease, the allele for normal cells is dominant and the allele for sickle-shaped cells is recessive. This is good news for Leslie: As long as either she or Glenn contribute the allele for normal red blood cells, her baby will not develop sickle cell disease.

The diagram summarizes what we've learned about sickle cell disease. The letter *A* denotes the allele for normal blood cells and *a* denotes the allele for sickle-shaped cells. In the diagram, Glenn's genotype is homozygous dominant. From Leslie's family history, she could be homozygous dominant or heterozygous; in the diagram, I've assumed the latter. You can see that Leslie and Glenn cannot have a baby with sickle cell disease. However, their baby might be affected in another way. **Sometimes one allele does not dominate another completely, a situation known as *incomplete dominance*.** In incomplete dominance, the phenotype that results often falls between the phenotype associated with either allele. This is the case for the genes that control red blood cells. **Individuals with one dominant and one recessive allele have *sickle cell trait*: In most situations they have no problems but when they are seriously short of oxygen, they suffer a temporary, relatively mild form of disease.** Thus, sickle cell trait is likely to appear when the person exercises vigorously or is at high altitudes (Sullivan, 1987). Leslie and Glenn's baby would have sickle cell trait if it inherited a recessive gene from Leslie and a dominant gene from Glenn.

One aspect of sickle cell disease that we haven't considered so far is why this disorder primarily affects African American children. The Cultural Influences feature addresses this point and, in the process, tells more about how heredity operates.

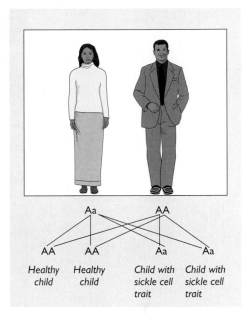

FIG 3–2

CULTURAL INFLUENCES

Why Do African Americans Inherit Sickle Cell Disease?

Sickle cell disease affects about 1 in 400 African American children. In contrast, virtually no European American children have the disorder. Why? Surprisingly, because the sickle cell allele has a benefit: Individuals with this allele are more resistant to malaria, an infectious disease that is one of the leading causes of childhood death worldwide. Malaria is transmitted by mosquitos, so it is most common in warm climates, including many parts of Africa. Compared to Africans who have alleles for normal blood cells, Africans with the sickle cell allele are less likely to die from malaria, which means that the sickle cell allele is passed along to the next generation.

This explanation of sickle cell disease has two implications. First, sickle cell disease should be common in any group of people living where malaria is common. In fact, sickle cell disease affects Hispanic Americans who trace their roots to malaria-prone regions of the Caribbean, Central America, and South America. Second, malaria is rare in the United States, which means that the sickle cell allele has no survival value to African Americans. Accordingly, the sickle cell allele should become less common in successive generations of African Americans, and research indicates that this is happening.

There is an important general lesson here. The impact of heredity depends on the environment. An allele may have survival value in one environment but not in others. ■

The simple genetic mechanism responsible for sickle cell disease, involving a single gene pair, with one dominant allele and one recessive allele, is also responsible for numerous other common traits, as shown in the table on page 56.

In each of these instances, individuals with the recessive phenotype have two recessive alleles, one from each parent. Individuals with the dominant phenotype have at least one dominant allele.

Some Common Phenotypes Associated with Single Pairs of Genes	
Dominant Phenotype	**Recessive Phenotype**
Curly hair	Straight hair
Normal hair	Pattern baldness (men)
Dark hair	Blond hair
Thick lips	Thin lips
Cheek dimples	No dimples
Normal hearing	Some types of deafness
Normal vision	Nearsightedness
Farsightedness	Normal vision
Normal color vision	Red-green color blindness
Type A blood	Type O blood
Type B blood	Type O blood
Rh-positive blood	Rh-negative blood

Source: McKusick, 1995.

TABLE 3–1

You'll notice that the table includes many biological and medical phenotypes but lacks behavioral and psychological phenotypes. Behavioral and psychological characteristics can be inherited, but the genetic mechanism is more elaborate, as we'll see in the next section.

Behavioral Genetics

Behavioral genetics is the branch of genetics that deals with inheritance of behavioral and psychological traits.** Behavioral genetics is complex, in part because behavioral and psychological phenotypes are complex. The traits controlled by single genes usually represent "either-or" phenotypes. That is, the genotypes are usually associated with two (or sometimes three) well-defined phenotypes. For example, a person either has normal color vision or has red-green color blindness; a person has blood that clots normally, has sickle cell trait, or has sickle cell disease.

Most important behavioral and psychological characteristics are not either-or cases but represent an entire range of different outcomes. Take extroversion as an example. You probably know a few extremely outgoing individuals and a few intensely shy persons but most of your friends and acquaintances are somewhere in between. Classifying your friends would produce a distribution of individuals across a continuum, from extreme extroversion at one end to extreme introversion at the other.

Many behavioral and psychological characteristics are distributed in this fashion, including intelligence and many aspects of personality. **When phenotypes reflect the combined activity of many separate genes, the pattern is known as *polygenic inheritance.*** Because so many genes are involved in polygenic inheritance, we usually cannot trace the effects of each gene. But we can use a hypothetical example to show how many genes work together to produce a behavioral phenotype that

> Many behavioral and psychological characteristics reflect polygenic inheritance in which the phenotype depends on the combined actions of many different genes.

spans a continuum. Let's suppose that four pairs of genes contribute to extroversion, that the allele for extroversion is dominant, and that the total amount of extroversion is simply the sum of the dominant alleles. If we continue to use uppercase letters to represent dominant alleles and lowercase letters to represent the recessive allele, the four gene pairs would be Aa, Bb, Cc, and Dd.

These four pairs of genes produce 81 different genotypes and 9 distinct phenotypes. For example, a person with the genotype AABBCCDD has 8 alleles for extroversion (the proverbial party animal). A person with the genotype aabbccdd has no alleles for extroversion (the proverbial wall flower). All other genotypes involve some combinations of dominant and recessive alleles, so these are associated with phenotypes representing intermediate levels of extroversion. In fact, the diagram shows that the most common outcome is for people to inherit exactly 4 dominant and 4 recessive alleles: 19 of the 81 genotypes produce this pattern (e.g., AABbccDd, AaBbcCDd). A few extreme cases (very outgoing or very shy), when coupled with many intermediate cases, produce the familiar bell-shaped distribution that characterizes many behavioral and psychological traits.

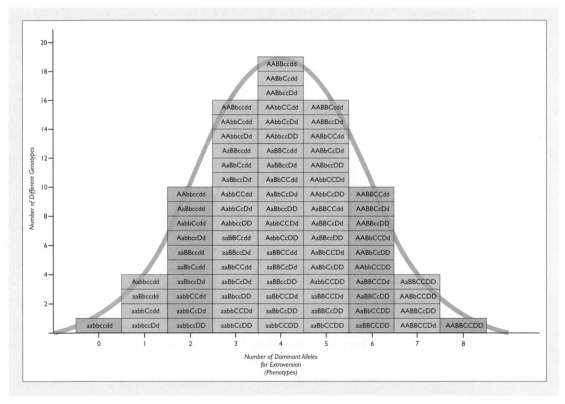

FIG 3–3

Remember, this example is completely hypothetical. Extroversion is not based on the combined influence of eight pairs of genes. I merely want to show how several genes working together could produce a continuum of phenotypes. Something like our example is probably involved in the inheritance of numerous human behavioral traits, except that many more pairs of genes are involved and the environment also influences the phenotype (Plomin et al., 1997).

Methods of Behavioral Genetics. If many behavioral phenotypes involve countless genes, how can we hope to unravel the influence of heredity? Twins provide some important clues. **Identical twins are called *monozygotic twins* because they come from a single fertilized egg that splits in two.** Because identical twins come from the same fertilized egg, they have the same genes that control body structure, height, and facial features, which explains why identical twins like those in the photo look alike. **In contrast, fraternal or *dizygotic* twins come from two separate eggs fertilized by two separate sperm.** Genetically, fraternal twins are just like any other siblings on average; about half their genes are the same. In twin studies, scientists compare identical and fraternal twins to measure the influence of heredity. If identical twins are more alike than fraternal twins, this implicates heredity.

An example will help illustrate the logic underlying comparisons of identical and fraternal twins. Suppose we want to determine whether extroversion is inherited. We would first measure extroversion in a large number of identical and fraternal twins. We might use a questionnaire with scores ranging from 0 to 100 (100 indicating maximal extroversion). Some of the results are shown in the table.

Twins' Scores on a Measure of Extroversion					
Fraternal Twins			**Identical Twins**		
Family	*One Twin*	*Other Twin*	*Family*	*One Twin*	*Other Twin*
Aikman	80	95	Bettis	100	95
Fernandez	70	50	Harbaugh	32	30
Herrod	10	35	Park	18	15
Stewart	25	5	Ramirez	55	60
Tomczak	40	65	Robinson	70	62

TABLE 3–2

Look first at the results for the fraternal twins. Most have similar scores: The Aikman twins both have high scores but the Herrod twins have low scores. Looking at the identical twins, their scores are even more alike, typically differing by no more than 5 points. This greater similarity among identical twins than fraternal twins would be evidence that extroversion is inherited, just as the fact that identical twins look more alike than fraternal twins is evidence that facial appearance is inherited.

Adopted children are another important source of information about heredity. In this case, adopted children are compared with their biological parents and their adoptive parents. The idea is that biological parents provide the child's genes but adoptive parents provide the child's environment. Consequently, if a behavior has genetic roots, then adopted children should resemble their biological parents even though they have never met them. But if the adopted children resemble their adoptive parents, we know that family environment affects behavior.

If we wanted to use an adoption study to determine whether extroversion is inherited, we would measure extroversion in a large sample of adopted children, their biological mothers, and their adoptive mothers. (Mothers are studied because obtaining data from biological fathers of adopted children is often difficult.) The results of this hypothetical study are shown in the table.

Scores from an Adoption Study on a Measure of Extroversion			
Child	**Child's Score**	**Biological Mother's Score**	**Adoptive Mother's Score**
Anita	60	70	35
Jerome	45	50	25
Kerri	40	30	80
Michael	90	80	50
Troy	25	5	55

TABLE 3–3

First, compare children's scores with their biological mothers' scores. Overall, they are related: Extroverted children like Michael tend to have extroverted biological mothers. Introverted children like Troy tend to have introverted biological mothers. In contrast, children's scores don't show any clear relation to their adoptive mothers' scores. For example, although Michael has the highest score and Troy has the lowest, their adoptive mothers have very similar scores. Children's greater similarity to biological than to adoptive parents would be evidence that extroversion is inherited.

Twin studies and adoption studies are not foolproof, however. Maybe you thought of a potential flaw in twin studies: Parents and other people may treat identical twins more similarly than they treat fraternal twins. This would make identical twins more similar than fraternal twins in their experiences as well as in their genes. Adoption studies have their own Achilles heel. Adoption agencies sometimes try to place youngsters with adoptive parents who are like their biological parents. For example, if an agency believes that the biological parents are bright, the agency may try harder to have the child adopted by parents that the agency believes are bright. This can bias adoption studies because biological and adoptive parents end up being similar.

The problems associated with twin and adoption studies are not insurmountable. Because twin and adoption studies have different faults, if the two kinds of studies produce similar results on the influence of heredity, we can be confident of those results. In addition, behavior geneticists are moving beyond traditional methods such as twin and adoption studies (Plomin et al., 1997; Plomin & Rutter, 1998). Today, it is possible to isolate particular segments of DNA in human chromosomes. These segments then serve as markers for identifying specific alleles. The procedure is complicated but the basic approach often begins by identifying people who differ in the behavior or psychological trait of interest. For example, researchers might identify children who are outgoing and children who are shy. Or they might identify children who read well and children who read poorly. The children rub the inside of their mouth with a cotton swab, which yields cheek cells that contain DNA. The cells are analyzed in a lab and the DNA markers for the two groups are compared. If the markers differ consistently, then the alleles near the marker probably contribute to the differences between the groups.

Heredity is implicated when identical twins are more alike than fraternal twins and when adopted children resemble their biological parents more than their adoptive parents.

Techniques like these have the potential to identify the many different genes that contribute to complex behavioral and psychological traits. Of course, these new methods have limits. Some require very large samples of children, which can be hard to obtain for rare disorders. Also, some require that an investigator have an idea, before even beginning the study, about which chromosomes to search and where. These can be major hurdles. But, when used with traditional methods of behavior genetics (e. g., adoption studies), the new methods promise a much greater understanding of how genes influence behavior and development.

Which psychological characteristics are affected by heredity? Research to date indicates that genetic influence is strongest in three psychological areas: intelligence, psychological disorders, and personality (Goldsmith et al., 1999; Neiderhiser et al., 1999). In the case of intelligence, identical twins' scores on IQ tests are consistently more alike than fraternal twins' scores (Plomin et al., 1997). Research also shows that heredity is an important component of two major psychological disorders. **In *depression*, individuals have pervasive feelings of sadness, are irritable, and have low self-esteem. In *schizophrenia*, individuals hallucinate, have confused language and thought, and often behave bizarrely.** Twin studies show remarkable similarity for identical twins for these disorders. In depression, for example, if one identical twin is depressed, the other twin has roughly a 70 percent chance of being depressed. For fraternal twins, the odds are much lower—only 25 percent (Gottesman, 1993; Rowe, 1994).

> ## Intelligence, psychological disorders, and personality are all strongly influenced by heredity.

Research that demonstrates the influence of heredity on personality is the topic of the Focus on Research feature.

FOCUS ON RESEARCH

Hereditary and Environmental Roots of Infants' Social Behavior

Who were the investigators and what was the aim of the study? Toddlers differ in the ways they interact with others, especially people they don't know well. Some toddlers interact easily and with little hesitation. Other toddlers are reluctant to interact and seem wary of people. This dimension of personality is known as sociability. Robert Plomin and David Rowe (1979) wanted to find out whether a toddler's sociability is determined, in part, by heredity.

How did the investigators measure the topic of interest? Plomin and Rowe decided to study sociability in identical and fraternal twins using structured observation. In the twins' home, an adult not known to the twins spent 5 minutes talking with the mother while the twins were nearby. Then the adult approached the twins and offered them a toy. During this time, two observers recorded the twins' behavior. Each observer was assigned one twin, so that the twins' behavior was assessed independently. The observers recorded many behaviors, but for simplicity, I'll focus on three:

1. the number of times the child spoke positively to the stranger (for example, describing himself or herself),

2. the amount of time spent looking at the stranger, and

3. how quickly the child approached the stranger when he offered the toy.

Who were the children in the study? The researchers obtained measures for 21 pairs of identical twins and 25 pairs of same-sex fraternal twins. Their average age was 22 months.

What was the design of the study? This study was correlational: Plomin and Rowe measured many variables, such as time spent looking at the stranger, and compared twins' similarity on these measures. The study focused on a single age group, so it was neither longitudinal nor cross-sectional.

Were there ethical concerns with the study? No. The situations that Plomin and Rowe created were routine in the toddlers' real life, so the children were not at risk. Plomin and Rowe obtained permission from the mothers for the twins to participate in the study.

What were the results? The primary results were expressed as correlations, which are shown in the graph. Each bar shows the size of the correlation for either identical or fraternal twins on one measure. For example, the first bar shows that the correlation for talking to the stranger was nearly 0.6 for identical twins. This means that if one identical twin talked often to the stranger, the other usually did, too; if one identical twin was quiet, the other usually was also.

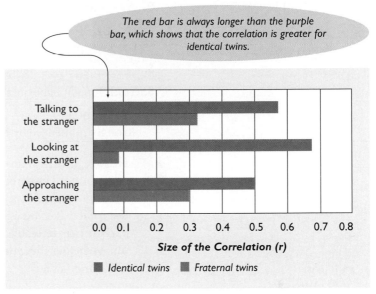

The red bar is always longer than the purple bar, which shows that the correlation is greater for identical twins.

FIG 3–4

The important pattern in the graph is that, for each measure, the correlation is greater for identical twins than for fraternal twins. That is, as I described on page 58, the greater similarity among identical twins than fraternal twins is evidence that a behavior is inherited.

What did the investigators conclude? Sociability, at least as reflected in the measures that Plomin and Rowe devised, is influenced by heredity.

What converging evidence would strengthen these conclusions? Plomin and Rowe tested children at one age—22 months. Their conclusions would be strengthened if they also tested older twins and found that sociability was influenced by heredity at, for example, 4 years of age. Strictly speaking, the results of this study only show that heredity influences sociability at 22 months. ■

We will look at personality in greater detail later. For now, keep in mind two conclusions from twin studies like Plomin and Rowe's and from adoption studies. On the one hand, the impact of heredity on behavioral development is substantial and widespread. Research shows that heredity has a sizable influence on such different aspects of development as intelligence and personality. In understanding children and their development, we must always think about how heredity may contribute. On the other hand, heredity is never the sole determinant of behavioral development. For example, 50 percent of the differences among children's scores on intelligence tests is due to heredity. But the remaining 50 percent is due to environment. Throughout this book, we'll see that the course of development is controlled by both heredity and environment.

Check Your Learning

1. In _____, an egg is fertilized by a sperm in a laboratory dish, then placed in the uterus.

2. The first 22 pairs of chromosomes are called _____.

3. A person is _____ when the alleles in a pair of chromosomes differ.

4. In _____, the phenotype often falls between the dominant and the recessive phenotype.

5. _____ reflects the combined activity of a number of distinct genes.

6. Traditionally, behavioral geneticists relied on twin and _____ studies.

7. Intelligence, _____, and personality are the psychological traits most strongly influenced by heredity.

Nature and Nurture The goal of twin and adoption studies is to reveal the contributions of heredity and environment to development. However, a problem in twin studies is that identical twins may be treated more similarly than fraternal twins and a problem in adoption studies is that children's biological parents may resemble their adoptive parents. How could an investigator determine whether these problems were present in his or her research?

Answers: (1) in vitro fertilization, (2) autosomes, (3) heterozygous, (4) incomplete dominance, (5) Polygenic inheritance, (6) adoption, (7) psychological disorders

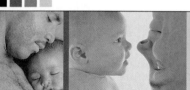

Genetic Disorders

3.2

Genetic Disorders

├ Inherited Disorders

└ Abnormal Chromosomes

Learning Objectives

■ **What disorders are inherited?**

■ **What disorders are caused by too many or too few chromosomes?**

Carolyn and Doug, both 46, hadn't planned to have a baby, but Carolyn soon discovered that her lingering case of the flu was actually morning sickness. She and Doug both knew that with Carolyn's age they risked having a baby with Down syndrome, but they decided not to worry about this. When Carolyn gave birth to a baby boy, they learned that he did have Down syndrome. Carolyn and Doug were startled by the news, but it didn't change their joy at being parents. They did, however, want to know more about the special challenges their son would face.

Like Carolyn and Doug's baby, some children are affected by heredity in a special way: They have genetic disorders that disrupt the usual pattern of development. Genetics can derail development in two ways. First, some disorders are inherited. Sickle cell disease is one example of an inherited disorder. Second, sometimes eggs or sperm have more or fewer than the usual 23 chromosomes. In this module, we'll see how inherited disorders and abnormal numbers of chromosomes can alter a child's development. **We'll also learn more about *Down syndrome*, a genetic disorder caused by an extra 21st chromosome that results in mental retardation.**

Inherited Disorders

In Module 3.1, we saw that sickle cell disease is a disorder that affects people who inherit two recessive alleles. In fact, sickle cell disease is one of many disorders that are homozygous recessive—triggered when a child inherits recessive alleles from both parents. Table 3-4 lists four of the more common disorders that are inherited in this manner.

Relatively few serious disorders are caused by dominant alleles. Why? If the allele for the disorder is dominant, every person with at least one of these alleles would have the disorder. Individuals affected with these disorders typically do not live long enough to reproduce, so dominant alleles that produce fatal disorders soon vanish from the species. **An exception is _Huntington's disease_, a fatal disease characterized by progressive degeneration of the nervous system.** Huntington's disease is caused by a dominant allele found on chromosome 4. Individuals who inherit this disorder develop normally through childhood, adolescence, and young adulthood. However, during middle age, nerve cells begin to deteriorate, causing muscle spasms, depression, and significant changes in personality (Shiwach, 1994). By the time symptoms of Huntington's disease appear, adults who are affected may already have produced children, many of whom go on to develop the disease themselves.

Inherited disorders that affect development are usually carried by recessive alleles, not dominant alleles.

Common Disorders Associated with Recessive Alleles		
Disorder	**Frequency**	**Characteristics**
Albinism	1 in 10,000 to 1 in 20,000 births	Skin lacks melanin, which causes visual problems and extreme sensitivity to light.
Cystic Fibrosis	1 in 2,500 births among European Americans; less common in African and Asian Americans	Excess mucus clogs digestive and respiratory tracts. Lung infections common.
Phenylketonuria (PKU)	1 in 10,000 births	Phenylalanine, an amino acid, accumulates in the body and damages the nervous system, causing mental retardation.
Tay-sachs disease	1 in 3,000 births among Jews of European descent	The nervous system degenerates in infancy, causing deafness, blindness, mental retardation, and, during the preschool years, death.

Based on Committee on Genetics, 1996; McKusick, 1995.

TABLE 3-4

Fortunately, most inherited disorders are rare. Phenylketonuria, for example, occurs once in every 10,000 births and Huntington's disease occurs even less frequently. Nevertheless, adults who believe that these disorders run in their family want to know if their children are likely to inherit the disorder. The Making Children's Lives Better feature shows how these couples can get help in deciding whether to have children.

MAKING CHILDREN'S LIVES BETTER
Genetic Counseling

Family planning is not easy for couples who fear that children they have may inherit serious or even fatal diseases. The best advice, though, is to seek the help of a genetic counselor before the woman becomes pregnant. With the couple's help, a genetic counselor constructs a detailed family history that can be used to decide whether it's likely that either the man or the woman has the allele for the disorder that concerns them.

A family tree for Leslie and Glenn, the couple from Module 3.1, would confirm that Leslie is likely to carry the recessive allele for sickle cell disease. The genetic counselor would then take the next step, obtaining a sample of Leslie's cells (probably from a blood test). The cells would be analyzed to determine if the 11th chromosome carries the recessive allele for sickle cell disease. If Leslie learns she has the dominant allele for healthy blood cells, then she and Glenn can be assured their children will not have sickle cell disease. If Leslie learns that she has the recessive allele, then she and Glenn will know they have a 25 percent risk of having a baby with sickle cell disease and a 50 percent risk of having a baby with sickle cell trait. Tests can also be administered after a woman is pregnant to determine whether the child she is carrying has an inherited disorder. ■

More common than inherited diseases are disorders caused by the wrong number of chromosomes, as we'll see in the next section.

Abnormal Chromosomes

Sometimes individuals do not receive the normal complement of 46 chromosomes. If they are born with extra, missing, or damaged chromosomes, development is always disturbed. The best example is Down syndrome, the disorder that affects Carolyn and Doug's son. Like the child in the photo, persons with Down syndrome have almond-shaped eyes and a fold over the eyelid. Their head, neck, and nose are usually smaller than normal. During the first several months, babies with Down syndrome seem to develop normally. Thereafter, though, their mental and behavioral development begins to lag behind the average child's. For example, a child with Down syndrome might not sit up without help until about 1 year, not walk until 2, or not talk until 3, months or even years behind children without Down syndrome. By childhood, mental retardation is apparent.

Carolyn and Doug are right in believing that rearing a child with Down syndrome presents special challenges for parents. During the preschool years, children with Down syndrome need special programs to prepare them for school. **In elementary and secondary school, children with Down syndrome (and other children with disabilities) are typically placed in regular classes, a practice known as *mainstreaming*.** Educational achievements of children with Down syndrome are likely to be limited. Nevertheless, many persons with Down syndrome lead fulfilling lives.

What causes Down syndrome? Individuals with Down syndrome typically have an extra 21st chromosome that is usually provided by the egg (Antonarakis & the Down Syndrome Collaborative Group, 1991). Why the mother provides two 21st chromosomes is unknown. However, the odds that a woman will bear a child with

Down syndrome increase markedly as she gets older. For a woman in her late 20s, the risk of giving birth to a baby with Down syndrome is about 1 in 1,000; for a woman in her early 40s, the risk is about 1 in 50. The increased risk may be because a woman's eggs have been in her ovaries since her own prenatal development. Eggs may deteriorate over time as part of aging or because an older woman has a longer history of exposure to hazards in the environment, such as X rays, that may damage her eggs.

An extra autosome (as in Down syndrome), a missing autosome, or a damaged autosome always has far-reaching consequences for development because the autosomes contain huge amounts of genetic material. In fact, nearly half of all fertilized eggs abort spontaneously within 2 weeks, primarily because of abnormal autosomes. Thus, most eggs that could not develop normally are removed naturally (Moore & Persaud, 1993).

Abnormal sex chromosomes can also disrupt development. The chart lists four of the more frequent disorders associated with atypical numbers of X and Y chromosomes. Keep in mind that "frequent" is a relative term; although these disorders are more frequent than PKU or Huntington's disease, the chart shows that most are rare. Notice that no disorders consist solely of Y chromosomes. The presence of an X chromosome appears to be necessary for life.

> Damaged autosomes always affect development because autosomes contain so much genetic material.

Common Disorders Associated with the Sex Chromosomes			
Disorder	**Sex Chromosomes**	**Frequency**	**Characteristics**
Klinefelter's syndrome	XXY	1 in 500 male births	Tall, small testicles, sterile, below-normal intelligence, passive
XYY complement	XYY	1 in 1,000 male births	Tall, some cases apparently have below-normal intelligence
Turner's syndrome	X	1 in 2,500-5,000 female births	Short, limited development of secondary sex characteristics, problems perceiving spatial relations
XXX syndrome	XXX	1 in 500-1,200 female births	Normal stature but delayed motor and language development

Based on Bancroft et al., 1982; Downey et al., 1991; Linden et al., 1988; Plomin et al., 1990.

TABLE 3–5

These genetic disorders demonstrate the remarkable power of heredity. Nevertheless, to fully understand how heredity influences development, we need to consider the environment, which we'll do in Module 3.3.

Check Your Learning

1. _____ is an inherited disorder caused by the accumulation of a particular amino acid, resulting in mental retardation.

2. Genetic disorders involving dominant alleles are rare because _____.

3. Down syndrome usually is caused by _____.

4. Many fertilized eggs are aborted spontaneously, primarily because of

_____.

5. Disorders involving abnormal numbers of sex chromosomes suggest that the presence of _____ chromosome is necessary for life.

Connections Children with Down syndrome have retarded mental development. How might this retarded cognitive development affect their social relationships with parents, siblings, and peers?

Answers: (1) PKU, (2) individuals with these disorders often do not live long enough to have children, (3) an extra 21st chromosome, (4) abnormal autosomes, (5) an X.

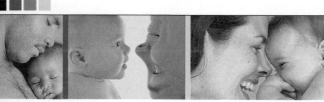

Heredity Is Not Destiny

3.3

Heredity Is Not Destiny

├ Paths from Genes to Behavior

├ Reaction Range

├ Changing Relations Between
  Nature and Nurture

└ The Nature of Nurture

Learning Objectives

■ **How do genes affect behavior?**

■ **Does a genotype always lead to the same phenotype?**

■ **How does the relation between heredity and environment change as children develop?**

■ **How do family environments influence children's development?**

> *Sadie and Molly are fraternal twins. As babies, Sadie was calm and easily comforted, but Molly was fussy and hard to soothe. Their parents wondered if they'd always differ or if they'd become more alike as they grew older.*

Many people mistakenly view heredity as a set of phenotypes that unfold automatically from the genotypes that are set at conception. Nothing could be further from the truth. Although genotypes are fixed when the sperm fertilizes the egg, phenotypes are not fixed. Instead, heredity and environment combine to direct a child's behavioral and psychological development. In this module, we'll look at links between heredity and environment. In the process, we'll learn if Sadie and Molly became more alike as they grew.

Paths from Genes to Behavior

You know, from Module 3.1, that there is no single intelligence gene and no one shyness gene; instead, many genes work togther to influence these and other aspects of behavioral development. But, how do genes work together to make some children brighter than others and some children more outgoing than others? That is, how does the information in strands of DNA end up influencing a child's behavioral and psychological development?

The specific paths from genes to behavior are largely uncharted, but some of their general properties are known. The most important is that genes never cause behavior directly; instead, they influence behavior indirectly, by making behaviors more or less likely. For example, there is no gene for dunking a basketball but genes do regulate bone length. As a consequence, some people grow taller than others and they are therefore more capable of dunking. Similarly, there is no gene for alcoholism, but genes do regulate how the body breaks down alcohol that is consumed. Consequently, some people become nauseated because their bodies cannot break down alcohol and they are therefore less likely to become alcoholics. These examples show that genes for height and breaking down alcohol affect behavior indirectly, by changing the odds that a person can dunk a basketball or become an alcoholic.

The influence of genes on behavior is always indirect and depends on the environment in which the genetic instructions are carried out.

Another important property of gene-behavior paths is that the behavioral consequences of genetic instructions depend on environments. In a basketball-less world, the gene for height would still produce taller people but they would no longer be more likely to dunk. In other words, to understand how heredity affects behavior, we must consider the environment in which genetic instructions are carried out.

In the remaining sections of this module, we'll look at other aspects of links between heredity and environment.

Reaction Range

If you read the fine print on a can of diet soda (and some other food products), you'll see the following warning:

> *"Phenylketonurics: contains phenylalanine."*

Children with PKU are missing an enzyme needed to break down phenylalanine. When phenylalanine accumulates, it damages the nervous system. But why the warning on diet soda? Today, most American hospitals check for PKU at birth—with a blood or urine test. Newborns who have the disease are immediately placed on a diet that limits intake of high-protein foods (e.g., meat, fish, dairy products), which tend to be high in phenylalanine, and mental retardation is avoided. Thus, an individual who has the genotype for PKU but is not exposed to phenylalanine has normal intelligence. PKU illustrates that development depends upon heredity and environmental factors, in this case, diet. And as you'll see in the Child Development and Family Policy feature, PKU represents an exciting example of how research has influenced family policy.

CHILD DEVELOPMENT AND FAMILY POLICY
Screening for PKU

PKU was first discovered in 1934 when a Norwegian mother asked a physician, Dr. Asbjørn Følling, to help her two children, both of whom suffered from mental retardation. Dr. Følling discovered that the children had large amounts of phenylpyruvic acid in their urine and phenylalanine in their blood. By the 1950s, other scientists had determined that the build-up of phenylalanine damaged the nervous system and had shown that a low-protein diet would leave the nervous system unharmed. The missing link was an effective way to diagnose PKU in newborns, before phenylalanine had a chance to accumulate and cause damage. In 1959, Dr. Robert Guthrie devised a quick and inexpensive way to determine levels of phenylalanine in a newborn's blood. Studies soon proved that the test was effective. Armed with this information and aided by a complimentary story in *Life* magazine, Dr. Guthrie and the National Association for Retarded Children lobbied vigorously for laws that required newborns to be screened for PKU. In 1965, New York became the first state to require mandatory screening; by the end of the 1960s, most U.S. states required screening. Today, all states require PKU screening and require health insurance providers to cover the cost of low-protein formula for infants with PKU. Thus, research revealed the mechanisms of PKU and led to a simple screening test; public policy that required mandatory screening and low-protein diets means that hundreds of children who are born each year with PKU can lead healthy, normal lives. ■

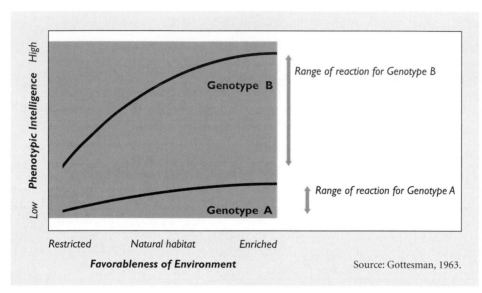

FIG 3–5

In general, heredity and environment jointly determine the direction of development. Therefore, a genotype can lead to a range of phenotypes. **Reaction range refers to this fact that a genotype is manifested in reaction to the environment where development takes place.** The diagram illustrates this fact by showing how phenotypic intelligence might vary, depending on the environment. Look first at genotypic intelligence A, which has a small reaction range. This genotype leads to much the same phenotypic intelligence, no matter whether development takes place in an enriched environment filled with stimulation from parents, siblings, and books or in an impoverished environment that lacks all such stimulation. In contrast, genotype B has a larger reaction range: The enriched environment leads to a much greater phenotypic intelligence than the impoverished environment. Thus, a single genotype can lead to a range of phenotypes, depending on the quality of the rearing environment.

The conclusion to be drawn from the example is obvious: One genotype leads to quite different phenotypes, depending upon the level of intellectual stimulation in the environment. Of course, what makes a "good" or "rich" environment is not the same for all facets of behavioral or psychological development. Throughout this book, you will see how specific kinds of environments influence very particular aspects of development (Wachs, 1983).

Changing Relations Between Nature and Nurture

How nature (genetics) and nurture (environment) work together partly depends on a child's age. Sandra Scarr (1992, 1993; Scarr & McCartney, 1983) describes three types of relations between heredity and environment. **In the first, a *passive gene-environment relation*, parents pass on genotypes to their children and provide much**

of the early environment for their young children. For example, bright parents are likely to transmit genes that make for bright children. Bright parents are also likely to provide books, museum visits, and discussions that are intellectually stimulating. In this case, heredity and environment are positively related: Both foster brighter children. In both respects, children are passive recipients of heredity and environment. This passive type of relation is most common with infants and young children.

In the second type of relation, an *evocative gene-environment relation,* **different genotypes evoke different responses from the environment.** For example, children who are bright (due in part to their genes) may pay greater attention to their teachers and ask more questions and, in turn, receive greater positive attention in school than children who are not as bright. Or, children who are friendly and outgoing (again, due in part to their genes) may elicit more interactions with others (and, in particular, more satisfying interactions) than children who are not as friendly and outgoing. In the evocative relation, which is common in young children, a child's genotype evokes or prompts people to respond differently to the child.

In the third type of relation, an *active gene-environment relation,* **individuals actively seek environments related to their genetic makeup.** Children who are bright (due in part to heredity) may actively seek peers, adults, and activities that strengthen their intellectual development. Similarly, youths like the ones in the photo, who are outgoing (due in part to heredity), seek the company of other people, particularly extroverts like themselves. **This process of deliberately seeking environments that fit one's heredity is called** *nichepicking.* Niche-picking is first seen in childhood and becomes more common as children get older and can control their environments. The Real Children feature shows niche-picking in action.

REAL CHILDREN

Sadie and Molly Pick Their Niches

Did Sadie and Molly, the twins in the module-opening vignette, become more alike as they grew? No. Even as a young baby, Sadie was always a "people person." She relished contact with other people and preferred play that involved others. Molly was more withdrawn and was quite happy to play alone. When they entered school, Sadie enjoyed making friends while Molly looked forward to the new activities and barely noticed the new faces. These differences reveal heredity in action because sociability is known to have important genetic components (Braungart et al., 1992).

As adolescents, Sadie and Molly continued to seek environments that fit their differing needs for social stimulation. Sadie was in school plays and sang in the school choir. Molly developed a serious interest in crafts, which she pursued by herself. Sadie was always doing something with friends. Molly enjoyed the company of some longtime friends, but she was just as happy to be working alone on some new craft project. Sadie and Molly chose distinctive and very different niches, choices that were influenced by the genes that regulate sociability. ■

The description of Sadie and Molly illustrates that genes and environment rarely influence development alone. Instead, nature and nurture interact. Experiences determine which phenotypes emerge, and genotypes influence the nature of children's experiences. The story of Sadie and Molly also makes it clear that, to understand how genes influence development, we need to look carefully at how environments work, which is our next topic.

The Nature of Nurture

Traditionally, psychologists have considered some environments as beneficial for children and others as detrimental. This view has been especially strong in regard to family environments. Some parenting practices were thought to be more effective than others and parents who used these effective practices were believed to have children who were, on average, better off than children of parents who don't use these practices. This view leads to a simple prediction: Children within a family should be similar because they all receive the same type of effective (or ineffective) parenting. However, dozens of behavioral genetic studies show that, in reality, siblings are not very much alike in their cognitive and social development (Dunn & Plomin, 1990).

Does this mean that family environment is not important? No. **These findings point to the importance of *nonshared environmental influences,* the forces within a family that make children different from one another** (Deater-Deckard, 2000). The family environment is important but it usually affects each child in a unique way, which makes siblings differ. Each of the children in the photo is likely to have different experiences in daily family life. For example, parents may be more affectionate with one child than another, they may use more physical punishment with one child than another, or they may have higher expectations for school achievement for one child than another. All these contrasting parental influences tend to make siblings different, not alike. Family environments are important, but, as I describe their influence throughout this book, you should remember that families create multiple unique environments, one for each child.

Much of what I have said about genes, environment, and development is summarized in the diagram (Lytton, 2000). Parents are the source of children's genes and, at least for young children, the primary source of children's experiences. Children's genes also influence the experiences that they have and the impact of those experiences on them. However, to capture the idea of nonshared environmental influences, we would need a separate diagram for each child, reflecting the fact that parents provide unique genes and a unique family environment for each of their offspring.

Most of this book explains the links among nature, nurture, and development. We can first see the interaction of nature and nurture during prenatal development, which is the topic of Chapter 4.

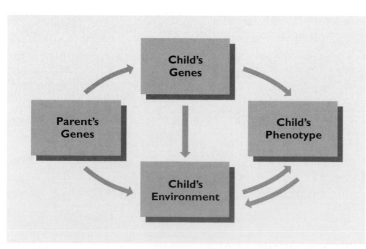

FIG 3–6

Check Your Learning

1. The path from genes to environment is always _____.

2. _____ refers to the fact that the same genotype can be associated with many different phenotypes.

3. In _____ gene-environment relations, children's genotypes cause others to respond differently to them.

4. Older children and adolescents often deliberately seek environments that match their heredity, a process known as _____.

5. Nonshared environmental influences tend to make siblings _____.

■■ **Active Children** Leslie and Glenn, the couple from Module 3.1 who were
■■ concerned that their baby could have sickle cell disease, are already charting their baby's life course. Leslie, who has always loved to sing, is confident that her baby will be a fantastic musician and easily imagines a regular routine of music lessons, rehearsals, and concerts. Glenn, a pilot, is just as confident that his child will share his love of flying; he is already planning trips the two of them can take together. Are Leslie's and Glenn's ideas more consistent with the active or passive views of children? What advice might you give to Leslie and Glenn about factors they are ignoring?

Answers: (1) indirect, by making some behaviors more or less likely, (2) Reaction range, (3) evocative, (4) niche-picking, (5) different rather than similar

Chapter Critical Review

1. Discuss the benefits and drawbacks of assisted reproduction methods, such as in vitro fertilization, surrogate parenting, and egg donation. Are these techniques changing our definition of "parent" and of "environment"?

2. A woman with curly dark hair and a man with straight blond hair have two children, one with straight blond hair and one with straight dark hair. Explain how this is possible (hint: refer back to Table 3–1, Some Common Phenotypes Associated with Single Pairs of Genes).

3. Explain why psychologists use twin studies and adoption studies for research in behavioral genetics. What general insights have such studies provided to the nature-nurture question?

4. How do genes influence behavior? Describe the general process and give a specific example.

5. How does the concept of nonshared environment help explain some of the links among, nature, nurture, and development?

For more review material, log on to www.prenhall.com/kail

See For Yourself

The Human Genome Project, launched in the late 1980s by U.S. scientists, aims to identify the exact location of all human genes. It is a vast undertaking that first requires determining the sequence of roughly 3 billion pairs of nucleotides like those shown in the diagram on page 54. The Project has produced maps of each chromosome showing the location of known genes. You can see these maps at a Web site maintained by the Human Genome Project. The address is http://www.ncbi.nlm.nih.gov/science96. At this site, you can select a "favorite" chromosome and see which genes have been located on it. See for yourself!

For More Information About . . .

human heredity, try Robert Shapiro's *The Human Blueprint: The Race to Unlock the Secrets of Our Genetic Script* (St. Martin's Press, 1991), which describes progress in genetics research by focusing on the Human Genome Project.

 children with Down syndrome, visit the Down syndrome Web site:

http://www.nas.com/downsyn

Key Terms

active gene-environment relation 69
allele 54
autosomes 53
behavioral genetics 56
chromosomes 52
deoxyribonucleic acid (DNA) 54
depression 60
dizygotic (fraternal) twins 58
dominant 54
Down syndrome 62

evocative gene-environment
  relation 69
gene 54
genotype 54
heterozygous 54
homozygous 54
Huntington's disease 63
incomplete dominance 55
in vitro fertilization 53
mainstreaming 64
monozygotic (identical) twins 58

niche-picking 69
nonshared environmental
  influences 70
passive gene-environment relation 68
phenotype 54
polygenic inheritance 56
reaction range 68
recessive 54
schizophrenia 60
sex chromosomes 54
sickle cell trait 55

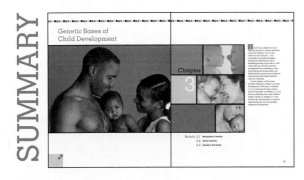

SUMMARY

3.1 Mechanisms of Heredity

The Biology of Heredity

At conception, the 23 chromosomes in the sperm merge with the 23 chromosomes in the egg. The 46 chromosomes that result include 22 pairs of autosomes plus two sex chromosomes. Each chromosome is one molecule of DNA, which consists of nucleotides organized in a structure that resembles a spiral staircase. A section of DNA that provides specific biochemical instructions is called a gene. All of a person's genes make up a genotype; phenotype refers to the physical, behavioral, and psychological characteristics that develop when the genotype is exposed to a specific environment.

Single Gene Inheritance

Different forms of the same gene are called alleles. A person who inherits the same allele on a pair of chromosomes is homozygous; in this case, the biochemical instructions on the allele are followed. A person who inherits different alleles is heterozygous; in this case, the instructions of the dominant allele are followed whereas those of the recessive allele are ignored. In incomplete dominance, the person is heterozygous but the phenotype is midway between the dominant and recessive phenotypes.

Behavioral Genetics

Behavioral and psychological phenotypes that reflect an underlying continuum (such as intelligence) often involve polygenic inheritance. In polygenic inheritance, the phenotype reflects the combined activity of many distinct genes. Polygenic inheritance has been examined traditionally by studying twins and adopted children, and more recently by identifying DNA markers. These studies indicate substantial influence of heredity in three areas: intelligence, psychological disorders, and personality.

3.2 Genetic Disorders

Inherited Disorders

Most inherited disorders are carried by recessive alleles. Examples include sickle cell disease, albinism, cystic fibrosis, PKU, and Tay-sachs disease. Inherited disorders are rarely carried by dominant alleles because individuals with such a disorder usually don't live long enough to have children. An exception is Huntington's disease, which doesn't become symptomatic until middle age.

Abnormal Chromosomes

Most fertilized eggs that do not have 46 chromosomes are aborted spontaneously soon after conception. One exception is Down syndrome, caused by an extra 21st chromosome. Down syndrome individuals have a distinctive appearance and are mentally retarded. Disorders of the sex chromosomes, which are more common because these chromosomes contain less genetic material than autosomes, include Klinefelter's syndrome, XYY complement, Turner's syndrome, and XXX syndrome.

3.3 Heredity Is Not Destiny

Paths from Genes to Behavior

Genes never influence behavior directly. Instead, they affect behavior indirectly by increasing the odds that a child will behave in a particular way. Also, the impact of a gene on behavior depends on the environment in which the genetic instructions are carried out.

Reaction Range

PKU does not lead to mental retardation when individuals with the disorder maintain a diet low in phenylalanine. This demonstrates the concept of reaction range—the same genotype can lead to different phenotypes. The outcome of heredity depends upon the environment in which development occurs.

Changing Relations Between Nature and Nurture

In infants and young children, the gene-environment relation is passive: parents pass on genotypes to their children and provide much of the early environment for their young children. An evocative gene-environment relation increasingly occurs during development as the child's genotype evokes responses from the environment. In older children and adolescents, an active gene-environment relation is common: Individuals actively seek environments related to their genetic makeup.

The Nature of Nurture

Family environments affect siblings differently, which is known as nonshared environmental influences. Parents provide a unique environment for each child in the family as well as providing a unique genotype for each child.

Prenatal Development and Birth

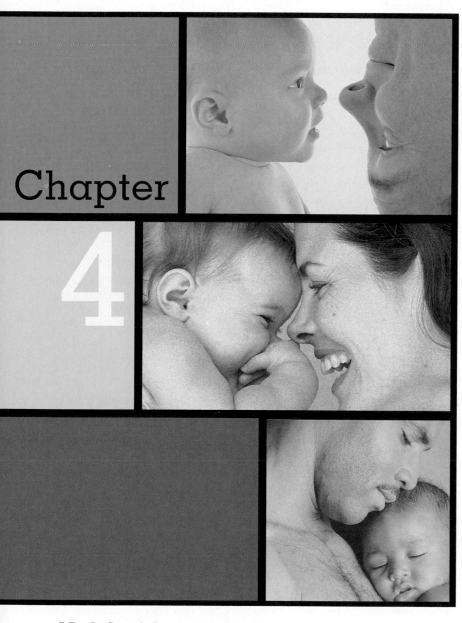

Chapter 4

I f you ask parents to name some of the most memorable experiences of their lives, many mention events associated with pregnancy and childbirth. From the exciting news that a woman is pregnant through birth 9 months later, the entire experience evokes awe and wonder. The events of pregnancy and birth provide the foundation upon which all child development is built. In Module 4.1, we'll trace the events of prenatal development that transform sperm and egg into a living, breathing human being. In Module 4.2, we'll learn about some developmental problems that can occur before birth. In Module 4.3, we'll turn to birth. We'll see what happens during labor and delivery and see what newborns are like.

From Conception to Birth

4.1

From Conception to Birth

Learning Objectives

■ **What happens to a fertilized egg in the first 2 weeks after conception?**

■ **When do body structures and internal organs emerge in prenatal development?**

■ **When do body systems begin to function well enough to support life?**

Eun Jung has just learned that she is pregnant with her first child. Like many other parents-to-be, she and her husband, Kinam, are ecstatic. But they also realize how little they know about "what happens when" during pregnancy. Eun Jung is eager to visit her obstetrician to learn more about the normal timetable of events during pregnancy.

Prenatal development begins when a sperm fertilizes an egg. **The changes that transform the fertilized egg into a newborn human make up *prenatal development*.** Prenatal development takes an average of 38 weeks. (Perhaps you've heard that pregnancy lasts 40 weeks. The difference is that health professionals measure pregnancy from the start of the last menstrual period, which is usually two weeks *before* conception.)

The 38 weeks of prenatal development are divided into three stages: the period of the zygote, the period of the embryo, and the period of the fetus. Each period gets its name from the term used to describe the baby-to-be at that point in prenatal development.

In this module, I'll trace the major developments during each period. As we go, you'll learn the answer to the "what happens when" question that intrigues Eun Jung.

Period of the Zygote (Weeks 1–2)

The diagram at the top of page 77 traces the major events of the first period of prenatal development, which begins with fertilization and lasts about 2 weeks. **It ends when the fertilized egg, called a *zygote*, implants itself in the wall of the uterus.** During these 2 weeks, the zygote grows rapidly through cell division. The zygote travels down the fallopian tube toward the uterus. Within hours, the zygote divides for the first time; then division occurs every 12 hours. Occasionally, the zygote separates into two clusters that develop into identical twins. Fraternal twins, which are more common, are created when two eggs are released and each is fertilized by a different sperm cell. After about 4 days, the zygote consists of about 100 cells and resembles a hollow ball.

By the end of the first week, the zygote reaches the uterus. **The next step is *implantation*: The zygote burrows into the uterine wall and establishes connections with the mother's blood vessels.** Implantation takes about a week to complete and triggers hormonal changes that prevent menstruation, letting the woman know she has conceived.

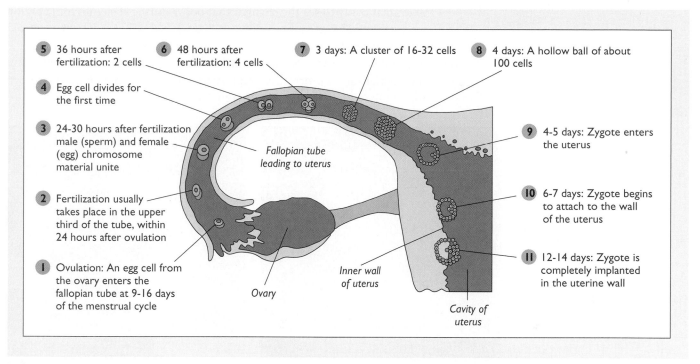

5 36 hours after fertilization: 2 cells

6 48 hours after fertilization: 4 cells

7 3 days: A cluster of 16-32 cells

8 4 days: A hollow ball of about 100 cells

4 Egg cell divides for the first time

3 24-30 hours after fertilization male (sperm) and female (egg) chromosome material unite

Fallopian tube leading to uterus

9 4-5 days: Zygote enters the uterus

2 Fertilization usually takes place in the upper third of the tube, within 24 hours after ovulation

10 6-7 days: Zygote begins to attach to the wall of the uterus

1 Ovulation: An egg cell from the ovary enters the fallopian tube at 9-16 days of the menstrual cycle

Ovary

Inner wall of uterus

11 12-14 days: Zygote is completely implanted in the uterine wall

Cavity of uterus

FIG 4–1

The implanted zygote, shown in the photo, is less than a millimeter in diameter. Yet its cells have already begun to differentiate. In the diagram on page 78, which shows a cross-section of the zygote and the wall of the uterus, you can see different layers of cells. **A small cluster of cells near the center of the zygote, the *germ disc*, eventually develops into the baby.** The other cells are destined to become structures that support, nourish, and protect the developing organism. **The layer of cells closest to the uterus becomes the *placenta*, a structure for exchanging nutrients and wastes between the mother and the developing organism.**

Implantation and differentiation of cells mark the end of the period of the zygote. Comfortably sheltered in the uterus, the zygote is well prepared for the remaining 36 weeks of the marvelous journey to birth.

Period of the Embryo (Weeks 3–8)

Once the zygote is completely embedded in the uterine wall, it is called an *embryo*. This new period typically begins the third week after conception and lasts until the end of the eighth week. During the period of the embryo, body structures and internal organs develop. At the beginning of the period, three layers form in the embryo. **The outer layer or *ectoderm* will become hair, the outer layer of skin, and the nervous system; the middle layer or *mesoderm* will form muscles, bones, and the circulatory system; the inner layer or *endoderm* will form the digestive system and the lungs.**

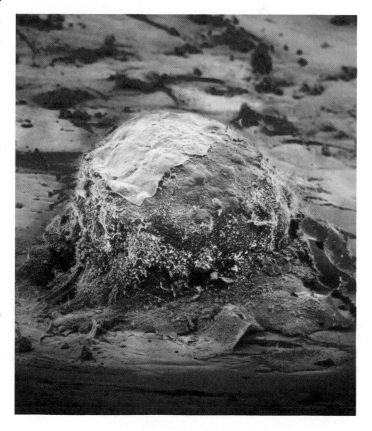

One dramatic way to see the changes that occur during the embryonic period is to compare a 3-week-old embryo with an 8-week-old embryo. The 3-week-old embryo shown in the left photo is about 2 millimeters long. Cell specialization is underway, but the organism looks more like a salamander than a human being. But growth and specialization proceeds so rapidly that an 8-week-old embryo—shown in the photo on the right—looks very different. You can see eyes, jaw, arms, and legs.

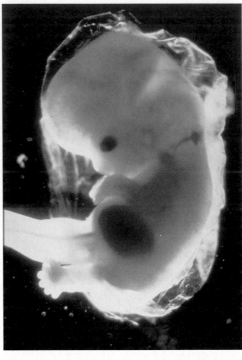

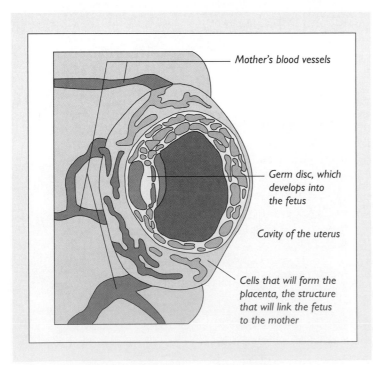

FIG 4–2

Mother's blood vessels

Germ disc, which develops into the fetus

Cavity of the uterus

Cells that will form the placenta, the structure that will link the fetus to the mother

The brain and the nervous system are also developing rapidly, and the heart has been beating for nearly a month. Most of the organs found in a mature human are in place, in some form. (The sex organs are a notable exception.) Yet, being only an inch long and weighing a fraction of an ounce, the embryo is much too small for the mother to feel its presence.

The embryo's environment is shown in the figure at the top of page 79. **The embryo rests in a sac called the *amnion*, which is filled with *amniotic fluid* that cushions the embryo and maintains a constant temperature.** The embryo is linked to the mother by two structures. **The *umbilical cord* houses blood vessels that join the embryo to the placenta.** In the placenta, the blood vessels from the umbilical cord run close to the mother's blood vessels, but aren't actually connected to them. Instead, the blood flows through villi, finger-like projections from the umbilical blood vessels that are shown in the enlarged view in the figure on page 79. As you can see, villi lie in close proximity to the mother's blood vessels, which allows nutrients, oxygen, vitamins, and waste products to be exchanged between mother and embryo.

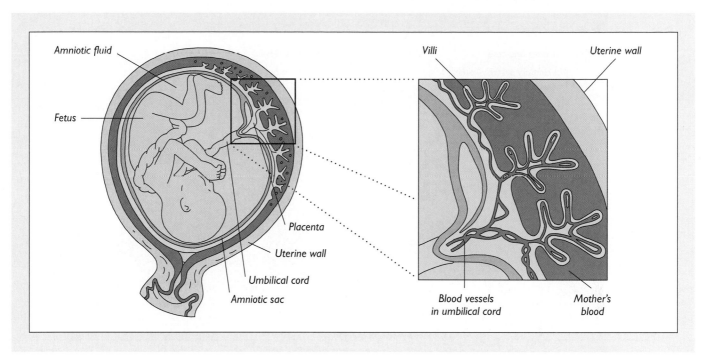

FIG 4–3

Growth in the period of the embryo follows two important principles. First, the head develops before the rest of the body. **Such growth from the head to the base of the spine illustrates the *cephalocaudal principle*.** Second, arms and legs develop before hands and feet. **Growth of parts near the center of the body before those that are more distant illustrates the *proximodistal principle*.** Growth after birth also follows these principles.

With body structures and internal organs in place, another major milestone passes in prenatal development. What's left is for these structures and organs to begin working properly. This is accomplished in the final period of prenatal development, as we'll see in the next section.

Period of the Fetus (Weeks 9–38)

The final and longest phase of prenatal development, the *period of the fetus*, extends from the ninth week after conception until birth. During this period, the baby-to-be becomes much larger and its bodily systems begin to work. The increase in size is remarkable. At the beginning of this period, the fetus weighs less than an ounce. At about 4 months, the fetus weighs roughly 4 to 8 ounces, enough for the mother to feel its movements. In the last 5 months of pregnancy, the fetus gains an additional 7 or 8 pounds before birth. The chart on page 80, which depicts the fetus at one-eighth of its actual size, shows these incredible increases in size.

During the fetal period, the finishing touches are put on the body systems that are essential to human life, such as the nervous system, respiration, and digestion. Some highlights of this period include the following:

- In the fifth and sixth months after conception, eyebrows, eyelashes, and scalp hair emerge. **The skin thickens and is covered with a thick greasy substance, *vernix*, that protects the fetus during its long bath in amniotic fluid.**

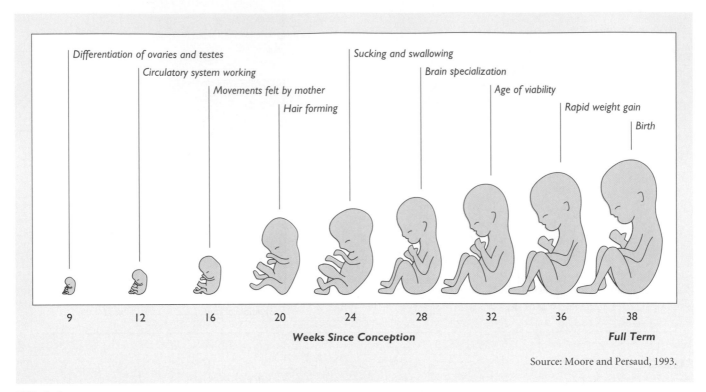

| Differentiation of ovaries and testes | Circulatory system working | Movements felt by mother | Hair forming | | Sucking and swallowing | Brain specialization | Age of viability | Rapid weight gain | Birth |

Weeks Since Conception

9   12   16   20   24   28   32   36   38   **Full Term**

Source: Moore and Persaud, 1993.

FIG 4–4

• Near the end of the embryonic period, male embryos develop testes and female embryos develop ovaries. In the third month, the testes in a male fetus secrete a hormone that causes a set of cells to become a penis and scrotum; in a female fetus, this hormone is absent, so the same cells become a vagina and labia.

• At 4 weeks after conception, a flat set of cells curls to form a tube. One end of the tube swells to form the brain; the rest forms the spinal cord. By the start of the fetal period, the brain has distinct structures and has begun to regulate body functions. **During the period of the fetus, all regions of the brain grow, particularly the *cerebral cortex*, the wrinkled surface of the brain that regulates many important human behaviors.**

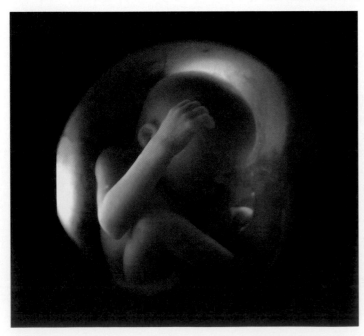

With these and other rapid changes, by 22 to 28 weeks most systems function well enough that a fetus born at this time has a chance to survive, which is why this age range is called the *age of viability*. By this age, the fetus has a distinctly baby-like look, as you can see in the photo. However, babies born this early have trouble breathing because their lungs are not yet mature. Also, they cannot regulate their body temperature very well because they lack the insulating layer of fat that appears in the eighth month after conception. With modern neonatal intensive care, infants born this early can survive, but they face other challenges, as I'll describe in Module 4.3.

The changes of the fetal period also mean that the fetus actually starts to behave (Joseph, 2000). The fetus responds to stimulation (Birnholz & Benaccrraf, 1983; Kisilcvsky & Low, 1998). For cxamplc, although we can't observe it directly, the man's guitar playing in the photo probably causes the fetal heart rate to increase and may cause the fetus to move. Also, the fetus develops regular periods of activity: Most mothers report times when the fetus is moving and other times when the fetus is still (DiPietro et al., 1996). And, as we'll see in the Looking Ahead feature, some fetuses are more active than others and these differences predict infants' behavior at 6 months of age.

LOOKING AHEAD

Fetal Activity Predicts Infant Fussiness

Some pregnant women say that the fetus is active constantly, almost as if it's exercising to prepare for birth! Yet, other women report little movement; the fetus seems to be perpetually quiet. Are these differences in the activity level of a fetus related to later aspects of an infant's development? Janiet DiPietro and her colleagues (1996) addressed this question by measuring fetal activity level approximately 1 month before birth. Pregnant women lay quietly for about an hour with a device attached to their abdomen that recorded motor activity (e.g., moving an arm or leg) but not breathing or hiccupping. When babies were 6 months old, mothers completed a questionnaire that assessed many aspects of infants' behavior. DiPietro and her colleagues found a correlation of 0.6 between fetal activity level and fussiness at 6 months. That is, a more active fetus tends to be fussier at 6 months, which means that the infant cries more often and more intensely, is more difficult to soothe when upset, and is moodier overall. In other words, an active fetus is more likely than an inactive fetus to become an unhappy, difficult baby. This finding suggests that infant fussiness may reflect nature more than nurture. If fussiness were due primarily to an infant's experiences after birth, then measures taken before birth should not predict fussiness. Because fussiness relates to fetal activity, biology rather than experiences after birth would seem to be the key factor in the onset of fussy behavior in babies. ■

> During the last period of prenatal development, the fetus becomes much larger and body systems begin to function.

Remarkably, newborns apparently can recognize some of the sounds they hear during prenatal development. DeCasper and Spence (1986) had pregnant women read aloud the famous Dr. Seuss story *The Cat in the Hat* twice a day for the last 2 months of pregnancy. As newborns, then, these babies had heard *The Cat in the Hat* for more than 3 hours. The newborns were then allowed to suck on a mechanical nipple connected to a tape recorder so that the baby's sucking could turn the tape on or off. The investigators discovered that babies would suck to hear a tape of their mother reading *The Cat in the Hat* but not to hear her reading other stories. Evidently, newborns recognized the familiar, rhythmic quality of *The Cat in the Hat* from their prenatal story-times.

These and other important prenatal changes are summarized in Table 4-1 on page 82.

■■■■ SUMMARY TABLE

Changes During Prenatal Development

Stage	Duration (after conception)	Principal Changes
1. Period of the Zygote	0–2 weeks	Egg is fertilized, zygote becomes implanted in wall of uterus
2. Period of the Embryo	2–8 weeks	Period of rapid growth, most body structures begin to form
3. Period of the Fetus	9–38 weeks	Huge increase in size, most body systems begin to function

TABLE 4–1

The milestones listed in the table make it clear that prenatal development does a remarkable job of preparing the fetus for independent living as a newborn baby. But these astonishing prenatal changes can only take place when a woman provides a healthy environment for her baby-to-be. The Making Children's Lives Better feature describes what pregnant women should do to provide the best foundation for prenatal development.

MAKING CHILDREN'S LIVES BETTER

Five Steps Toward a Healthy Baby

1. Visit a health-care provider for regular prenatal checkups. You should have monthly visits until you get close to your due date, when you will have a checkup every other week or maybe even weekly.

2. Eat healthy foods. Be sure your diet includes foods from each of the five major food groups (cereals, fruits, vegetables, dairy products, and meats and beans). Your health-care provider may recommend that you supplement your diet with vitamins, minerals, and iron, to be sure you are providing your baby with all the nutrients he or she needs.

3. Stop drinking alcohol and caffeinated beverages. Stop smoking. Consult your health-care provider before taking any over-the-counter medications or prescription drugs.

4. Exercise throughout pregnancy. If you are physically fit, your body is better equipped to handle the needs of the baby.

5. Get enough rest, especially during the last 2 months of pregnancy. Also, attend childbirth education classes so that you'll be prepared for labor, delivery, and your new baby.

As critically important as these steps are, they unfortunately do not guarantee a healthy baby. In Module 4.2, we'll see how prenatal development can sometimes go awry. ■

Check Your Learning

1. Fraternal twins develop when _____.

2. The period of the zygote ends _____.

3. Body structures and internal organs form during the period of the
   _____.

4. The embryo rests in a fluid-filled sac called the _____.

5. _____ is called the age of viability because at this time most body
   systems function well enough to support life.

6. In the last few months of prenatal development, the fetus has regular periods of
   activity and _____, which are the first signs of fetal behavior.

■ **Active Children** Suppose a fetus is extremely active before birth and is a
fussy, demanding baby after birth. How might these behaviors affect the baby's
parents and other family members?

Answers: (1) two eggs are fertilized by two sperm, (2) at 2 weeks after conception (when the zygote
is completely implanted in the wall of the uterus), (3) embryo, (4) amnion, (5) Between 22 and 28
weeks, (6) the eyes and ears respond to stimulation.

Influences on Prenatal Development

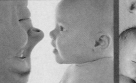

Learning Objectives

■ **How is prenatal development influenced by a pregnant woman's nutrition, the
stress she experiences while pregnant, and her age?**

■ **What is a teratogen, and what specific diseases, drugs, and environmental hazards
can be teratogens?**

■ **How exactly do teratogens affect prenatal development?**

■ **How can prenatal development be monitored? Can abnormal prenatal development be corrected?**

4.2

**Influences on Prenatal
Development**

├ General Risk Factors

├ Teratogens: Diseases, Drugs,
  and Environmental Hazards

├ How Teratogens Influence
  Prenatal Development

└ Prenatal Diagnosis and
  Treatment

*Chloe was barely 2 months pregnant at her first prenatal checkup. As she waited
for her appointment, she looked at the list of questions that she wanted to ask
her obstetrician. "I spend much of my workday at a computer. Is radiation from
the monitor harmful to my baby?" "When my husband and I get home from
work, we'll have a glass of wine to help unwind from the stress of the day. Is
moderate drinking like this okay?" "I'm 38. I know older women more often give
birth to mentally retarded babies. Is there any way I can know if my baby will be
mentally retarded?"*

All of Chloe's questions concern potential harm to her baby-to-be. She worries
about the safety of her computer monitor, about her nightly glass of wine, and about
her age. Chloe's concerns are well-founded. Beginning with conception, environmental factors influence the course of prenatal development, and they are the focus
of this module, which covers problems that sometimes arise in pregnancy.

General Risk Factors

As the name implies, general risk factors can have widespread effects on prenatal development. Scientists have identified three general risk factors: nutrition, stress, and a mother's age.

Nutrition. The mother is the developing child's sole source of nutrition, so a balanced diet that includes foods from each of the five major food groups is vital. Most pregnant women need to increase their intake of calories by about 10 to 20 percent to meet the needs of prenatal development. A woman should expect to gain between 25 and 35 pounds during pregnancy, assuming that her weight was normal before pregnancy. A woman who was underweight before becoming pregnant may gain as much as 40 pounds; a woman who was overweight should gain at least 15 pounds (Institute of Medicine, 1990). Of this gain, about one-third reflects the weight of the baby, the placenta, and the fluid in the amniotic sac; another third comes from increases in a woman's fat stores; yet another third comes from the increased volume of blood and increases in the size of her breasts and uterus (Whitney & Hamilton, 1987).

Sheer amount of food is only part of the equation for a healthy pregnancy. What a pregnant woman eats is also very important. Proteins, vitamins, and minerals are essential for normal prenatal development. For example, folic acid, one of the B vitamins, is important for the baby's nervous system to develop properly (Shaw et al., 1995). **When mothers do not consume adequate amounts of folic acid, their babies are at risk for *spina bifida*, a disorder in which the embryo's neural tube does not close properly during the first month of pregnancy.** Since the neural tube develops into the brain and spinal cord, when it does not close properly the result is permanent damage to the spinal cord and the nervous system. Many children with spina bifida need crutches, braces, or wheelchairs. Other prenatal problems have also been traced to inadequate proteins, vitamins, or minerals, so health-care providers typically recommend that pregnant women supplement their diet with additional proteins, vitamins, and minerals.

When a pregnant woman does not provide adequate nourishment, the infant is likely to be born prematurely and to be underweight. Inadequate nourishment during the last few months of pregnancy can particularly affect the nervous system, because this is a time of rapid brain growth. Finally, babies who do not receive adequate nourishment are vulnerable to illness (Guttmacher & Kaiser, 1986).

Stress. Does a pregnant woman's mood affect the zygote, embryo, or fetus in her uterus? Is a woman who is happy during pregnancy more likely to give birth to a happy baby? Is a pregnant woman like the harried office worker in the photo more likely to give birth to an irritable baby? **These questions address the impact on prenatal development of chronic *stress*, which refers to a person's physical and psychological responses to threatening or challenging situations.** We can answer these questions with some certainty for nonhumans. When pregnant female animals experience constant stress—such as repeated electric shock or intense overcrowding—their offspring are often smaller than average and prone to other physical and behavioral problems (Schneider, 1992). In addition, stress seems to cause greater harm when experienced early in pregnancy (Schneider et al., 1999).

Determining the impact of stress on human pregnancy is more difficult because we must rely solely on correlational studies. (It would be unethical to do an experiment that assigned some pregnant women to a condition of extreme stress.) Studies typically show that women who report greater anxiety during pregnancy more often give birth early or have babies who weigh less than average (Copper et al., 1996; Paarlberg et al., 1995).

Increased stress can harm prenatal development in several ways. First, when a pregnant woman experiences stress, her body secretes hormones that reduce the flow of oxygen to the fetus while increasing its heart rate and activity level (Monk et al., 2000). Second, stress can weaken a pregnant woman's immune system, making her more susceptible to illness (Cohen & Williamson, 1991), which can, in turn, damage fetal development. Third, pregnant women under stress are more likely to smoke or drink alcohol and less likely to rest, exercise, and eat properly. All these behaviors endanger prenatal development.

> Problems during pregnancy are more common when a woman's nutrition is inadequate and when she is under chronic stress.

I want to emphasize that the results described here apply to women who experience prolonged, extreme stress. Virtually all women sometimes become anxious or upset while pregnant. But occasional, relatively mild anxiety is not thought to have any harmful consequences for prenatal development.

Mother's Age. Traditionally, the 20s were thought to be the prime childbearing years. Teenage women as well as women who were 30 or older were considered less fit for the rigors of pregnancy. Is being a 20-something really important for a successful pregnancy? Let's answer this question separately for teenage and older women. Compared to women in their 20s, teenage women are more likely to have problems during pregnancy, labor, and delivery. This is largely because pregnant teenagers do not get good prenatal care, usually because they are unaware of the need and do not seek it out. For example, research done on African American adolescents suggests that when differences in prenatal care are taken into account, teenagers are just as likely as women in their 20s to have problem-free pregnancies and give birth to healthy babies (Goldenberg & Klerman, 1995).

Nevertheless, even when a teenager receives adequate prenatal care and gives birth to a healthy baby, all is not rosy. Children of teenage mothers generally do less well in school and more often have behavioral problems (Dryfoos, 1990). The problems of teenage motherhood—incomplete education, poverty, and marital difficulties—affect the child's later development (Furstenberg, Brooks-Gunn, & Morgan, 1987).

Of course, not all teenage mothers and their infants follow this dismal life course. Some teenage mothers finish school, find good jobs, and have happy marriages; their children do well in school, academically and socially. However, teenage pregnancies with happy endings are definitely the exception; for most teenage mothers and their children, life is a struggle. Educating teenagers about the true consequences of teen pregnancy is crucial.

Are older women better suited for pregnancy? This is an important question because today's American woman is waiting longer than ever to have her first child. Completing an education and beginning a career often delay childbearing. In fact, the birthrate in the 1990s among 30- to 34-year-olds was nearly triple what it was in the early 1970s (U.S. Department of Health and Human Services, 1995).

Traditionally, older women like the one in the photo were thought to have more difficult pregnancies and more complicated labor and deliveries. Today, we know that women in their 30s who are in good health are no more risk-prone during pregnancy, labor, and delivery than women in their 20s (Ales, Druzin, & Santini, 1990). Women in their 40s, however, are more liable to give birth to babies with Down syndrome.

In general, then, prenatal development is most likely to proceed normally when women are healthy and eat right, get good health care, and lead lives that are free of chronic stress. But even in these optimal cases, prenatal development can be disrupted, as we'll see in the next section.

Teratogens: Diseases, Drugs, and Environmental Hazards

In the late 1950s, many pregnant women in Germany took thalidomide, a drug to help them sleep. Soon, however, came reports that many of these women were giving birth to babies with deformed arms, legs, hands, or fingers (Jensen, Benson, & Bobak, 1981). **Thalidomide was a powerful *teratogen*, an agent that causes abnormal prenatal development.** Ultimately, more than 7,000 babies worldwide were harmed before thalidomide was withdrawn from the market (Moore & Persaud, 1993).

Prompted by the thalidomide disaster, scientists began to study teratogens extensively. Today, we know a great deal about many teratogens, which form three broad categories: diseases, drugs, and environmental hazards. Let's look at each.

Diseases. Sometimes women become ill while pregnant. Most diseases, such as colds and many strains of flu, do not affect the developing organism. However, several bacterial and viral infections can be very harmful and in some cases fatal to the embryo or fetus; five of the most common are listed in the table.

■■■■ SUMMARY TABLE

Teratogenic Diseases and Their Consequences

Disease	Potential Consequences
AIDS	Frequent infections, neurological disorders, death
Cytomegalovirus	Deafness, blindness, abnormally small head, mental retardation
Genital herpes	Encephalitis, enlarged spleen, improper blood clotting
Rubella (German measles)	Mental retardation; damage to eyes, ears, and heart
Syphillis	Damage to the central nervous system, teeth, and bones

TABLE 4-2

Some of these diseases pass from the mother through the placenta to attack the embryo or fetus directly. They include cytomegalovirus (a type of herpes), rubella, and syphilis. Other diseases attack at birth: The virus is present in the lining of the birth canal, and the baby is infected as it passes through to be born. Genital herpes is transmitted this way. AIDS is transmitted both ways—through the placenta and during passage through the birth canal.

The only way to guarantee that these diseases do not harm prenatal development is for a woman not to contract the disease before or during her pregnancy. Medication may help the woman, but does not prevent the disease from damaging the developing baby.

Drugs. Thalidomide illustrates the harm that drugs can cause during prenatal development. The table lists other drugs that are known teratogens.

■■■ SUMMARY TABLE

Teratogenic Drugs and Their Consequences

Drug	Potential Consequences
Alcohol	Fetal alcohol syndrome, cognitive deficits, heart damage, retarded growth
Aspirin	Deficits in intelligence, attention, and motor skill
Caffeine	Lower birth weight, decreased muscle tone
Cocaine and heroin	Retarded growth, irritability in newborns
Marijuana	Lower birth weight, less motor control
Nicotine	Retarded growth, possible cognitive impairments

TABLE 4-3

Notice that most of the drugs in the list are substances that you may use routinely—alcohol, aspirin, caffeine, nicotine. Nevertheless, when consumed by pregnant women, they present special dangers (Behnke & Eyler, 1993).

Cigarette smoking is typical of the potential harm from these drugs (Cornelius et al., 1995; Day et al., 2000; Fried, O'Connell, & Watkinson, 1992). The nicotine in cigarette smoke constricts blood vessels, which reduces the oxygen and nutrients that can reach the fetus over the placenta. Therefore, pregnant women who smoke are more likely to miscarry (abort the fetus spontaneously) and to bear children who are smaller than average at birth. Birth complications are also more frequent. And, as children develop, they are more likely to show signs of impaired attention, language, and cognitive skills. Finally, even secondhand smoke harms the fetus. When pregnant women don't smoke but fathers do, babies tend to be smaller at birth (Friedman & Polifka, 1996). The message is clear and simple: Pregnant women shouldn't smoke and they should avoid others who do.

Alcohol also carries serious risk. **Pregnant women who consume large quantities of alcoholic beverages often give birth to babies with *fetal alcohol syndrome (FAS)*.** Children with FAS usually grow more slowly than normal and have heart problems and misshapen faces. Like the child in the photo, youngsters with FAS often have a small head, a thin upper lip, a short nose, and widely spaced eyes. They are often mentally retarded and may have limited motor skills (Niebyl, 1991).

Fetal alcohol syndrome is most likely when pregnant women drink 3 or more ounces of alcohol daily. Does this mean that moderate drinking is safe? No. When women drink moderately throughout pregnancy, their children often have lower scores on tests of attention, memory, and intelligence (Streissguth et al., 1994).

Is there any amount of drinking that's safe during pregnancy? Maybe, but that amount is yet to be determined. Gathering definitive data is complicated by two factors. First, researchers usually determine the amount a woman drinks by her own responses to interviews or questionnaires. If for some reason she does not accurately report her consumption, it is impossible to estimate accurately the amount of harm associated with drinking. Second, any safe level of consumption is probably not the same for all women. Based on their health and heredity, some women may be able to consume more alcohol more safely than others.

These factors make it impossible to guarantee safe levels of alcohol or any of the other drugs listed in Table 4-3. The best policy, therefore, is for woman to avoid all drugs throughout pregnancy.

Environmental Hazards. As a by-product of life in an industrialized world, people are often exposed to toxins in food they eat, fluids they drink, and air they breathe. Chemicals associated with industrial waste are the most common environmental teratogens, and the quantities involved are usually minute. However, as was true for drugs, amounts that go unnoticed by an adult can cause serious damage to prenatal development (Dietrich, 2000). Several environmental hazards that are known teratogens are listed in the table.

■■■■ SUMMARY TABLE

Environmental Teratogens and Their Consequences

Hazard	Potential Consequences
Lead	Mental retardation
Mercury	Retarded growth, mental retardation, cerebral palsy
PCBs	Impaired memory and verbal skill
X-rays	Retarded growth, leukemia, mental retardation

TABLE 4–4

You'll notice that although X rays are included in this table, radiation associated with computer monitors and video display terminals (VDTs) is not. Several major studies have examined the impact of exposure to the electromagnetic fields that are generated by VDTs, and found no negative results. For example, Schnorr and her colleagues (1991) compared the pregnancies in telephone operators who worked at VDTs at least 25 hours weekly with operators who never used VDTs. For both groups of women, about 15 percent of the pregnancies ended in miscarriage. Other studies have not found a connection between exposure to VDTs and birth defects (Parazzini et al., 1993). Evidently, VDTs can be used safely by pregnant women.

In the Focus on Research feature, we look at one of these environmental teratogens in detail.

FOCUS ON RESEARCH

Impact of Prenatal Exposure to PCBs on Cognitive Functioning

Who were the investigators and what was the aim of the study? For many years, polychlorinated biphenyls (PCBs) were used in electrical transformers and paints, but the U.S. government banned them in the 1970s. Like many industrial by-products, they seeped into the waterways where they contaminated fish and wildlife. The amount of PCB in a typical contaminated fish does not affect adults, but Joseph Jacobson, Sandra Jacobson, and Harold Humphrey (1990) wanted to determine if this level of exposure was harmful to prenatal development. In particular, they knew from earlier work that substantial prenatal exposure to PCBs affected infants' cognitive skills; they hoped to determine if prenatal exposure similarly affected preschoolers' cognitive skills.

How did the investigators measure the topic of interest? Jacobson and his colleagues needed to measure prenatal exposure to PCBs and cognitive skill. To measure prenatal exposure, they measured concentrations of PCBs in (a) blood obtained from the umbilical cord and (b) breast milk of mothers who were breast-feeding. To measure cognitive skill, they used a standardized test, the McCarthy Scales for Children's Abilities. The McCarthy Scales measure children's abilities in five areas: verbal, perceptual, quantitative, memory, and motor abilities.

Who were the children in the study? The sample included 236 children who were born in western Michigan between 1980 and 1981. This region was chosen because, at the time, Lake Michigan contained many contaminated salmon and lake trout.

What was the design of the study? The study was correlational because Jacobson and his colleagues were interested in the relation that existed naturally between two variables: exposure to PCB and cognitive skill. The study was longitudinal because children were tested twice: Their exposure to PCBs was measured immediately after birth and their cognitive skill was measured at age 4 years.

Were there ethical concerns with the study? No. The children had been exposed to PCBs naturally, prior to the start of the study. (Obviously, it would not have been ethical for researchers to do an experiment that involved asking pregnant women to eat contaminated fish.) The investigators obtained permission from the parents for the children to participate.

What were the results? PCB exposure was unrelated to performance on the perceptual, quantitative, and motor scales of the McCarthy tests. That is, children with high levels of PCB exposure were just as likely to get high scores on these tests as children with low levels of PCB exposure. However, PCB exposure did affect scores on the verbal and memory scales. Looking at the graphs, you can see that verbal and memory scores were highest in children who had the least prenatal exposure to PCBs and lowest for the 4-year-olds who had the greatest prenatal exposure. In other words, as prenatal exposure to PCBs increased, verbal and memory skills decreased.

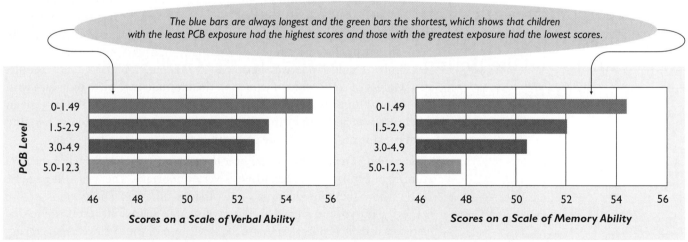

FIG 4–5

What did the investigators conclude? Prenatal exposure to PCBs affects at least two aspects of cognitive development—memory and verbal skill. Though children's scores were in the normal range, their reduced memory and verbal skills will probably cause some trouble in school, such as in learning to read.

What converging evidence would strengthen these conclusions? The results show that PCBs affect children's scores on standardized tests. More convincing would be longitudinal results showing that children exposed to PCBs were, during the elementary-school years, more likely to be diagnosed with a learning disability or with a language impairment. ■

Environmental teratogens are treacherous because people are unaware of their presence in the environment. The women in the Jacobson, Jacobson, and Humphrey (1990) study, for example, did not realize that they were eating PCB-laden fish. This invisibility makes it more difficult for a pregnant woman to protect herself from environmental teratogens. Pregnant women need to be particularly careful of the foods they eat and the air they breathe. They should try to be mindful of the following: (1) be sure all foods are cleaned thoroughly to rid them of insecticides, (2) avoid convenience foods that often contain many chemical additives, and (3) stay away from air that's been contaminated by household products such as cleansers, paint strippers, and fertilizers. Women in jobs that require contact with potential teratogens (e.g., housecleaners, hairdressers) should switch to less potent chemicals. For example, they should use baking soda instead of more chemically-laden cleansers. They should also wear protective gloves, aprons, and masks to reduce their contact with potential teratogens. Finally, because environmental teratogens continue to increase, pregnant women should check with a health-care provider to learn if other materials should be avoided.

How Teratogens Influence Prenatal Development

By assembling all the evidence of harm caused by diseases, drugs, and environmental hazards, scientists have identified four important general principles about how teratogens usually work (Hogge, 1990; Vorhees & Mollnow, 1987).

> The impact of teratogens depends on the genotype of the organism and the timing of exposure to the teratogen.

1. *The impact of a teratogen depends upon the genotype of the organism.* A substance may be harmful to one species but not to another. To determine its safety, thalidomide had been tested on pregnant rats and rabbits and their offspring had normal limbs. Yet, when pregnant women took the same drug in comparable doses, many had children with deformed limbs. Thalidomide was harmless to rats and rabbits but not people. Moreover, some women who took thalidomide gave birth to babies with normal limbs while others, taking comparable doses at the same time in their pregnancies, gave birth to babies with deformities. Apparently, heredity makes some individuals more susceptible than others to a teratogen.

2. *The impact of teratogens changes over the course of prenatal development.* The timing of exposure to a teratogen is very important. The chart on page 91 shows how the consequences of teratogens differ for the periods of the zygote, embryo, and fetus. During the period of the zygote, exposure to teratogens usually results in spontaneous abortion of the fertilized egg. During the embryonic period, exposure produces major defects in body structure. For example, women who took thalidomide during the embryonic period had babies with ill-formed or missing limbs. Women who contract rubella during the embryonic period have babies with heart defects. During the fetal period, exposure to teratogens produces either minor defects in body structure or causes body systems to function improperly. For example, when women drink large quantities of alcohol during the fetal period, the fetus develops fewer brain cells.

   Even within the different periods of prenatal development, developing body parts and systems are more vulnerable at some times than others. The blue shading in the chart indicates a time of maximum vulnerability; orange shading indicates a time when the developing organism is less vulnerable.

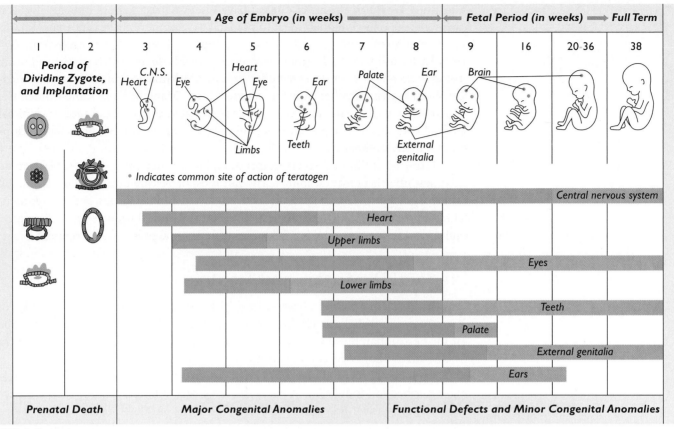

FIG 4-6

The heart, for example, is most sensitive to teratogens during the first two-thirds of the embryonic period. Exposure to teratogens before this time rarely produces heart damage; exposure after this time results in milder damage.

3. *Each teratogen affects a specific aspect (or aspects) of prenatal development.* Said another way, teratogens do not harm all body systems; instead, damage is selective. If a woman contracts rubella, the baby may have problems with its eyes, ears, and heart but its limbs will be normal. If a mother consumes PCB-contaminated fish, the baby typically has normal body parts and normal motor skills but below-average memory and verbal skills.

4. *Damage from teratogens is not always evident at birth but may appear later in life.* In the case of malformed limbs or babies born addicted to cocaine, the effects of a teratogen are obvious immediately. A cocaine baby goes through withdrawal—shaking, crying, and being unable to sleep. Sometimes, however, the damage from a teratogen becomes evident only as the child develops. For example, between 1947 and 1971, many pregnant women in North America and Europe took the drug diethylstilbestrol (DES) to prevent miscarriages. Their babies appeared normal at birth, but as adults, daughters are more likely to have a rare cancer of the vagina and to have difficulty becoming pregnant themselves (Friedman & Polifka, 1996). Sons of women who took DES may be less fertile and at risk for cancer of the testes (Sharpe & Skakkebaek, 1993). Here is a case in which the impact of the teratogen is not evident until decades after birth.

The Real World of Prenatal Risk. I have discussed risk factors individually, as if each were the only potential threat to prenatal development. In reality, many infants are exposed to multiple general risks and multiple teratogens (Giberson & Weinberg, 1992; Richardson, 1998). Pregnant women who drink alcohol often smoke and drink coffee. Pregnant women who are under stress often drink alcohol, and may self-medicate with aspirin or other over-the-counter drugs. Many of these same women live in poverty, which means they may have inadequate nutrition and receive minimal medical care during pregnancy. When all the risks are combined, prenatal development is rarely optimal.

From what I've said so far in this module, you may think that the developing child has little chance of escaping harm. But most babies are born in good health. Of course, a good policy for pregnant women is to avoid diseases, drugs, and environmental hazards that are known teratogens. This, coupled with thorough prenatal medical care and adequate nutrition, is the best recipe for normal prenatal development.

Prenatal Diagnosis and Treatment

I really don't care whether I have a boy or girl, just as long as it's healthy." Legions of parents worldwide have felt this way, but until recently, all they could do was hope for the best. Today, however, advances in technology give parents a much better idea whether their baby is developing normally.

Even before a woman becomes pregnant, a couple may go for genetic counseling, described in Module 3.2. A counselor constructs a family tree for each prospective parent to check for heritable disorders. If it turns out that one (or both) carries a disorder, further tests can determine the person's genotype. With this more detailed information, a genetic counselor can discuss choices with the prospective parents. They may choose to go ahead and conceive "naturally," taking their chances that the child will be healthy. Or, they could decide to use sperm or eggs from other people. Yet another choice would be to adopt a child.

After a woman is pregnant, how can we know if prenatal development is progressing normally? Traditionally, obstetricians gauged development by feeling the size

and position of the fetus through a woman's abdomen. This technique was not very precise and, of course, couldn't be done at all until the fetus was large enough to feel. Today, however, new techniques have revolutionized our ability to monitor prenatal growth and development. **A standard part of prenatal care in North America is *ultrasound*, a procedure using sound waves to generate a picture of the fetus.** As the photo shows, an instrument about the size of a hair dryer is rubbed over the woman's abdomen; the image is shown on a nearby TV monitor. The pictures that are generated are hardly portrait quality; they are grainy and it takes an expert's eye to distinguish what's what. Nevertheless, the procedure is painless and parents are thrilled to be able to see their baby and watch it move.

Ultrasound can be used as early as 4 or 5 weeks after conception; before this time the fetus is not large enough to generate an interpretable image. Ultrasound pictures are useful for determining the position of the fetus in the uterus and, at 16 to 20 weeks after conception, its sex. Ultrasound can also help in detecting twins or other multiple pregnancies. Finally, ultrasound can be used to identify gross physical deformities, such as abnormal growth of the head.

When a genetic disorder is suspected, two other techniques are particularly valuable because they provide a sample of fetal cells that can be analyzed. **In *amniocentesis*, a needle is inserted through the mother's abdomen to obtain a sample of the amniotic fluid that surrounds the fetus.** Amniocentesis is typically performed at approximately 16 weeks after conception. As you can see in the top diagram, ultrasound is used to guide the needle into the uterus. The fluid contains skin cells that can be grown in a laboratory dish and then analyzed to determine the genotype of the fetus.

In *chorionic villus sampling (CVS)*, a sample of tissue is obtained from the chorion, which is part of the placenta, and analyzed. The bottom diagram shows that a small tube, inserted through the vagina and into the uterus, is used to collect a small plug of cells from the placenta. CVS is often preferred over amniocentesis because CVS can be done about 8 weeks after conception, nearly two months earlier than amniocentesis. In both cases, results are returned from the lab within several days.

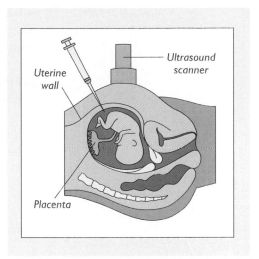

FIG 4–7

With samples obtained from either amniocentesis or CVS, about 200 different genetic disorders can be detected. These procedures are virtually error-free but at a price: Miscarriages are slightly more likely—1 or 2 percent—after amniocentesis or CVS (Cunningham, MacDonald, & Gant, 1989). A woman must decide if the information gained from amniocentesis or CVS justifies the slight risk of a miscarriage.

Ultrasound, amniocentesis, and CVS have made it much easier to determine if prenatal development is progressing normally. But what happens when it is not? Until recently a woman's options were limited: she could continue the pregnancy or end it. But options are expanding. **A whole new field called *fetal medicine* is concerned with treating prenatal problems before birth.** One approach in fetal medicine is to treat disorders medically, by administering drugs or hormones to the fetus. In one case, when ultrasound pictures showed a fetus with an enlarged thyroid gland that would have made delivery difficult, a hormone was injected into the amniotic fluid to shrink the thyroid gland and allow normal delivery (Davidson et al., 1991). In another case, amniocentesis revealed that a fetus had inherited an immune system disorder that would leave the baby highly vulnerable to infections, so healthy immune cells were injected into the umbilical cord (Elmer-DeWitt, 1994).

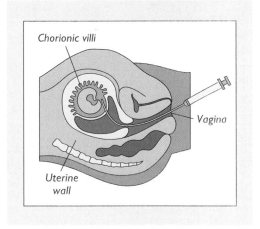

FIG 4–8

Another way to correct prenatal problems is fetal surgery. Doctors partially remove the fetus from the uterus, perform corrective surgery, then return the fetus to the uterus. Some cases of spina bifida have been corrected with fetal surgery in the seventh or eighth month of pregnancy. Surgeons cut through the mother's abdominal wall to expose the fetus, then cut through the fetal abdominal wall; the spinal cord is repaired and the fetus is returned to the uterus (Grovak, 1999).

Fetal surgery has also been used to correct some heart defects and urinary tract blockages (Ohlendorf-Moffat, 1991). Fetal surgery holds great promise but it is still highly experimental and therefore considered as a last resort.

Yet another approach to treating prenatal problems is genetic engineering, replacing defective genes with synthetic normal genes. Take phenylketonuria as an example. Remember, from Module 3.2, that when a baby inherits the recessive allele for PKU from both parents, and PKU is not detected at birth, toxins accumulate that cause mental retardation. In theory, it should be possible to take a sample of cells from the fetus, remove the recessive genes from the twelfth pair of chromosomes and replace them with the dominant genes. These "repaired" cells could then be injected into the fetus, where they would multiply and cause enough enzyme to be produced to break down phenylalanine, thereby avoiding PKU (Verma, 1990).

As with fetal surgery, however, translating idea into practice has been difficult and there are many problems yet to be solved (Marshall, 1995). Nevertheless, gene therapy has been successful in a few cases.

Fetal medicine may sound like science fiction, but these techniques have been used with humans. Granted, they are highly experimental and failures occur, but just as the end of the twentieth century has seen huge progress in prenatal diagnosis, prenatal treatment should be more common in the twenty-first century.

Answers to Chloe's questions: Return to Chloe's questions in the module-opening vignette (page 83) and answer them for her. Pages in this module where the answers appear are given:

- Question about her computer monitor—page 88
- Question about her nightly glass of wine—page 87
- Question about giving birth to a baby with mental retardation—page 85

Check Your Learning

1. Important general risk factors in pregnancy include a woman's nutrition, _____, and her age.

2. Adolescent girls can have problem-free pregnancies and give birth to healthy babies if _____.

3. When it comes to drugs, the best advice for a pregnant woman is _____.

4. Some of the most dangerous teratogens are _____ because a pregnant woman is often unaware of their presence.

5. During the period of the zygote, exposure to a teratogen typically _____.

6. Cases of women who took DES during pregnancy show that _____.

7. Two techniques used to determine if a fetus has a hereditary disorder are amniocentesis and _____.

8. In fetal medicine, health-care professionals treat problems of prenatal development with drugs and hormones, surgically, and _____.

■ ■ **Nature and Nurture** Describe how the impact of teratogens on the fetus
■ ■ shows nature and nurture in action during prenatal development.

Answers: (1) prolonged stress, (2) they receive adequate prenatal care, (3) to avoid all drugs, including aspirin, caffeine, and nicotine, (4) environmental hazards, (5) results in miscarriage (spontaneous abortion of the fertilized egg), (6) the damage from some teratogens is not evident until later in life, (7) chorionic villus sampling (CVS), (8) through genetic engineering

Happy Birthday!

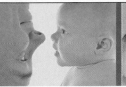

■ **What are the stages in labor and delivery?**

■ **What arc "natural" ways of coping with the pain of childbirth? Is childbirth at home safe?**

■ **How do we determine if a baby is healthy? What behavioral states are common in newborns?**

■ **What are some complications that occur during birth?**

■ **What is postpartum depression and what are its effects?**

> *Marlena is about to begin classes to prepare for her baby's birth. She is relieved that the classes are finally starting because this means the end of pregnancy is in sight. But all the talk she has heard about breathing exercises and coaching sounds pretty silly to her. Marlena would prefer to get knocked out for the delivery and wake up when everything is over.*

As women like Marlena near the end of pregnancy, they find that sleeping and breathing become more difficult, they tire more rapidly, they become constipated, and their legs and feet swell. Women look forward to birth, both to relieve their discomfort and, of course, to see their baby. In this module, we'll see the different stages involved in birth, review various approaches to childbirth, and look at problems that can arise. We'll also look at childbirth classes like the one Marlena is taking.

Labor and Delivery

In a typical pregnancy, a woman goes into labor about 38 weeks after conception. Scientists don't know all the events that initiate labor but one key element seems to be a "ready" signal from an area of the fetal brain that tracks the progress of developing body organs and systems (Palca, 1991).

"Labor" is named appropriately, for it is the most intense, prolonged physical effort that humans experience. Labor is usually divided into the three stages shown in the diagram on page 96. The first stage of labor begins when the muscles of the uterus start to contract. These contractions force amniotic fluid up against the cervix, the opening at the bottom of the uterus that is the entryway to the birth canal. The wavelike motion of the amniotic fluid with each contraction causes the cervix to enlarge gradually.

In the early phase of Stage 1, the contractions are weak and spaced irregularly. By the end of the early phase, the cervix is about 5 centimeters (2 inches) in diameter. In the late phase of Stage 1, contractions are stronger and occur at regular intervals. By the end of the late phase, the cervix is about 7 to 8 centimeters (3 inches) in diameter. In the transition phase of Stage 1, contractions are intense and sometimes occur without interruption. Women report that the transition phase is the most painful part of labor. At the end of transition, the cervix is about 10 centimeters (4 inches) in diameter.

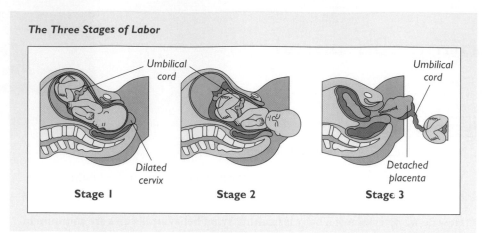

FIG 4–9

Stage 1 typically lasts from 12 to 24 hours for the birth of a first child, and most of the time is spent in the relative tranquility of the early phase. Stage 1 is usually shorter for subsequent births, with 3 to 8 hours being common. However, as the wide ranges suggest, these times are only rough approximations; the actual times vary greatly among women and are virtually impossible to predict.

> In the first stage of labor, contractions cause the cervix to expand; in the second, the baby is born; and in the third, the placenta is expelled.

When the cervix is fully enlarged, the second stage of labor begins. Most women feel a strong urge to push the baby out, using their abdominal muscles. This pushing, along with uterine contractions, propels the baby down the birth canal. **Soon the top of the baby's head appears, an event known as *crowning*.** In about an hour for first births and less for later births, the baby passes through the birth canal and emerges from the mother's body. **Most babies arrive headfirst, but a small percentage come out feet-first or bottom-first, which is known as a *breech presentation*.** The baby's birth marks the end of the second stage of labor.

With the baby born, you might think that labor is over, but it's not. There is a third stage, in which the placenta (also called, appropriately, the afterbirth) is expelled from the uterus. The placenta becomes detached from the wall of the uterus and contractions force it out through the birth canal. This stage is quite brief, typically lasting 10 to 15 minutes.

You can see the growing intensity of labor in this typical account. For Ximena, a 27-year-old pregnant for the first time, the early phase of Stage 1 labor lasted 18 hours. For the first 4 hours, Ximena averaged one contraction every 20 minutes. Each contraction lasted approximately 30 seconds. Then the contractions became longer, lasting 45 seconds. They came about every 15 minutes for 3 hours, and then every 8 to 10 minutes for another 11 hours. At this point, Ximena's cervix was 5 centimeters in diameter—the early phase was over.

The late phase of Stage 1 lasted 3 hours. For 2 hours Ximena had one 60-second contraction every 5 minutes. Then for 1 hour she had a 75-second contraction every 3 minutes. At this point, her cervix was 8 centimeters in diameter and she entered the transition phase. For the next 30 minutes she had a 90-second contraction every 2 minutes. Finally, her cervix was a full 10 centimeters and she could push. Thirty minutes later, David was born.

The stages of labor are summarized in the table.

■■■■ SUMMARY TABLE

Stages of Labor		
Stage	Duration	Primary Milestone
1	12-24 hours	cervix enlarges to 10 cm
2	1 hour	baby moves down the birth canal
3	10-15 minutes	placenta is expelled

TABLE 4-5

Approaches to Childbirth

When my mother went into labor (with me), she was admitted to a nearby hospital where she soon was administered a general anesthetic. My father went to a waiting room where he and other fathers-to-be anxiously awaited news of their babies. Some time later my mother recovered from anesthesia and learned that she had given birth to a healthy baby boy. My father, who had grown tired of waiting, had gone back to work, so he got the good news in a phone call.

These were standard hospital procedures in 1950 and virtually all American babies were born this way. No longer. Since the 1960s, many women have used more "natural" or prepared approaches to childbirth, viewing labor and delivery as life events to be celebrated, not medical procedures to be endured. One of the fundamental beliefs of all prepared approaches is that birth is more likely to be problem-free and rewarding when mothers and fathers understand what's happening during pregnancy, labor, and delivery. Consequently, prepared childbirth means going to classes to learn basic facts about pregnancy and childbirth (not unlike the material presented in this chapter).

Childbirth classes also spend considerable time showing women how to handle the pain of childbirth. Natural methods of dealing with pain are emphasized over medication. Why? When a woman is anesthetized—either with general anesthesia or local anesthesia (only the lower body is numbed)—she can't use her abdominal muscles to help push the baby through the birth canal. Without this pushing, the obstetrician may have to use mechanical devices to pull the baby through the birth canal, which involves some risk to the baby (Johanson et al., 1993). Also, drugs that reduce the pain of childbirth cross the placenta and can affect the baby. Consequently, when a woman receives large doses of pain-relieving medication, her baby is often withdrawn or irritable for days or even weeks (Brazelton, Nugent, & Lester, 1987). These effects are temporary, but they may give the new mother the impression that she has a difficult baby. It is best, therefore, to minimize the use of pain-relieving drugs during birth.

Childbirth classes emphasize three strategies to counter birth pain without drugs. First, because pain often feels greater when a person is tense, pregnant women learn ways to relax during labor. One technique is deep breathing. Second, women are taught visual imagery, picturing in detail a reassuring, pleasant scene or experience. Whenever they begin to experience pain during labor, they focus intensely on this image instead of the pain. A third strategy is to involve a supportive coach. The father-to-be, a relative, or close friend attends childbirth classes with the mother-to-be. The coach learns the techniques for coping with pain and, like the men in the

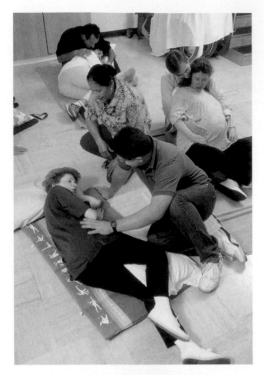

photo, practices them with the pregnant woman. During labor and delivery, the coach is present to help the woman use the techniques she has learned and offer support and encouragement.

Although Marlena, the pregnant woman in the vignette at the beginning of the module, may have her doubts about childbirth classes, research shows that they are useful (Hetherington, 1990). Although most mothers who attend childbirth classes use some medication to reduce the pain of labor, they typically use less than mothers who do not attend childbirth classes. Also, mothers and fathers who attend childbirth classes feel more positive about labor and birth compared to mothers and fathers who do not attend classes.

Another basic premise of the trend to natural childbirth is that birth need not always take place in a hospital. Virtually all babies in the United States are born in hospitals—only 1 percent are born at home. However, home birth is a common practice in Europe. In the Netherlands, for example, about one-third of all births take place at home. Advocates note that home delivery is less expensive and that most women are more relaxed during labor in their homes. Many women also enjoy the greater control they have over labor and birth in a home delivery. A health-care professional is present for home labor and delivery. Sometimes this is a doctor, but more often, it is a trained nurse-midwife like the one in the photo.

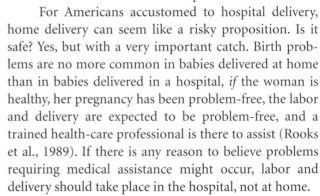

For Americans accustomed to hospital delivery, home delivery can seem like a risky proposition. Is it safe? Yes, but with a very important catch. Birth problems are no more common in babies delivered at home than in babies delivered in a hospital, *if* the woman is healthy, her pregnancy has been problem-free, the labor and delivery are expected to be problem-free, and a trained health-care professional is there to assist (Rooks et al., 1989). If there is any reason to believe problems requiring medical assistance might occur, labor and delivery should take place in the hospital, not at home.

Another alternative to home or hospital birth is the freestanding birth center. Birthing centers are typically small, independent clinics. A woman, her coach, and other family members and friends are assigned a birthing room that is often decorated to look homelike rather than institutional. A doctor or nurse-midwife assists in labor and delivery, which takes place entirely in the birthing room, where it can be observed by all. Like home deliveries, birthing centers are best for deliveries that are expected to be trouble-free.

Birth Complications

Women who are healthy when they become pregnant usually have a normal pregnancy, labor, and delivery. When women are not healthy or don't receive adequate prenatal care, problems can surface during labor and delivery. (Of course, even healthy women face these problems, but not as often.) In this section, we'll look at problems associated with lack of oxygen, being born too early, and being born underweight.

Lack of Oxygen. Until birth, the fetus obtains oxygen from the mother's blood that flows through the placenta and umbilical cord. **If this flow of blood is disrupted, infants do not receive adequate oxygen, a condition known as *anoxia.*** Anoxia sometimes occurs during labor and delivery because the umbilical cord is pinched or squeezed shut, cutting off the flow of blood. **Anoxia may also reflect *placental abruption,* which occurs when the placenta becomes detached from the wall of the uterus, severing the connection to the mother's blood supply.** Anoxia is very serious because it can lead to mental retardation or death (Petrie, 1991).

To guard against anoxia, fetal heart rate is monitored during labor, either by ultrasound or with a tiny electrode that is passed through the vagina and attached to the scalp of the fetus. An abrupt change in heart rate can be a sign that the fetus is not receiving enough oxygen. If heart rate does change suddenly, a health-care professional will try to confirm that the fetus is in distress, perhaps by measuring fetal heart rate with a stethoscope on the mother's abdomen.

When a fetus is in distress, a doctor may decide to remove it from the mother's uterus surgically (Guillemin, 1993). **In a *cesarean section* (or *C-section*) an incision is made in the abdomen to remove the baby from the uterus.** A C-section is riskier for mothers than a vaginal delivery because of increased bleeding and greater danger of infection. A C-section poses little risk for babies, although they are often briefly depressed from the anesthesia that the mother receives before the operation. And mother-infant interactions are much the same for babies delivered vaginally or by planned or unplanned C-sections (Durik, Hyde, & Clark, 2000).

In the United States, about 25 percent of babies are delivered by C-section, up from only 5 percent 30 years ago (Ventura et al., 1997). Many health-care professionals believe C-sections are often performed unnecessarily. Methods for monitoring fetal heart rate are not foolproof, so many C-sections are performed when the fetus is not really in distress. C-sections are also frequently used to end a slow or difficult labor. The U.S. Public Health Service has urged doctors to reduce the number of C-sections, saving the procedure only for emergencies that demand immediate delivery (Ventura et al., 1997).

Prematurity and Low Birth Weight. Normally, gestation takes 38 weeks from conception to birth. ***Premature infants* are born less than 38 weeks after conception. *Small-for-date infants* are substantially smaller than would be expected based on the length of time since conception.** Sometimes these two complications coincide, but not necessarily. Some, but not all, small-for-date infants are premature. And some, but not all, premature infants are small-for-date. In other words, an infant can go the full 9-month term and be under the average 7- to 8-pound birth weight of newborns; the child is therefore small-for-date but not premature. Similarly, an infant born at 7 months that weighs 3 pounds (the average weight of a 7-month fetus) is only premature. But if the baby born after 7 months weighs less than the average, it is both premature and small-for-date.

Of the two complications, prematurity is the less serious. In the first year or so, premature infants often lag behind full-term infants in many facets of development, but by age 2 or 3 years, differences vanish and most premature infants develop normally thereafter (Greenberg & Crnic, 1988).

Prospects are usually not so optimistic for small-for-date babies like the one shown in the photo on page 100. These infants are most often born to women who smoke or drink alcohol frequently during pregnancy or who do not eat enough

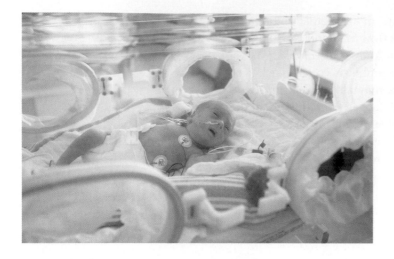

nutritious food (Chomitz, Cheung, & Lieberman, 1995). Babies that weigh less than 1,500 grams (3.3 pounds) at birth often do not survive; when they do, they are usually delayed in their cognitive and motor development (Ventura et al., 1997).

Small-for-date babies who weigh more than 1,500 grams have better prospects, though some do not reach as high a developmental level as others (Zubrick et al., 2000). (This is also true but to a lesser extent for babies who weigh less than 1,500 grams.) Why? Environmental factors turn out to be critical. Development of small-for-date infants depends upon the quality of care they receive in the hospital and at home. These babies can thrive if they receive excellent medical care and their home environment is supportive and stimulating. Unfortunately, not all at-risk babies have these optimal experiences. Many receive inadequate medical care because their families are living in poverty and can't afford it. Others experience stress or disorder in their family life. In these cases, development is usually delayed.

The importance of a supportive environment for at-risk babies was demonstrated dramatically in a longitudinal study of all children born in 1955 on the Hawaiian island of Kauai (Werner, 1995). At-risk newborns who grew up in stable homes were indistinguishable from children born without birth complications. ("Stable family environment" was defined as two supportive, mentally healthy parents present throughout childhood.) When at-risk newborns had an unstable family environment because of divorce, parental alcoholism, or mental illness, for example, they lagged behind their peers in intellectual and social development.

The Hawaiian study underscores a point I have made several times in this chapter: Development is best when pregnant women receive good prenatal care and children live in a supportive environment. Unfortunately, some babies do not fare well. ***Infant mortality* is the number of infants out of 1,000 births who die before their first birthday.** In the United States, about 9 babies out of 1,000—roughly 1 percent—live less than a year. As you can see in the graph, this figure places the United States near the bottom of the industrialized countries of the world (Wegman, 1994).

One reason so many American babies die is low birth weight. The United States has more babies with low birth weight than virtually all other industrialized countries, and we've already seen that low birth weight

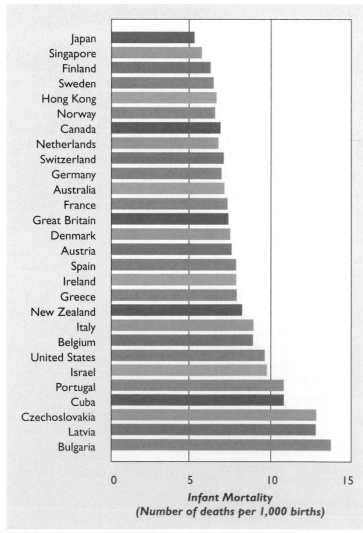

FIG 4-10

places an infant at risk. Low birth weight can usually be prevented if a pregnant woman gets regular prenatal care, but many pregnant women in the United States receive inadequate or no prenatal care. Virtually all the countries that rank ahead of the United States provide complete prenatal care at little or no cost. Many of these countries also provide for paid leaves of absence for pregnant women (Kamerman, 1993).

Prenatal development is the foundation of all development, and only with regular prenatal checkups can we know if this foundation is being laid properly. Pregnant women and the children they carry need this care, and countries need to be sure that they receive it.

The Newborn

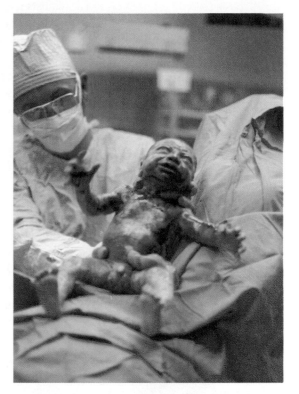

Newborn babies are actually rather homely, as this photo of my son Ben shows. I took it when he was 20 seconds old. Like other newborns, Ben is covered with blood and vernix, the white-colored "grease" that protects the fetus's skin during the many months of prenatal development. His head is temporarily distorted from coming through the birth canal, he has a beer belly, and he is bow-legged. Still, to us he was beautiful, and we were glad he'd finally arrived.

How can we tell if a newborn baby is healthy? **The *Apgar score*, a measure devised by Virginia Apgar, is used to evaluate the newborn baby's condition.** Health professionals look for five vital signs including breathing, heartbeat, muscle tone, presence of reflexes such as coughing, and skin tone. As you can see in the table, each of the five vital signs receives a score of 0, 1, or 2, with 2 being optimal.

	Five Signs Evaluated in the Apgar Score				
Points	Activity (muscle tone)	Pulse	Grimace (response to irritating stimulus)	Appearance (skin color)	Respiration
2	Baby moves limbs actively	100 beats per minute or more	Baby cries intensely	Normal color all over	Strong breathing and crying
1	Baby moves limbs slightly	Fewer than 100 beats per minute	Baby grimaces or cries	Normal color except for extremities	Slow, irregular breathing
0	No movement; muscles flaccid	Not detectable	Baby does not respond	Baby is blue-gray, pale all over	No breathing

TABLE 4–6

The five scores are added together, with a score of 7 or more indicating a baby in good physical condition. A score of 4 to 6 means the newborn will need special attention and care. A score of 3 or less signals a life-threatening situation that requires emergency medical care (Apgar, 1953).

The Apgar score provides a quick, approximate assessment of the newborn's status by focusing on the body systems needed to sustain life. For a comprehensive evaluation of the newborn's well-being, pediatricians and child-development specialists use the Neonatal Behavioral Assessment Scale, or NBAS for short (Brazelton, 1984). The NBAS evaluates a broad range of newborn abilities and behaviors that the infant needs to adjust to life outside the uterus. It measures reflexes, hearing, vision, alertness, irritability, and consolability (how easily the infant is soothed). The NBAS, along with a thorough physical examination, is particularly helpful in diagnosing disorders of the central nervous system (Brazelton et al., 1987).

Newborn States. Newborns spend most of their day alternating among four states (St. James-Roberts & Plewis, 1996; Wolff, 1987):

- *Alert inactivity.* The baby is calm with eyes open and attentive; the baby looks as if he is deliberately inspecting his environment.
- *Waking activity.* The baby's eyes are open, but they seem unfocused; the baby moves her arms or legs in bursts of uncoordinated motion.
- *Crying.* The baby cries vigorously, usually accompanied by agitated but uncoordinated motion.
- *Sleeping.* The baby's eyes are closed and the baby drifts back and forth from periods of regular breathing and stillness to periods of irregular breathing and gentle arm and leg motion.

Crying. Of these states, crying captures the attention of parents and researchers alike. Newborns spend 2 to 3 hours each day crying or on the verge of crying. If you've not spent much time around newborns, you might think that all crying is pretty much alike. In fact, scientists and parents can identify three distinctive types of cries (Snow, 1998). **A *basic cry* starts softly, then gradually becomes more intense and usually occurs when a baby is hungry or tired; a *mad cry* is a more intense version of a basic cry; and a *pain cry* begins with a sudden, long burst of crying, followed by a long pause, and gasping.**

Crying is actually the newborn's first attempt to communicate with others. When a baby like the one in the photo cries, it tells its parents that it's hungry, tired, angry, or hurt. By responding, parents encourage their newborn's efforts to communicate.

Parents are naturally concerned when their baby cries, and if they can't quiet a crying baby, their concern mounts and can easily give way to frustration and annoyance. It's no surprise, then, that parents develop little tricks for soothing their babies. The Real Children feature shows what one mother did when her baby cried.

REAL CHILDREN
Calming Jake

Whenever 4-week-old Jake cried, Peggy's first reaction was to try to figure out why he was crying. Was he hungry? Was his diaper wet? Simply addressing the needs that caused Jake to cry in the first place usually worked. If he continued to cry, she found that the best way to quiet Jake was to lift him to her shoulder and rock him or walk with him. The combination of being upright, restrained, in physical contact with her, and moving all helped to calm him. Sometimes Peggy would swaddle Jake—wrap him tightly in a blanket—and then rock him in a cradle or take him for a ride in a stroller. Another method Peggy used sometimes was to give Jake a pacifier to suck; sucking seemed to allow Jake to calm himself. Sometimes, as a last resort, she'd strap Jake in his car seat and go on a drive. The motion of the car seemed to soothe him.

Peggy's techniques weren't foolproof. Some would work one day but not another. Sometimes Peggy combined these techniques, for example, taking a swaddled Jake to her shoulder. Sometimes, nothing seemed to work, so she'd just put Jake in his crib. And sometimes, as if he were teasing Peggy, Jake would stop crying spontaneously and go right to sleep! ■

Sleeping. Crying may get parents' attention but sleep is what newborns do more than anything else. They sleep 16 to 18 hours daily. The problem for tired parents like the mom in the photo is that newborns sleep in naps taken around-the-clock. Newborns typically go through a cycle of wakefulness and sleep about every 4 hours. That is, they will be awake for about an hour, sleep for 3 hours, then start the cycle anew. During the hour when newborns are awake, they regularly move between the different waking states several times. Cycles of alert inactivity, waking activity, and crying are common.

As babies grow older, the sleep-wake cycle gradually begins to correspond to the day-night cycle (St. James-Roberts & Plewis, 1996). Most babies will begin sleeping through the night at about 3 or 4 months of age, a major milestone for bleary-eyed parents.

Roughly half of newborns' sleep is *irregular* or *rapid-eye-movement (REM) sleep*, a time when the body is quite active. During REM sleep, newborns move their arms and legs, they may grimace, and their eyes may dart beneath their eyelids. Brain waves register fast activity, the heart beats more rapidly, and breathing is more rapid. **In *regular* or *non-REM sleep*, breathing, heart rate, and brain activity are steady and newborns lie quietly without the twitching associated with REM sleep.** REM sleep becomes less frequent as infants grow. By 4 months, only 40 percent of sleep is REM sleep. By the first birthday, REM sleep drops to 25 percent, not far from the adult average of 20 percent (Halpern, MacLean, & Baumeister, 1995).

The function of REM sleep is still debated. Older children and adults dream during REM sleep and brain waves during REM sleep resemble those of an alert, awake person. Consequently, many scientists believe that REM sleep stimulates the brain in some way that helps foster growth in the nervous system (Halpern et al., 1995; Roffwarg, Muzio, & Dement, 1966).

Sudden Infant Death Syndrome. For many parents of young babies, sleep is sometimes a cause of concern. **In *sudden infant death syndrome* (SIDS), a healthy baby dies suddenly, for no apparent reason.** Approximately 1 to 3 of every 1,000 American babies dies from SIDS. Most of them are between 2 and 4 months old.

Scientists don't know the exact causes of SIDS, but they do know several contributing factors. Babies are more vulnerable to SIDS if they were born prematurely or with low birth weight. They are also more vulnerable if their parents smoke. SIDS is more likely when a baby sleeps on its stomach (facedown) than when it sleeps on its back (faceup). Finally, SIDS is more likely during winter when babies sometimes become overheated from too many blankets and too heavy sleepwear (Carroll & Loughlin, 1994). Evidently, SIDS infants, many of whom were born prematurely or with low birth weight, are less able to withstand physiological stresses and imbalances that are brought on by cigarette smoke, breathing that is temporarily interrupted, or by overheating.

As evidence about causes of SIDS accumulated, child advocates called for action. The result is described in the "Child Development and Family Policy" feature.

CHILD DEVELOPMENT AND FAMILY POLICY

Back to Sleep!

In 1992, based on mounting evidence that SIDS more often occurred when infants slept on their stomachs, the American Academy of Pediatrics (AAP) began advising parents to put babies to sleep on their backs or sides. In 1994, the AAP

joined forces with the U.S. Public Health Service to launch a national program to educate parents about the dangers of SIDS and the importance of putting babies to sleep on their backs. The "Back to Sleep" campaign was widely publicized through brochures, posters, like the one shown here, and videos. Since the "Back to Sleep" campaign began, research shows that far more infants are now sleeping on their backs and that the incidence of SIDS has dropped (National Institutes of Health, 2000). The best advice for parents—particularly if their babies were premature or small-for-date—is to keep their babies away from smoke, put them on their backs to sleep, and not overdress them or wrap them too tightly in blankets (Willinger, 1995). ■

Postpartum Depression

For parents, the time immediately after a trouble-free birth is full of excitement, pride, and joy—the much anticipated baby is finally here! Yet roughly half of all new mothers find that their initial excitement gives way to irritation, resentment, and crying spells. These feelings usually last a week or two and probably reflect both the stress of caring for a new baby and physiological changes as a woman's body returns to a nonpregnant state (Brockington, 1996).

For 10 to 15 percent of new mothers, however, irritability continues for months and is often accompanied by feelings of low self-worth, disturbed sleep, poor appetite, and apathy—a condition known as *postpartum depression.* Postpartum depression does not strike randomly. Biology contributes: Particularly high levels of hormones during the later phases of pregnancy place women at risk for postpartum depression (Harris et al., 1994). Experience also contributes: Women are more likely to experience postpartum depression when they were depressed before pregnancy, are coping with other life stresses (e.g., death of a loved one, moving), did not plan to become pregnant, and lack other adults (e.g., the father) to support their adjustment to motherhood (Brockington, 1996; Campbell et al., 1992).

Women who are lethargic and emotionless do not mother warmly and enthusiastically. They don't touch and cuddle their new babies much or talk to them. If the depression lasts only a few weeks, babies are unaffected. However, if postpartum depression lasts for months and months, children of depressed mothers are more likely to become depressed themselves and are also at risk for other behavioral problems (Murray, Fiori-Cowley, & Hooper, 1996).

All new mothers need support from family and friends, but if depression doesn't lift after a few weeks, the mother should see a mental-health professional.

Check Your Learning

1. The first (and longest) stage of labor includes early, late, and _____ phases.

2. Two problems with using anesthesia during labor are that a woman can't use her abdominal muscles to help push the baby down the birth canal and

   _____ .

3. To help women cope with labor pain without drugs, childbirth classes emphasize the importance of relaxation, a soothing visual image, and

   _____ .

4. Home delivery is safe when a pregnant woman is healthy, has had a problem-free pregnancy, expects to have a problem-free delivery, and _____ .

5. The supply of oxygen to the fetus can be disrupted because the umbilical cord is squeezed shut or because _____ .

6. High infant mortality rates in the United States reflect low birth weight, which has been linked to _____ .

7. Newborns spend more time asleep than awake and about half of this time asleep is spent in _____ , a time thought to foster central nervous system growth.

8. The campaign to reduce SIDS emphasizes that infants should _____ .

9. After giving birth, women who suffer _____ often feel irritable, have poor appetite and disturbed sleep, and are apathetic.

■■ **Continuity** Do studies on the long-term effects of prematurity and low birth weight provide evidence for continuity in development or discontinuity in development? Why?

Answers: (1) transition, (2) medication crosses the placenta and affects the baby, (3) a supportive coach, (4) a trained health-care professional is present to deliver the baby, (5) the placenta detaches from the wall of the uterus (placental abruption), (6) inadequate prenatal care, (7) REM sleep, (8) sleep on their backs, (9) postpartum depression

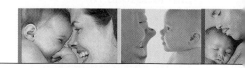

Chapter Critical Review

1. Consider two research studies discussed in Module 4.1, the DiPietro study of fetal activity and infant fussiness, and the DeCasper and Spence study of reading aloud during pregnancy. What do these studies suggest about connections between prenatal and postnatal development?

2. Design a public health program to alert women that lifestyle can affect the development of a fetus even before a woman knows she is pregnant. What groups of women might find special benefit from your program?

3. Explain how the four principles about how teratogens affect development, explained in this chapter, are related to the principles of reaction range and gene-environment relations, explained in Chapter 3.

For more review material, log on to http://www.prenhall.com/kail

See For Yourself

Words can hardly capture the miracle of a newborn baby. If you have never seen a newborn, you need to see one, or even better, a roomful. Arrange to visit the maternity ward of a local hospital, which will include a nursery for newborns. Through a large viewing window, you will be able to observe a few or as many as 15 to 20 newborns. These babies will no longer be covered with blood or vernix, but you will be able to see how the newborn's head is often distorted by its journey from the birth canal.

As you watch the babies, look for reflexive behavior and changes in states. Watch while a baby sucks its fingers. Find a baby who seems to be awake and alert, then note how long the baby stays this way. When alertness wanes, watch for the behaviors that replace it. Finally, observe how different the newborns look and act from each other. The wonderful variety and diversity found among human beings is already evident in humans who are hours or days old. See for yourself!

For More Information About . . .

 prenatal development, try Lennart Nilsson and Lars Hamberger's *A Child is Born* (Delacorte, 1990), which is the source of some of the remarkable photographs of the zygote, embryo, and fetus that appear in this chapter.

 virtually any aspect of pregnancy, visit the New York Online Access to Health (NOAH) Web site: http://www.noah-health.org/english/pregnancy/pregnancy.html

Key Terms

age of viability 80
amniocentesis 93
amnion 78
amniotic fluid 78
anoxia 99
Apgar score 101
basic cry 102
breech presentation 96
cephalocaudal principle 79
cerebral cortex 80
cesarean section (C-section) 99
chorionic villus sampling (CVS) 93
crowning 96
ectoderm 77
embryo 77

endoderm 77
fetal alcohol syndrome (FAS) 87
fetal medicine 93
germ disc 77
implantation 76
infant mortality 100
mad cry 102
mesoderm 77
non-REM sleep 103
pain cry 102
period of the fetus 79
placenta 77
placental abruption 99
postpartum depression 104
premature infants 99

prenatal development 76
proximodistal principle 79
rapid-eye-movement (REM) sleep 103
small-for-date infants 99
spina bifida 84
stress 84
sudden infant death syndrome (SIDS) 103
teratogen 86
ultrasound 92
umbilical cord 78
vernix 79
zygote 76

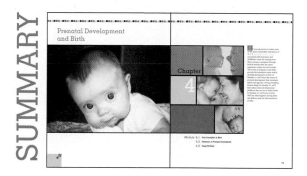

SUMMARY

4.1 From Conception to Birth

Period of the Zygote (Weeks 1–2)

The first period of prenatal development lasts 2 weeks. It begins when the egg is fertilized by the sperm in the fallopian tube and ends when the fertilized egg has implanted in the wall of the uterus. By the end of this period, cells have begun to differentiate.

Period of the Embryo (Weeks 3–8)

The second period of prenatal development begins 2 weeks after conception and ends 8 weeks after conception. This is a period of rapid growth when most major body structures are formed.

Period of the Fetus (Weeks 9–38)

The third period of prenatal development begins 8 weeks after conception and lasts until birth. This period is marked by an increase in the size of the fetus and changes in the body systems necessary for life.

4.2 Influences on Prenatal Development

General Risk Factors

Prenatal development can be harmed if a pregnant mother does not provide adequate nutrition for the developing organism and when women experience considerable stress during pregnancy.

A mother's age also is a factor in prenatal development. Teenagers often have problem pregnancies because they rarely receive adequate prenatal care. Women in their 30s are likely to have problem-free pregnancies if they are in good health before becoming pregnant.

Teratogens: Diseases, Drugs, and Environmental Hazards

Teratogens are agents that can cause abnormal prenatal development. Several diseases are teratogens. Only by avoiding these diseases entirely can a pregnant woman escape their harmful consequences. Many drugs that adults take are teratogens. Environmental teratogens are particularly dangerous because a pregnant woman may not know when these substances are present.

How Teratogens Influence Prenatal Development

The effect of teratogens depends upon the genotype of the organism, when during prenatal development the organism is exposed to the teratogen, and the amount of exposure. The impact of a teratogen may not be evident until later in life.

Prenatal Diagnosis and Treatment

Many techniques are used to track prenatal development. Ultrasound uses sound waves to generate a picture of the fetus. This picture can be used to determine the position of the fetus, its sex, and whether there are gross physical deformities. When genetic disorders

are suspected, amniocentesis or chorionic villus sampling (CVS) is used to determine the genotype of the fetus. The new field of fetal medicine seeks to correct problems of prenatal development medically, surgically, or through genetic engineering.

4.3 Happy Birthday!

Labor and Delivery

Labor consists of three stages. In Stage 1, the muscles of the uterus contract, causing the cervix to enlarge. In Stage 2, the baby moves through the birth canal. In Stage 3, the placenta is delivered.

Approaches to Childbirth

Prepared childbirth assumes that parents should understand what takes place during pregnancy and birth. In natural childbirth, pain-relieving medications are avoided because they prevent women from pushing during labor and because they affect the fetus. Instead, women learn to cope with pain through relaxation, visual imagery, and the help of a supportive coach.

Home birth is safe when the mother is healthy, labor and birth are expected to be trouble-free, and a health-care professional is present to deliver the baby.

Birth Complications

During labor and delivery, the flow of blood to the fetus can be disrupted, either because the umbilical cord is squeezed shut or because the placenta becomes detached from the wall of the uterus. Interrupted blood flow causes anoxia, a lack of oxygen to the fetus. If the fetus is endangered, the doctor may do a cesarean section, removing it from the uterus surgically.

Some babies are born prematurely and others are small-for-date. Premature babies develop more slowly at first but catch up by 2 or 3 years of age. Small-for-date babies often do not fare well, particularly if they weigh less than 1,500 grams at birth and if their environment is stressful.

Infant mortality is relatively high in the United States, primarily because of low birth weight and inadequate prenatal care.

The Newborn

The Apgar score measures five vital signs to determine a newborn baby's physical well-being. The Neonatal Behavioral Assessment Scale (NBAS) provides a comprehensive evaluation of a baby's behavioral and physical status.

Newborns spend their day in one of four states: alert inactivity, waking activity, crying, and sleeping. Newborns spend approximately two-thirds of every day asleep and go through a complete sleep–wake cycle once every 4 hours. By 3 or 4 months, babies sleep through the night. Newborns spend about half their time in REM sleep, a time characterized by active brain waves.

Some healthy babies die from sudden infant death syndrome (SIDS). Contributing to SIDS are prematurity and low birth weight. Babies are also vulnerable to SIDS when they sleep on their stomachs, are overheated, and are exposed to cigarette smoke. A national campaign to encourage parents to have babies sleep on their backs has reduced the number of SIDS cases.

Postpartum Depression

After giving birth, many women briefly experience irritation and crying spells. A few experience postpartum depression—they are irritable, have poor appetite and disturbed sleep, and are apathetic.

Prenatal Development
IN PERSPECTIVE

■ Continuity
Early development is related to later
development but not perfectly

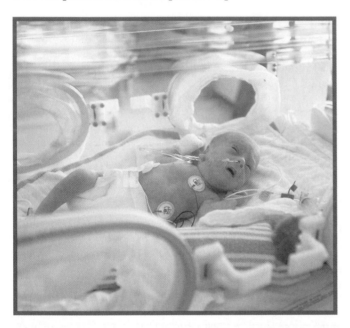

Remember the Hawaiian study of at-risk infants
(Chapter 4)? This study showed that outcomes for
such infants are not uniform. When at-risk infants receive
excellent medical care and they grow up in a stable, supportive environment, they become quite normal children.
But when they grow up in stressful environments, they lag
intellectually and socially. Similarly, SIDS is more likely to
affect babies who are born prematurely and with low birth
weight, yet not all of these babies die of SIDS. When premature and low birth weight babies sleep on their backs,
are not overheated, and their parents don't smoke, they're
unlikely to die from SIDS. Traumatic events early in development, such as being born early or underweight, do not
predetermine the rest of a child's life, but they do make
some developmental paths more likely than others.

■ Nature and Nurture
Development is always jointly influenced
by heredity and environment

We first encountered this theme in Chapter 1 in discussing ethological theory. Ethologists describe critical periods in development—times when animals
(including humans) are biologically programmed so that
certain types of experiences are particularly influential. In
other words, experiences can lead to learning only at certain
times in development. Newborn chicks, for example, are
strongly influenced by the experience of seeing large moving objects. This inborn tendency is shaped by the environment, because the chicks will follow the first large moving
object they see, whether it is their mother or a soccer ball.

Then in Chapter 3 we repeatedly saw how heredity
and environment are essential ingredients in all developmental recipes, though not always in equal parts. In sickle
cell disease, a gene that has survival value in malaria-prone
environments is harmful in environments where malaria
has been eradicated. In this case, nature and nurture are
intimately connected. In the case of PKU, infants who
inherit the defective gene become retarded when their
dietary environment includes foods with phenylalanine
but not when they avoid phenylalanine. We also saw that
children with genes for normal intelligence may develop
below-average, average, or above-average intelligence,
depending upon the environment in which they grow up.

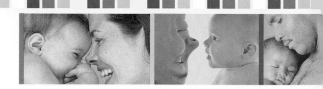

■ Active Child

Children help determine
their own development

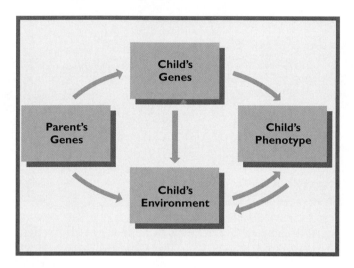

This theme is integral to the notion of gene-environment interaction, described in Chapter 3. Children who are bright may pay greater attention to their teachers and ask more questions and, as a result, receive greater positive attention in school than children who are not as bright. Or, children who are friendly and outgoing may elicit more interactions, and more satisfying interactions, with others than children who are not as friendly and outgoing. Bright or outgoing children will receive more intellectual stimulation or social attention than others, and these initial differences in intelligence or friendliness will become magnified as a result of that attention. In such a case, the children themselves are at least in part determining the way people react to them.

This theme is also central to the concept of niche picking, described in Chapter 3. As children grow, they actively seek environments that suit them. Thus, bright, inquisitive children deliberately look for environments that will challenge them, but less bright children find such environments threatening or boring and avoid them. Similarly, friendly, outgoing children seek socially rich environments, but shy children are intimidated by such environments and go elsewhere.

■ Connections

Development in different
domains is connected

Connections in development are central to many of the developmental theories that were introduced in Chapter 1. In particular, we will see this repeatedly as we revisit the theory of cognitive Jean Piaget throughout this book. Piaget believed that, beginning in infancy, children act like scientists, trying to create integrative theories of the physical and social worlds. And, in Chapter 2, we saw that the Schools of the 21st Century program is built on the idea that schools should meet more than children's intellectual growth; schools need to provide for children's physical health and be a safe haven for children before and after school.

In Chapter 3, we saw that links between different domains are often most evident when development is delayed or disrupted. For example, when children have Down syndrome, their motor skills develop more slowly, as do their cognitive skills. In other words, a genetic defect leads to delays in all developmental domains. A similar pattern is found with babies who are small-for-date. Their physical development is delayed, as is their cognitive development. Each of these examples underscores links between different domains of development.

Physical Development in Infants and Toddlers

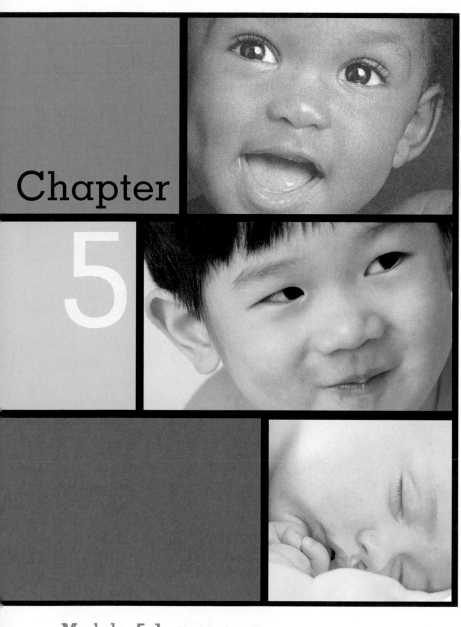

Chapter 5

Many first-time parents are stunned when, after just two or three wearings, a special outfit must be replaced because the infant can no longer wear it comfortably. The reason for a baby's ever-changing wardrobe, of course, is that infancy is a time of extraordinarily rapid physical growth. Infants typically double their birth weight by 3 months of age and triple it by their first birthday. If children continued this rate of growth for 10 years, they would weigh nearly as much as a jet airliner (McCall, 1979)! As you'll see in this chapter, these changes in physical growth are accompanied by important changes in infants' motor and perceptual skills. We'll begin tracing these changes, in Module 5.1, by looking at some of the factors that contribute to physical growth. In Module 5.2, we'll study the development of the brain. In Module 5.3, we'll discover how motor development provides youngsters with greater control of their body movements. Finally, in Module 5.4, we'll examine the origins of sensory and perceptual processes in infancy.

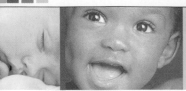

Healthy Growth

Learning Objectives

■ **What are the important features of physical growth in infants and toddlers? How do they vary from child to child?**

■ **How do heredity, hormones, and nutrition contribute to physical growth?**

■ **How do malnutrition, disease, and accidents affect infants' and toddlers' physical growth?**

When Sandy takes 18-month-old Luke with her in the car, she has always insisted that he be securely strapped in his car seat. However, as Luke has gotten older— more active and more independent—he has started to resist. Luke cries and thrashes wildly when Sandy tries to attach the straps. Sandy wonders if the car seat is worth all the aggravation it causes. Maybe she should just let him sit free in the back seat, so he could entertain himself. He'd be safe back there, wouldn't he?

For parents and children alike, physical growth is a topic of great interest. Parents marvel at how quickly babies add pounds and inches; 2-year-olds proudly proclaim, "I bigger now!" And parents like Sandy worry about the potential harm to their children from accidents.

In this module, we'll examine some of the basic features of physical growth and variations in growth patterns. We'll also consider the mechanisms responsible for growth. Finally, we'll end the module by seeing how malnutrition, disease, and accidents are, for some children, special obstacles to healthy growth.

Features of Human Growth

Probably the most obvious way to measure physical growth is in terms of sheer size—height and weight. The growth charts show the average changes in height and weight that take place from birth to 2 years. Average height increases

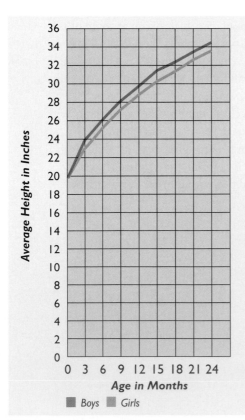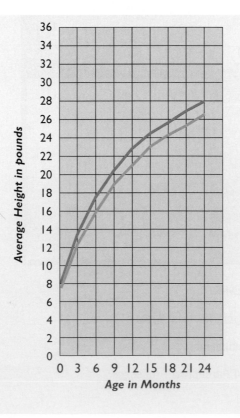

Boys ■ Girls

FIG 5–1

from 20 to 34 inches; average weight increases from 8 to about 27 pounds. (An interesting rule of thumb is that boys achieve half their adult height by 2 years and girls, by 18 months.)

Human growth follows the cephalocaudal principle that was introduced in Module 4.1 (page 79). That is, the head and trunk develop first; infants and toddlers are not simply scaled-down versions of adults. As you can see in the photo, the toddler has a disproportionately large head and trunk, making him look top-heavy compared to the older boy. As growth of the hips, legs, and feet catches up later in childhood, bodies take on more adult proportions.

Another important feature of physical growth takes place inside the body, with the development of muscle, fat, and bones. Virtually all the body's muscle fibers are present at birth. During childhood, muscles become longer and thicker as individual fibers fuse together. This process accelerates during adolescence, particularly for boys.

A layer of fat first appears under the skin near the end of the fetal period of prenatal development. Fat continues to accumulate rapidly during the first year after birth, producing the familiar look we call "baby fat." During the preschool years, children actually become leaner but in the early elementary-school years they begin to acquire more fat again. This happens gradually at first, then more rapidly during adolescence. The increase in fat in adolescence is more pronounced in girls than in boys.

Bone begins to form during prenatal development. What will become bone starts as cartilage, a soft flexible tissue. During the embryonic period, the center of the tissue turns to bone. **Then, shortly before birth, the ends of the cartilage structures, known as *epiphyses*, turn to bone.** Now the structure is hard at each end and in the center. Working from the center, cartilage turns to bone until finally the enlarging center section reaches the epiphyses, ending skeletal growth.

If you combine the changes in muscle, fat, and bone with changes in body size and shape, you have a fairly complete picture of physical growth during childhood. What's missing? The central nervous system, which we cover separately in Module 5.2.

Of course, the picture of children's physical growth that I have described in these pages is a typical profile; there are important variations on this prototype, as you'll see in the next section.

Variations on the Average Profile

When the University of Oregon Ducks won the first NCAA basketball tournament, in 1939, the average height of their starting lineup was 6 feet 2 inches. When the Duke University Blue Devils won the tournament in 2001, the average height of their starting lineup was 6 feet 6 inches, a difference of 4 inches. Of course, the changing heights of basketball players simply correspond to changes in the U.S. population at large. Today, adults and children are taller and heavier than previous generations. **Changes in physical development from one generation to the next are known as *secular growth trends*.** Secular trends have been quite large. A medieval knight's armor would fit today's 10- to 12-year-old boy; the average height of American sailors in the War of 1812 was 5 feet 2 inches!

> Physical growth includes change in height and weight as well as change in muscle, fat, and bone.

We also need to remember that "average" and "normal" are not the same. Many children are much taller or shorter than average and perfectly normal, of course. For example, among American 18-month-old girls, normal weights range from approximately 20 pounds to 29 pounds. In other words, an extremely light but normal 18-month-old girl would weigh only about two-thirds as much as her extremely heavy but normal peer. What is normal can vary greatly, and this applies not only to weight and other aspects of physical growth but to all aspects of development. Whenever a typical or average age is given for a developmental milestone, you should remember that the normal range for passing the milestone is much wider. Some children pass the milestone sooner than the stated age and some later, but all are normal.

We've seen that children's heights vary considerably. What accounts for these differences? To answer this question, we need to look at the mechanisms that are responsible for human growth.

Mechanisms of Physical Growth

It's easy to take physical growth for granted. Compared to other milestones of child development, such as learning to read, physical growth seems to come easily. Children, like weeds, seem to sprout without any effort at all. In reality, of course, physical growth is complicated; to understand it, we need to consider three factors: heredity, hormones, and nutrition.

Heredity. Dave and Doug are identical twins. Throughout childhood, they never differed in height by more than 3 inches. In contrast, Sam and Max, who are fraternal twins, usually differed by at least 2 inches and sometimes by as much as 12 inches. These variations are typical for identical and fraternal twins: The correlation between heights of identical twins is usually larger than 0.9 whereas the correlation for fraternal twins is approximately 0.5 (Wilson, 1986). This finding indicates that heredity plays a role in determining both a person's adult height as well as the rate at which the person achieves adult height.

Both parents contribute equally to their children's height. The correlation between the average of the two parents' height and their child's is about 0.7 (Plomin, 1990). Obviously, as a general rule, two tall parents will have tall children; two short parents will have short children; and, one tall parent and one short parent will have average-height offspring.

Hormones. How are genetic instructions translated into actual growth? **Part of the answer involves *hormones*, chemicals that are released by glands and travel in the bloodstream to act on other body parts.** One of these glands, the pituitary, is located deep in the brain. A few times each day, the pituitary secretes growth hormone (GH). This usually happens during sleep but sometimes after exercise. From the pituitary, GH travels to the liver, where it triggers the release of another hormone, somatomedin, which causes muscles and bones to grow (Tanner, 1990).

Without adequate amounts of GH, a child develops into a dwarf. As adults, dwarfs have normal proportions but they are quite short, measuring about 4 to $4\frac{1}{2}$ feet tall. Dwarfism can be treated with injections of GH, and children grow to normal height.

Another hormone, *thyroxine*, released by the thyroid gland in the neck, is essential for the proper development of nerve cells. Without thyroxine, nerve cells do not develop properly and mental retardation is the

Heredity, hormones, and nutrition all play important roles in children's physical growth.

result. Thyroxine also seems to be essential for most cells in the body to function properly, so deficiencies in thyroxine can retard physical growth by making the pituitary gland itself ineffective.

Nutrition. The third factor affecting physical growth is nutrition. Nutrition is particularly important during infancy, when physical growth is so rapid. In a 2-month-old, roughly 40 percent of the body's energy is devoted to growth. Most of the remaining energy fuels basic bodily functions, such as digestion and respiration.

Because growth requires so much high energy, young babies must consume an enormous number of calories in relation to their body weight. While an adult needs to consume only 15 to 20 calories per pound, depending upon level of activity (National Research Council, 1989), a 12-pound 3-month-old should eat about 50 calories per pound of body weight, or 600 calories. What's the best way for babies to receive the calories they need? The Making Children's Lives Better feature has some answers.

MAKING CHILDREN'S LIVES BETTER

What's the Best Food for Babies?

Breast-feeding is the best way to ensure that babies get the nourishment they need. Human milk contains the proper amounts of carbohydrates, fats, protein, vitamins, and minerals for babies.

Breast-feeding also has several other advantages compared to bottle-feeding (Shelov, 1993; Sullivan & Birch, 1990). First, breast-fed babies are ill less often because breast milk contains the mother's antibodies. Second, breast-fed babies are less prone to diarrhea and constipation. Third, breast-fed babies typically make the transition to solid foods more easily, apparently because they are accustomed to changes in the taste of breast milk that reflect a mother's diet. Fourth, breast milk cannot be contaminated, which is a significant problem in developing countries when formula is used to bottle-feed babies. Because of these many advantages, the American Academy of Pediatrics recommends that children be breast-fed for the first year, with iron-enriched solid foods introduced gradually. One suggested "menu" for the first year is shown in the table.

Ages When Solid Foods Can Be Introduced into an Infant's Diet	
Age (months)	**Food**
4–6	rice cereal, then other cereals
5–7	strained vegetables, then strained fruits
6–8	protein foods (cheese, yogurt, cooked beans)
9–10	finely chopped meat, toast, crackers
10–12	egg

Source: Whitney, Cataldo, & Rolfes, 1987

TABLE 5–1

A good rule is to introduce only one food at a time. A 7-month-old having cheese for the first time, for instance, should have no other new foods for a few days. In this way, allergies that may develop—skin rash or diarrhea—can be linked to a particular food, making it easier to prevent reoccurrences.

The many benefits of breast-feeding do not mean that bottle-feeding is harmful. Formula, when prepared in sanitary conditions, provides generally the same nutrients as human milk, but infants are more prone to develop allergies from formula and formula does not protect infants from disease. However, bottle-feeding has advantages of its own. A mother who cannot readily breast-feed can still enjoy the intimacy of feeding her baby, and other family members can participate in feeding. In fact, long-term longitudinal studies typically find that breast- and bottle-fed babies are similar in physical and psychological development (Fergusson, Horwood, & Shannon, 1987), so women in industrialized countries can choose either method and know that their babies' dietary needs will be met.

In developing nations, bottle-feeding is potentially disastrous. Often the only water available to prepare formula is contaminated; the result is that infants have chronic diarrhea, leading to dehydration and sometimes death. Or, in an effort to conserve valuable formula, parents may ignore instructions and use less formula than indicated in making milk; the resulting weak milk leads to malnutrition. For these reasons, the World Health Organization strongly advocates breast-feeding as the primary source of nutrition for infants and toddlers in developing nations. ■

By 2 years, growth slows, so children need less to eat. This is also a time when many children become picky eaters. Like the little girl in the photo, toddlers and preschool children find foods that they once ate willingly "yucky." As a toddler, my daughter loved green beans. When she reached 2, she decided that green beans were awful and adamantly refused to eat them. Though such finickiness can be annoying, it may actually be adaptive for increasingly independent preschoolers. Because toddlers don't know what is safe to eat and what isn't, eating only familiar foods protects them from potential harm (Birch & Fisher, 1995).

Challenges to Healthy Growth

Sadly, an adequate diet is only a dream to many of the world's children. In addition, many children worldwide are affected by diseases and accidental injuries. We'll look at these many challenges to healthy growth in this last section of Module 5.1.

Malnutrition. **Worldwide, about one in three children under age 5 is *malnourished*, as indicated by being small for their age** (World Health Organization, 1995). Many, like the little girl in the photo on page 117, are from Third World countries. But malnutrition is regrettably common in industrialized countries, too. Many American children growing up homeless and in poverty are malnourished. Approximately 20 percent of American children receive inadequate amounts of iron, and 10 percent go to bed hungry (Children's Defense Fund, 1996; Pollitt, 1994).

Malnourishment is especially damaging during infancy because growth is so rapid during these years. A longitudinal study conducted in Barbados in the West Indies (Galler & Ramsey, 1989; Galler, Ramsey, & Forde, 1986) followed a group of children who were severely malnourished as infants and a group from similar family environments who had adequate nutrition as infants. As older children, the two groups were indistinguishable physically: Children who were malnourished as infants were just as tall and weighed just as much as their peers. However, the children with a history of infant malnutrition had much lower scores on intelligence tests. They also had difficulty maintaining attention in school; they were easily distracted. Malnutrition during rapid periods of growth apparently damages the brain, affecting a child's intelligence and ability to pay attention (Morgane et al., 1993).

Malnutrition would seem to have a simple cure—an adequate diet. But the solution is more complex than that. Malnourished children are frequently listless and inactive (Ricciuti, 1993), behaviors that are useful because they conserve energy. At the same time, when children are routinely unresponsive and lethargic, parents may provide fewer and fewer experiences that foster their children's development. For example, parents who start out reading to their children at night may stop because their malnourished children seem uninterested and inattentive. The result is a self-perpetuating cycle in which malnourished children are forsaken by parents who feel that nothing they do gets a response, so they quit trying. A biological influence—lethargy stemming from insufficient nourishment—causes a profound change in the experiences—parental teaching—that shape a child's development.

To break the vicious cycle, children need more than an improved diet. Their parents must also be taught how to foster their children's development. Programs that combine dietary supplements with parent training offer promise in treating malnutrition (Valenzuela, 1997). Children in these programs often catch up with their peers in physical and intellectual growth, showing that the best way to treat malnutrition is by addressing both biological and sociocultural factors (Super, Herrera, & Mora, 1990).

Diseases. Around the world an estimated 11 million children aged 4 years and younger die every year. These are staggering numbers—roughly the equivalent of *all* U.S. 1-, 2-, and 3-year-olds dying in a single year. The leading killers of young children are infectious diseases—acute respiratory infections (including pneumonia and influenza) and diarrheal diseases each kill 2 million children annually (World Health Organization, 1999). The majority of these deaths can be prevented with proven, cost-effective treatments. For example, measles kills nearly 1 million children annually but can be prevented with vaccinations. Similarly, diarrhea kills by dehydrating youngsters, yet children can be saved by promptly providing water that contains salt and potassium.

The table at the top of page 118 shows the schedule of immunizations recommended by the American Academy of Pediatrics.

■ ■ ■ ▨ SUMMARY TABLE

Recommended Schedule of Immunizations for U.S. Children

Vaccine	Suggested Age for Immunization
Hepatitis B	1st: birth to 2 months
	2nd: 1 to 4 months
	3rd: 6 to 18 months
Diphtheria, tetanus, and acellular pertussis	1st: 2 months
	2nd: 4 months
	3rd: 6 months
	4th: 15 to 18 months
	5th: 4 to 6 years
Haemophilus influenzae and pneumococcal conjugate	1st: 2 months
	2nd: 4 months
	3rd: 6 months
	4th: 12 to 15 months
Polio	1st: 2 months
	2nd: 4 months
	3rd: 6 to 18 months
	4th: 4 to 6 years
Measles, mumps, rubella	1st: 12 to 15 months
	2nd: 4 to 6 years

TABLE 5-2

As part of a vigorous effort to prevent childhood illness, for the past two decades the World Health Organization (WHO) has worked to vaccinate children worldwide. Due to these efforts, vaccination rates have skyrocketed in many developing countries. More recently, WHO has joined with the United Nations Children's Fund (UNICEF) to create Integrated Management of Childhood Illness (IMCI), a program to combat the five conditions that account for the vast majority of childhood deaths: pneumonia, diarrhea, measles, malaria, and malnutrition (World Health Organization, 1997). Because many children who are ill have symptoms related to two or more of these five conditions, IMCI takes an integrated strategy that focuses on the overall health of the child. One component of IMCI is training health-care professionals to become more skilled in dealing with childhood illnesses. A second component is improving health-care systems so that they are better able to respond to childhood illness (e.g., ensuring that required medicines are available). A third component involves changing family and community practices to make them more conducive to healthy growth. For example, to protect children from mosquitos that carry malaria, children are encouraged to sleep in netting, as the child in the photo is doing. IMCI has been adopted in more than 60 countries and is playing a pivotal role in improving children's health worldwide.

Accidents. During the first year of life, the most common causes of infant mortality in the United States are medical conditions associated with birth defects or low birth weight. By age 1, however, toddlers and preschoolers are more than 3 times more likely to die from accidents than from any other single cause (Center for Disease Control and Prevention, 2000). Motor vehicle accidents are the most common cause of accidental death in infants and toddlers. Regrettably, many of these deaths could have been prevented had the youngsters been restrained properly, like the child in the photo, in an approved infant car seat. Without such restraint, infants and toddlers typically suffer massive head injuries when thrown through the windshield or onto the road. Sandy, the mom in the vignette, needs to stick with her "Luke rides in the car seat" policy; it *will* protect him in case of an accident.

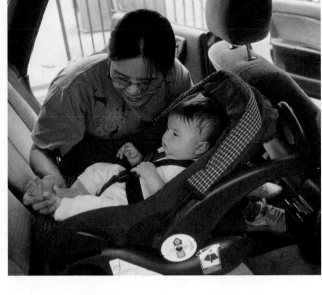

Many infants and toddlers also drown, die from burns, or suffocate. Often these deaths occur because young children are supervised inadequately. All too common, for example, are reports of toddlers who wander away, jump or fall into a swimming pool that lacks protective fencing, then drown. Parents and others who supervise toddlers and preschool children need to remember that young children are often eager to explore their environs yet they are unable to recognize many hazards. Parents, preschool teachers, and child-care workers must constantly keep a protective eye on their young children.

Check Your Learning

1. Physical growth involves increases in height and weight, changes in _____, and changes in bone, muscle, and fat.

2. Changes in physical development from one generation to the next are called _____.

3. Normal physical growth depends upon heredity, hormones, and _____.

4. Compared to bottle-fed babies, breast-fed babies are ill less often, _____, and make the transition to solid foods more readily.

5. Malnourishment is particularly damaging during infancy because _____.

6. The leading killer of children worldwide is _____.

7. More American toddlers and preschoolers are likely to die from _____ than any other cause.

Connections How does the operating philosophy of IMCI illustrate connections among physical, cognitive, and emotional development?

Answers: (1) body proportions, (2) secular growth trends, (3) nutrition, (4) are less prone to diarrhea and constipation, (5) growth is so rapid during this period, (6) infectious disease, (7) accidents

The Developing Nervous System

5.2

The Developing Nervous System

├─ Organization of the Mature Brain

└─ The Developing Brain

Learning Objectives

- What are the parts of a nerve cell? How is the brain organized?

- When is the brain formed in prenatal development? When do different regions of the brain begin to function?

> *Three days before his second birthday, Martin fell down the front steps and hit his head on a concrete block at the base of the steps. Martin was in a coma for a week, but then gradually became more alert, and now he seems to be aware of his surroundings. Needless to say, Martin's mother is grateful that he survived the accident, but she wonders what the future holds for her son.*

The physical changes we see in the first years are impressive, but even more awe-inspiring are the changes we cannot see, those involving the brain and the nervous system. An infant's feelings of hunger and a toddler's laugh both reflect the functioning brain and the rest of the nervous system. All the information that children learn—including language and other cognitive skills—are stored in the brain.

How does the brain accomplish these many tasks? How is the brain affected by an injury like the one that Martin suffered? To begin to answer these questions, let's look at how the brain is organized in adults.

Organization of the Mature Brain

The basic unit of the brain and the rest of the nervous system is the *neuron*, a cell that specializes in receiving and transmitting information. Neurons come in many different shapes, as shown in the photos at the top of page 121. The diagram below makes it easier to understand the basic parts found in all neurons. **The *cell body* at the center of the neuron contains the basic biological machinery that keeps the neuron alive. The receiving end of the neuron, the *dendrite*, looks like a tree with many branches.** The highly branched dendrite allows one neuron to receive input from many thousands of other neurons (Morgan & Gibson, 1991). **The tubelike structure at the other end of the cell body is the *axon*, which sends information to other neurons. The axon is wrapped in *myelin*, a fatty sheath that allows it to transmit information more rapidly.** The boost in neural speed from myelin is like the difference between driving and flying: from about 6 feet per second to 50 feet per second. **At the end of the axon are small knobs called *terminal buttons*, which release *neurotransmitters*, chemicals that carry information to nearby neurons.** Finally, you'll see that the terminal buttons of one axon don't actually touch the dendrites of other neurons. **The gap between one neuron and the next is a *synapse*.** Neurotransmitters cross synapses to carry information between neurons.

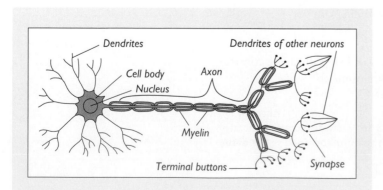

FIG 5–2

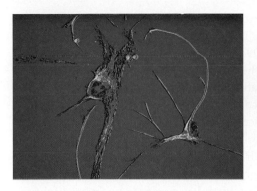
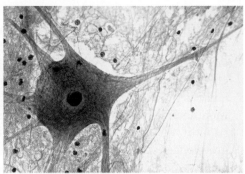
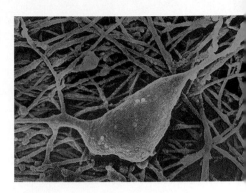

Take 50 to 100 billion neurons like these and you have the beginnings of a human brain. An adult's brain weighs a little less than 3 pounds and it easily fits into your hands. The wrinkled surface of the brain is the cerebral cortex; made up of about 10 billion neurons, the cortex regulates many of the functions that we think of as distinctly human. **The cortex consists of left and right halves, called *cerebral hemispheres*, that are linked by millions of axons in a thick bundle called the *corpus callosum*.** The characteristics that you value most—your engaging personality, your way with words, your uncanny knack for reading others—are all controlled by specific regions of the cortex, many of which are shown in the diagram.

Personality and your ability to make and carry out plans are largely functions of an area at the front of the cortex that is called, appropriately, the *frontal cortex*. For most people, the abilities to produce and understand language, to reason, and to compute are largely due to neurons in the cortex of the left hemisphere. For most people, artistic and musical abilities, perception of spatial relationships, and ability to recognize faces and emotions come from neurons in the right hemisphere.

Now that we know a bit of the organization of the mature brain, let's look at how the brain develops and begins to function.

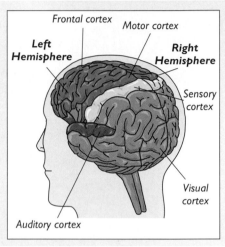

FIG 5–3

The Developing Brain

Scientists who study the brain's development are guided by several key questions: How and when do brain structures develop? When do different brain regions begin to function? Why do brain regions take on different functions? In this section, we'll see how research has answered each question.

Emerging Brain Structures. We know from Module 4.1 that the beginnings of the brain can be traced to the period of the zygote. **At roughly 3 weeks after conception, a group of cells form a flat structure known as the *neural plate*.** At 4 weeks, the neural plate folds to form a tube that ultimately becomes the brain and spinal cord. When the ends of the tube fuse shut, neurons are produced in one small region of the neural tube. Production of neurons begins about 10 weeks after conception, and by 28 weeks the developing brain has virtually all the neurons it will ever have. During these weeks, neurons form at the incredible rate of more than 4,000 per second (Kolb, 1989).

From the neuron-manufacturing site in the neural tube, neurons migrate to their final positions in the brain. The brain is built in stages, beginning with the innermost layers. Neurons in the deepest layer are positioned first, followed by neurons in the second layer, and so on. This layering process continues until all six layers of the mature brain are in place, which occurs about 7 months after conception (Rakic, 1995).

In the fourth month of prenatal development, axons begin to acquire myelin, the fatty wrap that speeds neural transmission. This process continues through infancy and into childhood and adolescence (Casaer, 1993). Neurons that carry sensory information are the first to acquire myelin; neurons in the cortex are among the last. You can see the effect of more myelin in improved coordination and reaction times. The older the infant and, later, the child, the more rapid and coordinated his or her reactions. (We'll talk more about this phenomenon when we discuss fine-motor skills in Module 5.3.)

In the months after birth, the brain grows rapidly. Axon and dendrites grow longer, and, like a maturing tree, dendrites quickly sprout new limbs. As the number of dendrites increases, so does the number of synapses; this rapid neural growth is shown in the diagram. **Soon after the first birthday, synapses begin to disappear gradually, a phenomenon known as *synaptic pruning*.** Thus, beginning in infancy and continuing into early adolescence, the brain goes through its own version of "downsizing," weeding out unnecessary connections between neurons (Johnson, 1998).

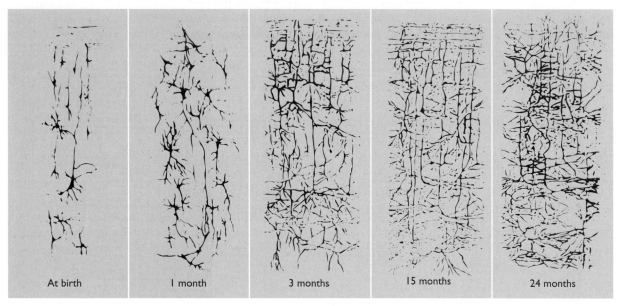

| At birth | 1 month | 3 months | 15 months | 24 months |

FIG 5–4

Structure and Function. Because the mature brain is specialized, with different psychological functions localized in particular regions, a natural question for developmental researchers is, How early in development does brain functioning become localized? To answer this question, scientists have used many different methods to map functions onto particular brain regions.

- *Studies of children with brain damage:* Children who suffer brain injuries provide valuable insights into brain structure and function. If a region of the brain regulates a particular function (e.g., understanding speech), then damage to that region should impair the function.

- *Studies of electrical activity:* **Metal electrodes placed on an infant's scalp, as shown in the photo, produce an *electroencephalogram (EEG)*, a pattern of brain waves.** If a region of the brain regulates a function, then the region should show distinctive EEG patterns while a child is using that function.

- *Studies using imaging techniques:* **One method, *functional magnetic resonance imaging (F-MRI),* uses magnetic fields to track the flow of blood in the brain. Another method, *positron emission tomography (PET-scan),* traces use of glucose in the brain.** If a region of the brain helps to regulate a function, then blood flow and use of glucose (a sugar that is a source of energy) should be higher in that region when a child is performing that function.

None of these methods is perfect; each has drawbacks. When studying children with brain injuries, for example, multiple areas of the brain may be damaged, making it hard to link impaired functioning to a particular brain region. Most imaging techniques are used sparingly because of potential hazards. PET-scan, for example, requires injecting children with a radioactive form of glucose.

Despite these limitations, the combined outcome of research using these different approaches indicates that many areas of the cortex begin to function early in life. EEG studies, for example, show that a newborn infant's left hemisphere generates more electrical activity in response to speech than the right hemisphere (Molfese & Burger-Judisch, 1991). Thus, by birth, the cortex of the left hemisphere is already specialized for language processing. This specialization allows for language to develop rapidly during infancy.

Is the right hemisphere equally well prepared to function at birth? This is a difficult question to answer, in part because the right hemisphere influences so many nonlinguistic functions. Music elicits greater electrical activity in the infant's right hemisphere than in the left. Furthermore, children who suffer brain damage to the right hemisphere often have difficulty integrating parts to form an integrated whole (Stiles, 2000), implicating the right hemisphere in understanding spatial relations. Other functions, such as recognizing faces, come more gradually but are under the right hemisphere's control by the preschool years (Hahn, 1987).

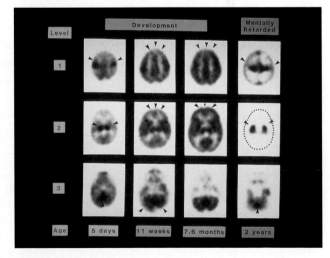

The Frontal Cortex. Like the left and right hemispheres, the frontal cortex begins to function early. The photo shows PET-scans for infants at several different ages. There is little activity in the frontal cortex of 5-day-old babies. Activity increases considerably by 11 weeks and approaches adult levels 7 or 8 months after birth (Chugani & Phelps, 1986). Obviously, 8-month-olds cannot plan and function as adults do, but their frontal cortex has become very active.

What is the frontal cortex regulating in PET-scans like the ones in the photo? Deliberate, goal-oriented behavior is a good bet. To understand research that leads to this conclusion, think back to a time when you had to change your regular routine. At the start of a new school year, perhaps you were assigned a new locker. For the first few days, you might have turned down the old hallway, reflecting last year's habit, instead of walking on to your new locker. To override your old response, maybe you deliberately reminded yourself to walk past the old hallway and turn at the new one.

Overriding responses that become incorrect or inappropriate is an important part of deliberate, goal-directed behavior. Children and adults with damage to the frontal cortex often have difficulty inhibiting responses that are no longer appropriate (Diamond et al., 1997). The frontal cortex begins to regulate inappropriate responding at about 1 year and gradually achieves greater control throughout the preschool and

school-age years (Welsh, Pennington, & Groisser, 1991). Thus, children gradually become better able to regulate their behavior to achieve cognitive and social goals.

Not only does the frontal cortex regulate responses, it also regulates feelings such as happiness, sadness, and fear. Nathan Fox (1991) believes that "emotional experience arises from two opposing innate action tendencies in the organism: approach and exploration of the novel versus freezing, fleeing, or withdrawal from harmful or dangerous stimuli." (p. 865) That is, emotions like happiness and curiosity stem from an organism's desire to approach a stimulus, and emotions like distress, disgust, or fear come from the desire to avoid a stimulus.

Fox and his co-investigators have shown that the left frontal cortex tends to regulate emotions stemming from the tendency to approach, while the right frontal cortex regulates emotions stemming from avoidance. For example, when babies display joy, the EEG reveals more activity in the left frontal area, and when babies like the one in the photo display stress or disgust, the right frontal area is more electrically active.

Babies also differ in their typical patterns of brain activity. These differences in brain activity are the subject of the Looking Ahead feature.

LOOKING AHEAD

Reactivity to Novel Stimuli Predicts Frontal Cortex Activity

Some babies have more spontaneous activity in the left frontal area of the brain, whereas other babies have greater right frontal activity. Infants with greater right frontal activity do not cope as well with stressful situations, such as being separated from their mothers. Susan Calkins, Nathan Fox, and Timothy Marshall (1996) wanted to know whether there was a connection between infants' responses to novel stimuli at 4 months and their brain activity at 9 months. The investigators expected that infants who responded negatively to the mild stress of a novel stimulus at 4 months (by fussing and crying) would have more right frontal activity at 9 months; infants who responded positively to novelty at 4 months (by smiling and vocalizing) would have more left frontal activity at 9 months.

> The left frontal cortex regulates emotions like happiness and curiosity; the right frontal cortex regulates emotions like distress and fear.

Calkins and her colleagues measured 4-month-olds' response to novelty by presenting novel sights, sounds, and odors. For each baby, they determined the degree of positive emotions (smiling, vocalizing) and negative emotions (fussing, crying). At 9 months, Calkins and her colleagues recorded electrical activity at different brain sites, including the frontal cortex, while the infant sat quietly on the mother's lap.

Based on their response to novelty as 4-month-olds, infants were divided into those who responded positively and infants who responded negatively. Then Calkins and her colleagues looked at patterns of brain activity at 9 months. They found that infants who responded negatively to novelty as 4-month-olds had relatively more right frontal activity as 9-month-olds. That is, babies who respond to novelty by fussing and crying had a more active right frontal cortex, the region that regulates emotions linked to avoidance. In contrast, infants who responded positively to novelty as 4-month-olds had relatively more left frontal activity as 9-month-olds. In other words, babies who respond to novelty by smiling had a more active left frontal cortex, the region that regulates emotions linked to approach. These differences indicate that the left frontal cortex regulates infants' tendency to approach or explore stimuli and the right frontal cortex regulates infants' tendency to avoid or escape stimuli. ■

The Looking Ahead feature highlights an important point in this module: The brain begins to specialize early in life. Language processing is associated primarily with the left hemisphere; recognizing nonspeech sounds, emotions, and faces is associated with the right hemisphere; and regulating emotions and intentional behavior is a function of the frontal cortex. Of course, this early specialization does not mean that the brain is functionally mature. Over the remainder of childhood and into adulthood, these and other regions of the brain continue to become more specialized.

I have described the typical pattern of brain localization, but it is not the only pattern. In some left-handed individuals, for example, the assignment of function to left and right hemispheres is reversed from the usual pattern (Springer & Deutsch, 1998). And when individuals suffer brain injury, some cognitive functions are usually impaired. But, over months and years, some functioning (less often, all functioning) is restored (Kolb & Whishaw, 1998). These examples raise the issue of how certain functions come to be localized in brain regions and how readily they are transferred to other regions. The next section will address these issues.

> When children suffer brain damage, cognitive processes are usually impaired; over time, these processes often recover, showing the brain's plasticity.

Brain Plasticity. *Neuroplasticity* **refers to the extent to which brain organization is flexible.** How plastic is the human brain? Answers to this question reflect the familiar views on the nature-nurture issue (Nelson, 1999; Stiles, 1998). Some theorists believe that organization of brain function is predetermined genetically; it's simply in most children's genes that, for example, the left hemisphere will specialize in language processing. In this view, the brain is like a house—a structure that's specialized from the very beginning, with some rooms designed for cooking, others for sleeping, others for bathing. Other theorists believe that few functions are rigidly assigned to specific brain sites at conception. Instead, experience helps determine the functional organization of the brain. In this view, the brain is more like an office building—an all-purpose structure with rooms designed to be used flexibly to meet the different business needs of the companies with offices in the building.

Research designed to test these views shows that the brain has some plasticity. Remember Martin, the toddler whose brain was damaged when he fell down the steps and hit his head? His language skills were impaired after the accident. This was not surprising because the left hemisphere of Martin's brain had absorbed most of the force of the fall. But within several months Martin had completely recovered his language skills. Apparently other neurons took over language-related processing from the damaged neurons. This recovery of function is not uncommon—particularly for young children—and shows the brain is plastic (Witelson, 1987).

However, the brain is not completely plastic—brains have a similar structure and similar mapping of functions on those structures. Visual cortex, for example, is almost always near the back of the brain. Sensory and motor cortex always run across the middle of the brain. But if a neuron's function is not specified at conception, how do different neurons take on different functions and in much the same pattern for most people? Researchers are trying to answer this question and many details still need to be worked out. The answer probably lies in complex biochemical processes (Barinaga, 1997; Kunzig, 1998). You can get an idea of what's involved by imagining people arriving for a football game at a stadium where there are no reserved seats. As fans enter the stadium, they see others wearing their own school colors and move in that direction. Of course, not everyone does this. Some fans sit with friends from the other team. Some pick seats based on other factors (e.g., to avoid looking into the sun, to be close to the concession stand). In general, though, by game time, most fans have taken seats on their respective sides of the field.

In much the same way, as neurons are created and begin migrating through the layers of cortex, cellular biochemistry makes some paths more attractive than others. Yet, just as each fan can potentially sit anywhere because there are no reserved seats, an individual neuron can end up in many different locations because genetic instructions do not assign specific brain regions. Thus, the human brain is plastic—its organization and function can be affected by experience—but its development follows some general biochemical instructions that ensure most people end up with brains organized along similar lines.

Check Your Learning

1. The _____ is the part of the neuron containing the basic machinery that keeps the cells alive.

2. Terminal buttons release _____, chemicals that carry neural transmissions to nearby neurons.

3. The wrinkled surface of the brain is the _____.

4. During prenatal development, the brain forms from a flat group of cells called the _____.

5. During the first year, axons and dendrites grow and many synapses form; however, starting at about the first birthday, _____.

6. To study brain organization, researchers study children with brain damage, _____, and use imaging techniques.

7. Human speech elicits more electrical activity from the _____ of an infant's brain.

8. A good example of brain plasticity is the fact that, although infants and toddlers who suffer brain damage often have impaired cognitive processes, _____.

Connections How does the pattern of development of the brain, described in this module, compare to the general pattern of physical growth described in Module 5.1?

Answers: (1) cell body, (2) neurotransmitters, (3) cerebral cortex, (4) neural plate, (5) unnecessary synapses disappear, a phenomenon known as synaptic pruning, (6) measure electrical activity in children's brains (EEGs), (7) left hemisphere, (8) over time, they often regain their earlier skills

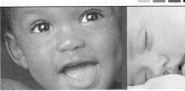

Motor Development

Learning Objectives

▪ How do reflexes help infants interact with the world?

▪ What are the component skills involved in learning to walk, and at what age do infants typically master them?

▪ How do infants learn to coordinate the use of their hands? When and why do most children begin to prefer to use one hand?

▪ How do maturation and experience influence children's acquisition of motor skills?

Nancy is 14 months old and a world-class crawler. Using hands and knees, she gets nearly anywhere she wants to go. Nancy does not walk and seems to have no interest in learning how. Her dad wonders whether he should be doing something to help Nancy progress beyond crawling. And down deep, he worries that perhaps he should have provided more exercise or training for Nancy when she was younger.

These photos have a common theme. **Each depicts an activity involving** *motor skills*—**coordinated movements of the muscles and limbs.** In each activity, success demands that each movement be done in a precise way and in a specific sequence. Similarly, to use a stick shift properly, you need to move the clutch pedal, gas pedal, and the stick shift in specific ways and in exactly the right sequence. If you don't give the car enough gas as you let out the clutch, you'll kill the engine. If you give it too much gas, the engine races and the car lurches forward.

If new activities are demanding for adults, think about the challenges infants face. **Infants must learn** *locomotion*, **that is, to move about in the world.** Newborns are relatively immobile, but infants soon learn to crawl, stand, and walk. Learning to move through the environment upright leaves the arms and hands free. Taking full advantage of this arrangement, the human hand has fully independent fingers (instead of a paw), with the thumb opposing the remaining four fingers. An opposable thumb makes it possible for humans to grasp and manipulate objects. **Infants must learn the *fine-motor skills* associated with grasping, holding, and manipulating objects.** In the case of feeding, for example, infants progress from being fed by others to holding a bottle, to feeding themselves with their fingers, to eating with a spoon. Each new skill requires incredibly complex physical movements.

In this module, we'll look first at infants' reflexes—unlearned responses that help protect infants and pave the way for later motor development. Then we'll see how children acquire locomotor and fine-motor skills. As we do, we'll find out if Nancy's dad should be worrying about her lack of interest in walking.

The Infant's Reflexes

Most newborns are well prepared to begin interacting with their world. **The newborn is endowed with a rich set of *reflexes*, unlearned responses that are triggered by a specific form of stimulation.** The table shows the many reflexes commonly found in newborn babies.

■ ■ ■ ■ SUMMARY TABLE

Some Major Reflexes Found in Newborns

Name	Response	Significance
Babinski	A baby's toes fan out when the sole of the foot is stroked from heel to toe.	Unknown
Blink	A baby's eyes close in response to bright light or loud noise.	Protects the eyes
Moro	A baby throws its arms out and then inward (as if embracing) in response to loud noise or when its head falls.	May help a baby cling to its mother
Palmar	A baby grasps an object placed in the palm of its hand.	Precursor to voluntary walking
Rooting	When a baby's cheek is stroked, it turns its head toward the stroking and opens its mouth.	Helps a baby find the nipple
Stepping	A baby who is held upright by an adult and is then moved forward begins to step rhythmically.	Precursor to voluntary walking
Sucking	A baby sucks when an object is placed in its mouth.	Permits feeding
Withdrawal	A baby withdraws its foot when the sole is pricked with a pin.	Protects a baby from unpleasant stimulation

TABLE 5-3

Some reflexes pave the way for newborns to get the nutrients they need to grow: Rooting and sucking ensure that the newborn is well prepared to begin a new diet of life-sustaining milk. Other reflexes protect the newborn from danger in the environment. The blink and withdrawal reflexes, for example, help newborns avoid unpleasant stimulation. Other reflexes serve as the foundation for larger, voluntary patterns of motor activity. For example, the stepping reflex looks like a precursor to walking. In fact, we'll see later that babies who practice the stepping reflex learn to walk earlier (Zelazo, 1983).

Reflexes indicate whether the newborn's nervous system is working properly. For example, infants with damage to their sciatic nerve, which is found in the spinal cord, do not show the withdrawal reflex, and infants who have problems with the lower part of the spine do not show the Babinski reflex. If these or other reflexes are weak or missing altogether, a thorough physical and behavioral assessment is called for.

Locomotion

In little more than a year, advances in posture and locomotion change the newborn from an almost motionless being into an upright, standing individual who walks through the environment. The chart shows some of the important milestones in motor development and the age by which most infants achieve them. By about 4 months, most babies can sit upright with support. By 7 months, they can sit without support, and by 9 months, they can stand if they hold on to an object for support. A typical 14-month-old can stand alone briefly and walk with assistance. Of course, not all children walk at exactly the same age. Some walk before their first birthday; others, like Nancy, the world-class crawler in the module-opening vignette, take their first steps as late as 17 or 18 months of age. By 24 months, most children can climb steps, walk backwards, and kick a ball.

Researchers once thought these developmental milestones reflected maturation (e.g., McGraw, 1935). Walking, for example, emerged naturally when the necessary muscles and neural circuits matured. Today, however, locomotion—and, in fact, all of motor development—is viewed from a new perspective. **According to *dynamic systems theory*, motor development involves many distinct skills that are organized and reorganized over time to meet demands of specific tasks.** For example, walking includes maintaining balance, moving limbs, perceiving the environment, and having a reason to move. Only by understanding each of these skills and how they are combined to allow movement in a specific situation can we understand walking (Thelen & Smith, 1998).

In the remainder of this section, we'll see how learning to walk reflects the maturity and coalescence of many component skills.

FIG 5–5

Source: Based on Shirley, 1931 and Bayley, 1969.

To master walking, infants must acquire distinct skills of standing upright, maintaining balance, stepping alternately, and using perceptual information to evaluate surfaces.

Posture and Balance. The ability to maintain an upright posture is fundamental to walking. But upright posture is virtually impossible for newborns and young infants because of the shape of their body. Cephalocaudal growth means that an infant is top-heavy. Consequently, as soon as a young infant starts to lose her balance, she tumbles over. Only with growth of the legs and muscles can infants maintain an upright posture (Thelen, Ulrich, & Jensen, 1989).

Once infants can stand upright, they must continuously adjust their posture to avoid falling down. By a few months after birth, infants begin to use visual cues and an inner-ear mechanism to adjust their posture. To show use of visual cues for balance, researchers had babies sit in a room with striped walls that move. When adults sit in such a room, they perceive themselves as moving (not the walls) and adjust their posture accordingly; so do infants, which shows that they use vision to maintain upright posture (Bertenthal & Clifton, 1998). In addition, when 4-month-olds who are propped in a sitting position lose their balance, they try to keep their head upright. They do this even when blindfolded, which means they are using cues from their inner ear to maintain balance (Woollacott, Shumway-Cook, & Williams, 1989).

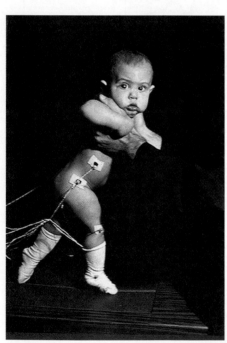

Stepping. Another essential element of walking is moving the legs alternately, repeatedly transferring the weight of the body from one foot to the other. Children don't step spontaneously until approximately 10 months because they must be able to stand to step.

Can younger children step if they are held upright? Thelen and Ulrich (1991) devised a clever procedure to answer this question. Infants were placed on a treadmill and held upright by an adult. When the belt on the treadmill started to move, infants could respond one of several ways. They might simply let both legs be dragged rearward by the belt. Or they might let their legs be dragged briefly, then move them forward together in a hopping motion. Many 6- and 7-month-olds demonstrated the mature pattern of alternating steps on each leg that is shown in the photo. Even more amazing is that when the treadmill was equipped with separate belts for each leg that moved at different speeds, babies adjusted, stepping more rapidly on the faster belt.

Apparently, the alternate stepping motion that is essential for walking is evident long before infants walk alone. Walking unassisted is not possible, though, until other component skills are mastered.

Perceptual Factors. Many infants learn to walk in the relative security of flat, uncluttered floors at home. But they soon discover that the environment offers a variety of surfaces, some more conducive to walking than others. Infants use perceptual information to judge whether a surface is suitable for walking. When placed on a surface that gives way underfoot (e.g., a waterbed), they quickly judge it unsuitable for walking and resort to crawling (Gibson et al., 1987). And when toddlers encounter a surface that slopes down steeply, few try to walk down, which would result in a fall. Instead, they slide or scoot backwards (Adolph, Eppler, & Gibson, 1993; Adolph, 1997). Results like these show that infants use perceptual cues to decide whether a surface is safe for walking.

Coordinating Skills. Dynamic systems theory emphasizes that learning to walk demands orchestration of many individual skills. Each component skill must first be mastered alone and then integrated with the other skills (Werner, 1948). **That is, mastery of intricate motions requires both *differentiation*—mastery of component skills—and their *integration*—combining them in proper sequence into a coherent, working whole.** In the case of walking, not until 12 to 15 months of age has the child mastered the component skills so that they can be coordinated to allow independent, unsupported walking.

Beyond Walking. If you can recall the feeling of freedom that accompanied your first driver's license, you can imagine how the world expands for infants and toddlers as they learn to move independently. The first tentative steps soon are followed by others that are more skilled. Most children learn to run a few months after they walk alone. Like walking, running requires moving the legs alternately. But running is more complicated because a runner actually becomes airborne briefly. To progress beyond walking to running, children must learn to propel themselves into the air and to maintain balance and to maintain their balancing while landing (Bertenthal & Clifton, 1998).

> Motor development involves mastering individual skills and integrating them into a coherent, working whole.

Fine-Motor Skills

A major accomplishment of infancy is skilled use of the hands (Bertenthal & Clifton, 1998). Newborns have little apparent control of their hands, but 1-year-olds are extraordinarily talented.

Reaching and Grasping. At about 4 months, infants can successfully reach for objects (Bertenthal & Clifton, 1998). These early reaches often look clumsy and for a good reason. When infants reach, they don't move their arm and hand directly and smoothly to the desired object (as older children and adults do). Instead, the infant's hand moves like a ship under the direction of an unskilled navigator—it moves a short distance, slows, then moves again in a slightly different direction, a process that's repeated until the hand finally contacts the object (McCarty & Ashmead, 1999). As infants grow, their reaches have fewer movements, though they are still not as continuous and smooth as older children's and adults' reaches (Berthier, 1996).

Grasping, too, becomes more efficient during infancy. Most 4-month-olds just use their fingers to hold objects. Like the baby in the photo, they wrap an object tightly with their fingers alone. Not until 7 or 8 months do most infants use their thumbs to hold objects (Siddiqui, 1995). At about this same age, infants begin to position their hands to make it easier to grasp an object. If trying to grasp a long thin rod, for example, infants place their fingers perpendicular to the rod, which is the best position for grasping (Bertenthal & Clifton, 1998).

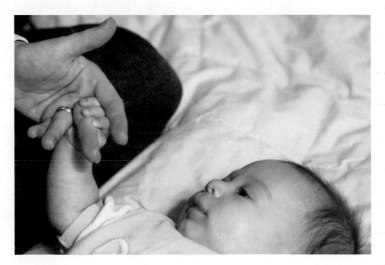

Infants' growing control of each hand is accompanied by greater coordination of the two hands. Although 4-month-olds use both hands, their motions are not coordinated; rather, each hand seems to have a mind of its own. Infants may hold a toy motionless in one hand while shaking a rattle in the other. At roughly 5 to 6 months of age, infants can coordinate the motions of their hands so that each hand performs different actions that serve a common goal. So a child might, for example, hold a toy animal in one hand and pet it with the other (Karniol, 1989).

These many changes in reaching and grasping are well illustrated as infants learn to feed themselves. At about 6 months, they are often given finger foods such as sliced bananas and green beans. Infants can easily pick up such foods, but getting them into their mouths is another story. The hand grasping the food may be raised to the cheek, then moved to the edge of the lips, and, finally, shoved into the mouth. Mission accomplished, but only with many detours along the way! Eye-hand coordination improves rapidly, so, before long, foods varying in size, shape, and texture reach the mouth directly.

At about the first birthday, youngsters are usually ready to try eating with a spoon. At first, they simply play with the spoon, dipping it in and out of a dish filled with food or sucking on an empty spoon. With a little help, they learn to fill the spoon with food and place it in their mouth, though the motion is awkward because they don't rotate their wrist. Instead, most 1-year-olds fill a spoon by placing it directly over a dish, and lowering it until the bowl of the spoon is full. Then, like the child in the photo, they raise the spoon to the mouth, all the while keeping the wrist rigid. In contrast, 2-year-olds rotate the hand at the wrist while scooping food from a dish and placing the spoon in the mouth—the same motion that adults use.

In each of these actions, the same principles of dynamic systems theory apply as applied to locomotion. Complex acts involve many component movements. Each must be performed correctly and in the proper sequence. Development involves first mastering the separate elements and then assembling them to form a smoothly functioning whole. Eating finger food, for example, requires grasping food, moving the hand to the mouth, then releasing the food. As the demands of tasks change and as children develop, the same skills are often reassembled to form a different sequence of movements.

Handedness. When young babies reach for objects, they don't seem to prefer one hand over the other; they use their left and right hands interchangeably. They may shake a rattle with their left hand and, moments later, pick up blocks with their right. In one study, infants and toddlers were videotaped as they played with toys that could be manipulated with two hands, such as a pinwheel (Cornwell, Harris, & Fitzgerald, 1991). The 9-month-olds used their left and right hands equally, but by 13 months, most grasped the toy with their right hand. Then, like the toddler in the photo, they used their left hand to steady the toy while the right hand manipulated the object. This early preference for one hand becomes stronger and more consistent during the preschool years. By the time children are ready to enter kindergarten, handedness is well established and very difficult to reverse (McManus et al., 1988).

What determines whether children become left- or right-handed? Heredity plays a role (Corballis, 1997). Parents who are both right-handed tend to have right-handed children. Children who are left-handed generally have a parent or grandparent who was also left-handed. But experience also contributes to handedness. Modern industrial cultures favor right-handedness. School desks, scissors, and can openers, for example, are designed for right-handed people and can be used by left-handers only with difficulty.

Sometimes cultural values influence handedness. The Islam religion dictates that the left hand is unclean, and so forbids its use in eating and greeting others. And traditionally in China, writing with the left hand was a cultural taboo; however, when children of Chinese parents grow up elsewhere, left-handers like the youngster in the photo are common (Harris, 1983). In the United States, elementary-school teachers used to urge left-handed children to use their right hands. As this practice has diminished in the last 50 years, the percentage of left-handed children has risen steadily (Levy, 1976). Thus, handedness seems to have both hereditary and environmental influences.

Maturation, Experience, and Motor Skill

For locomotion and fine-motor skill, the big picture is much the same: Progress is rapid during the first year as fundamental skills are mastered and combined to generate even more complex behaviors. Is the progress that we observe due primarily to maturation? That is, do skills gradually unfold, regardless of the child's upbringing? Or do motor skills develop only with training, practice, and experience? As you might imagine, maturation and experience both contribute.

Let's begin with the impact of maturation on motor development, which is well documented. The sequence of motor development that we have described for locomotion and fine-motor skill holds for most cultures. That is, despite enormous variation across cultures in child-rearing practices, motor development proceeds in much the same way and at roughly the same rate worldwide. This general point is well illustrated in the Cultural Influences feature.

CULTURAL INFLUENCES
Learning to Walk in a Native American Culture

Traditionally, infants in the Hopi culture are secured to cradle boards, like the one shown in the photo. Cradle boards prevent babies from moving hands or legs, rolling over, or raising their bodies. Infants feed and sleep while secured to the board; they are removed from the cradle board only for a change of clothes. This practice begins the day the infant is born and continues for the first 3 months. Thereafter, infants are allowed time off the boards so they can move around. Time off the cradle board increases gradually, but for most of the first year, infants sleep on the boards and spend some part of their waking time on them as well.

Obviously, the cradle board strictly limits the infant's ability to locomote during much of the first year, a time when most infants are learning to sit, creep, and crawl. Nevertheless, Dennis and Dennis (1940) discovered that infants reared with cradle boards learn to walk at approximately 15 months—about the same age as Hopi children reared by parents who had adopted Western practices and no longer used cradle boards.

Thus, a restrictive environment that massively reduces opportunities for practice has no apparent effect on the age of onset for walking. This suggests that the timing of an infant's first steps is determined more by an underlying genetic timetable than by specific experiences or practice. So, the worried father of Nancy, our world-class crawler in the opening vignette, can be reassured that his daughter's motor development is perfectly normal. ■

When the Dennis and Dennis (1940) study was repeated more than 40 years later, the story remained the same. Chisholm (1983) studied Navajo infants who spent much of their infancy secured to cradle boards. They, too, began to walk at about the same age as infants whose parents did not use cradle boards, confirming the importance of maturation in learning to walk.

Of course, maturation and experience are not mutually exclusive. Just because maturation figures importantly in the development of one motor skill, walking, does not imply that experience plays no role. In fact, practice and training do affect children's mastery of many motor skills. Here, too, studies of other cultures are revealing. In some African countries, young infants are given daily practice walking under the tutelage of a parent or sibling. In addition, infants are commonly carried by their parents in the piggyback style shown in the photo, which helps develop muscles in the infants' trunk and legs. These infants walk months earlier than American infants (Super, 1981).

Experience can improve the rate of motor development, but the improvement is limited to the specific muscle groups that are involved. In other words, just as daily practice kicking a soccer ball won't improve your golf game, infants who receive much practice in one motor skill usually don't improve in others. For example, in a study by Zelazo and her colleagues (1993), parents had their 6-week-olds practice stepping. Other parents had their infants practice sitting. After 7 weeks of practice, the two groups of infants, as well as a control group of 6-week-olds who had had no practice of any kind, were tested in their ability to step and sit. For both stepping and sitting, infants showed improvement in the skill they had practiced. When infants were tested on the skill they had not practiced, they did no better than infants in the control group. Thus, the impact of practice is specific, not widespread.

Similarly, when infants practice crawling on their bellies, this helps them crawl on hands and feet because many of the motions are the same (Adolph, Vereijken, & Denny, 1998). But when infants practice crawling on steep slopes, there is no transfer to walking on steep slopes, because the motions differ (Adolph, 1997).

Maturation and experience both contribute to the development of motor skills.

Experience becomes even more important in complex actions. Mastering discrete skills, connecting them in the correct sequence, and then timing them properly requires more than a few simple repetitions. Observing others, repeated practice, and getting feedback on errors is required. Of course, learning a complex behavior must build upon maturational changes. But with biological readiness and practice, youngsters learn a gamut of complex motor behaviors, from hitting a tennis ball to playing a violin to signing to communicate with people who do not hear.

Check Your Learning

1. Motor skill refers to coordinated movements of the muscles and _____.

2. Some reflexes help infants get necessary nutrients; other reflexes protect infants from danger; and still other reflexes _____.

3. According to _____, motor development involves many distinct skills that are organized and reorganized over time, depending on task demands.

4. Skills important in learning to walk include maintaining upright posture and balance, stepping, and _____.

5. Motor development involves differentiation of individual skills and their _____ into a cohesive whole.

6. Not until age _____ do children rotate their wrists while using a spoon.

7. Handedness is determined by heredity and _____.

8. Compared to infants reared in less restrictive environments, infants reared on cradle boards learn to walk _____.

9. When infants practice motor skills, the impact of this practice is _____.

Active Child Some children begin walking before their first birthday; others don't begin until a few months after. Describe some ways in which a child who starts walking early might then have different experiences than a child who starts walking late.

Answers: (1) limbs, (2) serves as the basis for later motor behavior, (3) dynamic systems theory, (4) using perceptual information, (5) integration, (6) 2 years, (7) environmental influences, (8) at about the same time, (9) limited to the practiced skill and there is no widespread effect

Sensory and Perceptual Processes

5.4

Sensory and Perceptual Processes

- Smell, Taste, and Touch
- Hearing
- Seeing
- Integrating Sensory Information

Learning Objectives

■ Are newborn babies able to smell, taste, and respond to touch?

■ How well do infants hear? How do they use sounds to understand their world?

■ How accurate is infants' vision? Do infants perceive color and depth?

■ How do infants integrate information from different senses?

Darla adores her 3-day-old daughter, Olivia. She loves holding her, talking to her, and simply watching her. Darla is certain that Olivia is already getting to know her, coming to recognize her face and the sound of her voice. Darla's husband, Steve, thinks she is crazy. He tells her, "Everyone knows that babies are born blind. And they probably can't hear much either." Darla doubts that Steve is right, but she wishes someone would tell her about babies' vision and hearing.

Darla's questions are really about her newborn daughter's sensory and perceptual skills. To help her, we need to remember that humans have different kinds of sense organs, each receptive to a unique kind of physical energy. The retina at the back of the eye, for example, is sensitive to some types of electromagnetic energy, and sight is the result. The eardrum detects changes in air pressure, and hearing is the result. Cells at the top of the nasal passage detect airborne molecules, and smell is the result. In each case, the sense organ translates the physical stimulation into nerve impulses that are sent to the brain.

Researchers study perception by presenting several distinct stimuli, then determining if infants respond the same to all or differently.

How can we know what an infant senses? Since infants can't tell us what they smell, hear, or see, researchers have had to devise other ways to find out. In many studies, an investigator presents two stimuli to a baby, such as a high-pitched tone and a low-pitched tone or a sweet-tasting substance and a sour-tasting substance. Then the investigator records the baby's physiological responses, such as heart rate or facial expression or head movement. If the baby consistently responds differently to the two stimuli, the baby must be distinguishing between them.

Another approach is based on the fact that infants usually prefer novel stimuli over familiar stimuli. Researchers use this fact to study perception by repeatedly presenting one stimulus (e.g., a low-pitched tone) until an infant barely responds. Then they present a second stimulus (e.g., a higher-pitched tone). If the infant responds strongly, then it can distinguish the two stimuli.

In this module, you'll learn what researchers using these techniques have discovered about infants' perception. We begin with smell, taste, and touch because these senses are particularly mature at birth.

Smell, Taste, and Touch

Newborns have a keen sense of smell. Infants respond positively to pleasant smells and negatively to unpleasant smells (Mennella & Beauchamp, 1997). They have a relaxed, contented-looking facial expression when they smell honey or chocolate but frown, grimace, or turn away when they smell rotten eggs or ammonia. Young babies can also recognize familiar odors. Newborns will look in the direction of a pad that is saturated with their own amniotic fluid (Schaal, Marlier, & Soussignan, 1998). They will also turn toward a pad saturated with the odor of their mother's breast or her perfume (Porter et al., 1991).

Newborns also have a highly developed sense of taste. They readily differentiate salty, sour, bitter, and sweet tastes (Rostenstein & Oster, 1997). Most infants seem to have a "sweet tooth." They react to sweet substances by smiling, sucking, and licking their lips. In contrast, infants grimace when fed bitter- or sour-tasting substances (Kaijura, Cowart, & Beauchamp, 1992). Infants are also sensitive to changes in the taste of breast milk that reflect a mother's diet. Infants will nurse more after their mother has consumed a sweet-tasting substance such as vanilla (Mennella & Beauchamp, 1996).

Newborns are sensitive to touch. As I described in Module 5.3, many areas of the newborn's body respond reflexively when touched. Touching an infant's cheek, mouth, hand, or foot produces reflexive movements, documenting that infants perceive touch.

If babies react to touch, does this mean they experience pain? This is difficult to answer because pain has such a subjective element to it. The same pain-eliciting stimulus that leads some adults to complain of mild discomfort causes others to report that they are in agony. Since infants cannot express their pain to us directly, we must use indirect evidence.

The infant's nervous system definitely is capable of transmitting pain: Receptors for pain in the skin are just as plentiful in infants as they are in adults (Anand & Hickey, 1987). Furthermore, babies' behavior in response to apparent pain-provoking stimuli also suggests that they experience pain (Buchholz et al., 1998). Look, for example, at the baby in the photo who is receiving an inoculation. She lowers her eyebrows, purses her lips, and, of course, opens her mouth to cry. Although we can't hear her, the sound of her cry is probably the unique pattern associated with pain. The pain cry begins suddenly, is high-pitched, and is not easily soothed. This baby is also agitated, moving her hands, arms, and legs (Craig et al., 1993). All together, these signs strongly suggest that babies experience pain.

Perceptual skills are extraordinarily useful to newborns and young babies. Smell and touch help them recognize their mothers. Smell and taste make it much easier for them to learn to eat. Early development of smell, taste, and touch prepare newborns and young babies to learn about the world.

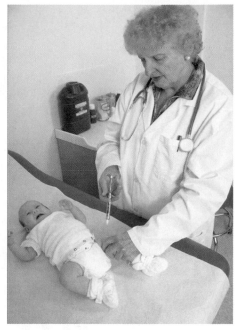

Hearing

Do you remember, from Module 4.1, the study with mothers in late pregnancy who read *The Cat in the Hat* aloud every day? This research showed that the fetus can hear at 7 or 8 months. As you would expect from these results, newborns typically respond to sounds in their surroundings. If a parent is quiet but then coughs, an infant may startle, blink his eyes, and move his arms or legs. These responses may seem natural, but they do indeed indicate that infants are sensitive to sound.

Not surprisingly, infants do not hear as well as adults. *Auditory threshold* **refers to the quietest sound that a person can hear.** An adult's auditory threshold is fairly easy to measure: A tone is presented, and the adult simply tells when he or she hears it. To test auditory thresholds in infants, who obviously cannot report what they hear, researchers have devised a number of clever techniques (Aslin, Jusczyk, & Pisoni, 1998). For example, in one simple method, the infant is seated on a parent's lap. Both parent and baby wear headphones, as does an observer seated in another room who watches the baby through an observation window. When the observer believes the baby is attentive, he signals the experimenter, who sometimes presents a tone over the baby's headphones and sometimes does nothing. Neither the observer nor the parent knows when tones are going to be presented, and they can't hear the tones through their headphones. On each trial, the observer simply judges if the baby responds in any fashion, such as turning its head or changing its facial expression or activity level. Afterwards, the experimenter determines how well the observer's judgments match the trials: If a baby can hear the tone, the observer should have noted a response only when a tone was presented.

This type of testing reveals that, overall, adults can hear better than infants; adults can hear some very quiet sounds that infants can't (Aslin et al., 1998). More importantly, this testing shows that infants best hear sounds that have pitches in the range of human speech—neither very high- nor very low-pitched. Infants can differentiate vowels from consonant sounds, and by 4½ months they can recognize their own names (Jusczyk, 1995; Mandel, Jusczyk, & Pisoni, 1995).

Infants also use sound to locate objects, determining whether they are left or right and near or far. In one study (Clifton, Perris, & Bullinger, 1991), 7-month-olds were shown a rattle. Then the experimenters darkened the room and shook the rat-

> Infants can distinguish different sounds and use sounds to judge the distance and location of objects.

tle, either 6 inches away from the infant or about 2 feet away. Infants often reached for the rattle in the dark when it was 6 inches away but seldom when it was 2 feet away. These 7-month-olds were quite capable of using sound to estimate distance, in this case distinguishing a toy they could reach from one they could not.

Thus, by the middle of the first year, most infants respond to much of the information provided by sound.

Seeing

If you've watched infants you've probably noticed that, while awake, they spend a lot of time looking around. Sometimes they seem to be scanning their environment broadly, and sometimes they seem to be focusing on nearby objects. But what do they actually see? Is their visual world a sea of gray blobs? Or do they see the world essentially as adults do? Actually, neither is the case, but, as you'll see, the second is closer to the truth.

FIG 5–6

From birth, babies respond to light and can track moving objects with their eyes. But what is the clarity of their vision and how can we measure it? ***Visual acuity* is defined as the smallest pattern that can be distinguished dependably.** You've undoubtedly had your visual acuity measured by trying to read rows of progressively smaller letters or numbers from a chart. The same basic logic is used in tests of infants' acuity, which are based on two premises. First, most infants will look at patterned stimuli instead of plain, nonpatterned stimuli. For example, if we were to show the two stimuli in the top diagram to infants, most would look longer at the striped pattern than the gray pattern. Second, as we make the lines narrower (along with the spaces between them), there comes a point at which the black and white stripes become so fine that they simply blend together and appear gray, just like the all gray pattern.

FIG 5–7

To estimate an infant's acuity, then, we pair the gray square with squares that differ in the width of their stripes, like those in the bottom diagram: When infants look at the two stimuli equally, it indicates that they are no longer able to distinguish the stripes of the patterned stimulus. By measuring the width of the stripes and their distance from an infant's eye, we can estimate acuity (detecting thinner stripes indicates better acuity).

Measurements of this sort indicate that newborns and 1-month-olds see at 20 feet what normal adults see at 200 to 400 feet. Infants' acuity improves rapidly and by the first birthday is essentially the same as a normal adult's (Kellman & Banks, 1998).

Not only do infants begin to see the world with greater acuity during the first year, they also begin to see it in color! How do we perceive color? The wavelength of light is the source of color perception. The diagram at the top of page 139 shows that lights we see as red have a relatively long wavelength, whereas violet, at the other end of the color spectrum, has a much shorter wavelength. **We detect wavelength—and therefore color—with specialized neurons called *cones* that are in the retina of the eye.** Some cones are particularly sensitive to short-wavelength light (blues and violets), others are sensitive to medium-wavelength light (greens and yellows), and still others to long-wavelength light (reds and oranges). These different kinds of cones are linked in complex circuits of neurons in the eye and in the brain, and this neural circuitry allows us to see the world in color.

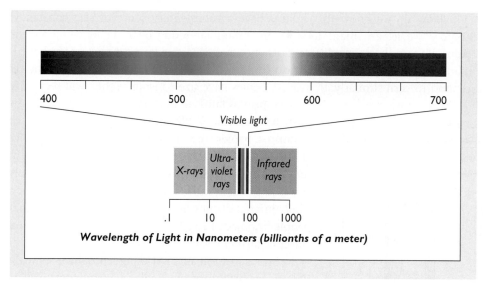

FIG 5-8

These circuits gradually begin to function in the first few months after birth. Newborns and young babies can perceive few colors, but by 3 months, the three kinds of cones and their associated circuits are working—infants are able to see the full range of colors (Kellman & Banks, 1998).

In fact, by 3 to 4 months, infants' color perception seems similar to adults' (Adams & Courage, 1995). In particular, infants, like adults, tend to see categories of color. For example, if a yellow light's wavelength is gradually increased, the infant will suddenly perceive it as a shade of red rather than a shade of yellow.

To study infants' perception of color categories, researchers use the same technique used to test visual acuity. First, infants are repeatedly shown the same colored light; it might be a light with a wavelength of 600 nanometers (billionths of a meter), which adults call yellow. Infants look intently at first, then look less. When this happens, a new light is shown. The wavelength of the new light always differs from the original by the same amount—20 nanometers, for example. For some babies, the wavelength is *decreased* 20 nanometers; adults still consider this a yellow light. For other babies, the wavelength is *increased* 20 nanometers; adults judge this a green light. Infants look longer at a new light from a new color category than a new light from the same, familiar color category. This result indicates that infants view the stimuli as adults do—in categories of color (Dannemiller, 1998; Teller & Bornstein, 1987).

The ability to perceive color, along with rapidly improving visual acuity, gives infants great skill to make sense out of their visual experiences.

> Infants not only perceive color and depth, they soon achieve many perceptual constancies.

Perceptual Constancies. The scene comes straight out of one of those lousy black-and-white horror movies that Hollywood used to crank out in the 1950s and 1960s: From its normal size, your mother's head begins to shrink, getting ever smaller until it finally vanishes altogether. Ee-e-e-e-ek!! Actually, for a baby, this scene might be a daily event. After all, any time a mother moves away from her baby, the image that she casts on the retinas of her baby's eyes gets smaller. Do babies have this nightmare? No. **Early on, infants master *size constancy*, the realization that an object's actual size remains the same despite changes in the size of its retinal image.**

How do we know that infants have a rudimentary sense of size constancy? Suppose we let an infant look at an unfamiliar teddy bear. Then we show the infant the same bear, at a different distance, paired with a larger replica of the bear. If infants lack size constancy, the two bears will be equally novel and babies should respond to each similarly. If, instead, babies have size constancy, they will recognize the first bear as familiar, the larger bear as novel, and be more likely to respond to the novel bear. In fact, by 4 or 5 months, babies treat the bear that they've seen twice at different distances—and, therefore, with different retinal images—as familiar (Granrud, 1986). This outcome is possible only if infants have size constancy. Thus, infants do not believe that mothers (and other people or objects) constantly change size as they move closer or farther away.

Size is just one of several perceptual constancies. Others are brightness and color constancy as well as shape constancy, shown in the diagram. All these constancies are achieved, at least in rudimentary form, by 4 months (Aslin, 1987; Dannemiller, 1998).

If you think about it, the message from the perceptual constancies is that "seeing is not believing," at least not always. A good part of perception, therefore, is knowing how to make sense out of what we see. Another important part of making sense out of what we see is deciding how near or far an object is.

Shape Constancy: Even though the door appears to change shape as it opens, we know that it really remains a rectangle.

FIG 5–9

Depth. People see objects as having three dimensions: height, width, and depth. The retina of the eye is flat, so height and width can be represented directly on its two-dimensional surface. But the third dimension, depth, cannot be represented directly on a surface, so how do we perceive depth? How do we decide if objects are nearby or far away? We use perceptual processing to infer depth.

Can infants perceive depth? Eleanor Gibson and Richard Walk (1960) addressed this question using a special apparatus. **The *visual cliff* is a glass-covered platform; on one side a pattern appears directly under the glass, but on the other it appears several feet below the glass.** Consequently, one side looks shallow but the other appears to have a steep drop-off, like a cliff.

As you can see in the photo, in the experiment the baby is placed on the platform and the mother coaxes her infant to come to her. Most babies willingly crawl to their mother when she stands on the shallow side. But virtually all babies refuse to cross the deep side, even when the mother calls the infant by name and tries to lure him or her with an attractive toy. Clearly, infants can perceive depth by the time they are old enough to crawl.

What about babies who cannot yet crawl? When babies as young as 1½ months are simply placed on the deep side of the platform, their heartbeat slows down. Heart rate often decelerates when people notice something interesting, so this would suggest that 1½-month-olds notice that the deep side is different. At 7 months, infants' heart rate accelerates, a sign of fear. Thus, although young babies can detect a difference between the shallow and deep sides of the visual cliff, only older, crawling babies are actually afraid of the deep side (Campos et al., 1978).

How do infants infer depth, on the visual cliff or anywhere? They use several kinds of cues. **One,** *retinal disparity,* **is based on the fact that the left and right eyes often see slightly different versions of the same scene.** When objects are distant, the images appear in very similar positions on the retina; when objects are near, the images appear in much different positions. Thus, greater disparity in positions of the image on the retina signals that an object is close. By 4 to 6 months, infants use retinal disparity as a depth cue, correctly inferring that objects are nearby when disparity is great (Kellman & Banks, 1998; Yonas & Owsley, 1987).

Other cues for depth that depend on the arrangement of objects in the environment include texture gradient, relative size, and interposition.

Texture gradient: **The texture of objects changes from coarse but distinct for nearby objects to finer and less distinct for distant objects.** In the photo, we judge the distinct flowers to be close and the blurred ones, distant.

Relative size: **Nearby objects look substantially larger than objects in the distance.** Knowing that the runners in the photo are really about the same size, we judge the ones that look smaller to be farther away.

Interposition: **Nearby objects partially obscure more distant objects.** In the photo, the glasses obscure the bottle, so we decide the glasses are closer (and use this same cue to decide the grapes are closer than the left glass).

By 7 months, infants use most of these cues to judge distance (Kellman & Banks, 1998). In one study (Arterberry, Yonas, & Bensen, 1989), for example, babies saw what appeared to be two toys resting on a checkered surface that gave linear perspective and texture gradients as depth cues. In fact, the checkered surface was a flat photograph. Infants were tested with one eye covered so that retinal disparity would not provide a cue to depth. Most 7-month-olds reached for the toy that looked closer, but 5-month-olds reached for the two toys equally often. Evidently, 7-month-olds use linear perspective and texture gradient to infer depth, but 5-month-olds do not.

Perceiving Objects. When you look at this pattern, what do you see? You probably recognize it as part of a human eyeball, even though all that's physically present in the photograph are many different colored dots. In this case, perception actually creates an object from sensory stimulation.

How do perceptual processes define objects? Edges play an important role (Kellman & Banks, 1998). ***Edges* are lines that mark the boundaries of objects.** We use edges to distinguish an object from another and from background. In the photo of the eyeball, for example, two circles of blue dots define the inner and outer edges of the iris; these edges cause us to see all the other blue dots as part of the same "thing"—the iris.

Early in the first year, infants use edges to identify objects. Infants' perception of edges is shown in some fascinating research involving patterns like the one in the figure at the top of page 143. When you see this pattern, it's almost impossible to not see a square. Of course, there's no actual physical stimulus that corresponds to the square. Instead, the cut-out portions of each circle are corners that define lines, creating an edge. It's this created edge that allows our perceptual system to "see" a square.

When infants view these circles, do they, too, "see" a square? The answer seems to be yes. In one study (Ghim, 1990), 3-month-olds were shown a real square. After six presentations of the square, one of the four patterns in the diagram below was shown. You can see that all consist of four circles, but only Pattern A creates the subjective experience of "seeing" a square. Having seen squares repeatedly, 3-month-olds looked much longer at Patterns B, C, and D than at Pattern A. Evidently, Pattern A looked familiar, so they looked less. Of course, the only way that Pattern A could be familiar is if infants "saw" a square created by the four circles and interpreted this as yet another presentation of the actual square they had seen previously.

Edges are most useful in distinguishing stationary objects. When motion is present, we use it to help define objects by following a simple

FIG 5–10

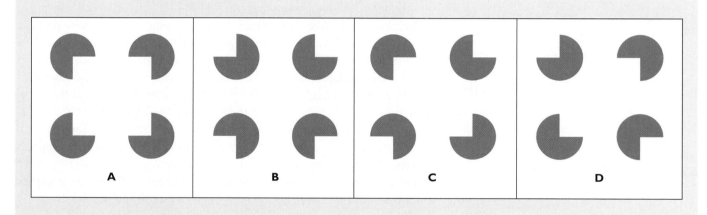

Source: Ghim, 1990.

FIG 5–11

rule: Elements that move together are usually part of the same object (Kellman & Banks, 1998). For example, at the left of the diagram, a pencil appears to be moving back and forth behind a colored square. If the square were removed, you would be surprised to see a pair of pencil stubs, as shown on the right side of the diagram. The common movement of the pencil's eraser and point lead us to believe that they're part of the same pencil.

By 2 to 4 months of age, infants, too, are surprised by demonstrations like this. If they see a display like the moving pencils, they will then look very briefly at a whole pencil, apparently because they expected it. In contrast, if after seeing the moving pencil they're shown the two pencil stubs, they look much longer, as if trying to figure out what happened (Eizenman & Bertenthal, 1998; Johnson & Aslin, 1995). Evidently, even very young babies use common motion to create objects from different parts.

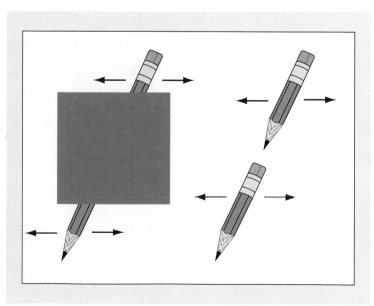

FIG 5–12

1-Month-Olds

Finish

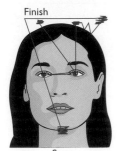

Start

3-Month-Olds

Start

Finish

FIG 5–13

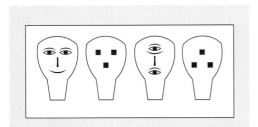

FIG 5–14

Source: Morton & Johnson, 1990.

One object that's particularly important for infants is the human face. Young babies readily look at faces. From the diagram on the right, which shows a pattern of eye fixations, you can see that 1-month-olds look mostly at the outer edges of the face. Three-month-olds, however, focus almost entirely on the interior of the face, particularly the eyes and lips.

Some scientists believe that general principles of perception explain how infants perceive faces (Aslin, 1987). They argue that infants are attracted to faces because faces have stimuli that move (the eyes and mouth) and stimuli with dark and light contrast (the eyes, lips, and teeth). Research by Dannemiller and Stephens (1988) supports this view. They found that when face and nonface stimuli are matched for a number of important variables (such as the amount of black/white contrast, the size and number of elements), $1\frac{1}{2}$-month-olds typically look at face and nonface stimuli equally. In other words, infants look at faces because of general perceptual principles (for example, babies like contrasting stimuli), not because faces are intrinsically attractive to infants.

Other theorists, however, argue that babies are innately attracted to stimuli that are facelike. The claim is that some aspect of the face—perhaps two eyes and a mouth in the correct arrangement—constitutes a distinctive stimulus that is readily recognized, even by newborns. For example, look at the different facelike stimuli in the diagram. In one study (Morton & Johnson, 1991), newborns turned their eyes to follow a moving face (at the left in the figure) more than they turned their eyes for stimuli that had either facial elements or a facial configuration but not both (the remaining three stimuli in the figure). Infants preferred faces over facelike stimuli, which supports the view that infants are innately attracted to faces.

More research is needed to decide whether face perception follows general perceptual principles or represents a special case. What is clear, though, is that by 3 or 4 months, babies have the perceptual skills that allow them to begin to distinguish individual faces (Carey, 1992). This ability is essential for it provides the basis for social relationships that infants form during the rest of the first year.

Integrating Sensory Information

So far, we have discussed infants' sensory systems separately. In reality, of course, most infant experiences are better described as "multimedia events." A nursing mother provides visual and taste cues to her baby. A rattle stimulates vision, hearing, and touch. From experiences like these, infants learn to integrate information from different senses.

Research shows that by 1 month—and possibly at birth—infants can integrate sensory information (Bahrick, 1992). For example, 1-month-olds can recognize an object visually that they had only touched previously (Gibson & Walker, 1984). By 4 months, infants are quite skilled at integrating sights and sounds: They can connect the characteristic sounds of male and female voices with the characteristic appearances of male and female faces (Poulin-Dubois et al., 1994).

Another example of how infants integrate vision and hearing is the topic of the Focus on Research feature.

FOCUS ON RESEARCH

Do Infants Integrate Sight and Sound When Others Speak?

Who were the investigators and what was the aim of the study? Compared to adults, children have a distinctive facial appearance and a distinctive sound when speaking. Children's faces tend to be more rounded, their eyes look larger, and their skin is softer. Children's voices tend to be higher-pitched, more variable in loudness, and often not as well controlled. Thus, adults know that individuals with rounded, soft-skinned faces (children) tend to have quavering, high-pitched voices; individuals with more angular, rougher-skinned faces (adults) tend to have steady, lower-pitched voices. Can infants, too, make connections with faces and voices? Lorraine Bahrick, Dianelys Netto, and Maria Hernandez-Reif (1998) conducted a study to answer this question.

How did the investigators measure the topic of interest? Bahrick and her colleagues created the setup shown in the diagram. They presented pairs of 20-second videotapes on two video monitors placed side by side. One monitor showed a close-up of a boy's face; the other, a close-up of a man's face. Both the boy and the man appeared to be talking. When the videos started, a separate audiotape began with a boy or a man reciting one particular nursery rhyme. As the infants heard the audiotape, research assistants recorded which video the infant watched. Infants saw 12 pairs of videotapes.

FIG 5–15

What should infants do when they see these videos? If infants know the rules,

boyish face = boyish voice

manlike face = manlike voice

then they should look at the video that matches the sound: They'll watch the video of the man when they hear the man's voice and the video of the boy when they hear the boy's voice.

Who were the children in the study? Bahrick and her colleagues tested sixteen 4-month-olds and sixteen 7-month-olds.

What was the design of the study? This study was experimental. One independent variable was the infant's age. Another was the grouping of the pairs of videos—the first six pairs of videos versus the last six pairs. The dependent variable was the amount of time the infants spent watching the video depicting a person who was the same age as the person speaking on the audiotape. The study included two age groups tested at the same point in time, so it was cross-sectional.

Were there ethical concerns with the study? No. Most infants seemed to enjoy watching the videos. All parents agreed to allow their infants to participate.

What were the results? If infants had no preference for the videotape that matched the audiotape, they should look at the two videos equally. In other words, they would spend about 50 percent of the time looking at the video that matched the audio. The bars in the graph at the top of page 146 show the percentage of time that infants actually spent watching the video showing a person who was the same age as the person speaking. The 4-month-olds had no preference on the first 6 videos, but looked longer at the matching videos on the second 6 videos. For 7-month-olds, the pattern was reversed: they looked longer at the matching video during the first 6 videos, but not on the second 6.

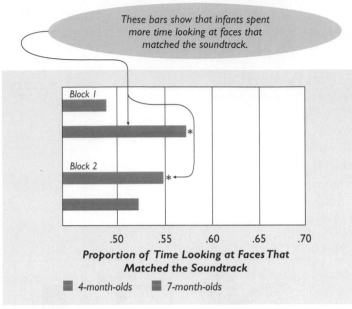

These bars show that infants spent more time looking at faces that matched the soundtrack.

Block 1

Block 2

.50   .55   .60   .65   .70

Proportion of Time Looking at Faces That Matched the Soundtrack

■ 4-month-olds   ■ 7-month-olds

FIG 5–16

What did the investigators conclude? Both 4- and 7-month-olds are able to integrate the typical appearances of face and typical sounds of voices. That is, infants know that childish faces tend to have childish voices and adult-like faces tend to have adult-like voices. The fact that these outcomes were found in different sets of videos also shows the obstacles of doing experimentation with young infants: Apparently the 4-month-olds took longer to figure out what was involved in the study and the 7-month-olds lost interest more quickly.

What converging evidence would strengthen these conclusions? Linking faces and voices based on age is but one of many cases in which sight and sound are related to each other. For example, when objects are nearby, their sound is louder than when objects are distant. And when objects move from left to right, their sound appears to move, too. Showing that infants discern these connections, too, would provide additional evidence of infants' ability to integrate vision and hearing. ■

Integrating sight and sound is yet another variation on the theme that has dominated this module: Infants' sensory and perceptual skills are impressive. Darla's newborn daughter, from the opening vignette, can definitely smell, taste, and feel pain. She can distinguish sounds, and at about 7 months she will use sound to locate objects. Her vision is a little blurry now but will improve rapidly, and in a few months, she'll see the full range of colors. Within only a month, she'll be making connections between sights and sounds and between other senses. In short, Darla's daughter, like most infants, is well prepared to make sense out of her environment.

> Infants readily integrate information from different senses, linking seeing to hearing and seeing to touch.

Check Your Learning

1. Babies react to sweet substances by smiling and sucking but grimace when fed substances with a _____ taste.

2. Babies probably experience pain because their nervous system is capable of transmitting pain and because _____.

3. Studies of auditory thresholds reveal that adults can hear better than infants, particularly _____.

4. Infants use sound to judge the distance and _____ of objects.

5. By age _____, infants have approximately the same visual acuity as adults.

6. At 3 months, infants see the full range of colors and, like adults, perceive colors as _____.

7. In the first few months of life, infants integrate what they see with what they _____ and what they see with what they hear.

Nature and Nurture Are infants' sensory and perceptual skills primarily the effect of nature, nurture, or both?

Answers: (1) bitter or sour, (2) they respond to pain-provoking stimulation, (3) softer sounds, (4) location, (5) 1 year, (6) categories, (7) feel

Critical Review

1. Explain how the example of malnutrition (Module 5.1) illustrates at least two of the four themes of child development first explored in Chapter 1.

2. Based on the research described in Module 5.2, explain the relation between emotional experience and response to stimuli. Why are both located in the frontal cortex?

3. Given the information presented in Module 5.3, summarize what parents can do to enhance their child's motor development.

4. Speculate on the survival benefits to infants of the perceptual abilities described in Module 5.4. Why should infants be able to distinguish between tastes and odor, react to sounds, and process visual information?

5. How would a psychologist from the learning perspective (described in Module 1.2) explain the research on sensory integration? How would the explanation of psychologists from the information-processing perspective differ?

For more review material, log on to www.prenhall.com/kail

See For Yourself

How can you decide if a toddler is left- or right-handed? Adults can tell us which hand they use in writing or throwing, but we need a more concrete approach with toddlers who don't even know left from right. Ask some toddlers to do the following tasks (derived from McManus et al., 1988):

    1. Color a square

    2. Throw a ball

    3. Thread a bead onto a string

4. Turn over cards placed on a table

5. Brush their teeth

6. Blow their nose with a tissue

7. Pick a piece of candy from a bag

8. Comb their hair

You should see that most toddlers use their right hand on many tasks but not on others. Few will show a strong preference for one hand over the other. See for yourself!

For More Information About . . .

 infant development in general, including perceptual development, try Charles W. Snow's *Infant Development,* 2nd ed. (Prentice-Hall, 1998).

 children's nutrition, visit the Web site of the American Medical Association:
http://www.ama-assn.org/insight/h_focus/nemours/nutritio/index.htm

Key Terms

auditory threshold 137
axon 120
cell body 120
cerebral hemispheres 121
cones 138
corpus callosum 121
dendrite 120
differentiation 131
dynamic systems theory 129
edges 142
electroencephalogram (EEG) 122
epiphyses 113
fine-motor skills 128
frontal cortex 121
functional magnetic resonance
  imaging (F-MRI) 123

hormones 114
integration 131
interposition 142
locomotion 127
malnourished 116
motor skills 127
myelin 120
neural plate 121
neuron 120
neuroplasticity 125
neurotransmitters 120
positron emission tomography
  (PET-scan) 123
reflexes 128
relative size 141
retinal disparity 141

secular growth trends 113
size constancy 139
synapse 120
synaptic pruning 122
terminal buttons 120
texture gradient 141
thyroxine 114
visual acuity 138
visual cliff 140

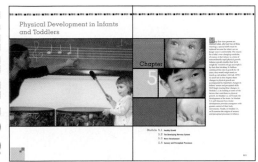

SUMMARY

5.1 Healthy Growth

Features of Human Growth
Physical growth is particularly rapid in infants and toddlers. Growth follows the cephalocaudal principle, with head and trunk developing before the limbs. Physical growth refers to not only height and weight but also to development of muscles, fat, and bones.

Variations on the Average Profile
Children are larger today than in previous generations. And children of the same age vary considerably in height and weight.

Mechanisms of Physical Growth
A person's height and weight as an adult are influenced by heredity. Growth hormone (GH) affects bone and muscle growth, and thyroxine affects nerve cells.

Nutrition is particularly important during infancy because it is a period of rapid growth. Breast-feeding provides babies with all the nutrients they need and has other advantages as well.

Challenges to Healthy Growth
Many children face serious obstacles on the road to healthy development. Malnutrition is a problem worldwide that is particularly harmful during infancy, when growth is so rapid. Treating malnutrition requires improving children's diet and helping parents to provide stimulating environments. Millions of children around the world die annually from infectious diseases. Integrated Management of Childhood Illness is a new integrated approach designed to promote children's health. In the United States, toddlers are more likely to die from accidents than any other single cause.

5.2 The Developing Nervous System

Organization of the Mature Brain
Nerve cells are composed of a cell body, a dendrite, and an axon. The mature brain consists of billions of neurons organized into nearly identical left and right hemispheres connected by the corpus callosum. The frontal cortex is associated with personality and goal-directed behavior; the cortex in the left hemisphere, with language; and the cortex in the right hemisphere, with nonverbal processes.

The Developing Brain
Brain structure begins in prenatal development, when neurons form at an incredible rate. After birth, neurons in the central nervous system become wrapped in myelin, allowing them to transmit information more rapidly. Throughout childhood, unused synapses disappear gradually, through a process of pruning.

Methods used to investigate brain functioning in children include (a) studying children with brain damage, (b) recording electrical activity, and (c) using imaging techniques. An infant's brain begins to function early in life. The cortex in the left hemisphere specializes in language processing at (or soon after) birth. The cortex in the right hemisphere controls some nonverbal functions, such as perception of music, very early in infancy; control of other right hemisphere functions, such as understanding spatial relations, is achieved by the preschool years. The frontal cortex has begun to regulate goal-directed behavior and emotions by the first birthday.

5.3 Motor Development

The Infant's Reflexes
Babies are born with many reflexes. Some help them adjust to life outside the uterus, some protect them, and some are the basis for later motor behavior.

Locomotion
Infants progress through a sequence of motor milestones during the first year, culminating in walking a few months after the first birthday. Like most motor skills, learning to walk involves differentiation of individual skills, such as maintaining balance and stepping on alternate legs, and then integrating these skills into a coherent whole. This is the dynamic systems theory of motor development.

Fine-Motor Skills
Reaching and grasping become more precise in the first year, reflecting principles of dynamic systems theory.

Most people are right-handed, a preference that emerges after the first birthday. Handedness is determined by heredity but can be influenced by experience and cultural values.

Maturation, Experience, and Motor Skill
Biology and experience both shape the mastery of motor skills. The basic timetable for motor milestones is similar around the world, which indicates underlying biological causes. Specific experience can accelerate motor development, particularly for complex motor skills.

5.4 Sensory and Perceptual Processes

Smell, Taste, and Touch
Newborns can smell and taste, preferring sweet substances over bitter and sour tastes. Infants respond to touch and they experience pain.

Hearing
Babies can hear, although they are less sensitive to higher- and lower-pitched sounds than adults. Babies can distinguish different sounds and use sound to locate objects in space.

Seeing
A newborn's visual acuity is relatively poor, but 1-year-olds can see as well as an adult with normal vision. By 3 or 4 months, children see color as well as adults. Infants use edges and motion to distinguish objects. Infants perceive faces early in the first year but it is not clear whether this is based on specific perceptual mechanisms or based on the same processes used to see other objects.

Integrating Sensory Information
Soon after birth, infants coordinate information from different senses. They recognize by sight an object that they've felt previously. And infants integrate what they see with what they hear.

Cognition in Infants
and Toddlers

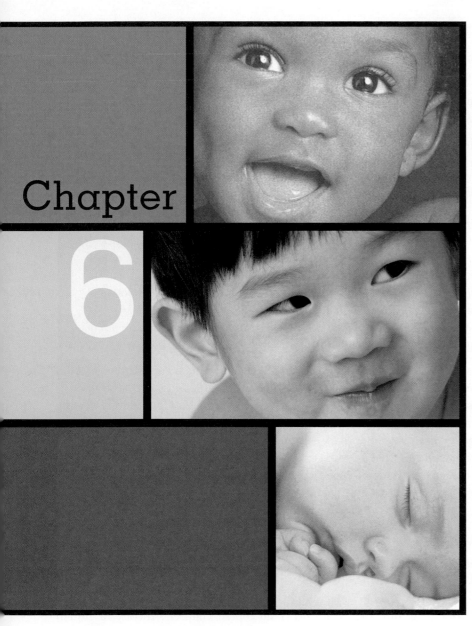

Chapter 6

In the movie *Look Who's Talking* we are privy to an infant's thoughts on everything from his birth and diaper changes to his mother's boyfriends. The humor, of course, turns on the idea that babies are capable of sophisticated thinking—they just can't express it. But what thoughts do lurk in the mind of an infant who is not yet speaking? And how do an infant's fledgling thoughts blossom into the powerful reasoning skills that older children, adolescents, and adults use daily?

For many years, the best answers to these questions came from the theory proposed by Jean Piaget. We begin, in Module 6.1, with some background on Piaget's theory and his description of the first stage of cognitive development. In Module 6.2, we look at information processing in infants and toddlers. Finally, in Module 6.3, we examine changes in language during the first 2 years.

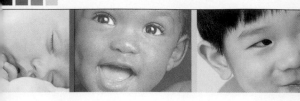

Piaget's Theory

6.1

Piaget's Theory

Learning Objectives

- How do assimilation, accommodation, and equilibration explain how children's thinking changes with age?

- How does thinking become more advanced as infants progress through the six substages of the sensorimotor stage?

- What are some criticisms of Piaget's account of cognitive processes in infants and toddlers?

- What are young children's naive theories of physics and biology?

When John, an energetic 2½-year-old, saw a bright orange monarch butterfly for the first time, his mother, Patrice, told him, "Butterfly, butterfly; that's a butterfly, John." A few minutes later, a yellow striped zebra swallowtail landed on a nearby bush and John shouted in excitement, "Butterfly, Mama, butterfly!" A bit later, a moth flew out of another bush; with even greater excitement in his voice, John shouted, "Butterfly, Mama, more butterfly!" As Patrice was telling John, "No, honey, that's a moth, not a butterfly," she marveled at how rapidly John seemed to grasp new concepts with so little direction from her. How was this possible?

For many years, our best answer to Patrice's question came from Jean Piaget, who began work on his theory of mental development in the 1920s. Piaget was trained as a biologist but he developed a keen interest in the branch of philosophy dealing with the nature and origins of knowledge. He decided to investigate the origins of knowledge not as philosophers had—through discussion and debate—but by doing experiments with children.

We'll begin our study of Piaget's work by looking at some key principles of his theory and, as we do, discover why John understands as quickly as he does.

Basic Principles of Piaget's Theory

Piaget believed that children are naturally curious. They constantly want to make sense out of their experience and, in the process, construct their understanding of the world. For Piaget, children at all ages are like scientists in that they create theories about how the world works. Of course, children's theories are often incomplete. Nevertheless, their theories are valuable because they make the world seem more predictable.

According to Piaget, children come to understand the world by using *schemes*, psychological structures that organize experience. That is, schemes are mental categories of related events, objects, and knowledge. During infancy, most schemes are based on actions. Infants group objects based on the actions they can perform on them. For example, infants suck and grasp, and they use these actions to create categories of objects that can be sucked and objects that can be grasped.

> Schemes are mental categories that organize experience, based on actions in infancy and abstract properties in adolescence.

Schemes are just as important after infancy, but then they are based primarily on functional or conceptual relationships, not actions. For example, preschoolers learn that forks, knives, and spoons form a functional category of "things I use to eat." Or they learn that dogs, cats, and goldfish form a conceptual category of "pets."

Like preschoolers, older children and adolescents use schemes based on functional and conceptual schemes, but they also have schemes that are based on increasingly abstract properties. For example, an adolescent might put fascism, racism, and sexism in a category of "ideologies that I despise."

Thus, children use schemes of related objects, events, and ideas throughout development. But as children develop, their basis for creating schemes shifts from physical activity to functional, conceptual, and, later, abstract properties of objects, events, and ideas.

Assimilation and Accommodation. Schemes change constantly, adapting to children's experiences. In fact, intellectual adaptation involves two processes working together: assimilation and accommodation. ***Assimilation occurs when new experiences are readily incorporated into existing schemes.*** Imagine a baby who is familiar with the grasping scheme. Like the baby in the photo, she will soon discover that the grasping scheme works not only on toys but also on blocks, balls, and other small objects. Extending the existing grasping scheme to new objects illustrates assimilation. ***Accommodation occurs when schemes are modified based on experience.*** Soon the infant learns that some objects can only be lifted with two hands and that some can't be lifted at all. Changing the scheme so that it works for new objects (e.g., using two hands to grasp a big stuffed animal) illustrates accommodation.

Assimilation and accommodation are easy to understand if you remember Piaget's belief that infants, children, and adolescents create theories to understand the world around them. The infant whose theory is that objects can be lifted with one hand finds that her theory is confirmed when she tries to pick up small objects, but she's in for a surprise when she tries to pick up a big stuffed animal. The unexpected result forces the infant, like a good scientist, to revise her theory to include this new finding.

Assimilation and accommodation are illustrated in the vignette at the beginning of the module. Piaget would say that when Patrice named the monarch butterfly for John, he formed a scheme something like "butterflies are bugs with big wings." The second butterfly differed in color but was still a bug with big wings, so it was readily assimilated into John's new scheme for butterflies. However, when John referred to the moth as a butterfly, Patrice corrected him. Presumably, John was then forced to accommodate to this new experience; the result was that he changed his scheme for butterflies to make it more precise; the new scheme might be something like "butterflies are bugs with thin bodies and big, colorful wings." He also created a new scheme, something like "a moth is a bug with a bigger body and plain wings."

Equilibration and Stages of Cognitive Development. Assimilation and accommodation are usually in balance, or equilibrium. That is, children find they can readily assimilate most experiences into their existing schemes, but occasionally they need to accommodate their schemes to adjust to new experiences. This balance between assimilation and accommodation is illustrated both by the baby grasping larger objects and John's understanding of butterflies.

Periodically, however, the balance is upset and a state of disequilibrium results. Children discover that their current schemes are not adequate because they are spending much more time accommodating than assimilating. **When disequilibrium occurs, children reorganize their schemes to return to a state of equilibrium, a process that Piaget called** *equilibration.* To restore the balance, current but now-outmoded ways of thinking are replaced by a qualitatively different, more advanced set of schemes.

One way to understand equilibration is to return to the metaphor of the child as a scientist. As discussed in Module 1.2, good scientific theories readily explain some phenomena but usually must be revised to explain others. Children's theories allow them to understand many experiences by predicting, for example, what will happen ("It's morning, so it's time for breakfast") or who will do what ("Mom's gone to work, so Dad will take me to school"), but they too must be modified when predictions go awry ("Dad thinks I'm old enough to walk to school, so he won't take me").

Sometimes scientists find that their theories contain critical flaws, so they can't simply revise; they must create a new theory that draws upon the older theory but is

> All children pass through all four of Piaget's stages in the same order, but some do so more rapidly than others.

fundamentally different. For example, when Copernicus realized that the earth-centered theory of the solar system was wrong, he retained the concept of a central object but proposed that it was the sun, a fundamental change in the theory. In much the same way, children periodically reach a point when their current theories seem to be wrong much of the time, so they abandon these theories in favor of more advanced ways of thinking about their physical and social worlds.

According to Piaget, these revolutionary changes in thought occur three times over the life span, at approximately 2, 7, and 11 years of age. This divides cognitive development into the four stages shown in the table.

Piaget's Four Stages of Cognitive Development		
Stage	**Approximate Age**	**Characteristics**
Sensorimotor	Birth to 2 years	Infant's knowledge of the world is based on senses and motor skills. By the end of the period, infant uses mental representations.
Preoperational thought	2 to 6 years	Child learns how to use symbols such as words and numbers to represent aspects of the world, but relates to the world only through his or her perspective.
Concrete operational thought	7 to 11 years	Child understands and applies logical operations to experiences, provided they are focused on the here and now.
Formal operational thought	Adolescence and beyond	Adolescent or adult thinks abstractly, speculates on hypothetical situations, and reasons deductively about what may be possible.

TABLE 6–1

Each of these stages is marked by a distinctive way of thinking about and understanding the world. The ages listed are only approximate: Some youngsters move through the stages more rapidly than others, depending on their ability and their experience. However, Piaget held that all children go through all four stages and in exactly this sequence. Sensorimotor thinking always gives rise to preoperational thinking; a child cannot "skip" preoperational thinking and move directly from sensorimotor to concrete operational thought.

In the rest of this module, we will look at the first of the four stages of cognitive development in detail. (We'll consider the other stages in Chapters 9, 12, and 15.)

Piaget's Sensorimotor Stage

We know, from Modules 5.3 and 5.4, that infants' perceptual and motor skills improve quickly throughout the first year. Piaget proposed that these rapidly changing skills in the first 2 years of life form a distinct phase in child development: **The *sensorimotor stage*, which spans birth to 2 years, consists of 6 substages during which the infant progresses from simple reflex actions to symbolic processing.** All infants move through the 6 substages in the same order. However, they progress at different rates, so the ages listed here are only approximations.

Substage 1: Exercising reflexes (roughly birth to 1 month). You know from Module 5.3 that newborns respond reflexively to many stimuli. As infants use their reflexes during the first month, they become more coordinated. Just as major-league players swing a bat with greater power and strength than Little Leaguers, 1-month-olds suck more vigorously and steadily than newborns.

Substage 2: Learning to adapt (roughly 1 to 4 months). During these months, reflexes become modified by experience. **The chief mechanism for change is the *primary circular reaction*, which occurs when an infant accidentally produces some pleasing event and then tries to recreate the event.** For example, an infant may inadvertently touch her lips with her thumb, thereby initiating sucking and the pleasing sensations associated with sucking. Later, the infant tries to recreate these sensations by guiding her thumb to her mouth. Sucking no longer occurs only reflexively when a mother places a nipple at the infant's mouth; instead, the infant has found a way to initiate sucking herself.

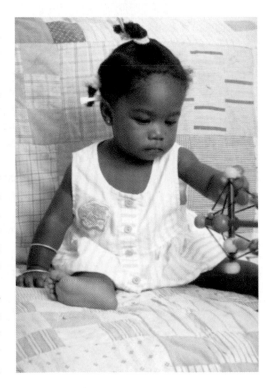

Substage 3: Making interesting events (roughly 4 to 8 months). Primary circular reactions are centered on the infant's own body, typically involving reflexes like sucking or grasping. However, beginning in Substage 3, the infant shows greater interest in the world; now objects are more often the focus of circular reactions. For example, the infant shown in the photo accidentally shook a new rattle. Hearing the interesting noise, the infant grasped the rattle again, tried to shake it, and expressed great pleasure at the noise. This sequence was repeated several times.

Novel actions that are repeated with objects are called *secondary circular reactions*. Secondary circular reactions are significant because they represent an infant's first efforts to learn about the objects in his or her environment, to explore their properties and their actions. No longer are infants grasping objects "mindlessly," simply because something is in contact with their hands. Instead, they are learning about the sights and sounds associated with objects.

Substage 4: Using means to achieve ends (roughly 8 to 12 months). This substage marks the onset of deliberate, intentional behavior. Why? For the first time, the "means" and "end" of activities are distinct. If, for example, a father places his hand in front of a toy, an infant will move his hand to be able to play with the toy. "The moving the hand" scheme is the means to achieve the goal of "grasping the toy." Using one action as a means to achieve another end is the first indication of purposeful, goal-directed behavior during infancy.

Substage 5: Experimenting (roughly 12 to 18 months). The infant at this stage is an active experimentalist. **An infant will repeat old schemes with novel objects, what Piaget called a *tertiary circular reaction*, as if she is trying to understand why different objects yield different outcomes.** An infant in Substage 5 may deliberately shake a number of different objects trying to discover which produce sounds and which do not. Or an infant may decide to drop different objects to see what happens. An infant in a crib will discover that stuffed animals land quietly whereas bigger toys often make a more satisfying clunk when they hit the ground.

Tertiary circular reactions represent a significant extension of the intentional behavior that emerged in Substage 4. Now babies repeat actions with different objects solely for the purpose of seeing what will happen.

Substage 6: Using symbols (roughly 18 to 24 months). By 18 months, most infants have begun to talk and gesture, evidence of the emerging capacity to use symbols. Words and gestures are symbols that stand for something else. When the baby in the photo waves, it is just as effective and symbolic as saying goodbye to bid farewell. Children also begin to engage in pretend play, another use of symbols. A 20-month-old may move her hand back and forth in front of her mouth, pretending to brush her teeth.

Once infants can use symbols, they can begin to anticipate the consequences of actions mentally, instead of having to perform them. Imagine that an infant and parent construct a tower of blocks next to an open door. Leaving the room, a baby in Substage 5 might close the door, knocking over the tower, because he cannot foresee the outcome of closing the door. But a baby in Substage 6 can anticipate the consequence of closing the door and move the tower beforehand.

Using symbols is the crowning achievement of the sensorimotor period. In just 2 years, the infant progresses from reflexive responding to symbolic processing. A summary of these changes is shown in the table at the top of page 157.

The ability to use mental symbols marks the end of sensorimotor thinking and the beginning of preoperational thought, which we'll examine in Chapter 9.

Evaluating Piaget's Account of Sensorimotor Thought

Despite the success of many aspects of Piaget's work, some features of his account of infants' thinking have held up better than others. For example, Piaget explained cognitive development with constructs like accommodation, assimilation, and equilibration. Subsequent researchers, however, have found other ways to explain children's performance on Piaget's tasks. **For example, Piaget thought**

Six Substages of Sensorimotor Development			
Substage	**Age (months)**	**Accomplishment**	**Distinguishing Features**
1	0–1	Reflexes become coordinated.	Sucking a nipple
2	1–4	Primary circular reactions appear—an infant's first learned adaptations to the world.	Thumb sucking
3	4–8	Secondary circular reactions emerge, allowing infants to learn about objects.	Shaking a toy to hear it rattle
4	8–12	Means–end sequencing develops, marking the onset of intentional behavior.	Moving an obstacle to reach a toy
5	12–18	Tertiary circular reactions appear, allowing children to experiment.	Shaking different toys to hear the sounds they make
6	18–24	Symbolic processing is revealed in language, gestures, and pretend play.	Eating pretend food with a pretend fork

TABLE 6–2

that a fundamental task of infancy was mastering *object permanence*—understanding that objects exist independently of oneself and one's actions. He claimed that 1- to 4-months-olds believe that objects no longer exist when they disappear from view—out of sight means out of mind. If you take a favorite toy from a 3-month-old and hide it under a cloth directly in front of her, she will not look for it even though the shape of the toy is clearly visible under the cloth and within reach!

At 8 months, infants search for objects, but their understanding of object permanence remains incomplete. If 8- to 10-month-olds see an object hidden under one container, then see it hidden under a second container, they routinely look for the toy under the first container. Piaget claimed that this behavior showed only a fragmentary understanding of objects because infants did not distinguish the object from the actions they used to locate it, such as lifting a particular container. Not until approximately 18 months do infants apparently have full understanding of object permanence.

> A criticism of Piaget's theory is that researchers have discovered better ways to explain children's performance on Piaget's tasks.

Investigators have since questioned Piaget's conclusions (Smith et al., 1999). Some fairly minor changes in procedures can affect 8- to 10-month-olds' success on the hidden object task. An infant is more likely to look under the correct container if, for example, the interval between hiding and looking is brief and if the containers are easily distinguished from each other. Therefore, infants who are unsuccessful on this task may be showing poor memory rather than inadequate understanding of the nature of objects (Marcovitch & Zelazo, 1999; Wellman, Cross, & Bartsch, 1986).

In addition, by devising some clever procedures, other investigators have shown that babies understand objects much earlier than Piaget claimed. Renée Baillargeon (1987, 1994), for example, assessed object permanence using the procedure shown in the diagram at the top of page 158. Infants first saw a silver screen that appeared to be rotating back and forth. When they were familiar with this display, one of two new displays was shown. In the *possible event*, a yellow box appeared in a

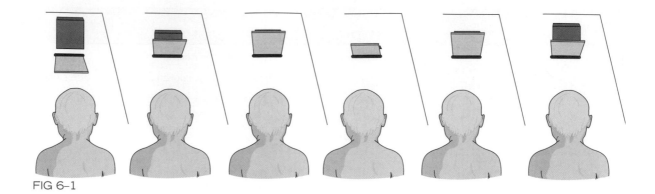

FIG 6–1

position behind the screen, making it impossible for the screen to rotate as far back as it had previously. Instead, the screen rotated until it made contact with the box, then rotated forward. In the *impossible event*, shown in the diagram, the yellow box appeared, but the screen continued to rotate as before. The screen rotated back until it was flat, then rotated forward, again revealing the yellow box. The illusion was possible because the box was mounted on a movable platform that allowed it to drop out of the way of the moving screen. However, from the infant's perspective, it appeared as if the box vanished behind the screen, only to reappear.

The disappearance and reappearance of the box violates the idea that objects exist permanently. Consequently, an infant who understands the permanence of objects should find the impossible event a truly novel stimulus and look at it longer than the possible event. Baillargeon found that $4\frac{1}{2}$-month-olds consistently looked longer at the impossible event than the possible event. Infants apparently thought that the impossible event was novel, just as we are surprised when an object vanishes from a magician's scarf. Evidently, then, infants have some understanding of object permanence early in the first year of life.

Alternative explanations for infants' performance on object permanence tasks do not mean that Piaget's theory is fundamentally wrong. They merely mean that the theory needs some revision to include important constructs that Piaget overlooked.

The Child as Theorist

Piaget believed that children, like scientists, formulate theories about how the world works. Children's theories are usually called "naive theories" because, unlike real scientific theories, they are not created by specialists and they are rarely evaluated by formal experimentation. Naive theories are, nevertheless, valuable in allowing children (and adults) to understand new experiences and predict future events.

Infants create specialized theories in domains such as physics and biology.

In Piaget's view, children formulate a grand, comprehensive theory that attempts to explain an enormous variety of phenomena—including reasoning about objects, people, and morals, for example—within a common framework. More recent views cling to the idea of children as theorists, but propose that children, like real scientists, develop specialized theories about much narrower areas. Some of the theories that young children first develop concern physics and biology. That is, based on their experiences, young children rapidly develop theories that organize their knowledge about properties of objects and living things (Wellman & Gelman, 1998). Let's look at children's naive theories in each of these areas.

Naive Physics. We know from Module 5.4 that young babies are able to distinguish objects. From their perceptions, what do infants learn about the properties of objects? A lot! Child-development researchers have discovered that, by 3 or 4 months, infants have already mastered some important basic facts about objects. They know, for instance, that objects move along connected, continuous paths and that objects cannot move "through" other objects (Spelke, 1994; von Hofsten et al., 1998). Infants look longer at moving objects that violate these properties (e.g., a ball that somehow rolls "through" a solid wall) than moving objects that are consistent with them, suggesting that infants are surprised when objects move in ways not predicted by their naive theory of physics.

By the middle of the first year, babies also understand that one object striking a second object will cause the latter to move (Kotovsky & Baillargeon, 1998; Spelke, 1994). This understanding is demonstrated in the study described in the Focus on Research feature.

FOCUS ON RESEARCH

What Do Infants Understand About Colliding Forces?

Who were the investigators and what was the aim of the study? When a moving object collides with a stationary object, the latter moves. How far it moves depends on a number of factors, such as the speed of the moving object. Laura Kotovsky and Renée Baillargeon conducted their research to determine whether infants understand that the size of a moving object affects how far the stationary object moves.

How did the investigators measure the topic of interest? For several trials, infants viewed a display box like the one at the top of the diagram (labeled familiarization event). A blue medium-sized cylinder (diameter of about 2½ inches) rolled down a ramp, colliding with a brightly colored bug. After the collision, the bug moved about 18 inches from the base of the ramp. When infants' looking had dropped 50 percent from its initial levels, infants were shown the test trials depicted in the bottom panels of the diagram. On some trials, the medium-sized cylinder was replaced with either a small orange cylinder (diameter of about 1 inch) or a large yellow cylinder (diameter of about 4 inches). When either of these cylinders collided with the bug, it traveled more than twice as far as it had previously (about 38 inches). If infants know that, after a collision, larger objects propel a stationary object farther, they should expect that the larger cylinder propels the bug farther than the medium cylinder but be surprised (and hence look longer) when the small cylinder propels the bug farther than the medium cylinder.

Who were the children in the study? Kotovsky and Baillargeon tested 27 5½-month-olds and 32 6½-month-olds.

What was the design of the study? This study was experimental. One independent variable was the infant's age. Another was the size of the cylinder (large versus small) that rolled down the ramp during the test trials. The dependent variable was the amount of time the infants spent watching the collision during the test events. The study included two age groups tested at the same point in time, so it was cross-sectional.

Familiarization Event

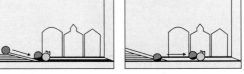

Test Events

Large-cylinder Event

 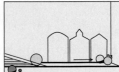

Small-cylinder Event

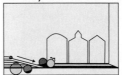 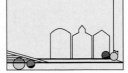

FIG 6–2

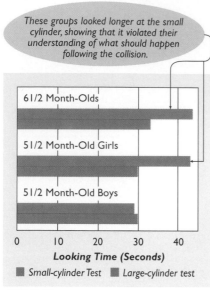

These groups looked longer at the small cylinder, showing that it violated their understanding of what should happen following the collision.

FIG 6–3

Were there ethical concerns with the study? No. Most infants apparently liked watching the objects roll down the ramp and collide with the bug.

What were the results? If infants do not understand that the size of a moving object affects the distance the stationary object will travel, they should look equally long at the large- and small-cylinder test events. If, instead, they understand that larger objects propel a stationary object farther, they should look longer at the small-cylinder test event because this violates that understanding. In fact, the graph shows 6½-month-olds and 5½-month-old girls looked longer at the small-cylinder test event but that 5½-month-old boys looked equally at the two events.

What did the investigators conclude? By approximately 6 months of age, infants expect a stationary object to move following a collision and they understand that the distance traveled depends on the size of the colliding object.

What converging evidence would strengthen these conclusions? Kotovsky and Baillargeon's results seem to suggest that understanding of this sort of collision emerges at about 6 months of age. This would be an ideal situation in which to conduct a microgenetic study: Infants could be tested repeatedly, perhaps weekly, beginning at about 5 months of age. According to Kotovsky and Baillargeon's findings, most infants should begin to show surprise (looking longer at the small-cylinder test event) at about 6 months. ■

Later in the first year, infants come to understand the importance of gravity. At this time, but not before, infants will look intently at an object that appears to float in midair with no obvious means of support, because it violates their understanding of gravity (Baillargeon, 1998).

These amazing demonstrations attest to the fact that the infant is, indeed, an accomplished naive physicist. Of course, the infant's theories are far from complete; naive understanding of physics takes place throughout the preschool years and later (e.g., Au, 1994). However, the important point is that infants rapidly create a reasonably accurate theory of some basic properties of objects, a theory that helps them understand why objects in their world such as toys act as they do.

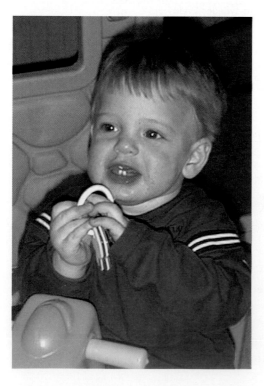

Naive Biology. When your computer crashes, do you think to yourself, "Oh, it must be feeling ill"? When you accidentally break your coffee mug, do you say, "Gosh, its parents will be terribly upset"? Of course not. Computers and coffee cups are inanimate but illness and parenthood are properties of animate objects. In fact, the difference between animate and inanimate objects is so fundamental that knowing an object is animate, our naive theory of biology allows us to infer many properties of the object.

Even toddlers apparently have some basic understanding of different properties of animate and inanimate objects. Toddlers understand, for example, that animate objects drink but inanimate objects do not. And they understand that keys are used to open inanimate objects but not animate objects. The youngster in the photo might use the key to open a toy car, a toy house, or a toy boat, but she would not use it to open a toy cow or a toy fish (Mandler & McDonough, 1998). Evidently, the distinction between animate and inanimate objects is established fairly early.

Young children's naive theory of biology, when joined with their naive theory of physics, provide powerful tools for making sense of their world and for understanding new experiences.

Check Your Learning

1. In Piaget's theory, a _____ is a mental structure that is used to organize information.

2. _____ takes place when a scheme is modified based on experience.

3. A toddler who has a scheme for flowers sees a tulip for the first time and says, "flower!" This demonstrates _____.

4. Piaget believed that when _____ occurs, children reorganize their schemes so that assimilation and accommodation are again in balance.

5. Sensorimotor thought begins with reflexive responding and ends with _____.

6. In a _____, an infant accidentally produces something pleasant, then tries to recreate that pleasing event.

7. One criticism of Piaget's theory is that infants' performance on tasks like object permanence is _____.

8. By 3 or 4 months, most infants know that objects move along _____.

Continuity Based on what you've learned so far, what would Piaget's position have been on the continuity-discontinuity issue discussed in Module 1.3?

Answers: (1) scheme, (2) Accommodation, (3) assimilation, (4) disequilibrium, (5) symbolic processing, (6) primary circular reaction, (7) better explained by ideas that are not part of Piaget's theory, (8) connected, continuous paths

Information Processing

6.2

Information Processing

- **What are the basic characteristics of the information-processing approach?**

- **How do infants learn and remember?**

- **What do infants and toddlers understand about number and about their environments?**

- **How is intelligence measured in infants and toddlers?**

> *Linda was only 36 hours old when John and Jean brought her home from the hospital. They quickly noticed that loud noises startled Linda, which worried them because their apartment was near an entrance ramp to a freeway. Trucks accelerating to enter the freeway made an incredible amount of noise that caused Linda to "jump" and sometimes cry. John and Jean wondered if Linda would get enough sleep. However, within days, the trucks no longer disturbed Linda; she slept blissfully. Why was a noise that had been so troubling no longer a problem?*

After just a few days, truck sounds no longer bothered newborn Linda. Her information processing had changed so that she ignored sounds that once startled her. In this module we'll learn more about information processing as a general framework, then learn more about information processing in infants and toddlers. As we do, we'll see how Linda "tunes out" distracting noise.

Basic Features of the Information-Processing Approach

A few weeks ago, Jim bought a new computer for his office. Jim was eager to use the new machine to handle his correspondence, prepare graphs for sales meetings, and, when his boss wasn't looking, surf the Web. But enthusiasm soon turned to disappointment: Although Jim's computer could do all these things, it was incredibly slow and time-consuming. The word processing software seemed to take forever to load, and it seemed to Jim that he'd spent hours staring at the screen while waiting for Web pages to appear. It gradually dawned on Jim that saving a few hundred dollars by getting a slower processor and less memory was probably a mistake. His computer simply lacked the hardware necessary to make the software run efficiently.

This simple distinction between computer hardware and computer software is the basis of an approach to human thinking known as *information processing*. The information-processing approach arose in the 1960s and is now one of the principal approaches to cognitive development (Kail & Bisanz, 1992; Klahr & MacWhinney, 1998). You remember, from Module 1.2, that information-processing theorists believe human thinking is based on both mental hardware and mental software. Mental hardware refers to mental and neural structures that are built-in and that allow the mind to operate. If the hardware in a personal computer refers to random-access memory, the central processor, and the like, what does mental hardware refer to? Information-processing theorists generally agree that mental hardware has three components: sensory memory, working memory, and long-term memory. The diagram shows how they are related.

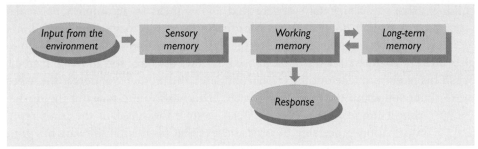

FIG 6–4

Sensory memory **is where information is held in raw, unanalyzed form very briefly (no longer than a few seconds).** For example, look at your hand as you clench your fist, then rapidly open your hand (so that your fingers are extended) and then rapidly reclench your fist. If you watch your fingers, you'll see an image of your fingers that lasts momentarily after you reclench your hand. What you're seeing is an image stored in sensory memory.

Working memory **is the site of ongoing cognitive activity.** Some theorists liken working memory to a carpenter's workbench that includes space for storing the materials for a current project as well as space for the carpenter to do the sawing, nailing, and painting involved in the project (Klatzky, 1980). In much the same way, working memory includes both ongoing cognitive processes and the information that they require (Baddeley, 1996). For example, as you read these sentences, part of working memory is allocated to the cognitive processes responsible for determining the meanings of individual words; working memory also stores the results of these analyses briefly while they are used by other cognitive processes to give meaning to sequences of words.

> In the information-processing view, mental hardware includes sensory, working, and long-term memories.

This description of working memory probably has a familiar ring to it. If you're familiar with personal computers, you'll recognize that working memory resembles random-access memory (RAM) because that's where we load programs we want to run and temporarily store the data those programs are using.

Long-term memory **is a limitless, permanent storehouse of knowledge of the world.** Long-term memory is like a computer's hard drive, a fairly permanent storehouse of programs and data. Long-term memory includes facts (Charles Lindbergh flew the Atlantic in the *Spirit of St. Louis*), personal events (I moved to Maryland in July 1999), and skills (how to swim the back stroke).

Information rarely is forgotten from long-term memory, though it is sometimes hard to access. For example, do you remember the name of the African American agricultural chemist who pioneered crop-rotation methods and invented peanut butter? If his name doesn't come to mind, look at this list: *Marconi Carver Fulton Luther.* Now do you know the answer? (If not, it appears before Check Your Learning, on page 170.) Just as books are sometimes misplaced in a library, you sometimes cannot find a fact in long-term memory. Given a list of names, though, you can go directly to the location in long-term memory associated with each name and determine which is the famed chemist.

Mental hardware allows us to "run" mental software, so the next question is, What is mental software? To answer this question, think about personal computer software you've used, such as programs for word processing, spreadsheets, or graphing. In each case, the software was designed to accomplish a specific function. In much the same way, mental software refers to mental programs that are the basis for performing particular tasks. According to information-processing psychologists, children have special mental software that allows them to accomplish particular tasks, such as reading, doing arithmetic, or finding their way to and from school.

Let's look at a simple example to see how information-processing psychologists analyze cognitive processes. Suppose a mother asks her son to make his bed, brush his teeth, and take out the trash. A bit later, the mother wonders if she asked her son about the trash, so she says, "Did I ask you to take out the trash?" Almost immediately, he says, "Yes." Despite the speed of the boy's reply, information-processing theorists believe that his mental software has gone through four general steps to answer the question, as shown in the diagram. First, the mental software must understand the mother's question. That is, the software must decode the sounds of the mother's speech and give them meaning. Next, the software searches working memory and long-term memory for the mother's earlier requests. When that list is located and retrieved, the software compares "take out the trash" with each of the items on the list. Finding a match, the software selects "yes" as the appropriate answer to the question. Thus, the processes of understanding, searching, comparing, and responding create a mental program that allows the boy to answer his mother.

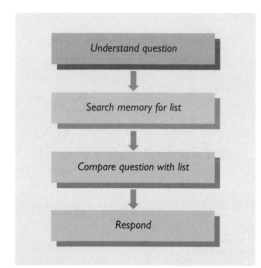

FIG 6–5

In the next section, we'll see how child-development researchers use these ideas to understand how thinking changes during the infant and toddler years.

Learning

An infant is always learning. For example, a 5-month-old learns that a new toy makes a noise every time she shakes it. Infants are born with many mechanisms that allow them to learn from experience. This learning can take many forms, including habituation, classical conditioning, operant conditioning, and imitation.

Habituation. Remember Linda, the newborn in the vignette, who jumped when trucks accelerated past her home? Her response was normal not only for infants but also for children and adolescents. **When presented with a strong or unfamiliar stimulus, an *orienting response* usually occurs: A person starts, fixes the eyes on the stimulus, and shows changes in heart rate and brain wave activity.** Collectively, these responses indicate that the infant has noticed the stimulus. Remember, too, that Linda soon ignored the sounds of trucks. After repeated presentations of a stimulus, people recognize it as familiar and the orienting response gradually disappears. ***Habituation* is the diminished response to a stimulus as it becomes more familiar.**

The orienting response and habituation are both useful to infants. On the one hand, orienting makes the infant aware of potentially important or dangerous events in the environment. On the other hand, constantly responding to insignificant stimuli is wasteful, so habituation keeps infants like the one in the photo from wasting too much energy on biologically nonsignificant events (Rovee-Collier, 1987).

Classical Conditioning. Some of the most famous experiments in psychology were conducted with dogs by a Russian physiologist, Ivan Pavlov. Dogs salivate when fed. Pavlov discovered that if something always happened just before feeding—for example, a bell sounded—dogs would begin to salivate to that event. **In *classical conditioning*, a neutral stimulus elicits a response that was originally produced by another stimulus.** In Pavlov's experiments, the bell was a neutral stimulus that did not naturally cause dogs to salivate. However, by repeatedly pairing the bell with food, the bell began to elicit salivation. Similarly, infants will suck reflexively when sugar water is placed in their mouth with a dropper; if a tone precedes the drops of sugar water, infants will suck when they hear the tone (Lipsitt, 1990).

Classical conditioning is important because it gives infants a sense of order in their worlds. That is, through classical conditioning, infants learn that a stimulus is a signal for what will happen next. An infant like the one in the photo may smile when she hears the family dog's collar because she knows the dog is coming to play with her. Or a toddler may smile when he hears water running in the bathroom because he realizes this means it's time for a bath.

Infants and toddlers are definitely capable of classical conditioning when the stimuli are associated with feeding or other pleasant events. It is much more difficult to demonstrate classical conditioning in infants and toddlers when the stimuli are aversive, such as loud noises or shock (Fitzgerald & Brackbill, 1976). Because adults care for very young children, learning about aversive stimulation is not a common biological problem for infants and toddlers (Rovee-Collier, 1987).

Operant Conditioning. In classical conditioning, infants form expectations about what will happen in their environment. ***Operant conditioning* focuses on the relation between the consequences of behavior and the likelihood that the behavior will reoccur.** When a child's behavior leads to pleasant consequences, the child will probably behave similarly in the future; when the child's behavior leads to unpleasant consequences, the child will probably not repeat the behavior. When a baby smiles, an adult may hug the baby in return; this pleasing consequence makes the baby more likely to smile in the future. When a baby grabs a family heirloom, an adult may become angry and shout at the baby; these unpleasant consequences make the baby less likely to grab the heirloom in the future.

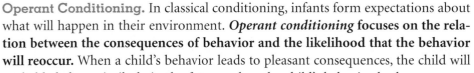

Infants learn through habituation, classical conditioning, operant conditioning, and imitation.

Imitation. Older children, adolescents, and young adults learn much simply by watching others behave. For example, children learn new sports moves by watching pro athletes, they learn how to pursue romantic relationships by watching TV, and they learn how to play new computer games by watching peers. Infants, too, are capable of imitation (Barr & Hayne, 1999). A 10-month-old may imitate an adult waving her finger back and forth or imitate another infant who knocks down a tower of blocks.

More startling is the claim that even newborns imitate. As shown in the photos at the top of page 166, Meltzoff and Moore (1989, 1994) found that 2- to 3-week-olds would stick out their tongue or open and close their mouth to match an adult's acts. This work is controversial because other researchers do not consistently obtain these results. In addition, because the newborns' behavior is not novel—

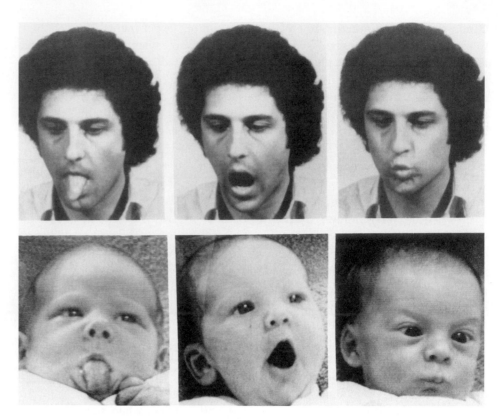

newborns are already capable of sticking out their tongues as well as opening and closing their mouths—some researchers do not consider this to be a "true" form of imitation (Anisfeld, 1991, 1996). This work may well represent an early, limited form of imitation; over the course of the first year of life, infants are able to imitate a rapidly expanding range of behavior.

Memory

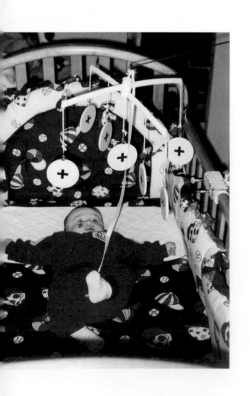

Young babies remember events for days or even weeks at a time. Some of the studies that opened our eyes to the infant's ability to remember used the method shown in the photo, which was devised by Carolyn Rovee-Collier (1997, 1999). A ribbon from a mobile is attached to a 2- or 3-month-old's leg; within a few minutes, the babies learn to kick to make the mobile move. When Rovee-Collier brought the mobile to the infants' homes several days or a few weeks later, babies would still kick to make the mobile move. If Rovee-Collier waited several weeks to return, most babies forgot that kicking moved the mobile. When that happened, Rovee-Collier gave them a reminder—she moved the mobile herself without attaching the ribbon to their foot. Then she would return the next day, hook up the apparatus, and the babies would kick to move the mobile.

Rovee-Collier's experiments show that three important features of memory exist as early as 2 and 3 months of age: (1) an event from the past is remembered, (2) over time, the event can no longer be recalled, and (3) a cue can serve to dredge up a memory that seems to have been forgotten.

Although memory begins in infancy, children, adolescents, and adults remember little from these years (Kail, 1990). *Infantile amnesia* **refers to the inability to remember events from early in one's life.** Adults recall nothing from infancy but they remember an ever-increasing number of events from about age 3 or 4 years (Eacott,

1999; Schneider & Bjorklund, 1998). For example, when the 2-year-old in the photo is older, he won't remember his brother's birth (Peterson & Rideout, 1998; Quas et al., 1999).* But there's a good chance the 2-year-old will remember his brother's third, or certainly his fourth, birthday.

Infantile amnesia has several possible explanations. One emphasizes language: Once children learn to talk, they tend to rely on language to represent their past (Nelson, 1993). Consequently, their earlier, prelingual experiences may be difficult to retrieve from memory.

Another explanation for infantile amnesia is based on a child's sense of self. I describe this in detail in Module 7.3, but the key idea is that 1- and 2-year-olds rapidly acquire a sense that they exist independently and are someone. Some theorists (Harley & Reese, 1999; Howe & Courage, 1997) argue that a child's sense of self provides an organizing framework for children's memories of events from their own lives. Infants and toddlers lack a sense of self, so they can't organize memories of life events, which is why they can't be recalled later in life.

Understanding the World

Powerful learning and memory skills allow infants and toddlers to learn much about their worlds. This rapid growth is well illustrated by research on their understanding of number and the environment.

Understanding Number. Basic number skills originate in infancy, long before babies learn names of numbers. Many babies experience daily variation in quantity. They play with two blocks and see that another baby has three; they watch as a father sorts laundry and finds two black socks but only one blue sock, and they eat one hot dog for lunch while an older brother eats three.

From these experiences, babies apparently come to appreciate that quantity or amount is one of the ways in which objects in the world can differ. This conclusion is based on research in which babies are shown pictures like those shown below. The actual objects in the pictures differ, as do their size, color, and position in the picture. The only common element is that at first each picture always depicts two of something.

  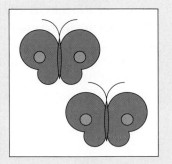 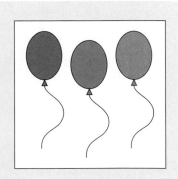

FIG 6–6

*Perhaps you're not convinced, because you can vividly recall significant events that occurred when you were 2, such as the birth of a sibling, a move to a different home, or the death of a relative. In reality, you are probably not remembering the actual event. Instead, I can almost guarantee that you're remembering others' retelling of these events and your role in them, not the events themselves. Events like these are often socially shared memories and that's what you're remembering.

When the first of these pictures is shown, an infant will look at it for several seconds. After several have been shown, an infant habituates; he or she will glance at the picture briefly, then look away, as if saying, "Enough of these pictures of two things, let's move on to something else." And, in fact, if a picture of a single object or of three objects is then shown, infants will again look for several seconds, their interest apparently renewed. Because the only systematic change is the number of objects depicted in the picture, we know that babies can distinguish stimuli on the basis of number. Typically, 5-month-olds can distinguish two objects from three and, less often, three objects from four (Canfield & Smith, 1996; Wynn, 1996).

How do infants distinguish differences in quantity? Older children might count, but, of course, infants have not yet learned names of numbers. Instead, the process is probably more perceptual in nature. As we saw in Module 5.4, the infant's perceptual system is sensitive to characteristics such as shape and color (Bornstein, 1981). Quantity may well be another characteristic of stimuli to which infants are sensitive. That is, just as colors (reds, blues) and shapes (triangles, squares) are basic perceptual properties, small quantities ("twoness" and "threeness") may be perceptually obvious (Strauss & Curtis, 1984).

Exploring the Environment. Learning about environments begins very early in life. Before infants can walk, they travel through environments in parents' arms, in strollers, and in automobiles. As soon as infants can crawl, they begin to explore their environments. Even when they are still, infants see people and objects move in their environments. According to Piaget (Piaget & Inhelder, 1967), an infant's early understanding of the environment is quite limited. **Infants first think of the positions of objects in space exclusively in terms of the objects' positions relative to the child's own body—what Piaget called an *egocentric frame of reference*. Only later do children acquire an *objective frame of reference* in which an object's location is thought of relative to the positions of other objects in space.**

The shift from egocentric to objective frames of reference is shown in research in which youngsters are seated in a room in which there are two identical windows, one to the child's left and one to the right. When the child is looking straight ahead, an experimenter sounds a buzzer. Shortly thereafter, a person appears always in the left window, saying the infant's name and showing toys (Acredolo, 1978, 1979). Infants and toddlers quickly learn to anticipate the appearance of the person in this window when they hear the buzzer.

After infants have learned to anticipate the face, they are turned 180 degrees, so that they are facing exactly the opposite direction. Once again the buzzer sounds. The crucial question is, Which way will the infant look? Up to about 12 months, infants consistently look left—as they had before but now incorrectly—showing an egocentric frame of reference. After 12 months, toddlers increasingly look to the right—a different direction but toward the correct window. Now infants realize that even though they have moved, the object has not. So, infants look to the same window as before, even though this means turning in a different direction (Acredolo, 1978; Wishart & Bower, 1982).

Individual Differences in Ability

So far in this chapter, I have emphasized patterns of cognitive development that apply to most infants and toddlers; I have ignored the fact that individual infants and toddlers often differ considerably in the ease and skill with which their cognitive processes function. These individual differences are, however, measured in mental tests devised for infants and toddlers. For example, the Bayley Scales of Infant Development (Bayley, 1970, 1993), designed for 2- to 42-month-olds, consist of mental and motor scales. The mental scale assesses adaptive behavior, such as attending to visual and auditory stimuli, following directions, looking for a fallen toy, and imitating. The motor scale assesses an infant's control of its body, its coordination, and its ability to manipulate objects. For example, 6-month-olds should turn their head toward an object that the examiner drops on the floor, 12-month-olds should imitate the examiner's actions, and 16-month-olds should build a tower from three blocks. The scales also assess habituation, memory, and problem solving.

In general, scores from infant intelligence tests like the Bayley Scales are not related to IQ scores obtained later in childhood, adolescence, or adulthood (McCall, 1989). Apparently, children must be at least 18 to 24 months old before their Bayley scores, or scores from similar scales, can predict later IQ scores on the Wechsler or Stanford-Binet scales (Kopp & McCall, 1982).

> Infant intelligence tests emphasize sensorimotor skills and, consequently, do not predict adult intelligence accurately.

Why don't scores on infant intelligence tests predict childhood or adult IQ more accurately? One reason is that infant tests measure different abilities than tests administered to children and adolescents: Infant tests place more emphasis on sensorimotor skills and less on tasks involving cognitive processes such as language, thinking, and problem solving.

According to this reasoning, a measure of infant cognitive processing might yield more accurate predictions of later IQ. In fact, habituation, described on page 164, does predict later IQ more effectively than scores from the Bayley. The average correlation between habituation and later IQ is approximately 0.5 (Bornstein, 1997). That is, 1- to 6-month-olds who habituate to visual stimuli more rapidly tend to have higher IQs as children. Apparently, infants who rapidly make sense of their world—in this case, thinking "I've seen this picture before, so let's see something new!"—are smarter during the elementary-school years. The Looking Ahead feature describes one study in which this relation was discovered.

LOOKING AHEAD

Predicting Intelligence in Childhood

Susan Rose and her colleagues (1997) wanted to determine whether a measure of infants' information processing would predict intelligence in childhood. Consequently, in their study 109 7-month-olds were given a series of visual recognition tasks. In each one, infants would see a stimulus such as a face or abstract pattern for 5 to 20 seconds. Immediately after, they were shown that stimulus paired with a novel stimulus from the same category (e.g., another face or another abstract pattern). The experimenters measured the amount of time that infants spent looking at the novel stimulus; infants who showed a stronger preference for novelty were assumed to have more effectively processed the familiar stimulus when it was presented originally. (Because, after all, it is that effective processing that makes the stimulus seem familiar.) At 11 years, 90 of the original children (83 percent) were tested on a variety of tasks, including a standard measure of children's intelligence, the Wechsler Intelligence Scale for Children—Revised. (I describe this test in more detail in Module 12.3.) The correlation between novelty preference at 7 months and intelligence at 11 years was 0.41. That is, 7-month-olds who tended to spend more time looking at a novel stimulus (apparently because their initial processing of the other face was more complete, making it seem more familiar and thus less interesting) had, more than 10 years later, higher scores on a common intelligence test. Stated more generally, more efficient information processing in infancy is associated with more efficient information processing in childhood. ■

If scores on the Bayley Scales do not predict later IQs, why are these tests used at all? The answer is that they are important diagnostic tools: They can be used to determine if development is progressing normally. For example, the Bayley mental scale can detect the impact of prenatal exposure to teratogens (Bellinger et al., 1987). It can also assess whether the infant's home environment provides sufficient stimulation for mental development (Bradley et al., 1987).

Response to question on page 163: The agricultural chemist who pioneered crop rotation while on the faculty of Tuskegee Institute of Technology is George Washington Carver.

Check Your Learning

1. Information-processing psychologists believe that mental hardware includes sensory memory, working memory, and _____.

2. _____ refers to specialized processes that allow children to complete particular tasks, such as reading or arithmetic.

3. Infants are capable of classical conditioning but not when the stimuli are _____.

4. Four-month-old Tanya has forgotten that kicking moves a mobile. To remind her of the link between kicking and the mobile's movement, we could _____.

5. Infantile amnesia, the ability to remember events from early in life, may be due to infants' and toddlers' limited language skills or to their lack of a _____.

6. Infants distinguish differences in quantity (2 from 3, for example) based on _____.

7. Before 12 months of age, infants have an egocentric frame of reference in which objects in space are located in relation to _____.

8. Infant intelligence tests, such as the Bayley Scales, do not predict childhood IQ scores but they are useful for _____.

Nature and Nurture What elements of the information-processing approach seem to emphasize nature? What elements emphasize nurture? How does information processing's emphasis on nature and nurture compare with Piaget's emphasis?

Answers: (1) long-term memory, (2) Mental software, (3) aversive, (4) show her a moving mobile, (5) sense of self, (6) perceptual processes, (7) their own bodies, (8) determining whether development is progressing normally

Language

- When can infants hear and produce basic speech sounds?

- What is babbling and how do children make the transition from babbling to talking?

- What different styles of language learning do young children use?

- How do children learn new words?

Stephanie is 20 months old and loves to talk. What amazes her parents is how quickly she adds words to her vocabulary. For example, the day her parents brought home a computer, Stephanie watched as they set it up. The next day, she spontaneously pointed to the computer and said, "puter." This happens all the time—Stephanie hears a word once or twice, then uses it correctly herself. Stephanie's parents wonder how she does this, particularly because learning vocabulary in a foreign language is so difficult for them!

From birth, infants make sounds: They laugh, cry, and, make some sounds that resemble speech. At about their first birthday, most youngsters say their first words and by age 2, most children have a vocabulary of a few hundred words. Like Stephanie, most children achieve these milestones with extraordinary ease and speed. How do they do it? The first answers to this question came from theories that were based on the learning perspective (from Module 1.2) that emphasized imitation and reward. Although these factors contribute to language acquisition, modern theories view language acquisition from a cognitive perspective and, as you'll see in the rest of this module, describe language acquisition in terms of mastering many distinct skills.

Perceiving Speech

To be able to learn a language, infants need to be able distinguish the basic speech sounds. **The basic building blocks of language are *phonemes*, unique sounds that can be joined to create words.** Phonemes include consonant sounds such as the sound of *t* in *toe* and *tap* along with vowel sounds such as the sound of *e* in *get* and *bed*. Infants can distinguish many of these sounds, some of them by as early as 1 month after birth (Aslin, Jusczyk, & Pisoni, 1998).

How do we know that infants can distinguish different vowels and consonants? Researchers have devised a number of clever techniques to determine if babies respond differently to distinct sounds. One approach is illustrated in the diagram. A rubber nipple is connected to a tape recorder so that sucking turns on the tape and sound comes out of a loudspeaker. In just a few minutes, 1-month-olds learn the relation between their sucking and the sound: They suck rapidly to hear a tape that consists of nothing more than the sound of *p* as in *pin*, *pet*, and *pat* (pronounced "puh").

FIG 6–7

After a few more minutes, infants seemingly tire of this repetitive sound and they suck less often, which represents the habituation phenomenon described in Module 6.2. But, if the tape is changed to a different sound such as the sound of *b* in *bed*, *bat*, or *bird* (pronounced "buh") babies begin sucking rapidly again. Evidently, they recognize that the sound of *b* is different from *p* because they suck more often to hear the new sound (Jusczyk, 1995).

Infants can even discriminate speech sounds that they have never heard before. Not all languages use the same set of phonemes; a distinction that is important in one language may be ignored in another. For example, unlike English, French and Polish differentiate between nasal and non-nasal vowels. To hear the difference, say the word *rod*. Now repeat it, while holding your nose. The subtle difference between the two sounds illustrates a non-nasal vowel (the first version of *rod*) and a nasal one (the second).

Babies growing up in homes where English is spoken have no systematic experience with nasal versus non-nasal vowels, but they can still hear differences like this one. Interestingly, toward their first birthday, infants apparently lose this competence and no longer readily distinguish sounds that are not part of their own language environment. For example, Werker and Lalonde (1988) found that 6- to 8-month-old infants of English-speaking parents could distinguish speech sounds that are used in Hindi but not in English. By 11 to 13 months of age, the infants, like their parents, could no longer tell the difference.

Findings like these suggest that newborns are biologically capable of hearing the entire range of phonemes in all languages worldwide. But as babies grow and are more exposed to a particular language, they only notice the linguistic distinctions that are meaningful in that environment. For example, the Japanese youngster in the photo will learn language sounds used in Japanese but will have difficulty hearing sounds used in other languages, such as English. Specialization in one language apparently comes at a cost; the potential to hear other language sounds easily is lost (Best, 1995; Kuhl, 1993).

Of course, hearing individual phonemes is only the first step in perceiving speech. One of the biggest challenges for infants is identifying recurring patterns of sounds—words. Imagine, for example, an infant overhearing this conversation between a parent and an older sibling:

SIBLING: Jerry got a new *bike*.

PARENT: Was his old *bike* broken?

SIBLING: No. He'd saved his allowance to buy a new mountain *bike*.

An infant listening to this conversation hears *bike* three times. Can the infant learn from this experience? Yes. When 7- to 8-month-olds hear a word repeatedly in different sentences, they later pay more attention to this word than to words they haven't heard previously. Evidently, 7- and 8-month-olds can listen to sentences and recognize the sound patterns that they hear repeatedly (Jusczyk & Aslin, 1995; Saffran,

Aslin, & Newport, 1996). And by 6 months infants looked at the correct parent when they heard "mommy" or "daddy" (Tincoff & Jusczyk, 1999).

In normal conversation, there are no silent gaps between words, so how do infants pick out words? Stress is an important clue in all languages. English contains many one-syllable words that are stressed and many two-syllable words that have a stressed syllable followed by an unstressed syllable (e.g., *dough´-nut, tooth´-paste, bas´-ket*). Infants pay more attention to stressed syllables than unstressed syllables, which is a good strategy for identifying the beginnings of words (Aslin et al., 1998; Mattys et al., 1999).

Of course, stress is not a foolproof sign, because many two-syllable words have stress on the second syllable (e.g., *gui-tar´, sur-prise´*), so infants need other methods to identify words in speech. One method is statistical. Infants notice syllables that go together frequently. For example, in a study by Aslin, Saffran, and Newport (1998), 8-month-olds heard the following sounds, which consisted of four 3-syllable artificial words, said over and over in a random order.

> Young infants can hear a wide range of phonemes but older infants can only hear those used in their native language.

> *pa bi ku go la tu da ro pi ti bu do da ro pi go la tu pa bi ku da ro pi …*

I've inserted gaps between the syllables and words so that you can see them more easily but in the study there were no breaks at all—just a steady flow of syllables for 3 minutes. Later, infants listened to these words less than to new words that were novel combinations of the same syllables. They had detected *pa bi ku, go la tu, da ro pi,* and *ti bu do* as familiar patterns and listened to them less than words like *tu da ro,* a new word made up from syllables they'd already heard.

Detecting stressed syllables and syllables that occur together provide infants with two powerful tools for identifying words in speech. Of course, they don't yet understand the meanings of these words; they just recognize a word as a distinct configuration of sounds.

Parents (and other adults) often help infants master language sounds by talking in a distinctive style. **In *infant-directed speech,* adults speak slowly and with exaggerated changes in pitch and loudness.** If you could hear the mother in the photo talking to her baby, you would notice that she alternates between speaking softly and loudly and between high and low pitches. (Infant-directed speech was once known as *motherese* until it became clear that most caregivers, not just mothers, talk this way to infants.)

Infant-directed speech may attract infants' attention more than adult-directed speech (Kaplan et al., 1995) because its slower pace and accentuated changes provide infants with more—and more salient—language clues. Similarly, it's easier to understand people speaking a foreign language when they talk slowly and carefully.

Infant-directed speech, then, helps infants perceive the sounds that are fundamental to their language. But how do infants accomplish the next step, producing speech? We answer this question in the next section of this module.

First Steps to Speaking

As any new parent can testify, newborns and young babies use sound to communicate: They cry to indicate discomfort or distress. At 2 months, though, babies begin to make sounds that are language-based. **They begin to produce vowel-like sounds, such as "ooooooo" or "ahhhhhh," a phenomenon known as** *cooing.* Sometimes infants become quite excited as they coo, perhaps reflecting the joy of simply playing with sounds.

After cooing comes *babbling,* **speechlike sound that has no meaning.** A typical 5- or 6-month-old might say "dah" or "bah," utterances that sound like a single syllable consisting of a consonant and a vowel. Over the next few months, babbling becomes more elaborate as babies apparently experiment with more complex speech sounds. Older infants sometimes repeat a sound as in "bahbahbah" and begin to combine different sounds, "dahmahbah" (Oller & Lynch, 1992).

At roughly 7 months, infants' babbling includes *intonation,* **a pattern of rising or falling pitch.** In English declarative sentences, for example, pitch first rises, then falls towards the end of the sentence. In questions, however, the pitch is level, then rises toward the end of the question. Older babies' babbling reflects these patterns: Babies who are brought up by English-speaking parents have both the declarative and question patterns of intonation in their babbling. Babies exposed to a language with different patterns of intonation, such as Japanese or French, reflect their language's intonation in their babbling (Levitt & Utman, 1992).

The appearance of intonation in babbling indicates a strong link between perception and production of speech: Infants' babbling is influenced by the characteristics of the speech that they hear. If hearing is crucial for the development of babbling, then can deaf children babble? The Real Children feature has the answer.

> Babbling appears at 5 or 6 months with a single consonant and vowel, then combines different speech sounds, and, later, adds intonation.

REAL CHILDREN

Lorraine Learns to Babble

Lorraine, now 22 months old, has been deaf since birth. She has worn a hearing aid since she was 7 months old and receives language therapy weekly from a speech-language therapist. At 11 months, Lorraine occasionally made simple sounds consisting of a consonant and a vowel, such as "bah." Her babbling remained very simple until about 15 months, when she began uttering longer, repetitive sequences of syllables. Thus, compared to children with normal hearing, Lorraine's babbling was delayed by several months.

In another respect, Lorraine's language skills developed right on schedule: As soon as Lorraine's parents learned of her deafness, they began using American Sign Language to communicate with her. They noticed that, at about 8 months, Lorraine began to imitate parts of the signs they used with her. At 13 months, she began to produce sequences of signs that were meaningless but matched the tempo and duration of real signing. In other words, Lorraine was going through different phases of babbling with her signing. ■

Lorraine is typical of deaf children: Compared to children with normal hearing, her babbling was much delayed as spoken language but right on schedule as sign language (Oller & Eilers, 1988; Pettito & Marentette, 1991). Evidently, in the middle of the first year, infants try to reproduce the sounds of language that others use in trying to communicate with them (or, in the case of deaf infants, the signs that others use). Hearing "dog," an infant may first say "dod," then "gog" before finally saying "dog" correctly. In the same way that beginning typists gradually link movements of their fingers with particular keys, through babbling, infants learn to use their lips, tongue, and teeth to produce specific sounds, gradually making sounds that approximate real words (Poulson et al., 1991). Fortunately, learning to produce language sounds is easier for most babies than the cartoon suggests!

B.C.   **by johnny hart**

Reprinted by permission of Johnny Hart and Creators Syndicate, Inc.

First Words

The ability to produce sound, coupled with the 1-year-old's advanced ability to perceive speech sounds, sets the stage for the infant's first true words. Soon after the first birthday, most infants begin to talk. Typically their first words are an extension of advanced babbling, consisting of a consonant-vowel pair that may be repeated. For example, when my daughter, Laura, was 9 months old she sometimes babbled "bay-bay." A few months later, she still said "bay-bay" but with an important difference. As a 9-month-old, "bay-bay" was simply an interesting set of sounds that she made for no reason (at least, none that was obvious to us). As a 13-month-old, "bay-bay" was her way of saying baby. *Mama* and *dada* are probably the most common first words that stem from advanced babbling. Other early vocabulary words include animals, food, and toys (Nelson, 1973).

An infant's first words represent an important insight: Speech is more than just entertaining sound; instead, sounds form words that refer to objects, actions, and properties. That is, infants apparently understand that words are symbols, entities that stand for other entities. From their experiences, infants form concepts such as "round, bouncy things" and "furry things that bark" and "little humans that adults carry." With the insight that speech sounds can denote these concepts, they begin to match words and concepts (Reich, 1986).

If this argument is correct, we should find that children use symbols in other areas, not just in language. They do. Gestures are symbols, and like the baby in the photo, infants begin to gesture shortly before their first birthday (Goodwyn & Acredolo, 1993). Young children may smack their lips to indicate hunger or wave "bye-bye" when leaving. In these cases, gestures and words convey a message equally well. Both reflect the child's developing ability to use symbols to represent actions and objects, which is one of the grand achievements of human development.

Fast Mapping Meanings to Words

Once children have the insight that a word can symbolize an object or action, their vocabularies grow slowly at first. A typical 15-month-old, for example, may learn 2 to 3 new words each week. **However, at about 18 months, many children experience a *naming explosion* during which they learn new words, particularly names of objects, much more rapidly than before.** Children now learn 10 or more new words each week (Fenson et al., 1994).

This rapid rate of word learning is astonishing when we realize that most words have many plausible but incorrect referents. To illustrate, imagine what's going through the mind of the child in the photo. The mother has just pointed to the flowers and said, "Flowers. These are flowers. See the flowers." To the mother (and you), this all seems crystal clear and incredibly straightforward. But what might a child learn from this episode? Perhaps the correct referent for "flowers." But a youngster could, just as reasonably, conclude that "flowers" refers to the petals, to the color of the flowers, or to the mother's actions in pointing to the flowers.

Surprisingly, though, most youngsters learn the proper meanings of simple words in just a few presentations. **Children's ability to connect new words to referents so rapidly that they cannot be considering all possible meanings for the new word is termed *fast mapping*.** Fast mapping meaning onto new words means that children must use rules to link words with their meanings (Carey, 1978). Researchers have found that young children use different fast-mapping strategies to help learn word meanings (Deak, 2000; Woodward & Markman, 1998).

Joint Attention. Parents encourage word learning by carefully watching what interests their children. When toddlers touch or look at an object, parents often label it for them. When a youngster points to a banana, a parent may say, "Banana, that's a banana." Of course, to take advantage of this help, infants must be able to tell when parents are labeling instead of just conversing. In fact, when adults label an unfamiliar object, 18- to 20-month-olds assume that the label is the object's name only when adults show signs that they are referring to the object. For example, toddlers are more likely to learn an object's name when adults look at the object while saying its name than when adults look elsewhere while labeling (Baldwin et al., 1996; Moore, Angelopoulos, & Bennett, 1999). Thus, beginning in the toddler years, parents and children work together to create conditions that foster word learning: Parents label objects and youngsters rely on adults' behavior to interpret the words they hear.

Constraints on Word Names. Joint attention simplifies word learning for children, but the problem still remains: How does a toddler know that *banana* refers to the object that she's touching, as opposed to her activity (touching) or to the object's color? Many researchers believe that young children follow several simple rules that limit their conclusions about what labels mean.

A study by Au and Glusman (1990) identified one of the rules that young children use. Au and Glusman presented preschoolers with a stuffed animal with pink horns that otherwise resembled a monkey and called it a *mido*. *Mido* was then repeated several times, always referring to the monkeylike stuffed animal with pink horns. Later, these youngsters were asked to find a *theri* in a set of stuffed animals that included several *mido*. Never having heard of a *theri*, what did the children do? They never picked a *mido*; instead, they selected other stuffed animals. Knowing that *mido* referred to monkeylike animals with pink horns, evidently they decided that *theri* had to refer to one of the other stuffed animals.

Apparently children were following this simple but effective rule for learning new words: If an unfamiliar word is heard in the presence of objects that already have names and objects that don't, the word refers to one of the objects that doesn't have a name. Researchers have discovered several other simple rules that help children match words with the correct referent (Hall & Graham, 1999; Waxman & Markow, 1995; Woodward & Markman, 1998):

> ### Children use joint attention, constraints, and sentence cues to help them learn the meanings of words.

- A name refers to a whole object, not its parts or its relation to other objects, and refers not just to this particular object but to all objects of the same type. For example, when a grandparent points to a stuffed animal on a shelf and says "dinosaur," children conclude that *dinosaur* refers to the entire dinosaur, not just its ears or nose, not to the fact that the dinosaur is on a shelf, and not to this specific dinosaur but to all dinosaurlike objects.

- If an object already has a name and another name is presented, the new name denotes a subcategory of the original name. If the child who knows the meaning of *dinosaur* sees a brother point to another dinosaur and hears the brother say "T-rex," the child will conclude that T-rex is a special type of dinosaur.

- Given many similar category members, a word applied consistently to only one of them is a proper noun. If a child who knows the term *dinosaur* sees that one of a group of dinosaurs is always called "Dino," the child will conclude that Dino is the name of that dinosaur.

Rules like these make it possible for children like Stephanie, the child in the vignette, to learn words rapidly because they reduce the number of possible referents. The child in the photo on page 176 follows these rules to decide that *flowers* refers to the entire object, not its parts or the action of pointing to it.

Sentence Cues. Children hear many unfamiliar words embedded in sentences containing words they already know. The other words and the overall sentence structure can be helpful clues to a word's meaning.

For example, when a parent describes an event using familiar words but an unfamiliar verb, children often infer that the verb refers to the action performed by the subject of the sentence (Fisher, 1996; Woodward & Markman, 1998). When the youngsters in the

photograph hear, "The man is juggling," they will infer that *juggling* refers to the man's actions with the balls, because they already know *man*.

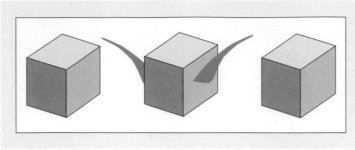

FIG 6–8

As another example of how sentence context aids word learning, look at the blocks in the diagram and point to the *boz* block. I imagine you pointed to the middle block. Why? In English, adjectives usually precede the nouns they modify, so you inferred that *boz* is an adjective describing *block*. Since *the* before *boz* implies that only one block is *boz*, you picked the middle one, having decided that *boz* means "winged." Preschool children, too, use sentence cues like these to judge word meanings (Gelman & Markman, 1985; Hall, Waxman, & Hurwitz, 1993).

Naming Errors. Of course, these rules for learning new words are not perfect. **A common mistake is *underextension*, defining a word too narrowly.** Using *car* to refer only to the family car and *ball* to a favorite toy ball are examples of underextension. **Between 1 and 3 years, children sometimes make the opposite error, *overextension*, defining a word too broadly.** Children may use *car* to also refer to buses and trucks or use *doggie* to refer to all four-legged animals.

The overextension error occurs more frequently when children are producing words than when they are comprehending words. Two-year-old Jason may say "doggie" to refer to a goat but nevertheless will correctly point to a picture of a goat when asked. Because overextension is more common in word production, it may actually reflect another fast-mapping rule that children follow: "If you can't remember the name for an object, say the name of a related object" (Naigles & Gelman, 1995).

Both underextension and overextension disappear gradually as youngsters refine meanings for words based on the feedback they receive from parents and others.

Styles of Learning Language

As youngsters expand their vocabulary, they often adopt a distinctive style of learning language (Bates, Bretherton, & Snyder, 1988). **Some children have a *referential style*; their vocabularies mainly consist of words that name objects, persons, or actions.** For example, Rachel, a referential child, had 41 name words in her 50-word vocabulary but only 2 words for social interaction or questions. **Other children have an *expressive style*; their vocabularies include some names but also many social phrases that are used like a single word, such as "go away," "what'd you want?" and "I want it."** Elizabeth, an expressive child, had a more balanced vocabulary: 24 name words and 14 for social interactions and questions.

> Language is primarily an intellectual tool for referential children and primarily a social tool for expressive children.

Children with the referential style primarily use language as an intellectual tool—a means of learning and talking about objects (Masur, 1995). In contrast, children with an expressive style use language as more of a social tool—a way of enhancing interactions with others. Of course, both of these functions—intellectual and social—are important functions of language, and as you might expect, most children blend the referential and expressive styles of learning language.

Check Your Learning

1. Young infants can distinguish many language sounds, but older infants are more likely to notice only _____ .

2. Adults using infant-directed speech speak slowly and exaggerate the loudness and _____ of their speech.

3. At about 7 months, most infants' babbling includes phrases that sound like questions, which shows infants are learning about patterns of _____ .

4. Deaf children babble later than average in spoken language but _____ in sign language.

5. Children begin to _____ at about the same age that they begin to talk, and both apparently reflect children's growing understanding of symbols.

6. Many strategies help children learn words, including joint attention, constraints on word learning, and _____ .

7. Sometimes children define a word too broadly, an error known as _____ .

8. When children have a referential style of language learning, they tend to use language primarily as a(n) _____ tool.

■ **Active Children** How does the research on language acquisition described in this module support the view that children actively try to interpret and understand the world?

Answers: (1) sounds that they hear in their language environment, (2) pitch, (3) intonation, (4) right on schedule, (5) gesture, (6) sentence cues, (7) overextension, (8) intellectual

Critical Review

1. Explain what Piaget meant when he referred to children as scientists.

2. Compare and contrast the Piagetian and information processing views of cognition, as described in Modules 6.1 and 6.2.

3. If Piaget created an intelligence test, how would it differ from the tests described in Module 6.2?

4. In some cultures, parents encourage children's speech development by such means as talking to them constantly and consciously naming objects. In other cultures, children's language development is taken for granted. Based on what you learned in Module 6.3, which approach makes more sense?

For more review material, log on to www.prenhall.com/kail

See For Yourself

It's eye-opening to observe infants performing simple versions of the learning tasks described on pages 164–166. For example, ring a bell every 15 seconds. The baby should orient to the first few rings, but then habituate. Or, if the infant has a mobile in its crib, tie a ribbon from the infant's leg to the mobile. In a few minutes, the infant should be kicking frequently, demonstrating operant conditioning (kicking recurs because it produces pleasant consequences). From watching infants perform these and other learning tasks, you will appreciate that even very young infants are surprisingly capable learners! See for yourself!

For More Information About . . .

 activities for babies that promote cognitive development, read S. H. Jacobs's *Your Baby's Mind* (Bob Adams, 1992), which describes learning games and exercises for babies that are derived from Piaget's view of sensorimotor intelligence.

 American Sign Language (ASL), visit the Animated American Sign Language Dictionary Web site: http://www.bconnex.net/~randys/index_nf.html

Key Terms

accommodation 153
assimilation 153
babbling 174
classical conditioning 165
cooing 174
egocentric frame of reference 168
equilibration 154
expressive style 178
fast mapping 176
habituation 164
infant-directed speech 173

infantile amnesia 166
information-processing theory 162
intonation 174
long-term memory 163
naming explosion 176
objective frame of reference 168
object permanence 157
operant conditioning 165
orienting response 164
overextension 178
phonemes 171

primary circular reaction 155
referential style 178
schemes 152
secondary circular reaction 155
sensorimotor stage 155
sensory memory 163
tertiary circular reaction 156
underextension 178
working memory 163

SUMMARY

6.1 Piaget's Theory

Basic Principles of Piaget's Theory

In Piaget's view, children construct their understanding of the world by creating schemes—mental categories of related events, objects, and knowledge. Infants' schemes are based on actions, but older children's and adolescents' schemes are based on functional, conceptual, and abstract properties.

Schemes change constantly. In assimilation, experiences are readily incorporated into existing schemes. In accommodation, experiences cause schemes to be modified. When accommodation becomes much more frequent than assimilation, children reorganize their schemes. This reorganization produces four different stages of mental development from infancy through adulthood.

Piaget's Sensorimotor Stage

The first 2 years of life constitute Piaget's sensorimotor stage, which is divided into 6 substages. By 8 to 12 months, one scheme is used in the service of another; by 12 to 18 months, infants experiment with schemes; and by 18 to 24 months, infants begin to engage in symbolic processing.

Evaluating Piaget's Account of Sensorimotor Thought

Piaget's theory has been criticized because children's performance on tasks, such as object permanence, is sometimes better explained by ideas that are not part of his theory.

The Child as Theorist

In contrast to Piaget's idea that children create a comprehensive theory that integrates all their knowledge, the modern view is that children are specialists, generating naive theories in particular domains, including physics and biology.

6.2 Information Processing

Basic Features of the Information-Processing Approach

According to the information-processing approach, cognitive development involves changes in mental hardware and mental software. Mental hardware includes sensory, working, and long-term memories. Mental software refers to mental programs that allow people to perform specific tasks.

Learning

Infants habituate, that is, they respond less as stimuli become more familiar. They also are capable of classical conditioning, operant con-

ditioning, in which the consequences of behavior determine whether the behavior is likely to be repeated, and imitation, in which they learn from watching others.

Memory

Studies of kicking show that infants can remember, forget, and be reminded of events that occurred in the past. Infantile amnesia, children's and adults' inability to remember events from early in life, may reflect the acquisition of language or their lack of a sense of self.

Understanding the World

Infants can distinguish quantities, probably by means of basic perceptual processes. By 12 months, they are more likely to know positions of objects relative to other objects, which is known as an objective frame of reference.

Individual Differences in Ability

Infant tests like the Bayley Scales include mental and motor scales. Typically, scores on these tests are not highly correlated with adult IQ but they are useful for determining if development is progressing normally. Habituation predicts later IQ more accurately.

6.3 Language

Perceiving Speech

Phonemes are the basic units of sound that make up words. Infants can hear phonemes, including those not used in their native language, but this ability is lost by the first birthday. Before they speak, infants can recognize words, apparently by noticing stress and syllables that go together. Infants prefer infant-directed speech because it provides them additional language clues.

First Steps to Speaking

At about 3 months, babies coo. Babbling soon follows, consisting of a single syllable; over several months, infants' babbling includes longer syllables and intonation. Deaf children babble later than children with normal hearing, but they make partial signs that are thought to be analogous to babbling.

First Words

Children's first words represent a cognitive accomplishment that is not specific to language. Instead, the onset of language is due to a child's ability to interpret and use symbols. Consistent with this view, there are parallel developments in the use of gestures.

Fast Mapping Meanings to Words

Children use several fast-mapping rules to determine probable meanings of new words: joint attention, constraints, and sentence cues. The rules do not always lead to the correct meaning. An underextension denotes a child's meaning that is narrower than an adult's meaning; an overextension denotes a child's meaning that is broader.

Styles of Learning Language

Some youngsters use a referential style in learning words that emphasizes words as names and views language as an intellectual tool. Other children use an expressive style that emphasizes phrases and views language as a social tool.

Social Behavior and Personality in Infants and Toddlers

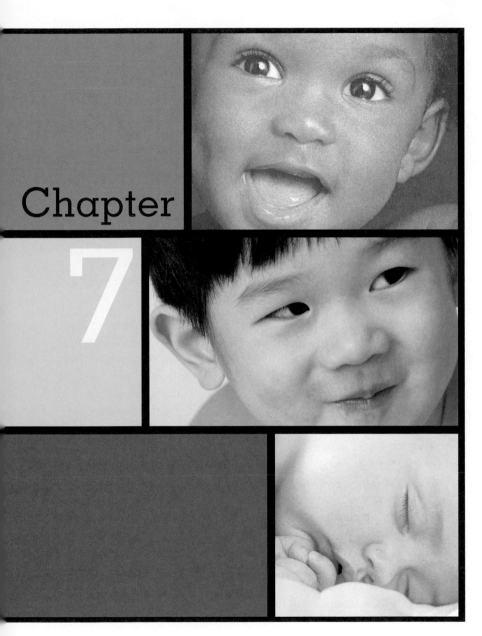

Chapter 7

In the years after World War II, many European infants and toddlers lived in orphanages. They were well fed and clothed but were typically cared for by a constantly changing cast of adults, sometimes as many as 50 by age 4. Lacking a strong social-emotional relationship with an adult during their formative years, the development of these children was disrupted, sometimes severely (Tizard & Hodges, 1978).

A social-emotional relationship with a parent is the foundation for much of a child's later development; we'll examine it in detail in Module 7.2. First, however, we'll see how emotions emerge in infancy and how they affect infants' and toddlers' behavior. In Module 7.2, we'll study young children's relationships with their parents and with their peers. In Module 7.3, we'll learn how infants and toddlers first come to understand themselves as people. And finally, in Module 7.4, we'll discover that infants have different behavioral styles that reflect, in part, emotions.

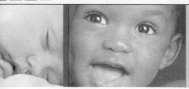

Emotions

7.1

Emotions

Learning Objectives

■ **When do infants begin to express basic emotions?**

■ **What are complex emotions and when do they develop?**

■ **When do infants begin to understand other people's emotions? How do they use this information to guide their own behavior?**

■ **When do infants and toddlers begin to regulate their own emotions?**

Nicole was ecstatic that she was finally going to see her 7-month-old nephew, Claude. She rushed into the house and, seeing Claude playing on the floor with blocks, swept him up in a big hug. After a brief, puzzled look, Claude burst into angry tears and began thrashing around, as if saying to Nicole, "Who are you? What do you want? Put me down! Now!" Nicole quickly handed Claude to his mother, who was surprised by her baby's outburst and even more surprised that he continued to sob while she rocked him.

Nicole's initial happiness, Claude's anger, and his mother's surprise illustrate three basic human emotions. Happiness, anger, and surprise, along with fear, disgust, and sadness are considered basic emotions because people worldwide experience them and because each consists of three elements: a subjective feeling, a physiological change, and an overt behavior (Izard, 1991). For example, suppose you wake to the sound of a thunderstorm and then discover your roommate has left for class with your umbrella. Subjectively, you might feel ready to explode with anger; physiologically, your heart would beat faster; and behaviorally, you would probably be scowling.

> Basic emotions—including happiness, anger, and fear—are experienced in much the same way by infants worldwide.

In addition to basic emotions, people feel complex emotions such as pride, guilt, and embarrassment. Unlike basic emotions, complex emotions have an evaluative component to them. For example, a 2-year-old who has spilled juice all over the floor may hang his head in shame; another 2-year-old who has, for the first time, finished a difficult puzzle by herself will smile in a way that radiates pride. Also, in contrast to basic emotions, complex emotions are not experienced the same way in all cultures.

In this module, we look at when children first express basic and complex emotions, how children come to understand emotions in others, and, finally, how children regulate their emotions.

Basic Emotions

If you're a fan of *Star Trek,* you know that Mr. Spock feels little emotion because he's half Vulcan, and people from the planet Vulcan don't have emotions. Is there a time when infants are like Mr. Spock, relatively free of emotion? No; emotions are with us from the first few months of life. To see for yourself, look at the photos of young babies on page 185. Which one is angry? Which are the sad and happy babies? The

  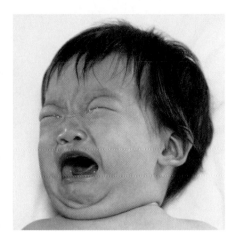

facial expressions are so revealing that I'm sure you guessed that the babies are, in order, sad, happy, and angry. But, do these distinctive facial expressions mean the infants are actually experiencing these emotions? Not necessarily. Remember that facial expressions are only one component of emotion—the behavioral manifestation. Emotion also involves physiological responses and subjective feelings. Of course, infants can't express their feelings to us verbally, so we don't know much about their subjective experiences. We're on firmer ground with the physiological element. At least some of the physiological responses that accompany facial expressions are the same in infants and adults. For example, when infants and adults smile—which suggests they're happy—the left frontal cortex of the brain tends to have more electrical activity than the right frontal cortex (Fox, Kimmerly, & Schafer, 1991).

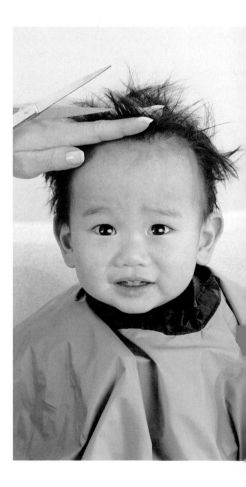

Many scientists use this and similar findings to argue that facial expressions are reliable clues to an infant's emotional state. For example, research also shows that infants and adults worldwide express basic emotions in much the same way (Izard, 1991). The child in the photo on the right shows the universal signs of fear. His eyes are open wide, his eyebrows are raised, and his mouth is relaxed but slightly open. The universality of emotional expression suggests that humans are biologically programmed to express emotions in a specific way; it's simply in our genes to smile when we're happy and scowl when we're unhappy.

Another finding linking infants' facial expressions to emotions is that, by 5 to 6 months, infants' facial expressions change predictably and meaningfully in response to events. When a happy mother greets her baby, the baby usually smiles in return; when a tired, distracted mother picks up her baby roughly, the baby usually frowns at her. These findings suggest that by the middle of the first year (and maybe earlier) facial expressions are fairly reliable indicators of an infant's emotional state (Izard et al., 1995; Weinberg & Tronick, 1994).

If facial expressions provide a window on a baby's emotions, what do they tell us about the early phases of emotional development? Let's start with happiness.

Happiness During the first few weeks after birth, infants begin to smile, but this seems to be related to internal physiological states. An infant may smile after feeding or while asleep, for example. **At about 2 months, *social smiles* first appear: Infants smile when they see another human face.** Sometimes social smiling is accompanied by cooing, the early form of vocalization described in Module 5.3 (Sroufe & Waters, 1976). Smiling and cooing seem to be the infant's way of expressing pleasure at seeing another person.

At about 4 months, smiling is joined by laughter, which usually occurs when a baby experiences vigorous physical stimulation (Sroufe & Wunsch, 1972). Tickling 4-month-olds or bouncing them on your knee is a good way to prompt a laugh. Toward the end of the first year, infants often laugh when familiar events take a novel turn. For example, a 1-year-old will laugh when her mother pretends to drink from a baby bottle or her father drapes a diaper around his waist. Laughter is now a response to psychological stimulation as well as physical stimulation.

The early stages of positive feelings, like happiness, are fairly clear: An infant's experience of happiness is first linked primarily to physical states, such as feeling full after a meal or being tickled. Later, feelings of happiness reflect psychological states, such as the pleasure of seeing another person or an unusual event.

Negative Emotions We know much less about the development of negative emotions such as fear, anger, and sadness. Certainly, newborns express distress, but specific negative emotions are hard to verify. Anger emerges gradually, with distinct displays appearing between 4 and 6 months. Infants will become angry, for example, if a favorite food or toy is taken away (Sternberg & Campos, 1990). Reflecting their growing understanding of goal-directed behavior (see Module 5.1), infants also become angry when their attempts to achieve a goal are frustrated. For example, if a parent restrains an infant trying to pick up a toy, the guaranteed result is a very angry baby.

Like anger, fear seems to be rare in newborns and young infants. **The first distinct signs of fear emerge at about 6 months when infants become wary in the presence of an unfamiliar adult, a reaction known as *stranger wariness.*** When a stranger approaches, a 6-month-old typically looks away and begins to fuss (Mangelsdorf, Shapiro, & Marzolf, 1995). The baby in the photo is showing the signs of stranger wariness. The grandmother has picked him up without giving him a chance to warm up to her, and the outcome is as predictable as it was with Claude, the baby boy in the opening vignette who was frightened by his aunt: He cries, looks frightened, and reaches with arms outstretched in the direction of someone familiar.

How wary an infant feels around strangers depends on a number of factors (Thompson & Limber, 1991). First, infants tend to be less fearful of strangers when the environment is familiar and more fearful when it is not. Many parents know this firsthand from traveling with their infants: When they enter a friend's house for the first time, the baby clings tightly to its mother. Second, the amount of anxiety depends on the stranger's behavior. Instead of rushing to greet or pick up the baby, as Nicole did in the vignette, a stranger should talk with other adults and, in a while, perhaps offer the baby a toy (Mangelsdorf, 1992). Handled this way, many infants will soon be curious about the stranger instead of afraid.

Wariness of strangers is adaptive because it emerges at the same time that children begin to master creeping and crawling (described in Module 5.3). Like Curious George, the monkey in a famous series of children's books, babies are inquisitive and want to use their new locomotor skills to explore their worlds. Being wary of strangers provides a natural restraint against the tendency to wander away from familiar caregivers. During the second year, wariness of strangers gradually declines as toddlers learn to interpret facial expressions and recognize when a stranger is friendly and not hostile.

Although children worldwide express basic emotions, there are cultural differences in the frequency of emotional expression. In one study (Camras et al., 1998), European American 11-month-olds cried

Infants have greater fear of strangers in unfamiliar environments and when strangers don't allow infants to warm up to them.

and smiled more often than Chinese 11-month-olds. In another study (Zahn-Waxler et al., 1996), U.S. preschoolers were more likely than Japanese preschoolers to express anger in interpersonal conflicts. Thus, even though basic emotions are rooted in biology, the way they are expressed is influenced by culture.

Complex Emotions

Basic emotions emerge early in infancy but complex emotions such as feelings of guilt, embarrassment, and pride don't surface until 18 to 24 months of age (Lewis, 1992). Complex emotions depend on the child having some understanding of the self, which typically occurs between 15 and 18 months (as we'll see in Module 7.3). Children feel guilty or embarrassed, for example, when they've done something that they know they shouldn't have done: A child who breaks a toy is thinking, "You told me to be careful. But I wasn't!" Similarly, children feel pride when they've done something that was challenging: The toddler in the photo is probably thinking something like, "This was hard, but I did it, all by myself!" For children to experience complex emotions, they need to be more advanced cognitively, which explains why complex emotions don't appear until the very end of infancy (Lewis, Alessandri, & Sullivan, 1992).

In sum, complex emotions like guilt and pride require more sophisticated understanding than basic emotions like happiness and fear, which are more biologically based. By age 2, however, children express both basic and complex emotions. Of course, expressing emotions is only part of the developmental story. Children must also learn to recognize others' emotions, which is our next topic.

Recognizing and Using Others' Emotions

When can infants first identify emotions in others? By 6 or 7 months, infants begin to distinguish facial expressions associated with different emotions. A 6-month-old can, for example, distinguish a happy, smiling face from a sad, frowning face (Ludemann, 1991; Ludemann & Nelson, 1988). Typically, baby girls are more accurate than baby boys at recognizing adults' facial expressions of emotion (McClure, 2000).

Strictly speaking, these studies tell us only that infants can discriminate facial expressions, not emotions *per se*. Other research, however, indicates that 6-month-olds have indeed begun to recognize the emotions themselves. The best evidence is that infants often match their own emotions to other people's emotions. When happy mothers smile and talk in a pleasant voice, infants express happiness themselves. If mothers are angry or sad, infants become distressed, too (Haviland & Lelwica, 1987). In addition, infants look longer at happy faces when they hear happy-sounding talk and longer at angry faces when they hear angry-sounding talk (Soken & Pick, 1999).

Also like adults, infants use others' emotions to direct their behavior. **Infants in an unfamiliar or ambiguous environment often look at their mother or father, as if searching for cues to help them interpret the situation, a phenomenon known as** *social referencing.* For example, in a study by Hirshberg and Svejda (1990), 12-month-olds were shown novel toys that made sounds, such as a stuffed alligator that hissed. For some toys, parents were told to look happy; for others, parents were to look afraid. When parents looked afraid, their infants, too, appeared distressed and moved away from the toys.

In other studies of social referencing, infants watch an adult express happiness when looking inside one box but disgust when looking inside another. Infants are more likely to explore the box that elicited happiness (Repacholi, 1998). Furthermore, facial expressions or vocal expressions alone provide infants with enough information to decide if they want to explore an unfamiliar object (Mumme, Fernald, & Herrera, 1996). Thus, social referencing shows that infants rely on their parents' emotions to help them regulate their own behavior.

Regulating Emotions

Think back to a time when you were *really* angry at a good friend. Did you shout at the friend? Did you try to discuss matters calmly? Or did you simply ignore the situation altogether? Shouting is a direct expression of anger, but calm conversation and overlooking a situation are purposeful attempts to regulate emotion. People often regulate emotions; for example, we routinely try to suppress fear (because we know there's no real need to be afraid of the dark), anger (because we don't want to let a friend know just how upset we are), and joy (because we don't want to seem like we're gloating over our good fortune).

> Infants regulate their emotions by looking away from frightening events or moving closer to a parent.

Child-development researchers have discovered that emotion regulation clearly begins in infancy. By 4 to 6 months, infants use simple strategies to regulate their emotions (Buss & Goldsmith, 1998; Mangelsdorf, Shapiro, & Marzolf, 1995). When something frightens or confuses an infant—for example, a stranger or a mother who suddenly stops responding—they often look away (just as older children and even adults often turn away or close their eyes to block out disturbing stimuli). Frightened infants also move closer to a parent, another effective way of helping to control their fear (Parritz, 1996). As children get older, they devise even more effective strategies for dealing with emotions (e.g., reassuring themselves that there's no reason to be afraid of the dark) but the effort to control emotions (instead of being swept away by them) emerges in infancy.

Check Your Learning

1. Basic emotions include a subjective feeling, a physiological change, and _____.

2. During infancy, happiness is first linked to physical states and later to _____.

3. The first detectable form of fear is _____, which emerges at about 6 months.

4. Wariness of strangers is adaptive because it emerges at about the same time that _____.

5. Complex emotions, such as guilt and shame, emerge later than basic emotions because _____.

6. In social referencing, infants use a parent's facial expression _____.

7. Infants often control fear by looking away from a frightening event or by _____.

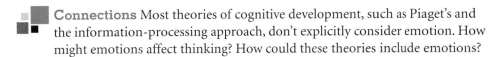

■■ **Connections** Most theories of cognitive development, such as Piaget's and
■ ■ the information-processing approach, don't explicitly consider emotion. How
might emotions affect thinking? How could these theories include emotions?

Answers: (1) an overt behavior, (2) psychological states, (3) wariness of strangers, (4) infants master creeping and crawling, (5) complex emotions require more advanced cognitive skills, (6) to
direct their own behavior (e.g., deciding if an unfamiliar situation is safe or frightening), (7) moving closer to a parent

Relationships with Others

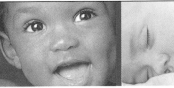

7.2

Relationships with Others
├ The Growth of Attachment
├ Quality of Attachment
└ Onset of Peer Interactions

Learning Objectives

■ **How does an attachment relationship develop between an infant and primary
caregiver?**

■ **What different types of attachment relationships are there? What are the consequences of different types of relationships? How does child care affect attachment
relationships?**

■ **How do infants and toddlers first interact with peers?**

*Ever since Samantha was a newborn, Karen and Dick looked forward to going
to their favorite restaurant on Friday night. Karen enjoyed the break from child-
care responsibilities and Dick liked being able to talk to Karen without interrup-
tions. But recently they've had a problem. When they leave her with a sitter,
8-month-old Sam gets a frightened look on her face and usually begins to cry
hysterically. Karen and Dick wonder if Sam's behavior is normal and if their
Friday night dinners might be coming to an end.*

The social-emotional relationship that develops between an infant and a parent
(usually, but not necessarily, the mother) is special. This is a baby's first social-emotional relationship, so scientists and parents alike believe it should be satisfying and
trouble-free to set the stage for later relationships. In this module, we'll look at the
steps involved in creating the baby's first emotional relationship. Along the way, we'll
see why 8-month-old Sam has begun to cry when Karen and Dick leave her with a
sitter. And we'll also examine children's first interactions with peers.

The Growth of Attachment

Sigmund Freud was the first modern theorist to emphasize the importance of
emotional ties to the mother for psychological development. Today, the dominant view of early human relationships comes from John Bowlby (1969, 1991). His
work originated in ethology, a branch of biology (described in Module 1.1) concerned with adaptive behaviors of different species. **According to Bowlby, children
who form an *attachment* to an adult—that is, an enduring social-emotional rela-**

Many infant behaviors are designed to elicit caregiving from adults and thus promote an attachment bond.

tionship—are more likely to survive. This person is usually the mother but need not be; the key is a strong emotional relationship with a responsive, caring person so attachments can form with fathers, grandparents, or someone else.

Bowlby (1969) argued that evolutionary pressure favored behaviors likely to elicit caregiving from an adult, such as clinging, sucking, crying, and smiling. That is, over the course of human evolution, these behaviors have become a standard part of the human infant's biological heritage, and the responses they evoke in adults create an interactive system that leads to the formation of attachment relationships.

The attachment relationship develops gradually over the first several months after birth, reflecting the baby's growing perceptual and cognitive skills described in Chapters 5 and 6. The first step is for the infant to learn the difference between people and other objects. Typically, in the first few months, babies begin to respond differently to people and to objects—for example, smiling more and vocalizing more to people—suggesting that they have begun to identify members of the social world.

During these months, mother and infant begin to synchronize their interactions. Remember from Module 3.3 that young babies' behaviors go through cycles. Infants move between states of alertness and attentiveness to states of distress and inattentiveness. Caregivers begin to recognize these states of behavior and adjust their own behavior accordingly. A mother who notices that her baby is awake and alert will begin to smile at and talk to her baby. These interactions often continue until the baby's state changes, which prompts the mother to stop. In fact, by 3 months of age, if a mother does not interact with her alert baby (but, instead, stares silently), babies become at least moderately distressed, looking away from her and sometimes crying (Toda & Fogel, 1993).

Thus, like the mom and baby in the photo, mothers and infants gradually synchronize their behaviors so that they are both "on" at the same time (Gable & Isabella, 1992). These interactions provide the foundation for more sophisticated communication and foster the infant's trust that the mother will respond predictably and reassuringly.

By approximately 6 or 7 months, most infants have singled out the attachment figure—usually the mother—as a special individual. An infant will smile at the mother and cling to her more than to other people. The attachment figure is now the infant's stable social-emotional base. For example, a 7-month-old like the one in the photo will explore a novel environment but periodically look toward his mother, as if seeking reassurance that all is well. The behavior suggests the infant trusts his mother and indicates the attachment relationship has been established. In addition, this behavior reflects important cognitive growth: It means that the infant has a mental representation of the mother, an understanding that she will be there to meet the infant's needs (Lewis et al., 1997).

The formation of the attachment bond also explains why 8-month-old Sam cries whenever Karen and Dick try to leave her with a sitter. Sam is attached to Karen, expects her to be nearby, and is upset when separated from her.

Attachment typically first develops between infants and their mothers because mothers are usually the primary caregivers of American infants. Most babies soon become attached to their fathers, too, but they interact differently with fathers. Fathers typically spend much more time playing with their babies than taking care of them. In countries around the world—Australia, India, Israel, Italy, Japan, and the United States—"playmate" is the customary role for fathers (Roopnarine, 1992). Fathers even play with infants differently than mothers. Physical play is the norm for fathers, particularly with sons, whereas mothers spend more time reading and talking to babies, showing them toys, and playing games like patty-cake (Parke, 1990). Given the opportunity to play with mothers or fathers, infants more often choose their fathers. However, when infants are distressed, mothers are preferred (Field, 1990). Thus, although most infants become attached to both parents, mothers and fathers typically have distinctive roles in their children's early social development.

Quality of Attachment

Attachment between infant and mother usually occurs by 8 or 9 months of age, but the attachment can take on different forms. Mary Ainsworth (1978, 1993) pioneered the study of attachment relationships using a procedure that has come to be known as the Strange Situation. As shown in the diagram, the Strange Situation involves a series of episodes, each about 3 minutes long. The mother and infant enter an unfamiliar room filled with interesting toys. The mother leaves briefly, then mother and baby are reunited. Meanwhile, the experimenter observes the baby, recording its response to both events.

Based on how the infant reacts to separation from the mother and then reunion, Ainsworth (1993) and other researchers (Main & Cassidy, 1988) have identified four primary types of attachment relationships. One is a secure attachment and three are insecure attachments (avoidant, resistant, disorganized).

1. Observer shows the experimental room to mother and infant, then leaves the room.

2. Infant is allowed to explore the playroom for 3 minutes; mother watches but does not participate.

3. A stranger enters the room and remains silent for 1 minute, then talks to the baby for a minute, and then approaches the baby. Mother leaves unobtrusively.

4. The stranger does not play with the baby but attempts to comfort it if necessary.

5. After 3 minutes, the mother returns, greets, and consoles the baby.

6. When the baby has returned to play, the mother leaves again, this time saying "bye-bye" as she leaves.

7. Stranger attempts to calm and play with the baby.

8. After 3 minutes, the mother returns and the stranger leaves.

FIG 7–1

- *Secure attachment:* **The baby may or may not cry when the mother leaves, but when she returns, the baby wants to be with her and if the baby is crying, it stops.** Babies in this group seem to be saying, "I missed you terribly, but now that you're back, I'm okay." Approximately 60 to 65 percent of American babies have secure attachment relationships.

- *Avoidant attachment:* **The baby is not upset when the mother leaves and, when she returns, may ignore her by looking or turning away.** Infants with an avoidant attachment look as if they're saying, "You left me again. I always have to take care of myself!" About 20 percent of American infants have avoidant attachment relationships, which is one of the three forms of insecure attachment.

- *Resistant attachment:* **The baby is upset when the mother leaves and remains upset or even angry when she returns, and is difficult to console.** Like the baby in the photo, these babies seem to be telling the mother, "Why do you do this? I need you desperately and yet you just leave me without warning. I get so angry when you're like this." About 10 to 15 percent of American babies have this resistant attachment relationship, which is another form of insecure attachment.

- *Disorganized (disoriented) attachment:* **The baby seems confused when the mother leaves and, when she returns, seems as if it doesn't really understand what's happening.** The baby often has a dazed look on its face as if wondering, "What's going on here? I want you to be here, but you left and now you're back. I don't know whether to laugh or cry!" About 5 to 10 percent of American babies have this disorganized attachment relationship, the last of the three kinds of insecure attachment.

Secure attachments and the different forms of insecure attachments are observed worldwide. As you can see in the graph, secure attachments are the most common throughout the world (van Ijzendoorn & Kroonenberg, 1988). This is fortunate because, as we'll see, a secure attachment provides a solid base for later social development.

Infants typically form the same type of attachment relationships with both parents (Fox, Kimmerly, & Schafer, 1991). An infant who is securely attached to its mother is usually securely attached to its father, too. In addition, siblings usually have the same type of attachment relationships with their parents (Rosen & Burke, 1999).

Consequences of Quality of Attachment Erikson, Bowlby, and other theorists (Sroufe & Fleeson, 1986) believe that attachment, as the first social relationship, lays the foundation for all of an infant's later social relationships. In this view, infants who experience the trust and compassion of a secure attachment should develop into preschool children who interact confidently and successfully with their peers. In contrast, infants who do not experience a successful, satisfying first relationship should be more prone to problems in their social interactions as preschoolers.

Both of these predictions are supported by research, as the following findings demonstrate:

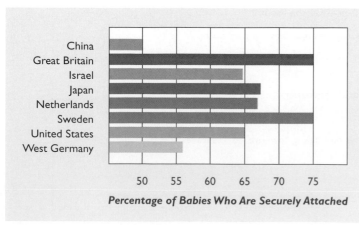

Percentage of Babies Who Are Securely Attached

FIG 7–2

- Children with secure attachment relationships have higher-quality friendships and fewer conflicts in their friendships than children with insecure attachment relationships (Lieberman, Doyle, & Markiewicz, 1999).

- School-age children are less likely to have behavior problems if they have secure attachment relationships and more likely if they have insecure attachment relationships (Carlson, 1998; Wakschlag & Hans, 1999).

- At a summer camp, 11-year-olds who had secure attachment relationships as infants interacted more skillfully with their peers and had more close friends than 11-year-olds who had insecure attachment relationships (Elicker, Englund, & Sroufe, 1992).

Infants with secure attachment relationships tend to have more successful peer relationships.

The conclusion seems inescapable: As infants who have secure attachment relationships develop, their social interactions tend to be more satisfying. Why? Secure attachment evidently promotes trust and confidence in other humans, which leads to more skilled social interactions later in childhood. Of course, attachment is only one step along the long road of social development. Infants with insecure attachments are not doomed, but this initial misstep can interfere with their social development.

Factors Determining Quality of Attachment Because secure attachment is so important to a child's later development, researchers have tried to identify the factors involved. Undoubtedly the most important is the interaction between parents and their babies (De Wolff & van Ijzendoorn, 1997). A secure attachment is most likely when parents respond to infants predictably and appropriately. For example, the mother in the photo has promptly responded to her baby's crying and is trying to reassure her baby. The mother's behavior evidently conveys that social interactions are predictable and satisfying, and apparently this behavior instills in infants the trust and confidence that are the hallmark of secure attachment.

Why does predictable and responsive parenting promote secure attachment relationships? To answer this question, think about your own friendships and romantic relationships. These relationships are usually most satisfying when we believe we can trust the other people and depend on them in times of need. The same formula seems to hold for infants. **Infants develop an *internal working model,* a set of expectations about parents' availability and responsivity, generally and in times of stress.** When parents are dependable and caring, babies come to trust them, knowing they can be relied upon for comfort. That is, babies develop an internal working model in which they believe their parents are concerned about their needs and will try to meet them (Bretherton, 1992).

Many research findings attest to the importance of a caregiver's sensitivity for developing secure attachment:

- In a longitudinal study, infants were more likely to have a secure attachment relationship at 12 months when their parents were sensitive, responding quickly and appropriately to their infant at 3 months (Cox et al., 1992).

- In a study conducted in Israel, infants were less likely to develop secure attachment when they slept in dormitories with other children under 12, where they received inconsistent (if any) attention when they became upset overnight (Sagi et al., 1994).

- In a study conducted in the Netherlands, infants were more likely to form a secure attachment when their mother had three months of training that emphasized monitoring an infant's signals and responding appropriately and promptly (van den Boom, 1994, 1995).

> ## The key to a secure attachment relationship is sensitive, responsive parenting.

Thus, secure attachment is most likely when parents are sensitive and responsive. Of course, not all caregivers react to babies in a reliable and reassuring manner. Some respond intermittently or only after the infant has cried long and hard. And when these caregivers finally respond, they are sometimes annoyed by the infant's demands and may misinterpret the infant's intent. Over time, these babies tend to see social relationships as inconsistent and often frustrating, conditions that do little to foster trust and confidence.

Why are some parents more responsive (and thus more likely to foster secure attachment) than others? In modern attachment theory (e.g., Cassidy, 1994), parents have internal working models of the attachment relationship with their own parents, and these working models guide interactions with their own infants. When questioned about attachment relationships with the Adult Attachment Interview (George, Kaplan, & Main, 1985), adults can be classified into one of three groups:

- *Autonomous adults* describe childhood experiences objectively and mention both positive and negative aspects of their parents.

- *Dismissive adults* describe childhood experiences in very general terms and often idealize their parents.

- *Preoccupied adults* describe childhood experiences emotionally and often express anger or confusion regarding relationships with their parents.

According to attachment theory, only parents with autonomous attachment representations are likely to provide the sensitive caregiving that promotes secure attachment relationships. In fact, many studies show that parents' autonomous attachment representations are associated with sensitive caregiving, and, in turn, with secure attachment in their infants (Aviezer et al., 1999; van Ijzendoorn, 1995; Pederson et al., 1998). Furthermore, longitudinal research (Beckwith, Cohen, & Hamilton, 1999) shows that infants with secure attachment relations tend to become adults with autonomous attachment representations, completing the circle.

The sensitive and responsive caregiving that is essential for secure attachments is often taxing, particularly for babies with difficult temperaments. That is, babies who fuss often and are difficult to console are more prone to insecure attachment (Goldsmith & Harman, 1994; Seifer et al., 1996). Insecure attachment may also be more likely when a difficult, emotional infant has a mother whose personality is rigid and traditional than when the mother is accepting and flexible (Mangelsdorf et al., 1990). Rigid mothers do not adjust well to the often erratic demands of their difficult babies; instead, they want the baby to adjust to them. This means that rigid mothers less often provide the responsive, sensitive care that leads to secure attachment.

Fortunately, even brief training for mothers of newborns can help them respond to their babies more effectively (Wendland-Carro, Piccinini, & Millar, 1999). Mothers can be taught how to interact more sensitively, affectionately, and responsively, paving the way for secure attachment and the lifelong benefits associated with a positive internal working model of interpersonal relationships.

Attachment, Work, and Child Care Since the 1970s, more women in the work-force and more single-parent households have made child care a fact of life for many American families. Today, approximately 6 million U.S. infants and toddlers are cared for by someone other than their mother. About one-third of America's infants and preschoolers are cared for in their home, typically by the father or a grandparent. Another third receive care in the provider's home. The provider is often but not always a relative. Finally, another third attend day-care or nursery-school programs. The patterns are very similar for European American, African American, and Hispanic American youngsters (Singer et al., 1998; U.S. Bureau of the Census, 1995).

Parents and policy makers alike have been concerned about the impact of such care on children generally and specifically its impact on attachment. Is there, for example, a maximum amount of time per week that infants should spend in care outside the home? Is there a minimum age below which infants should not be placed in care outside the home? The Child Development and Family Policy feature describes work that has attempted to answer these and other questions about the impact of early child care on children's development.

CHILD DEVELOPMENT AND FAMILY POLICY

Determining Guidelines for Child Care for Infants and Toddlers

Because so many American families need child care for their infants and toddlers, a comprehensive study of early child care was required to provide parents and policy makers with appropriate guidelines. The task fell to the National Institute of Child Health and Human Development, which was created in 1962 to study children's physical, emotional, and cognitive development. Planning for the Early Child Care study began in 1989 and by 1991 the study was underway. Researchers recruited 1,364 mothers and their newborns from 12 U.S. cities. Both mothers and children have been tested repeatedly (and the testing continues, since the study is ongoing).

One of the first reports from this project concerned the impact of early child care on 15-month-olds' attachment to their mothers (NICHD Early Child Care Research Network, 1997). The results indicated no overall effects of child-care experience on mother-infant attachment, which was measured with the Strange Situation (described on pages 191–192). A secure mother-infant attachment was just as likely, regardless of the quality of child care, the amount of time the child spent in care, the age when the child began care, how frequently the parents changed child-care arrangements, and the type of child care (e.g., child-care center, in the home with a non-relative).

However, when the effects of child care were considered along with character-istics of mothers, an important pattern was detected: When mothers who were less sensitive and less responsive placed their infants in low-quality child care, insecure attachments were more common. As the investigators put it, "poor quality, unstable, or more than minimal amounts of child care apparently added to the risks already inherent in poor mothering, so that the combined effects were worse than those of low maternal sensitivity and responsiveness alone." (p. 877)

These results provide clear guidelines for parents. They can enroll their infants and toddlers in high-quality day-care programs with no fear of harmful consequences. As long as the quality is good, other factors (e.g., the type of child care or the amount of time the child spends in child care) typically do not affect the mother-child attachment relationship.

> ## Parents can enroll their children in high-quality day care without fear of harmful consequences.

The results of the Early Child Care Study are reassuring for parents, who often have misgivings about their infants and toddlers spending so much time in the care of others. Nevertheless, they raise another, equally important question: What are the features of high-quality child care? That is, what should parents look for when trying to find care for their children? In general, high-quality child care has (Burchinal et al., 2000; Lamb, 1999; Rosenthal & Vandell, 1996):

- a low ratio of children to caregivers;
- a well-trained, experienced staff;
- low staff turnover;
- ample opportunities for educational and social stimulation; and
- effective communication between parents and day-care workers concerning the general aims and routine functioning of the day-care program.

Collectively, these variables do *not* guarantee that a child will receive high-quality care. Sensitive, responsive caregiving—the same behavior that promotes secure attachment relationships—is the real key to high-quality child care. Centers that have well-trained, experienced staff caring for a relatively small number of children are more likely to provide good care but the only way to know the quality of care with certainty is to see for yourself (Lamb, 1998).

Fortunately, employers have begun to realize that convenient, high-quality child care makes for a better employee. In Flint, Michigan, for example, child care was part of the contract negotiated between the United Auto Workers and General Motors. Many cities have modified their zoning codes so that new shopping complexes and office buildings must include child-care facilities, like those in the photograph. Businesses are realizing that the availability of excellent child care helps attract and retain a skilled labor force. With effort, organization, and help from the community and business, full-time employment and high-quality caregiving can be compatible. ■

Onset of Peer Interactions

First social relationships are usually with parents, but infants rapidly expand their social horizons. Peer interactions begin surprisingly early in infancy. Two 6-month-olds together will look, smile, and point at one another. Over the next few months, infants laugh and babble when with other infants (Hartup, 1983; Rubin, Bukowski, & Parker, 1998).

Beginning at about the first birthday and continuing through the preschool years, peer relations rapidly become more complex. **In a classic early study, Parten (1932) identified a developmental sequence that began with *nonsocial play*—children playing alone or watching others play but not playing themselves.** Later, children progressed to more elaborate forms of play with each child having a well-defined role. Today, researchers no longer share Parten's view that children move through each stage of play in a rigid sequence, but the different forms of play that she distinguished are useful nonetheless.

The first type of social play to appear—soon after the first birthday—is *parallel play*: youngsters play alone but maintain a keen interest in what other chil-

dren are doing. For example, each boy in the photo has his own toy but is watching the other play, too. During parallel play, exchanges between youngsters begin to occur. When one talks or smiles, the other usually responds (Howes, Unger, & Seidner, 1990).

Beginning at roughly 15 to 18 months, toddlers no longer just watch one another at play. **In *simple social play,* youngsters engage in similar activities, talk or smile at one another, and offer each other toys.** Play is now truly interactive (Howes & Matheson, 1992). An example of simple social play would be two 20-month-olds pushing toy cars along the floor, making "car sounds," and periodically trading cars.

Toward the second birthday, *cooperative play* begins: Now children organize their play around a distinct theme and take on special roles based on the theme. For example, children may play "hide-and-seek" and alternate roles of hider and finder, or they may have a tea party and alternate being the host and guest.

This rapid progression toward more complex play continues during the pre-school years, as we'll see in Module 10.1.

Check Your Learning

1. By approximately _____ months of age, most infants have identified a special individual, typically but not always the mother, as the attachment figure.

2. Around the world, _____ is the customary role for fathers.

3. Joan, a 12-month-old, was separated from her mother for about 15 minutes. When they were reunited, Joan would not let her mother pick her up. When her mother approached, Joan looked the other way and toddled to another part of the room. This behavior suggests that Joan has a(n) _____ attachment relationship.

4. _____ is the most common form of attachment worldwide.

5. The single most important factor in fostering a secure attachment relationship is _____ .

6. Adults with _____ representations of the attachment relationships with their own parents are most likely to have secure attachments with their own children.

7. An insecure attachment is likely when an infant receives poor-quality child care and _____ .

■ **Active Children** How do an infant's behaviors contribute to the formation
■■ of attachment? How do the caregiver's behaviors contribute?

Answers: (1) 8 or 9, (2) playmate, (3) avoidant, (4) Secure attachment, (5) responsive parenting that fosters an infant's trust and confidence, (6) autonomous, (7) insensitive, unresponsive parenting

Self-Concept

7.3

Self-Concept
└ Origins of Self-Recognition
└ Moving Beyond
   Self-Recognition

Learning Objectives

■ **When do infants first recognize themselves?**

■ **Following self-recognition, how do infants acquire a self-concept?**

Mark loves to look through photo albums with Meagan, his 20-month-old daughter. Until recently, Meagan seemed to treat photo albums like any other book that was filled with interesting pictures. In the past few weeks, though, she's begun to pay special attention to pictures of herself, often pointing to them while gleefully shouting, 'Meagan! Meagan!' It's obvious that something has happened to make Meagan much more interested in pictures of herself. Mark wonders what it is.

Child-development researchers would tell Mark that Meagan has taken the first step in the long journey toward a self-concept. **A person's *self-concept* refers to the attitudes, behaviors, and values that a person believes make him or her a unique individual.** Part of one teenage girl's self-concept is evident in her answer to the question "Who are you?"

I'm sensitive, friendly, outgoing, popular, and tolerant, though I can also be shy, self-conscious, and even obnoxious! I'd like to be friendly and tolerant all of the time. That's the kind of person I want to be, and I'm disappointed when I'm not. I'm responsible, even studious now and then, but on the other hand, I'm a goof-off, too, because if you're too studious, you won't be popular (Harter, 1990, p. 352).

As an adult, your answer is probably even more complex because, after all, most people are complex creatures. But how did you acquire this complex self-concept? We'll answer that question in this module, beginning with the origins of an infant's sense of self.

Origins of Self-Recognition

What is the starting point for self-concept? Following the lead of the nineteenth century philosopher and psychologist William James, modern researchers believe that the foundation of self-concept is the child's awareness that he or she exists. At some point early in life, children must realize that they exist independently of other people and objects in the environment and that their existence continues over time.

Measuring the onset of this awareness is not easy. Obviously, we can't simply ask a 3-year-old, "So, tell me, when did you first realize that you existed and that you weren't simply part of the furniture?" A less direct approach is needed, and the photo shows one route that many investigators have taken. Like many babies his age, the 9-month-old in the photo is looking at the face he sees in the mirror. Babies at this age sometimes touch the face in the mirror or wave at it, but none of their behaviors indicates that they recognize themselves in the mirror. Instead, babies act as if the face in the mirror is simply a very interesting stimulus.

How would we know that infants recognize themselves in a mirror? One clever approach is to have the mother place a red mark on her infant's nose; she does this surreptitiously, while wiping the baby's face. Then the infant is returned to the mirror. Many 1-year-olds touch the red mark on the mirror, showing that they notice the mark on the face in the mirror. By 15 months, however, an important change occurs: Babies see the red mark in the mirror, then reach up and touch *their* own noses. By age 2, virtually all children do this (Bullock & Lütkenhaus, 1990; Lewis & Brooks-Gunn, 1979). When these older toddlers notice the red mark in the mirror, they understand that the funny-looking nose in the mirror is their own.

Do you doubt that the mirror task shows an infant's emerging sense of self? Perhaps you think it tells more about an infant's growing understanding of mirrors than the baby's self-awareness. One way to examine this possibility would be to test infants who have never seen mirrors previously. Priel and deSchonen (1986) took this approach, testing infants from Israeli desert communities. These babies had never seen mirrors or, for that matter, virtually any reflective surfaces because they lived in tents. Nevertheless, the same developmental trend appeared in the desert infants as in a comparison group of infants living in a nearby city. No 6- to 12-month-olds in either group touched their noses after they saw the mark, some 13- to 19-month-olds did, and nearly all the 20- to 26-month-olds did.

We don't need to rely solely on the mirror task to know that self-awareness emerges between 18 and 24 months. During this same period, toddlers look more at photographs of themselves than at photos of other children. Like Meagan in the vignette, they also refer to themselves by name or with a personal pronoun, such as "I" or "me," and sometimes they know their age and their gender. These changes suggest that self-awareness is well established in most children by age 2 (Lewis, 1987).

As you might imagine, toddlers' self-awareness is quite fragile initially. To illustrate, in one study (Povinelli & Simon, 1998), 3-year-olds were videotaped playing a game, during which an experimenter surreptitiously placed a sticker on the child's head. A few minutes later children watched a videotape of themselves playing the game. Although almost all children recognized themselves in the videotape, fewer than half reached up to take the sticker off their head. (In contrast, virtually all 4-year-olds reached.) The results suggest that toddlers' self-awareness is not strongly linked across time but is, instead, focused largely on the present. Young children seemingly don't make the connection between the current self ("I am watching a videotape") and previous self ("just a few minutes ago, there was a sticker on my head").

Youngsters' growing self-recognition probably reflects cognitive development. For example, when children with Down syndrome achieve a mental age of approximately 18 months, they typically recognize themselves in the mirror task (Loveland, 1987a, b). Apparently, self-recognition requires cognitive skills that usually emerge sometime in the middle of the second year.

> Most children are self-aware by age 2: They recognize themselves in mirrors and photos, and refer to themselves by name or with *I* and *me*.

Moving Beyond Self-Recognition

Once self-awareness is established, children begin to acquire a self-concept. That is, once children fully understand that they exist and that they have a unique mental life, they begin to wonder who they are. They want to define themselves. How do children develop a self-concept?

Some important insights into the early phases of this process came from work by Laura Levine (1983), who studied 20- to 28-month-olds. This is the period when children are just beginning to become self-aware. Children were tested on several measures of self-awareness, including the mirror recognition task. They were also observed as they interacted with an unfamiliar peer in a playroom filled with toys. The key finding was that children who were self-aware were much more likely to say,

"Mine!" while playing with toys than children who were not yet self-aware.

Maybe you think these self-aware children were being confrontational in saying "Mine" as in, "This car is mine and don't even think about taking it." But they weren't. Actually, self-aware children were more likely to say positive things during their interactions with peers. Levine argued that "Claiming toys was not simply a negative or aggressive behavior, but appeared to be an important part of the child's definition of herself within her social world." (p. 547) In other words, the girl in the photo saying "Mine!" is not trying to deny the doll to the other girl; she is simply saying that playing with dolls is part of who she is.

As toddlers grow, their self-concepts rapidly move beyond possessions and become much more elaborate. We'll examine these changes more in Chapters 10, 13, and 16.

Check Your Learning

1. Apparently children become self-aware by age 2 because at this age they recognize themselves in a mirror and in photographs and they _____.

2. Children with Down syndrome don't recognize themselves on the mirror task until they have a mental age of approximately 18 months, which indicates that _____.

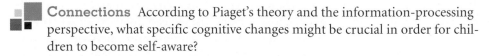

Connections According to Piaget's theory and the information-processing perspective, what specific cognitive changes might be crucial in order for children to become self-aware?

Temperament

Learning Objectives

■ What are the different features of temperament?

■ How do heredity and environment influence temperament?

■ How stable is a child's temperament across childhood?

■ What are the consequences of different temperaments?

> *Soon after Sueko arrived in the United States from Japan to begin graduate studies, she enrolled her 5-month-old son in day care. She was struck by the fact that, compared to her son, the European American babies in the day-care center were "wimps" (slang she had learned from American TV). The other babies cried often and with minimal provocation. Sueko wondered whether her son was unusually "tough" or whether he was just a typical Japanese baby.*

When you've observed young babies—perhaps as part of See for Yourself in Chapter 3—were some babies like Sueko's, quiet most of the time, while others cried often and impatiently? Maybe you saw some infants who responded warmly to strangers and others who seemed very shy. **An infant's consistent mood and style of behavior is referred to as *temperament*.** Temperament does not refer so much to *what* babies do as to *how* they do what they do. For example, all babies become upset occasionally and cry. However, some, like Sueko's son, recover quickly while others are very hard to console. These differences in emotion and style of behavior are evident in the first few weeks after birth and are important throughout life.

Let's start this module by looking at different ways that scientists define temperament.

What Is Temperament?

Alexander Thomas and Stella Chess (Chess & Thomas, 1986; Thomas, Chess, & Birch, 1968) pioneered the study of temperament. In 1956, they began the New York Longitudinal Study, tracing the lives of 141 individuals from infancy through adulthood. Thomas and Chess gathered their initial data by interviewing the babies' parents and asking individuals unfamiliar with the children to observe them at home. Based on these interviews and observations, Thomas and Chess evaluated the behavior of the 141 infants along the nine temperamental dimensions listed in the table at the top of page 202.

Using these nine dimensions, Thomas and Chess could place most infants into one of three groups. About 40 percent of the babies were categorized as "easy" babies. These infants were usually happy and cheerful, tended to adjust well to new situations, and had regular routines for eating, sleeping, and toileting. About 10 percent of the babies were categorized as "difficult." As you might imagine, in many respects they were the opposite of the easy babies: Difficult babies were often unhappy, did not adjust well to new situations, and had irregular routines for eating and sleeping.

7.4

Temperament

├─ What Is Temperament?

├─ Hereditary and Environmental
│   Contributions to
│   Temperament

├─ Stability of Temperament

└─ Temperament and Other
    Aspects of Development

Most infants in the New York Longitudinal Study had "easy," "difficult," or "slow-to-warm-up" temperaments.

Dimensions of Temperament in the New York Longitudinal Study	
Dimension	**Description**
Activity level	Amount of physical and motor activity in daily situations
Rhythmicity	Regularity in eating, sleeping, toileting
Approach/withdrawal	Response to a novel object (accepting vs. rejecting)
Distractibility	Ease with which ongoing activity is disrupted by competing stimuli
Adaptability	Ease with which the child adjusts to changes in the environment
Intensity of reaction	Energy level of the child's responses
Mood	Balance between happy and unhappy behavior
Threshold	Level of stimulation needed for the child to respond
Attention span and persistence	Amount of time devoted to an activity, particularly with obstacles or distractions present

TABLE 7–1

In addition, difficult babies tended to withdraw from novel experiences and they responded intensely to novel stimulation. About 15 percent of the babies were categorized as "slow-to-warm-up." Like difficult babies, slow-to-warm-up babies tended to be unhappy and did not adjust well when placed in new situations. But unlike difficult babies, slow-to-warm-up babies did not respond intensely and they tended to be relatively inactive. The remaining babies—roughly one-third—did not fit into any of the groups; in general, they were average on most of the nine dimensions.

Although the New York Longitudinal Study launched the modern study of infant temperament, not all investigators agree with Thomas and Chess's nine dimensions and three groups. For example, Arnold Buss and Robert Plomin (1975, 1984) propose that temperament involves three primary dimensions—emotionality, activity, and sociability. *Emotionality* **refers to the strength of the infant's emotional response to a situation, the ease with which that response is triggered, and the ease with which the infant can be returned to a nonemotional state.** At one extreme are infants whose emotional responses are strong, easily triggered, and not easily calmed; at the other extreme are infants whose responses are subdued, relatively difficult to elicit, and readily soothed. *Activity* **refers to the tempo and vigor of a child's movements.** Active infants are always busy, like to explore their environment, and enjoy vigorous play. Inactive infants have a more controlled behavioral tempo and are more likely to enjoy quiet play. *Sociability* **refers to a preference for being with other people.** Some infants relish contact with others, seek their attention, and prefer play that involves other people. Other infants, like the girl in the photo, enjoy solitude and are quite content to play alone with toys.

If you compare these three dimensions with the nine listed in Table 7.1, you'll see a great deal of overlap. For example, Buss and Plomin's emotionality dimension combines the intensity and threshold dimensions of the New York Longitudinal Study. In fact, the major theories of temperament include many of the same elements (Shiner, 1998).

Hereditary and Environmental Contributions to Temperament

Most theories agree that temperament reflects both heredity and experience. The influence of heredity is shown in twin studies: Identical twins are more alike in most aspects of temperament than fraternal twins. For example, Goldsmith, Buss, and Lemery (1997) found that the correlation for identical twins' activity level was 0.72 but the correlation for fraternal twins was only 0.38. In other words, like the youngsters in the photo, if one identical twin is temperamentally active, the other usually is, too. Goldsmith et al. (1997) also found that identical twins were more alike than fraternal twins on social fearfulness (shyness), persistence, and proneness to anger.

Recently, scientists looking for links between genes and temperament came up with a surprising finding: Infants and toddlers who are upset by novel stimulation (and who often become shy preschoolers) have narrower faces than youngsters who respond calmly to novel stimulation (Arcus & Kagan, 1995). This observation is provocative because the brain and the facial skeleton originate in the same set of cells in prenatal development. Thus, one fascinating hypothesis is that genes influence levels of hormones that affect both facial growth and temperament.

The environment also contributes to children's temperament. Positive emotionality—youngsters who laugh often, seem to be generally happy, and often express pleasure—seems to reflect environmental influences (Goldsmith et al., 1997). Conversely, infants more often develop intense, difficult temperaments when mothers are abrupt in dealing with them and lack confidence (Belsky, Fish, & Isabella, 1991).

Heredity and experience may also explain why Sueko, the Japanese mother in the vignette, has such a hardy son. The Cultural Influences feature tells the story.

CULTURAL INFLUENCES

Why Is Sueko's Son So Tough?

If you've ever watched an infant getting a shot, you know the inevitable response. After the syringe is removed, the infant's eyes open wide and then the baby begins to cry, as if saying, "Wow, that hurt!" Infants differ in how intensely they cry and in how readily they are soothed, reflecting differences in the emotionality dimension of temperament, but virtually all European American babies cry. It's easy to suppose that crying is a universal response to the pain from the inoculation, but it's not.

In stressful situations like getting a shot, Japanese and Chinese infants are less likely to become upset (Kagan et al., 1994). Lewis, Ramsay, and Kawakami (1993) found that most European American 4-month-olds cried loudly within 5 seconds of an injection, but only half the Japanese babies in their study cried. Furthermore, when Japanese and Chinese babies become upset, they are soothed more readily than European American babies. Lewis and his colleagues found that about three-fourths of the Japanese babies were no longer crying 90 seconds after the injection compared to fewer than half of the European American babies. The conclusion seems clear: Sueko's son appears to be a typical Japanese baby in crying less often and less intensely than the European American babies at his day-care center.

Why are Asian infants less emotional than their European American counterparts? Heredity may be involved. Perhaps the genes that contribute to emotionality are less common among Asians than among European Americans. But we can't overlook experience. Compared to European American mothers, Japanese mothers spend more time in close physical contact with their babies, constantly and gently soothing them; this may reduce the tendency to respond emotionally. ■

There's no question that heredity and experience cause babies' temperaments to differ, but how stable is temperament across infancy and the toddler years? We'll find out in the next section.

Stability of Temperament

Do calm, easygoing babies grow up to be calm, easygoing children, adolescents, and adults? Are difficult, irritable infants destined to grow up to be cranky, whiny children? The first answers to these questions came from the Fels Longitudinal Project, a study of many aspects of physical and psychological development from infancy. Although not a study of temperament per se, Jerome Kagan and his collaborators (Kagan, 1989; Kagan & Moss, 1962) found that fearful preschoolers in the Fels project tended to be inhibited as older children and adolescents.

Spurred by findings like this one, later investigators attempted to learn more about the stability of temperament. Their research shows that temperament is somewhat stable during the infant and toddler years. An active fetus is more likely to be an active infant, and is also more likely to be a difficult, unadaptive infant (DiPietro et al., 1996). Newborns who cry under moderate stress tend, as 5-month-olds, to cry when they are placed

in stressful situations (Stifter & Fox, 1990). And, as I mentioned before, infants who are frightened or upset by novel stimulation tend to be inhibited and less sociable as preschoolers (Kagan, Snidman, & Arcus, 1998).

Thus, evidence suggests that temperament is at least somewhat stable throughout infancy and the toddler years (Lemery et al., 1999). Of course, the links are not perfect. For example, some fearful infants became sociable preschoolers, and some infants who responded calmly to novel stimulation were inhibited as preschoolers.

Though temperament is only moderately stable during infancy and toddlerhood, it can still shape development in important ways. For example, an infant's temperament may determine the experiences that parents provide. Parents may read more to quiet babies but, like the father in the photo, play more physical games with their active babies. These different experiences, driven by the infants' temperaments, contribute to each infant's development, despite the fact that the infants' temperaments may change over the years. In the next section, we'll see some of the connections between temperament and other aspects of development.

Temperament and Other Aspects of Development

One of the goals of Thomas and Chess's New York Longitudinal Study was to discover temperamental features of infants that would predict later psychological adjustment. In fact, Thomas and Chess discovered that about two-thirds of the preschoolers with difficult temperaments had developed behavioral problems by the time they entered school. In contrast, fewer than one-fifth of the children with easy temperaments had behavioral problems (Thomas et al., 1968).

Other scientists have followed the lead of the New York Longitudinal Study in looking for links between temperament and outcomes of development, and they've found that temperament is an important influence on development. Here are some illustrative examples:

- Persistent children are likely to succeed in school whereas active and distractible children are less likely to succeed (Martin, Olejnik, & Gaddis, 1994).

- Shy, inhibited children often have difficulty interacting with their peers and often do not cope effectively with problems (Eisenberg et al., 1998; Kochanska & Radke-Yarrow, 1992).

- Anxious, fearful children are more likely to comply with a parent's rules and requests, even when the parent is not present (Kochanska, 1995).

- Extroverted, uninhibited toddlers are more likely to have accidents that cause injury (Schwebel & Plumert, 1999).

The Focus on Research feature shows that temperament is also related to a child's tendency to help people in distress.

> **Temperament is linked to school success, good peer relations, and compliance with parents' requests.**

FOCUS ON RESEARCH

Temperament Influences Helping Others

Who were the investigators and what was the aim of the study? When people are in obvious distress, some children readily step forward to help but others seem reluctant to help. Why are some children so helpful but others aren't? Shari Young, Nathan Fox, and Carolyn Zahn-Waxler (1999) argued that temperament may be part of the answer. Specifically, inhibited, shy youngsters may find it difficult to overcome their reticence to help another, particularly when they do not know the person and when the other person does not specifically request help. Young and her colleagues examined this hypothesis by studying inhibition and helping in 2-year-olds.

How did the investigators measure the topic of interest? The researchers videotaped children as they interacted with their mother and a stranger during free play. At some point during the session, the experimenter feigned injury (e.g., she pretended that she had caught her fingers in the clipboard). Later in the session, the mother also feigned injury (e.g., she pretended to bump into a chair). While feigning injury, the experimenter and the mother did not solicit the child's help in any way, either directly (e.g., by saying, "Help me, help me") or indirectly (e.g., by calling the child's name). Later, observers scored children's behaviors on several dimensions, including:

- Inhibition: The extent to which children avoided the experimenter, even when he began playing with a novel, attractive toy.

- Concerned expression: The extent to which children displayed obvious concern for the injured experimenter or mother, as shown by, for example, expressions of sadness.

- Helpful behavior: The extent to which children acted in ways apparently aimed at reducing distress, such as sharing a toy or stroking the injured body part.

Who were the children in the study? The study involved fifty 2-year-olds. Children were tested within two weeks of their second birthday.

What was the design of the study? This study was correlational because Young and her colleagues were interested in the relation that existed naturally between inhibition and helping. The study was actually longitudinal (children were also tested at 4 months) but I'm only describing the results from the second testing session, which took place at age 2 years.

Were there ethical concerns with the study? No. The children enjoyed most of the free play session. The experimenters and mothers "recovered" quickly from their feigned injuries—in approximately one minute—and no children were visibly upset by the injury.

What were the results? The graph shows some correlations between inhibition and (a) expressing concern and (b) helping behavior, separately for helping the mother and helping the experimenter. Let's begin with the correlations for mothers. Neither correlation is significant, which indicates that when interacting with their moms shy and outgoing children were equally likely to express concern and to provide help. The results differ for helping the experimenter. The correlation between inhibition and expressing concern is again small, indicating that shy and outgoing youngsters were equally likely to express concern when the experimenter feigned injury. However, the correlation between inhibition and helping was negative: Shy, inhibited 2-year-olds were less likely than outgoing 2-year-olds to help an experimenter who appeared to be hurt.

What did the investigators conclude? A young child's temperament helps to determine whether that child will help. When mothers and experimenters feigned injury, both shy and outgoing children noticed and were disturbed by their distress. Outgoing children typically translated this concern into action, helping both mothers and experimenters. In contrast, shy youngsters helped mothers but could not overcome their reticence to help an unfamiliar adult who did not specifically ask for help. Even though shy children see that a person is suffering, their apprehensiveness in unfamiliar social settings often prevents them from helping.

What converging evidence would strengthen these conclusions? One way to test the generality of these results would be to repeat the experiment, replacing the mother and adult experimenter with an older sibling and unfamiliar child who is the same age as the older sibling. The prediction is that shy and outgoing children would help the familiar older sibling but only outgoing children would help the unfamiliar older child. ■

Even more impressive are the findings from longitudinal studies showing that children's temperament predicts important aspects of adults' lives. In a study conducted in Sweden (Kerr, Lambert, & Bem, 1996), shy boys and girls married later than nonshy children. In addition, shy boys became fathers later than nonshy boys and shy girls were less educated than nonshy girls.

Although these findings underscore that temperament is an important force in infants' and toddlers' development, temperament rarely acts alone. Instead, the influence of temperament often depends on the environment in which children develop. To illustrate, let's consider the link between temperament and behavior problems. Infants and toddlers who temperamentally resist control—they are difficult to manage, often unresponsive, and sometimes impulsive—tend to be prone to behavior problems, particularly aggression, when they are older. However, more careful analysis shows that resistant temperament leads to behavior problems primarily when mothers do not exert much control over their children. Among mothers who do exert control—they prohibit, warn, and scold their children when necessary—resistant temperament is not linked to behavior problems (Bates et al., 1998).

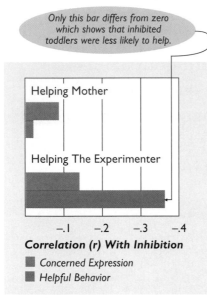

Only this bar differs from zero which shows that inhibited toddlers were less likely to help.

Helping Mother

Helping The Experimenter

−.1   −.2   −.3   −.4
Correlation (r) With Inhibition
■ *Concerned Expression*
■ *Helpful Behavior*

FIG 7–3

Similarly, young children who are anxious and fearful tend to be more compliant. But, again, careful analysis shows this is true only when parents encourage compliance with discipline that elicits mild distress (Kochanska, 1997). When a parent asks a child to pick up toys promptly or be punished, fearful, anxious children are more likely to comply than fearless children because fearful children worry about the possibility of punishment. However, when parents seek compliance by encouraging their children to cooperate, anxious temperament is no longer linked to compliance: If a parent asks a child to pick up toys because it will be helpful to the parent, fearful and fearless children are equally likely to comply.

Thus, the relation between temperament and compliance to a parent's request depends very much on how that request is framed. Only by considering these other factors can we understand links between temperament and development.

Check Your Learning

1. In their New York Longitudinal Study, Thomas and Chess identified infants with easy, difficult, and _____ temperaments.

2. Buss and Plomin's theory has three temperamental dimensions, including emotionality, _____, and sociability.

3. Compared to European American infants, Asian infants are calmer and _____.

4. An active fetus is more likely to be an active infant, and is also more likely to be a _____.

5. Research on the stability of temperament during infancy and the toddler years typically finds that _____.

6. Thomas and Chess found that by the time difficult babies had entered school, many had _____.

7. Although temperament is an important developmental force, the influence of temperament often depends on _____.

■ ■
■ **Nature and Nurture** What are the biological bases of temperament? How does the environment influence temperament? How do nature and nurture interact to influence temperament?

Answers: (1) slow-to-warm-up, (2) activity, (3) are soothed more readily when upset, (4) difficult, unadaptive infant, (5) temperament is only moderately stable, (6) developed behavioral problems, (7) the environment in which children develop

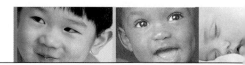

Chapter Critical Review

1. Explain why stranger wariness (Module 7.1) and attachment (Module 7.2) are adaptive responses.

2. How does an infant's or child's temperament (Module 7.4) affect the development of attachments (Module 7.2) and the development of social behavior (Module 7.3)? Give several examples of your own to demonstrate the interactions between the various factors discussed in the text.

3. Imagine that your best friend is the mother of a 3-month-old. Your friend is about to return to her job as a social worker, but she's afraid that she'll harm her baby by going back to work. What could you say to reassure her?

4. How might the sensory and perceptual skills described in Module 5.4 contribute to the formation of attachment between infants and caregivers?

For more review material, log on to www.prenhall.com/kail

See For Yourself

Arrange to visit a local day-care center where you can unobtrusively observe toddlers for several days. As you watch the children, see if you can detect the temperamental differences that are described in Module 7.4. Can you iden-tify an emotional child, an active child, and a social child? Also, notice how adults respond to the youngsters. See if the same behaviors lead to different responses from adults, depending on the child's temperament. See for yourself!

For More Information About . . .

 the development of the attachment relationship, read T. Berry Brazelton and Bertrand Cramer's *The Earliest Relationship* (Addison-Wesley, 1990), which illustrates the drama of attachment through lively case studies.

 temperament, visit the following Web site of a publisher of questionnaires and software used to measure temperament.
http://www.temperament.com

Key Terms

activity 202
attachment 189
autonomous attachment
  representation 194
avoidant attachment 192
cooperative play 197
dismissive attachment
  representation 194
disorganized (disoriented)
  attachment 192

emotionality 202
internal working model 193
parallel play 196
preoccupied attachment
  representation 194
nonsocial play 196
resistant attachment 192
secure attachment 192
self-concept 198
simple social play 197

sociability 202
social referencing 187
social smiles 185
stranger wariness 186
temperament 201

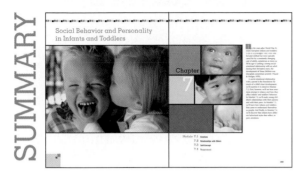

SUMMARY

7.1 Emotions

Basic Emotions

Scientists often use infants' facial expressions to judge when different emotional states emerge in development. The earliest indicator of happiness is the social smile, which emerges at about 2 months. Laughter appears at 4 months. Anger and fear are both evident by about 6 months of age. Fear first appears in infancy as stranger anxiety.

Complex Emotions

Complex emotions have an evaluative component and include guilt, embarrassment, and pride. They appear between 18 and 24 months, requiring more sophisticated cognitive skills than basic emotions like happiness and fear.

Recognizing and Using Others' Emotions

By 6 months, infants have begun to recognize the emotions associated with different facial expressions. They use this information to help them evaluate unfamiliar situations.

Regulating Emotions

Infants use simple strategies (e.g., looking away) to regulate emotions such as fear.

7.2 Relationships with Others

The Growth of Attachment

Attachment is an enduring social-emotional relationship between infant and parent. Many behaviors that contribute to the formation of attachment are biologically programmed. By about 6 or 7 months, infants have identified an attachment figure, typically the mother. In the ensuing months, infants often become attached to other family members, including fathers, whose usual role is playmate.

Quality of Attachment

Research with the Strange Situation, in which infant and mother are separated briefly, reveals four primary forms of attachment. Most common is a secure attachment, in which infants have complete trust in the mother. In avoidant relationships, infants deal with the lack of trust by ignoring the mother; in resistant relationships, infants often seem angry with her; in disorganized (disoriented) relationships, infants seem to not understand the mother's absence.

Children with secure attachment relationships during infancy often interact with their peers and more skillfully. Secure attachment is most likely to occur when mothers respond sensitively and consistently to their infants. Adults who have autonomous representations of attachment to their own parents are most likely to use the sensitive caregiving that promotes secure attachments.

Many U. S. children are cared for at home by a father or other relative, in a day-care provider's home, or in a day-care center. Attachment relationships in infants and toddlers are not harmed by such arrangements as long as the care is high quality and parents remain responsive to their children.

Onset of Peer Interactions

Children's first real social interactions, at about 12 to 15 months, take the form of parallel play, in which infants play alone while watching each other. A few months later, simple social play emerges, in which toddlers engage in similar activities and interact with one another. At about 2 years, cooperative play organized around a theme becomes common.

7.3 Self-Concept

Origins of Self-Recognition

At about 15 months, infants begin to recognize themselves in the mirror, one of the first signs of self-recognition. They also begin to prefer to look at pictures of themselves, to refer to themselves by name and with personal pronouns, and sometimes to know their age and gender. Evidently, by 2 years most children have the rudiments of self-awareness, but this early understanding is fragile.

Moving Beyond Self-Recognition

After toddlers become self-aware, they begin to acquire a self-concept. Possessions are one of the first elements in young children's self-concepts.

7.4 Temperament

What Is Temperament?

Temperament refers to stable patterns of behavior that are evident soon after birth. The New York Longitudinal Study suggests three temperamental patterns: easy, difficult, and slow-to-warm-up; other research suggests that the dimensions of temperament are emotionality, activity, and sociability. The major theories of temperament include many of the same elements, organized differently.

Hereditary and Environmental Contributions to Temperament

The major theories agree that both heredity and environment contribute to temperament. For many dimensions of temperament, identical twins are more alike than fraternal twins. Positive emotionality reflects environmental influences and difficult temperament is linked to abrupt parenting.

Stability of Temperament

Temperament is somewhat stable during infancy and the toddler years and moderately stable into childhood and adolescence. The correlations are not very strong, which means that, for many children, temperament does change as they develop.

Temperament and Other Aspects of Development

Many investigators have shown that temperament is related to other aspects of development. Difficult babies are more likely to have behavioral problems by the time they are old enough to attend school. Persistent children are more successful in school, shy children sometimes have problems with peers, anxious children are more compliant with parents, and inhibited children are less likely to help a stranger in distress. However, the impact of temperament always depends on the environment in which children develop.

Development in Infants and Toddlers
IN PERSPECTIVE

■ Continuity

Early development is related to later development but not perfectly

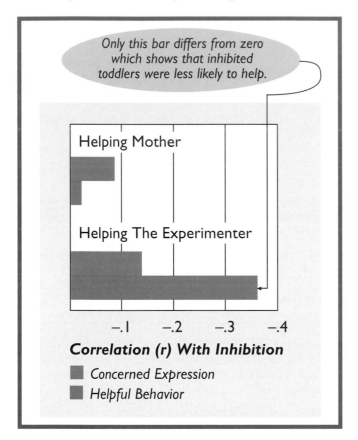

Only this bar differs from zero which shows that inhibited toddlers were less likely to help.

Helping Mother

Helping The Experimenter

−.1   −.2   −.3   −.4

Correlation (r) With Inhibition

■ *Concerned Expression*
■ *Helpful Behavior*

Remember the Hawaiian study in Chapter 4? This study showed that outcomes for at-risk infants are not uniform. When at-risk infants grow up in a stable, supportive environment, they become quite normal children. But when they grow up in stressful environments, they lag intellectually and socially. Similarly, SIDS is more likely to affect babies born prematurely and with low birth weight, yet, not all of these babies die of SIDS. When premature and low birth weight babies sleep on their backs, are not overheated, and their parents don't smoke, they're unlikely to die from SIDS. Traumatic events early in development, such as being born early or underweight, do not predetermine the rest of a child's life, but they do make some developmental paths easier to follow than others.

■ Nature and Nurture

Development is always jointly influenced by heredity and environment

In Chapter 3, we saw, again and again, how heredity and environment are essential ingredients in all developmental recipes, though not always in equal parts. In sickle cell disease, an allele has survival value in malaria-prone environments but not in environments where malaria has been eradicated. In PKU, persons who inherit the disorder become retarded when their dietary environment includes foods with phenylalanine but not when they avoid phenylalanine. And children with genes for normal intelligence develop below-average, average, or above-average intelligence, depending upon the environment in which they grow. In Chapter 5, we saw that physical growth is shaped both by hereditary factors and by an environment that includes adequate nutrition. Finally, in Chapter 7, it was clear that infants inherit mechanisms that facilitate language learning but that learning also depends critically on the child's language environment. Nature and nurture . . . development always depends on both.

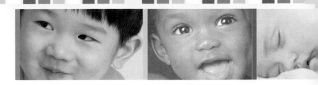

■ Active Children
Children help determine
their own development

This idea is the cornerstone of Piaget's theory. Beginning in infancy, children constantly try to make sense of what goes on around them. Their understanding—and the shortcomings therein—propels cognitive development to more sophisticated levels. Thus, as children take their developmental journeys, Piaget's child is a busy navigator, trying to understand the routes available and trying to decide among them.

Temperament also shows how children determine their own development. Temperament helps determine how parents, peers, and other adults respond to children. Parents and peers, for example, usually respond positively to temperamentally easy children. Peers get along better with easy children than with shy, inhibited children. Children's temperament does not alone dictate the direction of their development, but it makes some directions much easier to follow than others.

■ Connections
Development in different
domains is connected

Links between different domains are often evident when development is delayed or disrupted. In Chapter 3, for example, we saw that when children have Down syndrome, their motor skills develop more slowly, as does their cognitive skills. This, in turn, limits their social skills. The impact of malnutrition, described in Chapter 5, also shows these connections. Malnourished youngsters are often listless, which affects how their parents interact with them (parents are less likely to provide stimulating experiences). Less stimulation, in turn, slows the children's intellectual development. Finally, think about the impact of improved motor skills. Being able to locomote and to grasp gives children access to an enormous amount of information about their environment. They can explore objects that look interesting and they can keep themselves close to parents. Improved motor skills promote children's cognitive and social development, not to mention make a child's life more interesting! Physical, cognitive, social, and emotional development are linked: Change in one area almost always leads to change of some kind in the others.

Physical Growth in Preschool Children

Chapter 8

On April 13, 1997, millions of people around the world watched in awe as Tiger Woods won the Masters golf tournament in Augusta, Georgia. Tiger's performance was extraordinary. He was the youngest golfer, at age 21, ever to win the Masters and did so with the lowest score (270) and the biggest margin of victory (12 strokes) ever. In 2000, Tiger become only the fifth player ever to achieve golf's Grand Slam—winning the U.S. Open, the Masters, the Professional Golf Association, and the British Open tournaments. And he was the youngest player ever to accomplish this feat!

As astonishing as it may sound, Tiger's golf career began during the preschool years. As a 2-year-old, he showed his putting skill on TV, as a 3-year-old he shot 48 for 9 holes, and as a 5-year-old, he was featured in an article in *Golf Digest* magazine. Of course, Tiger's preschool accomplishments are extreme, but most youngsters show remarkable changes in their physical and motor development between 2 and 5 years of age, which we'll examine in Modules 8.1 and 8.2. In Module 8.3, we'll look at factors that promote healthy development as well as some threats to healthy development. Finally, in Module 8.4, we'll consider maltreatment of children.

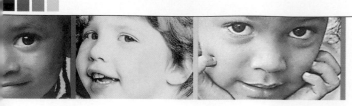

Physical Growth

8.1

Physical Growth

└ Body Growth

├ Brain Development

└ Sleep

■ **What changes take place in preschool children's growing bodies?**

■ **How does the brain become more powerful during the preschool years?**

■ **How much do preschool children sleep? What problems sometimes disrupt their sleep?**

Tomeka and LaToya both have 3-year-old sons. Tomeka's son is about 3 inches taller than average and LaToya's son is about 3 inches shorter than average. Tomeka loves to tease LaToya about this. "My boy is gonna be a basketball star but yours is gonna be the waterboy!" Latoya knows that Tomeka is just kidding but privately she wonders if her son is destined to be a shorter-than-average man.

The preschool years are a time of continued physical growth and individual differences in growth, like those that interest Tomeka and Latoya, become obvious. We'll begin this module by examining these changes, then look at changes in brain functioning. We'll end the module with an important contributor to children's growth, sleep.

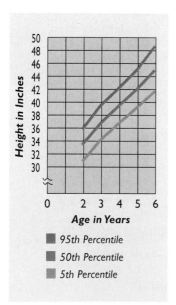

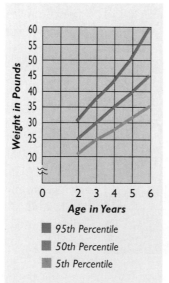

FIG 8–1

Body Growth

Growth during the preschool years is not nearly as rapid as during the infant and toddler years. The average 2-year-old boy or girl is about 34 inches tall and weighs 28 pounds; over the next 4 years, both gain about 2 to 3 inches and 4 pounds a year, so that as 6-year-olds they're about 44 inches tall and weigh 45 pounds.

As was true for infants and toddlers, the range of individual normal growth is amazing. The graphs show height and weight for children at the 5th and 95th percentiles, which represent the limits of what's considered normal growth; they also show height and weight for average children. (These are combined for boys and girls because gender differences in physical development are negligible during the preschool years.) A 4-year-old child in the 95th percentile for weight is half-again heavier (14 pounds) than a child in the 5th percentile. Both are normal but the difference is huge (particularly when you see it in real live 4-year-olds, not as an abstract point on a chart).

Because growth is stable during the preschool years, we can more accurately predict a child's height as an adult. Table 8-1 shows how to predict height at maturity for children at different ages.

Multipliers Used to Predict a Preschool Child's Height as an Adult		
Age (yrs)	Multiplier for Boys	Multiplier for Girls
2	2.06	2.01
3	1.86	1.76
4	1.73	1.62
5	1.62	1.51
6	1.54	1.43

Based on Garn, 1966

TABLE 8–1

Using these multipliers, I predicted the adult height of both of my sons within an inch. For example, Matt was 33 inches at age 2; his predicted height of 68 inches (2.06 x 33) was only an inch from his actual height of 69 inches. (Weight isn't nearly as easy to predict because it's based on more factors than height and is more variable through adulthood.) And, if LaToya uses these same multiplier with her son, she'll discover that he will probably (but not necessarily) be shorter than average as an adult.

Increases in height and weight are accompanied by changes in body shape and appearance that make the preschool child's body more mature looking. The legs begin to catch up to the trunk. As you can see in the diagram, older preschoolers have the body proportions of older children instead of the infant's top-heavy look. Also, preschoolers lose baby fat, which makes their bodies appear more slender and less like the chubby look of an infant.

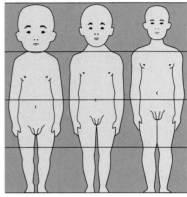

Newborn   2-year-old   6-year-old

FIG 8–2

Over the preschool years, muscles develop and more cartilage turns to bone. These changes help to make children stronger. However, as bone becomes harder it becomes more likely to break, not bend. Consequently, a hard fall that would have only bruised a toddler is more likely to fracture an older child's bone.

The preschool years also produce remarkable changes in children's teeth. Although teeth begin forming in prenatal development, the first tooth—usually one of the lower front teeth—does not appear until 6 or 10 months of age. By 1 year, many infants have 4 teeth and by age 3 children typically have all 20 primary (baby) teeth that are shown in the diagram. From 3 to 6 years is a quiet time on the teeth front, but at about 5 or 6 years children begin to lose primary teeth and permanent teeth begin to erupt.

Proper dental care should begin as soon as the first tooth appears. Parents can wipe these teeth with a clean cloth and, at about 18 months, graduate to a soft-bristled toothbrush. The American Academy of Pediatric Dentistry recommends that children see a dentist as soon as the first tooth emerges and visit a dentist twice a year thereafter for a checkup, cleaning, and, beginning at 2½ to 3 years, fluoride treatment. Because preschool children's teeth are usually widely spaced and unlikely to trap food, flossing isn't necessary. It may seem odd to devote so much time to teeth that are going to fall out anyway, but diseased primary teeth can harm the development of permanent teeth.

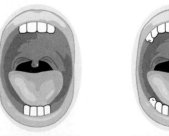

1-Year-Old's Teeth   2-Year-Old's Teeth

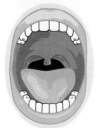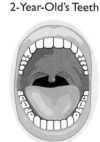

3-Year-Old's Teeth   Adult's Teeth

FIG 8–3

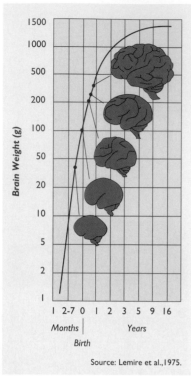

Source: Lemire et al., 1975.

FIG 8–4

Brain Development

The preschool years are a time of rapid growth in the brain. The chart shows increases in brain weight from birth to adolescence. You can see that the brain has achieved 80 percent of its mature weight by age 3 and more than 90 percent by age 5. To put these numbers in perspective, typical 5-year-old children have achieved only 30 percent of their overall body weight. Thus, the brain grows much more quickly than the body overall.

The preschool brain also changes in several ways that help it to operate more efficiently. Synaptic pruning—the weeding out of underused neurons—continues throughout the preschool years. As axons grow and reach their target, such as another neuron or a muscle, not all make functional contact. Those that don't are eliminated.

Myelinization—the wrapping of neurons with fat so they transmit information more rapidly—also progresses throughout these years. One region that becomes myelinated during the preschool years is the corpus callosum. As you can see in the diagram below, the corpus callosum consists of bundles of neurons that link the left and right hemispheres. Myelinization of the corpus callosum is important because it allows the hemispheres to communicate more effectively with each other (Witelson & Kigar, 1988). Neurons in the sensory and motor regions of the brain also become myelinated during these years, which helps to account for the young child's rapidly improving perceptual-motor coordination (Todd et al., 1995).

The brain also continues to become more specialized. Language-related skills such as speaking and comprehending speech become more localized in the brain's left hemisphere; skills associated with understanding emotions and comprehending spatial relations become more localized in the right hemisphere (Hellige, 1994). Such specialization allows the brain to operate more efficiently but at a price—the more specialized brain is less able to recover from injury.

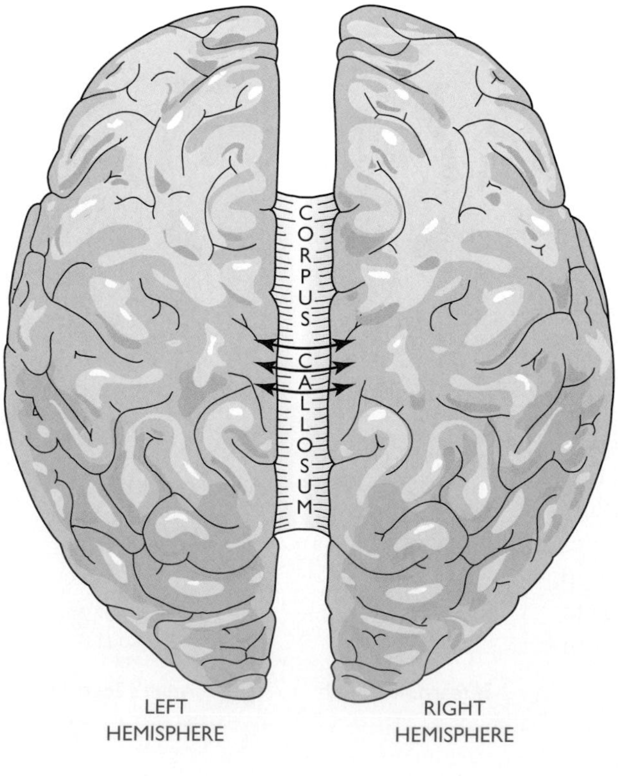

Sleep

Sleep is an important element in children's growth because, as I described in Module 5.1, most growth hormone (GH) is secreted when children are sleeping. In fact, sleep routines are well established by the preschool years. In the chart on page 217, you can see that 2-year-olds spend about 13 hours sleeping, compared to just under 11 hours for 6-year-olds. The chart also shows an important transition that typically occurs at about age 4. Most youngsters give up their afternoon nap and sleep longer at nighttime to compensate. This can be a challenging time for parents and caregivers who use naptime as an opportunity to complete some work or to relax.

Following an active day, most preschool children drift off to sleep easily. However, most children will have an occasional night when bedtime is a struggle. Furthermore, for approximately 20 to 30 percent of preschool children, bedtime struggles occur nightly (Lozoff, Wolf, & Davis, 1985). More often than not, these bedtime problems reflect the absence of a regular bedtime routine that's followed consistently. The Making Children's Lives Better feature shows how such a routine can avoid bedtime problems.

LEFT HEMISPHERE

RIGHT HEMISPHERE

CORPUS CALLOSUM

FIG 8–5

MAKING CHILDREN'S LIVES BETTER

Avoiding Bedtime Struggles

Getting children ready for bed can be a wonderful end to the day—a private, quiet time that's enjoyed by parent and child. But bedtime can also be frustrating and trying when children resist going to bed. The key to a pleasant bedtime is to establish a night-time routine that helps children to wind down from busy daytime activities. This routine should start at about the same time every night ("It's time to get ready for bed.") and end at about the same time (when the parent leaves the child and the child tries to fall asleep). A typical routine might include the following events:

- The child completes bathroom tasks, such as bathing, toileting, and brushing teeth.

- The child puts on sleepwear. (Children should have special clothing that they wear only at night so that wearing them is another cue to the child that it's bedtime.)

- The parent and child spend time together in quiet activities, such as the parent reading to the child, singing lullabies, or saying prayers.

- The parent checks that the child has the favorite blanket or stuffed animal, hugs the child, then leaves the room.

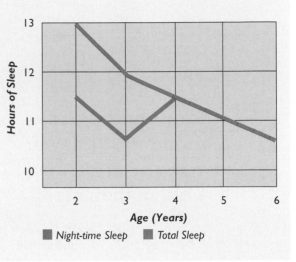

FIG 8-6

This nighttime routine may be anywhere from 15 to 45 minutes long, depending on the child. Also, as children get older, parents can expect them to perform more of these tasks independently. A 2-year-old will need help all along the way but, like the girl in the photo, a 6-year-old can do them alone. But remember to follow the routine consistently; this way children know that each step is getting them closer to bedtime and falling asleep.

After children are in bed, they sometimes cry or call out for parents—"I need a glass of water." "I'm scared." "It's too dark!" What should parents do? If they believe the child's request is legitimate—it concerns something that truly makes it hard for them to fall asleep—then parents should respond promptly. If, however, the child's request is a delaying tactic to avoid falling asleep (or being alone), it's better ignored. When parents respond to every bedtime request, they're reinforcing such requests (making them more likely that night and on subsequent nights). Of course, parents are fallible too and when they've had a hard day or have other tasks to finish before day's end, they may want to rush through the bedtime routine. Parents should resist the temptation. Obviously, since the point is to help children relax, rushing them from one step to the next is counterproductive. ■

After preschool children are asleep, they will sleep peacefully through most nights. **Many children have *nightmares*, vivid, frightening dreams occurring toward morning that usually wake the child.** Occasional nightmares are normal and need nothing more than on-the-spot parental comforting and reassurance. Should nightmares occur repeatedly or trouble the child during waking hours, parents should try to pinpoint the cause of the nightmare and, if need be, seek professional help (Mindell & Cashman, 1995).

Two other sleep disturbances are much rarer than nightmares but are quick to capture a parent's attention. **In *night terrors*, children appear to wake in a panicked state and are often breathing rapidly and perspiring heavily.** Nevertheless, children often don't respond to parents (because they are not fully awake), typically go back to sleep quickly, and, unlike nightmares, don't remember the episode the following morning. Night terrors usually occur early in the night and seem to be a by-product of wakening too rapidly from a deep sleep. Although often very frightening to parents, night terrors rarely indicate any underlying problem in children; parents can usually safely ignore the episode (Adair & Bauchner, 1993).

> Many children have nightmares; far fewer have night terrors and walk in their sleep.

A second sleep disturbance is sleep walking, in which during deep sleep children get out of bed and walk. For example, 4-year-old Ricky once sleepwalked into his sister's bedroom, opened the closet door, and squared off as if to pee into the closet. Fortunately, his mom got him directed to the bathroom just in time! The only real danger in sleepwalking is that children can injure themselves. Consequently, parents should wake sleepwalking children and get them back in bed. And, if children sleepwalk regularly, parents should be sure that the child's environment has no special hazards, such as unguarded stairways.

A final disturbance is bedwetting. Most U.S. children are toilet trained as 2- or 3-year-olds. Once trained, they are usually quite successful at staying dry during the day. At nighttime, however, many preschoolers—more boys than girls—wet the bed. For example, about 25 percent of 4-year-olds wet their bed occasionally (Wille, 1994). Such bedwetting in preschool children is perfectly normal; almost all preschool children grow out of the problem by age 5 or 6. If the problem persists, there a number of simple, effective methods to help children stay dry at night, such as bedwetting alarms that alert sleeping children when they are starting to urinate and exercises to help children control the sphincter muscles that regulate urination (American Psychiatric Association, 1994; Rappaport, 1993).

Check Your Learning

1. During the preschool years, boys' and girls' height and weight are _____.

2. A preschooler's body begins to look more adultlike because _____ and because they lose some baby fat.

3. Much of the cartilage in a preschooler's body changes to bone, which makes _____ more likely.

4. The first tooth typically emerges late in the first year and most children have all 20 primary teeth by approximately _____ years of age.

5. Changes in the brain between 2 and 5 years include pruning of unnecessary neurons, continued myelinization of more neurons, and _____.

6. An important transition in sleeping occurs at approximately age 4 when most children _____.

7. The most important step in preventing bedtime struggles is to _____.

8. Unlike nightmares, night terrors are fairly uncommon, they usually occur early in the evening, and _____.

Continuity Does change in height and weight during the preschool years provide evidence for continuity of development or discontinuity of development?

Answers: (1) about the same, (2) the legs catch up with the trunk, (3) fractures (broken bones), (4) 3, (5) greater specialization (localizing functions in specific brain regions), (6) no longer nap in the afternoon but sleep longer at night, (7) always follow a bedtime routine that allows a child to wind down gradually, (8) children don't remember them in the morning

Motor Development

8.2

Motor Development

├─ Gross-Motor Skills

├─ Fine-Motor Skills

├─ Handedness

└─ Gender Differences in
   Motor Skills

Learning Objectives

■ **How do children's gross and fine-motor skills improve during the preschool years? How do preschool children draw?**

■ **How similar are left- and right-handed children?**

■ **Do preschool boys and girls differ in their motor skills?**

Jessica and Kevin are 5-year-old fraternal twins. Their dad, Bill, isn't surprised that Kevin can throw a softball farther than Jessica can. But he is stunned (and, to be honest, a little worried) that Jessica can hop and skip farther and faster than Kevin. And Jessica usually dresses herself but Kevin needs help, particularly tying his shoes. Bill always thought his son would be the athlete of the two but it sure looks to him as if Jessica is the one with all the coordination.

Because preschool children get bigger, their muscles become stronger, and their brains become more powerful, motor skills show some amazing improvements during these years. We'll trace these improvements in this module. We'll see how gross- and fine-motor skills improve, then we'll look at handedness. We'll end by examining gender differences in motor development, where we'll learn whether Kevin and Jessica are typical for young boys and girls.

Gross-Motor Skills

Most infants have learned to walk by 18 months of age. Through the preschool years, children move beyond simple walking to running and jumping and other complex motor skills that require ever greater coordination and more precise timing of the components.

Children's growing skill is evident in their running and hopping. Most 2-year-olds have a hurried walk instead of a true run; they move their legs stiffly (rather than bending them at the knees) and are not airborn as is the case when running. By 5 or 6 years, children run easily, quickly changing directions or speed. Similarly, an average 2- or 3-year-old will hop a few times on one foot, typically keeping the upper body very stiff; by 5 or 6, children can hop long distances on one foot or alternate hopping first on one foot a few times, then on the other.

In addition, preschool children become much more proficient at coordinating the motions of their arms and legs. This is particularly apparent when youngsters try to throw or catch a ball. In the diagram on page 220, you can see that 2- and 3-year-olds throw using the forearm almost exclusively; in contrast, 6-year-olds step into a throw, rotating their upper body to help propel the ball. Similarly, a 2-year-old can catch a ball only if it happens to land squarely on the extended forearms; by age 6, children use their legs to move to the ball, then adjust their upper body and forearms to absorb the force of the ball.

Throwing   Catching

Age 2-3

Age 3-5

Age 6+

FIG 8–7

With their advanced motor skills, older preschoolers delight in unstructured play. Like the youngsters in the photo, they enjoy swinging, climbing over jungle gyms, and balancing on a beam. Some learn to ride a tricycle or ski downhill. Others begin to participate in organized sports: Many communities have soccer and baseball or softball programs in which the game is simplified to require only age-appropriate skills.

Fine-Motor Skills

Changes in fine-motor skill go hand-in-hand (pardon the pun) with the changes in gross-motor skills that I've just described. Preschool children become much more dextrous, able to make many precise and delicate movements with their hands and fingers. Greater fine-motor skill means that preschool children can begin to care for themselves. No longer must they rely primarily on parents to feed and clothe them; instead, they become increasingly skilled at feeding and dressing themselves. A 2- or 3-year-old, for example, can put on some simple clothing and use zippers but not buttons; by 3 or 4 years, children can fasten buttons and take off their clothes when going to the bathroom; most 5-year-olds can dress and undress themselves, except for tying shoes, which children typically master at about age 6.

Greater fine-motor coordination also leads to improvements in preschool children's printing. Part of this improvement comes because young children hold pens and pencils more efficiently. The Focus on Research feature tells how.

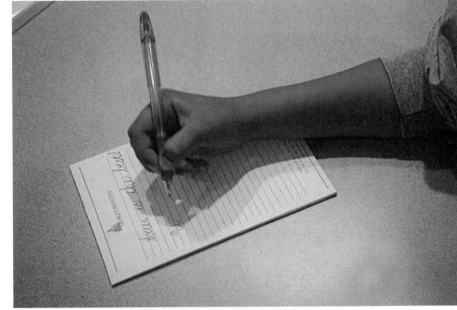

FOCUS ON RESEARCH

Learning to Grip a Pen

Who were the investigators and what was the aim of the study? When adults hold a pen or pencil, they usually rest it on the middle finger, then keep it there with the thumb and the index finger (top photo). In contrast, when they mix batter or paint, they are more likely to wrap the spoon tightly with the thumb and all four fingers (bottom photo). Each grip is well suited for its task because writing or drawing requires precise motions with relatively little strength but mixing requires more strength and less precision.

Tammy Greer and Jeffrey Lockman (1998) wanted to determine whether preschool children grip a pen adaptively. They hypothesized that 3-year-olds would use a greater variety of grips because they were more likely to still be experimenting with different ways to hold a pen. They also hypothesized that 3-year-olds might be more likely to vary their grip depending on the size of the pen or the type of writing task (e.g., drawing a vertical line versus drawing a horizontal line).

How did the investigators measure the topic of interest? The experimenter placed pieces of paper in the front of the participant. Each piece had a rectangle—placed vertically or horizontally—in one of the four corners of the paper. There was a dot at one end of the rectangle; participants were handed a felt-tip pen and asked to draw a line to the far side of the rectangle. Each participant drew a total of 16 lines. The participant's behavior was videotaped with two cameras—one in front and one above.

Who were the children in the study? Greer and Lockman tested 16 3-year-olds, 16 5-year-olds, and 16 college students.

What was the design of the study? The study was experimental because Greer and Lockman examined the impact of several variables on the way that participants gripped the pens. That is, the independent variables included the participant's age, the diameter of the pen (27 mm versus 73 mm) and whether the participant drew horizontal or vertical lines. The dependent variable was the participant's grip. The study was cross-sectional because it included participants at three ages (3 years, 5 years, adults), each tested once.

Were there ethical concerns? No. The procedures were harmless and the experimenters received written permission from the college students and from the parents of the preschool children.

What were the results? The study produced three main results. First, the size of pen and the type of writing task did not influence grips at any age. Second, use of the most efficient grip, labeled "Adult, 1-finger", in the graph, increased steadily with age, from 10 percent among 3-year-olds to more than 80 percent among adults. Third, as predicted, 3-year-olds were much more likely than the two older groups to be experimenting with different grips. A few used the mixing grip and a few used the efficient adult, 1-finger grip. Many more, however, used variants of the mature grip, either resting the pen on the ring finger and placing two fingers on top or resting the pen on the pinkie and placing three fingers on top. And about 25 percent of the 3-year-olds, who are not represented in the graph, used other idiosyncratic grips!

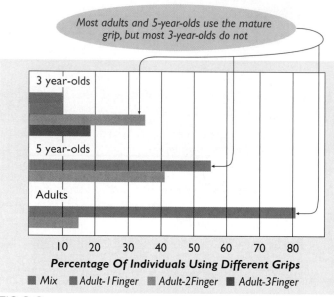

FIG 8–8

What did the investigators conclude? By age 5, children are well on their way to gripping pens in the effective manner that adults use. In contrast, 3-year-olds are still experimenting with different ways to hold a pen. As Greer and Lockman phrase it, "The variability that we observed in young 3-year-old children may indicate not just that the motor skill of writing is immature, but that these children are in the process of discovering forms of writing that maximize stability and efficiency." (p. 899)

What converging evidence would strengthen these conclusions? Greer and Lockman's study was cross-sectional and experimental. Their results would be strengthened by conducting research that was longitudinal and observational (not necessarily in a single study). That is, because 5-year-olds grip pens in the mature form but 3-year-olds do not, a longitudinal study from 3 to 5 years would establish the actual developmental paths that children follow as they learn to grip pens. They could also complement their work by doing observational research—videotaping children as they spontaneously gripped markers, pencils, pens, and paintbrushes. This sort of work, when combined with the present cross-sectional, experimental findings, would provide a very comprehensive account of the development of mature forms of holding a writing implement. ■

A better grip also improves preschoolers' drawing. Given a crayon or marker, most preschool children love to draw. My son Matt would spend hours drawing cars and other vehicles. Rhoda Kellogg (1970) analyzed millions of drawings by preschool children and found that they follow a common developmental pattern as they become progressively more complex.

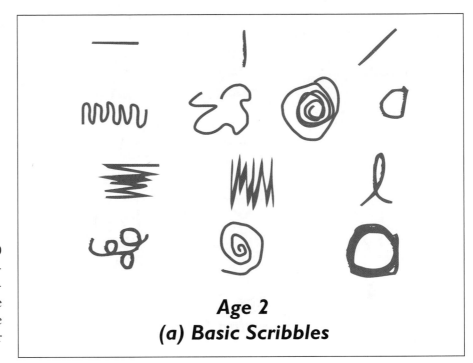

Age 2
(a) Basic Scribbles

At age 2, children scribble; about 20 different scribbles are common, including vertical, horizontal, zig-zag, and circular lines. At this age, children are delighted by the simple lines that are created just by moving a crayon or marker across paper.

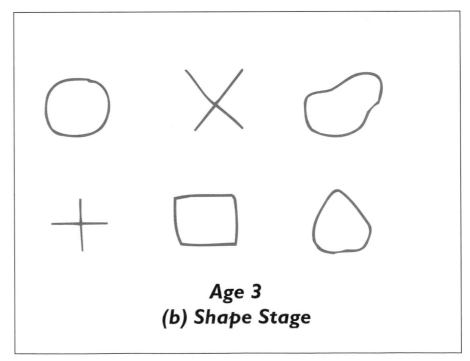

Age 3
(b) Shape Stage

At age 3, most children are in the *shape stage*, in which they draw six basic shapes: circles, rectangles, triangles, crosses, X's, and odd-shaped forms.

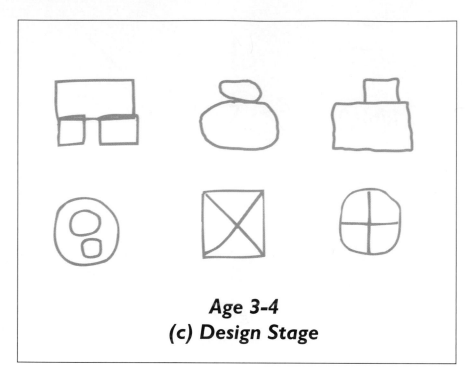

Age 3-4
(c) Design Stage

At age 3 or 4, most children move into the *design stage*, in which they combine the six basic shapes to create more complex patterns.

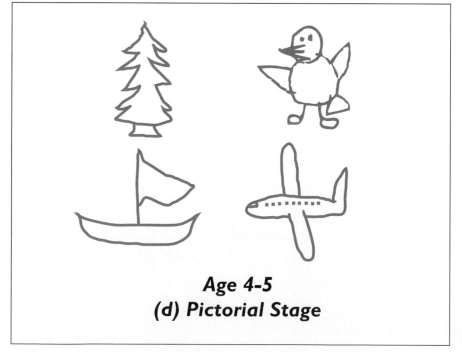

Age 4-5
(d) Pictorial Stage

At age 4 or 5, children typically enter the *pictorial stage* in which they begin to depict recognizable objects such as people, animals, plants, or vehicles.

This progression reflects more than the growth of fine-motor skills; it also reflects cognitive growth that allows children to understand more of what they see about them. Also, compared to younger preschool children, older preschool children often have a plan before they start to draw; they want to draw Mom or, like my son Matt, a car. And, older children are more concerned that their art be realistic, depicting objects accurately. Ironically, many accomplished artists strive to create styles that are not linked to representing reality (Winner, 1989).

Improved drawing skills are due to cognitive and motor development.

Handedness

By age 2, a child's hand preference is clear; most children—about 90 percent—use their right hand in fine-motor skills such as coloring, brushing teeth, or zipping a jacket. At this age, youngsters occasionally use their nonpreferred hand for tasks but by age 5 children typically use their nonpreferred hand only when the preferred hand is busy doing something else.

Movements of the right hand (as well as right arm and right leg) are controlled by regions in the brain's left hemisphere; movements of the left hand, arm, and leg are controlled by regions in the brain's right hemisphere. In right-handed people, the left hemisphere is often called the dominant hemisphere because the left hemisphere and right hand are associated with greater dexterity than the right hemisphere and left hand. Interestingly, although language functions (e.g., speaking and comprehension) are almost always localized in the left (dominant) hemisphere of right handers, the pattern is more varied in left handers. Most show the same pattern as right handers but language is localized in the right (dominant) hemisphere in some left-handed people and more evenly distributed between the two hemispheres in others (Coren, 1992; Hiscock & Kinsbourne, 1987).

Many adults view being left handed as a disadvantage. (In fact, *gauche*, which means awkward and *sinister*, meaning evil, are derived from foreign words that mean *left*.) It is true that the industrialized world favors right-handed people: desks, can openers, scissors, and guitars are designed for right handers, not left handers. Moreover, left-handed children and adults are more likely to have migraine headaches and allergies and are more likely to suffer from language-based problems such as stuttering and reading disability (Coren & Halpern, 1991). Yet, left-handed individuals like the child in the photo are often more talented artistically and spatially: Michelangelo, Leonardo da Vinci, and Pablo Picasso, for example, were all left handed. And, overall, left-handed children have greater mathematical talent. In one study of mathematically gifted children, 20 percent were left handed, which is about twice the number that would have been expected based on the number of left-handed children in the population (Bower, 1985).

Gender Differences in Motor Skills

Although preschool boys and girls don't differ much in height and weight, preschool boys tend to be a bit more muscular. Consequently, boys often have the advantage on motor tasks that rely on strength, such as running or throwing (Garai & Scheinfeld, 1968). And, boys tend to be more active (Eaton & Yu, 1986). During quiet activities such as story time, preschool boys are more often the ones who are squirming around or tickling each other while the girls are listening attentively.

When activities require that children coordinate the movements of their limbs—balancing on one foot, hopping, or skipping—young girls tend to be more skilled than boys. Similarly, in activities that require fine-motor coordination—fastening buttons, stringing beads on a thread, printing legibly—girls are usually more skilled than boys (Cratty, 1979). Thus, Jessica and Kevin, the twins in the opening vignette, are showing typical gender differences in motor skills.

Because young boys and girls don't differ much physically, gender differences in motor skill may reflect social encouragement to participate in gender stereotyped activities. A parent may buy a jump rope for a daughter and a football for a son. The daughter practices skipping rope, which improves her gross-motor coordination; like the boy in the photo, the son practices throwing the football, which strengthens the muscles in his arms and chest (Golombok & Fivush, 1994).

Check Your Learning

1. Not until approximately age _____ do children use their upper body while throwing and catching a ball.

2. At about 3 or 4 years, children's drawings often include _____.

3. In most left-handed persons language is localized in the left hemisphere, in others language is _____.

4. Left-handed children and adults tend to be better at art, spatial relationships, and _____.

5. Young boys are more active than girls and have an advantage on tasks that require _____.

■ ■
■ ■   **Nature and Nurture** How might an ethologist explain gender differences in motor skills? How might a social cognitive theorist explain these differences?

Answers: (1) 6 years, (2) complex patterns that are derived from basic shapes such as circles and rectangles, (3) either localized in the right hemisphere or represented equally in both hemispheres, (4) math, (5) greater strength

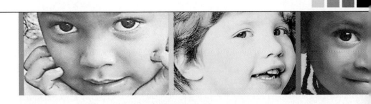

Health and Wellness

Learning Objectives

■ **What should preschool children eat to grow? What can parents do if their preschool children become picky eaters?**

■ **What illnesses and accidents are common during the preschool years?**

■ **How do preschool children react to being hospitalized?**

> *Chuck always loved having dinner with his 3-year-old daughter, but no longer. Kara turns up her nose at everything Chuck serves. She used to eat peanut butter sandwiches but now screams, "No! I hate them." She used to love mashed potatoes but now just pushes them around into little piles on her plate. Mealtimes have become confrontations. Chuck worries that Kara isn't getting enough to eat and he wonders what he can do to restore Kara's interest in eating.*

Compared to many childhood tasks, physical growth seems easy. To paraphrase a famous line from the movie *Field of Dreams*, "If you feed them, they will grow." But of course it's not this simple. As we'll see in the first part of this module, *what* children are fed matters a great deal. We'll also learn what Chuck can do to coax Kara into eating more. In the second part of this module, we'll look at some of the factors that can threaten healthy development in preschool children.

Nutrition

The foods that children eat and the liquids they drink fuel the growth that I described in Module 8.1. Because preschoolers grow more slowly than infants and toddlers, they need to eat less per pound than before. One rule of thumb is that preschoolers should consume about 40 calories per pound of body weight, which works out to be roughly 1,500 to 1,700 calories daily for many preschool children.

More important than the sheer number of calories, however, is a balanced diet that includes all five major food groups. Table 8-2 shows a healthy diet that provides adequate calories and nutrients for preschool children.

Eating to Meet Preschoolers' Nutritional Needs		
Group	**Number of Servings**	**What Counts as a Serving?**
Grains	6	1 slice of bread, 1 cup of cereal
Vegetables	3	1 cup of raw leafy vegetables, 3/4 cup of vegetable juice
Fruits	2	1 medium apple, 2 cups of canned fruit
Milk	2	1 cup of milk, $1\frac{1}{2}$ ounces of natural cheese
Meat and beans	2 (5 ounces total)	2 to 3 ounces of cooked lean meat, 2 tablespoons of peanut butter

From USDA (2000)

TABLE 8-2

The servings listed in the table are definitely not a complete a list of the foods good for young children; they simply are examples of healthy choices (and quantities) for children. Many, many other foods could have been listed, too. A healthy diet doesn't mean that children must eat the same foods over and over again.

Not only does a healthy diet draw upon all five food groups, it also avoids too much sugar and, especially, too much fat. For preschool children, no more than approximately 30 percent of the daily caloric intake should come from fat, which works out to be roughly 500 calories from fat. Unfortunately, too many preschool children, like the ones in the photo, become hooked on fast-food meals, which are notoriously high in fat. A Whopper, fries, and shake has nearly 600 calories from fat, 100 more than children should consume all day! Excessive fat intake is the first step toward obesity (which I'll discuss in Module 11.1), so parents need to limit their preschool children's fat intake (Whitaker et al., 1997).

Encouraging preschool children to eat healthy foods is tough for parents because, as I mentioned in Module 5.1, some preschoolers become notoriously picky eaters. Like Kara in the opening vignette, they often seem to refuse virtually everything, especially nutritious foods that health-conscious parents want them to eat. Parents should not be overly concerned about this finicky period. Although some children do eat less than before (in terms of calories per pound), virtually all picky eaters get adequate food for growth.

Nevertheless, picky-eating children can make mealtime miserable for all. What's a parent to do? Experts (Leach, 1991; American Academy of Pediatrics, 1992) recommend several guidelines for encouraging children to be more open-minded about foods and to deal with them when they aren't:

> ## Parents should not be overly concerned when their preschool children become picky eaters.

- When possible, allow children to pick among different healthy foods (e.g., milk versus yogurt).
- Allow children to eat foods in any order they want.
- Offer children new foods one at a time and in small amounts; encourage but don't force children to eat new foods.
- Don't force children to clean their plates.
- Don't spend mealtimes talking about what the child is or is not eating; instead, talk about other topics that interest the child.
- Never use food to reward or punish children.

By following these guidelines, mealtimes can be pleasant and children can receive the nutrition they need to grow.

Threats to Children's Development

If you ask a group of parents about their preschool children's health-related problems, you're likely to get a long list. Some items on the list, like colds and coughs, are mainly annoying. (Many parents would claim that a runny nose is a permanent state in their preschool children!) Others on the list are much more serious, sometimes requiring hospitalization. In the next few pages, we'll look at the gamut of illness and injuries that affect preschool children's health.

Minor Illnesses. Most preschoolers are all too familiar with coughs, runny noses, and colds. The average preschool child has 7 or 8 colds a year. Preschool children, like the youngster in the photo, are particularly vulnerable to colds (and other respiratory illnesses) because their lungs are still developing. Fortunately, most children are only ill for a few days and rarely need to visit a health-care professional. And, the cloud of minor illness actually has a silver lining—two of them, in fact. First, minor illness helps the child's body to develop immunity to more serious diseases. Second, by being ill and recovering, young children begin to learn about the way that their bodies work and may be better prepared to deal with future, more serious illness (Parmalee, 1986). In other words, when children spend a day or two in bed, feeling lousy, then recover, they gain insight into the nature of illness and healing; consequently, they are less frightened later by other more serious illnesses that make them feel worse, for longer periods of time.

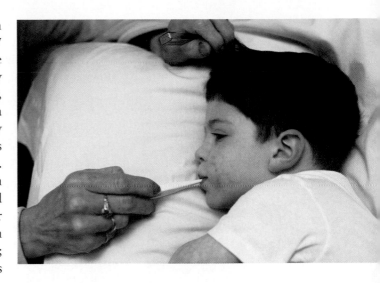

Chronic Illnesses. Many children suffer from chronic illnesses, such as asthma, diabetes, and cancer. Unlike colds, flu, and measles, with chronic illness children are not simply bedridden for a few days, before recovering to full health. Instead, they must contend with their illness routinely; it is part of the fabric of their daily living, like eating and sleeping. Children with leukemia must receive periodic treatments of chemotherapy over 2 to 3 years. Children with diabetes, for example, need daily injections of insulin. The Real Children feature shows how diabetes affects the life of one 4-year-old.

REAL CHILDREN

David Lives with Diabetes

David was diagnosed with Type I (juvenile) diabetes just after his second birthday. David's body does not produce insulin, a hormone used to convert sugar in the blood into energy. David is now 4. His parents give him three shots of insulin each day. Like the parent in the photo, they prick his finger several times daily to check the level of sugar in his blood. David's parents constantly watch for signs that his blood sugar may be low (e.g., trembling or dizziness) or that his blood sugar may be too high (e.g., increased thirst, frequent urination) and they often give him snacks between meals to help regulate his blood sugar.

In other respects, however, David's life is typical for 4-year-olds. He goes to preschool every morning, he's constantly playing with his next-door neighbor, and he often argues with his older sister. Although he knows that he has diabetes and sometimes worries about it, most of the time he enjoys just being a regular kid. ■

Fortunately, most chronic illnesses are uncommon. An exception is asthma, the most common chronic disease of childhood, affecting approximately 5 to 6 million American children. In asthma, passages in the lungs that carry air become inflamed temporarily, narrowing them and interfering with their ability to transport air. Allergies, smoke, a cold, pet hair, mold, and dust mites can all trigger asthma attacks, which may be as brief as a few minutes or as long as several days. An attack can become life-threatening when the flow of oxygen is blocked completely. Severe asthma attacks account for nearly a half-million visits by children to hospital emergency rooms and kill a few hundred children and adolescents each year.

Asthma has no cure but when managed effectively, there are virtually no limits to what children with asthma can do, including vigorous physical activities. To manage asthma effectively, the National Institutes of Health (1997) recommends the following guidelines:

- Visit a physician every 6 months.
- Take proper medications for long-term control and quick relief and, if using a medicine that is inhaled, be sure to use the inhaler properly.
- Monitor your health and watch for symptoms that your asthma is getting worse.
- Avoid things that may trigger an asthma attack, such as tobacco smoke, dust mites, animal hair, and mold.

By following these guidelines, most children with asthma learn that they can control the disease and that they can do almost everything that their friends do. Parents contribute too; when parents adjust to asthma (and other chronic diseases) as a problem that can be solved, their children are better able to handle the challenges of their chronic illness (Kazak et al., 1997).

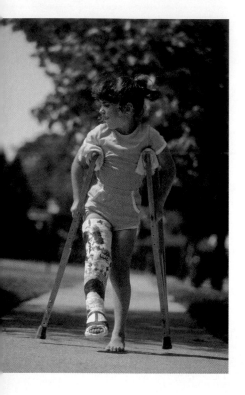

Accidents. Preschool children are often eager to explore the unknown but often lack the cognitive skills to determine whether they are endangering themselves. As a consequence, many preschoolers, like the youngster in the photo, are hurt in accidents. Many childhood accidents are falls or cuts that produces bruises, some bleeding, and a few tears but no lasting harm. However, some are more serious. In fact, accidents are the leading cause of death in preschool children. Thousands of young children die every year in auto accidents, drownings, and fires.

The term *accident* implies that the event happened by chance and no one was to blame. In reality, many of the accidents that hurt or kill young children can be foreseen and could be prevented. The table lists some of the common accidents that hurt young children, along with some effective methods of prevention. Following these practices is easy and substantially reduces the chance that a child will be harmed in an accident.

Ways to Reduce Accident Risk for Young Children	
Type of Accident	**Ways to Reduce Risk**
auto accidents	Children should always ride in an approved car seat that has been properly installed in the back seat.
drowning	Children should never be left unattended near sources of water, particularly swimming areas but also bathtubs and buckets filled with water.
poisoning	Keep all medications in child-resistant containers; keep them and all other harmful substances (e.g., animal poisons, cleansers) out of children's way (out of reach, locked, or both).
cycling	When a child rides in a seat on a bicycle, be sure that the seat is installed properly and that the child is strapped in securely and wearing a helmet. When riding a tricycle or bicycle, the child should stay off streets, be supervised by a parent, and wear a helmet.
firearms	All firearms should be locked, with ammunition stored in a separate locked location. Children should not have access to keys.
fires	Install smoke detectors and check them regularly. Keep fire extinguishers handy. Tell children how to leave the house in case of a fire and practice leaving the house.

TABLE 8–3

Environmental Contributions to Illness and Injury. Not all children are equally prone to illness and injury. Instead, some are more likely to be ill and others are more injury-prone. Why? Stress is one factor. Many children experience serious stress at some point in their lives—coping with a move to an unfamiliar neighborhood, their parents' marital conflicts, or the death of a friend or relative. In these circumstances, children are more likely to be ill, perhaps because stress reduces their resistance to disease (Beautrais, Fergusson, & Shannon, 1982). And when parents are under stress, their children are at greater risk for illness and injury. Caught up in their own stress, parents may be less cautious in dealing with hazardous situations or they may pay less attention to the symptoms of their children with chronic illness (Craft, Montgomery, & Peters, 1992).

> Children are more prone to illness and injury when they live in stress and poverty.

More important than stress is poverty. For children living in poverty, health-related problems often begin before birth, when their mothers receive inadequate prenatal care and have an inadequate diet. After birth, many youngsters living in poverty do not eat adequately. Because their families cannot afford it, they often do not get regular medical care, such as immunizations, which makes them more susceptible to disease (Children's Defense Fund, 1997). And, of course, poverty is stressful for children and parents alike, accentuating the impact it has on children's health.

Among industrialized countries, the United States is unusual in not guaranteeing basic health care for young children. In many European countries, for example, health care is available to all children for little or no cost (Lie, 1990; Verbrugge, 1990). In these countries, healthy disease-free growth is seen in the same light as an education—a fundamental right of all children, regardless of income or race. Regrettably, most U.S. children have no such guarantee when it comes to health care; the country bears a substantial medical, psychological, and economic burden as a consequence (Children's Defense Fund, 1997).

Impact of Hospitalization. Sometimes children with asthma and other chronic illnesses must be hospitalized to receive the care they need. Few adults enjoy being hospitalized, so it's no surprise that young children often find the experience difficult. Preschool children are usually upset at being separated from parents (sometimes for the first time). They're often afraid of what's going to happen to them in this unfamiliar setting and they dislike the lack of control that's customary in the hospital environment (Whaley & Wong, 1991).

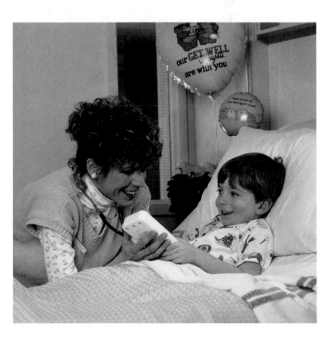

Working together, parents and health-care professionals can make a hospital stay less traumatic for children. Parents can be encouraged to spend as much time as possible with their hospitalized child. Some hospitals even allow rooming in—parents can sleep in the same room with their child. And, for times when a parent can't be present, a warm and caring nurse like the one in the photo can be assigned to the child to act as a parental substitute. Health-care professionals should explain—in simple, straightforward language—what's going to happen in the hospital so that children know what to expect. And health-care professionals can allow children some choices—what to eat, when to bathe, when to do physical therapy—so they don't feel powerless in the hospital environment (Whaley & Wong, 1991). By addressing preschool children's concerns in this manner, the hospital stay can become much less stressful for the child.

Check Your Learning

1. For healthy growth, most preschoolers need about 1,500 to 1,700 calories per day, taken from _____.

2. By allowing children to pick from different foods, to eat in any order they want, and to eat new foods in small amounts, parents can _____.

3. One benefit of minor illness is that the child's body begins to develop immunities to more serious diseases; another benefit is that _____.

4. The essential elements in managing asthma effectively are routine visits to a physician, proper medication, monitoring asthma symptoms, and

   _____.

5. _____ are the leading cause of death in preschool children.

6. Children are more prone to injury and illness when they experience stress and when they _____.

7. Hospitalization is difficult for children because they dislike being separated from their parents, they're afraid of what might happen to them, and

   _____.

Connections Environmental factors such as family stress and poverty place some children at greater risk for injury. How might a child's temperament (discussed in Module 7.4) also make some preschool children more susceptible to injury?

Answers: (1) the five basic food groups, (2) make it less likely that their preschoolers will become picky eaters, (3) children learn more about the nature of illness and recovery, preparing them for future, more serious diseases, (4) avoiding things that might trigger an asthma attack, such as smoke, (5) Accidents, (6) live in poverty, (7) they dislike the lack of control that's customary in hospitals

Child Neglect and Maltreatment

Learning Objectives

■ **What are the consequences of child maltreatment?**

■ **What factors cause parents to mistreat their children?**

■ **How can maltreatment be prevented?**

The first time 5-year-old Max came to preschool with bruises on his face, he said he'd fallen down the basement steps. When Max had similar bruises a few weeks later, his teacher spoke with the school's director, who contacted local authorities. They discovered that Max's mother hit him with a paddle for even minor misconduct; for serious transgressions, she beat Max and made him sleep alone in an unheated, unlighted basement.

Unfortunately, cases like Max's occur far too often in modern America. Maltreatment comes in many forms (Goodman et al., 1998). The two that often first come to mind are physical abuse involving assault that leads to injuries and sexual abuse involving fondling, intercourse, or other sexual behaviors. Another form of maltreatment is neglect, not giving children adequate food, clothing, or medical care. And, as the poster reminds us, children can also be harmed by psychological abuse—ridicule, rejection, and humiliation.

The frequency of these various forms of maltreatment is difficult to estimate because so many cases go unreported. According to the National Center on Child Abuse and Neglect (1997), approximately 1 million children annually suffer maltreatment or neglect. About 50 percent are neglected, about 25 percent are abused physically, and about 15 percent are abused sexually (National Center on Child Abuse and Neglect, 1997).

We'll begin this module by looking at the consequences of maltreatment, then look at some causes, and, finally, examine ways to prevent maltreatment.

Consequences of Maltreatment

You probably aren't surprised to learn that the prognosis for youngsters like Max is not very good. Some, of course, suffer permanent physical damage. Even when there is no lasting physical damage, the children's social and emotional development is often disrupted. They tend to have poor relationships with peers, often because they are too aggressive (Bolger, Patterson, & Kupersmidt, 1998; Parker & Herrera,

1996). Their cognitive development and academic performance is also disturbed. Abused youngsters tend to get lower grades in school, score lower on standardized achievement tests, and be retained in a grade rather than promoted. Also, school-related behavior problems are common, such as being disruptive in class (Goodman et al., 1998; Trickett & McBride-Chang, 1995).

Adults who were abused as children often experience emotional problems such as depression or anxiety, are more prone to think about or attempt suicide, and are more likely to abuse spouses and their own children (Malinosky-Rummell & Hansen, 1993). In short, when children are maltreated, virtually all aspects of their development are affected and these effects do not vanish with time.

Some children are less affected by maltreatment than others. In the Looking Ahead feature, I describe some factors that seem to protect children from long-term harm from abuse.

LOOKING AHEAD

Factors that Reduce the Impact of Child Abuse

Childhood sexual abuse is tragic and many children who are abused sexually suffer long-term harm. Lynsky and Fergusson (1997), for example, found that when children were abused sexually, approximately 75 percent of these children as adults had psychiatric disorders or adjustment difficulties, such as depression, anxiety, and substance abuse. However, 25 percent reported no problems of this sort. Lynsky and Fergusson (1997) tried to determine why these individuals escaped the harm that was typical for sexual abuse. They discovered two factors: One was the adolescent peer group and the other was the relationship with the father. Specifically, sexually abused children were more likely to avoid long-term difficulties when (a) as adolescents they avoided delinquent or substance-abusing peers, and (b) their father was supportive, caring, and nurturant. Thus, the type of peers and the type of father-child relationship can help to mitigate the long-term consequences of childhood sexual abuse. ∎

Causes of Maltreatment

Why would a parent abuse a child? Maybe you think parents would have to be severely disturbed or deranged to harm their own flesh and blood. Not really. Today, we know that the vast majority of abusing parents cannot be distinguished from nonabusing parents in terms of standard psychiatric criteria (Wolfe, 1985). That is, adults who mistreat their children are not suffering from any specific mental or psychological disorder, and they have no distinctive personality profile.

Modern accounts of child abuse no longer look to a single or even a small number of causes. Instead, a host of factors put some children at risk for abuse and protect others; the number and combination of factors determine if the child is a likely target for abuse (Belsky, 1993). Let's look at three of the most important factors: cultural context, the parents, and the children themselves.

Children are most likely to be abused when their culture condones physical punishment, their parents lack effective child-rearing skills, and their own behavior is often aversive.

The most general category of contributing factors has to do with cultural values and the social conditions in which parents rear their children. For example, a culture's view of physical punishment contributes to child maltreatment. Many countries in Europe and Asia have strong cultural prohibitions against physical punishment. It simply isn't done and would be viewed in much the same way we would view an American parent who punished by not feeding the child for a few days. In Sweden, for example, spanking is against the law. But the scene in the photo, a mother spanking her child, is common in the United States. Countries that do not condone physical punishment tend to have lower rates of child maltreatment than the United States (Zigler & Hall, 1989).

What social conditions seem to foster maltreatment? Poverty is one: Maltreatment is more common in families living in poverty, in part because lack of money increases the stress of daily life (Goodman et al., 1998). When parents worry if they can buy groceries or pay the rent, they are more likely to punish their children physically instead of making the extra effort to reason with them.

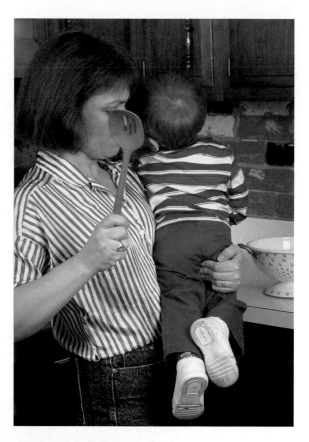

Social isolation is a second force. Abuse is more likely when families are socially isolated from other relatives or neighbors. When a family like the one in the bottom photo lives in relative isolation, it deprives the children of adults who could protect them and deprives parents of social support that would help them cope with life stresses (Garbarino & Kostelny, 1992; Korbin, 1987).

Work by Claudia Coulton and her colleagues (1995) shows the influence of poverty and isolation on child maltreatment. They obtained data from 177 U.S. census tracts in Cleveland, Ohio. (A typical census tract includes about 2,000 residents.) Child maltreatment was more common in census tracts that were poorer, as indicated by more people living in poverty, higher unemployment, more vacant housing, and greater population loss. In addition, maltreatment was more common in census tracts that had fewer elderly residents, a greater ratio of children to adults, and fewer males. Thus, maltreatment is more common in neighborhoods that are poor and that have few other adults to help with child rearing. Apparently, maltreatment often occurs when parents are unable to cope with the financial and psychological burdens that child rearing entails.

Social factors like those studied by Coulton and her colleagues (1995) clearly contribute to child abuse, but they are only part of the puzzle. Although maltreatment is more common among families living in poverty, it does not occur in a majority of these families and it does occur in middle-class families, too. Consequently, we need to look for additional factors to explain why abuse occurs in some families but not others.

Today, we know that parents who abuse their children

- were, as children, sometimes maltreated themselves (Simons et al., 1991).
- have high expectations for their children but do little to help them achieve these goals (Trickett et al., 1991).
- rely upon physical punishment to control their children (Trickett & Kuczynski, 1986).

Overall, then, the typical abusing parent often had an unhappy childhood and has limited understanding of effective parenting techniques.

Cultural, parental, and child factors all contribute to child abuse.

To place the last few pieces in the puzzle, we must look at the abused children themselves. Children may inadvertently, through their behavior, bring on their own abuse. In fact, infants and preschoolers are more often abused than older ones. Why? They are easier targets of abuse and they are less able to regulate aversive behaviors that elicit abuse (Belsky, 1993). You've probably heard stories about a parent who shakes a baby to death because the baby won't stop crying. Because younger children are more likely to cry or whine excessively—behaviors that irritate all parents sooner or later—they are more likely to be the targets of abuse.

For much the same reason, children who are frequently ill are more often abused. When children are sick, they're more likely to cry and whine, annoying their parents. Also, when children are sick, they need medical care, which means additional expense, and they can't go to school, which means that parents must arrange alternate child care. By increasing the level of stress in a family, sick children can inadvertently become the targets of abuse (Sherrod et al., 1984).

Stepchildren form another group at risk for abuse (Daly & Wilson, 1996). Just as Cinderella's stepmother doted on her biological children but abused Cinderella, stepchildren are more at risk for abuse and neglect than biological children. Adults are less invested emotionally in their stepchildren and this lack of emotional investment leaves stepchildren more vulnerable.

Obviously the children are not at fault and do not deserve the abuse. Nevertheless, normal infant or child behavior can provoke anger and maltreatment from some parents.

Thus, cultural, parental, and child factors all contribute to child maltreatment. These are summarized in the table.

◼◼◼◻ SUMMARY TABLE

Factors that Contribute to Child Abuse

General Category	Specific Factor
Cultural and Social Contributions	• Abuse is more common in cultures that tolerate physical punishment.
	• Abuse is more common when families live in poverty because of the stress produced by inadequate income.
	• Abuse is more common when families are socially isolated because parents lack social supports.
Parents' Contributions	• Parents who abuse their children were often maltreated themselves as children.
	• Parents who abuse their children often have poor parenting skills (e.g., unrealistic expectations, inappropriate punishment).
Children's Contributions	• Young children are more likely to be abused because they cannot regulate their behavior.
	• Ill children are more likely to be abused because their behavior while ill is often aversive.
	• Stepchildren are more likely to be abused because stepparents are less invested in their stepchildren.

TABLE 8–4

Any single factor will usually not result in abuse. For instance, a sick infant who cries constantly would not be maltreated in countries where physical punishment is not tolerated. Maltreatment is likely only when cultures condone physical punishment, parents lack effective skills for dealing with children, and a child's behavior is frequently aversive.

Preventing Maltreatment

The complexity of child abuse dashes any hopes for a simple solution. Because maltreatment is more apt to occur when several contributing factors are present, eradicating child maltreatment would entail a massive effort.

American attitudes toward "acceptable" levels of punishment and poverty would have to change. American children will be abused as long as physical punishment is considered acceptable and effective and as long as poverty-stricken families live in chronic stress from simply trying to provide food and shelter. Parents also need counseling and training in parenting skills. Abuse will continue as long as parents remain ignorant of effective methods of parenting and discipline.

It would be naive to expect all of these changes to occur overnight. However, by focusing on some of the more manageable factors, the risk of maltreatment can be reduced, if not eliminated entirely. For example, families can be taught more effective ways of coping with situations that might otherwise trigger abuse (Wicks-Nelson & Israel, 1991). Parents can learn the more effective modes of regulating their children's behavior. (I'll describe these in Module 10.2.) In role-playing sessions that recreate problems from home, for example, child-development professionals can demonstrate more effective means of solving problems, and then parents can practice these themselves.

Social supports also help. When parents know that they can turn to other helpful adults for advice and reassurance, they better manage the stresses of child rearing that might otherwise lead to abuse. Finally, we need to remember that most parents who have mistreated their children deserve compassion, not censure. In most cases, parents and children are attached to each other; maltreatment is a consequence of ignorance and burden, not malice.

Check Your Learning

1. Maltreatment includes physical abuse, sexual abuse, psychological abuse, and
   _____ .

2. Adults who were abused as children are more likely to have emotional problems, to be suicide-prone, and _____ .

3. Children who are maltreated frequently have poor peer relationships, sometimes because they are _____ .

4. Social factors that contribute to child maltreatment include cultural views toward physical punishment, poverty, and _____ .

5. Children who are at special risk for maltreatment include infants and toddlers, children who are ill frequently, and _____ .

6. Programs for preventing maltreatment often try to help families learn
   _____ .

Active Children How does child abuse illustrate, in an unfortunate way, that children are sometimes active contributors to their own development?

Answers: (1) neglect, (2) to abuse spouses and children, (3) too aggressive, (4) social isolation, (5) stepchildren, (6) new ways of coping with situations that might trigger maltreatment

Critical Review

1. Your sister is very upset because her 4-year-old son is the smallest boy in his preschool class. Most of the other boys weigh 8 to 10 pounds more than he does. Should she be concerned about his weight? What would you say to her?

2. Based on the material described in Modules 5.4 and 8.1, are young children's early efforts to draw limited primarily by their perceptual skills or by their motor skills?

3. You saw in Module 8.1 that children's brains reach their adult size and weight much sooner than their bodies do. What are the implications of this fact for social policy? In what way is the rapid growth of brain tissue adaptive for human infants and preschoolers?

4. A sociologist claims that child maltreatment would vanish if poverty were eliminated. Do you agree? Why or why not?

For more review material, log on to www.prenhall.com/kail

See For Yourself

Arrange to visit a preschool program—one that enrolls children as young as age 2 as well as some as old as 6. Ask if you can watch the children as they color or simply observe the drawings that are probably displayed around the classroom. Take the descriptions of the different types of children's drawings (from pages 223-224) and find examples of each. You should be struck by the rapid progress that children make in their drawings. See for yourself!

For More Information About . . .

 child abuse, read David J. Pelzer's *A Child Called It—One Child's Courage to Survive* (Bob Adams, 1992), which is an often shocking and heart-wrenching first-hand memoir of child abuse by a man who became a writer and advocate for abused children and who, in 1994, was the only American to be named one of the Outstanding Young Persons of the World.

 many of the topics in this chapter, including physical growth, nutrition, and chronic illness, visit the Web site of the American Academy of Pediatrics: http://www.aap.org

Key Terms

design stage 224
nightmares 217
night terrors 217
pictorial stage 224
shape stage 223

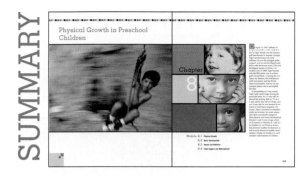

Physical Growth in Preschool
Children

8.1 Physical Growth

Body Growth
Preschool children grow steadily, adding about 2 to 3 inches and 4 pounds each year. Preschool children begin to look more mature because their bodies have more adultlike proportions and less fat. During these years, much cartilage turns to bone and children acquire, typically by age 3, all 20 primary teeth.

Brain Development
Between 2 and 5 years unnecessary neurons are pruned and neurons in the corpus callosum and sensory and motor regions of the brain are wrapped in myelin. In addition, the brain becomes more specialized with specific functions (e.g., comprehending speech) becoming localized in particular brain regions.

Sleep
Preschool children typically sleep about 12 hours each night. Many children occasionally have problems falling asleep. The best approach is to follow a consistent bedtime routine. Many children experience occasional nightmares; less common are night terrors and sleep walking. Normally none of these sleep disturbances poses a special problem for children. Many preschool children wet their beds during the night; this, too, is not a problem unless it persists into the elementary-school years.

8.2 Motor Development

Gross-Motor Skills
Children's gross-motor skills improve steadily throughout the preschool years. Children become more skilled at running and hopping as well as at throwing and catching a ball. Most 2- or 3-year-olds, for example, throw a ball using only their forearms but 6-year-olds use their arm, upper body, and legs.

Fine-Motor Skills
Preschool children become much more dextrous, which makes it possible for them to feed and clothe themselves. Their greater fine-motor coordination also means that their drawing becomes much more complex. Children's first drawings—at about age 2—consist of scribbles; youngsters rapidly progress to shapes and combining shapes. At about age 4 or 5, children begin to draw recognizable objects such as people and animals.

Handedness
Most preschool children use their right hand most of the time. For most children, language functioning is typically localized in the left hemisphere. However, language is localized in the right hemisphere for some left-handed children and in both hemispheres for other left-handed children. Left-handed children and adults are more prone to some health problems and language disorder but are more talented artistically, spatially, and mathematically.

Gender Differences in Motor Skills
Young boys tend to be more active than girls and have an advantage on tasks that rely on strength. However, girls usually perform better than boys on tasks that require coordinated movements of the limb or fine-motor coordination.

8.3 Health and Wellness

Nutrition
Most preschool children need a diet of roughly 1,500 to 1,700 calories, from each of the five food groups, that is low in sugar and fat. To discourage "picky eating," parents should allow children to choose their food, allow them to eat in any sequence, and not force children to eat everything on their plate.

Threats to Children's Development
Preschool children frequently have minor illnesses, such as colds. Having a minor illness benefits children by helping them develop immunities and teaching them about the nature of illness and recovery.

Most chronic illnesses are rare, but several million U.S. children are afflicted with asthma, in which they have difficulty breathing because air passages in their lungs are inflamed. Children with asthma can lead normal lives as long as they follow several guidelines, such as taking proper medications.

More preschool children die from accidents than any other cause. Parents can either avoid most accidents entirely (e.g., by ensuring that children cannot get to poisons) or they can reduce the chance for injury from an accident (e.g., by having children always ride in a car seat).

Children are more prone to illness and injury when they are living in stress and when they live in poverty. Hospitalization disturbs children because of the separation from parents, the fear of the unknown, and the loss of control.

8.4 Child Neglect and Maltreatment

Consequences of Maltreatment
Children who are maltreated sometimes suffer permanent physical damage. Their peer relationships are often poor, and they tend to lag in cognitive development and academic performance.

Causes of Maltreatment
A culture's views on violence, poverty, and social isolation can foster child maltreatment. Parents who abuse their children are often unhappy, socially unskilled individuals. Younger, unhealthy children are more often targets of maltreatment, as are stepchildren.

Preventing Maltreatment
Prevention should target each of the factors that contribute to child maltreatment. In reality, prevention programs often focus on providing families with new ways of coping with problems and providing parents with resources to help them cope with stress.

Cognitive Development in Preschool Children

Chapter

9

I remember playing the card game "war" with my son Ben when he was a preschooler. In this game, each player turns a card over from the top of his or her deck. The player with the high card wins the hand; the game is over when one player has all the cards. For an adult, the game is boring because there is no room for strategies—the outcome is based purely on luck. But I remember being impressed by the many skills necessary for 4-year-old Ben to play. He had to know the numbers 2–10 (plus jack, queen, king, and ace) to determine the high card, he had to know the special rules that applied when the cards played had the same value, and he had to know the rule for deciding when the game was over. Simple for an adult, yet Ben clearly could not have played the game when he was 2.

In this module, we'll look at the cognitive skills that allow preschoolers like Ben to play games and to accomplish many other impressive intellectual feats. We begin, in Module 9.1, by examining several different accounts of cognitive processing during the preschool years. In Module 9.2, we'll trace language development during this period. In Module 9.3, we'll look at young children's growing communication skills. Finally, in Module 9.4, we'll study different ways of educating preschool children.

Cognitive Processes

9.1

Cognitive Processes

Learning Objectives

■ **What are the distinguishing features of thinking during the preoperational stage?**

■ **How does children's information processing improve during the preschool years?**

■ **Why did Vygotsky view development as an apprenticeship?**

> *Three-year-old Jamila loves talking to Grandma Powell on the telephone, but sometimes these conversations get derailed: When Grandma Powell asks a question, Jamila often replies by nodding her head. Jamila's dad has explained that Grandma Powell (and others on the phone) can't see her nodding, that she needs to say "yes" or "no." But, no luck. Jamila invariably returns to head-nodding. Her dad can't understand why such a bright and talkative child doesn't realize that nodding is meaningless over the phone.*

By the time children enter the preschool years, an extraordinary amount of cognitive development has taken place. Yet, as the vignette reminds us, preschoolers have a long way to travel on the road to cognitive maturity. In this module, we'll look at preschoolers' thinking from three perspectives: Piaget's, information processing, and that of Lev Vygotsky, a Russian psychologist.

Piaget's Account

In Piaget's theory, preschoolers have just made the transition from sensorimotor thinking to preoperational thinking. **The *preoperational stage*, which spans ages 2 to 7, is marked by the child's use of symbols to represent objects and events.** Throughout this period, preschool children gradually become proficient at using common symbols, such as words, gestures, graphs, maps, and models. In the first part of this section, I'll describe Piaget's original account of preoperational thinking. Then I'll describe newer research that complements Piaget's account.

Characteristics of Preoperational Thinking. Although preschool children's ability to use symbols represents a huge advance over sensorimotor thinking, preschool children's thinking is quite limited compared to that of school-age children. Why? To answer this question, we need to look at three important characteristics of thought during the preoperational stage: *egocentrism, centration,* and *appearance as reality.*

Preoperational children typically believe that others see the world—both literally and figuratively—exactly as they do. *Egocentrism* **refers to young children's difficulty in seeing the world from another's outlook.** When youngsters stubbornly cling to their own way, they are not simply being contrary. Instead, preoperational children do not comprehend that other people have different ideas and feelings.

In the drawing, the man is asking the preschooler to select the photograph that shows how the objects on the table look to him. Most will select photo 3, which shows how the objects look to the child, not photo 1, the correct choice. Preoperational youngsters evidently suppose that the mountains are seen the same way by all;

FIG 9–1

they presume that theirs is the only view, not one of many possible views (Piaget & Inhelder, 1956).

Egocentrism also explains why Jamila, the 3-year-old in the vignette, nods her head when talking on the phone. Jamila assumes that because she is aware that her head is moving up and down (or side to side), her grandmother must be aware of it, too. In the Real Children feature, we'll set yet another manifestation of this egocentrism.

> Preoperational children often ignore others' perspectives, focus on one aspect of a problem, and confuse appearance with reality.

REAL CHILDREN

Christine, Egocentrism, and Animism

Because of their egocentrism, preschool children sometimes attribute their own thoughts and feelings to others. **Preoperational children sometimes credit inanimate objects with life and lifelike properties, a phenomenon known as *animism* (Piaget, 1929).** A 3½-year-old I know, Christine, illustrated preoperational animism in a conversation we had on a rainy day:

RK:	Is the sun happy today?
CHRISTINE:	No. It's sad today.
RK:	Why?
CHRISTINE:	Because it's cloudy. He can't shine. And he can't see me!
RK:	What about your trike? Is it happy?
CHRISTINE:	No, he's very sad, too.
RK:	Why is that?
CHRISTINE:	Because I can't ride him. And because he's all alone in the garage.

Caught up in her egocentrism, Christine believes that objects like the sun and her tricycle think and feel as she does. ■

A second characteristic of preoperational thinking is that children seem to have the psychological equivalent of tunnel vision: They often concentrate on one aspect of a problem but totally ignore other equally relevant aspects. ***Centration* is Piaget's term for this narrowly focused thought that characterizes preoperational youngsters.**

Piaget demonstrated centration in his experiments involving conservation. In the conservation experiments, Piaget wanted to determine when children realize that important characteristics of objects (or sets of objects) stay the same despite changes in their physical appearance. Some tasks that Piaget used to study conservation are shown in the diagram on page 244. Each begins with identical objects (or sets of objects). Then one of the objects (or sets) is transformed and children are asked if the objects are the same in terms of some important feature.

A typical conservation problem, involving conservation of liquid quantity, is shown the photo. Children are shown identical beakers filled with the same amount of juice. After children agree that the two beakers have the same amount of juice, the juice is poured from one beaker into a taller, thinner beaker. The juice looks different in the tall, thin beaker—it rises higher—but of course the amount is unchanged. Nevertheless, preoperational children claim that the tall, thin beaker has more juice than the original beaker. (And, if the juice is poured into a wider beaker, they believe it has less.)

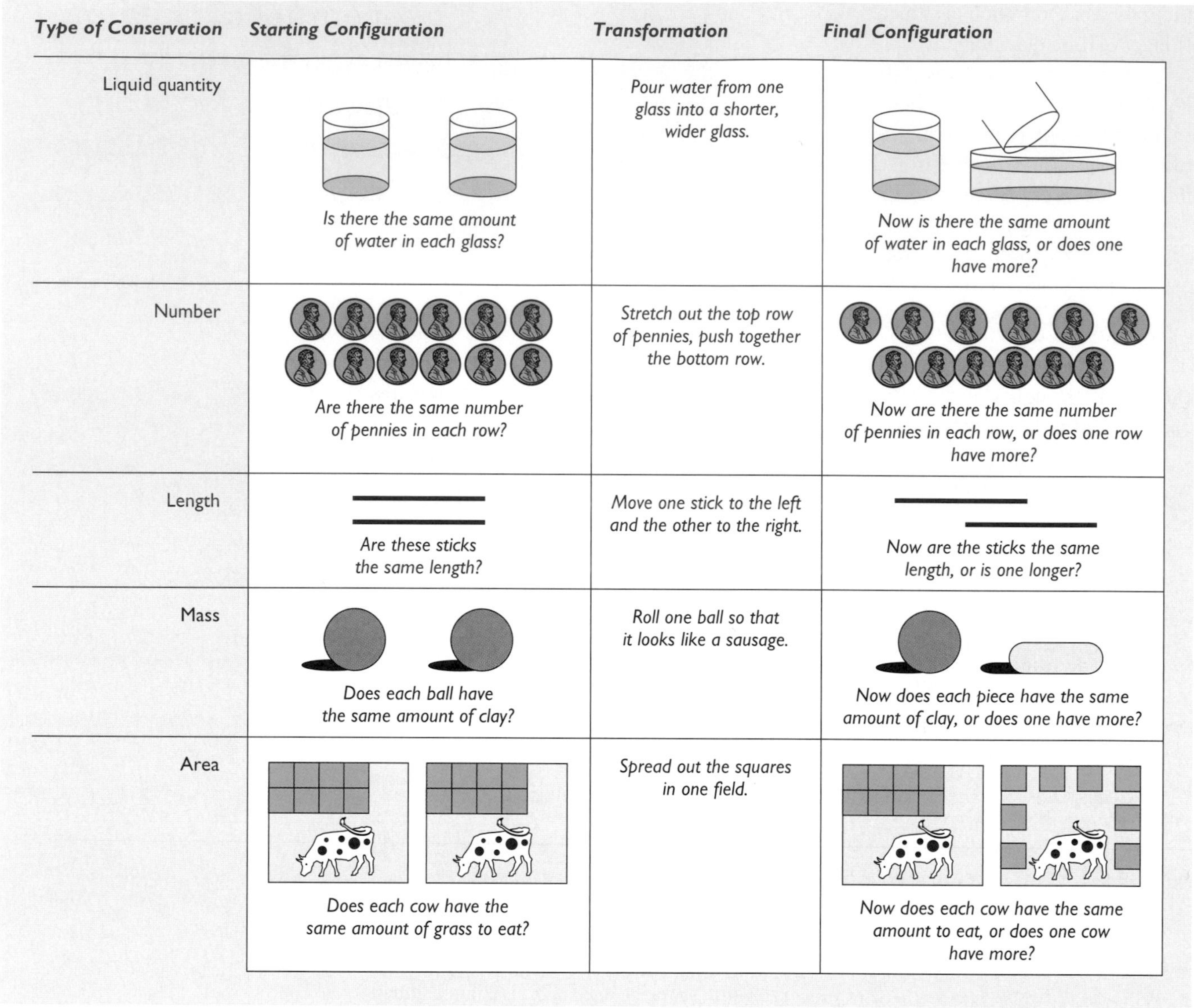

Type of Conservation	Starting Configuration	Transformation	Final Configuration
Liquid quantity	Is there the same amount of water in each glass?	Pour water from one glass into a shorter, wider glass.	Now is there the same amount of water in each glass, or does one have more?
Number	Are there the same number of pennies in each row?	Stretch out the top row of pennies, push together the bottom row.	Now are there the same number of pennies in each row, or does one row have more?
Length	Are these sticks the same length?	Move one stick to the left and the other to the right.	Now are the sticks the same length, or is one longer?
Mass	Does each ball have the same amount of clay?	Roll one ball so that it looks like a sausage.	Now does each piece have the same amount of clay, or does one have more?
Area	Does each cow have the same amount of grass to eat?	Spread out the squares in one field.	Now does each cow have the same amount to eat, or does one cow have more?

FIG 9–2

What is happening here? According to Piaget, preoperational children center on the level of the juice in the beaker. If the juice is higher after it is poured, preoperational children believe that there must be more juice now than before. Because preoperational thinking is centered, these youngsters ignore the fact that the change in the level of the juice is always accompanied by a change in the diameter of the beaker.

In other conservation problems, preoperational children also tend to focus on only one aspect of the problem. In conservation of number, for example, preoperational children concentrate on the fact that, after the transformation, one row of objects is now longer than the other. In conservation of length, preoperational children concentrate on the fact that, after the transformation, the end of one stick is farther to the right than the end of the other. Preoperational children's centered thinking means that they overlook other parts of the problem that would tell them the quantity is unchanged.

A final feature of preoperational thinking is that preschool children believe an object's appearance tells what the object is really like. For instance, many a 3-year-old has watched with quiet fascination as an older brother or sister put on a ghoulish costume only to erupt in frightened tears when their sibling put on scary make-up. For the youngster in the photo, the scary made-up face is reality, not just something that looks frightening but really isn't.

Confusion between appearance and reality is not limited to costumes and masks. It is a general characteristic of preoperational thinking. Consider the following cases where appearances and reality conflict:

- a boy is angry because a friend is being mean but smiles because he's afraid the friend will leave if he reveals his anger
- a glass of milk looks brown when seen through sunglasses
- a piece of hard rubber looks like food (e.g., like a piece of pizza)

Older children and adults know that the boy looks happy, the milk looks brown, and the object looks like food but that the boy is really angry, the milk is really white, and the object is really rubber. Preoperational children, however, confuse appearance and reality, thinking the boy is happy, the milk is brown, and the piece of rubber is edible.

Distinguishing appearance and reality is particularly difficult for children in the early years of preoperational thinking. This difficulty is evident in research on children's use of scale models, which are objects that also symbolize some much larger object. A model of a house, for example, can be an interesting object in its own right as well as a representation of an actual house. The ability to use scale models develops early in the preoperational period. If young children watch an adult hide a toy in a full-size room, then try to find the toy in a scale model of the room that contains all the principal features of the full-scale room (e.g., carpet, window, furniture), 3-year-olds find the hidden toy readily but 2½-year-olds do not (DeLoache, Miller, & Rosengren, 1995, 1997).

Why is this task so easy for 3-year-olds and so difficult for 2½-year-olds? Judy DeLoache believes that 2½-year-olds' "…attention to a scale model as an interesting and attractive object makes it difficult for them to simultaneously think about its relation to something else." (DeLoache, Miller, & Rosengren, 1997, p. 308) In other words, for young children the appearance of the object is reality and, consequently, they find it hard to think about the model as a symbol of something else (i.e., the full-size room).

If this argument is correct, 2½-year-olds should be more successful using the model if they don't have to think of it as a symbol for the full-size room. DeLoache tested this hypothesis in the study described in the Focus on Research feature. (This is one of my 10 favorite studies of all time, for reasons that will soon be obvious.)

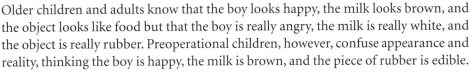

FOCUS ON RESEARCH

Finding Toys in a Shrunken Room

Who were the investigators and what was the aim of the study? Judy DeLoache, Kevin Miller, and Karl Rosengren (1997) believed that 2½-year-olds could not find the toy in the model because it was difficult for them to think of the model as an object *and* as a symbol of the full-size room. To test this argument, they created

a condition designed to eliminate the need for children to think of the model as an object and as a symbol. Children were told that a machine could shrink the full-size room. In this case, the model is no longer a symbol of the full-size room; it *is* the room, just shrunken. Consequently, DeLoache and her colleagues expected 2½-year-olds to find the hidden toy because they believed the model was the full-size room shrunken to miniature size.

How did the investigators measure the topic of interest? Some children were tested with the usual procedures: hiding the toy in the full-size room and asking children to find it in the scale model. Other children were tested in the new condition designed to help them find the toy. Children were shown the oscilloscope shown in the photograph, which was described as a shrinking machine. They saw a toy doll—Terry the Troll—placed in front of the oscilloscope; then the experimenter and child left the room briefly while a tape-recorder played sounds that were described as noise "the machine makes when it's shrinking something." When experimenter and child returned, Terri had shrunk from 8 inches to 2 inches. Next, Terry was hidden in the full-size room, the experimenter aimed the "shrinking machine" at the full-size room, then experimenter and child left the room. While the tape recorder played shrinking sounds, research assistants quickly removed everything from the full-size room and substituted the model. Experimenter and child returned and the child was asked to find Terri. This procedure was repeated, so that children searched for Terri on four separate trials.

Who were the children in the study? DeLoache and her colleagues tested 32 children whose average age was 2½ years.

What was the design of the study? The study was experimental. The independent variable was the presence or absence of the shrinking machine. The dependent variable was the percentage of trials on which the children found Terri.

Were there ethical concerns with the study? For children tested with the "shrinking machine," the study involved deception. Parents were fully informed about the shrinking machine before they gave consent, and parents were present throughout the experiment. Immediately after the experiment, children were told that the machine could not really shrink objects. They were shown the model, the full-size room and both small and large versions of Terri. The deception seemed warranted and no children seemed upset when they were told what really happened.

What were the results? The top part of the graph shows the percentage of trials when children found the toy. Children rarely found the toy in the standard condition, but they did frequently in the "shrinking machine" condition. The bottom part of the graph shows the percentage of children who found Terry on at least three of the four trials. No children in the standard condition were this accurate, but most children in the "shrinking machine" condition were.

What did the investigators conclude? When 2½-year-olds must think of the model as an object *and* as a symbol, they find this very difficult and, conse-

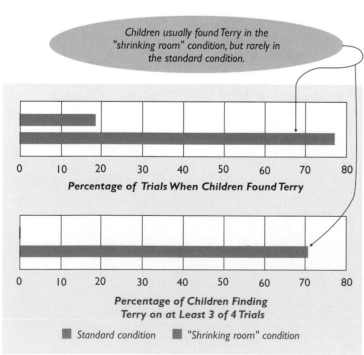

Children usually found Terry in the "shrinking room" condition, but rarely in the standard condition.

Percentage of Trials When Children Found Terry

Percentage of Children Finding Terry on at Least 3 of 4 Trials

■ Standard condition ■ "Shrinking room" condition

FIG 9–3

quently, cannot find the hidden toy, even though the model is an exact replica of the full-size room. When children need only think of the model *as* the original room, but much smaller, they readily find the toy. Thus, the scale model task shows young children's limits in distinguishing appearance from reality.

What converging evidence would strengthen these conclusions? Because the changes observed by DeLoache and her colleagues appeared across a fairly narrow age range, this would be an ideal opportunity to conduct a microgenetic study: The goal would be to show, for individual children, the age at which they understand that the model is a symbol of something else. Additional useful research would be to compare the results with other situations in which an object also serves a symbolic function (e.g., children's understanding that a map is a colorful piece of paper as well as symbol of a much larger physical space). ■

Are you skeptical that young children can be this confused? Many researchers shared your skepticism when these findings were first reported and they went to great lengths to show that young children were somehow being misled by some minor aspects of the experiment. But most of the follow-up experiments failed; rewording the instructions, using different materials, or even training children all had relatively little effect (Siegler, 1998). Confusion about appearance and reality is a deep-seated characteristic of preoperational thinking (especially in the early years of this stage), as are egocentrism and centration.

The defining characteristics of preoperational thought are summarized in the table.

■■■■ SUMMARY TABLE

Characteristics of Preoperational Thinking

Characteristic	Definition	Example
Egocentrism	Child believes that all people see the world as he or she does.	A child gestures during a telephone conversation, not realizing that the listener cannot see the gestures.
Centration	Child focuses on one aspect of a problem or situation but ignores other relevant aspects.	In conservation of liquid quantity, child pays attention to the height of the liquid in the beaker but ignores the diameter of the beaker.
Appearance as reality	Child assumes that an object really is what it appears to be.	Child believes that a person smiling at another person is really happy even though the other person is being mean.

TABLE 9–1

Extending Piaget's Account: Children's Naive Theories. In Chapter 5, I described how researchers have expanded Piaget's account to show that infants create naive theories of physics and biology. These theories become more elaborate in the preschool years. For example, preschool children's naive theories of biology come to include many of the specific properties associated with animate objects (Wellman & Gelman, 1998). Many 4-year-olds' theories of biology include the following elements:

- *Movement:* Children understand that animals can move themselves but inanimate objects can only be moved by other objects or by people. Shown an animal and a toy hopping across a table in exactly the same manner, preschoolers claim that only the animal can move itself (Gelman & Gottfried, 1996).

- *Growth:* Children understand that, from their first appearance, animals get bigger and physically more complex but that inanimate objects do not change in this way. They believe, for example, that sea otters and termites become larger as time goes by but that tea kettles and teddy bears do not (Rosengren et al., 1991).

- *Internal parts:* Children know that the insides of animate objects contain different materials than the insides of inanimate objects. Preschool children judge that blood and bones are more likely to be inside an animate object but that cotton and metal are more likely to be inside an inanimate object (Simons & Keil, 1995).

- *Inheritance:* Children realize that only living things have offspring that resemble their parents. Asked to explain why a dog is pink, preschoolers believe that some biological characteristic of the parents probably made the dog pink; asked to explain why a can is pink, preschoolers rely on mechanical causes (e.g., a worker used a machine), not biological ones (Springer & Keil, 1991; Weissman & Kalish, 1999).

- *Healing:* Children understand that when injured, animate things heal by regrowth whereas inanimate things must be fixed by humans. Preschoolers know that hair will grow back when cut from a child's head but must be repaired by a person when cut from a doll's head (Backschedier, Shatz, & Gelman, 1993).

Findings like these make it clear that preschoolers' naive theories of biology are complex. Of course, their theories aren't complete; they don't know, for instance, that genes are the biological basis for inheritance (Springer & Keil, 1991). And preschoolers' theories include some misconceptions: They believe, for example, that adopted children will physically resemble their adoptive parents (Solomon et al., 1996).

As toddlers and preschoolers, children form a naive theory in another area—psychology! In many situations, adults try to explain to children why people act as they do and these explanations often emphasize that desires or goals cause people's behavior. Just as naive physics allows us to predict how objects act, naive psychology allows us to predict how people act (Lillard, 1999).

> During the preschool years, children form a theory of mind—a naive understanding of connections between thoughts, beliefs, and behavior.

Collectively, a person's ideas about connections between thoughts, beliefs, and behavior form a *theory of mind*, a naive understanding of the relations between mind and behavior. One of the leading researchers on theory of mind, Henry Wellman (1991, 1992), believes that children's theory of mind moves through three phases during the preschool years. In the earliest phase, common in 2-year-olds, children are aware of desires, and they often speak of their wants and likes, as in "Lemme see" or "I wanna sit." And they often link their desires to their behavior, such as "I happy there's more cookies" (Wellman, 1991). Thus, by age 2, children understand that they and other people have desires and that desires can cause behavior.

By about age 3, an important change takes place. Now children clearly distinguish the mental world from the physical world. For example, if told about one girl who has a cookie and another girl who is thinking about a cookie, 3-year-olds know that only the first girl's cookie can be seen, touched, and eaten (Harris et al., 1991). And, most 3-year-olds use "mental verbs" like *think, believe, remember,* and *forget,* which suggests that they have a beginning understanding of different mental states (Bartsch & Wellman, 1995). Although 3-year-olds talk about thoughts and beliefs, they nevertheless emphasize desires when trying to explain why people act as they do.

Not until age 4 do mental states really take center stage in children's understanding of their and others' actions. That is, by age 4, children understand that their and others' behavior is based on their beliefs about events and situations, even when those beliefs are wrong.

This developmental transformation is particularly evident when children are tested on false belief tasks like the one shown in the figure. In all false belief tasks, a situation is set up so that the child being tested has accurate information, but someone else does not. For example, in the story in the figure, the child being tested knows that the marble is really in the box, but Sally, the girl in the story, believes that the marble is still in the basket. Remarkably, although 4-year-olds correctly say that Sally will look for the marble in the basket (acting on her false belief), most 3-year-olds say she will look in the box. The 4-year-olds understand that Sally's behavior is based on her beliefs, despite the fact that her beliefs are incorrect (Frye, 1993). As Bartsch and Wellman (1995) phrase it, 4-year-olds "…realize that people not only have thoughts and beliefs, but also that thoughts and beliefs are crucial to explaining why people do things; that is, actors' pursuits of their desires are inevitably shaped by their beliefs about the world." (p. 144)

Thus, naive psychology flourishes in the preschool years. Armed with this theory, children see that other people's behavior is not unpredictable but follows regular patterns.

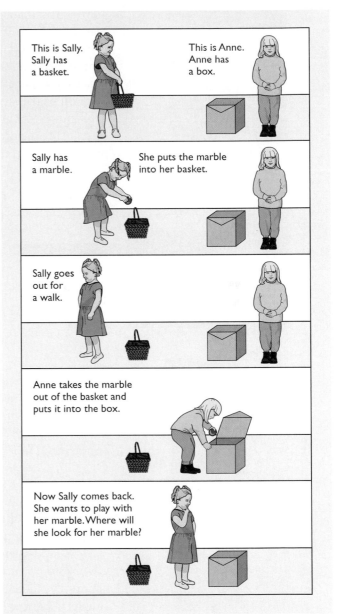

FIG 9-4

Information-Processing Perspectives on Preschool Thinking

Unlike Piaget's theory, the preschool years are not a separate stage in the information-processing approach. Instead, these years show continued growth of many cognitive skills. In the next few pages, we'll look at preschool children's improving skills of attention, memory, and counting.

Attention. Have you ever been in a class where you knew you should be listening and taking notes, but the lecture was just so boring that you started noticing other things—the construction going on outside or an attractive person seated nearby? After a while, maybe you reminded yourself to "Pay attention!" We get distracted because our perceptual systems are marvelously powerful. They provide us with far more information at any time than we could possible interpret. **Attention is the process by which we select information that will be processed further.** In a class, for example, where the task is to direct your attention to the lecture, it is easy to ignore other stimuli if the lecture is interesting. But if the lecture is not interesting, other stimuli intrude and capture your attention.

The roots of attention can be seen in infancy. Remember Linda, the newborn in the vignette in Module 6.2, who jumped when trucks accelerated past her home? Linda soon began to ignore the sounds of trucks, a sign of habituation, which we discussed on page 164. Habituation indicates that attention is selective: A stimulus that once captured attention no longer does.

During the preschool years, children gradually become better able to regulate their attention. You can see these changes in the results of a study of 2½- to 4½-year-olds by Ruff, Capozzoli, and Weissberg (1998). These investigators observed preschoolers in several settings. In one, children sat at a table watching hand puppets and dolls enact brief skits. In another, children were told they could play with an assortment of toys on a table top. Ruff and her colleagues videotaped children in both settings, then analyzed the tapes for many behaviors. Children who were actively engaged in the puppet show or free play—as inferred by their posture, facial expressions, spontaneous comments, and the like—exhibited *focused attention*. Children who left the table exhibited *active inattention*.

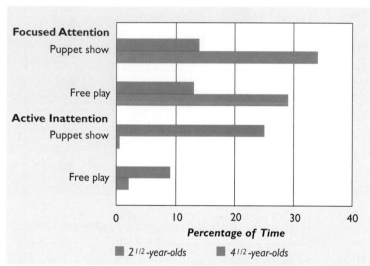

FIG 9–5

The results, shown in the graph, illustrate two important characteristics of attention during the preschool years. First, attention improved markedly in this period. In both settings, the 4½-year-olds spent much more time than the 2½-year-olds in focused attention and much less time in active inattention. Second, the 4½-year-olds, though much more attentive than the younger children, still spent less than half the time in a state of focused attention. Maintaining focused attention is a demanding skill, one that emerges gradually beyond the preschool and school-age years (Enns, 1990).

Why does attention improve with age? For one thing, older children and adolescents are simply more likely to remind themselves that they need to pay attention. They are also more likely to have mastered some attentional "tricks of the trade." For example, if asked to determine if two objects are the same, older children and adolescents are more likely to compare them feature by feature until they find features that do not match or they run out of features to check (Vurpillot, 1968). By directing their attention in this manner, children are guaranteed that they will do the task accurately and in the least amount of time possible. Asked if the two houses in the diagram at the top of page 251 are the same, older children typically start by comparing the top windows and work down until they have compared all six pairs of windows. In contrast, younger children direct their attention haphazardly—not systematically checking corresponding windows—so they often don't find the differing windows.

Young children need help to pay attention better. One approach is to make relevant information more salient than irrelevant information. For example, closing a classroom door may not eliminate competing sounds and smells entirely, but it will make them less salient. Or, when preschoolers are working at a table or desk, we can remove all objects that are not necessary for the task. It's also very helpful, particularly for young children, to remind them periodically to pay attention only to relevant information and ignore the rest.

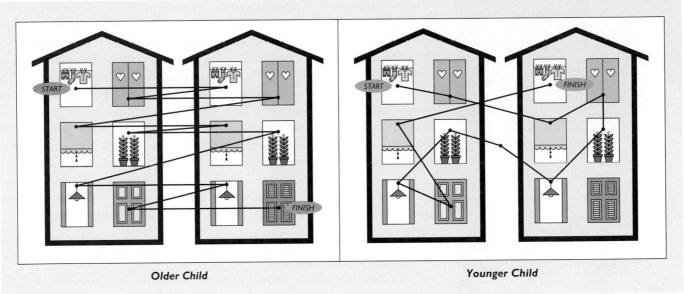

Older Child　　　　　Younger Child

FIG 9–6

Memory. We know, from Module 6.2, that infants are able to remember. However, a novel feature of memory, autobiographical memory, emerges in the preschool years. *Autobiographical memory* **refers to people's memory of the significant events and experiences of their own lives.** You can see your own autobiographical memory by answering these questions:

> *Who was your teacher in fourth grade?*
> *Where (and with whom!) was your first kiss?*
> *Was your high school graduation indoors or outdoors?*

In answering these questions, you searched memory, just as you would search memory to answer questions such as "What is the capital of Ohio?" and "Who invented the sewing machine?" However, answers to questions about Ohio and sewing machines are based on general knowledge that you have not experienced personally; answers to questions about *your* fourth-grade teacher, *your* first kiss, and *your* high school graduation are based on knowledge unique to your own life. Autobiographical memory is important because it helps people construct a personal life history. In addition, autobiographical memory allows people to relate their experiences to others, creating socially shared memories (Nelson, 1993).

Autobiographical memory originates in the preschool years, when parents encourage children to think about the past by asking them to recall recent events. Picking up a 3-year-old from preschool, a parent may ask, "Whom did you play with?" "What did you have for snack?" In questions like these, parents usually focus on *who, what, where, when,* and *why*. In this way, they teach their children the aspects of events that are important. Their questions also emphasize the importance of temporal and causal order in organizing the past (Schneider & Bjorklund, 1998).

Research on children's autobiographical memory has played a central role in cases of suspected child abuse. When abuse is suspected, the victim is usually the sole witness. To prosecute the alleged abuser, the child's testimony is needed. But can preschoolers accurately recall these events? One obstacle to accurate testimony is that young children are often interviewed repeatedly during legal proceedings,

> Autobiographical memory, which helps people to construct a life history, begins in the preschool years.

which can cause them to confuse what actually happened with what others suggest may have happened. When, as in the situation in the photo, the questioner is an adult in a position of authority, children often believe that what is suggested by the adult actually happened (Ceci & Bruck, 1995, 1998; Lampinen & Smith, 1995). They will tell a convincing tale about what happened simply because adults have led them to believe things must have happened that way. Young children's story-telling can be so convincing that law-enforcement officials, caseworkers, and developmental psychologists cannot reliably distinguish children who are telling the truth from children who are describing events that did not happen (Leichtman & Ceci, 1995).

Preschoolers can provide reliable testimony, but many commonly used legal procedures can undermine their credibility. Here are guidelines for improving the reliability of child witnesses (Ceci & Bruck, 1997, 1998):

- Warn children that interviewers may sometimes try to trick them or suggest things that didn't happen.

- Interviewers' questions should evaluate alternative explanations of what happened and who was involved.

- Children should not be questioned repeatedly on a single issue.

Following these guidelines will foster the conditions under which preschoolers (and older children, too) are likely to recall the past more accurately and thereby be better witnesses.

Counting. We know from Module 6.2 that infants are able to discriminate quantities long before they can count. However, by 2 years, most youngsters know some number words and they have begun to count. Usually, their counting is full of mistakes. They might count—"1, 2, 6, 7"—skipping 3, 4, and 5. Gelman and Meck (1986) charted preschoolers' understanding of counting. They simply placed several objects in front of a child and asked, "How many?" By analyzing children's answers to many of these questions, Gelman and Meck discovered that by age 3 most children have mastered three basic principles of counting, at least when it comes to counting up to five objects.

- *One-to-one principle:* **There must be one and only one number name for each object that is counted.** A child who counts three objects as "1, 2, a" understands this principle because the number of number words matches the number of objects to be counted.

- *Stable-order principle:* **Number names must be counted in the same order.** A child who counts in the same sequence—for example, consistently counting four objects as "1, 2, 4, 5"—shows understanding of this principle.

- *Cardinality principle:* **The last number name differs from the previous ones in a counting sequence by denoting the number of objects.** Typically, 3-year-olds reveal their understanding of this principle by repeating the last number name, often with emphasis: "1, 2, 4, 8 . . . EIGHT!"

During the preschool years, children master the one-to-one, stable-order, and cardinality principles of counting.

During the preschool years, children master these basic principles and apply them to ever larger sets of objects. By age 5, most youngsters apply these counting principles to as many as nine objects. Of course, children's understanding of these principles does not mean that they always count accurately. To the contrary, children can apply all these principles consistently while counting incorrectly. They must master the conventional sequence of the number names and the counting principles to learn to count accurately.

Learning the number names beyond 9 is easier because the counting words can be generated based on rules for combining decade number names (20, 30, 40) with unit names (1, 2, 3, 4). And later, similar rules are used for hundreds, thousands, and so on. By age 4, most youngsters know the numbers to 20 and some can count to 99. Usually, they stop counting at a number ending in 9 (29, 59), apparently because they don't know the next decade name (Siegler & Robinson, 1982).

Learning to count beyond 10 is more complicated in English than in other languages. For example, *eleven* and *twelve* are completely irregular names, following no rules. Also, the remaining "teen" number names differ from the 20s, 30s, and the rest in that the decade number name comes after the unit (thir-*teen*, four-*teen*) rather than before (*twenty*-three, *thirty*-four). Also, some decade names only loosely correspond to the unit names on which they are based: twenty, thirty, and fifty resemble two, three, and five but are not the same.

In contrast, the Chinese, Japanese, and Korean number systems are almost perfectly regular. *Eleven* and *twelve* are expressed as ten-one and ten-two. There are no special names for the decades: *Two-ten* and *two-ten-one* are names for 20 and 21. These simplified number names help explain why youngsters growing up in Asian countries count more accurately than U.S. preschool children of the same age (Miller et al., 1995). Furthermore, the direct correspondence between the number names and the base-ten system makes it easier for Asian youngsters like the girl in the photo to learn base-ten concepts (Miura et al., 1988).

Vygotsky's Theory of Cognitive Development

Like many authors, I often refer to child development as a journey that can proceed along many different paths. For Piaget and neo-Piagetian theorists, children make the journey alone. Other people (and culture, in general) certainly influence the direction that children take, but the child is seen as a solitary explorer-adventurer boldly forging ahead.

Lev Vygotsky (1896–1934), a Russian psychologist, proposed a very different account. Vygotsky saw development as an apprenticeship in which children advance when they collaborate with others who are more skilled. According to Vygotsky (1978), children rarely make much headway on the developmental path when they walk alone; they progress when they walk hand in hand with an expert partner.

Vygotsky died of tuberculosis when he was only 37 years old, so he never had the opportunity to formulate a complete theory of cognitive development as Piaget did. Nevertheless, his ideas are influential because they fill some gaps in the Piagetian and neo-Piagetian accounts. Three of Vygotsky's most important contributions are the zone of proximal development, scaffolding, and private speech.

The Zone of Proximal Development. Four-year-old Ian and his dad often work on puzzles together. Ian does most of the work; like the father in the photo at the top of page 254, his dad sometimes finds a piece that Ian needs or correctly orients a piece. When Ian tries to do the same puzzles himself, he rarely can complete them. **The difference between what Ian can do with assistance and what he can do alone defines the *zone of proximal development*.** That is, the zone refers to the difference between the level of performance a child can achieve when working independently and the higher level of performance that is possible when working under the guidance of more skilled adults or peers (Wertsch & Tulviste, 1992).

Think, for example, about a preschooler who is asked to clean her bedroom. She doesn't know where to begin. By structuring the task for the child—"start by putting away your books, then your toys, then your dirty clothes"—an adult can help the child accomplish what she cannot do by herself. Just as training wheels help children learn to ride a bike by allowing them to concentrate on other aspects of bicycling, collaborators help children perform effectively by providing structure, hints, and reminders.

The idea of a zone of proximal development follows naturally from Vygotsky's basic premise that cognition develops first in a social setting and only gradually comes under the child's independent control. Understanding how the shift from social to individual learning occurs brings us to the second of Vygotsky's key contributions.

Scaffolding. Have you ever had the good fortune to work with a master teacher, one who seemed to know exactly when to say something to help you over an obstacle but otherwise let you work uninterrupted? *Scaffolding* **refers to a teaching style that matches the amount of assistance to the learner's needs.** Early in learning a new task, when a child knows little, the teacher provides a lot of direct instruction. But, as the child begins to catch on to the task, the teacher provides less instruction and only occasional reminders (McNaughton & Leyland, 1990).

We saw earlier how a parent helping a preschooler clean her room must provide detailed structure. But as the child does the task more often, the parent needs to provide less structure. Similarly, when high school students first try to do proofs in geometry, the teacher must lead them through each step; as the students begin to understand how proofs are done and can do more on their own, the teacher gradually provides less help.

The defining characteristic of scaffolding—giving help but not more than is needed—clearly promotes learning (Plumert & Nichols-Whitehead, 1996). Youngsters do not learn readily when they are constantly told what to do or when they are simply left to struggle through a problem unaided. However, when teachers collaborate with them—allowing children to take on more and more of a task as they master its different elements—they learn more effectively (Pacifici & Bearison, 1991). Scaffolding is an important technique for transferring cognitive skills from others to the child.

Private Speech. The little girl in the photo is talking to herself as she is playing. **This behavior demonstrates *private speech*, comments not directed to others but intended to help children regulate their own behavior.** Vygotsky (1934/1986) viewed private speech as an intermediate step toward self-regulation of cognitive skills. At first, children's behavior is regulated by speech from other people that is directed toward them. When youngsters first try to control their own behavior and thoughts, without others present, they instruct themselves by speaking aloud. **Finally, as children gain ever-greater skill, private speech becomes *inner speech*, Vygotsky's term for thought.**

If children use private speech to help control their behavior, then we should see children using it more often on difficult tasks than on easy tasks, and more often after a mistake than after a correct response. These predictions are generally supported in research (Berk, 1992), documenting the power of language in helping children learn to control their own behavior and thinking.

The key components of Vygotsky's theory are summarized in the table. His view of cognitive development as an apprenticeship, a collaboration between expert and novice, complements the other views described in this module. Each perspective—Piaget's theory, the information-processing approach, and Vygotsky's work—provides a unique lens for viewing thinking during the preschool years.

Vygotsky viewed cognitive development as a collaboration between a novice child and more skilled teachers who scaffold children's learning.

■■■ SUMMARY TABLE

Key Concepts in Vygotsky's Theory

Concept	Defined	Example
Zone of proximal development	The difference between what children can do alone and what they can do with assistance	A child makes little progress cleaning his room alone but accomplishes the task readily when a parent provides structure (e.g., "Start by getting stuff off the floor").
Scaffolding	Providing instruction that matches the learner's needs exactly—neither too much instruction nor too little	A teacher provides much help when a child is first learning to distinguish "b" from "d" but then provides less help as the child learns the difference.
Private speech	Speech that is not directed at others but instead guides the child's own behavior	A child working on a puzzle says to herself, "Start with the edges. Look for pieces with straight sides."

TABLE 9-2

Check Your Learning

1. An important characteristic of preoperational thought is _____, which refers to children's inability to see the world as others do.

2. Because of their egocentrism, preoperational children sometimes attribute life-like properties to inanimate objects, a phenomenon known as _____.

3. According to Wellman's theory, the basic element of 2-year-olds' theory of mind is that _____.

4. Older children and adolescents have better attentional skills because they remind themselves to pay attention more often and because _____.

5. Preschoolers' testimony is more likely to be reliable when interviewers test alternate hypotheses and avoid repeated questioning and when children are warned that _____.

6. The _____ refers to the difference between what children can do alone and what they can do with skilled help.

7. Children use private speech more on difficult tasks than on easy tasks and more often after _____.

■■■ **Nature and Nurture** Compare the role of cultural influences on cognitive development in Piaget's theory, information-processing approaches, and Vygotsky's theory.

Answers: (1) egocentrism, (2) animism, (3) people have desires that cause behaviors, (4) they have mastered more attentional "tricks of the trade," (5) interviewers may try to trick them, (6) zone of proximal development, (7) they've made a mistake

Language

9.2

Language

├─ Encouraging Word Learning

├─ From Two-Word Speech to Complex Sentences

└─ How Children Acquire Grammar

Learning Objectives

■ What conditions help preschoolers to expand their vocabulary?

■ How do children progress from speaking single words to complicated sentences?

■ How do children acquire the grammar of their native language?

Jaime's daughter, Luisa, is a curious 2½-year-old who bombards her father with questions. Jaime enjoys Luisa's questioning but he is bothered by the way she phrases her questions. Luisa will say, "What you are doing?" and "Why not she sleep?" Obviously, Jaime doesn't talk this way, so he wonders where Luisa learned to ask questions like this. Is it normal, or is it a symptom of some type of language disorder?

Not long after children begin to talk, they start combining words to form simple sentences. A typical 2-year-old has a vocabulary of a few hundred words and speaks in sentences that are 2 or 3 words long. At the end of the preschool years, a typical 5-year-old has a vocabulary of several thousand words and speaks in sentences that are 5 or more words long. These impressive changes in language are the focus of this module. We'll begin with word learning, then look at how children master rules for combining words to create sentences, where we'll see that Luisa's way of asking questions is quite normal for youngsters learning English.

Encouraging Word Learning

Children's vocabularies increase steadily during the preschool years. For children to expand their vocabularies, they need to hear others speak. Not surprisingly, then, children learn words more rapidly if their parents speak to them frequently (Roberts, Burchinal, & Durham, 1999). Of course, sheer quantity of parental speech is not all that matters. Parents can foster word learning by naming objects that are the focus of a child's attention (Dunham, Dunham, & Curwin, 1993). Parents can name different products on store shelves as they point to them. During a walk, parents can label the objects—birds, plants, vehicles—that the child sees.

Parents can also help children learn words by reading books with them. Reading together is fun for parents and children alike, and provides opportunities for children to learn new words. However, the way that parents read makes a difference. When parents carefully describe pictures as they read, preschoolers' vocabularies increase (Reese & Cox, 1999). Asking children questions also helps. In a study of 4-year-olds (Sénéchal, Thomas, & Monker, 1995), some parents simply read the story and children listened. Other parents read the story but stopped periodically to ask a "what" or "where" question that the child could answer with the target word. Later, the researchers tested children's abilities to recognize the target words and produce them. The graph shows that children who answered questions recognized more target words than children who only listened. Children who answered questions were also much more likely to produce the target words.

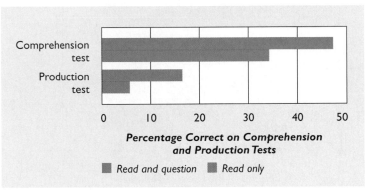

FIG 9–7

Why is questioning effective? When an adult reads a sentence (e.g., Arthur is angling), then asks a question (e.g., What is Arthur doing?), a child must match the new word (*angling*) with the pictured activity (*fishing*) and say the word aloud. When parents read without questioning, children can ignore words they don't understand. Questioning forces children to identify meanings of new words and practice saying them.

Viewing television can also help word learning under some circumstances. For example, preschool children who regularly watch *Sesame Street* usually have larger vocabularies by the time they enter kindergarten than preschoolers who watch *Sesame Street* only occasionally (Rice et al., 1990). Other television programs, notably cartoons, do not have this positive influence. What accounts for the difference? *Sesame Street* involves children in language activities to help them learn words (in the photo, words with *E*). Cartoons, however, require no interaction at all.

Research on reading to children, along with research on television and parents' influence, points to a simple but powerful conclusion: Children are most likely to learn new words when they participate in activities that force them to understand the meanings of new words and use those new words. Is learning new words (and other aspects of language) more difficult for children learning two languages? The Cultural Influences feature has the answer.

CULTURAL INFLUENCES
Growing Up Bilingual

The United States is truly a multicultural nation. In some states, 25 percent or more of the children are bilingual, and the percentages are even higher in some urban areas (U.S. Bureau of the Census, 1995). These youngsters usually speak English and another language, such as Spanish or, like the children in the photo, Chinese.

Is learning two languages easier or harder than learning just one language? For much of the twentieth century, the general view was that bilingualism harmed children's development. One child psychology text published in 1952 surveyed the research and concluded, "There can be no doubt that the child reared in a bilingual environment is handicapped in his language growth." (Thompson, 1952, p. 367) Today, we know that this conclusion is wrong because it was based on studies of poor, immigrant children's scores on intelligence tests. In retrospect, immigrant children's test scores had more to do with their poverty and unfamiliarity with a new culture than with their bilingualism.

In fact, modern studies lead to a different picture. When 1- and 2-year-olds learn two languages simultaneously, they often progress somewhat slowly at first because they mix words from the two languages. By age 3 or 4, however, children separate the languages; and by the time they begin elementary school, most are as proficient as monolinguals in both languages (Baker, 1993; Lanza, 1992).

Furthermore, bilingual children actually *surpass* monolingual children in some language skills. Bilingual preschoolers are more likely to understand that the printed form of a word is unrelated to the meaning of the word (Bialystok, 1997). For example, bilingual preschoolers are less likely to believe that words denoting large objects (e.g., car) are longer than words denoting small objects (e.g., spider).

Bilingual children also better understand that words are simply arbitrary symbols. Bilingual youngsters, for instance, are more likely than monolingual children to understand that, as long as all English speakers agreed, *dog* could refer to cats and *cat* could refer to dogs (Bialystok, 1988; Campbell & Sais, 1995).

Of course, many children in America can't speak English at the time when they should begin school. How to teach these children has prompted much national debate. One view is that all Americans should speak English and so all teaching should be in English. Another view is that children learn more effectively in their native tongue and so all teaching should be done in that language.

Bilingual children learn language as rapidly as monolingual children and they better understand the symbolic nature of words.

Much of the debate over the proper language of instruction is political, reflecting people's desire for a society with a universal cultural heritage and language rather than a society with pluralistic heritages and languages. Ignoring the political aspects, research shows that the best method uses the child's native language *and* English (Padilla et al., 1991; Wong-Fillmore et al., 1985). Initially, children receive basic English-language teaching while they are taught other subjects in their native language. Gradually, more instruction is in English, in step with children's growing proficiency in the second language. When instruction is in children's native language and English, they are most likely to master academic content and English, outcomes that are less likely when instruction is solely in the native language or English. ■

From Two-Word Speech to Complex Sentences

At about 1½ years, children begin to combine individual words to create two-word sentences, like *more juice, gimme cookie, truck go, my truck, Daddy go, Daddy bike.* **Researchers call this kind of talk *telegraphic speech* because, like telegrams of days gone by, it consists of only words directly relevant to meaning.** Before phones and e-mail, people sent urgent messages by telegraph, and the charge was based on the number of words. Consequently, telegrams were brief and to the point, containing only the important nouns, verbs, adjectives, and adverbs, much like children's two-word speech.

In their two-word speech, children follow rules to express different meanings. For example, the sentences *truck go* and *Daddy eat* are both about agents—people or objects that do something and the actions they perform. Here the rule is "agent + action." In contrast, *my truck* is about a possessor and a possession; the rule for creating these sentences is "possessor + possession."

When children are in the two-word stage, they use several basic rules to express meaning (Brown, 1973). These are listed in the table.

Rules Used to Express Meaning During the Two-Word Stage	
Rule	**Example**
agent + action	"Daddy eat"
possessor + possession	"my truck"
action + object	"gimme cookie"
agent + object	"boy car" (meaning the boy is pushing the car)
action + location	"put chair" (meaning put the object on the chair)
entity + location	"truck chair" (meaning the truck is on the chair)
attribute + entity	"big car"
demonstrative + entity	"that cup"
Based on Brown, 1973	

TABLE 9-3

Of course, not all children use all eight rules, but most do. And this is true of children around the world (Tager-Flusberg, 1993). Regardless of the language they learn, children's two-word sentences follow a common set of rules that are very useful in describing ideas concerning people and objects, their actions, and their properties.

When children move beyond two-word sentences, they quickly begin to use much longer sentences. For example, at 1½ years, my daughter Laura would say, "gimme juice" or "bye-bye Mom." As a 2½-year-old, she had progressed to, "When I finish my ice cream, I'll take a shower, okay?" and "Don't turn the light out—I can't see better!" Her improvement was characteristic of most children.

Beginning at about the second birthday, children move to three-word and even longer sentences. **Their longer sentences are filled with *grammatical morphemes*, words or endings of words (such as *-ing*, *-ed*, or *-s*) that make a sentence**

grammatical. To illustrate, a 1½-year-old might say, "kick ball," but a 3-year-old would be more likely to say, "I am kicking the ball." Compared to the 1½-year-old's telegraphic speech, the 3-year-old has added several elements including a pronoun, *I*, to serve as the subject of the sentence, the auxiliary verb *am*, *-ing* to the verb *kick*, and an article, *the*, before *ball*. Each of these grammatical morphemes makes the older child's sentence slightly more meaningful and much more grammatical.

How do children learn all of these subtle nuances of grammar? Conceivably, a child might learn that *kicking* describes kicking that is ongoing and that *kicked* describes kicking that occurred in the past. Later, the child might learn that *raining* describes current weather and *rained* describes past weather. But learning different tenses for individual verbs—one by one—would be remarkably slow going. More effective would be to learn the general rules that "verb + *-ing*" denotes an ongoing activity and "verb + *-ed*" denotes a past activity. In fact, this is what children do: They learn general rules about grammatical morphemes.

Jean Berko (1958) conducted one of the first studies showing that children's use of grammatical morphemes is based on their growing knowledge of grammatical rules, not simply memory for individual words. She showed preschoolers pictures of nonsense objects like the one in the diagram. The experimenter labeled it saying, "This is a wug." Then youngsters were shown pictures of two of the objects while the experimenter said, "Now there is another one. There are two of them. There are two…" Most children spontaneously said, "Wugs." Because *wug* is a novel word, children could answer correctly only by applying the rule of adding *-s* to indicate plural.

Sometimes, of course, applying the general rule can lead to very creative communication. As a 3-year-old, my daughter would say, "unvelcro it," meaning detach the Velcro. She had never heard *unvelcro*, but she created this word from the rule that "*un-* + verb" means to reverse or stop the action of a verb. Creating such novel words is, in fact, evidence that children learn grammar by applying rules, not learning individual words.

Additional evidence that children master grammar by learning rules comes from preschoolers' *overregularization*, **applying rules to words that are exceptions to the rule.** Youngsters learning English may incorrectly add an *s* instead of using an irregular plural—*two mans* instead of *two men* or *two foots* instead of *two feet*. With the past tense, children may add *-ed* instead of using an irregular past tense—*I goed* instead of *I went* or *she runned* instead of *she ran* (Marcus et al., 1992). Children apparently know the general rule but not all the words that are exceptions.

The rules governing grammatical morphemes range from fairly simple to very complex. The rule for plurals—add *-s*—is simple to apply and, as you might expect, it's one of the first grammatical morphemes that children master. Adding *-ing* to denote ongoing action is also simple and it, too, is mastered early. More complex forms, such as the various forms of the verb *to be* are mastered later; but, remarkably, by the end of the preschool years, children typically have mastered most of the rules that govern grammatical morphemes.

At the same time that preschoolers are mastering grammatical morphemes, they extend their speech beyond the subject-verb-object construction that is basic in English. You can see these changes in the way children ask questions. Children's questions during two-word speech are marked by intonation alone. Soon after a child can declare, "My ball," he can also ask "My ball?" Children quickly discover *wh*-words (*who, what, when, where, why*), but they don't use them correctly. Like

This is a wug.

Now there is another one.
There are two of them.
There are two_____ .

FIG 9–8

Luisa, the 2½-year-old in the module-opening vignette, many youngsters merely attach the *wh*-word to the beginning of a sentence without changing the rest of the sentence: *What he eating? What we see?* But by 3 or 3½ years, youngsters insert the required auxiliary verb before the subject, creating *What is he eating?* or *What did we see?* (deVilliers & deVilliers, 1985).

Between ages 3 and 6 years, children also learn to use negation ("That isn't a butterfly") and embedded sentences ("Jennifer thinks that Bill took the ball"). They begin to comprehend passive voice ("The ball was kicked by the girl") as opposed to the active voice ("The girl kicked the ball"), although full understanding of this form continues into the elementary-school years (Tager-Flusberg, 1993). In short, by the time most children enter kindergarten, they use most of the grammatical forms of their native language with great skill.

> As children move beyond two-word speech, they begin to master questions, negation, and other more complex sentence forms.

Ponder these accomplishments for a moment, particularly in light of what else you know about 5-year-old children. Most can neither read nor do arithmetic and some don't know the letters of the alphabet, but virtually all have mastered the grammar of their native tongue. How do they do it? Some answers to this question are in the next section.

How Children Acquire Grammar

If you were asked to explain how children master grammar, where would you begin? You might propose that children learn to speak grammatically by listening to and then copying adult sentences. In fact, B. F. Skinner (1957) and other learning theorists once claimed that all aspects of language—sounds, words, grammar, and communication—were learned through imitation and reinforcement (Whitehurst & Vasta, 1975).

Critics were quick to point to some flaws in the learning explanation of grammar, however. One problem is that children produce many more sentences than they have ever heard. In fact, most of children's sentences are novel, which is difficult to explain in terms of simple imitation of adults' speech. For example, when children create questions by inserting a *wh*-word at the beginning of a sentence ("What she doing?"), who are they imitating?

Also troublesome for the learning view is that even when children imitate adult sentences, they do not imitate adult grammar. In simply trying to repeat, "I am drawing a picture," young children will say, "I draw picture." Furthermore, linguists, particularly Noam Chomsky (1957, 1995), argued that grammatical rules are far too complex for toddlers and preschoolers to infer them solely on the basis of speech that they hear.

If grammatical rules are not acquired through imitation and reinforcement, what is the answer? Perhaps children are born with mechanisms that simplify the task of learning grammar (Slobin, 1985). According to this view, children are born with neural circuits in the brain that allow them to infer the grammar of the language that they hear. That is, grammar itself is not built into the child's nervous system, but processes that guide the learning of grammar are.

This proposal that inborn mechanisms help children learn grammar might not be as intuitively appealing as imitation, but many findings indirectly support this view:

1. *Specific regions of the brain are known to be involved in language processing.* If children are born with a "grammar-learning processor," it should be possi-

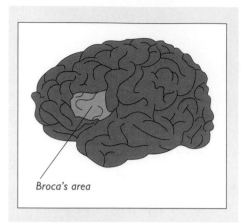

FIG 9-9

ble to locate a specific region or regions of the brain that are involved in learning grammar. In fact, you may remember from Module 5.2 that for most people the left hemisphere of the brain plays a critical role in understanding language. Some functions of language have been located even more precisely. For example, the shaded area in the diagram is Broca's area: a region in the left frontal cortex that is necessary for combining words into meaningful sentences. The fact that specific areas in the brain, such as Broca's area, have well-defined functions for language make it plausible that children have specialized neural circuits that help them learn grammar.

2. *Only humans learn grammar readily.* If grammar is learned solely through imitation and reinforcement, then it should be possible to teach rudimentary grammar to nonhumans. If, instead, learning grammar depends upon specialized neural mechanisms that are unique to humans, then efforts to teach grammar to nonhumans should fail. This prediction has been tested many times by trying to teach grammar to chimpanzees, the species closest to humans on the evolutionary ladder. Chimpanzees like the one in the photo have been taught to communicate using gestures taken from sign language or with plastic chips to stand for words. The result? Chimps master only simple grammatical rules governing two-word speech, but only with massive effort that is completely unlike the preschool child's learning of grammar (Savage-Rumbaugh et al., 1993; Seyfarth & Cheney, 1996). Since numerous efforts to teach grammar to chimps have failed, this suggests that children rely upon some type of inborn mechanism specific to humans to master grammar.

3. *There is a critical period for learning language.* You recall, from Module 1.2, that a critical period refers to a time in development when children master skills or behaviors readily. Apparently, the period from birth to about 12 years is critical to acquiring language generally and mastering grammar particularly. If children do not acquire language in this period, they will never truly master language later. Evidence of a critical period for language comes from studies of isolated children. In one tragic instance, a baby girl named Genie was restrained by a harness during the day and a straightjacket-like device at night. No one was permitted to talk to Genie, and she was beaten when she made any noise. When Genie was discovered, at age 13, her language was very primitive. After several years of language training, her mastery of grammar remains limited, resembling the telegraphic speech of a 2-year-old (Curtiss, 1989; Rymer, 1993).

Further evidence for a critical period for language comes from studies of individuals learning second languages. Individuals master the grammar of a foreign language at the level of a native speaker only if they are exposed to the language prior to adolescence (Newport, 1991). Why is it that one period of time can be so much more influential for language than others? Why can't missed language experiences be made up after age 12? A critical period for language answers these questions. That is, just as females ovulate for only a limited portion of the life span, the neural mechanisms involved in learning grammar may function only during infancy and childhood.

The evidence in favor of an inborn grammar-learning device is impressive but only indirect. As yet, there is no definitive finding that makes an airtight case for the existence of a grammar-learning device (Maratsos, 1998). Consequently, scientists have continued to look for other explanations.

Some theorists (e.g., Braine, 1992) believe that children learn grammar using the same cognitive skills that allow them to learn other rules and regularities in their environments. **According to the *semantic bootstrapping hypothesis*, children rely upon their knowledge of the meanings of words to discover grammatical rules (Bates & MacWhinney, 1987).** That is, children notice that some words (nouns) typically refer to objects, and others (verbs) to actions. They also notice that nouns and verbs have distinct functions in sentences. By detecting such regularities in speech, children gradually infer the grammatical rules that provide structure for their language.

Both the grammar-learning device and the bootstrapping hypothesis could be correct: Children may learn grammar using some mechanisms that are specific to language as well as some that are not (Maratsos, 1998). And both views agree that language experience is important because it provides the information from which grammatical rules are inferred. After all, children growing up in a home where Japanese is spoken master Japanese grammar, not Russian or English grammar.

For many children, parents' speech is the prime source of information about language. Parents fine-tune their speech so that it includes examples of the speech that their children are attempting to master (Hoff-Ginsberg, 1990). For example, when 2- and 3-year-olds begin to experiment with pronouns like *you, I, she,* and *he,* their parents provide many examples of how to use pronouns correctly. Similarly, as these children begin to use auxiliary verbs such as *have, has, was,* and *did,* parents use speech that is especially rich in these verbs (Sokolov, 1993). By providing extra instances of the parts of speech that children are mastering, parents make it easier for children to unearth new grammatical rules.

> Some researchers believe that built-in neural circuits help children infer the grammar of their native language; other researchers believe children use cognitive skills to find regular patterns in speech they hear.

Parents also provide feedback to help children evaluate their tentative grammatical rules. Most of the feedback is indirect. When a child's speech is incorrect or incomplete, parents don't say, "That's wrong!" or "How ungrammatical!" Instead, they rephrase or elaborate the child's remark. For example, if a child were to say, "Sara eating cookie," a parent might reply, "Yes, Sara is eating a cookie." "Doggie go" might lead to "Yes, the doggie left." A parent's reply captures the meaning of the child's remark while demonstrating correct grammatical forms (Bohannon, MacWhinney, & Snow, 1990). At the same time, when a child's grammar is accurate, a parent will often simply repeat it or continue the conversation. Thus, when parents rephrase their children's speech, it means that some aspect of the remark was ungrammatical; if they continue the conversation, it means that the remark was grammatical.

Parents don't provide feedback for all utterances; in fact, a majority of children's errors go uncorrected. However, the amount of feedback is sufficient for children to reject incorrect hypotheses about grammatical rules and retain correct ones (Bohannon et al., 1996).

Which of these different ideas about how children learn grammar is correct? As yet, there is no single, comprehensive theory of how grammar is mastered. But there is general agreement that such a theory will include some mechanisms that are specific to learning grammar, children actively seeking to identify regularities in their environment, and an environment that is rich in language. All three factors keep children on the trail that leads to mastering grammar (MacWhinney, 1998).

The Making Children's Lives Better feature suggests some ways parents and other adults can help children master grammar and other aspects of language.

MAKING CHILDREN'S LIVES BETTER
Promoting Language Development

Adults eager to promote children's language development can follow a few guidelines:

1. Talk with children frequently and treat them as partners in conversation. That is, try talking with children interactively, not directively.

2. Use a child's speech to show new language forms. Expand a child's remark to introduce new vocabulary or new grammatical forms. Rephrase a child's ungrammatical remark to show the correct grammar.

3. Encourage children to go beyond minimal use of language. Have them answer questions in phrases and sentences, not single words. Have them replace vague words such as "stuff" or "somebody" with more descriptive ones.

4. Listen. This guideline has two parts. First, because children often talk slowly, it's tempting for adults to complete their sentences for them. Don't. Let children express themselves. Second, pay attention to what children are saying and respond appropriately. Let children learn that language works.

5. Make language fun. Use books, rhymes, songs, jokes, and foreign words to increase a child's interest in learning language.

Of course, as children's language improves during the preschool years, others can understand it more readily, which means that children become better at communicating. The emergence and growth of communication skills is the topic of the next module. ■

Check Your Learning

1. Young children are most likely to learn new words when parents label objects, when they regularly watch TV programs like *Sesame Street*, and when parents _____.

2. Compared to monolingual children, bilingual children are more likely to know that the printed form of a word is unrelated to the meaning of a word and to know that _____.

3. Children's two-word sentences are based on a common set of rules that are useful in describing _____.

4. As children move beyond two-word sentences, _____ appear in their speech, beginning with those that follow simple rules.

5. Evidence that children learn grammatical rules comes from overregularization, in which children _____.

6. One flaw in the learning explanation of grammar is that children say many novel sentences; another is that _____.

7. Evidence that children are born with specialized neural circuits for learning grammar includes the facts that specific brain regions are associated with

language processing, _____, and there is a critical period for learning language.

8. According to the semantic bootstrapping hypothesis, children _____ to discover grammatical rules.

9. Parents help their children learn grammar by _____ and by providing them with feedback.

■ **Connections** Children master grammar during the preschool years. How well does this feat match Piaget's view of the preschool child's thinking?

Answers: (1) ask questions while reading to them, (2) words are arbitrary symbols, (3) ideas about people and objects, their actions, and their properties, (4) grammatical morphemes, (5) apply grammatical rules to words that are exceptions to the rule, (6) young children trying to imitate adults' speech do not imitate adults' grammar, (7) only humans learn grammar, (8) use their knowledge of word meanings, (9) providing extra examples of the parts of speech that children are trying to master.

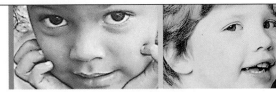

Communicating with Others

9.3
Communicating with Others
├ Taking Turns
├ Speaking Effectively
└ Listening Well

Learning Objectives

■ **When and how do children learn to take turns in conversation?**

■ **What are the skills required to be an effective speaker?**

■ **What is involved in becoming a good listener?**

Marla and Kitty, both 5-year-olds, usually are good friends, but right now they're boiling mad at each other. Marla was going to the mall with her dad to buy some new markers. Kitty found out and gave Marla money to buy some markers for her, too. Marla returned with the markers, but they weren't the kind that Kitty liked, so she was angry. Marla was angry because she didn't think Kitty should be mad; after all, it was Kitty's fault for not telling her what kind to buy. Meanwhile, Marla's dad hopes they come to some understanding soon and cut out all the racket.

Arguments like the one between Marla and Kitty illustrate how easily people can miscommunicate. Often two people talk at the same time, their remarks may be rambling or incoherent, and neither person listens to the other. In contrast, effective oral communication relies upon several simple guidelines:

- People should take turns, alternating as speaker and listener.
- A speaker's remarks should relate to the topic and be understandable to the listener.
- A listener should pay attention and let the speaker know if his or her remarks don't make sense.

Complete mastery of these pragmatic skills is a lifelong pursuit; after all, even adults often miscommunicate with one another because they don't observe one or more of these rules. However, youngsters grasp many of the basics of communication early in life. Let's see.

Taking Turns

Many parents begin to encourage turn-taking long before infants say their first words (Field & Widmayer, 1982):

PARENT:	Can you see the bird?
INFANT (COOING):	ooooh
PARENT:	It is a pretty bird.
INFANT:	ooooh
PARENT:	You're right, it's a cardinal.

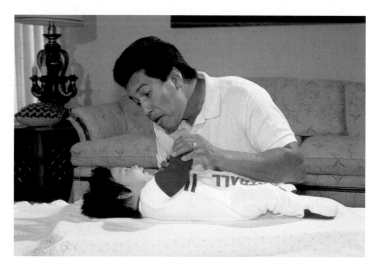

Soon after 1-year-olds begin to speak, parents, like the father in the photo, encourage their youngsters to participate in conversational turn-taking. To help children along, parents often carry both sides of a conversation to demonstrate how the roles of speaker and listener alternate (Shatz, 1983):

PARENT (TO INFANT):	What's Amy eating?
PARENT (ILLUSTRATING REPLY):	She's eating a cookie.

Parents and other caregivers seem to do whatever is necessary to allow infants and toddlers to fit in to a conversation. That is, caregivers scaffold youngsters' attempts to converse, making it more likely that children will succeed.

By age 2, spontaneous turn-taking is common in conversations between youngsters and adults (Barton & Tomasello, 1991). And by age 3, children have progressed to the point that if a listener fails to reply promptly, the child repeats his or her remark in order to elicit a response (Garvey & Berninger, 1981). A 3-year-old might say, "Hi, Paul" to an older sibling who's busy reading. If Paul doesn't answer in a few seconds, the 3-year-old might say, "Hi, Paul" again. When Paul remains unresponsive, the 3-year-old is likely to shout, "PAUL!"—showing that by this age children understand the norm that a comment deserves a response. Preschool children seem to interpret the lack of a response as, "I guess you didn't hear me, so I'll say it again, louder!"

Speaking Effectively

When do children first try to initiate communications with others? Wanting to tell something to someone else is a deliberate act, and, based on Piaget's description of sensorimotor thinking (pages 155–156), we wouldn't expect much communication until near the first birthday. In fact, what appears to be the first deliberate attempts to communicate typically emerge at 10 months (Bates et al., 1979; Golinkoff, 1993). Infants at this age may, like the infant in the photo, point to an object, or they may touch an object. They continue this behavior until the person acknowledges them.

After the first birthday, children begin to use speech to communicate and often initiate conversations with adults (Bloom et al., 1996). Toddlers' first conversations are about themselves but their conversational scope expands rapidly to include objects in the environment (e.g., toys, food). Later, conversations begin to include more abstract notions, such as hypothetical objects and past or future events (Foster, 1986).

Of course, young children are not always skilled conversational partners. At times their communications are confusing, leaving a listener to wonder, "What was that all about?" Every message—whether an informal conversation or a formal lecture—should have a clear meaning. But saying something clearly is often difficult because clarity can only be judged by considering the listener's age, experience, knowledge of the topic, and the context of the conversation. For example, think about the simple request, "Please hand me the Phillips-head screwdriver." This message may be clear to older listeners familiar with different types of screwdrivers, but it won't mean much to younger listeners who think all screwdrivers are alike. And, if the tool box is filled with Phillips-head screwdrivers of assorted sizes, the message won't be clear even to a knowledgeable listener.

Constructing clear messages is a fine art, but, amazingly, by the preschool years, youngsters begin to adjust their messages to match the listener and the context. In a classic study, Marilyn Shatz and Rochel Gelman (1973) asked 4-year-olds to explain how a toy worked, once to a 2-year-old and once to an adult. Shatz and Gelman found that 4-year-olds talked more overall to adults than to 2-year-olds and used longer sentences with adult listeners than with 2-year-old listeners. Also, children used simpler grammar and more attention-getting words, such as *see, look, watch,* and *hey,* when speaking with 2-year-olds. Here, for example, is how one 4-year-old child explained the toy to her two different listeners. (By the way, the toy is a garage with drivers and trucks that carry marbles to a dumping station):

> **Young children adjust their messages based on a listener's age and knowledge.**

Adult listener: You're supposed to put one of these persons in, see? Then one goes with the other little girl. And then the little boy. He's the little boy and he drives. And then they back up. . . . And then the little girl falls out and then it goes backwards.

Two-year-old listener: Watch, Perry. Watch this. He's back in here. Now he drives up. Look, Perry. Look here, Perry. Those are marbles, Perry. Put the men in here. Now I'll do it. (Shatz & Gelman, 1973, p. 13)

Shatz and Gelman's findings show that preschoolers are already sensitive to the importance of the audience in formulating a clear message. In addition, preschool children give more elaborate messages to listeners who are unfamiliar with a topic than to listeners who are familiar with it (O'Neill, 1996). For example, a child describing where to find a toy will give more detailed directions to a listener whose eyes were covered when the toy was hidden.

Preschoolers clearly have begun to understand the factors that must be considered in creating clear messages. Even so, sometimes messages are not clear to listeners. Speakers need to pay attention to listeners; if they don't seem to understand the message, they need to try again. And, in fact, preschool children seem to understand that, when listeners misunderstand, speakers need to do something, such as repeating what they said (Shwe & Markman, 1997). In the grander scheme of things, repeating what you've just said is not a very good strategy. But it is a first step in trying to make oneself better understood.

Thus, preschool children express themselves to others and adjust their conversations to fit listeners. Are they equally adept at listening? We'll find out in the next section.

Listening Well

Listening well may seem easy but it's not—a skilled listener must continuously decide whether a speaker's remarks make sense. If they do, then a listener needs to make an appropriate reply, typically by extending the conversation with another remark that's on the topic.

Few toddlers master this fundamental conversation skill. Their replies are more likely to be unrelated to the topic than related to it (Bloom, Rocissano, & Hood, 1976). Asked, "Where's the sock?" a 1½-year-old may say something like, "I'm hungry!" By 3 years, children are more adept at continuing conversations by making remarks that relate to the topic being discussed.

If a message is vague or confusing, a listener should ask the speaker to clarify the message. This seems obvious enough, but young children do not always realize when a message is ambiguous. Told to find "the red toy," they may promptly select the red ball from a pile that includes a red toy car, a red block, and a red toy hammer. Instead of asking the speaker which specific red toy, young listeners often assume that they know which toy the speaker had in mind (Beal & Belgrad, 1990). Only when messages almost defy comprehension—they are too soft to be heard or give obviously ambiguous or even conflicting information—do youngsters detect a problem.

> Young children often ignore ambiguities in messages and assume they know what the listener intended.

Because young children's remarks often contain ambiguities and because, as listeners, they often do not detect ambiguities, young children often miscommunicate, just like Marla and Kitty in the opening vignette. Kitty probably didn't communicate exactly what kind of markers she wanted, and Marla didn't understand that the directions were unclear. Throughout the preschool and elementary-school years, youngsters gradually master the many skills involved in determining if a message is consistent and clear (Ackerman, 1993).

Sometimes messages are confusing because they conflict with what a listener thinks is true. For example, suppose a child is told that the family cat, who always stays indoors, has run away. Even preschoolers are more likely to believe such a message when told by a parent than by a classmate because they know the parent is better informed about this particular topic (Robinson, Champion, & Mitchell, 1999).

This discussion of listening skills completes our catalog of the important accomplishments that take place in communication during the preschool years. As children enter kindergarten, they have mastered many of the fundamental rules of communication.

Check Your Learning

1. If a listener doesn't respond promptly, a 3-year-old speaker will _____.

2. Before they can talk, infants often try to communicate by making noises or by _____.

3. Preschool children adjust their speech based on a listener's age and _____.

4. When listeners do not understand them, toddlers will sometimes _____.

5. When toddlers respond to a remark, their comment is often _____.

6. Young children often ignore ambiguities in messages because _____.

Active Children Preschool children are often poor communicators: Their comments often do not relate to a topic or may be incomprehensible to a listener. How might these limits in communication skill affect a parent's way of disciplining a preschool child?

Answers: (1) repeat the remark in an effort to elicit a reply, (2) touching or pointing at an object, (3) familiarity with the topic of conversation, (4) repeat their remark, (5) not relevant to the speaker's topic, (6) they assume that they know what the speaker means

Early Childhood Education

9.4

Early Childhood Education

├─ Varieties of Early Childhood Education

├─ Preschool Programs for Economically Disadvantaged Children

└─ Using TV to Educate Preschool Children

Learning Objectives

■ **What are the aims of preschool programs? How are they best achieved?**

■ **How effective is Head Start?**

■ **Can television be used to educate preschool children?**

> *Whenever Bill visits his 5-year-old granddaughter, Harmony, he is struck by the amount of time she spends watching TV. Many of the programs she watches are worthwhile. Nevertheless, Bill wonders if such a steady diet of TV-viewing might somehow be harmful. Images pop on and off the screen so rapidly that Bill wonders how Harmony will ever learn to pay attention. And he worries that she won't be as attentive in other settings that aren't as rich in video stimulation.*

More than 150 years ago, the German educator Friedrich Froebel argued that young children are like flowers: When cared for properly, they blossom and become beautiful. Based on this philosophy, Froebel created the first kindergarten, literally, a garden of children. Through play, Froebel believed that children learn what they can do and what they can become.

In the twentieth century, these same ideas were extended to even younger children, producing early childhood education. In this module, we'll look at the many different forms of early childhood education, and, as we do, we'll see if Bill's concern for his granddaughter is well founded.

Varieties of Early Childhood Education

According to Yahoo! Maps, there are 31 preschools within 5 miles of my home in West Lafayette, Indiana. Some are church-sponsored programs that operate a few mornings each week; others are part of national chains that are open several hours each day; and still others are really day-care facilities, not preschools per se. The situation in West Lafayette is common—American communities typically have a huge number and variety of programs for preschool children, like those shown in the photos at the top of page 270.

Let's begin by distinguishing day-care centers from preschools. The aim of day care is to care for children while their parents are at work; the aim of a preschool is to nurture children's intellectual, social, and emotional growth. The distinction between day care and preschool is no longer clear cut. Why? Most day-care centers typically provide, at some time in the day, the same kinds of growth-promoting activities that were once the trademark of preschools. And, as preschool programs have become more extensive—growing from 2 to 3 hours a few days each week to all morning or all afternoon 5 days each week—they have become a form of child care.

Programs of early childhood education vary in the extent to which the teacher provides a structured curriculum that has explicit instructional goals. In child-centered programs, the goal is to educate the whole child—physically, cognitively, socially, and emotionally. Children learn through play, typically in the context of activities that teachers have prepared for them. In more academically oriented programs, teachers follow an explicit curriculum to help preschool children achieve explicit goals for linguistic, cognitive, social, and emotional growth. These approaches are alike in using play to anchor teaching and learning. They differ primarily in the explicitness of instructional goals and their emphasis on achieving them.

Most U.S. parents agree with an emphasis on using preschool programs to educate the whole child. That is, American parents want preschools to help their youngsters to get a good start academically, to provide the experience of being part of a group, and to encourage children to become self-reliant. These goals are not shared worldwide. In China, parents emphasize academic preparation. In contrast, when Japanese parents send youngsters like those in the photo to preschool, they want them to learn the value of being a good group member (Tobin, Wu, & Davidson, 1989).

In creating preschool programs, many early childhood educators have found Piaget's theory a rich source of ideas (Siegler, 1998). Piaget's view of cognitive development has some straightforward implications for teaching practices that promote children's growth:

- Cognitive growth occurs as children construct their *own* understanding of the world, so the teacher's role is to create environments where children can discover *for themselves* how the world works. A teacher shouldn't simply try to tell children how the letters *a* and *b* differ, but instead should provide children with materials that allow them to discover the differences themselves.
- Children profit from experience only when they can interpret this experience with their current cognitive structures. It follows, then, that the best teaching

experiences are slightly ahead of the children's current skills. As a youngster begins to recognize letters, instead of jumping right to letter-sound skills, a teacher should go to slightly more difficult letter-discrimination problems.

- Cognitive growth can be particularly rapid when children discover inconsistencies and errors in their own thinking. Teachers should, therefore, encourage children to look at the consistency of their thinking but then let children take the lead in sorting out the inconsistencies. If a child is making mistakes in distinguishing letters, a teacher shouldn't correct the error directly but should encourage the child to look at a large number of these errors to discover what he or she is doing wrong.

Drawing upon these and other guidelines, the National Association for the Education of Young Children (NAEYC) has proposed a set of guidelines for developmentally appropriate practices for early childhood education. These practices are shown in Table 9-2.

> Although early childhood education programs vary in the structure of the curriculum, all anchor teaching in play.

NAEYC Recommendations for Developmentally Appropriate Practices in Early Childhood Education	
Practice	**Defined**
Create a caring community of learners	The early childhood setting functions as a community of learners in which all participants—children, families, teachers—contribute to each other's well-being and learning.
Teach to enhance development and learning	Teachers use their knowledge of child development to provide appropriate learning experiences that allow children to acquire important knowledge and skills.
Assess children's learning and development	Age-appropriate assessment of young children's progress is used to benefit children—in adapting teaching to meet children's needs, for communicating with the child's family, and for evaluating the program's effectiveness.
Establish reciprocal relationships with families	Early childhood teachers work in collaborative partnerships with families. Teachers acknowledge parents' goals for children and respond with respect to parents' preferences and concerns without abdicating professional responsibility to children.

Based on NAEYC, 1997.

TABLE 9-2

Preschool programs that embrace most of the guidelines tend to be more effective: Children who "graduate" from such programs tend to be better prepared for kindergarten and first grade. Their behavior in the classroom is more appropriate and they tend to work harder and do better in school (Hart et al., 1993). Consequently, parents should spend the extra time to find preschool programs that follow these guidelines.

Preschool Programs for Economically Disadvantaged Children

Effective preschool education is particularly important for children who are economically disadvantaged. Without preschool, children from low-income families often enter kindergarten or first grade lacking key readiness skills for academic success, which means they rapidly fall behind their peers who have these skills. Consequently, providing preschool experiences for children from poor families has long been a part of federal policies to eliminate poverty. The Child Development and Family Policy feature traces the beginnings of these programs.

CHILD DEVELOPMENT AND FAMILY POLICY

Providing Children with a Head Start for School

For more than 35 years, Head Start has been helping to foster the development of preschool children from low-income families. This program's origins can be traced to two forces. First, in the early 1960s, child-development researchers argued that environmental influences on children's development were much, much stronger than had been estimated previously. The year 1961 marked the appearance of *Intelligence and Experience* by psychologist Joseph McVicker Hunt. Hunt reviewed the scientific evidence concerning the impact of experience on intelligence and concluded that children's intellectual development could reach unprecedented heights once child-development scientists identified optimal environmental influences. In addition, a novel program in Tennessee directed by Susan Gray (Gray & Klaus, 1965) gave credibility to the argument by showing that a summer program coupled with weekly home visits throughout the school year could raise intelligence and language in preschool children living in poverty. Gray's findings suggested that Hunt's claims were not simply pipe dreams.

> The Head Start program was triggered, in part, by research suggesting powerful environmental influences on children's development.

The second force was a political twist of fate. When President Lyndon Johnson launched the War on Poverty in 1964, the Office of Economic Opportunity (OEO) was the command center. Sargent Shriver, OEO's first director, found himself with a huge budget surplus. Most of the War on Poverty programs targeted adults and many of these programs were politically unpopular and Shriver was reluctant to spend more money on these programs. Shriver realized that no programs were aimed at children per se and that such programs would be much less controversial politically. (After all, critics may try to argue that poor adults "deserve their fate" because they're lazy or irresponsible financially, but such arguments are not very convincing when applied to young children.) Furthermore, he was personally familiar with the potential impact of programs targeted at young children through his experience as the president of the Chicago School Board and his wife's work on the President's Panel on Mental Retardation (Zigler & Muenchow, 1992).

Shriver envisioned a program that would better prepare poor children for first grade. In December 1964, he convened a 14-member planning committee that included professionals from medicine, social work, education, and psychology. Over a 6-week period, the planning committee devised a comprehensive program that would, by involving professionals and parents, meet the health and educational needs of young children. In May of 1965, President Johnson announced the opening of Head Start and by that summer, a half-million American youngsters were enrolled. The program continues today and has now served the needs of millions of American children living in poverty. ■

How effectively do these programs meet the needs of preschool youngsters? This turns out to be a question that's hard to answer because of the very nature of Head Start. Since the beginnings in the 1960s, Head Start has been tailored to meet the needs of individual communities; no two Head Start programs are exactly alike. Because Head Start takes on different forms in different communities, this makes it difficult to make blanket statements about the overall effectiveness of the program. However, high-quality Head Start programs are effective overall. That is, Head Start programs that adhere to guidelines like those suggested by the NAEYC (page 271) are successful in many respects. Children are healthier and do better in school (Lazar & Darlington, 1982; Zigler & Styfco, 1994). For example, Head Start graduates *are* less likely to repeat a grade level or to be placed in special education classes. And they are more likely to graduate from high school. Thus, investing in Head Start pays real dividends in dollars not spent on special education or welfare and, more importantly, in improved quality of life for the children who participate.

Using TV to Educate Preschool Children

Nineteen hundred sixty-nine was a watershed in the history of children's television. That year marked the appearance of a program designed to use the power of video and animation to foster preschool skills, including recognizing letters and numbers, counting, and building vocabulary. The program achieved its goals. Preschoolers who watched the show regularly were more proficient at the targeted academic skills than preschoolers who watched infrequently. Regular viewers also adjusted to school more readily, according to teachers' ratings (Bogatz & Ball, 1972).

By now, of course, you know that I'm talking about Big Bird, Bert, Ernie, and other members of the cast of *Sesame Street*, shown in the photo. Since appearing in 1969, *Sesame Street*, produced by the Children's Television Workshop, has helped educate generations of preschoolers. Today, mothers and fathers who watched *Sesame Street* as preschoolers are watching it with their own youngsters.

More recent studies confirm that *Sesame Street* remains effective. Rice and her colleagues (1990), for example, found that children who had watched *Sesame Street* frequently at age 3 had larger vocabularies as 5-year-olds than children who watched infrequently.

Building on the success of *Sesame Street*, the Children's Television Workshop developed a number of other successful programs. The *Electric Company* taught reading skills; *3-2-1 Contact* focused on science and technology, and *Square One TV* taught mathematics (Fisch & McCann, 1993). Other public television programs include *Reading Rainbow*, to introduce children's books; *Where in Time is Carmen Sandiego?*, to teach history; and *Bill Nye the Science Guy*, to make science lessons fun and exciting. Programs like these leave little doubt that children can learn academic skills and useful social skills from TV.

Research with actual TV programs leads to the same conclusion. Youngsters who watch TV shows that emphasize prosocial behavior, such as *Mister Rogers' Neighborhood*, are more likely to behave prosocially (Huston & Wright, 1998). In fact, a comprehensive analysis revealed that the impact of viewing prosocial TV programs is much greater than the impact of viewing televised violence (Hearold, 1986). Boys, in particular, benefit from viewing prosocial TV, perhaps because they usually are much less skilled prosocially than girls.

Although research indicates that prosocial behavior can be influenced by TV watching, two important factors restrict the actual prosocial impact of TV viewing. First, prosocial behaviors are portrayed far less frequently than aggressive behaviors, so opportunities to learn prosocial behaviors from television are limited. Second, the relatively small number of prosocial programs compete with other kinds of television programs and other non-TV activities for children's time, so children simply may not watch the few prosocial programs that are televised. Consequently, we are far from harnessing the power of television for prosocial uses.

> The contents of TV programs can influence children's development, but TV-watching per se does not appear to be harmful.

Television has its critics. Although they concede that some TV programs help children learn, they also argue that the medium itself—independent of the contents of programs—has several harmful effects on viewers, particularly young children (Huston & Wright, 1998). One common criticism is that because TV programs consist of many brief segments presented in rapid succession, children who watch a lot of TV develop short attention spans and have difficulty concentrating in school. Another concern heard frequently is that because TV provides ready-made, simple-to-interpret images, children who watch a lot of TV become passive, lazy thinkers and become less creative.

In fact, as stated, neither these criticisms is consistently supported by research (Huston & Wright, 1998). The first criticism—TV watching reduces attention—is the easiest to dismiss. Research repeatedly shows that increased TV viewing does not lead to reduced attention, greater impulsivity, reduced task persistence, or increased activity levels. The contents of TV programs can influence these dimensions of children's behavior—children who watch impulsive models behave more impulsively themselves—but TV per se does not harm children's ability to pay attention. Bill, the grandfather, in the opening vignette, need not worry that his granddaughter's TV-viewing will limit her ability to pay attention later in life.

As for the criticism that TV viewing fosters lazy thinking and stifles creativity, the evidence is mixed. Many studies find no link between amount of TV viewing and creativity. Some find a negative relation in which, as children watch more TV, they tend to get lower scores on tests of creativity (Valkenburg & van der Voort, 1994, 1995). Child-development researchers don't know why the negative effects aren't found more consistently, although one idea is that the effects depend on what programs children watch, not simply the amount of TV watched.

In general, then, although the contents of TV programs can clearly influence children (positively or negatively, depending on what children watch), there is no strong evidence that TV watching per se has harmful effects on children.

Check Your Learning

1. In child-centered and academically oriented preschools alike, teaching and learning is often anchored in _____.

2. NAEYC guidelines for developmentally appropriate practice call for creating a caring community of learners, teaching that enhances development, _____, and establishing relationships with families.

3. Children who attend Head Start are healthier, less likely to repeat a grade or be placed in special education classes, and are _____.

4. Youngsters who are frequent viewers of *Sesame Street* typically improve their academic skills and, according to their teachers, _____.

5. Contrary to popular criticism, frequent TV-viewing is not consistently related to reduced attention or reduced _____.

■■ **Connections** How do successful Head Start programs demonstrate connec-
■■ tions between different domains of development?

Answers: (1) play, (2) assessing children's learning, (3) more likely to graduate from high school, (4) adjust to school more readily, (5) creativity

Critical Review

1. What, in your opinion, is the most important cognitive change that takes place during the preschool years? Support your opinion by explaining the adaptive importance of that change.

2. Compare three major explanations for how children acquire grammar: learning, inborn neural circuits, and semantic bootstrapping (Module 9.2). Which best fits each of the cognitive theories described in Module 9.1?

3. Piaget's theory provides some useful guidelines for effective preschool programs. What guidelines for such programs can you derive from the information-processing approach? From Vygotsky's theory?

4. Some policy-makers have argued that TV programs like *Sesame Street* could be used to achieve the goals of Head Start programs, but much less expensively. What are the strengths and weaknesses of such a policy?

For more review material, log on to www.prenhall.com/kail ■■■

See For Yourself

Berko's (1958) wugs test is fun to try with preschool children. Photocopy the drawing on page 260 and show it to a preschooler, repeating the instructions that appear on that page. You should find that the child quite predictably says,

two wugs. Create some pictures of your own to examine other grammatical morphemes, such as adding *-ing* to denote ongoing activity or adding *-ed* to indicate past tense. See for yourself!

For More Information About . . .

 Genie, the girl whose tragic childhood provides some fascinating insights into the critical period for language development, read Russ Rymer's *Genie* (HarperCollins, 1993), which describes Genie's childhood and the debates about how best to rehabilitate her.

 preschool children and early childhood education, visit the Web site of the National Association for the Education of Young Children: **http://www.naeyc.org/**

Key Terms

animism 243
attention 249
autobiographical memory 251
cardinality principle 252
centration 243
egocentrism 242
grammatical morphemes 259

inner speech 255
one-to-one principle 252
overregularization 260
preoperational stage 242
private speech 254
scaffolding 254

semantic bootstrapping
  hypothesis 263
stable-order principle 252
telegraphic speech 259
theory of mind 248
zone of proximal development 254

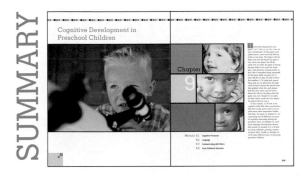

SUMMARY

9.1 Cognitive Processes

Piaget's Account

From 2 to 7 years, children are in Piaget's preoperational stage. Their thinking is limited by egocentrism, the inability to see the world as others do. They are also centered in their thinking and sometimes confuse appearance with reality. During these years, children's theories of biology distinguish properties of animate and inanimate objects and their theories of psychology gradually include the idea that behavior is based on people's beliefs about events and situations.

Information-Processing Perspectives on Preschool Thinking

Compared to older children, preschool children are less able to pay attention, primarily because they lack well-developed strategies for paying attention. Autobiographical memory emerges in the preschool years, often prompted by parents questioning children about past events. Young children's memory of the past is inaccurate because they cannot distinguish what actually happened from what adults suggest may have happened. Preschoolers begin to count at age 2 and by 3 most have mastered the one-to-one, stable-order, and cardinality principles when counting small sets of objects.

Vygotsky's Theory of Cognitive Development

Vygotsky believed that cognition develops first in a social setting and only gradually comes under the child's independent control. The difference between what children can do with assistance and what they can do alone defines the zone of proximal development. Control of cognitive skills is most readily transferred from others to the child through scaffolding, a teaching style that allows children to take on more and more of a task as they master its different components. Children often talk to themselves, particularly when the task is difficult or after they have made a mistake.

9.2 Language

Encouraging Word Learning

Children's word learning is fostered by being read to and by watching television. The key is making children think about the meanings of new words.

From Two-Word Speech to Complex Sentences

Not long after their first birthday, children produce two-word sentences that are based on simple rules for expressing ideas or needs. Moving from two-word to more complex sentences involves adding grammatical morphemes. Children first master grammatical morphemes that express simple relations, then those that denote complex relations.

As children acquire grammatical morphemes they also extend their speech to other sentence forms, such as questions, and, later, to more complex constructions, such as passive sentences.

How Children Acquire Grammar

Some researchers claim that the brain is prewired to help children learn grammar. Findings consistent with this argument are specialized regions in the brain for processing language, the inability of chimpanzees to master grammar, and critical periods in language acquisition. Other researchers believe that children use general cognitive skills to infer grammatical rules from regularities in the speech that they hear.

Language experience is important for learning grammar. Parents provide examples of the rules of speech that their children are trying to master, and they provide children with feedback concerning grammatical rules.

9.3 Communicating with Others

Taking Turns

Parents encourage turn-taking even before infants talk and, later, demonstrate both the speaker and listener roles. By age 3, children spontaneously take turns and prompt one another to speak.

Speaking Effectively

Before they can speak, infants use gestures and noises to communicate. During the preschool years, children gradually become more skilled at constructing clear messages, in part by adjusting their speech to fit the listener's needs. They also begin to monitor their listeners' comprehension, repeating messages if necessary.

Listening Well

Toddlers are not good conversationalists because their remarks don't relate to the topic. Preschoolers are unlikely to identify ambiguities in another's speech.

9.4 Early Childhood Education

Varieties of Early Childhood Education

Most early childhood education programs emphasize play but academically oriented programs embed play in explicit instructional goals. According to Piaget's theory, early childhood education is most effective when it emphasizes children's discovery, provides experiences that are just ahead of the child's current skills, and allows children to discover inconsistencies in their thinking. Guidelines by the NAEYC for developmentally appropriate teaching practice call for creating a caring community of learners, teaching that enhances development, assessing children's learning, and establishing relationships with families.

Preschool Programs for Economically Disadvantaged Children

Head Start was created in the 1960s as part of President Johnson's War on Poverty. Children from low-income families who participate in high-quality Head Start programs are healthier and do better in school.

Using TV to Educate Preschool Children

Children who watch *Sesame Street* regularly improve their academic skills and adjust to school more readily. When children watch programs that emphasize prosocial skills, they are more likely to behave prosocially. Although critics have suggested that frequent TV-viewing leads to reduced attention and reduced creativity, research does not consistently support these criticisms.

Social Behavior and Personality in Preschool Children

Chapter 10

During free play at a local preschool, Carolyn and Sui-Lan had decided they were a mom and dad and were trying to convince Superna, not very successfully, to be their baby. Luke and Aurellio were crawling under a table—pretending that it was a cave—trying to find an evil three-headed monster. Kerry was carefully drawing a picture of her bedroom, complete with her bed, her favorite toys, and her pet gerbil. Elaine and Keisha were arguing about which puzzle they should try to solve. These children at play show the richness of social behavior during the preschool years, a topic that we'll examine in this chapter.

We begin, in Module 10.1, by examining preschool children's growing understanding of self, including their identity as a boy or girl. In Modules 10.2 and 10.3, we look at children's social relationships with parents, siblings, and peers. Finally, in Module 10.4, we examine preschool children's initial efforts to regulate their own behavior to conform to others' requests.

Self

10.1

Self

└ Gender Roles

├ Gender Identity

└ Self-Esteem

Learning Objectives

- **What are gender stereotypes? How do they differ for males and females? What do preschoolers know about gender stereotypes?**

- **How do people, children themselves, and biology contribute to children's learning of gender roles?**

- **Do preschool children have high self-esteem?**

> *Taryn, who has just turned 4, knows that she's a girl but is convinced that she'll grow up to be a man. Taryn plays almost exclusively with boys and her favorite toys are trucks and cars. Taryn tells her parents that when she's bigger, she'll grow a beard and will be a daddy. Taryn's father is confident that his daughter's ideas are a natural part of a preschooler's limited understanding of gender, but her mother wonders if they've neglected some important aspect of Taryn's upbringing.*

In Module 7.3, we learned that, by 15 to 18 months, toddlers begin to acquire a concept of self. They begin to define themselves, a process that accelerates in the preschool years. Youngsters now are likely to define themselves in terms of physical characteristics ("I have blue eyes"), their preferences ("I like spaghetti"), and their competencies ("I can count to 50"). What these features have in common is a focus on a child's characteristics that are observable and concrete (Damon & Hart, 1988).

A particularly important element in the child's search for the self is identifying oneself as a boy or girl and learning the behaviors associated with each role. We'll examine this process in this module and, as we do, we'll learn whether Taryn's wish to grow up to be a man is typical for preschoolers. **We'll also look at children's *self-esteem*, which refers to a person's judgments and feelings about his or her own worth.**

Gender Roles

Like a role in a play, a *social role* is a set of cultural guidelines for how a person **should behave.** The social roles associated with gender are among the first that children learn. **During the preschool years, children learn about *gender roles*—the culturally prescribed roles that are considered appropriate for males and females. All cultures have *gender stereotypes*—beliefs about how males and females differ in personality traits, interests, and behaviors.** Of course, because stereotypes are beliefs, they may or may not be true. For example, read the following sentence:

> *Terry is active, independent, competitive, and aggressive.*

As you were reading this sentence, you probably assumed that Terry was a male. Why? Although Terry is a common name for both males and females, the adjectives used to describe Terry are more commonly associated with men than women. The table on page 281 lists traits that college students typically associate with males and females.

Features Judged by College Students to Be Characteristically Male or Female	
Male	**Female**
Independent	Emotional
Aggressive	Home-oriented
Not excitable	Kind
Skilled in business	Cries easily
Mechanical aptitude	Creative
Outspoken	Considerate
Acts as a leader	Devotes self to others
Self-confident	Needs approval
Ambitious	Gentle
Not easily influenced	Aware of others' feelings
Dominant	Excitable

Based on T. L. Ruble, 1983

TABLE 10–1

The traits associated with males are called *instrumental* because they describe individuals who act on the world and influence it. In contrast, the traits associated with females are called *expressive*, because they describe emotional functioning and individuals who value interpersonal relationships.

American men and women both believe that instrumental traits typify males whereas expressive traits typify females (Lutz & Ruble, 1995; T. L. Ruble, 1983; Williams & Best, 1990). However, these views are *not* shared by adults worldwide. John Williams and Deborah Best (1990) directed an ambitious project involving 300 different traits and participants in 30 countries. The graphs on page 282 present the results for just four traits and seven countries. You can see that each trait shows considerable cultural variation. For example, virtually all American subjects consider men aggressive, but only a slight majority of Nigerian subjects do. Thus, American views of men and women are not shared worldwide. In fact, what's notable about the research results is that Americans' gender stereotypes are more extreme than any other country listed. Keep this in mind as you think about what men and women can and cannot do and what they should and should not do. Your ideas about gender are shaped by your culture's beliefs, which are not held universally.

By the time American children are ready to enter elementary school, they have learned much about gender stereotypes. In a study by Deborah Best and her colleagues (1977), 5-year-olds were asked if 16 stereotypically masculine and 16 stereotypically feminine traits were more typical of boys or girls. Boys and girls judged one-third of the traits the way adults would. They believed, for example, that males were more likely to be assertive and ambitious but that females were more likely to be gentle and affectionate.

Preschool children's view of gender tend to be rigid, too. They do not yet understand that gender stereotypes sometimes do not apply. In one study (Martin, 1989), 4-year-olds were told about hypothetical children, some of whom had same-sex friends and gender-role typical interests. Others had other-sex friends and gender-role atypical interests: "Tommy is a 5-year-old boy whose best friend is a girl.

Compared to adults in other countries, American adults have more extreme stereotypes of men and women.

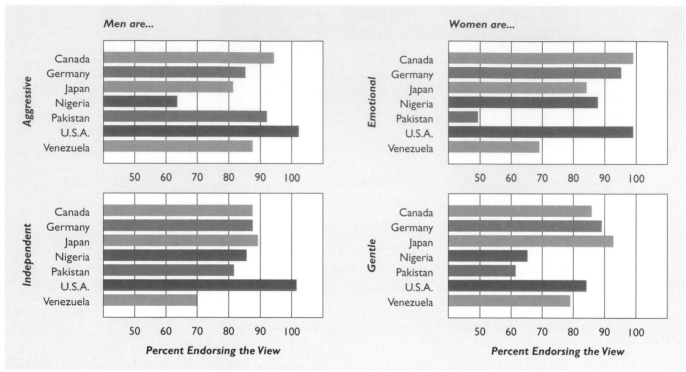

FIG 10–1

Tommy likes to iron with an ironing board." When children were asked how much the hypothetical child would like to play with masculine and feminine toys, they based their judgments solely on the hypothetical child's sex: The hypothetical boys would like masculine toys, the hypothetical girls, the feminine ones. Even though Tommy likes to play with a girl and pretend to iron, 4-year-olds thought he would want to play with masculine toys.

Thus, preschool children tend to see gender stereotypes as general guidelines for behavior that are binding for all boys and girls (Signorella, Bigler, & Liben, 1993; Taylor, 1996). It's important to recognize children's tendency to stereotype gender behavior because stereotypes are very limiting. If we have stereotyped views, we expect males to act in particular ways and females to act in other ways, and we respond to males and females solely on the basis of gender, not as individuals. For example, do you assume the youngster in the photo is a girl based on her taste in toys? Assuming the child is a girl, would, in turn, probably lead you to think she plays more quietly and is more easily frightened than if you assume the child is a boy (Stern & Karraker, 1989). Making stereotyped assumptions about gender leads to a whole host of inferences about behavior and personality that may not be true.

Gender Identity

As youngsters learn the behaviors assigned to males and females, they begin to identify with one of these groups. **Children forge a *gender identity*, the perception of oneself as either male or female.** How do children acquire their culture's roles for males and females? How do they develop a sense of identity as a male or female? We'll answer these questions in this section.

The Socializing Influences of People and the Media. Folklore holds that parents and other adults—teachers and television characters, for example—directly shape children's behavior towards the roles associated with their sex. Boys are rewarded for boyish behavior and punished for girlish behavior.

Parents treat sons and daughters similarly, except for gender-related behavior.

The folklore even has a theoretical basis: According to social learning theorists like Albert Bandura (1977, 1986) and Walter Mischel (1970), children learn gender roles in much the same way that they learn other social behaviors: through reinforcement and observational learning. Parents and others thus shape appropriate gender roles in children, and children learn what their culture considers appropriate behavior for males and females by simply watching how adults and peers act.

How well does research support social learning theory? An extensive analysis of 172 studies involving 27,836 children (Lytton & Romney, 1991) found that parents tend to treat sons and daughters similarly except when it comes to gender-related behavior. That is, parents interact equally with sons and daughters, are equally warm to both, and encourage both sons and daughters to achieve and be independent. But in behavior related to specific gender roles, parents respond differently to sons and daughters. Activities such as playing with dolls, dressing up, or helping an adult are more often encouraged in daughters than in sons; rough-and-tumble play and playing with blocks are more encouraged in sons than in daughters.

Fathers are more likely than mothers to treat sons and daughters differently. More than mothers, fathers like the one in the photo often encourage gender-related play. Fathers also push their sons more but accept dependence in their daughters (Snow, Jacklin, & Maccoby, 1983). A father, for example, may urge his frightened young son to jump off the diving board ("Be a man!") but not be so insistent with his daughter ("That's okay, honey"). Apparently mothers are more likely to respond based on their knowledge of the individual child's needs, but fathers respond based on gender stereotypes. A mother responds to her son knowing that he's smart but unsure of himself; a father may respond based on what he thinks boys should be like.

Peers are also influential. Preschoolers are critical of peers who engage in cross-gender play (Langlois & Downs, 1980). This is particularly true of boys who like feminine toys or who play at feminine activities. A boy who plays with dolls and a girl like the one in the photo who plays with trucks will both be ignored, teased, or ridiculed by their peers, but the boy more harshly than the girl (Levy, Taylor, & Gelman, 1995). Once children learn rules about gender-typical play, they often harshly punish peers who violate those rules.

Peers influence gender roles in another way, too. Between 2 and 3 years of age, children begin to prefer playing with same-sex peers. Little boys play together with cars, and little girls play together with dolls. This preference increases during childhood, reaching a peak in preadolescence. Then the tide begins to turn, but even in adulthood,

time spent at work and at leisure is, quite commonly, segregated by gender (Hartup, 1983). Men play sports or cards together; women shop or have lunch together. This tendency for boys to play with boys and girls with girls has several distinctive features (Maccoby, 1990):

- In some cultures, adults select playmates for children. However, in cultures where children choose playmates, boys select boys as playmates and girls select girls.

- Children spontaneously select same-sex playmates. Adult pressure ("James, why don't you play with John, not Amy") is not necessary.

- Children resist parents' efforts to get them to play with members of the opposite sex. Girls are often unhappy when parents encourage them to play with boys, and boys are unhappy when parents urge them to play with girls.

- Children's reluctance to play with members of the opposite sex is not restricted to gender-typed games, such as playing house or playing with cars. Boys and girls prefer same-sex playmates even in gender-neutral activities such as playing tag or doing puzzles.

Why do boys and girls seem so attracted to same-sex play partners? Eleanor Maccoby (1988, 1990) believes that two factors are critical. First, boys specifically prefer rough-and-tumble play and generally are more competitive and dominating in their interactions. Girls' play is not as rough and is less competitive, so Maccoby argues that boys' style of play may be aversive to girls.

Boys and girls don't play together often because girls don't like boys' style of play and because girls find that their enabling interaction style is ineffective with boys.

Second, when girls and boys play together, girls do not readily influence boys. **Girls' interactions with one another are typically *enabling*—their actions and remarks tend to support others and sustain the interaction. In contrast, boy's interactions are often *constricting*—one partner tries to emerge as the victor by threatening or contradicting the other, by exaggerating, and so on.** When these styles are brought together, girls find their enabling style is ineffective with boys. The same subtle overtures that work with other girls have no impact on boys. Boys ignore girls' polite suggestions about what to do and ignore girls' efforts to resolve conflicts with discussion.

Regardless of the exact cause, early segregation of playmates by style of play means that boys learn primarily from boys and girls from girls. This helps solidify a youngster's emerging sense of membership in a particular gender group and sharpens the contrast between their own gender and the other gender.

Television also influences children's gender-role learning. Women on television tend to be cast in romantic, marital, or family roles; they are depicted as emotional, passive, and weak. Men are more often cast in leadership or professional roles and are depicted as rational, active, and strong (Huston et al., 1992). Consequently, children who watch a lot of TV end up with more stereotyped views of males and females. For example, Kimball (1986) studied gender-role stereotypes in a small Canadian town that was located in a valley and could not receive TV programs until a transmitter was installed in 1974. Children's views of personality traits, behaviors, occupations, and peer relations were measured before and after TV was introduced.

The graphs on page 285 show changes in boys' and girls' views; positive numbers indicate a change toward more stereotyped views. Boys' views were more stereotyped on all four dimensions. For example, in their more stereotyped views of occupations, boys now believed that girls could be teachers and cooks whereas boys could be physicians and judges. Girls' views were more stereotyped only for traits and

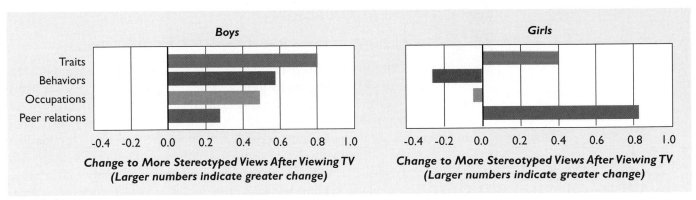

FIG 10-2

peer relations. After TV was introduced, girls believed that boasting and swearing were characteristic of boys and sharing and helping were characteristic of girls. Findings like these indicate that TV viewing causes children to adopt many of the stereotypes that dominate television programming (Signorielli & Lears, 1992).

Let's now return to our original question: How well does research support the social learning explanation of gender roles? Studies of parents, peers, and TV show that children learn much about gender roles simply by observing males and females. But simple observation of real-life models or television characters cannot be the entire explanation. You can see why if you think about young boys growing up. They traditionally have far more opportunities to observe their mother's behavior than their father's, yet boys are more likely to imitate their father (using hammer and saw) than their mother (cooking). Thus, an important element in learning about gender is identifying with one gender and then actively seeking out activities that are typical for that gender. This aspect of gender-role learning is the focus of cognitive theories, which we'll examine next.

Cognitive Theories of Gender Identity. According to Lawrence Kohlberg (1966; Kohlberg & Ullian, 1974), full understanding of gender develops gradually and involves three elements:

- *Gender labeling:* **By age 2 or 3, children understand that they are either boys or girls and label themselves accordingly.**
- *Gender stability:* **During the preschool years, children begin to understand that gender is stable: Boys become men and girls become women.** However, children in this stage believe that a girl who wears her hair like a boy will become a boy and that a boy who plays with dolls will become a girl (Fagot, 1985).
- *Gender consistency:* **Between 4 and 7 years, most children understand that maleness and femaleness do not change over situations or according to personal wishes.** They understand that a child's sex is unaffected by the clothing that a child wears or the toys that a child likes.

Taryn, the 4-year-old in the opening vignette, is in the first stage—she knows that she's a girl. However, she has yet to develop a sense of gender stability or gender consistency. **When children understand labels, stability, and consistency, they have mastered *gender constancy.***

According to Kohlberg's theory, only children who understand gender constancy should have extensive knowledge of sex-stereotyped activities (Newman, Cooper, & Ruble, 1995). That is, not until children understand that gender is constant do they begin to learn what is appropriate and possible for their gender and what is not, as you'll see in the Real Children feature.

REAL CHILDREN

Laura Trades Her Penis for Pom-Poms

When my daughter Laura was 2, she knew that she was a girl but she also insisted that she would grow up to be a daddy. She also claimed that she had a penis, which she would show by pulling her labia away from her body until they were extended about an inch. I have no idea why she did these things, but they clearly document her limited understanding of gender! At about the same time, my son Ben was on a school wrestling team. Laura often went with me to watch Ben wrestle. Afterwards, she thought it was great fun to wrestle on the living room floor, slapping her hand down on the carpet when she pinned me. Never did she comment on the fact that all the wrestlers were boys; evidently this was irrelevant.

By the time she turned 4, Laura's understanding of gender was much better. She knew that she would become a woman and that she did not have a penis. At this age, I remember vividly taking her to watch Ben play football. I wondered if she would become so bored and restless that we'd need to leave. Wrong. Laura immediately discovered the cheerleaders (all girls) and insisted we sit right in front of them. Throughout the game (and the rest of the season), Laura's eyes were riveted to the cheerleaders' every move, and when we'd get home, she'd imitate their routines. According to Kohlberg's theory, 4-year-old Laura knew that cheerleading was for girls and that because she was a girl, cheerleading was for her. ■

> According to cognitive theories, after children understand that gender is constant, they try to learn more about activities and behaviors typically associated with their gender.

Laura's interest in gender-typical behavior emerged only after she understood gender constancy. You can see this same pattern in findings from research (Szkrybalo & Ruble, 1999). For example, Martin and Little (1990) measured preschool children's understanding of gender and their knowledge of gender-typed activities (for example, that girls play with dolls and that boys play with airplanes). The youngest children in their study—3½- to 4-year-olds—did not understand gender constancy and they knew little of gender-stereotyped activities. By age 4, children understood gender constancy but still knew little of gender-stereotyped activities. By 4½ years, many children understood gender constancy *and* knew gender-typical and gender-atypical activities. Importantly, there were no children who lacked gender constancy but knew about gender-stereotyped activities, a combination that is impossible according to Kohlberg's theory.

Kohlberg's theory specifies *when* children begin learning about gender-appropriate behavior and activities (once they understand gender constancy) but not *how* such learning takes place. A theory proposed by Martin and Halverson (1987), illustrated in the diagram, addresses how children learn about gender. **In *gender-schema theory*, children first decide if an object, activity, or behavior is female or male, then use this information to**

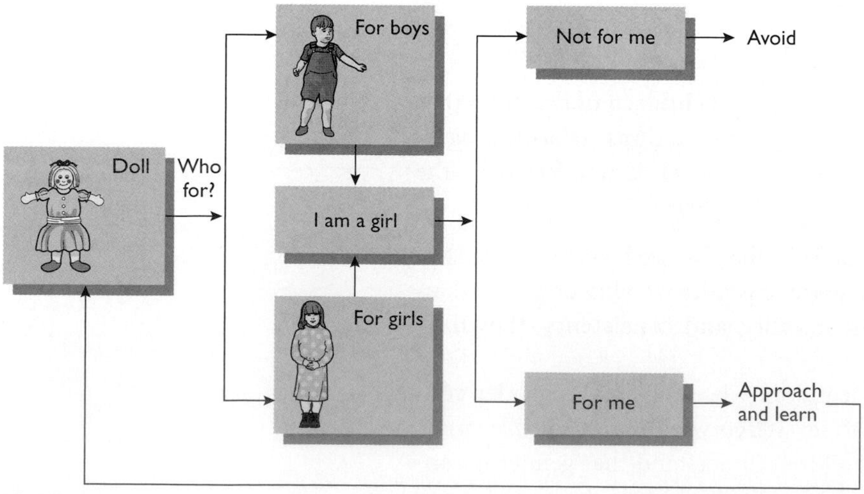

FIG 10-3

Source: Martin & Halvarson, 1981.

decide whether or not they should learn more about the object, activity, or behavior. That is, once children know their gender, they pay attention primarily to experiences and events that are gender appropriate (Martin & Halverson, 1987). According to gender-schema theory, the preschool boy in the photo who is watching a group of girls playing in the sand will decide that playing in the sand is for girls and that, because he is a boy, playing in the sand is not for him. Seeing a group of older boys playing football, he will decide that football is for boys, and because he is a boy, football is acceptable and he should learn more about it.

According to gender-schema theory, after children understand gender, it's as if they see the world through special glasses that allow only gender-typical activities to be in focus (Liben & Signorella, 1993). After children understand gender, their tastes in TV programs begin to shift along gender-specific lines (Luecke-Aleksa et al., 1995). In addition, they begin to use gender labels to evaluate toys and activities. Shown an unfamiliar toy and told that children of a specific gender *really* like this toy, children like the toy much more if others of their gender do, too (Martin, Eisenbud, & Rose, 1995).

This selective viewing of the world explains a great deal about children's learning of gender roles, but as we'll see in the next section, one final important element needs to be considered.

Biological Influences. A fertilized human egg has 23 pairs of chromosomes. If the 23rd pair includes an X and a Y chromosome, then testes develop about 6 weeks after conception; if the 23rd pair includes two X chromosomes, then ovaries appear about 10 weeks after conception. During prenatal development, the testes and ovaries secrete hormones that regulate the formation of male and female genitals and some features of the central nervous system. This raises an obvious question: Do these hormones also contribute to gender differences in behavior and, in turn, social roles? As you can imagine, this question is not easy to answer because scientists cannot experiment directly with hormones as they are secreted during prenatal development. We do know that hormones are a factor in gender differences in aggressive behavior; however, their role in other gender-based differences in behavior is less clear.

Let's look at some evidence that supports a role for biological influence:

- On questionnaires that measure instrumental traits associated with males (such as being independent, self-confident, aggressive) and expressive traits associated with females (such as being emotional, creative, considerate), identical twins' answers are more similar than fraternal twins' answers (Mitchell, Baker, & Jacklin, 1989). This result suggests that how expressive or instrumental a child is depends, in part, on heredity.

- During prenatal development the adrenal glands sometimes malfunction and, as a result, some females are inadvertently exposed to unusually large amounts of male hormones, such as androgen. In growing up, some of these girls prefer masculine activities (such as playing with cars instead of dolls) and male playmates to a much greater extent than girls not exposed to these amounts of androgen (Berenbaum & Snyder, 1995; Collaer & Hines, 1995), which suggests that androgen influences the development of masculine traits.

Neither of these findings provides ironclad evidence that biology promotes children's learning of gender roles. The studies of twins, at best, suggest hereditary influence but don't tell how biology promotes learning of gender roles. The studies of prenatal exposure to androgen are not completely convincing because the levels of hormones are so much greater than normal that it's risky to make judgments about normal hormone levels.

Perhaps the most accurate conclusion to draw is that biology, the socializing influence of people and media, and the child's own efforts to understand gender-typical behavior all help children to learn gender roles and to acquire a gender identity. In the next section, we'll see that as childen's identities become more well developed, they start to like some aspects of themselves more than others.

Self-Esteem

During the preschool years, children begin to take more responsibility for themselves. For example, they dress themselves. They also begin to identify with adults and begin to understand the opportunities that are available in their culture. Play begins to have purpose as children explore adult roles, such as mother, father, teacher, athlete, or musician. Youngsters start to explore the environment on their own, asking innumerable questions about the world, and imagine possibilities for themselves.

Erik Erikson, in the theory of psychosocial development that I described in Module 1.2, argued that young children soon realize their initiative may place them in conflict with others; they cannot pursue their goals and ambitions with abandon. **According to Erikson, *purpose* is achieved with a balance between individual initiative and a willingness to cooperate with others.**

Erikson claimed that achieving purpose was a normal developmental milestone, just as most infants become attached to caregivers. One of the byproducts of this psychosocial growth is that preschool children acquire self-esteem, the first feelings of their own worth. Children with high self-esteem judge themselves favorably and feel positive about themselves. In contrast, children with low self-esteem judge themselves negatively, are unhappy with themselves, and often would rather be someone else.

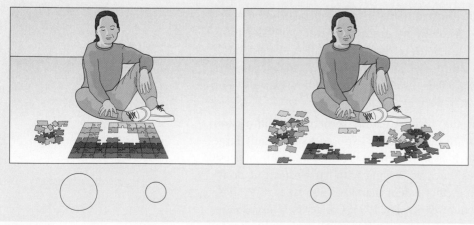

FIG 10–4

During the preschool years, self-esteem is often measured with an approach devised by Harter and Pike (1984). The sample pictures show a girl either solving a puzzle easily or having difficulty. During testing, children are first asked to point to the pictured child who is most like them. Then they point to the larger circle if they believe that they are "a lot" like the child in that picture or the smaller one if they believe they are "a little" like the child in that picture. Harter and Pike used 24 pairs of pictures like these to measure children's self-worth in four areas: cognitive competence, physical competence, acceptance by peers, and acceptance by mother.

When scientists use methods like these, they typically find preschool children have very positive views of themselves across many different domains. For example, when Harter and Pike (1984) used the pictures shown on page 288 to estimate kindergarten children's cognitive competence (e.g., the child solves puzzles easily), the average score was 3.6 out of a possible 4. In other words, virtually all the children said they were either a little or a lot like the competent child. Most preschool children have extraordinarily high self-esteem; they are full of self-confidence and eager to take on new tasks. In fact, self-esteem is at its peak at this age. As we'll see in Module 13.1, self-esteem drops when children begin school.

Self-esteem is at its peak in the preschool years.

Check Your Learning

1. Male gender stereotypes include instrumental traits while female gender stereotypes emphasize _____ traits.

2. Compared to adults from other countries, Americans' views on gender are _____.

3. When asked whether a child with gender-atypical interests would like to play with gender-typical or gender-atypical toys, most preschoolers say _____.

4. Parents treat sons and daughters similarly except when it comes to _____.

5. Same-sex play is common because most girls don't enjoy boys' rough-and-tumble play and because _____.

6. In Kohlberg's theory, during the preschool years, children master _____; that is, they understand that boys become men and girls become women.

7. According to cognitive theories, children want to learn about gender-typical activities only after _____.

8. One way to measure self-esteem in young children is to show pictures of children succeeding or failing in different domains and ask them _____.

9. For most preschoolers, self-esteem is quite _____.

■ ■ **Nature and Nurture** What evidence supports the role of the environment
■ ■ in the development of children's gender identities? What evidence shows the influence of biology?

Answers: (1) expressive, (2) more stereotyped, (3) the child will want to play with the gender-typical toy, (4) gender-related behavior, (5) girls find that their enabling style of interaction is ineffective with boys, (6) gender stability, (7) they have learned that gender is constant, (8) which picture is more like them, (9) high

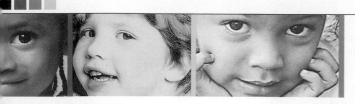

Relationships with Parents

10.2

Learning Objectives

■ **What is a systems view of family dynamics?**

■ **What are the primary dimensions of parenting?**

■ **What parental behaviors affect children's development?**

■ **How do children help determine how parents rear them?**

■ **What role does family configuration play in children's development?**

> *Kelly and Alexia, both 4-year-olds, wanted to have a snack. When Kelly asked her mom she said, "No way!" When Kelly asked, "Why not?" her mother exploded, "Because I said so. That's why. Stop pestering me." The next day the girls were at Alexia's house and they saw some chocolate chip cookies on the kitchen counter. When Alexia asked her mom if they could have some she said, "No," then explained that it was too close to dinner. But she said that each girl could pick one cookie and save it until after dinner.*

The vignette illustrates what we all know well from personal experience—parents go about child rearing in many different ways. In this module, you'll learn about different approaches that parents take to raising children. But let's begin by thinking about parents as an important element in the family system.

The Family as a System

A simple-minded view of child-rearing is that parents' actions are all that really matter. That is, through their behavior, parents directly and indirectly determine their children's development. This view of parents as all powerful was part of early psychological theories (e.g., Watson, 1925) and is held even today by some first-time parents. But most theorists now view families from an ecological perspective (described in Module 1.2). That is, families form a system of interacting elements—parents and children influence one another (Parke & Buriel, 1998).

In the systems view, parents still influence their children, both directly—for example, by encouraging them to study hard—and indirectly—for example, by being generous and kind to others. However, the influence is no longer exclusively from parent to children but is mutual: Children influence their parents, too. By their behaviors, attitudes, and interests, children affect how their parents behave toward them. When, for example, children resist discipline, parents may become less willing to reason and more inclined to use force (Ritchie, 1999).

Even more subtle influences become apparent when families are viewed as systems of interacting elements. For example, fathers' behaviors can affect mother-child relationships—a demanding husband may leave his wife with little time, energy, or interest in helping her daughter with her homework. Or, when siblings argue constantly, parents may become preoccupied with avoiding problems rather than encouraging their children's development.

These many examples show that narrowly focusing on parents' impact on children misses the complexities of family life. But there is even more to the systems view. The family itself is embedded in other social systems, such as neighborhoods and religious institutions (Parke & Buriel, 1998). These other institutions can affect family dynamics. Sometimes they simplify child rearing, as when neighbors are trusted friends and can help care for each others' children. Sometimes, however, they complicate child rearing. Grandparents who live nearby and visit constantly can create friction within the family. At times, the impact of the larger systems is indirect, as when work schedules cause a parent to be away from home or when schools must eliminate programs that benefit children.

The diagram summarizes the numerous interactive influences that exist in a systems view of families. In the remainder of this module, we'll describe parents' influences on children and then how children affect their parents' behavior. Finally, we'll consider how parent-child influences vary with culture and family configuration.

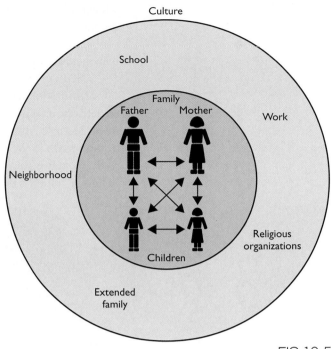

FIG 10–5

Dimensions and Styles

Parenting can be described in terms of general dimensions that are like personality traits in that they represent stable aspects of parental behavior—aspects that hold across different situations (Holden & Miller, 1999). Research consistently reveals two general dimensions of parental behavior. One is the degree of warmth and responsiveness that parents show their children. Another is the amount of control parents exert over their children.

Let's look first at warmth and responsiveness. At one end of the spectrum are parents who are openly warm and affectionate with their children. They are involved with them, respond to their emotional needs, and spend considerable time with them. At the other end of the spectrum are parents who are relatively uninvolved with their children and sometimes even hostile toward them. These parents often seem more focused on their own needs and interests than their children's. Warm parents enjoy hearing their children describe the day's activities; uninvolved or hostile parents aren't interested, considering it a waste of their time. Warm parents see when their children are upset and try to comfort them; uninvolved or hostile parents pay little attention to their children's emotional states and invest little effort comforting them when they're upset.

As you might expect, children benefit from warm and responsive parenting (Pettit, Bates, & Dodge, 1997). When parents are warm toward them, children typically feel secure and happy, and they're better behaved. In contrast, when parents are uninvolved or hostile, their children are often anxious and less controlled. And, children often have low self-esteem when their parents are uninvolved (Rothbaum & Weisz, 1994).

Children benefit from warm, responsive parenting.

A second general dimension of parental behavior concerns the control that parents exercise over their children's behavior. At one end of this spectrum are controlling, demanding parents. These parents virtually run their children's lives. Overcontrol is shown by parents who always want to know where their teenagers are and what they are doing. At the other end of the spectrum are parents who make few demands and rarely exert control. Their children are free to do almost anything without fear of parental reproach. Parents who undercontrol don't care where their teenagers are or what they are doing.

Neither of these extremes is desirable. Overcontrol deprives children of the opportunity to meet behavioral standards on their own, which is the ultimate goal of socialization. When parents direct every aspect of preschoolers' lives, their children never learn to make decisions for themselves. Undercontrol fails children because it doesn't teach them cultural standards for behavior. When parents allow preschoolers to do whatever they want, their children don't believe they are accountable for their behavior, which is definitely not true in the long run.

Parents need to strike a balance, maintaining adequate control while still allowing children freedom to make some decisions for themselves. This is often easier said than done, but a good starting point is setting standards that are appropriate for the child's age, then showing the child how to meet them, and, finally, rewarding the child for complying (Powers & Roberts, 1995; Rotto & Kratochwill, 1994). Suppose a mother wants her preschooler to fold and put away her socks. This is a reasonable request because the child is physically capable of this simple task and she knows where the socks should be stored. Like the mother in the photo, she should show her daughter how to complete the task, and then praise her when she does.

Once standards are set, they should be enforced consistently. For example, the mother should insist that her daughter always fold and put away her socks, not just occasionally. When parents enforce rules erratically, children come to see rules as optional instead of obligatory, and they try to avoid complying with them (Conger, Patterson, & Ge, 1995).

Effective control is also based on good communication. Parents should explain why they've set standards and why they reward or punish as they do. If a mother wants her son to clean his room, she should explain that a messy room is unsafe, makes it difficult to find toys that he wants, and makes it difficult for her to clean. Parents can also encourage children to ask questions if they don't understand or disagree with standards. If the son feels that his mother's standards for orderliness are so high that it's impossible to play in his room, he should feel free to raise the issue with his mother without fear of making her angry.

A balanced approach to control—based on age-appropriate standards, consistency, and communication—avoids the problems associated with overcontrol because the expectations more likely reflect the child's level of maturity and they are open to discussion. A balanced approach also avoids the problems of undercontrol because standards are set and parents expect children to meet those standards consistently.

Cultural Differences in Warmth and Control. Control and warmth are universal aspects of parents' behavior, but views about the "proper" amounts of each vary with particular cultures. European Americans want their children to be happy and self-reliant individuals, and they believe these goals can best be achieved when parents are warm and exert moderate control (Goodnow, 1992; Spence, 1985). In many Asian and Latin American countries, however, individualism is less important than cooperation and collaboration (Okagaki & Sternberg, 1993). In China, for example, Confucian principles dictate that parents are always right and that emotional restraint is the key to family harmony (Chao, 1994). In fact, consistent with their cultural values, mothers and fathers in China are more likely to emphasize parental control and less likely to express affection than are mothers and fathers in the United States (Lin & Fu, 1990).

Parenting Styles. Combining the dimensions of warmth and control produces four prototypic styles of parenting, as shown in the diagram (Baumrind, 1975, 1991).

	Parental Control	
	High	Low
High	Authoritative	Indulgent-Permissive
Low	Authoritarian	Indifferent-Uninvolved

Parental Involvement

FIG 10–6

- *Authoritarian parenting* **combines high control with little warmth.** These parents lay down the rules and expect them to be followed without discussion. Hard work, respect, and obedience are what authoritarian parents wish to cultivate in their children. There is little give-and-take between parent and child because authoritarian parents do not consider children's needs or wishes. This style is illustrated by Kelly's mother in the opening vignette and the mother in the photo. Neither feels any obligation whatsoever to explain her decisions.

- *Authoritative parenting* **combines a fair degree of parental control with being warm and responsive to children.** Authoritative parents explain rules and encourage discussion. This style is exemplified by Alexia's mother in the opening vignette. She explained why she did not want the girls eating cookies now and found a compromise that allowed them to have cookies later.

- *Indulgent-permissive parenting* **offers warmth and caring but little parental control.** These parents generally accept their children's behavior and punish them infrequently. An indulgent-permissive parent would readily agree to Kelly or Alexia's request to have a snack, simply because it is something the child wants to do.

- *Indifferent-uninvolved parenting* **provides neither warmth nor control.** Indifferent-uninvolved parents provide for their children's basic physical and emotional needs but little else. They try to minimize the amount of time spent with their children and avoid becoming emotionally involved with them. If Kelly or Alexia had parents with this style, she might have simply eaten the snack without asking, knowing that her parents wouldn't care and would rather not be bothered.

Overall, children are best served by the warmth and control associated with authoritative parenting.

Of these four styles, children are usually best served by the combination of warmth and control that is the hallmark of authoritative parenting (Baumrind, 1991; Maccoby & Martin, 1983). Children with authoritative parents tend to be responsible, self-reliant, and friendly. In contrast, children with authoritarian parents typically have lower self-esteem and are less skilled socially. Children with indulgent-permissive parents are often impulsive and easily frustrated. Children with indifferent-uninvolved parents have low self-esteem and are impulsive, aggressive, and moody.

The benefits of authoritative parenting are not restricted to European American children. They apply as well to children and parents from several different ethnic groups in the United States, including people of African, Asian, and Hispanic descent (Brody & Flor, 1998; Steinberg et al., 1992). However, some researchers find that authoritarian parenting can benefit children growing up in poverty (Furstenberg, 1993).Why? When youngsters grow up in neighborhoods with a lot of violence and crime, strict obedience to parents can protect children (Kelly, Power, & Wimbush, 1992).

As important as these different dimensions and styles are for understanding parenting, there is more to effective child rearing, as we'll see in the next section.

Parental Behavior

Dimensions and styles are general characterizations of how parents typically behave. If, for example, I describe a parent as warm or controlling, you immediately have a sense of that parent's usual style in dealing with his or her children. Nevertheless, the price for such a broad description is that it tells us little about how parents behave in specific situations and how these parental behaviors influence children's development. Put another way, what specific behaviors can parents use to influence their children? Researchers who study parents name three: direct instruction, modeling, and feedback.

Direct Instruction. Parents often tell their children what to do. But simply playing the role of drill sergeant in ordering children around—"Clean your room!" "Turn off the TV!"—is not very effective. **A better approach is *direct instruction*, telling a child what to do, when, and why.** Instead of just shouting, "Share your candy with your brother!" a parent should explain when and why it's important to share with a sibling.

> Parents can influence children through direct instruction, by acting as models, and by providing feedback.

In addition, just as coaches help athletes master sports skills, parents can help their youngsters master social and emotional skills. Parents can explain links between emotions and behavior—"Catlin is sad because you broke her crayon" (Gottman, Katz, & Hooven, 1996). They can also teach how to deal with difficult social situations—"When you ask Lindsey if she can sleep over, do it privately so you won't hurt Kaycee's or Hannah's feelings" (Mize & Pettit, 1997). In general, children who get this sort of parental "coaching" tend to be more socially skilled and, not surprisingly, get along better with their peers.

Direct instruction and coaching are particularly powerful when paired with modeling. Urging children to act in particular way, such as sharing with others, is more compelling when children also see others sharing. In the next section, we'll see how children learn by observing others.

Learning by Observing. Children learn a great deal from parents simply by watching them. The parents' modeling and the youngsters' observational learning thus leads to imitation, so children's behavior resembles the behavior they observe. **Observational learning can also produce *counterimitation*, learning what should not be done.** If an older sibling kicks a friend and parents punish the older sibling, the younger child may learn not to kick others.

Sometimes observational learning leads to *disinhibition*, an increase in all behaviors like those observed. Children who watch their parents shouting angrily, for example, are more likely to yell at or push a younger sibling. In other words, observation can lead to a general increase in aggression, or put still another way, aggressive responses became disinhibited. **The opposite effect, in which an entire**

class of behaviors is made less likely, is known as *inhibition.* When a child, like the one in the photo, sees parents punish a sibling, the child is less likely to behave in the ways that led the sibling to be punished.

So far, we've seen that parents influence their children's development by direct instruction and by acting as models that children can observe. In the next section, we'll see how parents use feedback to affect children's behavior.

Feedback. By giving feedback to their children, parents indicate whether a behavior is appropriate and should continue or is inappropriate and should stop. Feedback comes in two general forms. *Reinforcement* **is any action that increases the likelihood of the response that it follows.** Parents may use praise to reinforce a child's studying or give a reward for completing household chores. *Punishment* **is any action that discourages the reoccurrence of the response that it follows.** Parents may forbid children to watch television when they get poor grades in school or make children go to bed early for neglecting household chores.

Of course, parents have been rewarding and punishing their children for centuries, so what do psychologists know that parents don't know already? In fact, researchers have made some surprising discoveries concerning the nature of reward and punishment. **Parents often unwittingly reinforce the very behaviors they want to discourage, a situation called the** *negative reinforcement trap* (Patterson, 1980). The negative reinforcement trap occurs in three steps, most often between a mother and her son. In the first step, the mother tells her son to do something he doesn't want to do. She might tell him to clean up his room, to come inside while he's outdoors playing with friends, or to study instead of watching television. In the next step, the son responds with some behavior that most parents find intolerable: He argues, complains, or whines—not just briefly, but for an extended period of time. In the last step, the mother gives in—saying that the son needn't do as she told him initially—simply to get the son to stop the behavior that is so intolerable.

The feedback to the son is that arguing (or complaining or whining) works; the mother rewards that behavior by withdrawing the request that the son did not like. That is, although we usually think a behavior is strengthened when it is followed by the presentation of something that is valued, behavior is also strengthened when it is followed by the removal of something that is disliked.

As for punishment, research (Parke, 1977) shows that punishment works best when

- administered directly after the undesired behavior occurs, not hours later.
- an undesired behavior *always* leads to punishment, not usually or occasionally.
- accompanied by an explanation of why the child was punished and how punishment can be avoided in the future.
- the child has a warm, affectionate relationship with the person administering the punishment.

At the same time, research reveals some serious drawbacks to punishment. One is that punishment is primarily suppressive: Punished responses are stopped, but only temporarily if children do not learn new behaviors to replace those that were punished. For example, denying TV to brothers who are fighting stops the undesirable behavior, but fighting is likely to recur unless the boys learn new ways of solving their disputes.

A second drawback is that punishment can have undesirable side effects. Children become upset as they are being punished, which makes it unlikely that they will understand the feedback punishment is meant to convey. A child denied TV for misbehaving may become angry over the punishment itself and ignore why he's being punished. Furthermore, when children are punished physically, they often imitate this behavior with peers and younger siblings (Whitehurst & Vasta, 1977). Children who are spanked often use aggression to resolve their disputes with others.

One method combines the best features of punishment while avoiding its shortcomings. **In *time-out*, a child who misbehaves must briefly sit alone in a quiet, unstimulating location.** Some parents have children sit alone in a bathroom; others have children sit away from others, as shown in the photo. Time-out is punishing because it interrupts the child's ongoing activity and isolates the child from other family members, toys, books, and, generally, all forms of rewarding stimulation.

The period is sufficiently brief—usually just a few minutes—for a parent to use the method consistently. During time-out, both parent and child typically calm down. Then, when time-out is over, a parent can talk with the child and explain why the punished behavior is objectionable and what the child should do instead. Reasoning like this—even with preschool children—is effective because it emphasizes why a parent punished initially and how punishment can be avoided in the future.

Thus, parents can influence children by direct instruction, by modeling behavior that they value and not modeling what they don't want their children to learn, by giving feedback, and through the parenting styles that we examined in the first section of this module. In the next section, we'll switch perspectives and see how children affect their parents' behavior.

Children's Contributions

I emphasized earlier that the family is a dynamic, interactive system with parents and children influencing each other. In fact, children begin at birth to influence the way their parents treat them.

That is, parents behave differently depending upon a child's specific behavior (Kochanska, 1993). To illustrate the reciprocal influence of parents and children, imagine two children with different temperaments as they respond to a parent's authoritative style. The first child has an easy temperament and readily complies with parental requests and responds well to family discussions about parental expectations. These parent-child relations are a textbook example of successful authoritative parenting. But suppose, like the child in the photo, the second child has a difficult temperament and complies reluctantly and sometimes not at all. Over time, the parent becomes more controlling and less affectionate. The child in turn complies even less in the future, leading the parent to adopt an authoritarian parenting style (Bates et al., 1998).

As this example illustrates, parenting behaviors and styles often evolve as a consequence of the child's behavior. With a young child who is eager to please adults and less active, a parent may discover a modest amount of control is adequate. But for a child who is not as eager to please and very active, a parent may need to be more controlling and directive (Dumas, LaFreniere, & Serketich, 1995; Hastings & Rubin, 1999). Influence is reciprocal: Children's behavior helps determine how parents treat them and the resulting parental behavior influences children's behavior, which in turn causes parents to again change their behavior (Stice & Barrera, 1995).

As time goes by, these reciprocal influences lead many families to adopt routine ways of interacting with each other. Some families end up functioning smoothly: Parents and children cooperate, anticipate each other's needs, and are generally happy. Unfortunately, other families end up troubled: Disagreements are common, parents spend much time trying unsuccessfully to control their defiant children, and everyone is often angry and upset (Belsky, Woodworth, & Crnic, 1996; Kochanska, 1997).

> Parents' behavior and styles often evolve over time as a consequence of their children's behavior.

Over the long term, such troubled families do not fare well, so it's important that these negative reciprocal influences be nipped in the bud (Carrere & Gottman, 1999; Christensen & Heavey, 1999). When parents recognize the problem early on, they can modify their own behavior. For example, they can try to be less controlling, which sometimes causes children to be less defiant. I am *not* suggesting that parents allow children to do as they please. Instead, parents should decide aspects of children's lives where they need less control and relinquish it.

Parents should also discuss expectations for appropriate behavior with their preschoolers. Such discussions may seem odd for children so young, but, phrased properly, these conversations can help parents and children to better understand one another. And, just as importantly, they help to establish a style for dealing with family issues that will serve everyone well as the children grow.

Of course, many parents find it hard to view family functioning objectively because they are, after all, an integral part of that family. And parents often lack the expertise needed to change their children's behavior. In these circumstances, a family therapist can provide invaluable assistance, identifying the obstacles to successful family functioning and suggesting ways to eliminate them.

Family Configuration

Worldwide, families have primary responsibility for helping children become contributing members of their cultures—this aim is much the same worldwide (Whiting & Child, 1953). However, what constitutes a family differs widely around the world and within the United States. Beyond the traditional arrangement of a mother, father, and their children, many configurations are possible. We'll look at two of these in this section. You'll see that warm, supportive parenting is what matters most to children, not any particular family configuration.

The Role of Grandparents. In many cultures around the world, grandparents play important roles in children's lives. One influential analysis suggested five specific styles of grandparenting (Neugarten & Weinstein, 1964):

- *Formal grandparents* express strong interest in the grandchild but maintain a hands-off attitude toward child rearing.
- *Fun-seeking grandparents* see themselves as a primary source of fun for their grandchildren but avoid more serious interactions.
- *Distant grandparents* have little contact with children, except as part of holidays or other family celebrations.

- *Dispensing-family-wisdom grandparents* provide information and advice to parents and child alike.

- *Surrogate-parent grandparents* assume many of the normal roles and responsibilities of a parent.

Of these different styles, we know the most about the surrogate-parent style because it is particularly common in African American families. The Cultural Influences feature describes the important role of grandmothers in African American family life.

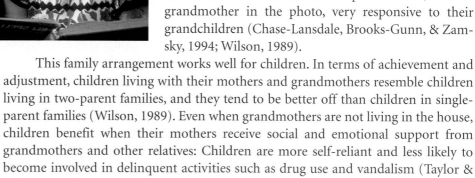

CULTURAL INFLUENCES

Grandmothers in African American Families

Approximately 1 in 8 African American children live with their grandmothers, compared to only 1 in 25 European American children (U.S. Bureau of the Census, 1994). Why is this? A quarter of all African American children grow up in chronic poverty and living with relatives is one way of sharing—and thereby reducing—the costs associated with housing and child care.

African American grandmothers who live with their daughters and their children frequently become involved in rearing their grandchildren, adopting the surrogate-parent style (Pearson et al., 1990). When the daughter is a teenage mother, the grandmother may be the child's primary caregiver, an arrangement that benefits both the adolescent mother and the child. Freed from the obligations of child rearing, the adolescent mother is able to improve her situation by, for example, finishing school. The child benefits because grandmothers are often more effective mothers than teenage mothers: Grandmothers are less punitive and, like the grandmother in the photo, very responsive to their grandchildren (Chase-Lansdale, Brooks-Gunn, & Zamsky, 1994; Wilson, 1989).

This family arrangement works well for children. In terms of achievement and adjustment, children living with their mothers and grandmothers resemble children living in two-parent families, and they tend to be better off than children in single-parent families (Wilson, 1989). Even when grandmothers are not living in the house, children benefit when their mothers receive social and emotional support from grandmothers and other relatives: Children are more self-reliant and less likely to become involved in delinquent activities such as drug use and vandalism (Taylor & Roberts, 1995).

Thus, grandmothers and other relatives can ease the burden of child rearing in African American families living in poverty, and not surprisingly, children benefit from the added warmth, support, and guidance of an extended family. ■

Children of Gay and Lesbian Parents. More than a million youngsters in the United States have a gay or lesbian parent. In most of these situations, children were born in a heterosexual marriage that ended in divorce when one parent revealed his or her homosexuality. Less frequent, but becoming more common, are children born to single lesbians or to lesbian couples or gay men.

Research on gay and lesbian parents and their children is scarce, and most has involved children who were born to a heterosexual marriage that ended in divorce when the mother came out as a lesbian. Most of these lesbian mothers are European American and well-educated.

As parents, gay and lesbian couples are more similar to heterosexual couples than different. There is no indication that gay and lesbian parents are less effective than heterosexual parents. In fact, some evidence suggests that gay men may be especially responsive to children's needs, perhaps because their self-concepts include emotional sensitivity that is traditionally associated with the female gender role (Bigner & Jacobsen, 1989).

> In most respects, children of gay and lesbian parents resemble children of heterosexual parents.

Children reared by gay and lesbian parents seem to develop much like children reared by heterosexual couples (Patterson, 1992; Chan, Raboy, & Patterson, 1998). Preschool boys and girls apparently identify with their own gender and acquire the usual accompaniment of gender-based preferences, interests, activities, and friends. In other respects—such as self-concept, social skill, moral reasoning, and intelligence—children of lesbian mothers resemble children of heterosexual parents.

Research on children reared by gay and lesbian couples, along with findings concerning African American grandmothers, challenge the traditional wisdom that a two-parent family with mother and father both present necessarily provides the best circumstances for development. Multiple adults *are* important (a fact that will become even clearer in Module 13.5 on divorce), but who the adults are seems to matter less than what they do. Young children benefit from good parenting skills, whether it's a mother and father or grandparents or two women or two men doing the parenting.

Check Your Learning

1. According to the systems approach, the family consists of interacting elements who influence each other and the family itself is _____.

2. Compared to American parents, Chinese parents tend to be more controlling and less _____.

3. Children who have low self-esteem and are impulsive, aggressive, and moody often have parents with an _____ style of parenting.

4. In a _____, parents unwittingly reinforce undesirable behaviors.

5. Parental behaviors that influence children include direct instruction, modeling (learning through observation), and _____.

6. The effectiveness of punishment depends on timing, consistency, the presence of an accompanying explanation, and _____.

7. _____ grandparents are very interested in their grandchildren but avoid becoming involved in child rearing.

Active Children Most descriptions of parenting focus on the impact of parents on their children's development. Think about the alternative: How do children's actions and characteristics affect a parent's behavior?

Answers: (1) embedded in other social systems, such as neighborhoods, (2) affectionate, (3) indifferent-uninvolved, (4) negative reinforcement trap, (5) feedback (reward and punishment), (6) the child's relationship with the person who is punishing, (7) Formal

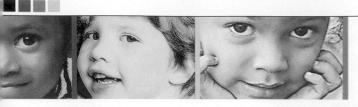

Relationships with Siblings and Peers

10.3

Relationships with Siblings and Peers

├─Sibling Relationships
└─Peer Relationships

Learning Objectives

■ How do firstborn, laterborn, and only children differ?

■ What determines how well siblings get along?

■ How do preschool children play together? How do parents influence their play?

Bob and Alice adored their 2-year-old son, Robbie, who was friendly, playful, and always eager to learn new things. In fact, Bob thought Robbie was nearly perfect and saw no reason to tempt fate by having another child. However, Alice had heard stories that only children were conceited, spoiled, and unfriendly. Alice was sure that Robbie would grow up like this unless she and Bob had another child. What to do?

Children's first social relationships are usually with parents, but their social horizons expand rapidly. In many families, children form relationships with siblings. We'll study these relationships in the first part of this module, where we'll see if Alice's fears about only children are well-founded. During the preschool years, most children's social relationships move beyond the family to include peers; we'll study these relationships in the second part of this module.

Sibling Relationships

For most of a year, all firstborn children are only children like Robbie. Some children remain "onlies" forever, but most get brothers and sisters. Some firstborns are joined by many siblings in rapid succession; others are simply joined by a single brother or sister. As the family acquires these new members, parent-child relationships become more complex. Parents can no longer focus on a single child but must adjust to the needs of multiple children. Just as important, siblings influence each other's development, not just during childhood but, as the cartoon reminds us, throughout life. To understand sibling influence, let's look at differences among firstborns, laterborns, and only children.

PEANUTS © 1993. Reprinted with permission of United Feature Syndicate.

Firstborn, Laterborn, and Only Children. Firstborn children are often "guinea pigs" for most parents, who have lots of enthusiasm but little practical experience rearing children. Parents typically have high expectations for their firstborns and are both more affectionate and more punitive with them. As more children arrive, parents become more adept at their roles, having learned "the tricks of the parent trade" with earlier children. With laterborn children, parents have more realistic expectations and are more relaxed in their discipline (e.g., Baskett, 1985).

The different approaches that parents take with their firstborns and laterborns help explain differences that are commonly observed between these children. Firstborn children generally have higher scores on intelligence tests and are more likely to go to college. They are also more willing to conform to parents' and adults' requests. Laterborn children, perhaps because they are less concerned about pleasing parents and adults but need to get along with older siblings, are more popular with their peers and more innovative (Eaton, Chipperfield, & Singbeil, 1989).

And what about only children? Alice, the mother in the opening vignette, was well acquainted with the conventional wisdom which says that parents, like the ones in the photo, dote on "onlies," with the result that they are selfish and egotistical. Is the folklore correct? From a comprehensive analysis of more than 100 studies, the answer is "no." In fact, only children were found more likely to succeed in school than other children and to have higher levels of intelligence, leadership, autonomy, and maturity (Falbo & Polit, 1986). Thus, contrary to the popular stereotype, only children are not "spoiled brats" who boss around parents, peers, and teachers. Instead, only children are, for the most part, much like children who grow up with siblings. Alice and Bob needn't have another child just to guarantee that Robbie will grow up to be generous and sensitive to others instead of selfish and egotistical.

This research has important implications for China, where only children are the norm due to government efforts to limit family size. The Child Development and Family Policy feature tells the story.

CHILD DEVELOPMENT AND FAMILY POLICY

Assessing the Consequences of China's One-Child Policy

With more than a billion citizens, the People's Republic of China has the largest population in the world. The Chinese make up roughly 20 percent of the world's population. For much of the twentieth century, Chinese leaders have recognized that a large, rapidly growing population was a serious obstacle to economic growth and an improved standard of living. Consequently, the Chinese government implemented several programs to limit family size and since 1979 has had a policy of one child per family. The policy was promoted with billboards like the one in the photo that advertised the benefits of having only one child. Parents were encouraged to use contraceptives and, more importantly, one-child families received many economic benefits: cash bonuses, better health and child care, and more desirable housing.

The policy has been effective in reducing the birth rate in China and now social scientists are evaluating the consequences of the one-child policy on children and their families. For example, traditionally the Chinese have valued well-behaved children who get along well with others. Would the only children in today's China be less cooperative and more self-centered than previous generations of Chinese youngsters? The answer seems to be no. Many studies have compared only and non-only children in China; most comparisons find no differences; when differences are found, the advantage often goes to the only child (Jiao, Ji, & Jing, 1996; Yang et al., 1995).

As Chinese only children enter adulthood, a new concern will be care of the elderly. Traditionally, children have been responsible for their aging parents. This task becomes more demanding—financially and psychologically—when it cannot be shared with other siblings. Research will be needed to determine whether older people receive adequate care and to determine the impact on only children of providing such care. Through this sort of research, psychologists and other social scientists will play an important role in helping to determine the long-term consequences of China's decision to limit family size. ■

In discussing firstborn, laterborn, and only children, we have ignored relationships that exist between siblings. These can be powerful forces on development, as we'll see next.

Qualities of Sibling Relationships. From the very beginning, sibling relationships are complicated. On the one hand, most expectant parents are excited by the prospect of another child and their enthusiasm is contagious: Their children, too, eagerly await the arrival of the newest family member. On the other hand, the birth of a sibling is often distressing for older children, who may become withdrawn or return to more childish behavior because of the changes that occur in their lives, particularly the need to share parental attention and affection (Gottlieb & Mendelson, 1990). However, distress can be avoided if parents remain responsive to their older children's needs (Howe & Ross, 1990). In fact, one of the benefits of a sibling's birth is that fathers become more involved with their older children (Stewart et al., 1987).

Many older siblings enjoy helping their parents take care of newborns (Wagner, Schubert, & Schubert, 1985). Like the sibling in the photo, older children play with the baby, console it, feed it, or change its diapers. As the infant grows, interactions between siblings become more frequent and more complicated. For example, toddlers tend to talk more to parents than to older siblings. But, by the time the younger sibling is 4 years old, the situation is reversed: Now young siblings talk more to older siblings than to their mother (Brown & Dunn, 1992). Older siblings become a source of care and comfort for younger siblings when they are distressed or upset (Garner, Jones, & Palmer, 1994).

As time goes by, some siblings grow close, becoming best friends in ways that nonsiblings can never be. Other siblings constantly argue, compete, and overall simply do not get along with each other. The basic pattern of sibling interaction seems to be established early in development and remains fairly stable. Dunn, Slomkowski, and Beardsall (1994), for example, interviewed mothers twice about their children's interaction, first when the children were 3- and 5-year-olds and again 7 years later, when the children were 10- and 12-year-olds. Dunn and her colleagues found that siblings who got along as preschoolers often continued to get along as young adolescents, whereas siblings who quarreled as preschoolers often quarreled as young adolescents.

Why are some sibling relationships so filled with love and respect, whereas others are dominated by jealousy and resentment? Put more simply, what factors contribute to the quality of sibling relationships? First, children's sex and temperament matter. Sibling relations are more likely to be warm and harmonious between siblings of the same sex than between siblings of the opposite sex (Dunn & Kendrick, 1981) and when neither sibling is temperamentally emotional (Brody, Stoneman, & McCoy, 1994). Age is also important: Sibling relationships generally improve as the younger child approaches adolescence because siblings begin to perceive one another as equals (Buhrmester & Furman, 1990).

> To reduce the stress associated with a sibling's birth, parents should remain responsive to their older children's needs.

Parents contribute to the quality of sibling relationships, both directly and indirectly (Brody, 1998). The direct influence stems from parents' treatment. Siblings more often get along when they believe that parents have no "favorites" but treat all siblings fairly (Kowal & Kramer, 1997). When parents lavishly praise one child's accomplishments while ignoring another's, children notice the difference and their sibling relationship suffers.

This doesn't mean that parents must treat all their children the same. Children understand that parents should treat their kids differently—based on their age or personal needs. Only when differential treatment is not justified do sibling relationships deteriorate (Kowal & Kramer, 1997).

The indirect influence of parents on sibling relationships stems from the quality of the parents' relationship with each other: A warm, harmonious relationship between parents fosters positive sibling relationships; conflict between parents is associated with conflict between siblings (Erel, Margolin, & John, 1998; Volling & Belsky, 1992). When parents don't get along, they no longer treat their children the same, leading to conflict among siblings (Brody et al., 1994).

One practical implication of these findings is that in their pursuit of family harmony (otherwise known as peace and quiet), parents can influence some of the factors affecting sibling relationships but not others. Parents can help reduce friction between siblings by being equally affectionate, responsive, and caring with all of their children and by caring for one another. At the same time, some dissension is natural in families, especially those with preschool boys and girls: Children's different interests lead to arguments, like the one in the photo. Faced with common simple conflicts—Who decides which TV show to watch? Who gets to eat the last cookie? Who gets to hold the new puppy?—a 3-year-old brother and a 5-year-old sister will argue because they lack the social and cognitive skills that allow them to find mutually satisfying compromises.

When siblings do fight—particularly young children—parents should intervene. Siblings often fight because they're competing for limited resources: They want to play with the same toy or they want to watch different programs on TV. Here parents can arrange for some form of cooperation. Siblings also fight because one child is bored and, for lack of anything else to do, begins to interfere with a sibling's activities. Parents can solve this problem by helping the first child become engaged in some activity of his or her own. And sometimes the best strategy simply is to separate feuding siblings.

By intervening in these ways, not only are parents resolving a dispute, they are also showing children more sophisticated ways to negotiate; later, children often try to use these techniques themselves instead of fighting (Kramer, Perozynski, & Chung, 1999; Pearlman & Ross, 1997).

Peer Relationships

In Module 7.2, we saw that peer interactions begin in infancy with the emergence of parallel play at about the first birthday. Cooperative play, in which children organize their play around a theme and take on special roles, appears toward the second birthday, but is not very common. However, by the time children are $3\frac{1}{2}$ to 4 years old, parallel play is much less common and cooperative play is the norm (Howes & Matheson, 1992). Cooperative play typically involves peers of the same gender, a preference that increases until, by the end of the preschool years, youngsters choose same-sex playmates about two-thirds of the time (LaFreniere, Strayer, & Gauthier, 1984).

Conflicts occur often in preschoolers' play and youngsters often use aggression to resolve their conflicts (Hay, Castle, & Davies, 2000). Among preschoolers, common aggressive behaviors included hitting, kicking, pushing, or biting the other child, or as shown in the photo, trying to grab a toy from another child. **By the end of the preschool years, some preschoolers resort to *bullying*, in which the aggression is unprovoked and seems to have as its sole goal to intimidate, harass, or humiliate another child.** Bullying is illustrated by a child who spontaneously says, "You're stupid!" and then kicks the child (Crick, Casas, & Ku, 1999).

Of course, preschoolers' interactions are not *always* aggressive; sometimes they act prosocially to peers. When preschool children see other people who are obviously hurt or upset, they appear concerned, like the child in the photo. They try to comfort the person by hugging them or patting them, and they try to determine why the person is upset (Zahn-Waxler et al., 1992). Apparently, at this early age, children recognize signs of distress but their attempts to be helpful are limited because their knowledge of what they can do to help is modest. As youngsters acquire more strategies to help others, their preferred strategies become more adultlike (Strayer & Schroeder, 1989). For example, if a sister was upset because her favorite toy was broken, a 3-year-old brother might comfort her by patting her on the back or giving her his favorite blanket. In contrast, a 9-year-old brother might reassure his sister that Mom will probably buy a replacement toy.

Make Believe. During the preschool years, cooperative play often takes the form of make believe. Preschoolers have telephone conversations with imaginary partners or pretend to drink imaginary juice. In early phases of make believe, children rely on realistic props to support their play. While pretending to drink, younger preschoolers use a real cup; while pretending to drive a car, they use a toy steering wheel.

In later phases of make believe, children no longer need realistic props; instead, they can imagine that a block is the cup, or, like the boys in the photo on page 305, that a paper plate is the steering wheel. Of course, this gradual movement toward more abstract make believe is possible because of cognitive growth that occurs during the preschool years (Harris & Kavanaugh, 1993).

As you might suspect, make believe reflects the values important in a child's culture (Bornstein et al., 1999). For example, Farver and Shin (1997) studied make-believe play of European American preschoolers and Korean American preschoolers. The Korean American children came from recently immigrated families, so they still held traditional Korean values, such as an emphasis on the family and on harmony over conflict. The two groups of children differed in the themes of their make-believe play. Adventure and fantasy were favorite themes for European American youngsters but family roles and everyday activities were favorites of the Korean American children.

In addition, the groups differed in their style of play during make believe. European American children were more assertive in their make believe and more likely to disagree with their play partner's ideas about pretending (*I* want to be the the king; *you* be the mom!). Korean American children were more polite and more likely to strive for harmony (Could I *please* be king?). Thus, cultural values influence both the content and the form of make believe.

Make-believe play is not only entertaining for children, it seems to promote cognitive development (Berk, 1994). Children who spend much time in make-believe play tend to be more advanced in language, memory, and reasoning. They also tend to have a more sophisticated understanding of other people's thoughts, beliefs, and feelings (Howe, Petrakos, & Rinaldi, 1998; Youngblade & Dunn, 1995).

Yet another benefit of make believe is that it allows children to explore topics that frighten them. Children who are afraid of the dark may reassure a doll who is also afraid of the dark. By explaining to the doll why she shouldn't be afraid, children come to understand and regulate their own fear of darkness. Or children may pretend that a doll has misbehaved and must be punished, which allows them to experience the parent's anger and the doll's guilt. Make believe allows children explore other emotions, too, including joy and affection (Gottman, 1986).

> Make-believe play promotes cognitive development and lets children explore emotional topics that frighten them.

For many preschool children, make-believe play involves imaginary companions. Children can usually describe their imaginary playmates in some detail, mentioning sex and age as well as the color of their hair and eyes. Imaginary companions were once thought to be fairly rare and a sign of possible developmental problems. But more recent research shows that nearly two-thirds of all preschoolers report imaginary companions (Taylor, Cartwright, & Carlson, 1993).

Moreover, an imaginary companion is associated with many positive social characteristics: Preschoolers with imaginary friends tend to be more sociable and have more real friends than other preschoolers. Furthermore, vivid fantasy play with imaginary companions does not mean that the distinction between fantasy and reality is blurred: Children with imaginary companions can distinguish fantasy from reality just as accurately as youngsters without imaginary companions (Taylor et al., 1993).

Solitary Play. At times throughout the preschool years, many children prefer to play alone. Should parents be worried? Usually, no. Solitary play comes in many forms and most are normal—even healthy. Spending free play time alone coloring, solving puzzles, or assembling Legos™ is not a sign of maladjustment. Many youngsters enjoy solitary activities and at other times choose very social play.

Parents promote children's play by acting as skilled playmates, mediating disputes, and coaching social skills.

However, some forms of solitary play *are* signs that children are uneasy interacting with others (Coplan et al., 1994; Harrist et al., 1997). One type of unhealthy solitary play is wandering aimlessly. Sometimes children go from one preschool activity center to the next, as if trying to to decide what to do. But really they just keep wandering, never settling into play with others or constructive solitary play. Another unhealthy type of solitary play is hovering: A child stands nearby peers who are playing, watching them play but not participating. Over time, these behaviors do not bode well for youngsters, so it's best for these youngsters to see a professional who can help them overcome their reticence in social situations (Ladd, 1998).

Parental Influence. Parents get involved in their preschool children's play in several ways (Isley et al., 1999). Sometimes they take the role of playmate (and many parents deserve an Oscar for their performances). They use the opportunity to scaffold (see Module 9.1) their children's play, often raising it to more sophisticated levels (Tamis-LeMonda, & Bornstein, 1996). For example, if a toddler is stacking toy plates, a parent might help the child stack the plates (play at the same level) or might pretend to wash each plate (play at a more advanced level). When parents demonstrate more advanced forms of play, their children often play at the more advanced levels later (Bornstein et al., 1996).

Another parental role during preschoolers' play is mediator. Preschoolers often disagree, argue, and sometimes fight. As shown in the photo, children play more cooperatively and longer when parents are present to help iron out conflicts (Mize, Pettit, & Brown, 1995; Parke & Bahvnagri, 1989). When young children can't agree on what to play, a parent can negotiate a mutually acceptable activity. When both youngsters want to play with the same toy, a parent can arrange for them to share. Here too, parents scaffold their preschoolers' play, smoothing the interaction by providing some of social skills that preschoolers lack.

Yet another parental role is coach. Preschool children often encounter social problems that, although minor from an adult's perspective, seem overwhelming to the child. For example, a child might be coloring when another child approaches and demands the crayon the child is using. Parents can help their preschoolers understand and handle such problems. When parents coach—and when their advice is constructive—their children tend to be skilled socially and less aggressive (Mize & Pettit, 1997).

Parents also influence the success of their children's peer interactions in a much less direct manner. Children's relationships with peers are most successful when, as infants, they had a secure attachment relationship with their mother (Ladd & LeSieur, 1995; Lieberman, Doyle, & Markiewicz, 1999).

Why does quality of attachment predict the success of children's peer relationships? One view is that a child's relationship with his or her parents is the internal working model for all future social relationships. When the parent-child relationship is high quality and emotionally satisfying, children are encouraged to form relationships with other people. Another possibility is that a secure attachment relationship with the mother makes an infant feel more confident about exploring the environment, which, in turn, provides more opportunities to interact with peers. These two views are not mutually exclusive; both may contribute to the relative ease with which securely attached children interact with their peers (Hartup, 1992b).

Check Your Learning

1. Compared to firstborn children, laterborn children are more innovative and more _____.

2. When compared to children who have siblings, only children are, for the most part, _____.

3. Siblings are more likely to get along when they are of the same sex, not temperamentally emotional, and when the younger child _____.

4. Sibling relationships are harmed when parents treat their children differently if _____.

5. Parents can influence sibling relationships directly by treating children fairly and indirectly by _____.

6. _____ play promotes cognitive development and helps children explore topics that may frighten them.

7. Solitary play is worrisome when children wander airmlessly or _____.

8. Parents influence a preschool child's play in their role as playmate, _____, and coach.

■■ **Connections** How does preschool children's play illustrate connections between physical, cognitive, social, and emotional development?

Answers: (1) popular, (2) similar, not different, (3) enters adolescence, (4) children believe the differential treatment is not justified, (5) getting along with each other, (6) Make-believe, (7) hover around other children who are playing, (8) negotiator

Moral Development: Learning to Control One's Behavior

10.4

Moral Development: Learning to Control One's Behavior

Learning Objectives

- **When does self-control begin and how does it change as children develop?**

- **How do parents influence their children's ability to maintain self-control?**

- **What strategies can children use to improve their self-control?**

- **When do preschoolers begin to understand that moral roles are different from other rules?**

> *Shirley returned from a long day at work tired but eager to celebrate her son Ryan's third birthday. Her excitement quickly turned to dismay when she discovered that Ryan had taken a huge bite of icing from the birthday cake while the baby-sitter fixed lunch. Before she had left for work that morning, Shirley had explicitly told Ryan not to touch the cake. Why couldn't Ryan wait? Why did he give in to temptation? What could she do to help Ryan control himself better in the future?*

In this vignette, Shirley wishes that Ryan had greater *self-control*, the ability to rise above immediate pressures and not give in to impulse. A child who saves her allowance to buy a much-desired object instead of spending it immediately on candy is showing self-control, as is an adolescent who studies for an exam instead of going to the mall with his friends, knowing that tomorrow he can enjoy the mall and a good grade on his exam.

Self-control is one of the first steps toward moral behavior because children must learn that they cannot constantly do whatever tempts them at the moment. Instead, society has rules for behavior in certain situations, and children must learn to restrain themselves.

In this module, we'll first see how self-control emerges during the preschool years. Then we'll learn some of the factors that determine how well children control themselves. Finally, we'll look at strategies that children use to improve their self-control and children's understanding of the special nature of moral rules.

Beginnings of Self-Control

In the cartoon on page 309, Calvin shows little self-control. Is he typical for his age? Thankfully, no. Self-control begins during infancy and the preschool years. Claire Kopp (1982, 1987) believes that self-control develops in three phases:

- At approximately the first birthday, infants become aware that people impose demands on them and they must react accordingly. They learn that they are not entirely free to behave as they wish; instead, others set limits on what they can do. These limits reflect both concern for their safety ("Don't touch! It's hot") as well as early socialization efforts ("Don't grab Ravisha's toy").

- At about 2 years, toddlers have internalized some of the controls imposed by others and they are capable of some self-control in parents' absence. For example, although the boy on the left in the photo certainly looks as if he wants to play with the toy that the other toddler has, so far he has inhibited his desire to grab the toy, perhaps because he remembers that his parents have told him not to take things from others.

- At about 3 years, children become capable of self-regulation, which "involves flexible and adaptive control processes that can meet quickly changing situational demands" (Kopp, 1987, p. 38). Children can devise ways to regulate their own behavior. To return to the example of a playmate's interesting toy, children might tell themselves that they really don't want to play with it, or they might turn to another activity that removes the temptation to grab it.

Of course, preschoolers have much to learn about regulating impulsive behavior, and control is achieved only gradually throughout the elementary-school years. And individual preschoolers differ tremendously in their degree of self-control. Some show greater restraint and control while others show little.

Individual differences are evident in research that examines consistency in self-control. Vaughn, Kopp, and Krakow (1984), for example, examined preschoolers' self-control on three different tasks. On one task, the child was told to not touch a novel telephone while the experimenter left the room; on a second task, the child was asked to wait for a signal before beginning to search for hidden food; on a third, the experimenter said that an attractively wrapped package was a gift for the child, who was not to touch it until the experimenter and mother had finished some paperwork. The correlations between children's performance on the different tasks ranged from 0.29 to 0.47. These correlations mean that, although children were far from perfectly consistent, in general a child who had good self-control on one task tended to have good control on other tasks, too.

Perhaps you wonder about the validity of these tasks. Are these tasks really measuring important aspects of self-control in children's natural environments?

> By age 3, children are capable of some self-regulation, largely because they can formulate simple plans for dealing with the demands of different situations.

Mothers' reports of their youngsters' self-control represent one source of evidence for the validity of these tasks. Children who are less likely to touch prohibited toys are, according to their mothers' reports, more likely to spontaneously confess to misdeeds at home and more likely to do as asked at home, without parental supervision (Kochanska et al., 1994).

The Looking Ahead feature provides some truly remarkable evidence that laboratory tasks measure important facets of children's self-control in their natural environments.

LOOKING AHEAD

Self-Control during the Preschool Years Predicts Personality and Achievement in Adolescence

Told not to touch a novel toy, some preschoolers patiently comply with the instruction for minutes on end; other preschoolers reach for the toy as soon as the experimenter leaves the room. These differences are striking while watching children and naturally makes one wonder if the differences persist over the years. Results from longitudinal studies on the long-term consistency of self-control suggest that the differences are, in fact, remarkably stable. Shoda, Mischel, and Peake (1990) tracked down nearly 200 15- to 18-year-olds who had participated in self-control experiments as 4-year-olds. In the original experiments, 4-year-olds were told that if they waited alone in a room until the experimenter returned, they would receive a big prize. If they rang a bell to signal the experimenter to return, they would receive a much smaller prize. Then the researchers simply recorded the length of time children waited until the experimenter returned. You may be surprised to learn that the length of time that 4-year-olds waited was related to a host of characteristics some 11 to 14 years later. The table shows some of the significant correlations between the 4-year-olds' ability to delay gratification and personality and SAT scores as adolescents.

Correlations between Preschoolers' Delayed Gratification and Measures of Coping, Personality, and Academic Achievement in Adolescence	
	Measure
Personality	
Is likely to yield to temptation	-.50
Distractibility when trying to concentrate	-.41
Is planful, thinks ahead	.36
Tends to go to pieces under stress, becomes rattled and disorganized	-.34
SAT scores	
Verbal scale	.42
Quantitative scale	.57
Source: Shoda, Mischel, and Peake, 1990	

TABLE 10–2

Incredibly, 4-year-olds who wait longer before calling the experimenter are still, as 15- to 18-year-olds, better able to exert self-control, more attentive and able to plan, and have higher SAT scores. ∎

Obviously, individuals differ in their ability to resist temptation, and this characteristic is remarkably stable over time. But why are some preschoolers (and, later, adolescents) better able than others to exert self-control? As you'll see in the next section of this module, parents play an important role in determining children's self-control.

Parental Influences

In the neighborhood where I grew up, there were next-door neighbors where both husbands had similar jobs with an engineering company, and both wives were full-time homemakers. Nevertheless, their lifestyles had little in common. One family always seemed to be the first on the block to own new toys: the first stereo record player, the first color TV, the first Ford Mustang in 1964, and so on. The other family was as frugal as the first family was free-spending: Occasional trips to the repair shop kept the black-and-white TV working, children wore hand-me-down clothes, and the dad rode a bus to work.

Obviously, the children growing up in these two families were exposed to very different models of self-control. Adults in the first family preferred immediate gratification, but those in the second family preferred to save their money for deferred goals. Children's self-control is influenced by their exposure to such models. Research in which children have the opportunity to imitate adults who model little or much self-control shows that children can show self-restraint or be incredibly impulsive, simply depending upon how they observe others behave (Bandura & Mischel, 1965).

> Children have greater self-control when parents show self-control and when parents are not overly strict.

In addition, correlational studies show that parents' behavior is related to their children's self-control, but not in a way that you may expect. Self-control is *lower* in children whose parents are very strict with them (Feldman & Wentzel, 1990). One interpretation of this finding is that strict parents "overcontrol" their children: By constantly directing them to do one thing but not another, parents do not give their children either the opportunity or the incentive to internalize control. Consistent with this argument is the finding that children have greater self-control when parents encourage them to be independent and make their own decisions (Silverman & Ragusa, 1990).

So far, the story seems reasonably straightforward: For children to gain self-control, parents must relinquish control. By gradually giving children more opportunities to regulate their own behavior and see the consequences of their choices, parents foster self-control. For example, instead of insisting that preschool children follow a set after-dinner routine, parents can allow children to choose between coloring, reading, or playing a quiet game.

But more recent research shows that the story is not so simple after all. Temperament affects children's responses to parents' efforts to promote self-control. We'll look at this research in the next section.

Temperamental Influences on Self-Control

Children's temperament helps determine their level of self-control. Emotional toddlers and preschoolers are less able to control themselves (Stifter, Spinrad, & Braungart-Rieker, 1999). That is, youngsters who have difficulty regulating their emotions usually have difficulty regulating their behavior.

Temperament also influences how children respond to parents' efforts to teach self-control. The aspect of temperament that's most important for self-control is children's anxiety and fearfulness (Kochanska, 1991, 1993). Some anxious and fearful children become nervous at the prospect of potential wrongdoing. When told not to eat a cookie until after dinner, fearful children may leave the room because they're afraid that otherwise they might give in to temptation. With these children, a simple parental reminder usually guarantees compliance because they are so anxious about not following instructions, or getting caught, or having to confess to a misdeed.

For children who are not naturally fearful at the thought of misdeeds, other approaches are necessary. More effective with these children are positive appeals to the child to cooperate, appeals that build on the strong attachment relationship between parent and child. Fearless children comply with parental requests out of positive feelings for a loved one, not out of distress caused by fear of misdeeds.

The Focus on Research feature describes a study that links temperament to different methods for fostering self-control in children.

FOCUS ON RESEARCH

Temperament, Parental Influence, and Self-Control

Who was the investigator and what was the aim of the study? Grazyna Kochanska (1997) wanted to evaluate proposed links between children's temperament, parents' influence, and children's self-control. In particular, she believed that temperamentally fearful children would have better self-control when parents used gentle discipline that elicited mild distress and that temperamentally fearless children would have better self-control when parents appealed to their strong mutual attachment.

How did the investigator measure the topic of interest? Kochanska's study included four key variables: children's fearful temperament, parents' use of gentle discipline, strength of parent-child attachment, and children's self-control and compliance. Temperament was measured by having mothers complete questionnaires and by recording children's anxiety as they were asked to do different novel acts (e.g., put a hand inside a large box, jump on a trampoline). Use of gentle discipline was measured by observing mothers interacting with their children and coding for the presence of guiding, gentle requests to comply (as opposed to threats or angry demands). Parent-child attachment was measured by having mothers complete questionnaires that assessed attachment security as described in Module 7.2. Finally, children's self-control and compliance was tested in two ways: with games that posed a strong temptation to cheat (because the games were impossible to win following the rules) and with stories that allowed children to support (or condemn) a story character who took desirable toys from another story character.

Who were the children in the study? Kochanska tested 103 $2\frac{1}{2}$- to 3-year-olds on the temperamental measures. At this time, mothers completed the attachment questionnaire and interacted with their children while experimenters observed their disciplinary styles. Kochanska retested 99 of these children as 4-year-olds and 90 of them as 5-year-olds. During these sessions, she administered the measures of self-control and compliance. (For simplicity, I'm only going to describe the results from the first two test sessions.)

> Parents foster children's self-control by using gentle discipline with temperamentally fearful children and by using appeals to cooperate with temperamentally fearless children.

What was the design of the study? This study was correlational because Kochanska was interested in relations that existed naturally between children's temperament, parental behaviors, and children's self-control and compliance. The study was longitudinal because children were tested three times, at approximately $2\frac{1}{2}$, 4, and 5 years of age.

Were there ethical concerns with the study? No. Most of the tasks that children performed were fun. The tasks to assess fearfulness—for example, putting a hand inside a large box—were designed to elicit concern, not fear.

What were the results? Kochanska used the measures of temperament obtained from the $2\frac{1}{2}$- to 3-year-olds to divide the sample into fearful and fearless toddlers. Next, she examined links between gentle discipline, attachment, and children's self-control. The correlations are shown in the graph and correspond to Kochanska's predictions. For fearful children, self-control was associated more strongly with a mother's gentle discipline than with attachment security. In contrast, for fearless children, self-control was associated more strongly with attachment security than gentle discipline.

What did the investigator conclude? Parents do influence their children's ability to maintain self-control, but the nature of that influence depends on children's temperament. Fearful children respond to gentle reminders to comply, apparently because such reminders elicit mild distress. Fearless children respond to requests to cooperate because they appeal to the strong attachment relationship.

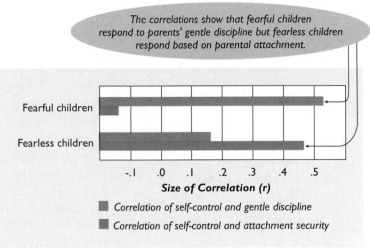

FIG 10–7

What converging evidence would strengthen these conclusions? Temperament and strength of attachment were two key constructs in this study. Temperament was measured by observing children's behavior directly and through questionnaires, but strength of attachment was measured only with questionnaires. It would be useful to replicate the study, but measuring strength of attachment through observational measures like the Strange Situation paradigm described on page 189. ■

Of course, regardless of their temperament, children are not perfectly consistent in their self-control. Children who are able to resist temptation on one occasion may give in the next time. Why do children show self-control on some tasks but not others? As we'll see in the next section, the answer lies in children's plans for resisting temptation.

Improving Self-Control

Imagine it's one of the first nice days of spring. You have two major exams that you should study for, but it's so-o-o-o tempting to spend the entire day with your friends, sitting in the sun. What do you do to resist this temptation and stick to studying? You might remind yourself that these exams are very important. You might also move to a windowless room to keep your mind off the tempting weather. Stated more generally, effective ways to resist temptation include (a) reminding yourself of the importance of long-term goals over short-term temptations and (b) reducing the attraction of the tempting event.

During the preschool years, some youngsters begin to use both of these methods spontaneously. In an experiment by Mischel and Ebbesen (1970), 3- to 5-year-olds were asked to sit alone in a room for 15 minutes. If they waited the entire time, they would receive a desirable reward. Children could call the experimenter back to the room at any time by a prearranged signal; in this case, they would receive a much less desirable reward.

Some children, of course, were better able than others to wait the full 15 minutes. How did they do it? Some children talked to themselves: "I've gotta wait to get the best prize!" As Vygotsky described (Module 9.1), these youngsters were using private speech to control their own behavior. Others sang and still others invented games. All were effective techniques for enduring 15 boring minutes to receive a desired prize.

Later studies show that children who have a concrete way of handling the situation are far better able to resist temptation (Mischel, Shoda, & Rodriguez, 1989). Effective plans include (a) reminders to avoid looking at the tempting object, (b) reminders of rules against touching a tempting object, and (c) activities designed to divert attention from the tempting object, such as playing with other objects. For example, in the module-opening vignette, Shirley could have helped Ryan make a plan to resist temptation. She might have told him, "When you feel like you want to eat some cake, tell yourself, 'No cake until Mom gets home' and go play in your bedroom." Any of these hints would have provided Ryan with a plan for regulating his own behavior.

Overall, then, how children think about tempting objects or outcomes makes all the difference. Even preschoolers can achieve self-control by making plans that include appropriate self-instruction. As children learn to regulate their own behavior, they also begin to learn about moral rules—cultural rights and wrongs—which are described in last section of this module.

Learning About Moral Rules

The foundation of moral thinking is set in the preschool years. For example, during these years children begin to understand that moral rules are special. **Many rules are actually *social conventions*, arbitrary standards of behavior agreed to by a cultural group to facilitate interactions within the group.** Thus, social convention says that we can eat french fries but not green beans with our fingers and

> Moral reasoning emerges in the preschool years when children distinguish moral rules from social conventions.

that children can address peers but not teachers by their first names. In contrast, moral rules, such as prohibitions against murder and rape, are designed to protect people and are not arbitrary. By age 3, most children distinguish moral rules from social conventions. They judge that hurting other people and taking their possessions are more serious transgressions than eating ice cream with one's fingers and not paying attention to a story (Nucci & Weber, 1995; Smetana & Braeges, 1990).

Other research shows that preschoolers know the difference between lies and mistakes (Siegal & Peterson, 1998). And, when led to believe that they damaged an object, preschoolers often show traditional signs of guilt, such as distress, apologizing, and trying to right their wrong (Kochanska, Casey, & Fukumoto, 1995). Collectively, these findings tell us that preschoolers have begun to understand the fundamental distinctions in the moral domain. This understanding provides the foundation for more sophisticated reasoning about moral issues, which we'll examine in more detail in Chapter 15.

Check Your Learning

1. At approximately age _____ , children first learn that other people make demands of them.

2. Fifteen- to 18-year-olds who were better able to resist temptation as preschoolers still have better self-control, are more attentive and planful, and have

   _____ .

3. Research in which children have the opportunities to imitate adults show that, after viewing adults who showed little self-control, children _____ .

4. When parents are very controlling, their children tend to _____ .

5. With fearful children, parents can foster self-control by using gentle discipline; with fearless children, parents can foster self-control by _____ .

6. Children can maintain self-control more effectively when they remind themselves to resist temptation and _____ .

7. Preschoolers' early moral thinking is revealed in their ability to distinguish moral rules from social conventions, in their ability to distinguish lies from mistakes, and _____ .

■■ **Continuity** Review the findings on delay of gratification described in the Looking Ahead feature on page 310. Are these results more consistent with the view that development is a continuous process or the view that development is a discontinuous process?

Answers: (1) 1, (2) higher SAT scores, (3) imitated the adults' poor self-control, (4) have poor self-control, (5) asking them to cooperate, which appeals to their strong attachment relationship, (6) they divert their attention from the tempting object or event, (7) in showing signs of guilt for misdeeds

Chapter Critical Review

1. Refer back to the graph on page 282 that displays information about gender stereotypes in other cultures. Use the information in the graphs to hypothesize how the types of games that preschoolers in Nigeria or Venezuela play would differ from those children play in the U.S.

2. Consider the parenting style in your cultural group. How would you characterize it, using the classification in Module 10.2? What was the primary cultural influence on your parents' style when you were growing up: that of the macroculture, or that of a specific cultural or ethnic group? Do you think that your parenting style will differ from that of your parents (or, if you are a parent, how does it differ)?

3. Suppose you heard the host of a radio talk show say, "What's wrong with American youth today is that parents don't discipline the way they used to. 'Spare the rod and spoil the child' made sense before and still makes sense today." If you called in, what would you say in response to the host's remarks?

4. Most research on sibling relationships is based on families with two children because these families are easier to find than families with three or more children and because there's only one sibling relationship to consider. Think how the conclusions about sibling relationships described in this module might need to be modified to apply to larger families.

5. Why does make-believe play become so important during the preschool years? In your answer, use what you learned about cognitive development in Module 9.1.

6. Compare and contrast the view of self-control presented in Module 10.1 with Vygotsky's ideas of self-control, which appeared in Module 9.1.

For more review material, log on to www.prenhall.com/kail

See For Yourself

Many students find it hard to believe that parents actually use the different styles described in Module 10.2. To convince yourself that parents really differ along these dimensions, visit a place where parents and young children interact together, such as a shopping mall, a fast-food restaurant, or a playground. Observe parents and their children, then judge their warmth and degree of control. For example, at the playground, see whether some parents eagerly play with children (warm parents) but others use this as an opportunity to read the newspaper (uninterested parents). See whether some parents allow children to choose their own activities or whether parents make all the decisions. As you watch, decide whether parents are using feedback and modeling constructively. You should observe an astonishing variety of parental behavior, some effective and some not. See for yourself!

For More Information About . . .

 the ways that biological, psychological, and cultural forces influence gender development, read *Gender Development* by S. Golombok and R. Fivush (Cambridge University Press, Adams, 1992), which provides a comprehensive account of how and why boys and girls develop differently.

 how to deal with all the different problems— large and small—that come up in rearing children, visit the *Today's Parents* Web site: **http://www.todaysparent.com**

Key Terms

authoritarian parenting 293
authoritative parenting 293
bullying 304
constricting style 284
counterimitation 294
direct instruction 294
disinhibition 294
dispensing-family-wisdom grandparents 298
distant grandparents 297
enabling style 284
expressive traits 281
formal grandparents 297

fun-seeking grandparents 297
gender consistency 285
gender constancy 285
gender identity 282
gender labeling 285
gender roles 280
gender-schema theory 286
gender stability 285
gender stereotypes 280
indifferent-uninvolved parenting 293
indulgent-permissive parenting 293
inhibition 295
instrumental traits 281

negative reinforcement trap 295
punishment 295
purpose 288
reinforcement 295
self-control 308
self-esteem 280
social conventions 314
social role 280
surrogate-parent grandparents 298
time-out 296

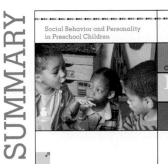

SUMMARY

10.1 Self

Gender Roles
Instrumental traits describe individuals who act on the world and are usually associated with males. Expressive traits describe individuals who value interpersonal relationships and are usually associated with females. By the end of the preschool years, children have learned many of the traits typically associated with males and females.

Gender Identity
Parents treat sons and daughters similarly, except in gender-related behavior. Peers influence gender-role learning by discouraging cross-gender play. Children who watch television frequently tend to have stereotyped views of men and women.

According to Kohlberg's theory, children learn that gender is constant over time. According to gender-schema theory, children learn about gender by paying attention to behaviors of same-sex people. Biological influence on gender roles is shown in twin studies and in the impact of male hormones on female prenatal development.

Self-Esteem
Self-esteem is assessed by asking preschoolers to compare themselves to hypothetical children. Self-esteem is very high during the preschool years.

10.2 Relationships with Parents

The Family as a System
According to the systems approach, parents and children influence each other. The family itself is influenced by other social systems, such as neighborhoods and religious organizations.

Dimensions and Styles
One dimension of parenting is parental warmth: Children clearly benefit from warm, caring parents. Another dimension is control. Effective parenting involves setting appropriate standards and enforcing them consistently. Combining warmth and control yields four styles: (a) authoritarian parents are controlling but uninvolved, (b) authoritative parents are controlling but responsive, (c) indulgent-permissive parents are loving but exert little control, and (d) indifferent-uninvolved parents are neither warm nor controlling. Authoritative parenting is usually best for children.

Parental Behavior
Parents influence development by direct instruction, coaching, and by serving as models for their children. Parents also use feedback to influence children's behavior. Sometimes parents fall into the negative reinforcement trap, inadvertently reinforcing behaviors they want to discourage. Effective punishment is prompt, consistent, accompanied by an explanation, and delivered by a person with whom the child has a warm relationship. Punishment suppresses behaviors but does not eliminate them, and often has side effects. Time-out is a useful form of punishment.

Children's Contributions
Parenting is influenced by characteristics of children themselves (e.g., temperament). Families develop routine ways of interacting, which can be harmful if based on negative mutual influences.

Family Configuration
Compared to American parents, Chinese parents are more controlling and less affectionate. African American grandmothers often live with their daughters, an arrangement that benefits children because grandmothers play an active role in child rearing. Gay and lesbian parents are more similar to heterosexual parents than different; their children develop much like children reared by heterosexual couples.

10.3 Relationships with Siblings and Peers

Sibling Relationships
Firstborn children are often more intelligent but less popular and innovative. Only children are generally comparable to children with siblings.

The birth of a sibling is stressful for children when parents ignore the older child's needs. Siblings get along better when they are of the same sex, parents treat them fairly, they enter adolescence, and they have parents who get along well.

Peer Relationships
Cooperative play is common among preschoolers. Make-believe play promotes cognitive development and allows children to explore frightening topics in a nonthreatening way. Most forms of solitary play are harmless. Parents foster children's play by acting as skilled playmates, mediating disputes, and coaching social skills.

10.4 Moral Development: Learning to Control One's Behavior

Beginnings of Self-Control
At 1 year, infants are first aware that others impose demands on them; by 3 years, youngsters can regulate their behavior. Preschoolers with good self-control tend to become adolescents with good self-control.

Parental Influences
When children observe adults who delay gratification, they more often delay gratification themselves. Children who have the best self-control tend to have parents who do not use harsh punishment and who encourage their children to make their own decisions.

Temperamental Influences on Self-Control
With fearful children, reminders help self-control; with fearless children, appeals to the attachment relationship help self-control.

Improving Self-Control
Children can regulate their own behavior when they have plans to help remember a goal and something to distract them from tempting objects.

Learning About Moral Rules
Preschool children distinguish moral rules from social conventions, distinguish lies from mistakes, and show signs of guilt.

Development in Preschoolers
IN PERSPECTIVE

■ Continuity

Early development is related to later development but not perfectly

We saw several instances of this theme in Chapter 8. For example, preschool children's height predicts their height as adults, but not perfectly. Some children end up being taller than expected and some shorter. Handedness represents another example. Handedness is well established by the end of the preschool years and left-handed people are more likely to become skilled artists or mathematicians. Yet we all know left-handers who are miserable at art and math! Finally, we saw that sexual abuse in childhood usually leads to adjustment problems in adulthood but some individuals escape these harmful consequences. In each case, characteristics or events early in life are related to outcomes later in life but not consistently. Other factors often intervene to affect outcomes, such as a nurturing, caring father in the case of childhood sexual abuse.

■ Nature and Nurture

Development is always jointly influenced by heredity and environment

In Chapter 9, we learned that children's mastery of grammar depends on innate mechanisms that simplify the task of detecting rules for combining words. Yet the environment also contributes. Parents provide extra examples of the grammatical rules their children are trying to master and parents provide feedback when children's speech is ungrammatical. Self-control, described in Chapter 10, also illustrates the combined effects of nature and nurture. Examples of environmental influence on self-control are numerous: Parents contribute to their children's self-control by showing self-control themselves and by gradually allowing children to make their own decisions. But the story does not end with environmental influence: Biological influences are important, in the form of children's temperament. Children who are temperamental tend to have poorer self-control. And temperament determines how children respond to parents' efforts to teach self-control. Anxious children tend to comply with parents' requests because they worry about the consequences of not complying.

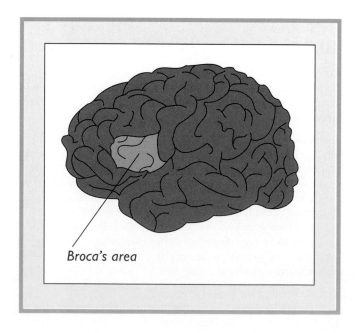

Broca's area

■ Active Child
Children help determine
their own development

The impact children have on their own lives was shown several times in the last few chapters. In Chapter 8, children's improved motor skills mean that parents and other adults treat them differently, allowing them to act more independently (e.g., dressing themselves). Also in Chapter 8, it was evident that some children unknowingly and unwittingly contribute to their own abuse. When children whine and cry constantly (because they're ill or simply too young to regulate their own behavior well), they increase the chances that they'll be abused. Finally, in Chapter 10, we learned that parents' discipline is driven, in part, by their children's response to prior discipline. When children do not comply, parents often resort to more severe forms of discipline, hoping that this will be more effective. In each instance, characteristics of children—their improving motor skills, their whining, or their response to parents' discipline—affect how adults treat them.

■ Connections
Development in different
domains is connected

This theme emerged many times in Chapters 8–10. It is central to Vygotsky's theory, which emphasizes that cognitive development takes place in a social setting and is promoted by social interactions with skilled teachers. And children's growing communication skills allow their social interactions with adults and peers to be more successful and more rewarding. Finally, we saw that learning gender roles is not simply a social phenomenon: Cognitive processes are essential. Kohlberg's theory shows that children don't really begin to learn about gender until they understand that they will remain a boy or girl for life. Once they understand gender constancy, gender-schema theory shows how children use this information to decide which experiences are relevant to them. Biology apparently contributes, too, although we still don't really understand how. Biology, cognition, and social forces are interwoven in children's development.

Physical Development in School-Age Children

Chapter 11

During the elementary-school years, millions of boys and girls around the world begin to participate in sports. Some play in organized basketball, baseball, or soccer leagues. Others play in pick-up games in a schoolyard or street. Regardless of the setting, though, such physical activity is a ubiquitous element of childhood signifying that children have reached important milestones in physical, motor, cognitive, and social growth. They now have enough control over their bodies to perform the complex skills that are essential to many sports, they have the cognitive processes that allow them to know when the skills are needed, and they have the interpersonal skills that allow them to be part of a team.

We'll examine the cognitive and social changes in Chapters 12 and 13. Here we'll concentrate on physical development. We start, in Module 11.1, by describing different aspects of physical growth. In Module 11.2, we'll look at children's growing motor skills. Finally, in Module 11.3, we consider some children whose development is not typical and thus presents them with special challenges.

Growth of the Body

11.1

Growth of the Body

├─Physical Growth

├─Nutrition

├─Tooth Development

└─Vision

> **Learning Objectives**
>
> ▪ **How much do school-age children grow?**
>
> ▪ **What are elementary-school children's nutritional needs? What are the best ways to approach malnutrition and obesity?**
>
> ▪ **When do children's primary teeth begin to come in?**
>
> ▪ **What vision problems are common in school-age children?**

Ricardo, age 12, has been overweight for most of his life. He dislikes the playground games that entertain most of his classmates during recess, preferring to stay indoors. He has relatively few friends and is not particularly happy with his lot in life. Many times Ricardo has lost weight from dieting, but he's always regained it quickly. His parents know that being overweight is a health hazard, and they wonder if there is anything that will help their son.

The body grows steadily during the elementary-school years. We'll look at the nature of this growth in the first part of this module, then examine the nutrition required to support this growth. There, we'll learn more about Ricardo's obesity. We'll end the module by focusing on changes in children's teeth and vision.

Physical Growth

Physical growth during the elementary-school years continues at the steady pace established during the preschool years. From the graphs, you can see that a typical 6-year-old weighs about 45 pounds and is 45 inches tall but grows to about 90 pounds and 60 inches by age 12. In other words, most children gain about 8 pounds and 2 to 3 inches per year. Many parents notice that their elementary-school children outgrow shoes and pants more rapidly than they outgrow sweaters, shirts, or jackets; this is because most of the increase in height comes from the legs, not the trunk.

Boys and girls are about the same size for most of these years (which is why they are

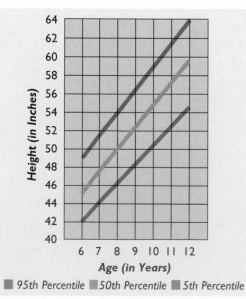

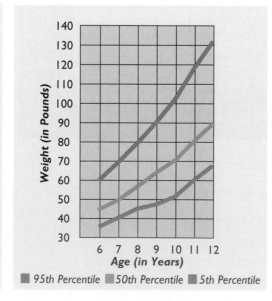

FIG 11–1

combined in the graph), but girls are much more likely than boys to enter puberty toward the end of the elementary-school years. Those who do, grow rapidly, becoming much bigger than boys. (I'll have more to say about this in Module 14.1.) Thus, at ages 11 and 12, the average girl is about a half-inch taller than the average boy.

As was true in the preschool years, individuals of the same age often differ markedly in their height and weight. For example, all the girls on my daughter's current soccer team are 10-year-olds, but the tallest is nearly a foot taller than the shortest and the heaviest weighs 45 pounds more than the lightest! This range of heights and weights is obvious in the photo. Ethnic differences are also evident in children's growth: In these years, African American children tend to be taller than European American children, who are taller than Asian American children (Webber et al., 1995).

Some children are unusually short because their body does not produce enough growth hormone (see Module 5.1). This condition, which affects about 1 child in 5,000, is treated by injecting children daily with synthetic growth hormone. These injections begin in childhood and continue through adolescence, when growth would stop normally. When treated with growth hormone therapy, children often have a brief growth spurt, followed by more rapid growth than before they started therapy.

Since synthetic growth hormone was first made available in 1985, growth hormone therapy has spread to children who are short but whose bodies do produce adequate amounts of natural growth hormone.* Kirk and Nora are typical of many parents who, being small themselves, have a son who has consistently been at the fifth percentile on height. Though tests make it clear that their son's body is producing normal amounts of growth hormone, Kirk and Nora have vigorously pursued hormone therapy for him.

Although this practice is widespread in the United States, many scientists and health-care professionals are skeptical. The treatments are very expensive, do not necessarily make children taller as adults (they may just help them reach their natural adult height sooner), and may make children more prone to infections. Furthermore, by itself being short is not consistently related to adjustment problems (Sandberg, Brook, & Campos, 1994). Given these many concerns, it's not surprising that the Committees on Drugs and Bioethics of the American Academy of Pediatrics (1997) suggests that growth hormone therapy be targeted primarily for children with known hormonal problems, not for all children who are short.

Nutrition

As children enter elementary-school, they need to eat more to support growth and to provide energy for their active lives. Although preschool children need only consume about 1,500 to 1,700 calories per day, the average 7- to 10-year-old needs about 2,400 calories each day. Of course, the exact figure depends on the child's age and size and can range anywhere from roughly 1,700 to 3,300 calories daily.

As was true for preschool children, elementary-school children need a well-balanced diet. They should eat regularly from each of the five food groups that I described on page 227. Too often children consume calories from sweets that are empty—they have very little nutritional value.

---

* Before it was synthesized in 1985, growth hormone was quite limited because it was available only from the brains of cadavers. In those days, only children with actual growth disorders could readily obtain growth hormone.

It's also important that school-age children eat breakfast. At this age, many children skip breakfast, often because they're too rushed in the morning. In fact, breakfast should provide about one-fourth of a child's daily calories. When children don't eat breakfast, they often have difficulty paying attention or remembering in school (Pollitt, 1995). Consequently, parents should organize their mornings so that, like the child in the photo, their children have enough time for breakfast.

Many American schoolchildren skip breakfast because they're living in poverty and their parents can't afford to feed them. For these youngsters, a missed breakfast is part of a much larger problem of malnutrition or subnutrition. As we've seen before (page 117), malnutrition is a problem worldwide and is disturbingly common in the United States. For school-age children, chronic malnutrition causes many problems. Children's growth can be slowed. In addition, children are more likely to be irritable and to be ill, causing them to miss school. And, even when they're in school, underfed children often have trouble concentrating on their schoolwork.

One attack on this problem is to provide free and reduced-price meals for children at school. Lunch programs are the most common, but breakfast and dinner are sometimes available, too. These programs have a tremendous positive impact on children. Because they are better fed, they are absent from school less often and their achievement scores improve (Gleason, 1995; Meyers et al., 1989). Sadly, many children who are eligible for these programs do not participate, typically because parents don't realize their children are eligible. Parents need to be encouraged to have their children participate and all adults need to support these programs as they provide immediate and lasting benefits to the children they serve.

Although many children do not receive adequate nutrition, others have the opposite problem: Some children and adolescents eat too much. We'll look at this problem in the next section of this module.

Obesity. Ricardo, the boy in the module-opening vignette, is typical of the 5 to 10 percent of American children and adolescents who are obese, at least 20 percent over the ideal body weight for their age and height. Overweight youngsters, like the boy in the photo, are often unpopular and have low self-esteem (Braet, Mervielde, & Vandereycken, 1997). Furthermore, they are at risk for many medical problems, including high blood pressure and diabetes, throughout life because the vast majority of overweight children and adolescents become overweight adults (Serdula et al., 1993).

Heredity plays an important role in juvenile obesity. In adoption studies, children and adolescents' weight is related to the weight of their biological parents, not to the weight of their adoptive parents (Stunkard et al., 1986). Genes may influence obesity by influencing a person's activity level. In other words, being genetically more prone to inactivity makes it more difficult to burn off calories and easier to gain weight. **Heredity may also help set *basal metabolic rate*, the speed at which the body consumes calories.** Children and adolescents with a slower basal metabolic rate burn off calories less rapidly, making it easier for them to gain weight (Epstein & Cluss, 1986).

One's environment is also influential. Television advertising, for example, encourages youth to eat tasty but fattening foods. Parents play a role, too. They may inadvertently encourage obesity by emphasizing external eating signals rather than internal. Infants eat primarily because of internal signals: They eat when they experience hunger and stop eating when they feel full. During the preschool years, this internal control of eating is often gradually replaced by external signals. Parents who urge their children to "clean their plates" even when they are no longer hungry are teaching their children to ignore internal cues to eating. Thus, obese children and adolescents may overeat because they rely on external cues and disregard internal cues to stop (Birch, 1991).

Obese youth *can* lose weight. The most effective programs have several features in common (Epstein et al., 1995; Foreyt & Goodrich, 1995; Israel et al., 1994):

- The focus of the program is to change obese children's eating habits, encourage them to become more active, and discourage sedentary behavior.

- As part of the treatment, children learn to monitor their eating, exercise, and sedentary behavior. Goals are established in each area and rewards are earned when the goals are met.

- Parents are trained to help children set realistic goals and to use behavioral principles to help children meet these goals. Parents also monitor their own lifestyles to be sure they aren't accidentally fostering their child's obesity.

> In effective programs for treating obesity, children and parents set eating and exercise goals and monitor progress toward those goals.

When programs incorporate these features, obese children do lose weight. However, even after losing weight, many of these children remain overweight. It is best to establish good eating and exercise habits in order to avoid obesity in the first place.

Tooth Development

Like the child in the photo, many 5- and 6-year-olds see the loss of a tooth as a sign of maturity. That's a good thing, because after children's primary teeth begin to fall out at this age, children lose teeth regularly—about four a year for the next 5 years! The primary teeth are steadily replaced by permanent teeth. By age 12, most children will have approximately 24 teeth. The four second molars usually erupt at 11 to 13 years and the third molars typically appear in late adolescence or early adulthood (which is why they're called *wisdom* teeth).

In the Cultural Influences feature, we'll see how the loss of teeth is celebrated in cultures around the world.

CULTURAL INFLUENCES

Shed-Tooth Rituals Around the World

In the United States, England, and Australia, many youngsters who have lost a baby tooth eagerly place it under their pillow and wait for the tooth fairy to replace it overnight with money. This practice apparently originated about 100 years ago but rituals celebrating the loss of baby teeth have existed throughout history. A common practice was to offer the tooth to an animal, often one with large teeth, with the hope that the child would grow strong teeth. In ancient times, children of Abyssinia offered the lost tooth to a hyena and, more recently, some Native American children offered teeth to a beaver. In many cultures, children offered teeth to mice; French children, for example, threw the lost tooth under their beds, hoping that a mouse would eat the tooth and provide them with a stronger new one (Wynbrandt, 1998).

In modern cultures, many variants of these practices are common. In Italy, children place their lost tooth under a pillow and a mouse replaces it with a coin. In Turkey, the tooth is buried at a site significant for the child's future: The tooth might be buried on a college campus if parents want their child to be well educated. In Korea, children throw their tooth onto the roof of their homes and ask a magpie (a bird thought to be the bearer of good news) to bring them a new tooth. In Japan, a lost lower tooth is thrown onto the roof but a lost upper tooth is buried. This is to

Good care for teeth includes frequent brushings, fluoride treatment, and regular checkups.

encourage adult teeth to grow in the right direction. Similarly, in Hong Kong, where most children live in high-rise buildings, children put their arm out the window and let the tooth fall to the street, a practice thought to help adult teeth grow straight.

What these various interesting customs have in common is the recognition that a lost tooth is a physical symbol of the child's progress toward maturity. With each lost tooth, the developing individual is a bit less childlike and a bit more adultlike. ■

Caring for permanent teeth is important throughout childhood and adulthood. Food that is not removed from the teeth combines with bacteria in the mouth to produce acid that eats through the tooth's enamel surface, creating a cavity. To avoid cavities, children (and adults) should brush and floss regularly. This is particularly important after eating foods high in starches and carbohydrates because these produce the acid that leads to decay. Fluoride in toothpaste and drinking water is an integral part of the fight against tooth decay. Fluoride interferes with the formation of tooth-damaging acids and helps to repair tooth surfaces that have been damaged by acid. Finally, decay prevention also involves regular visits to a dentist for a check-up and cleaning.

The United States has made remarkable progress in reducing tooth decay. Today, approximately half of school-age children and adolescents are cavity free, compared to only 25 percent 30 years ago. This improvement reflects better overall

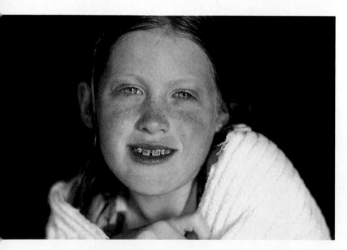

dental care, widespread use of fluoride, and more frequent sealing of the chewing surfaces of permanent teeth in plastic. However, sealing teeth is not always a routine part of children's dental care; if it were, cavities would become even less common (Brown et al., 1996).

When permanent teeth erupt, some children experience *malocclusion*—their upper and lower teeth don't meet properly. Malocclusion has many causes: heredity, early loss of primary teeth, an accident, or thumbsucking after the permanent teeth erupt. Another problem for many children is that the permanent teeth are crowded or overlap. Malocclusion can make chewing difficult and crowded teeth are prone to decay. The solution to both problems is treatment by an orthodontist. Braces like those that the child in the photo is wearing use steady pressure to move teeth into position. After 6 months to 2 years of braces, teeth are usually aligned properly.

Vision

Children's sensory systems—vision, hearing, and taste, for example—mature early in infancy and, for the most part, change little during childhood. One physical change during the elementary-school years that affects hearing concerns the eustachian tube, which links the inner ear to the upper part of the throat. In school-age children the eustachian tube becomes longer and more curvy, which helps to reduce the incidence of otitis media (ear infection) that causes temporary hearing loss and permanent loss if left uncorrected.

By far the most common sensory disorder in these years involves vision. **In *myopia* (nearsightedness) the lens projects images of distant objects in front of the retina instead of on it, which means they look fuzzy instead of sharp.** For example, Akilah, a fourth grader, often squinted when she tried to read the blackboard and complained that she didn't like being at a desk in the back of the room. A vision test revealed that Akilah suffered from myopia: Her near vision was clear but her distant vision wasn't. Approximately 25 percent of school-age children are myopic and it usually emerges between 8 and 12 years of age. Heredity clearly contributes, as myopia runs in families and identical twins are more likely than fraternal twins to be myopic (Sperduto et al., 1983). But experience is also a factor: Children who spend much time reading, working at a computer, or drawing—all activities that draw upon near vision—are more likely to become myopic. Happily, myopia is easily remedied with glasses; Akilah was fitted with glasses and she no longer squinted or complained about sitting in the back of the room.

Check Your Learning

1. Boys and girls grow at about the same rate during elementary-school years, but at the end of this period, girls _____.

2. Although synthetic growth hormone is sometimes administered to short children whose bodies produce adequate growth hormone, most scientists and health-care professionals _____.

3. When children skip breakfast, _____.

4. Effective programs for treating obesity in children focus on changing children's eating habits, changing their exercise habits, and _____.

5. Fluoride protects teeth by interfering with the formation of tooth-damaging acids and _____.

6. Approximately 25 percent of school-age children suffer from _____, in which they cannot see distant objects clearly.

Nature and Nurture Your friend Kim, who is overweight, is upset to find that her 10-year-old son is putting on weight. What can you tell Kim about the influence of genetics on childhood obesity? What would you suggest to help her son to avoid becoming obese?

Answers: (1) are more likely to enter puberty and grow rapidly, (2) believe that only children with known hormone disorders should receive growth hormone, (3) they often have difficulty paying attention and remembering in school, (4) training parents to help children set realistic goals, (5) helping to repair tooth surfaces damaged by acid, (6) myopia

Motor Development

11.2

Motor Development

Learning Objectives

■ How do motor skills improve during the elementary-school years? Do boys and girls differ in their motor skills?

■ Are American children physically fit?

■ What are the benefits of participating in sports? What are the optimal circumstances for children to participate?

■ What kinds of accidents are common in school-age children and how can they be prevented?

Miguel and Dan are 9-year-olds playing organized baseball for the first time. Miguel's coach is always upbeat. He constantly emphasizes the positive. When they lost a game 12 to 2, the coach complimented all the players on their play in the field and at bat. In contrast, Dan's coach was livid when the team lost and he was very critical of three players who made errors that contributed to the loss. Miguel thinks that baseball is great but Dan can hardly wait for the season to be over.

Motor skills improve remarkably over the elementary-school years. We'll trace these changes in the first part of this module, then see whether U.S. children are fit. Next, we'll examine children's participation in sports and see how coaches like those in the vignette influence children in organized sports. Finally, we'll see how children's improved motor skills sometimes place them at risk for injury.

Growth of Motor Skills

Elementary-school children's greater size and strength contributes to improved motor skills. During these years, children steadily run faster and jump farther. For example, the figure on page 329 shows how far a typical boy and girl can throw a ball and how far they can jump (in the standing long jump). By the time children are 11 years old, they can throw a ball three times farther than they could at age 6 and they can jump nearly twice as far.

Fine-motor skills also improve as children move through the elementary-school years. Children's greater dexterity is evident in a host of activities ranging from typing, writing, and drawing to working on puzzles, playing the piano, and building model cars. Children gain much greater control over their fingers and hands, making them much more nimble. This greater fine-motor coordination is obvious in children's handwriting.

Gender Differences in Motor Skills. In both gross-motor and fine-motor skills, there are gender differences in performance levels. Girls tend to excel in fine-motor skills; their handwriting tends to be better than boys', for example. And on a task in which pegs must be moved to different positions on a board, girls tend to be faster

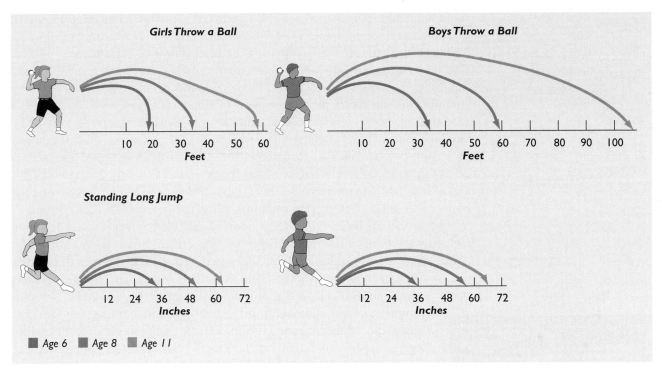

Girls Throw a Ball

10 20 30 40 50 60
Feet

Boys Throw a Ball

10 20 30 40 50 60 70 80 90 100
Feet

Standing Long Jump

12 24 36 48 60 72
Inches

12 24 36 48 60 72
Inches

■ Age 6   ■ Age 8   ■ Age 11

FIG 11–2

(Kail, 1991; Thomas & French, 1985). Girls also excel on gross-motor skills that require flexibility and balance, such as tumbling. On gross-motor skills that emphasize strength, boys usually have the advantage. The diagram, for example, shows that boys throw and jump farther than girls.

Some of the gender differences in gross-motor skills that require strength reflect the fact that as children approach and enter puberty, girls' bodies have proportionately more fat and less muscle than boys' bodies. This difference explains why, for example, boys can hang from a bar using their arms and hands much longer than girls can. However, for other gross-motor skills, such as running, throwing, and catching, body composition is much less important (Smoll & Schutz, 1990). In these cases, children's experience is crucial. During recess, elementary-school girls are more often found on a swingset, jumping rope, or perhaps talking quietly in a group; in contrast, boys are playing football or shooting baskets. Many girls and their parents believe that sports and physical fitness are less valuable for girls than boys (Eccles, Jacobs, & Harold, 1990). Consequently, girls spend less time in these sports and fitness-related activities than boys, depriving them of opportunities to practice, which is essential for developing motor skills (Eccles & Harold, 1991).

> Girls tend to excel on fine-motor skills that require dexterity and on gross-motor skills that require flexibility and balance; boys tend to excel on gross-motor skills that require strength.

Physical Fitness

Being active physically has many benefits for children—it helps to promote growth of muscles and bone, promotes cardiovascular health (National High Blood Pressure Education Program Working Group, 1996), and can help to establish a lifelong pattern of exercise. How fit are U.S. school-age children? According to their own reports, school children are quite active—they report spending more than 2 hours each day in moderate to vigorous activity (Simons-Morton et al., 1997). However, when children are tested against objective criteria, the picture is different. In studies that include a full battery of fitness tests, such as the mile run, pull-ups, and sit-ups, fewer than half the children usually meet standards for fitness on all tasks (Corbin & Pangrazi, 1992; Looney & Plowman, 1990).

Many factors contribute to low levels of fitness. In most elementary-schools, physical education classes meet only once or twice a week. And, even when children are in these classes, they spend a surprisingly large proportion of time—nearly half—standing around instead of exercising (Parcel et al., 1987). Television and other sedentary leisure-time activities may contribute, too. Children who watch TV often tend to be less fit physically, but the nature of this relation remains poorly understood: Children who watch TV a lot may have fewer opportunities to exercise but it may be that children who are in poor physical condition would rather watch TV than exercise.

Many experts believe that U.S. schools should offer physical education more frequently each week. And many believe that physical education classes should offer a range of activities in which all children can participate and that can be the foundation for a lifelong program of fitness. Thus, instead of emphasizing team sports such as touch football, physical education classes should emphasize activities like running, walking, racquet sports, and swimming; these can be done throughout adolescence and adulthood and either alone or with another person (American Academy of Pediatrics Committee on Sports Medicine and Committee on School Health, 1989). Families can encourage fitness, too. Instead of spending an afternoon watching TV and eating popcorn, they can go hiking or biking together.

Participating in Sports

Children's greater motor skill means they are able to participate in many team sports, including baseball, softball, basketball, and soccer. Obviously, when children, like the girls in the photo, play sports, they get exercise and improve their motor skills. But there are other hidden benefits as well. Sports can provide children a chance to learn important social skills, such as how to work effectively as part of a group, often in complementary roles. And playing sports allows children to use their emerging cognitive skills as they devise new playing strategies or modify the rules of a game.

Children differ in their reasons for participating in sports and in their beliefs about the benefits of sports participation. The Focus on Research feature compares boys' and girls' beliefs concerning the benefits of participating in sports.

FOCUS ON RESEARCH

Why Participate in Organized Sports?

Who were the investigators and what was the aim of the study? If you ask children and adults why youth should participate in sports, the range of answers is astonishing. Some answers emphasize the fun of playing, others emphasize the benefits to children's social relationships, and still others emphasize the competitive edge that children gain. Sally White, Joan Duda, and Michael Keller (1998) decided to determine whether boys and girls agree on the purposes of sports participation.

How did the investigators measure the topic of interest? The investigators administered the Perceived Purposes of Sport Questionnaire. Each of 46 items on this questionnaire is of the form "A very important thing sport should do is..." followed by a specific benefit (e.g., give us a chance to have fun, teach us to respect our bodies). After reading each item, children indicated their agreement on a scale ranging from 1 (strongly disagree) to 5 (strongly agree). The 46 items tapped beliefs in 7 general categories. The categories and example items from each are shown in the figure below.

Who were the children in the study? The children were recruited through a local youth athletic association and included 100 boys and 92 girls who were participating in organized swimming, soccer, basketball, or ice hockey. The children were 11-year-olds.

What was the design of the study? This study was correlational because White and her colleagues were interested in the relation that existed naturally between a child's gender and his or her beliefs about sports participation. The sample included only 11-year-olds and they were tested just once, so the study was not developmental (i.e., was neither longitudinal nor cross-sectional).

Were there ethical concerns with the study? No. The investigators obtained permission from the children, their parents, their coaches, and the athletic association.

What were the results? The graph shows how strongly children endorsed each of the seven general categories. What is most striking is that boys' and girls' are very similar concerning the most important reasons for participating in sports. Boys and girls both believe that the most important reasons for participating in sports are enhancing self-esteem, skill mastery and cooperation, and physical activity. And boys and girls agree that social status and deception are the least important reasons for participating. Thus, in the grander scheme of things, boys and girls have similar ideas. However, boys do see somewhat more benefit from sports participation than girls do in terms of social status, deception, and competitiveness.

Boys and girls agree that enhancing self-esteem, improving skills, and being active physically are the main reasons for participating in sports.

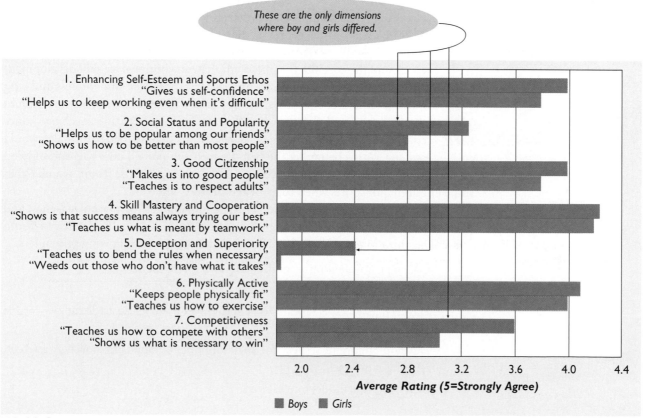

FIG 11-3

What did the investigators conclude? Boys and girls expect similar benefits from their participation in youth sports. They expect to gain self-confidence, learn about teamwork, and become physically fit. Although boys are more likely than girls to agree that sports will help them to be popular and to be competitive, they do not consider these the primary reasons for participating in sports.

What converging evidence would strengthen these conclusions? The chief weaknesses of this study are both associated with the sample. First, White and her colleagues tested only 11-year-olds. Adolescents and younger children might differ in their reasons for participating in sports, so it would be useful to conduct a developmental study comparing, for example, 7-, 11-, and 15-year-olds. Second, the 11-year-olds in the study were taken from organized sports programs. Obviously, such children do not constitute a random sample of 11-year-olds and you can imagine that this group might have different reasons for participating in sports. Consequently, it would also be useful to test a less restricted sample of children. ■

In days gone by, children gathered together informally—at a playground, a vacant lot, or someone's backyard—to play these sports. However, when today's children participate, the setting is often an official league, organized and run by adults. This turns out to be a mixed blessing. Adults' involvement in children's sports has several advantages: Children learn how to improve their skills and get knowledgeable feedback, and they can enjoy spending time with a positive role model. But there are disadvantages as well. Adults sometimes overemphasize competition instead of skill development, they can be so controlling that children have little opportunity to learn leadership skills, and they may so emphasize drills, strategy, and performance that the activity becomes more like work instead of play.

When adults like Miguel's coach (in the module-opening vignette) encourage their players and emphasize skill development, children usually enjoy playing, often improve their skills, and increase their self-esteem (Smith & Smoll, 1997; Smoll et al., 1993). In contrast, when adults like Dan's coach and the coach in the photo emphasize winning over skill development and criticize or punish players for bad plays, children lose interest and stop playing (Bailey & Rasmussen, 1996; Smith & Stoll, 1996). You may doubt that anyone coaching a young child could be as bad as Dan's coach but I once coached against a man who, when one of his players made a mistake, would *scream*, "You'd better get the ball the next time or I'll take you out and you won't play anymore!" His players were 8- and 9-year-old girls; it's no wonder that some children quit sports when coaches act this way.

Many youth sports organizations provide guidelines for players, coaches, and parents, so that children will enjoy participating. For example, the American Youth Soccer Organization has a code for coaches that includes the following principles:

- Coach positively: Praise children, don't criticize them.

- Be sure that children have fun!

- Have realistic expectations for children and use these to form reasonable demands.

- Develop children's respect for their opponents, opposing coaches, referees, and the game itself.

- Be a good role model for children.

When coaches (and parents) follow these guidelines, it's a good bet that their players will have fun and continue to play the sport. And everyone involved needs to remember that this is the whole point: Children (and adults) play games for recreation, to have fun!

Accidents

Elementary-school children's improved motor skills and greater independence places them at greater risk for injury. For example, children may walk to school unsupervised and need to cross busy streets. Or, like the youngster in the photo, they may ride a bike and need to share the street with much larger and faster vehicles.

Not surprisingly, then, accidents involving an automobile are the most common cause of injury and death for elementary-school children, either as a passenger or as a pedestrian. Bicycle accidents are the next most frequent cause of childhood injuries (U.S. Department of Health and Human Services, 1997). As I mentioned on page 119, parents need to be vigilant in requiring children to wear seat belts in cars and wear helmets on bikes, scooters, skateboards, and roller blades. Although seat belts and helmets won't prevent accidents, they dramatically reduce the risk of injury (Peterson & Oliver, 1995).

Preventing accidents is not easy, in part because school-age children often object to parents' efforts to ensure safety and in part because, in the process of taking advantage of their new skills and freedom, children often unknowingly endanger themselves. Parents can help by being good role models—by always fastening their own seat belts and wearing a helmet when biking. And they can insist that their children always wear seat belts and helmets, even when the trip is brief or otherwise seems safe. By these actions, parents are not only protecting themselves and their children from injury, they are also making their children much more safety-conscious and less prone to take risks themselves (Tuchfarber, Zins, & Jason, 1997).

Parents can also prevent accidents by being realistic in assessing their own children's skills. Too often parents overestimate their children's abilities, particularly their cognitive and motor skills. They may allow a 7-year-old to cross a busy street, when, in fact, most children younger than 9 or 10 years will not look consistently and cannot accurately judge the amount of time they have to cross a street. Or parents may allow a child to ride to school in a bike lane adjacent to a street filled with commuters, even though children may not consistently pay attention while biking or may be unable to maneuver their bike around unexpected hazards, such as a pothole.*

Parents need to be aware that these situations are ripe for injury and should be avoided. In the first instance, the parent could accompany the child to the busy street, help the child cross, then let the child continue alone; in the second, the parent could insist that the child find a less busy route or use another form of transportation. Parents need to remember that school-age children's cognitive and motor skills are, in many respects, still quite limited; these limits can expose children to danger and parents need to avoid these situations before accidents happen (Dunne, Asher, & Rivara, 1992).

> Parents can help protect their children from accidents by being good role models, by insisting that their children use protective devices, and by not overestimating their children's skills.

* While biking, my son Matt once crashed right into the back of a parked car because he was too busy watching the gears shift on his new bike. Fortunately, he escaped with just a few scrapes, but this illustrates how easily a childhood lapse in concentration can lead to a cycling accident.

Community- and school-based programs are important tools in efforts to reduce childhood accidents. Through such programs, children can learn safety-oriented behaviors that reduce their risk for injury. Successful programs often present material about safety to children but, more importantly, provide role-playing opportunities in which youngsters can practice safety skills. For example, children can be taught to "stop, drop, and roll" if their clothing is on fire, then be asked to practice this behavior. Or children might be taught ways to cross a street safely (e.g., pick a safe spot to cross, then look left, right, and left again before crossing), then be allowed to practice this skill, supervised by an adult. When programs like these are run in communities by schools or hospitals, children readily learn behaviors that promote safety (Zins et al., 1994).

Check Your Learning

1. Boys typically have the advantage on gross-motor skills that emphasize strength but girls tend to have the advantage on _____.

2. Although children often report that they spend much time in vigorous play, in fact, fewer than _____ percent of children typically meet all standards for fitness.

3. Most physical education classes do relatively little to help schoolchildren stay physically fit because the classes meet infrequently and because

   _____.

4. Boys and girls agree that the most important reasons for participating in sports are enhancing self-esteem, skill mastery and cooperation, and _____.

5. Having parents as coaches has many drawbacks; they sometimes overemphasize competition, they _____, and their emphasis on drills, strategy, and performance turns play into work.

6. The most common cause of injury and death for elementary-school children is

   _____.

7. Parents can help their children avoid accidents and be more safety conscious by always insisting that their children wear seat belts in cars and helmets when biking or roller blading, being good role models for safety behavior, and

   _____.

Connections   Discuss how participation in sports illustrates connections between motor, cognitive, and social development.

Answers: (1) fine-motor skills that emphasize dexterity, (2) 50, (3) children in physical education classes spend too little time actually exercising, (4) physical activity, (5) are so controlling that children do not have the opportunity to experience leadership, (6) the automobile, (7) not overestimating their children's cognitive and motor skills

Children with Special Challenges

Learning Objectives

- What are learning disabilities?

- What is attention deficit hyperactivity disorder?

- What are the different forms of mental retardation?

Sanjit, a second grader, has taken two separate intelligence tests and both times he had above-average scores. Nevertheless, Sanjit absolutely cannot read. Letters and words are as mysterious to him as Metallica's music would be to Mozart. His parents took Sanjit to an ophthalmologist who determined that nothing is wrong with his eyes. What is wrong?

Throughout history, societies have recognized children with atypical abilities and today we know much about these children. We'll begin this module with a look at learning disabilities, where we'll discover why Sanjit can't read. Then we'll consider children with attention deficit hyperactivity disorder. Finally, we'll end the module (and the chapter) by discussing children with mental retardation.

Children with Learning Disabilities

For some children with normal intelligence, learning is a struggle. **These young-sters have a *learning disability*, which refers to a child who (a) has difficulty mastering an academic subject, (b) has normal intelligence, and (c) is not suffering from other conditions that could explain poor performance, such as sensory impairment or inadequate instruction (Hammill, 1990).**

In the United States, about 5 percent of school-age children are classified as learning disabled, which translates into roughly 2 million youngsters (Moats & Lyon, 1993). The number of distinct disabilities and the degree of overlap among them is still debated (Stanovich, 1993). However, one common classification scheme distinguishes disability in language (including listening, speaking, and writing), in reading, and in arithmetic (Dockrell & McShane, 1993).

The variety of learning disabilities complicates the task for teachers and researchers because it suggests that each type of learning disability may have its own cause and treatment (Lyon, 1996). Take reading, the most common area of learning disability, as an example. Many children with a reading disability have problems in phonological awareness (described in Module 6.3), which refers to understanding and using the sounds in written and oral language. For a reading-disabled child like Sanjit (in the vignette) or the boy in the photograph, all vowels sound alike. Thus *pin* sounds like *pen* which sounds like *pan.* These youngsters benefit from explicit, extensive instruction on the connections between letters and their sounds (Lyon, 1996; Wise, Ring, & Olson, 1999).

In the case of arithmetic disability, children often have difficulty recognizing what operations are needed and how to perform them. Here, instruction emphasizes determining the goal of arithmetic problems, using goals to select correct arithmetic operations, and using operations accurately (Goldman, 1989).

The key to helping these children is to move beyond the generic label "learning disability" to pinpoint specific cognitive and academic deficits that hamper an individual child's performance in school. Then instruction can be specifically tailored to improve the child's skills (Moats & Lyon, 1993).

Planning effective instruction for children with learning disabilities is much easier said than done, however, because diagnosing a learning disability is very difficult. Some children have both reading and language disabilities; other children have reading and arithmetic disabilities. Despite these difficulties, with ingenuity, hard work, and care, children with learning disabilities—and all exceptional children, for that matter—can develop their full intellectual potential.

Attention Deficit Hyperactivity Disorder

Soon after Stephen entered kindergarten, his teacher remarked that he sometimes seemed to be out of control. Stephen was easily distracted, often moving aimlessly from one activity to another. He also seemed to be impulsive, and compared to other youngsters his age, he had much more difficulty waiting his turn. At first, Stephen's parents just attributed his behavior to boyish energy. But when Stephen progressed to first and second grade, his pattern of behavior continued. He began to fall behind in reading and arithmetic. Also, his classmates were annoyed by his behavior and began to avoid him. This just made Stephen mad, so he often got into fights with his classmates. Finally, Stephen's parents took him to a psychologist, who determined that Stephen had attention deficit hyperactivity disorder. ***Attention deficit hyperactivity disorder (ADHD)* is a condition in which a child exhibits overactivity, inattention, and/or impulsivity.**

- *Overactivity:* Children with ADHD are unusually energetic, fidgety, and unable to keep still, especially in situations like school classrooms where they need to limit their activity.

- *Inattention:* Youngsters with ADHD skip from one task to another. They do not pay attention in class and seem unable to concentrate on schoolwork.

- *Impulsivity:* Children with ADHD often act before thinking; they may run into a street before looking for traffic or interrupt others who are speaking.

Not all children with ADHD show all of these symptoms to the same degree. Some, like the boy in the photograph, may be primarily hyperactive. Others may be primarily impulsive and show no signs of hyperactivity; their disorder is often described simply as attention deficit disorder (Barkley, 1990). Furthermore, symptoms often vary with the setting. Some youngsters who are unable to maintain attention in school may sit still for hours playing a video game at home (Barkley, 1996).

In light of these inconsistencies, it probably won't surprise you that researchers disagree about the number of different subtypes of ADHD and the factors that give rise to ADHD (Barkley, 1996; Panksepp, 1998). However, it *is* clear that children with ADHD often have problems with conduct and academic performance. Like Stephen, many hyperactive children are aggressive and therefore are not liked by their peers (Barkley, 1990; McGee, Williams, & Feehan, 1992). Although youngsters with ADHD usually have normal intelligence, their scores on reading, spelling, and arithmetic achievement tests are often below average (Pennington, Groisser, & Welsh, 1993). Roughly 3 to 15 percent of all school-age children are diagnosed with ADHD; boys outnumber girls by a 3:1 ratio (Wicks-Nelson & Israel, 1991).

One myth about ADHD is that most children "grow out of it" in adolescence or young adulthood. More than half the children who are diagnosed with ADHD will have, as adolescents and young adults, problems related to overactivity, inattention, and impulsivity. Few of these young adults complete college and some will have work- and family-related problems (Fischer et al., 1993; Rapport, 1995). The Looking Ahead feature shows just how long lasting ADHD can be.

> Children with ADHD are overactive, inattentive, and impulsive; as a consequence, they often do poorly in school and are disliked by peers.

LOOKING AHEAD
Persistent Effects of ADHD

If children grow out of ADHD, then we should find that children diagnosed with ADHD turn out, as adults, to be like most adults. Research consistently suggests that they aren't, at least when ADHD is left untreated. Rasmussen and Gillberg (2000) compared a group of 55 22-year-olds who had been diagnosed with ADHD as 7-year-olds to a group of 22-year-olds who did not have ADHD as 7-year-olds. The graph shows the results: On all four measures, adults who had been diagnosed with ADHD fare poorly compared adults who had never been diagnosed with ADHD. Adults with ADHD were more likely to have attentional problems as adults, to complete fewer than 12 years of schooling, to have problems reading and writing, and to be involved in criminal activity. These longitudinal results show that ADHD diagnosed at age 7 does not go away and, unless treated, life outcomes are not very good for children with ADHD. ■

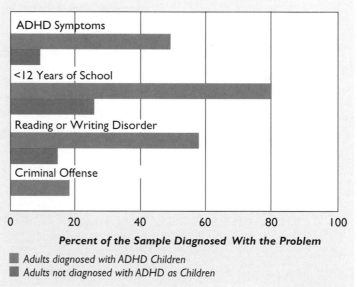

FIG 11–4

Why are some children afflicted with ADHD? Does too much sugar cause children to become "hyper"? Are food additives the culprit? In fact, except for a few children who are overly sensitive to sugar or allergic to food dyes, research shows no connection between children's diet and ADHD (McGee, Stanton, & Sears, 1993; Wolraich et al., 1994).

The primary causes of ADHD lie elsewhere. Heredity contributes: Identical twins more often both have ADHD than fraternal twins (Edelbrock et al., 1995). A stressful home environment also contributes: Youngsters with ADHD often come from families with parents in conflict or under great stress themselves (Bernier & Siegel, 1994). Some children evidently inherit a predisposition for the disorder, which can be triggered by stress at home.

Attention deficit hyperactivity disorder is often treated with stimulant drugs, such as Ritalin. It may seem odd that stimulants are given to children who are already overactive, but these drugs stimulate the parts of the brain that normally inhibit hyperactive and impulsive behavior. Thus, stimulants actually have a calming influence for many youngsters with ADHD, allowing them to focus their attention (Aman, Roberts, & Pennington, 1998).

By itself, though, medication does not improve children's performance in school because it ignores psychological and social influences on ADHD. Children with ADHD need to learn to regulate their behavior and attention. For example, children can be taught to remind themselves to read instructions before starting assignments. And they need reinforcement from others for inhibiting impulsive and hyperactive behavior (Barkley, 1994).

Parents can also encourage attention and goal-oriented behavior at home. Anastopoulos and his colleagues (1993) arranged for parents of children with ADHD to attend nine training sessions on using positive reinforcement to foster attention and compliance. Parents also learned effective ways to punish children for being inattentive. Following training, children had fewer symptoms of ADHD. Equally important, the parents felt that the training made them feel more competent in parenting. They also reported feeling significantly less parental stress.

The best approach for children with ADHD involves all of these techniques—medication, instruction, and parent training. Comprehensive treatment helps a child with ADHD become more attentive, less disruptive, and stronger academically (Carlson et al., 1992).

Children with Mental Retardation

"Little David" was the oldest of four children. He learned to sit only days before his first birthday, he began to walk at 2, and said his first words as a 3-year-old. By age 5, David was far behind his agemates developmentally. David had Down syndrome, described in Module 3.2. An extra 21st chromosome caused David's retarded mental development.

> Mental retardation is defined by below-average test scores along with problems adapting to the environment.

Mental retardation **refers to substantially below-average intelligence and problems adapting to an environment that emerge before the age of 18.** Below-average intelligence is defined as a score of 70 or less on an intelligence test such as the Stanford-Binet. Adaptive behavior is usually evaluated from interviews with a parent or other caregiver and refers to the daily living skills needed to live, work, and play in the community—skills for caring for oneself and social skills. Only individuals who are under 18, have problems in these areas, and IQ scores of 70 or less are considered mentally retarded (Baumeister & Baumeister, 1995).

Types of Mental Retardation. Your image of a mentally retarded child may be someone with Down syndrome, like the child shown on page 64. In reality, mentally retarded individuals are just as varied as nonretarded people. How, then, can we describe this variety? One approach is to distinguish the causes of mental retardation. **Some cases of mental retardation—no more than 25 percent—can be traced to a specific biological or physical problem and are known as *organic mental retardation*.** Down syndrome is the most common organic form of mental retardation. Other types of mental retardation apparently do not involve biological damage. *Familial mental retardation* **simply represents the lower end of the normal distribution of intelligence.**

Organic mental retardation is usually substantial, and familial mental retardation is usually less pronounced. The American Association on Mental Retardation identifies four levels of retardation. The levels, along with the range of IQ scores associated with each level, are shown in the chart. Also shown are the three levels of retardation typically used by educators in the United States (Cipani, 1991).

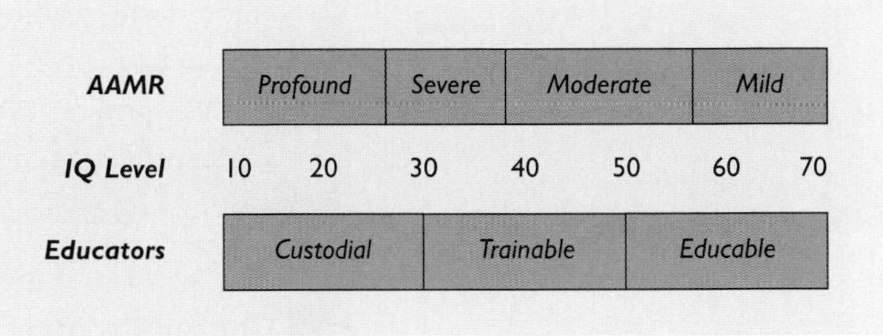

AAMR	Profound	Severe	Moderate	Mild	
IQ Level	10 20	30 40	50	60 70	
Educators	Custodial	Trainable		Educable	

FIG 11–5

The most severe forms of mental retardation are, fortunately, relatively uncommon. Profound, severe, and moderate retardation together make up only 10 percent of all cases. Profoundly and severely retarded individuals usually have so few skills that they must be supervised constantly. Consequently, they usually live in institutions for retarded persons, where they can sometimes be taught self-help skills such as dressing, feeding, and toileting (Reid, Wilson, & Faw, 1991).

Moderately retarded persons may develop the intellectual skills of a nonretarded 7- or 8-year-old. With this level of functioning, they can sometimes support themselves, typically at a sheltered workshop, where they perform simple tasks under close supervision.

The remaining 90 percent of individuals with mental retardation are classified as mildly or educably mentally retarded. These individuals go to school and can master many academic skills, but at an older age than a nonretarded child. Individuals with mild mental retardation can lead independent lives. Many mildly retarded people work. Some marry. Comprehensive training programs that focus on vocational and social skills help individuals with mild mental retardation be productive citizens and satisfied human beings (Ellis & Rusch, 1991), as you can see by learning more about "little David" in the Real Children feature.

REAL CHILDREN

Little David, the Rest of the Story

Little David, so named because he was named after his father, was the oldest of four children; none of his siblings was mentally retarded. As the children grew up, they interacted the way most siblings do—laughing and playing together and sometimes fighting and arguing. Beginning as a teenager and continuing into adulthood, each day David took a city bus from home to his job at a sheltered workshop. He worked 6 hours at such tasks as making bows for packages and stuffing envelopes. He saved his earnings to buy what became his prized possessions—a camera, a color TV, and a VCR.

As David's siblings entered adulthood, they began their own families. David relished his new role as Uncle David and looked forward to visits from nieces and nephews. As David entered his 40s, he began to suffer memory loss and was often confused. When he died, at age 47, family and friends grieved over their loss. Yet they all marveled at the richness of David's life. By any standards, David had led a full and satisfying life. ■

Check Your Learning

1. Children with a learning disability are unable to master an academic subject, have _____, and have no other condition, such as sensory impairment, that could explain their poor performance.

2. Children with reading disability often benefit from instruction on
   _____.

3. The three primary symptoms of ADHD are overactivity, inattention, and
   _____.

4. Cases of _____ mental retardation are due to specific biological or
   physical problems.

■ **Continuity**   What happens to children with ADHD when they become
   adults? How does this address the issue of continuity of development?

Answers: (1) normal intelligence, (2) connections between letters and their sounds, (3) impulsivity, (4) organic

Chapter Critical Review

1. Growth hormones are used widely in the United States. What cultural reasons account for this?

2. Daniel, a 10-year-old whose favorite activities are reading, watching TV, playing computer and video games, and playing with his dog, is beginning to gain too much weight. Devise an exercise program and a healthy diet for Daniel.

3. Your local parks and recreation department has started a basketball program for second grade children. Write a code of conduct for coaches and parents.

4. How might our definitions of mental retardation change if they were based on Jean Piaget's cognitive developmental theory?

For more review material, log on to www.prenhall.com/kail

See For Yourself

To see some of the developmental differences in physical growth and motor skill that I have described in this chapter, watch youth softball and baseball games. Most programs will have children grouped by age (e.g., third and fourth graders together). Try to observe one game at each age level. As you watch, you should see obvious age differences in *speed* (how fast children run the bases), *agility* (children's control and grace as they swing a bat or field a ball), and *strength* (how hard and how far balls are hit). The age differences in physical growth and motor skill should be obvious but also be sure to notice how much children of the same age differ in their size and ability. See for yourself!

For More Information About . . .

attention deficit hyperactivity disorder (ADHD), read Mark M. Jacobs's *A Dad's Nuts and Bolts Guide to Understanding Attention Deficit Disorder* (DD Clearinghouse, 2000). This book mixes solid information on ADHD with personal experience and humor.

 safety tips for children and ways to prevent accidents, visit the Web site of the National SAFE KIDS Campaign:
http://www.safekids.org

Key Terms

attention deficit
  hyperactivity disorder 336
basal metabolic rate 324

familial mental retardation 338
learning disability 335
malocclusion 326

mental retardation 338
myopia 327
organic mental retardation 338

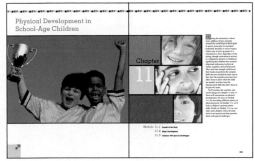

11.1 Growth of the Body

Physical Growth

Elementary-school children grow at a steady pace, more so in their legs than in the trunk. Boys and girls tend to be about the same size for much of these years, but there are large individual differences and ethnic differences.

Some children receive growth hormone because their bodies do not produce enough growth hormone naturally for normal growth. Other children with adequate natural growth hormone also receive synthetic growth hormone, but this practice is discouraged by scientists and health-care professionals.

Nutrition

School-age children need approximately 2,400 calories daily, preferably drawn from each of the five food groups. Children need to eat breakfast because this meal should provide approximately one-fourth of their calories and, without breakfast, they often have trouble concentrating in school.

Many children living in poverty do not eat breakfast and do not receive adequate nutrition overall. Programs for free and reduced-price meals are often available for these children but sometimes their parents do not realize that their children are eligible to participate.

Many obese children are unpopular, have low self-esteem, and are at risk for medical disorders. Obesity reflects both heredity and acquired eating habits. In the most effective programs for treating obesity in youth, both children and parents set eating and exercise goals and monitor their daily progress.

Tooth Development

Children start to lose primary teeth at 5 or 6 years of age and, by age 12, have 24 of their permanent teeth. The loss of a baby tooth is celebrated in most cultures worldwide as a sign of maturity. Good dental hygiene includes frequent brushing, fluoride treatments, and regular checkups.

Vision

Most sensory systems change little in childhood. An exception is vision: Many children have myopia, in which they can see nearby objects clearly but not distant objects. Myopia reflects heredity and experience and is easily remedied with glasses.

11.2 Motor Development

Growth of Motor Skills

Fine- and gross-motor skills improve substantially over the elementary-school years, reflecting children's greater size and strength. Girls tend to excel in fine-motor skills that emphasize dexterity (e.g., handwriting) as well as gross-motor skills that require flexibility and balance (e.g., tumbling); boys tend to excel in gross-motor skills that emphasize strength (e.g., throwing). Although some of these differences reflect differences in body makeup, they also reflect differing cultural expectations regarding motor skills for boys and girls.

Physical Fitness

Although children report spending much time being physically active, in fact, fewer than half of American schoolchildren meet all standards for physical fitness. Part of the explanation for the lack of fitness is physical education in elementary school: The classes are not taught often enough and involve too little activity. Television may also contribute. Physical education in the schools needs to be more frequent and more oriented toward developing patterns of lifetime exercise. Families can become more active, thereby encouraging children's fitness.

Participating in Sports

Many school-age children participate in team sports; both boys and girls believe that sports participation enhances their self-esteem, helps them to master skills and learn about cooperation, and is a means to stay physically fit. Adult coaches often can help children to improve their skills but they sometimes overemphasize competition, they are so controlling that children have little opportunity to experience leadership, and they overemphasize drills, strategy, and performance, which turns "play" into "work."

Accidents

Because elementary-school children are more mobile and more independent, they're at greater risk for injury than preschool children. The most common cause of injury and death at this age is the automobile—children are hurt either as a passenger or as a pedestrian. Parents can help to prevent accidents by being good role models (e.g., always wearing their own seat belt in a car), insisting that their children wear seat belts in cars and helmets when biking, and by not overestimating their children's cognitive and motor skills. Another way to prevent accidents is through community- and school-based programs in which children learn safety behaviors and have the opportunity to practice them.

11.3 Children with Special Challenges

Children with Learning Disabilities

Children with a learning disability have normal intelligence but have difficulty mastering specific academic subjects. The most common is reading disability, which often can be traced to inadequate understanding and use of language sounds.

Attention Deficit Hyperactivity Disorder

Children with ADHD are typically overactive, inattentive, and impulsive. They sometimes have conduct problems and do poorly in school. Attention deficit hyperactivity disorder is due to heredity and environmental factors, including a stressful home environment. A comprehensive approach to treatment—involving medication, instruction, and parent training—produces the best results.

Children with Mental Retardation

Individuals with mental retardation have IQ scores of 70 or lower and problems in adaptive behavior. Organic mental retardation is due to specific biological or physical causes; familial mental retardation reflects the lower end of the normal distribution of intelligence. Most persons with retardation are classified as mildly or educably retarded; they attend school, work, and have families.

Cognitive Development in School-Age Children

Chapter

12

Every fall, American 5- and 6-year-olds trot off to kindergarten, starting an educational journey that lasts 13 or more years. As the journey begins, many children can read only a few words and know little math; by the end, most can read complete books and many have learned algebra and geometry. In this chapter, we'll look carefully at school-age children's academic accomplishments and the cognitive skills that make them possible. The first three modules focus on cognitive and intellectual skills. We'll start, in Module 12.1, by examining cognitive processes from Piagetian and information-processing perspectives. In Module 12.2, we look at different definitions of intelligence. In Module 12.3, we discover some of the ways that children differ in their intellectual abilities. The last two modules focus on academic achievement. In Module 12.4, we look at children's ability to read, write, and use numbers. In Module 12.5, we consider some of the educational practices that foster students' learning.

12.1

Cognitive Processes
├─ Concrete Operational Thinking
└─ Memory Skills

Cognitive Processes

Learning Objectives

■ **What are the strengths and weaknesses of concrete operational thinking?**

■ **How do strategies and knowledge help school-age children to remember more effectively?**

At the end of the first day of school, 5-year-old Sabine and 10-year-old Melika each asked new friends for phone numbers and promised they would call that night. After dinner, both wanted to make the promised phone calls. Melika had written her friend's phone number in a notebook, so she found the number and called the friend. Sabine had done nothing special to remember the number and, not surprisingly, had forgotten it. To make matters worse, she couldn't remember the friend's last name, so she simply had to wait until the next day to talk to her new friend.

Piaget and information-processing theorists agree that school-age children's cognitive skills are remarkable, both in their own right and when compared to preschool children's skills. In this module, we'll look at both accounts, starting with Piaget's description of concrete operational thinking. Then, we'll look at information-processing accounts of memory skill, where we'll see that Melika's success in remembering the phone number and Sabine's failure are quite typical for children their age.

Concrete Operational Thinking

According to Piaget, elementary-school children enter a new stage of cognitive development that is distinctly more adultlike and much less childlike. **In the *concrete operational stage*, which spans ages 7 to 11, children first use mental operations to solve problems and to reason.** What are the mental operations that are so essential to concrete operational thinking? *Mental operations* **are strategies and rules that make thinking more systematic and more powerful.** Some mental operations apply to numbers. For example, addition, subtraction, multiplication, and division are familiar arithmetic operations that concrete operational children use. Other mental operations apply to categories of objects. For example, classes can be added (mothers + fathers = parents) and subtracted (parents − mothers = fathers). Still other mental operations apply to spatial relations among objects. For example, if point A is near points B and C, then points B and C must be close to each other.

> Concrete operational thinking is based on mental operations that yield consistent results and that can be be reversed.

Mental operations give concrete operational thinking a rule-oriented, logical flavor that is missing in preoperational thought. Applied properly, mental operations yield consistent results. Taking the familiar case of arithmetic operations, 4 + 2 is always 6, not just usually or only on weekends.

Another important property of mental operations is that they can be reversed. Each operation has an inverse that can "undo" or reverse the effect of an operation. If you start with 5 and add 3, you get 8; by subtracting 3 from 8, you reverse your steps and return to 5. For Piaget, reversibility of this sort applied to all mental operations.

Concrete operational children are able to reverse their thinking in a way that preoperational youngsters cannot. In fact, reversible mental operations is part of why concrete operational children pass the conservation tasks described on page 242: Concrete operational thinkers understand that if the transformation were reversed (for example, the juice was poured back into the original container), the objects would be identical.

Concrete operational thinking is much more powerful than preoperational thinking. Remember that preoperational children are egocentric (believing that others see the world as they do), are centered in their thinking, and confuse appearances with reality. None of these limitations applies to children in the concrete operational stage.

Egocentrism wanes as youngsters have more experiences with friends and siblings who assert their own perspectives on the world (LeMare & Rubin, 1987). Learning that events can be interpreted in different ways leads children to realize that many problems have different facets that must be considered (thereby avoiding centration) and that appearances can be deceiving.

Concrete operational thinking is a major cognitive advance, but it has its own limits. As the name implies, concrete operational thinking is limited to the tangible and real, to the here and now. The concrete operational youngster takes "an earthbound, concrete, practical-minded sort of problem-solving approach, one that persistently fixates on the perceptible and inferable reality right there in front of him" (Flavell, 1985, p. 98). That is, thinking abstractly and hypothetically is beyond the ability of concrete operational thinkers.

Memory Skills

In Module 6.2, we saw that memory skills take center stage in information-processing approaches to child development. Children's memory improves rapidly during the elementary-school years, due to two factors (Kail, 1990; Schneider & Bjorklund, 1998). First, as children grow, they use more effective strategies for remembering. Second, children's growing factual knowledge of the world allows them to organize information more completely and, therefore, remember better. We'll look at each of these factors in the next few pages.

Strategies for Remembering. Last week, I wrote four pages for this book that would have made Tom Clancy green with envy, when the unthinkable happened—a power failure knocked out my computer and all those wonderful words were lost. If I had only saved the text to the hard drive . . . but I hadn't.

This tale of woe sets the stage for understanding how strategies aid memory. Recall that working memory is used for briefly storing a small amount of information, such as the words in these sentences. However, as you read additional sentences, they displace words read earlier from working memory. For you to learn this information, it must be transferred to long-term memory. Anything not transferred from working memory to long-term memory is lost, just as my words vanished from the computer's memory with the power failure.

***Memory strategies* are activities that improve remembering.** Some strategies help maintain information in working memory. Others help transfer information to long-term memory. Still others help retrieve information from long-term memory. Obviously, there are many memory strategies.

Children begin to use memory strategies early. Preschool children look at or touch objects that they've been told to remember (DeLoache, 1984). Looking and touching aren't very effective, but they tell us that preschoolers understand that they should be doing something to try to remember; remembering doesn't happen automatically!

During the elementary-school years, children begin to use more powerful strategies. For example, 7- and 8-year-olds use rehearsal, a strategy of repetitively naming information that is to be remembered. As children get older, they learn other memory strategies and they learn when it is best to use them. That is, older children and (and adolescents) begin to identify different kinds of memory problems and which memory strategies are most appropriate. For example, Melika in the opening vignette wrote her friend's number in a notebook, an effective method for remembering the number until that evening.

When reading a textbook or watching a television newscast, the aim is to remember the main points, not the individual words or sentences. Rehearsal is ineffective for this task, but outlining or writing a summary are good strategies because they identify the main points and organize them (Kail, 1990). During the elementary-school years, children begin to use outlines to help them remember information in textbooks. Also, as children grow, they are more likely to write down information on calendars, so that, like the girl in the photo, they won't forget future events.

Thus, successful learning and remembering involves identifying the goals of memory problems and choosing suitable strategies (Schneider & Bjorklund, 1998). As you might expect, younger children sometimes misjudge the objectives of a memory task, which causes them to choose an inappropriate strategy. For example, young children may believe that they are supposed to remember a textbook passage verbatim whereas they really only need to remember its gist. Or, they may understand the memory task, but not pick the best strategy. For example, to remember the gist of a textbook paragraph, a younger child might rehearse it (a bad choice) while an older child would outline it (a good choice). Children gradually become more skilled at identifying task goals and selecting appropriate strategies, but even high school students do not always use effective learning strategies when they should (Lovett & Pillow, 1996; Slate, Jones, & Dawson, 1993).

After children choose a memory strategy, they need to monitor its effectiveness. That is, they need to decide if the strategy is working. If it's not, they need to begin anew—re-analyzing the memory task to select a better approach. If the strategy is working, they should determine the portion of the material they have not yet mastered and concentrate their efforts there.

Monitoring improves gradually with age. For example, elementary-school children can accurately identify which material they have not yet learned, but they do not consistently focus their study efforts on this material (Kail, 1990).

The diagram summarizes the sequence of steps in monitoring. Perhaps this diagram looks familiar. It should. Analyzing, strategizing, and monitoring are the key elements of productive studying. Study goals may change when you move from this book to your

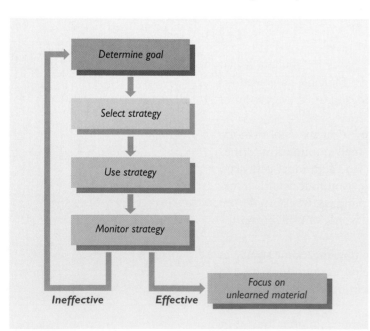

FIG 12–1

math text to a novel that you are reading for English, but the basic sequence still holds. Studying should always begin with a clear understanding of what goal you are trying to achieve, because this sets the stage for all the events that follow. Too often, students just read a text, without any clear idea of what they should be getting out of the material. Always plan a study session with a well-defined goal, such as "Become familiar with the basic contents of Module 12.1 in my child-development book." With this goal, you would start by carefully reading the outline, learning objectives, and vignette that begin the module. Then, skim the module, paying close attention to headings, sentences in the margins, boxes, and topic sentences of paragraphs. Now—before even reading the module—write an outline of its main topics. If you can't, then you need to skim again and try again—you don't yet understand the overall structure of the module. If you can write an outline, then you know you are familiar with the basic contents of the chapter, and you're ready to go on to reading the module carefully to master its details.

> As children develop, they begin to use different strategies to improve memory.

Skilled use of strategies is one aspect of effective remembering; as you'll see in the next few pages, knowledge is also an aid to memory.

Knowledge and Memory. Let's start our examination of how knowledge influences memory by looking at a study by Michelene Chi (1978). She asked 10-year-olds and adults to remember sequences of numbers. In the graph, you can see that adults remembered more numbers than children. Next she asked participants to remember the positions of objects in a matrix. This time 10-year-olds' recall was much better than adults'.

What was responsible for this unusual reversal of the expected age difference? Actually, the objects were chess pieces on a chessboard, and the children were skilled chess players but the adults were novices. The positions of the pieces were taken from actual games, so they were familiar configurations for the child chess players. For the adults, who lacked knowledge of chess, the patterns seemed arbitrary. But the children had the knowledge to organize and give meaning to the patterns, so they could recognize and then recall the whole configuration instead of many isolated pieces. It was as if the adults were seeing this meaningless pattern

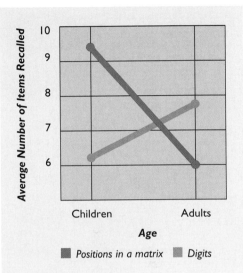

FIG 12-2

n n c c b a s b c c b n

while the children were seeing this

n b c   c b s   a b c   c n n.

The link between knowledge and memory is also illustrated in the Real Children feature.

REAL CHILDREN

Keith Visits the Air Force Museum

A few years ago, I went with a troop of Boy Scouts to visit the U.S. Air Force Museum in Dayton, Ohio. On the drive home, I asked James, a 10-year-old who likes computers and basketball but not airplanes, what he had seen in the museum. "Uh, lotsa planes. Some jets and prop jobs. Oh, and some rockets, too," was his reply. I posed the same question to Keith, another 10-year-old, whose father is a pilot and aeronautical engineer and who lives and breathes airplanes. Keith began, "This was so incredibly cool. I started in the Air Power Gallery and saw a Lightning, a Mustang, a Thunderbolt, a Mitchell, a Liberator, a Flying Fortress, and a Super Fort. Then we went to the Modern Flight hangar. They had a Stratojet, a Stratofort, and a Hustler. There was a Sabre and a Super Sabre there, too." Keith went on like this for another 5 minutes. When he was done, I estimated that Keith had remembered the names of 40 to 50 airplanes.

Amused, I asked Keith to try to remember the following words: table, green, rain, bus, spoon, dad, coal, doll, salt, doctor, hill, tennis, shirt, piano, nickel, robin. He paused for a moment, then began to remember words. He finished with 6 words from the list of 16. How could Keith recall so few words from my list when he had remembered 7 or 8 times that many planes? The key is Keith's extensive aeronautical knowledge, which allowed him to organize his recall of planes. He began by recalling World War II fighters (Lightning, Mustang, Thunderbolt), then World War II bombers (Mitchell, Liberator, Flying Fortress, Super Fortress). He continued this way, organizing his recall by category. However, when asked to recall my 16 words, where his knowledge of airplanes was useless, Keith had just an average 10-year-old's memory. For Keith, as for Chi's chess experts, knowledge is memory power. ■

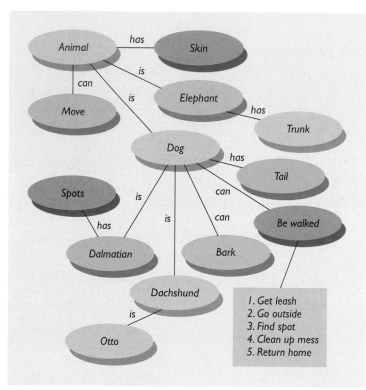

FIG 12–3

Source: Kail, 1990.

[Diagram labels: Animal — has — Skin; Animal — can — Move; Animal — is — Elephant; Elephant — has — Trunk; Dog — is — Elephant; Dog — has — Tail; Dog — can — Be walked; Dog — can — Bark; Dog — is — Dalmatian; Dalmatian — has — Spots; Dachshund — is — Dog; Otto — is — Dachshund; Be walked: 1. Get leash 2. Go outside 3. Find spot 4. Clean up mess 5. Return home]

Usually, of course, the knowledge that allows a child to organize information and give it meaning increases gradually with age (Schneider & Bjorklund, 1998). Researchers often depict knowledge as a network like the one in the diagram, which shows part of a 10-year-old's knowledge of animals. The entries in the network are linked by different types of associations. Some of the links denote membership in categories (dalmatian is a dog), and others denote properties (elephant has a trunk). **Still others denote a *script*, a memory structure used to describe the sequence in which events occur.** The list of events in walking the dog is a script.

A network diagram like this for a younger child would have fewer entries and fewer and weaker connecting links. Consequently, the youngster cannot organize information as extensively, which makes remembering more difficult than for an older child.

Nevertheless, the knowledge that young children have is organized, and this turns out to be a powerful asset. In the case of events that fit scripts, for example, they needn't try to remember each individual activity; instead, they simply remember the script. When the youngster in the photo wants to tell his dad about baking cookies, he can simply retrieve the "baking cookies" script and use it to organize his recall of the different events.

Though knowledge can improve memory, it can also distort memory. If a specific experience does not correspond to children's knowledge, the experience is likely to be forgotten or distorted so that it conforms to the child's knowledge. For example, when told a story about a female helicopter pilot, many youngsters will remember the pilot as a man because their network specifies that pilots are men (Levy & Boston, 1994).

Scripts, too, can distort memory because children cannot distinguish what they experienced from what is specified in the script. For example, the boy baking cookies may remember greasing the cookie sheet simply because this is part of the baking cookie script, not because he actually did the greasing (Hudson, 1988). Thus, although children's growing knowledge usually helps them to remember, sometimes it can interfere with accurate memory.

The different processes that affect children's remembering are summarized in the table.

> Children's knowledge can improve memory, but can also distort memory.

■■■□ SUMMARY TABLE

Information-Processing Elements that Aid Memory

Element	Definition	Example
Strategies	Deliberate acts used to help a person remember	Before Melika had a chance to write her friend's number in her notebook, she rehearsed it, "743-1423...743-1423."
Monitoring	Assessing the effectiveness of a strategy and one's progress toward a learning goal	Monique tested herself on the weekly spelling list, then spent 20 minutes studying the words she had missed.
Knowledge	Understanding of relations between items that promotes remembering by organizing information to be remembered	When Samer arrived at the grocery, he realized he'd lost the list his mom had given him. Rather than walk home for it, he decided to think about different food groups—dairy products, meats, and so on—to help him remember what he was supposed to buy.
Scripts	Memory structure that allows people to remember events that occur in a specified order	Asked by his grandpa to describe a day at summer camp, Hector explained that the day began with breakfast, followed by two activity periods. Lunch came next, then a rest period, and two more activity periods... and so on.

TABLE 12-1

Check Your Learning

1. Concrete operational children are capable of _____, which are actions that can be performed on objects or ideas.

2. During the concrete operational stage, children cannot reason _____.

3. Children and adolescents often select a memory strategy after they _____.

4. The term _____ refers to periodically evaluating a strategy to determine whether it is effective.

5. The knowledge that children acquire can distort their recall, either by causing them to forget information that does not conform to their knowledge or by _____.

6. A _____ is a memory structure that describes the sequence in which events occur.

 **Nature and Nurture** How might nature and nurture contribute to improvements in memory skills during the school-age years?

Answers: (1) mental operations, (2) abstractly and hypothetically, (3) determine the goal of a memory task, (4) monitoring, (5) causing them to recall events that are part of a script but that did not actually take place, (6) script

The Nature of Intelligence

12.2

The Nature of Intelligence

- Psychometric Theories
- Gardner's Theory of Multiple Intelligences
- Sternberg's Triarchic Theory

Learning Objectives

■ **What is the psychometric view of the nature of intelligence?**

■ **How does Gardner's theory of multiple intelligences differ from the psychometric approach?**

■ **What are the three components of Sternberg's triarchic theory of intelligence?**

Max is 12 years old and is moderately mentally retarded. That is, he performs most tasks at the level of a nonretarded 5- or 6-year-old. For example, he can't do many of Piaget's conservation tasks and he reads very slowly and with much effort. Nevertheless, if Max hears a song on the radio, he can immediately sit down at the piano and play the melody flawlessly, despite having had no musical training. Everyone who sees Max do this is astonished. How can a person who is otherwise so limited intellectually perform such an amazing feat?

Before you read further, how would you define intelligence? If you're typical of most Americans, your definition probably includes the ability to reason logically, connect ideas, and solve real problems. You might mention verbal ability, meaning the ability to speak clearly and articulately. You might also mention social competence, referring, for example, to an interest in the world at large and an ability to admit when you make a mistake (Sternberg & Kaufman, 1998).

As you'll see in this module, many of these ideas about intelligence are included in psychological theories of intelligence. We'll begin by considering the oldest theories of intelligence, those associated with the psychometric tradition. Then we'll look at two newer approaches and, along the way, get some insights into Max's uncanny musical skill.

Psychometric Theories

Psychometricians are psychologists who specialize in measuring psychological characteristics such as intelligence and personality. When psychometricians want to research a particular question, they usually begin by administering a large number of tests to many individuals. Then they look for patterns in performance across the different tests. The basic logic underlying this technique is similar to the logic a jungle hunter uses to decide whether some dark blobs in a river are three separate rotting logs or a single alligator (Cattell, 1965). If the blobs move together, the hunter decides they are part of the same structure, an alligator. If they do not move together, they are three different structures, three logs. Similarly, if changes in performance on one test are accompanied by changes in performance on a second test—that is, they move together—one could assume that the tests are measuring the same attribute or factor.

Suppose, for example, that you believe there is such a thing as general intelligence. That is, you believe that some people are smart regardless of the situation, task, or problem, whereas others are not so smart. According to this view, children's performance should be very consistent across tasks. Smart children should always receive high scores, and the less smart youngsters should always get lower scores. As early as 1904, Charles Spearman reported findings supporting the idea that a general factor for intelligence, or *g*, is responsible for performance on all mental tests.

Other researchers, however, have found that intelligence consists of distinct abilities. For example, Thurstone and Thurstone (1941) analyzed performance on a wide range of tasks and identified seven distinct patterns, each reflecting a unique ability: perceptual speed, word comprehension, word fluency, space, number, memory, and induction. Thurstone and Thurstone also acknowledged a general factor that operated in all tasks, but they emphasized that the specific factors were more useful in assessing and understanding intellectual ability.

These conflicting findings have led many psychometric theorists to propose hierarchical theories of intelligence that include both general and specific components. John Carroll (1993), for example, proposed the hierarchical theory with three levels that's shown in the diagram. At the top of the hierarchy is *g*, general intelligence. In the level underneath *g* are eight broad categories of intellectual skill, ranging from fluid intelligence to processing speed. Each of the abilities in the second level is further divided into the skills listed in the third and most specific level. Crystallized intelligence, for example, includes understanding printed language, comprehending language, and knowing vocabulary.

> Patterns of test scores provide evidence for general intelligence as well as for specific abilities.

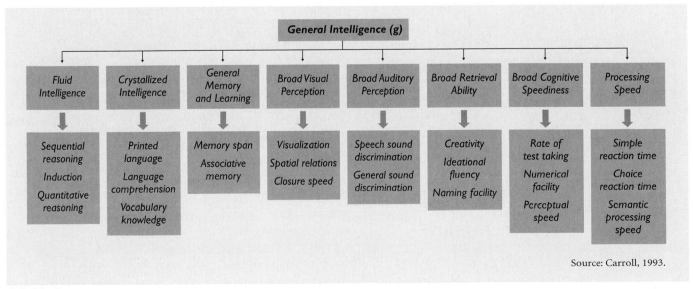

Source: Carroll, 1993.

FIG 12–4

Carroll's hierarchical theory is, in essence, a compromise between the two views of intelligence—general versus distinct abilities. But some critics find it unsatisfactory because it ignores the research and theory on cognitive development described in Module 12.1. They believe we need to look beyond the psychometric approach to understand intelligence. In the remainder of this module, then, we'll look at two newer theories that have gained a following.

Gardner's Theory of Multiple Intelligences

Only recently have developmental psychologists viewed intelligence from the perspective of Piaget's theory and information-processing psychology. These new theories present a much broader theory of intelligence and how it develops. Among the most ambitious is Howard Gardner's (1983, 1993) theory of multiple intelligences. Rather than using test scores as the basis for his theory, Gardner draws on research in child development, studies of brain-damaged persons, and studies of exceptionally talented people. He proposes seven distinct intelligences that are shown in Table 12–2. The first three intelligences in this list—linguistic intelligence, logical-mathematical intelligence, and spatial intelligence—are included in psychometric theories of intelligence. The last four intelligences are not: Musical, bodily-kinesthetic, interpersonal, and intrapersonal intelligences are unique to Gardner's theory. According to Gardner, a gifted athlete, a talented dancer, and a sensitive, caring child are showing intelligence as is the child who writes well or is skilled at math.

Gardner's Seven Intelligences	
Type of Intelligence	**Definition**
Linguistic	Knowing the meaning of words, having the ability to use words to understand new ideas, and using language to convey ideas to others
Logical-mathematical	Understanding relations that can exist among objects, actions, and ideas, as well as the logical or mathematical relations that can be performed on them
Spatial	Perceiving objects accurately and imagining in the mind's eye the appearance of an object before and after it has been transformed
Musical	Comprehending and producing sounds varying in pitch, rhythm, and emotional tone
Bodily-kinesthetic	Using one's body in highly differentiated ways, as dancers, craftspeople, and athletes do
Interpersonal	Identifying different feelings, moods, motivations, and intentions in others
Intrapersonal	Understanding one's emotions and knowing one's strengths and weaknesses

Source: Gardner, 1983, 1993

TABLE 12–2

How did Gardner arrive at these seven distinct intelligences? First, each has a unique developmental history. Linguistic intelligence, for example, develops much earlier than the other six. Second, each intelligence is regulated by distinct regions of the

brain, as shown in studies of brain-damaged persons. Spatial intelligence, for example, is regulated by particular regions in the brain's right hemisphere. Third, each has special cases of talented individuals. **Musical intelligence is often shown by** *savants***, individuals with mental retardation who are extremely talented in one domain (Miller, 1999).** Max, the 12-year-old in the module-opening vignette, is a savant whose special talent is music. Like Max, Eddie B., the 10-year-old savant in the photo, can play a tune correctly after a single hearing and without ever having had formal musical training (Shuter-Dyson, 1982).

Prompted by Gardner's theory, researchers have begun to look at nontraditional aspects of intelligence. **For example, one aspect of interpersonal intelligence is** *social-cognitive flexibility***, which refers to a person's skill in solving social problems with relevant social knowledge.** Jones and Day (1997) studied social-cognitive flexibility by presenting different social scenarios to adolescents. In one scenario, a man and a woman walk past each other; the woman says hello but the man ignores her. Following each scenario, adolescents were asked a series of questions about what happened in the scenario. Some adolescents were much better at understanding that each scenario might have many different interpretations (e.g., "The man ignored the woman because he's very shy." "The man was lost in thought and didn't see her.") and that a person's interpretation of the scenario would cause them to act differently.

Adolescents who understood the different interpretations of the scenarios were not more skilled in solving verbal or logical reasoning problems. But they were more competent socially (e.g., could deal more effectively with peers) and were less likely to have social problems (e.g., be shy or anxious). Thus, as Gardner's theory predicts, acting skillfully in social situations is an element of intelligence that is distinct from the linguistic and logical-mathematical intelligences of psychometric theories.

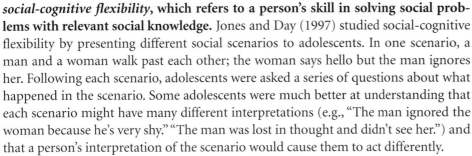

The theory of multiple intelligence has important implications for education. Gardner (1993, 1995) believes that schools should foster all intelligences, not just the traditional linguistic and logical-mathematical intelligences. Teachers should capitalize on the strongest intelligences of individual children. Some students may best understand unfamiliar cultures, for example, by studying their dance, while other students may understand these cultures by studying their music.

Some American schools have enthusiastically embraced Gardner's ideas (Gardner, 1993). Are these schools better? We don't really know because school performance is usually evaluated with tests, and there aren't acceptable tests to evaluate progress in all the areas covered by Gardner's theory. At this point, researchers are still evaluating the theory and the educational reforms it has inspired. However, there is no doubt that Gardner's work has helped liberate researchers from narrow psychometric-based views of intelligence. A comparably broad but different view of intelligence comes from another new theory that we'll look at in the next section.

Sternberg's Triarchic Theory

Robert Sternberg's (1977) early work included a theory of how adults solve problems on intelligence tests. **He later elaborated this theory into what he called the** *triarchic theory* **because it includes three parts or subtheories (Sternberg, 1985).**

According to the *componential subtheory*, **intelligence depends on basic cognitive processes called *components*.** A component is simply Sternberg's term for the different information-processing skills described in Module 12.1, such as monitoring. Whether the task is solving an item on an intelligence test, reading a newspaper, or understanding a conversation, components must be selected and organized in the proper sequence to complete the task successfully. In this subtheory, intelligence reflects more efficient organization and use of components.

> In the triarchic theory, intelligence reflects strategies children use to complete tasks plus the familiarity and relevance of those tasks.

The triarchic theory includes two other subtheories. **According to the *experiential subtheory*, intelligence is revealed in both novel and familiar tasks.** For novel tasks, intelligence is associated with the ability to apply existing knowledge to a new situation. At the start of a new school year, for example, readily adjusting to new tasks is a sign of intelligence. Bright children learning multiplication readily draw upon relevant math knowledge to grasp what's involved in multiplication.

For familiar tasks, intelligence is associated with automatic processing. Completing a task automatically means using few mental resources (i.e., less working memory capacity). At the end of a school year, performing now-familiar school tasks automatically rather than with effort is a sign of intelligence. Bright children now solve multiplication problems automatically, without thinking about the intermediate steps.

According to the *contextual subtheory*, intelligent behavior involves skillfully adapting to an environment. That is, intelligence is always partly defined by the demands of an environment or cultural context. What is intelligent for children growing up in cities in North America may not be intelligent for children growing up in the Sahara desert, the Australian outback, or on a remote island in the Pacific Ocean. Moreover, what is intelligent at home may not be intelligent in the neighborhood. The Cultural Influences feature illustrates how intelligent behavior is always defined by the context.

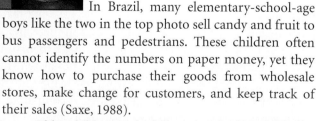

CULTURAL INFLUENCES

How Culture Defines What Is Intelligent

In Brazil, many elementary-school-age boys like the two in the top photo sell candy and fruit to bus passengers and pedestrians. These children often cannot identify the numbers on paper money, yet they know how to purchase their goods from wholesale stores, make change for customers, and keep track of their sales (Saxe, 1988).

Older children and adolescents who live on Pacific Ocean Islands near New Guinea learn to sail boats like the one in the bottom photo hundreds of miles across open seas to get from one small island to the next. They have no formal training in mathematics, yet they are able to use a complex navigational system based on the positions of stars and estimates of the boat's speed (Hutchins, 1983).

If either the Brazilian vendors or the island navigators were given the tests that measure intelligence in American students, they would fare poorly. Does this mean they are less intelligent than American children? Of course not. The skills that are important to American conceptions of intelligence and assessed on our intelligence tests are less valued in these other cultures and so are not cultivated in the young. Each culture defines what it means to be intelligent, and the specialized computing skills of vendors and navigators are just as important measures of intelligence in their cultural settings as verbal skills are in American culture (Sternberg & Kaufman, 1998). ■

The three subtheories are summarized in Table 12–3. In the table, you can see that, in contrast to the psychometric approach and to Gardner's theory, the triarchic theory does not identify specific contents of intelligence. Instead, Sternberg defines intelligence in terms of processes: the strategies people use to complete tasks (componential subtheory), the familiarity of those tasks (experiential subtheory), and the relevance of the tasks to personal and cultural goals (contextual subtheory).

Subtheories in Sternberg's Triarchic Theory of Intelligence		
Subtheory	**Definition**	**Example**
Componential	Intelligence depends upon basic processes called components	Asked how a peach and a piece of cheese were alike and how they differed, Terrence retrieved from long-term memory the facts that both were food and that a peach was a fruit but cheese was a dairy product.
Experiential	Intelligent behavior involves applying existing knowledge on novel tasks	When Jordan's friend taught her a new card game, she saw that it was a lot like solitaire and she could use many of the rules and strategies from that game.
	Intelligent behavior involves performing familiar tasks automatically	Mickey has spent so many hours practicing his multiplication tables that he doesn't even have to think about the problems anymore; the product simply pops into his mind effortlessly.
Contextual	Intelligent behavior involves adapting to one's environment	When Deshawn couldn't get a ride to the mall, he looked up the bus schedule on the Internet and he found when the bus to the mall would go by his house.

TABLE 12-3

Sternberg's theory also underscores the dangers of comparing test scores of different cultural, ethnic, or racial groups. Comparisons are usually invalid because the test items are not equally relevant in different cultures. In addition, most test items are not equally novel in different cultures. A vocabulary test, for example, is useful in assessing intelligence in cultures where formal education is essential to skilled adaptations (because skilled use of language is important for success in schools). In cultures where schooling is not a key to success, a vocabulary test would not provide useful information because it would be irrelevant to cultural goals and much too novel.

As with Gardner's theory, researchers are still evaluating Sternberg's theory. And, as you can see in the table that summarizes the different approaches, theorists are still debating the question of what intelligence is. But, however it is defined, the fact is that individuals differ substantially in intellectual ability, and numerous tests have been devised to measure these differences. The construction, properties, and limitations of these tests are the focus of the next module.

■■■□ SUMMARY TABLE

Features of Major Perspectives on Intelligence

Approach to Intelligence	Distinguishing Features
Psychometric	Intelligence as a hierarchy of general and specific skills
Gardner's theory of multiple intelligences	Seven distinct intelligences—linguistic, logical-mathematical, spatial, musical, bodily-kinesthetic, interpersonal, and intrapersonal intelligences
Sternberg's triarchic theory	Intelligence is defined by context, experience, and information-processing components

TABLE 12–4

Check Your Learning

1. If some children consistently have high scores on different intelligence tests while other children consistently have lower scores on the same tests, this would support the view that intelligence _____.

2. According to _____ theories, intelligence includes both general intelligence as well as more specific abilities, such as verbal and spatial skill.

3. Gardner's theory of multiple intelligences includes linguistic, logical-mathematical, and spatial intelligences, which are included in psychometric theories, as well as musical, _____, interpersonal, and intrapersonal intelligences, which are ignored in psychometric theories.

4. Based on Gardner's view of intelligence, teachers should _____.

5. According to Sternberg's _____ subtheory, intelligence refers to adapting to an environment to achieve goals.

6. Sternberg's theory emphasizes that comparing test scores of children from cultural groups is dangerous because _____.

■ ■
■ ■ **Connections** Compare and contrast the major perspectives on intelligence in terms of the extent to which they make connections between different aspects of development. That is, to what extent does each perspective emphasize cognitive processes versus integrating physical, cognitive, social, and emotional development?

Answers: (1) consists of a general factor, g, (2) hierarchical, (3) bodily-kinesthetic, (4) adjust their teaching to capitalize on a child's strongest intelligences, (5) contextual, (6) test items are neither equally relevant nor equally novel for children from different groups

Individual Differences in Intellectual Skills

Learning Objectives

- Why were intelligence tests devised initially? What are modern tests like?

- How well do modern intelligence tests work?

- What are the roles of heredity and environment in determining intelligence?

- How do ethnicity and social class influence intelligence test scores?

Charlene, an African American third grader, received a score of 75 on an intelligence test administered by a school psychologist. Based on the test score, the psychologist believes that Charlene is mildly mentally retarded and should receive special education. Charlene's parents are indignant; they believe that the tests are biased against African Americans and that the score is meaningless.

American schools faced a crisis at the beginning of the twentieth century. Between 1890 and 1915, school enrollment nearly doubled nationally as great numbers of immigrants arrived, and reforms restricted child labor and emphasized education (Chapman, 1988). Increased enrollment meant that teachers now had larger numbers of students who did not learn as readily as the "select few" students who had populated their classes previously. How to deal with these less capable children was one of the pressing issues of the day. In this module, you'll see how intelligence tests were devised initially to assess individual differences in intellectual ability. Then we'll look at a simple question: "How well do modern tests work?" Finally, we'll examine how race, ethnicity, social class, gender, environment, and heredity influence intelligence, and we'll learn how to interpret Charlene's test score.

Binet and the Development of Intelligence Testing

The problems facing educators at the beginning of the twentieth century were not unique to the United States. In 1904, the Minister of Public Instruction in France asked two noted psychologists, Alfred Binet and Theophile Simon, to formulate a way to recognize children who needed special instruction in school. Binet and Simon's approach was to select simple tasks that French children of different ages ought to be able to do, such as naming colors, counting backwards, and remembering numbers in order. Based on preliminary testing, Binet and Simon determined problems that normal 3-year-olds could solve, that normal 4-year-olds could solve, and so on. **Children's *mental age* or *MA* referred to the difficulty of the problems that they could solve correctly.** A child who solved problems that the average 7-year-old could pass would have an MA of 7.

Binet and Simon used mental age to distinguish "bright" from "dull" children. A "bright" child would have the MA of an older child; for example, a 6-year-old with an MA of 9 was considered bright. A "dull" child would have the MA of a younger child, for example, a 6-year-old with an MA of 4. Binet and Simon confirmed that

> **Binet and Simon created the first intelligence test by using simple tasks to distinguish children who would do well in school from children who wouldn't.**

"bright" children did better in school than "dull" children. Voilá— the first objective measure of intelligence!

Lewis Terman, of Stanford University, revised Binet and Simon's test and published a version known as the Stanford-Binet in 1916. **Terman described performance as an *intelligence quotient*, or IQ, which was simply the ratio of mental age to chronological age, multiplied by 100:**

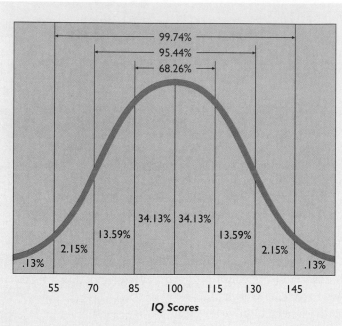

FIG 12–5

$$IQ = MA/CA \ x \ 100$$

At any age, children who are perfectly average will have an IQ of 100 because their mental age equals their chronological age. The figure shows the typical distribution of test scores in the population. You can see that roughly two-thirds of children taking a test will have IQ scores between 85 and 115 and that 95 percent will have scores between 70 and 130.

The IQ score can also be used to compare intelligence in children of different ages. A 4-year-old with an MA of 5 has an IQ of 125 (5/4 x 100), the same as an 8-year-old with an MA of 10 (10/8 x 100).

IQ scores are no longer computed in this manner. Instead, children's IQ scores are determined by comparing their test performance to others their age. When children perform at the average for their age, their IQ is 100. Children who perform above the average have IQs greater than 100; children who perform below the average have IQs less than 100. Nevertheless, the concept of IQ as the ratio of MA to CA helped popularize the Stanford-Binet test.

By the 1920s, the Stanford-Binet had been joined by many other intelligence tests. Educators enthusiastically embraced the tests as an efficient and objective way to assess a student's chances of succeeding in school (Chapman, 1988).

Today, more than 75 years later, the Stanford-Binet remains a popular test. It was last revised in 1986. Like the earlier versions, today's Stanford-Binet consists of various cognitive and motor tasks, ranging from the extremely easy to the extremely difficult. The test may be administered to individuals ranging in age from approximately 2 years to adulthood, but not every individual is given every question. For example, a kindergarten child, like the youngster in the photo, may be asked to name pictures of familiar objects, string beads, answer questions about everyday life, or fold paper into shapes. Older individuals may be asked to define vocabulary words, solve an abstract problem, or decipher an unfamiliar code. The examiner determines, according to specific guidelines, the appropriate starting place on the test and administers progressively more difficult questions until the child fails all the questions at a particular level. An IQ score is assigned on the basis of how many questions the child passed compared with the average number passed by children of the same age.

Another popular test, the WISC-III, includes subtests for verbal and perform-ance skills, some of which are shown in the figure. Children thus are assessed on ver-bal IQ, performance IQ, and a combination of the two, the full-scale IQ. Unlike the Stanford-Binet, on the WISC-III, each child receives the same subtests, with some adjustment for either age level or competence or both.

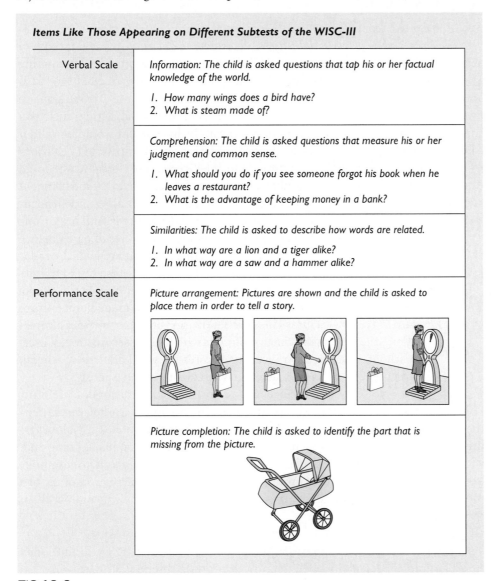

Items Like Those Appearing on Different Subtests of the WISC-III

Verbal Scale	*Information: The child is asked questions that tap his or her factual knowledge of the world.* *1. How many wings does a bird have?* *2. What is steam made of?*
	Comprehension: The child is asked questions that measure his or her judgment and common sense. *1. What should you do if you see someone forgot his book when he leaves a restaurant?* *2. What is the advantage of keeping money in a bank?*
	Similarities: The child is asked to describe how words are related. *1. In what way are a lion and a tiger alike?* *2. In what way are a saw and a hammer alike?*
Performance Scale	*Picture arrangement: Pictures are shown and the child is asked to place them in order to tell a story.*
	Picture completion: The child is asked to identify the part that is missing from the picture.

FIG 12–6

Source: Simulated items similar to those in the Wechsler Intelligence Scales for Adult and Children. Copyright 1949, 1955, 1974, 1981, and 1990 by the Psychological Corporation. Reproduced by permission. All rights reserved.

The Stanford-Binet and the WISC-III are administered to one per-son at a time, rather than to a group. Group tests of intelligence have the advantage of providing information about many individuals quickly and inexpensively, often without the need of highly trained psychologists. But individual testing optimizes the motivation and attention of the examinee and provides an opportunity for a sensitive examiner to assess factors that may influence test performance. The examiner may notice that the examinee is relaxed and that test performance is therefore a rea-sonable sample of the individual's talents. Or the examiner may observe

The Stanford-Binet and the WISC-III are both individual tests of intelligence; the Stanford-Binet measures overall IQ whereas the WISC-III measures verbal and performance IQ.

that intense anxiety is interfering with performance. Such determinations are not possible with group tests. Consequently, most psychologists prefer individualized tests of intelligence over group tests.

Do Tests Work?

What do test scores mean? Are they really measuring intelligence? **These questions raise the issue of** *validity*, **which refers to the extent that a test really measures what it claims to measure.** Validity is usually measured by determining the relation between test scores and other independent measures of what the test is thought to measure. For example, to measure the validity of a test of extroversion, we would have children take the test, then observe them in a social setting, such as a school recess, and record who is outgoing and who is shy. The test would be valid if scores correlated highly with our independent observations of extroverted behavior.

How would we extend this approach to intelligence tests? Ideally, we would administer the intelligence tests and then correlate the scores with other independent estimates of intelligence. Therein lies the problem. There are no other independent ways to estimate intelligence; the only way to measure intelligence is with tests. Consequently, many follow Binet's lead and obtain measures of performance in school, such as grades or teachers' ratings of their students. Correlations between these measures and scores on intelligence tests typically fall somewhere between 0.4 and 0.6 (Neisser et al., 1996). For example, the correlation between scores on the WISC-III and grade point average is 0.47 (Wechsler, 1991). This correlation is positive but far from a correlation of 1. Obviously, some youngsters with high test scores do not excel in school, whereas others with low scores get good grades. In general, however, tests do a reasonable job of predicting school success.

> Most test developers show that their tests are valid—actually measure intelligence—by showing that test scores are related to children's performance in school.

Not only are intelligence tests reasonable predictors of performance in school, they also predict performance in the workplace, particularly for more complex jobs (Gottfredson, 1997; Schmidt & Hunter, 1998). Workers with higher IQ scores tend to be more successful in their on-the-job training and, following training, more successful in their actual work performance. If, for example, two teenagers have summer jobs running tests in a biology lab, the smarter of the two will probably learn the procedures more rapidly and, once learned, conduct them more accurately.

Increasing Validity with Dynamic Testing. Traditional tests of intelligence such as the Stanford-Binet and the WISC-III measure knowledge and skills that a child has accumulated up to the time of testing. These tests do not directly measure a child's potential for future learning; instead, the usual assumption is that children who have learned more in the past will probably learn more in the future. Critics argue that tests would be more valid if they directly assessed a child's potential for future learning.

Dynamic testing **measures a child's learning potential by having the child learn something new in the presence of the examiner and with the examiner's help.** Thus, dynamic testing is interactive and measures new achievement rather than past achievement. It is based on Vygotsky's ideas of the zone of proximal development and scaffolding (page 254). Learning potential can be estimated by the amount of material the child learns during interaction with the examiner and/or from the amount of help the child needs to learn the new material (Grigorenko & Sternberg, 1998).

To understand the difference between traditional, static methods of intelligence testing and new, dynamic approaches, imagine a group of children attending a week-long soccer camp. On the first day, all children are tested on a range of soccer skills and receive a score that indicates their overall level of soccer skill. If this score were shown to predict later success in soccer, such as number of goals scored in a season, this would be a valid static measure of soccer skill. To make this a dynamic measure of soccer skill, children would spend all week at camp being instructed in new skills. At the end of the week, the test of soccer skills would be readministered. The amount of the child's improvement over the week would measure learning potential, with greater improvement indicating greater learning potential.

Dynamic testing is a recent innovation and is still being evaluated. Preliminary research does indicate, however, that static and dynamic testing both provide useful and independent information. If the aim is to predict future levels of a child's skill, it is valuable to know a child's current level of skill (static testing) as well as the child's potential to acquire greater skill (dynamic testing). By combining both forms of testing, we achieve a more comprehensive view of a child's talents than by relying on either method alone (Day et al., 1997).

Hereditary and Environmental Factors

Joanna, a 7-year-old girl, was administered the WISC-III and obtained a score of 112. Ted, a 7-year-old boy, took the same test and received a score of 92. What accounts for the 20-point difference in these youngsters' scores? Heredity and experience both matter.

Some of the evidence for hereditary factors is shown in the graph. If genes influence intelligence, then siblings' test scores should become more alike as siblings become more similar genetically (Plomin & Petrill, 1997). In other words, since identical twins are identical genetically, they typically have virtually identical test scores, which would be a correlation of 1. Fraternal twins have about 50 percent of their genes in common, just like non-twins of the same biological parents. Consequently, their test scores should be (a) less similar than scores for identical twins, (b) as similar as other siblings who have the same biological parents, and (c) more similar than scores of children and their adopted siblings. You can see in the graph that each of these predictions is supported.

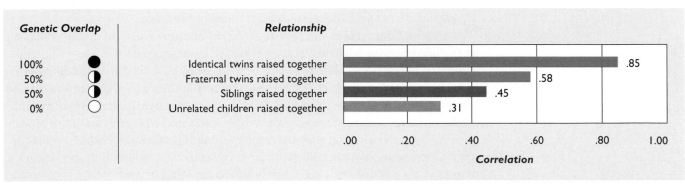

FIG 12-7

Heredity also influences patterns of developmental change in IQ scores (Wilson, 1983). Patterns of developmental change in IQ are more alike for identical twins than for fraternal twins. If one identical twin gets higher IQ scores with age, the other twin almost certainly will, too. In contrast, if one fraternal twin gets higher scores with age, the other twin may not necessarily show the same pattern. Thus, identical twins are not only more alike in overall IQ, but in developmental change in IQ as well.

Studies of adopted children suggest that the impact of heredity increases during childhood and adolescence: If heredity helps determine IQ, then children's IQs should be more like their biological parents' IQs than their adoptive parents' IQs. In fact, these correlations were computed in the Colorado Adoption Project (Plomin et al., 1997), which included adopted children as well as their biological and adoptive parents. Biological parents' IQ was measured before the child was born; adoptive parents' IQ was measured before the child's first birthday; children's IQs were tested repeatedly in childhood and adolescence. The results, shown in the graph, are clear. At every age, the correlation between children's IQ and their biological parents' IQ (shown by the blue line) is greater than the correlation between children's IQ and their adoptive parents' IQ (shown by the red line). In fact, children's IQ scores are essentially unrelated to their adoptive parents' IQs.

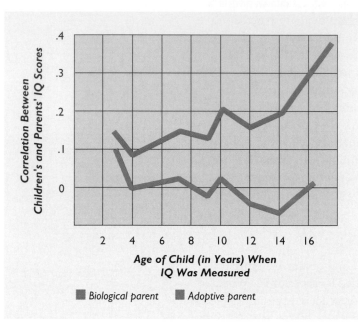

FIG 12-8

Notice, too, that the relation between children's IQs and their biological parents' IQ actually gets *stronger* as children get older. In other words, as adopted children get older, their test scores increasingly resemble their biological parents' scores. These results are evidence for the greater impact of heredity on IQ as a child grows.

Do these results mean that heredity is the sole determiner of intelligence? No. Two areas of research show the importance of environment on intelligence. The first is research on characteristics of families and homes. The second is research on the impact of preschool intervention or enrichment programs.

If intelligence were solely due to heredity, environment should have little or no impact on children's intelligence. But we know that many characteristics of parents' behavior and home environments are related to children's intelligence. Bettye Caldwell and Robert Bradley (1994) developed the Home Observation for Measurement of the Environment (HOME), an inventory for assessing parents' behavior as well as the quality and organization of the child's home environment.

Home Observation for Measurement of the Environment testing indicates that children with high test scores typically have parents who are stimulating, responsive, and involved (Bradley, Caldwell, & Rock, 1988). In addition, among European American children, an environment that includes plenty of variety and appropriate play materials is linked to high test scores. For African American children, a well-organized home environment is associated with higher scores (Bradley et al., 1989). That is, children tend to have higher IQs when their environments are well structured and predictable (e.g., meals are eaten at a regular time, homework is always done after dinner). Child-development scientists don't know why certain features of environments are particularly important for intelligence in different groups, but the more general point is that children's home environments clearly affect intelligence.

The importance of a stimulating environment for intelligence is also demonstrated by intervention programs that prepare economically disadvantaged children for school. When children grow up in never-ending poverty, the cycle is predictable and tragic: Youngsters have few of the intellectual skills to succeed in school, so they fail; lacking an education, they find minimal jobs (if they can work at all), guaranteeing that their children, too, are destined to grow up in poverty.

Since Project Head Start began in 1965, massive educational intervention has been an important tool in the effort to break this repeated cycle of poverty. Head Start and other intervention programs teach preschool youngsters basic school readiness skills and social skills and offer guidance to parents (Ramey & Ramey, 1990). When children participate in these enrichment programs, their test scores go up and school achievement improves, particularly when intervention programs are extended beyond preschool into the elementary-school years (Reynolds & Temple, 1998). In the Focus on Research feature, we look at one of these success stories in detail.

FOCUS ON RESEARCH

The Carolina Abecedarian Project

Who were the investigators and what was the aim of the study? Since the 1960s, many intervention programs have demonstrated that young children's intelligence test scores can be raised with enrichment, but the improvement is often short-lived. That is, within a few years after completing the intervention program, test scores are at the same level as before the program. Frances Campbell and Craig Ramey (1994; Ramey & Campbell, 1991) designed the Carolina Abecedarian Project to see if massive and sustained intervention could produce more long-lasting changes.

How did the investigators measure the topic of interest? Some children did not participate in any intervention program. Other children attended a special day-care facility daily from 4 months until 5 years. The curriculum emphasized mental, linguistic, and social development for infants, and prereading skills for preschoolers. Some children went on to participate in another intervention program during their first 3 years of elementary-school. During this phase, a teacher visited the home a few times each month, bringing materials for improving reading and math. The teachers taught parents how to use the materials with their child and acted as facilitators between home and school. Campbell and Ramey measured the impact of intervention in several ways, including scores on intelligence tests, scores on achievement tests, and children's need for special services in school.

> Massive, long-term intervention increases children's intelligence and achievement.

Who were the children in the study? At the start, the project included 111 children; most were born to African American mothers who had less than a high school education, an average IQ score of 85, and typically no income. Over the course of the study, 21 children dropped out of the project, leaving 90 children at the end.

What was the design of the study? This study was experimental because children were randomly assigned to an intervention condition (preschool intervention, elementary-school intervention, both, or no intervention). The independent variable was the intervention condition. The dependent variables included performance on intelligence and achievement tests. The study was longitudinal because children were tested repeatedly over an 8-year period.

Were there ethical concerns with the study? No. The nature of the study was explained fully to parents, including how their child was assigned to a particular intervention condition.

What were the results? The graph shows children's performance on three achievement tests that they took as 12-year-olds, 4 years after the elementary-school intervention had ended. In all three areas that were tested—written language, math, and reading—performance clearly reflects the amount of intervention. Youngsters who had a full 8 years of intervention generally have the highest scores; children with no intervention have the lowest scores.

What did the investigators conclude? Massive, continued intervention works. An improvement of 7 to 10 points may not strike you as very much, but it is a substantial improvement from a practical standpoint. For example, the written language scores of the youngsters with 8 years of intervention place them near the 50th percentile, meaning that their scores are greater than about half of the children taking the test. In contrast, children with no intervention have scores at the 20th percentile, making their scores greater than only 20 percent of the children taking the test. Thus, after intervention, children moved from being substantially below average to average, quite an accomplishment.

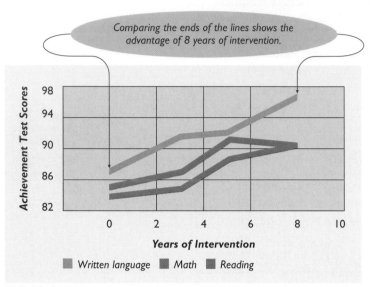

FIG 12–9

What converging evidence would strengthen these conclusions? The results of the Abecedarian Project show that massive intervention works. This conclusion would be strengthened by two kinds of evidence. First, the investigators could continue the longitudinal study to confirm that the benefits observed in elementary-school years last through middle school and high school. Second, they could show that the benefits extend beyond performance on achievement tests to other, more direct indicators of success in school such as grades, being promoted at the end of the school year to the next grade, avoiding learning disabilities, and, later, continuing education beyond high school. ■

Of course, massive intervention over 8 years is expensive. But so are the economic consequences of poverty, unemployment, and their byproducts. Programs like the Abecedarian Project show that the repetitive cycle of school failure and education can be broken. And, in the process, they show that intelligence is fostered by a stimulating and responsive environment.

Impact of Ethnicity and Social Class

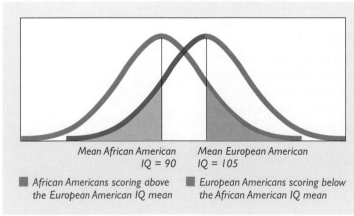

FIG 12–10

The results in the graph have been the source of controversy for decades. They show that on many intelligence tests, African Americans score about 15 points lower than European Americans (Brody, 1992). What accounts for this difference? Some of the difference is due to social class. Typically, children from lower social classes have lower scores on intelligence tests, and African American children are more likely than European American children to live in lower socioeconomic class homes. When European American and African American children of comparable social class are compared, the difference in IQ test scores is reduced but not eliminated

(Brooks-Gunn, Klebanov, & Duncan, 1996). So social class explains some but not all of the difference between European American and African American children's IQ scores.

Some critics contend that the difference in test scores reflects bias in the tests themselves. They argue that test items reflect the cultural heritage of the test creators, most of whom are middle-class European Americans, and so tests are biased against lower-class and African American children. They point to test items like this one:

A conductor is to an orchestra as a teacher is to what?
book   school   class   eraser

Children whose background includes exposure to orchestras are more likely to answer this question correctly than children who lack this exposure.

The problem of bias has led to the development of *culture-fair intelligence tests*, which include test items based on experiences common to many cultures. An example is Raven's Progressive Matrices, which consists solely of items like the one shown here. Examinees are asked to select the piece that would complete the design correctly (6, in this case).

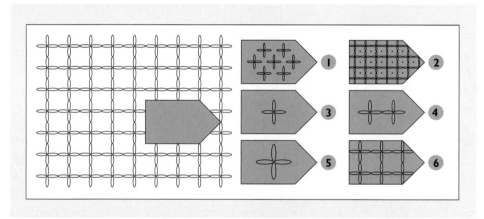

FIG 12–11

Culture-fair tests predict achievement in school, but do not eliminate group differences in test scores: European and African Americans still differ (Anastasi, 1988; Herrnstein & Murray, 1994). Why? Culture can influence a child's familiarity with the entire testing situation, not simply familiarity with particular items. A culture-fair test will underestimate a child's intelligence if, for example, the child's culture encourages children to solve problems in collaboration with others and discourages them from excelling as individuals.

Moreover, because they are wary of questions posed by unfamiliar adults, many African American and other economically disadvantaged children often answer test questions by saying, "I don't know." Obviously, this strategy guarantees an artificially low test score. When these children are given extra time to feel at ease with the examiner, they respond less often with "I don't know" and their test scores improve considerably (Zigler & Finn-Stevenson, 1992).

A low score on an intelligence test means that a child lacks some of the skills needed to succeed in school.

If all tests reflect cultural influences, at least to some degree, how should we interpret test scores? Remember that tests assess successful adaptation to a particular cultural context. Most intelligence tests predict success in a school environment, which usually espouses middle-class values. Regardless of ethnic group—African American, Hispanic American, or European American—a child with a high test score has the intellectual skills needed for academic work based on middle-class values. A child with a low test score, like Charlene in the module-opening vignette, lacks those skills. Does a low score mean Charlene is destined to fail in school? No. It simply means that, based on her current skills, she's unlikely to do well. As we saw in the Focus on Research feature on the Abecedarian Project, improving Charlene's skills will improve her school performance.

By focusing on groups of people, it's easy to lose sight of the fact that individuals within these group differ in intelligence. Look again at the graph on page 364; you'll see that the average difference in IQ scores between European Americans and African Americans is very small compared to the entire range of scores for these groups. Many African Americans achieve higher IQ scores than the average European American; many European Americans achieve lower IQ scores than the average African American.

Gender Differences in Intellectual Abilities and Achievement

Boys and girls are similar in most cognitive skills. However, researchers have identified gender differences in three intellectual skills: Girls tend to have greater verbal skill but boys tend to have greater mathematical and visual-spatial skill.

Verbal Ability. Janet Hyde and Marcia Linn (1988) summarized research on gender differences in verbal skill and found that females had greater verbal ability in 75 percent of the 165 studies that they analyzed. Usually the difference was small. But it was larger for general measures of verbal ability, unscrambling scrambled words, and quality of speech production. Girls also read, write, and spell better than boys (Feingold, 1993; Hedges & Nowell, 1995), and more boys have reading and other language-related problems such as stuttering (Halpern, 1986).

> ### Girls excel in verbal skills but boys excel in spatial skills.

Why are girls more talented verbally than boys? Part of the explanation may lie in biology. The left hemisphere of the brain, which is central to language (see Module 6.3), may mature more rapidly in girls than in boys (Diamond et al., 1983). But experience also contributes. Reading, for instance, is often stereotyped as an activity for girls (Huston, 1983). Consequently, girls are more willing than boys to invest time and effort in mastering verbal skills like reading.

Spatial Ability. In Module 12.2, you saw that spatial ability is a component of most models of intelligence. **One aspect of spatial ability is *mental rotation*, the ability to imagine how an object will look after it has been moved in space.** The items in the figure below test mental rotation: The task is to determine which of the figures labeled A through E are rotated versions of the figure in the box on the left. From childhood on, boys tend to have better mental rotation skill than girls (Vederhus & Krekling, 1996; Voyer, Voyer, & Bryden, 1995). (The correct answers are C and D.)

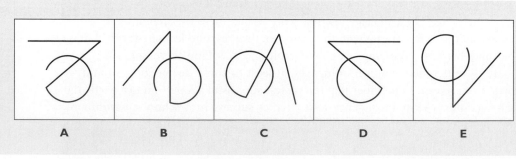

A   B   C   D   E

FIG 12–12

Source: Pellegrino & Kail, 1982.

Spatial ability also involves determining relations between objects in space while ignoring distracting information. For example, which of the tilted bottles of water in the figure has the waterline drawn correctly? In an upright bottle, the waterline is at right angles to the sides of the bottle, but selecting the correct answer for the tilted bottle (A, in this case) requires that you ignore the conflicting perceptual information provided by the sides of the bottle. From adolescence on, boys are more accurate than girls on these kinds of spatial tasks (Voyer, Voyer, & Bryden, 1995).

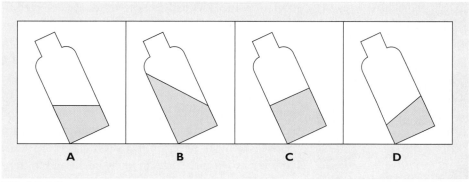

A   B   C   D

FIG 12–13

Explanations for gender differences in spatial ability abound:

- A recessive gene on the X chromosome may promote spatial ability (Thomas & Kail, 1991). In this type of inheritance, males only have to inherit a recessive gene from their mother to score high in spatial ability, but females must inherit the recessive gene from both parents.

- The right hemisphere of the brain may be more specialized for spatial processing in males than in females, perhaps because boys mature more slowly than girls (Waber, 1977).

- Boys are more likely than girls to participate in activities that foster spatial skill, such as estimating the trajectory of an object moving through space (e.g., a baseball), using two-dimensional plans to assemble an object such as a scale model (Baenninger & Newcombe, 1995), or, like the boys in the photo, playing video games that involve visual-perceptual skills (Okagaki & Frensch, 1994).

Each of these possible explanations of gender differences in spatial ability is supported by some studies but not by others. And, of course, the explanations are not necessarily mutually exclusive. Biological and experiential forces may both contribute to gender differences in spatial ability, just as both contribute to gender differences in verbal ability (Casey, Nuttall, & Pezaris, 1999). Thus, parents and others can foster verbal and spatial abilities in boys and girls because each is influenced considerably by experience.

Mathematics. Gender differences in math skill are complex. Let's start with performance on standardized math achievement tests. Standardized tests emphasize computational skills during the elementary- and middle-school years, and girls usually score higher than boys. Problem solving and applying math concepts are emphasized in high school and college; here boys often score higher than girls. Thus, initially girls excel in math computation, but later boys excel in math problem solving (Hyde,

Fennema, & Lamon, 1990). The gender difference remains even when boys and girls take an equal number of math courses (Kimball, 1989).

The gender difference in performance on math achievement tests is not restricted to the United States. Beller and Gafni (1996) analyzed math scores from the International Assessment of Educational Progress. For 9-year-olds, gender differences were inconsistent; for 13-year-olds, boys' scores exceeded girls' scores in 17 of the 20 countries studied, including Brazil, China, Ireland, and Israel.

Paradoxically, the results are different for grades in math courses. Often no differences are detected in boys' and girls' grades, but when a difference occurs, it invariably favors girls. This is even true for courses in high school and college—when males are getting higher scores on achievement tests (Kimball, 1989).

Why should females get lower scores on tests of math achievement but higher grades in math courses? One idea is that girls are confident when dealing with relatively familiar math problems on classroom tests. However, when girls, like the ones in the photo, take standardized achievement tests that have many novel problems, they are less confident and don't do as well. Boys are confident in their math skills and like the challenge of novel problems on standardized tests (Kimball, 1989). Because math is stereotyped as a masculine pursuit, girls tend to lack confidence in their math skills and are less likely to succeed in math (Casey, Nuttall, & Pezaris, 1997; Crawford, Chaffin, & Fitton, 1995).

This argument probably sounds familiar to you because the explanation is basically the same one used to explain gender differences in verbal skill: Boys succeed in math and girls succeed in language because children in each group are encouraged to pursue activities consistent with gender stereotypes.

Because of findings like these, educators have worked hard to reduce gender stereotypes associated with math (Secada, Fennema, & Adajian, 1995). Unfortunately, gender differences in math continue. Hedges and Nowell (1995) evaluated data from The National Assessment of Educational Progress (NAEP) which administers

Girls have better math grades than boys, but boys get higher scores on math achievement tests.

standardized tests in several areas to approximately 70,000 to 100,000 American students in grades 3, 7, and 11. The researchers found that the gender difference in math achievement has been remarkably constant since the NAEP test was first administered in 1978.

What does it mean that gender differences are just as large at the start of the twenty-first century as they were in the last quarter of the twentieth century? Perhaps stereotypes for language and math have not changed. Maybe math is still "a guy thing," despite decades of efforts to show girls that math is just as appropriate and interesting a subject for them and that girls can be just as successful in math as boys.

Another possibility is that biological factors contribute to the gender difference in math. In particular, spatial ability, which we just discussed, may play a role. Some aspects of math are easier to understand if they can be visualized mentally. For example, being able to imagine a three-dimensional space where lines and planes intersect simplifies learning geometry. Boys may be more successful in some areas of math because they more often have the spatial skills that promote understanding (Casey et al., 1997).

Most likely, the gender difference in math is due to multiple factors. Some have roots in biology (e.g., spatial skill) but others have roots in experience (e.g., stereotypes concerning math).

Check Your Learning

1. The Stanford-Binet introduced the idea of the intelligence quotient, which was _____, multiplied by 100.

2. The WISC-III provides a verbal IQ score and a _____.

3. Modern intelligence tests are typically validated by _____.

4. As identical twins develop, their IQ scores _____.

5. As adopted children get older, their IQ scores increasingly resemble the IQ scores of their _____ parents.

6. Evidence for the impact of environment on intelligence comes from studies of families and homes as well as from _____.

7. The problem of cultural bias on intelligence tests led to the development of _____.

8. Girls may excel in verbal ability because of gender differences in brain development and because _____.

9. In math, girls get better grades but boys _____.

■ ▨ **Nature and Nurture** Summarize gender differences in ability. How does
▨ ■ nature contribute to these differences? How does nurture contribute?

Answers: (1) MA/CA, (2) performance IQ score, (3) showing that test scores correlate with measures of performance in school, (4) follow the same developmental profile, (5) biological, (6) studies on the impact of intervention and enrichment programs, (7) culture-fair intelligence tests, which have test items common to many cultures, (8) verbal activities such as reading are stereotyped as being for girls, (9) get higher scores on standardized tests

Academic Skills

12.4

Academic Skills

├─Reading Skills

├─Writing Skills

└─Math Skills

Learning Objectives

■ **What are the components of skilled reading?**

■ **As children develop, how does their writing improve?**

■ **When do children understand and use quantitative skills?**

Angelique is a fifth grader who absolutely loves to read. As a preschooler, Angelique's parents read Dr. Seuss stories to her and now she has progressed to the point where she can read (and understand!) 400-page novels intended for teens. Her parents marvel at this accomplishment and wish they better understood the skills that were involved so they could help Angelique's younger brother learn to read as well as his sister does.

Reading is indeed a complex task and learning to read well is a wonderful accomplishment. Much the same can be said for writing and arithmetic. We'll examine each of these academic skills in this module. As we do, you'll learn about the skills that underlie Angelique's mastery of reading.

Reading Skills

Try reading the following sentence:

Sumisu-san wa nawa o naifu de kirimashita.

You probably didn't make much headway, did you? (Unless you know Japanese.) Now try this one:

Snore secretary green plastic sleep trucks.

These are English words and you probably read them quite easily, but did you get anything more out of this sentence than the one in Japanese? These examples show two important processes involved in skilled reading. **Word recognition is the process of identifying a unique pattern of letters.** Unless you know Japanese, your word recognition was not successful in the first sentence. You did not know that *nawa* means *rope* or that *kirimashita* is the past tense of the English verb *cut*. Furthermore, because you could not recognize individual words, you had no idea of the meaning of the sentence. **Comprehension is the process of extracting meaning from a sequence of words.** In the second sentence, your word recognition was perfect, but comprehension was still impossible because the words were presented in a random sequence. These examples remind us just how difficult learning to read can be.

In the next few pages, we'll look at some of the skills that children must acquire if they are to learn to read and to read well. We'll start with prereading skills, then move to word recognition and comprehension.

Prereading Skills. English words are made up of individual letters, so children need to know their letters before they can learn to read. Consequently, it's not surprising that kindergarten children who know most of their letters learn to read more easily than their peers who don't know their letters (Stevenson et al., 1976). **In addition, letters have distinctive sounds and readers need to be able to hear these different sounds, a skill known as** *phonological awareness.* The Looking Ahead feature shows that children who can readily distinguish these sounds learn to read more readily than children who do not.

> Prereading skills include knowing the letters of the alphabet and the sounds they make.

LOOKING AHEAD

Predicting Reading Skill

Reading well is an essential skill in modern society, yet many children never master it. Consequently, researchers have sought early indicators of children who will encounter difficulty learning to read. Phonological awareness is the best indicator available so far: Children who have trouble identifying different language sounds usually have problems learning to read.

For example, Wagner, Torgesen, and Rashotte (1997) measured kindergarten children's phonological awareness in a number of ways. In one task, the experimenter presented four words—*fun, pin, bun, gun*—and asked the child to pick the word that didn't rhyme with the others. In another task, children were asked to say the first, last, or middle sound of a word: "What's the first sound in cat?"

After these children entered first grade, the experimenters measured their ability to read individual words. The investigators found that the correlation between children's performance on phonological awareness tasks in kindergarten and their reading score in first grade was 0.82. That is, kindergarten children who were aware of letter sounds tended to be skilled readers in first grade whereas kindergarten children who were unaware of letter sounds tended to be unskilled readers in first grade. As the children in this longitudinal study get older, phonological skills continue to be the best predictor of their reading ability (Wagner et al., 1997). ■

Much other research confirms the idea that sensitivity to the sounds of language is an essential step in learning to read (e.g., Hatcher & Hulme, 1999). Furthermore, phonological skills are not only important in learning to read in alphabet-based languages such as English, they are also important in learning to read in non-alphabet based languages such as Chinese (Ho & Bryant, 1997).

If phonological skills are so essential, how can we help children master them? The Making Children's Lives Better feature describes one easy way.

MAKING CHILDREN'S LIVES BETTER

Rhyme Is Sublime Because Sounds Abound

The Cat in the Hat and *Green Eggs and Ham* are two books in the famous Dr. Seuss series. You probably know these stories for their zany plots and extensive use of rhyme. When parents frequently read rhymes—not just Dr. Seuss, but also Mother Goose and other nursery rhymes—their children become more

aware of word sounds. Passages like this draw children's attention to the different sounds that make up words:

> *I do not like them in a house. I do not like them with a mouse. I do not like them here or there. I do not like them anywhere. I do not like green eggs and ham. I do not like them, Sam-I-am.* (Geisel, 1960, p. 20)

The more parents read rhymes to their children, the greater their children's phonological awareness, which makes learning to read much easier (Goswami & Bryant, 1990; Reese & Cox, 1999).

So, the message is clear. Read to children—the more, the better. As the photo shows, children love it when adults read to them and learning more about word sounds is icing on the cake! ■

Recognizing Words. The first step in actual reading is identifying individual words. One way to do this is to say the sounds associated with each letter, and then blend the sounds to produce a recognizable word. Such "sounding out" is a common technique among beginning readers. Older children sometimes sound out words, but only when they are unfamiliar, which points to another common way of recognizing words (Coltheart et al., 1993). Words are recognized through direct retrieval from long-term memory: As the individual letters in a word are identified, long-term memory is searched to see if there is a matching sequence of letters. Knowing that the letters are, in sequence, *c-a-t*, long-term memory is searched for a match and the child recognizes the word as *cat*.

So far, word recognition may seem like a one-way street where readers first recognize letters and then recognize words. In reality, readers constantly use context to help them recognize letters and words. For example, readers typically recognize *t* faster in *cast* than in *asct*. That is, readers recognize letters faster when they appear in words than in nonwords. How do the nearby letters in *cast* help readers to recognize the *t*? As children recognize the first letters in the word as *c, a,* and *s,* the possibilities for the last letter become more limited. Because English only includes four 4-letter words that start with *cas* (well, five if you include *Cass*), the last letter can only be *e, h, k,* or *t*. In contrast, there are no four-letter words (in English) that begin with *acs,* so all 26 letters must be checked, which takes more time than just checking four letters. In this way, a reader's knowledge of words simplifies the task of recognizing letters, which in turn makes it easier to recognize words (Seidenberg & McClelland, 1989).

Readers also use the sentence context to speed word recognition. Read these two sentences:

> *The last word in this sentence is cat.*
> *The little girl's pet dog chased the cat.*

Most readers recognize *cat* more rapidly in the second sentence. The reason is that the first seven words put severe limits on the last word: It must be something "chaseable," and because the "chaser" is a *dog, cat* is a very likely candidate. In contrast, the first seven words in the first sentence put no limits on the last word; virtually any word could end the sentence. Beginning and skilled readers both use sentence context like this to help them recognize words (Kim & Goetz, 1994).

As you can imagine, most beginning readers, like the child in the photo, rely more heavily on "sounding out" because they know fewer words.

As they gain more reading experience, they are more likely to be able to retrieve a word directly from long-term memory. You might be tempted to summarize this as, "Beginning readers sound out and more advanced readers retrieve directly." Don't! From their very first efforts to read, most children use direct retrieval for a few words. From that point on, the general strategy is to try retrieval first and, if that fails, then children sound out the word or ask a more skilled reader for help (Booth, Perfetti, & MacWhinney, 1999; Siegler, 1986). For example, when my daughter Laura was just beginning to read, she knew *the, Laura,* and several one-syllable words that ended in *at,* such as *bat, cat,* and *fat.* Shown a sentence like

> *Laura saw the fat cat run,*

she would say, "Laura s-s-s. . . ah-h. . . wuh . . . saw the fat cat er-r-r. . . uh-h-h . . n-n-n . . . run." Familiar words were retrieved rapidly but the unfamiliar ones were slowly sounded out. With more experience, fewer words are sounded out and more are retrieved (Siegler, 1986), but even skilled readers sometimes fall back on sounding out when they confront unfamiliar words. Try reading

> *The rock star rode to the concert in a palanquin.*

You may well need to do some sounding out, then consult a dictionary (or look at the definition given prior to Check Your Learning) for the correct meaning.

Beginning readers often try to recognize a word through retrieval, but often resort to sounding out.

Comprehension. Once individual words are recognized, reading begins to have a lot in common with understanding speech. That is, the means by which people understand a sequence of words is much the same whether the source of words is printed text or speech or, for that matter, Braille or sign language (Crowder & Wagner, 1992). **In all of these cases, children derive meaning by combining words to form *propositions* or ideas and then combining propositions.** For example, as you read

> *The tall boy rode his bike,*

you spontaneously derive a number of propositions, including "There is a boy," "The boy is tall," and "The boy was riding." If this sentence were part of a larger body of text, you would derive propositions for each sentence, then link the propositions together to derive meaning for the passage as a whole (Perfetti & Curtis, 1986).

As children gain more reading experience, they better comprehend what they read. Several factors contribute to this improved comprehension (Siegler, 1998):

- *Working memory capacity increases, which means that older and better readers can store more of a sentence in memory as they try to identify the propositions it contains* (Nation et al., 1999; Siegel, 1994): This extra capacity is handy when readers move from sentences like "Kevin hit the ball" to "In the bottom of the ninth, with the bases loaded and the Cardinals down 7-4, Kevin put a line drive into the left-field bleachers, his fourth home run of the Series."

- *Children acquire more general knowledge of their physical, social, and psychological worlds, which allows them to understand more of what they read* (Bisanz et al., 1992; Graesser et al., 1994): For example, even if a 6-year-old could recognize all of the words in the longer sentence about Kevin's home run, the child would not fully comprehend the meaning of the passage because he or she lacks the necessary knowledge of baseball.

- *With experience, children use more appropriate reading strategies:* The goal of reading and the nature of the text dictate how you read. When reading a novel, for example, do you often skip sentences (or perhaps paragraphs or entire pages) to get to "the good parts"? This approach makes sense for pleasure reading but not for reading textbooks or recipes or how-to manuals. Reading a textbook requires attention to both the overall organization and the relation of details to that organization. Older, more experienced readers are better able to select a reading strategy that suits the material being read (Brown et al., 1996).

- *With experience, children better monitor their comprehension:* When readers don't grasp the meaning of a passage because it is difficult or confusing they read it again (Baker, 1994). Try this sentence (adapted from Carpenter & Daneman, 1981): "The Midwest State Fishing Contest would draw fishermen from all around the region, including some of the best bass guitarists in Michigan." When you first encountered "bass guitarists" you probably interpreted "bass" as a fish. This didn't make much sense, so you reread the phrase to determine that "bass" refers to a type of guitar. Older readers are better able to realize that their understanding is not complete and take corrective action.

Thus, several factors contribute to improved comprehension as children get older. And greater comprehension, along with improved word recognition skills, explain why children like Angelique are able to read ever-more complex text as they grow. These factors are summarized in the table.

■ ■ ■ ■ ■ SUMMARY TABLE

Component Skills Involved in Reading	
Skill	**Definition**
Prereading skills	Knowing letter names
	Linking names of letters to the sounds they make
Recognizing words	Sounding out individual syllables
	Retrieving familiar word names from long-term memory
Comprehension	Understanding of word combinations, based on interplay of working memory, understanding of the world, appropriate reading strategies, and effective monitoring of one's reading for sense

TABLE 12-5

In the next part of this module, you'll see how information-processing psychologists use similar ideas to explain children's developing ability to write.

Writing Skills

Though few of us end up being a Maya Angelou, a Sandra Cisneros, or a John Grisham, most adults do write, both at home and at work. The basics of good writing are remarkably straightforward (Williams, 1997), but writing skill develops very gradually during childhood, adolescence, and young adulthood. Research indicates a number of factors that contribute to improved writing as children develop (Adams, Treiman, & Pressley, 1998; Siegler, 1998).

Greater Knowledge and Access to Knowledge about Topics. Writing is about telling something to others. With age, children have more to tell as they gain more knowledge about the world and incorporate this knowledge into their writing (Benton et al., 1995). For example, asked to write about a mayoral election, 8-year-olds are apt to describe it as much like a popularity contest; 12-year-olds more often describe it in terms of political issues that are both subtle and complex. Of course, students are sometimes asked to write about topics quite unfamiliar to them. In this case, older children's and adolescents' writing is usually better because they are more adept at finding useful reference material and incorporating it into their writing.

Greater Understanding of How to Organize Writing. One difficult aspect of writing is organization, arranging all the necessary information in a manner that readers find clear and interesting. In fact, children and young adolescents organize their writing differently than older adolescents and adults (Bereiter & Scardamalia, 1987). **Young writers often use a *knowledge-telling strategy*, writing down information on the topic as they retrieve it from memory.** For example, asked to write about the day's events at school, a second grader wrote:

> *It is a rainy day. We hope the sun will shine. We got new spelling books. We had our pictures taken. We sang Happy Birthday to Barbara.* (Waters, 1980, p. 155)

The story has no obvious structure. The first two sentences are about the weather but the last three deal with completely independent topics. Apparently, the writer simply described each event as it came to mind.

Toward the end of the elementary-school years, children begin to use a *knowledge-transforming strategy*, deciding what information to include and how best to organize it for the point they wish to convey to their reader. This approach involves considering the purpose of writing (e.g., to inform, to persuade, to entertain) and the information needed to achieve this purpose. It also involves considering the needs, interests, and knowledge of the anticipated audience.

Asked to described the day's events, older children's writing can take many forms, depending on the purpose and audience. An essay written to entertain peers about humorous events at school would differ from one written to convince parents about problems in schoolwork. And both of these essays would differ from one written to inform an exchange student about a typical day in a U.S. middle school. In other words, although children's knowledge-telling strategy gets words on paper, the more mature knowledge-transforming strategy produces a more cohesive text for the reader.

Greater Ease in Dealing with the Mechanical Requirements of Writing. Soon after I earned my pilot's license, I took my son Matt for a flight. A few days later, he wrote the following story for his second grade weekly writing assignment.

> *This weekend I got to ride in a one propellered plane. But this time my dad was alone. He has his license now. It was a long ride. But I fell asleep after five minutes. But when we landed I woke up. My dad said, "You missed a good ride." My dad said, "You even missed the jets!" But I had fun.*

Matt spent more than an hour writing this story and the original (hanging in my office) is filled with erasures where he corrected misspelled words, ill-formed letters, and incorrect punctuation. Had Matt simply *described* our flight together aloud (instead of writing it), his task would have been much easier. In oral language, he could ignore capitalization, punctuation, spelling, and printing the individual letters. These many mechanical aspects of writing can be a burden for all writers, but particularly for young writers.

> Older children's writing is better because these children know more about the world, organize their writing more effectively, and are better able to handle the mechanical requirements of writing.

In fact, research shows that when youngsters, like the one in the photo, are absorbed by the task of printing letters correctly, the quality of their writing usually suffers (Jones & Christensen, 1999). As children master printed and cursive letters, they can pay more attention to other aspects of writing. Similarly, correct spelling and good sentence structure are particularly hard for younger writers; as they learn to spell and to generate clear sentences, they write more easily and more effectively (Graham et al., 1997; McCutchen et al., 1994).

Greater Skill in Revising. Few authors get it down right the first time. Instead, they revise and revise, then revise some more. In the words of one expert, "Experienced writers get something down on paper as fast as they can, just so they can revise it into something clearer...." (Williams, 1997, p. 11).

Unfortunately, young writers often don't revise at all—the first draft is usually the final draft. To make matters worse, when young writers revise, the changes do not necessarily improve their writing (Fitzgerald, 1987). Effective revising requires being able to detect problems and to know how to correct them (Baker & Brown, 1994; Beal, 1996). As children develop, they're better able to find problems and to know how to correct them, particularly when the topic is familiar to them (McCutchen, Francis, & Kerr, 1997).

The summary table lists the factors that contribute to better writing as children grow.

■■■□ SUMMARY TABLE

Factors Contributing to Improved Writing with Age

Factor	Defined
Greater knowledge	Older children know more about the world and thus have more to write about.
Better organization	Older children organize information to convey a point to the reader but younger children simply list topics as they come to mind.
Greater facility with mechanical requirements	Spelling, punctuation, and printing (or typing) are easier for older children, so they can concentrate on writing per se.
Greater skill in revising	Older children are better able to recognize and correct problems in their writing.

TABLE 12–6

Looking at the factors in the table, it's quite clear why good writing is so long in developing. Many different skills are involved and each is complicated in its own right. Mastering them collectively is a huge challenge, one that spans all of childhood, adolescence, and adulthood. Much the same could be said for mastering quantitative skills, as we'll see in the next section.

Math Skills

In Module 9.1 we saw that preschoolers understand many of the principles underlying counting, even if they sometimes stumble over the mechanics of counting.

By kindergarten, children have mastered counting and they use this skill as the starting point for learning to add. For instance, suppose you ask a kindergartner to solve the following problem: "John had four oranges. Then Mary gave him two more oranges. How many oranges does John have now?" Like the child in the photo, many 6-year-old children solve the problem by counting. They first count out four fingers on one hand, then count out two more on the other. Finally, they count all six fingers on both hands. To subtract, they do the same procedure in reverse (Siegler & Jenkins, 1989; Siegler & Shrager, 1984).

Youngsters soon abandon this approach for a slightly more efficient method. Instead of counting the fingers on the first hand, they simultaneously extend the number of fingers on the first hand corresponding to the larger of the two numbers to be added. Next, they count out the smaller number, with fingers on the second hand. Finally, they count all of the fingers to determine the sum (Groen & Resnick, 1977).

After children begin to receive formal arithmetic instruction in first grade, addition problems are less often solved by counting aloud or by counting fingers. Instead, children add and subtract by counting mentally. That is, children act as if they are counting silently, beginning with the larger number, and adding on. By age 8 or 9, children have learned the addition tables so well that sums of the single-digit integers (from 0 to 9) are facts that are simply retrieved from memory (Ashcraft, 1982).

These counting strategies do not occur in a rigid developmental sequence. Individual children use many or all of these strategies, depending upon the problem. Children usually begin by trying to retrieve an answer from memory. If they are not reasonably confident that the retrieved answer is correct, then they resort to counting aloud or on fingers (Siegler, 1988). Retrieval is most likely for problems with small addends (e.g., 1 + 2, 2 + 4) because these problems are presented frequently in textbooks and by teachers. Consequently, the sum is highly associated with the problem, which makes the child confident that the retrieved answer is correct. In contrast, problems with larger addends, such as 9 + 8, are presented less often. The result is a weaker link between the addends and the sum and, consequently, a greater chance that children will need to determine an answer by counting.

Children use many strategies to add, including counting on fingers and retrieving answers directly from memory.

Of course, arithmetic skills continue to improve as children move through elementary-school. They become more proficient in addition and subtraction, learn multiplication and division, and move on to the more sophisticated mathematical concepts involved in algebra, geometry, trigonometry, and calculus.

Comparing U.S. Students with Students in Other Countries. When compared to students worldwide in terms of math skills, U.S. students don't fare well. For example, the graph on page 378 shows the results of the Third International Mathematics and Science Study (National Center for Education Statistics, 1997), which compares math and science achievement of students in 41 different countries. Students in the United States have substantially lower scores than students in the leading nations. Phrased another way, the very best U.S. students only perform at the level of average students in Asian countries like Singapore and Korea. Furthermore, the cultural differences in math achievement hold for both math operations and math problem solving (Stevenson & Lee, 1990).

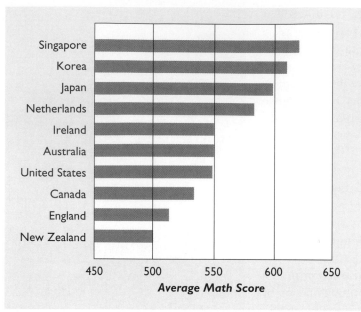

FIG 12-14

Why do American students rate so poorly? Consider a typical fifth grader's day in Taipei, the largest city in Taiwan. Students attend school from 8 A.M. until 4 P.M. daily. Most evenings, students spend 2 to 3 hours doing homework. This academic routine is grueling by U.S. standards, where fifth graders typically spend 6 to 7 hours in school each day and less than an hour doing homework. And, although many American schoolchildren are unhappy when schoolwork intrudes on time for play and television, students in China are enthusiastic about school and school-related activities, including homework.

In a comprehensive comparison of students in Japan, Taiwan, and the United States, Stevenson and Lee's findings (1990) found many substantial differences:

- *Time in school and how it is used.* By fifth grade, students in Japan and Taiwan spend 50 percent more time than American students in school, and more of this time is devoted to academic activities than in the United States.

- *Time spent in homework and attitudes toward it.* Students in Taiwan and Japan spend more time on homework and value homework more than American students.

- *Parents' attitudes.* American parents are more often satisfied with their children's performance in school; in contrast, Japanese and Taiwanese parents set much higher standards for their children.

- *Parents' beliefs about effort and ability.* Japanese and Taiwanese parents believe more strongly than American parents that effort, not native ability, is the key factor in school success.

Thus, students in Japan and Taiwan excel because they spend more time both in and out of school on academic tasks. Furthermore, their parents (and teachers) set loftier scholastic goals and believe that students can attain these goals with hard work. Japanese classrooms even post a motto describing ideal students—*gambaru kodomo*—they who strive the hardest.

Parents underscore the importance of schoolwork in many ways to their children. For example, even though homes and apartments in Japan and China are very small by U.S. standards, Asian youngsters, like the child in the photo, typically have a desk in a quiet area where they can study undisturbed (Stevenson & Lee, 1990). For Japanese and Taiwanese teachers and parents, academic excellence is paramount and it shows in their children's success.

What can Americans learn from Japanese and Taiwanese educational systems? From their experiences with Asian students, teachers, and schools, Stevenson and Stigler (1992) suggest several ways American schools could be improved:

- Give teachers more free time to prepare lessons and correct students' work.
- Improve teachers' training by allowing them to work closely with older, more experienced teachers.
- Organize instruction around sound principles of learning such as providing multiple examples of concepts and giving students adequate opportunities to practice newly acquired skills.
- Set higher standards for children, who need to spend more time and effort in school-related activities in order to achieve those standards.

> American schools could be improved by giving teachers better training and more time to prepare lessons, basing teaching on principles of learning, and setting higher standards.

Changing teaching practices and attitudes toward achievement would begin to reduce the gap between American students and students in other industrialized countries, particularly Asian countries. Ignoring the problem will mean an increasingly undereducated work force and citizenry in a more complex world—an alarming prospect for the twenty-first century.

Definition of word on page 373: A palanquin is a covered couch resting on two horizontal poles that are carried by four people, one at each end of the poles.

Check Your Learning

1. Important prereading skills include knowing letters and _____.

2. Beginning readers typically recognize words by sounding them out; with greater experience, readers are more likely able to _____.

3. Older and more experienced readers understand more of what they read because the capacity of working memory increases, they have more general knowledge of the world, _____, and they are more likely to use appropriate reading strategies.

4. Children typically use a _____ to organize their writing.

5. Children revise best when _____.

6. The simplest way of solving addition problems is to _____; the most advanced way is to retrieve sums from long-term memory.

7. Compared to students in U.S. elementary-schools, students in Japan and Taiwan spend more time in school, and a greater proportion of that time is _____.

■ **Active Children** Imagine two children just entering first grade. One has mastered prereading skills, can sound out many words, and recognizes a rapidly growing set of words. The second child knows most of the letters of the alphabet, but knows only a handful of letter-sound correspondences. How are these differences in reading skills likely to lead to different experiences in first grade?

Answers: (1) sounds associated with each letter, (2) retrieve words from long-term memory, (3) they monitor their comprehension more effectively, (4) knowledge-telling strategy, (5) the topic is familiar to them, (6) count on one's fingers, (7) devoted to academic activities

Effective Schools

Learning Objectives

■ **What are the hallmarks of effective schools and effective teachers?**

■ **How are computers used in school and what are their effects on instruction?**

Shalicia attends elementary school in a building that was opened in 1936. The building shows its age. The rooms are drafty, the desks are decorated with generations of graffiti, and new technology means an overhead projector. Nevertheless, attendance is good. Most students learn to read, and ultimately graduate from high school, and many continue their education at community colleges and state universities. Shalicia's cousin, Camille, attends a nearby elementary school that is about as old as Shalicia's school. Yet truancy is commonplace at Camille's school, many children never learn to read, and fewer than half the students graduate from high school. The girls' mothers, who are sisters, wonder why students in one school are so much more successful than students in the other.

How do schools influence children's development? Answering this question is difficult because American education is a smorgasbord, reflecting local control by communities throughout the United States. Schools differ on many dimensions, including their emphasis on academic goals and parent involvement. Teachers, too, differ in many ways, such as how they run their classrooms and how they teach. These and other variables affect how much students like Shalicia and Camille learn, as you'll see in the next few pages. Let's begin with school-based influences.

School-Based Influences on Student Achievement

Whether success is defined in terms of the percentage of students who are literate, graduate, or go to college, some schools are successful and some are not. Why? Researchers (Good & Brophy, 1994; Stevenson & Stigler, 1992; Walberg, 1995) have identified a number of factors associated with success in school:

Students succeed when their school emphasizes excellence, is safe and nurturing, monitors progress, and involves parents.

- *Staff and students alike understand that academic excellence is the primary goal of the school and of every student in the school.* The school day emphasizes instruction (not simply filling time from 8:30 to 3:30 with nonacademic activities), and students are recognized publicly for their academic accomplishments.

- *The school climate is safe and nurturant.* Students know that they can devote their energy to learning (instead of worrying about being harmed in school) and they know the staff truly wants to see them succeed.

- *Parents are involved.* In some cases, this may be through formal arrangements, such as parent-teacher organizations. Or it may be informal. Parents may spend some time each week in school grading papers or, like the father in the photo at the top of page 381, tutoring a child. Such involvement signals both teachers and students that parents are committed to students' success.

• *Progress of students, teachers, and programs is monitored.* The only way to know if schools are succeeding is by measuring performance. Students, teachers, and programs need to be evaluated regularly, using objective measures that reflect academic goals.

In schools that follow these guidelines, students usually succeed. In schools where the guidelines are ignored, students more often fail.

Of course, on a daily basis, individual teachers have the most potential for impact. Let's see how teachers can influence their students' achievement.

Teacher-Based Influences on Student Achievement

Take a moment to recall your teachers in elementary and middle school. Some you probably remember fondly, because they were enthusiastic and innovative, and they made learning fun. You may remember others with bitterness. They seemed to have lost their love of teaching and children, making class a living hell. Your experience tells you that some teachers are better than others, but what exactly makes a good teacher? Personality and enthusiasm are not the key elements. Although you may enjoy warm and eager teachers, research (Good & Brophy, 1994; Stevenson & Stigler, 1992; Walberg, 1995) shows several other factors are critical when it comes to students' achievement. Students tend to learn the most when teachers

• *manage the classroom effectively so they can devote most of their time to instruction.* When teachers, like the man in the photo, spend a lot of time disciplining students, or when students do not move smoothly from one class activity to the next, instructional time is wasted, and students are apt to learn less.

• *believe they are responsible for their students' learning and that their students will learn when taught well.* When students don't understand a new topic, these teachers repeat the original instruction (in case the student missed something) or create new instruction (in case the student heard everything but just didn't "get it"). These teachers keep plugging away because they feel at fault if students don't learn.

• *emphasize mastery of topics.* Teachers should introduce a topic, then give students many opportunities to understand, practice, and apply the topic. Just as you'd find it hard to go directly from driver's ed to driving a race car, students more often achieve when they grasp a new topic thoroughly, then gradually move on to other, more advanced topics.

- *teach actively.* They don't just talk or give students an endless stream of worksheets. Instead, they demonstrate topics concretely or have hands-on demonstrations for students. They also have students participate in class activities, and encourage students to interact, generating ideas and solving problems together.

- *pay careful attention to pacing.* They present material slowly enough that students can understand a new concept, but not so slowly that students get bored.

- *value tutoring.* They work with students individually or in small groups, so they can gear their instruction to each student's level and check each student's understanding. They also encourage peer tutoring, in which more capable students tutor less capable students. Children who are tutored by peers do learn, and so do the tutors, evidently because teaching helps tutors organize their knowledge.

- *teach children techniques for monitoring and managing their own learning.* Students are more likely to achieve when they are taught how to recognize the aims of school tasks and know effective strategies for achieving those aims (like those described on pages 345-347).

When teachers teach according to these guidelines, most of their students learn the material and enjoy school. When teachers don't observe these guidelines, their students often fail, or, at the very least, find learning difficult and school tedious (Good & Brophy, 1994; Stevenson & Stigler, 1992; Walberg, 1995).

> Computers are used in schools as tutors, for experiential learning, and to help children accomplish traditional academic goals more easily.

The Role of Computers. Some educational reformers argue that computers be used to improve students' learning. Computers can be used in schools as a tutor (Lepper & Gurtner, 1989). Children use computers to learn reading, spelling, arithmetic, science, and social studies. Computers allow instruction to be individualized and interactive. Students proceed at their own pace, receiving feedback and help when necessary. Computers are also a valuable medium for experiential learning (Lepper & Gurtner, 1989). Simulation programs allow students to explore the world in ways that would be impossible or dangerous otherwise. Students can change the law of gravity or see what happens to a city when no taxes are imposed. Finally, computers can help students achieve traditional academic goals more readily (Steelman, 1994). A graphics program can allow artistically untalented students to produce beautiful illustrations. A word-processing program can relieve much of the drudgery associated with revising, thereby encouraging better writing.

Not all researchers, educators, and policy-makers are enthusiastic about computers taking on a pivotal role in education. Some critics fear that computers eliminate an important human element in learning. However, all experts agree on the need for research-based policies concerning children and computer technology. The Child Development and Family Policy feature describes progress toward this goal.

CHILD DEVELOPMENT AND FAMILY POLICY

How Can Computers Promote Child Development?

Most U.S. children have access to computers at home and at school, and most adults agree that computer literacy is an important skill for children to acquire. Yet some adults worry that the benefits of computers for children are accompanied by some serious costs. Hearing these concerns, the Board on Children, Youth, and Families (BCYF) has worked to create constructive policies for children and computer technology. The BCYF is part of the National Academy of Sciences, a private organization that was chartered by the U.S. Congress in 1863. The BCYF provides nonpartisan critical analysis of policy-related issues concerning children, youth, and their families. Beginning in 2001, the BCYF summarized the existing research on children and computers to determine the additional research needed to help formulate public policy. The work has focused on three key issues, each of which has an associated question for public policy. These are summarized in Table 12–7.

Policy Issues Concerning Children and Computers	
Issue	**Policy Question**
Access to Computer Technology: Children from low-income families are less likely to have a computer at home; their schools usually have computers, but they tend to be older machines and there are fewer of them.	How can all children have ready access to modern computing equipment?
Use of Computers in Education: Simply putting computers in classrooms has little impact on quality of instruction. Instead, teachers need additional training, computerized instruction needs to be integrated into curriculums, computers need to have software that is instructionally effective, and software needs to be adjustable to the needs of individual students.	What are effective ways of using computers to improve students' learning?
Computers and Children's Well-Being: Outside the classroom, computers may have positive and negative effects on children. On the positive side, the Internet allows children to maintain friendship over distances, an asset in today's mobile society. On the negative side, the time that children devote to computers may come at the expense of other activities that promote children's well-being (e.g., physical play, interacting with peers, reading).	What can be done to increase the benefits of computers for children's lives while minimizing the potential harm?

TABLE 12-7

The BCYF does not have an in-house research team to conduct the necessary studies. Instead, the BCYF works to make these issues well known in the scientific community. In this spirit, in January 2001, BCYF conducted a workshop in which researchers and policy-makers met to discuss these issues and the type of research that is needed. The result of this workshop—along with other efforts by the BCYF and other interested organizations—will be to encourage child-development researchers in universities to conduct the studies necessary to provide policy-related information. ▪

Check Your Learning

1. In successful schools, academic excellence is a priority, the school is safe and nurturing, progress of students and teachers is monitored, and _____.

2. Effective teachers manage classrooms well, believe they are responsible for their students' learning, _____, teach actively, pay attention to pacing, value tutoring, and show children how to monitor their own learning.

3. Computers are used in schools as tutors, _____, and to help students accomplish traditional academic tasks more simply.

 Connections How do the factors associated with effective schools and effective teachers described in this module relate to the factors responsible for cultural differences in mathematics achievement described in Module 12.4?

Chapter Critical Review

1. If Jean Piaget were asked to define intelligence, how might his definition differ from a psychometrician's? How might it differ from Gardner's and Sternberg's definitions of intelligence?

2. Which perspective on intelligence best explains Max, the savant in the vignette that opens Module 12.2? Which best explains a person who is all-around gifted—good in all school subjects as well as socially skilled? Which best explains your personal intellectual gifts?

3. Explain why scores in intelligence tests do only a fair job of predicting school performance (see Module 12.3). What others factors might be involved in school success besides what intelligence tests are measuring?

4. A perennial debate in education is whether children should be taught to read with phonics (sounding out words) or with whole-word methods (recognizing entire words). Does the research described in Module 12.4 provide evidence that either method is more effective?

For more review material, log on to www.prenhall.com/kail

See For Yourself

The best way to understand the differences between good and bad teaching is to visit some actual school classrooms. Try to visit three or four classes in at least two different schools. (You can usually arrange this by speaking with the school's principal.) Take along the principles of good teaching that are listed on pages 381-382. Start by watching how the teachers and children interact. Then, decide how much the teacher relies upon each of the principles. If possible, ask the teachers about teaching philosophies and practices, including their opinions about the teaching principles listed on pages 381-382. You'll probably see that most teachers use some but not all of these principles. And you'll also see that, in today's classroom, consistently following all the principles is very challenging. See for yourself!

For More Information About . . .

 cultural differences in scholastic achievement, try Harold W. Stevenson and James W. Stigler's *The Learning Gap* (Summit Books, 1992), which describes research comparing schooling in the United States and in Asia.

tips and exercises to help develop better study skills for college, visit the Web site of the University Counseling Center of the Virginia Polytechnic Institute and State University:
http://www.ucc.vt.edu/stdysk/stdyhlp.html

Key Terms

concrete operational stage 344
componential subtheory 354
components 354
comprehension 370
contextual subtheory 354
culture-fair intelligence tests 365
dynamic testing 360
experiential subtheory 354

intelligence quotient (IQ) 358
knowledge-telling strategy 375
knowledge-transforming strategy 375
memory strategies 345
mental age (MA) 357
mental operations 344
mental rotation 366
phonological awareness 371

propositions 373
psychometricians 350
savants 353
script 348
social-cognitive flexibility 353
triarchic theory 353
validity 360
word recognition 370

SUMMARY

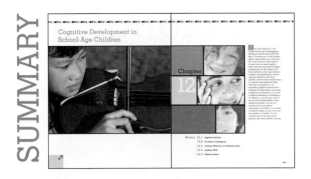

12.1 Cognitive Processes

Concrete Operational Thinking
Between ages 7 and 11 children use mental operations but their thinking is focused on the concrete and real.

Memory Skills
Preschool children use strategies to help remember. Using memory strategies well depends upon analyzing the goal of a task and monitoring the effectiveness of the strategy. Both skills improve during childhood.

A child's knowledge helps to organize information that is to be remembered. Knowledge can also distort memory by causing children to forget information that does not conform to their knowledge or to "remember" events that did not actually take place.

12.2 The Nature of Intelligence

Psychometric Theories
Psychometric approaches to intelligence include theories that describe intelligence as a general factor as well as theories that include specific factors. Hierarchical theories include general and specific factors.

Gardner's Theory of Multiple Intelligences
Gardner's theory includes linguistic, logical-mathematical, spatial, musical, bodily-kinesthetic, interpersonal, and intrapersonal intelligences. Gardner's theory has stimulated research on nontraditional forms of intelligence. The theory also implies that schools should teach to each child's unique intellectual strengths.

Sternberg's Triarchic Theory
Sternberg's triarchic theory includes (a) the contextual subtheory, which specifies that intelligent behavior is defined by the individual's culture, (b) the experiential subtheory, which specifies that intelligence is associated with task familiarity, and (c) the componential subtheory, which specifies that intelligent behavior involves organizing basic cognitive processes into an efficient strategy.

12.3 Individual Differences in Intellectual Skills

Binet and the Development of Intelligence Testing
Binet created the first intelligence test to identify students who would have difficulty in school. Using this work, Terman created the Stanford-Binet, which introduced the concept of IQ.

Do Tests Work?
Intelligence tests are reasonably valid measures of achievement in school and of performance in the workplace. Dynamic tests improve validity by measuring potential for future learning.

Hereditary and Environmental Factors
The impact of heredity on IQ is shown in findings that (a) siblings' IQ scores are more alike as siblings are more similar genetically, and (b) adopted children's IQ scores are more like their biological parents' test scores than their adoptive parents' scores. The role of the environment is shown by the impact on IQ of well-organized home environments and intervention programs.

Impact of Ethnicity and Social Class
The average IQ score for African Americans is lower than the average score for European Americans, a difference attributed to the fact that more African American children live in poverty and that the test assesses knowledge based on middle-class experiences. IQ scores remain valid predictors of school success because middle-class experience is often a prerequisite for school success.

Gender Differences in Intellectual Abilities and Achievement
Girls excel in verbal skills whereas boys excel in spatial ability. Girls get better grades in math; boys get better scores on math achievement tests.

12.4 Academic Skills

Reading Skills
Prereading skills include knowing letters and letter sounds. Beginning readers more often recognize words by sounding them out; advanced readers more often retrieve a word from long-term memory. Comprehension improves with age due to several factors: Working memory capacity increases, readers gain more world knowledge, and readers better monitor what they read and match reading strategies to the reading task.

Writing Skills
As children develop, their writing improves because they know more about the world, organize their writing better, master the mechanics of writing, and revise better.

Math Skills
Children first add and subtract by counting, but later retrieve addition facts directly from memory. In mathematics, American students lag behind students in other countries, chiefly because of differences in time spent on schoolwork and in parents' attitudes.

12.5 Effective Schools

School-Based Influences on Student Achievement
Successful schools emphasize academic excellence, are safe and nurturing, monitor progress, and urge parents to be involved.

Teacher-Based Influences on Student Achievement
Students succeed when teachers manage classrooms effectively, take responsibility for students' learning, teach mastery of material, pace material well, value tutoring, and show children how to monitor learning. Computers are used in school as tutors, to provide experiential learning, and as a tool to achieve traditional academic goals.

Social Behavior and Personality in School-Age Children

Chapter 13

I magine that you enter a hypothetical elementary-school classroom. The children look typical enough—some are following the teacher's lesson enthusiastically, others seem puzzled by it, and a handful aren't paying attention. However, the teacher introduces you to the students, who include Mother Teresa, Adolf Hitler, Mohandas Gandhi, and Martin Luther King Jr. Although seemingly identical now, three of the students will rank among the twentieth century's greatest figures and one will be guilty of unspeakable horrors. Why? What determines whether children care about others or take from others? Whether they become a Good Samaritan or follow a path of evil?

The modules in this chapter will provide some insights into these questions. In Module 13.1, we examine children's self-esteem because it is basic to children's ability to interact succesfully with others. In Module 13.2, we look at children's relationships with their peers. In Modules 13.3 and 13.4, we discover why children sometimes help and sometimes hurt others. Finally, in Module 13.5, we see how children are affected by after-school care and divorce.

Self-Esteem

13.1

Self-Esteem

| Learning Objectives |

■ **How is self-esteem measured in school-age children?**

■ **How does self-esteem change in the elementary-school years?**

■ **What factors influence the development of self-esteem?**

■ **How is children's development affected by low self-esteem?**

> *As a preschool child, Micah was brimming with self-confidence and was always enthusiastic about taking on new challenges and experiences. But as he progressed through the elementary-school years, Micah's confidence and enthusiasm waned. As a 5-year-old, he told his parents he was going to be a big league ball player; as an 11-year-old, he no longer said such things. As a 5-year-old, he loved looking at picture books, solving puzzles, and counting as high as he could; as an 11-year-old, he was much less interested in school-related activities. Don't get me wrong—Micah was still basically a happy kid. But he'd clearly lost the rampant self-confidence of his preschool years.*

This vignette charts change in self-esteem, which I first described in Chapter 10. In this module, we'll see how self-esteem is measured in elementary-school children, how it changes as children develop, and what forces shape it. And we'll see whether Micah's changing self-esteem is typical.

Measuring Self-Esteem

In Module 10.1, we saw that preschool children's self-esteem is typically measured by showing pictures and asking youngsters to judge which of two hypothetical children they resemble (e.g., a child who makes friends easily, or a child who does not make friends easily). With older children (and adolescents), self-esteem is often measured with questionnaires, in which children read statements like those in the diagram on page 389. The most widely used self-esteem questionnaire of this sort is the *Self-Perception Profile for Children* (SPPC for short) devised by Susan Harter (1985, 1988). The SPPC is designed to evaluate self-worth in children age 8 and older in five domains (Harter, 1988, p. 62):

- *Scholastic competence:* How competent or smart the child feels in doing schoolwork.

- *Athletic competence:* How competent the child feels at sports and games requiring physical skill or athletic ability.

- *Social acceptance:* How popular or accepted the child feels in social interactions with peers.

- *Behavioral conduct:* How adequate the child feels about behaving the way one is supposed to.

- *Physical appearance:* How good-looking the child feels and how much the child likes his or her physical characteristics, such as height, weight, face, and hair.

The SPPC includes six statements for each domain. For example, the diagram lists two of the statements used to evaluate scholastic competence, shown as they actually appear on the SPPC. In both statements, the child has checked the response that indicates the highest level of self-esteem. A child's answers to all six statements are used to create an average level of self-esteem in that domain. The averages for each of the five domains are then used to generate a self-perception profile for each child. Two profiles are illustrated in the figure. Allison's self-esteem is high across all five domains; Colleen's self-esteem is much more varied. She feels positive about her social acceptance and physical appearance and, to a lesser extent, about her conduct. However, she feels negative about her scholastic and athletic competence.

> The SPPC measures children's overall self-worth and their self-worth in five areas: scholastic and athletic competence, social acceptance, behavioral conduct, and physical appearance.

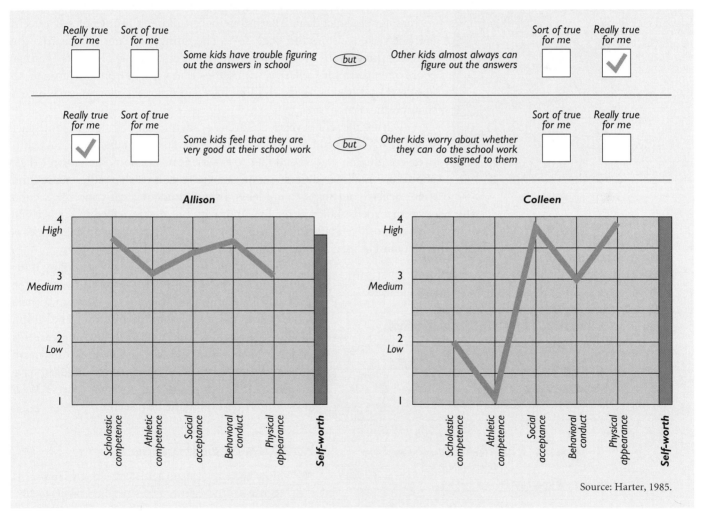

FIG 13-1

Notice that each profile ends with a bar graph depicting the child's overall self-worth. Overall self-worth is measured on the SPPC with six more items, such as "Some kids like the way they are leading their life" and "Some kids like the kind of person they are." Children's responses to these statements are then averaged to create a measure of overall self-worth.

Developmental Change in Self-Esteem

In the opening vignette, Micah's self-esteem dropped somewhat as he progressed through the elementary-school years. Such change is common. Why? Unlike Garrison Keillor's mythical Lake Wobegon, all children are not above average. During the elementary-school years, children begin to compare themselves with peers (Ruble et al., 1980). When they do, they discover that they are not necessarily the best reader or the fastest runner. They may realize, instead, that they are only an average reader. Or, like the girl in the background of the photo, they come to understand that they are one of the slowest runners in the class. This realization often produces a modest drop in those dimensions of self-esteem in which the child compares less favorably to peers.

Self-esteem changes in another important way during the elementary-school years: It becomes more differentiated as children become older (Boivin, Vitaro, & Gagnon, 1992). Children are able to evaluate themselves in more domains as they develop, and their evaluations in each domain are increasingly independent. That is, younger children's ratings of self-esteem are often like Allison's (on page 389): The ratings are consistent across the different dimensions. In contrast, older children's (and adolescents') ratings more often resemble Colleen's, with self-esteem varying from one domain to another. That is, school-age children have multiple self-esteems, each linked to a specific content area.

During the school years, children's academic self-concepts become particularly well defined (Byrne & Gavin, 1996; Marsh & Yeung, 1997). As children accumulate success and failure experiences in school, they form beliefs about their ability in different content areas (e.g., English, math, science) and these beliefs contribute to students' overall academic self-concept. A child who believes that she is skilled at reading and math but not so skilled in science will probably have a positive academic self-concept overall. But a child who believes he is untalented in most academic areas will have a negative academic self-concept.

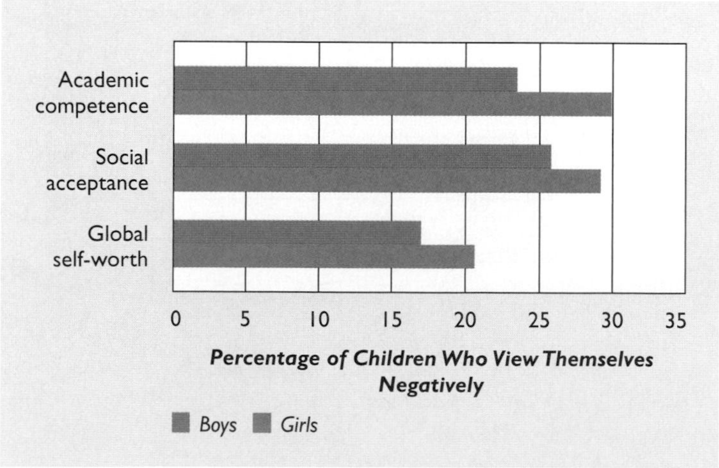

Sadly, at all ages and in all settings, many individuals do not view themselves very positively. Some children are ambivalent about who they are; others actually feel negative about themselves. The graph shows that roughly 25 percent of 9- and 10-year-olds in one study (Cole, 1991) had negative self-esteem on three scales of the SPPC. Why do these children have so little self-worth compared to their peers? We'll answer this question in the next section.

FIG 13–2

Sources of Self-Esteem

Think back to Allison and Colleen, the two girls whose self-perceptions are graphed on page 389. Both girls evaluated their overall self-worth very positively. In general, they were happy with themselves and with their lives. Why do these girls feel so positive while some children feel so negative about themselves? You won't be surprised to learn that parenting plays a key role.

Children are more likely to view themselves positively when their parents are affectionate toward them and involved with them (Lord, Eccles, & McCarthy, 1994).

Around the world, children have higher self-esteem when families live in harmony and parents nurture their children (Scott, Scott, & McCabe, 1991). A father who routinely hugs his daughter and gladly takes her to piano lessons is saying to her, "You are important to me." When children hear this regularly from parents, they evidently internalize the message and come to see themselves positively.

Parents' discipline also is related to self-esteem. Children with high self-esteem generally have parents who aren't afraid to set rules, but are also willing to discuss rules and discipline with their children (Coopersmith, 1967). Parents who fail to set rules are, in effect, telling their children that they don't care—they don't value them enough to go to the trouble of creating rules and enforcing them. In much the same way, parents who refuse to discuss discipline with their children are saying, "Your opinions don't matter to me." Not surprisingly, when children internalize these messages, the result is lower overall self-worth.

Allison's and Colleen's positive self-worth can therefore be credited, at least in part, to their parents for being warm and involved, for establishing rules, and for discussing these rules with them. But how can we account for the fact that Allison views herself positively in all domains whereas Colleen's self-perceptions are more varied? As I've suggested before, social comparisons are important (Butler, 1992). Both girls have many opportunities during each day to compare themselves with peers. Allison is almost always the first to finish assignments, usually gets one of the highest grades in the class on exams, and is often asked by her teacher to help classmates on math and science problems.

Meanwhile, Colleen is usually among the last to finish assignments, typically gets low grades on tests, and is one of the students Allison helps with math and science. Daily classroom routines give every student ample opportunities to discover everyone's academic standing within the room. Soon, everyone knows that Allison is one of the most capable students and Colleen, one of the least capable. Allison understands that her classmates see her as talented academically, so her academic self-esteem is quite high. Like the boy in the photo, Colleen knows that her classmates see her as not very talented academically, so her academic self-esteem is low.

The basic idea, then, is that children's self-esteem is based, in part, on how they are viewed by those around them. Children's self-esteem is high when others view them positively and low when others view them negatively (Hoge, Smit, & Hanson, 1990). This explanation has implications for academically talented youngsters, who might be placed in classes for gifted children. We'll look at these implications in the Making Children's Lives Better feature.

MAKING CHILDREN'S LIVES BETTER

Self-Esteem in Gifted Classes

In a traditional classroom of students with a wide range of ability, talented youngsters compare themselves with other students and develop positive academic self-esteem. But in classes for gifted students, many talented youngsters are only average and some are below average. The resulting social comparisons cause these children's academic self-esteem to drop (Marsh et al., 1995).

There is a clear lesson here for parents and teachers: When parents think about enrolling their child in classes for gifted children, they should understand that accelerated academic progress often comes at a price: Children's academic self-esteem often declines somewhat, even though their actual skills are improving.

What can parents do? First, they should look honestly at their child and decide whether he or she values learning per se versus being at the top of the class. Students who value being at the top of the class will be more affected by social comparisons in a gifted class than students who are more intent on mastering challenging academic material. Second, parents should find out whether common assignments and comparative evaluations are made, as in typical classrooms, or whether the gifted class emphasizes individualized work. The latter is more conducive to self-esteem. Carefully considering these factors can help parents decide if a gifted program is likely to lower their child's self-esteem, a very unwelcome side effect. ■

> Children have greater self-esteem when they work hard in school, get along with peers, avoid disciplinary problems, participate in extracurricular activities, and feel that teachers care about them.

In examining sources of self-esteem—not just for children in gifted classes, but for all children—several characteristics of teachers and schools should also be taken into account (Hoge et al., 1990). In general, self-esteem is greater when students work hard in school, get along with their peers, and avoid disciplinary problems. In addition, self-esteem is greater when students participate in extracurricular activities, such as music, student council, sports, and clubs. Finally, students' self-esteem is enhanced when the overall climate of the school is nurturing—when students believe that teachers care about them and listen to them. Grades matter, too, but good grades affect students' self-esteem in specific disciplines—in math or English—not their overall self-esteem (Hoge et al., 1990; Marsh & Yeung, 1997).

By encouraging students to work to the best of their ability and by being genuinely interested in their progress, teachers can enhance the self-esteem of all students, regardless of their talent. Parents can do the same and, by encouraging their children to participate in extracurricular activities that match their talents, further promote self-esteem.

Consequences of Low Self-Esteem

It is important that parents and teachers make an effort to enhance children's self-esteem because children with low self-esteem are at risk for many developmental problems. Children with low self-esteem are

- more likely to have problems with peers (Hymel et al., 1990),
- more prone to psychological disorders such as depression (Button et al., 1996; Garber, Robinson, & Valentiner, 1997),
- more likely to be involved in antisocial behavior (Dubow, Edwards, & Ippolito, 1997),
- more likely to do poorly in school (Marsh & Yeung, 1997).

In looking at these outcomes, we need to be cautious about stating that each is caused by low self-esteem. In fact, in many cases, low self-esteem contributes to the outcome but is itself also caused by the outcome. Poor school performance is a case in point: Over time, children who are unskilled academically do not keep up in school, which causes a drop in their academic self-esteem, making them less confident and probably less successful in future school learning (Marsh & Yeung, 1997). Much the same vicious circle probably applies to the poor peer relationships seen in children with low self-esteem. Poor social skills lead to peer rejection, reducing self-esteem in the peer context and disrupting future peer interactions.

Understanding this complex cause-effect-cause pattern is important in deciding how to help children with low self-esteem. Some children benefit directly from therapy that increases their low self-esteem. Others, however, need additional treatment, such as improving their social skills. And, we need to remember that all children have some talents that can be nurtured. Taking the time to recognize each child creates the feelings of "being special" that promote self-esteem.

Check Your Learning

1. Harter's *Self-Perception Profile for Children* (SPPC) is used to assess a child's self-esteem in five domains (scholastic competence, athletic competence, social acceptance, behavioral conduct, physical appearance) and the child's _____.

2. Over the elementary-school years, self-esteem often drops because _____.

3. As children develop, levels of self-esteem change and self-esteem becomes _____.

4. Children are more likely to have positive self-worth when parents are affectionate and involved with them and when parents _____.

5. A gifted child's self-esteem will not be harmed by a gifted class if the child values learning for its own sake or if the gifted class emphasizes _____.

6. Children with low self-esteem are more likely to have poor peer relations, _____, to be involved in antisocial activities, and to do poorly in school.

Connections How do the long-term consequences of low self-esteem show connections between cognitive, social, and emotional development?

Answers: (1) overall self-worth, (2) children compare themselves to peers and sometimes discover they are below average, (3) more differentiated, (4) set rules and discuss discipline with their children, (5) individualized work, (6) to be prone to psychological disorders such as depression

13.2

Relationships with Peers

Relationships with Peers

Learning Objectives

■ **Why do children become friends, and what are the benefits of friendship?**

■ **Why are some children more popular than others? What are the causes and consequences of being rejected?**

■ **What are the origins of prejudice?**

When 12-year-old Ian agreed to baby-sit for his 5-year-old bother, Kyle, their mother reminded Ian to keep Kyle out of the basement because Kyle's birthday presents were there, unwrapped. But as soon as their mother left, Kyle wanted to go to the basement to ride his tricycle. When Ian told him no, Kyle burst into angry tears and shouted, "I'm gonna tell Mom you were mean to me!" Ian wished he could explain to Kyle, but he knew that would just cause more trouble!

When children attend elementary-school, the context of peer relations changes dramatically. Not only does the sheer number of peers increase dramatically, children are often exposed to a far more diverse set of peers than before. In addition, children find themselves interacting with peers in situations that range from reasonably structured with much adult supervision (e.g., a classroom) to largely unstructured with minimal adult supervision (e.g., a playground during recess). In this module, we'll examine these changes in peer relationships. We'll see why children's interactions become smoother as they get older and learn more about Ian's growing understanding of what others are thinking. Then we'll look at friendship and popularity.

An Overview of Peer Interactions in School-Age Children

An obvious change in children's peer relations during the elementary-school years is that children get along better than when they were younger. When conflicts arise, elementary-school children are better able to resolve them because of their greater cognitive and social skills. Why? Perspective-taking is the key. As children move beyond the preschool years, they realize that others see the world differently, both literally and figuratively. Robert Selman (1980, 1981) drew upon Piaget's theory to explain how perspective-taking improves during childhood. According to Selman, preschool children sometimes know that two people can have different perspectives, but they may confuse the two perspectives. However, by the elementary-school years, children know that perspectives differ because people have access to different information. Imagine two classmates: One is excited about a class field trip but the second is sad because she knows the trip has been canceled. Elementary-school children understand that the children feel differently because only the second child knows that the trip has been canceled.

Later in the elementary-school years, children take another step forward in their perspective-taking. Now they can see themselves as others do. For example, in

> **Peer relations improve during the elementary-school years due to improved perspective-taking.**

the vignette, 12-year-old Ian knows that his brother thinks he is being bossy and mean. (And he understands that Kyle feels this because Kyle doesn't know what's in the basement and what their mother told Ian before she left.) Because children are able to take another's perspective and to see themselves in others' eyes, social interactions are easier and conflicts can be resolved when they do arise.

Because elementary-school children get along better, they spend more and more time with peers, without direct supervision from adults. What do they do together? In one study (Zarbatany, Hartmann, & Rankin, 1990), investigators asked Canadian students in grades 5 and 6 how they spent their time with peers. The students in the study indicated how often they participated with peers in each of 29 different activities. The results, shown in the graph, are not too surprising, eh? The most common activities with peers are simple—just being together and talking.

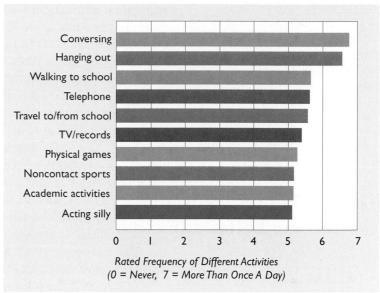

Rated Frequency of Different Activities
(0 = Never, 7 = More Than Once A Day)

FIG 13–3

The figure also highlights another important feature of peer relations during the elementary-school years. Children reported that they played physical games a few times each week, which reflects, in part, the emergence of a special type of play in school-age children. In rough-and-tumble play, children playfully chase, punch, kick, shove, fight, and wrestle with peers. Notice "playfully" in this definition: Unlike aggression, where the intention is to do harm, rough-and-tumble play is for fun. When children are involved in rough-and-tumble play, they are usually smiling and sometimes laughing (Pellegrini & Smith, 1998). When parents or teachers intervene, the youngsters usually explain that there's no problem, they're just playing. Rough-and-tumble play is more common among boys than girls, and girls' rough-and-tumble play tends to emphasize running and chasing over wrestling and fighting.

Friendship

Over time, children develop special relationships with certain peers. *Friendship* **is a voluntary relationship between two people involving mutual liking.** By the time children enter kindergarten, most children claim to have a "best friend." If you ask them how they can tell a child is their best friend, their response will probably resemble 6-year-old Katelyn's:

INTERVIEWER: Why is Heidi your best friend?

KATELYN: Because she plays with me. And she's nice to me.

INTERVIEWER: Are there any other reasons?

KATELYN: Yeah, Heidi lets me play with her dolls.

Like Katelyn and Heidi, and the girls in the photo, most friends are alike in age, gender, and race (Hartup, 1992a). Because friends are supposed to treat each other as equals, friendships are rare between an older, more experienced child and a younger, less experienced child. Because children typically play with same-sex peers (see Module 10.1), boys and girls rarely become friends.

Friendships are more common between children from the same race or ethnic group than between children from different groups, reflecting racial segregation in American society. Friendships among children of different groups are more common in schools where classes are smaller (Hallinan & Teixeira, 1987). Evidently, when classes are large, children select friends from the large number of available same-race peers. When fewer same-race peers are available in smaller classes, children more often become friends with other-race children. Interracial friendships are usually confined to school, unless children come from integrated neighborhoods. That is, when children live in different, segregated neighborhoods, their friendship does not extend to out-of-school settings (DuBois & Hirsch, 1990).

> When children have good friends, they are more likely to behave prosocially and are better adjusted.

Of course, friends are usually alike not only in age, sex, and race. Children and adolescents are also drawn together because they have similar attitudes toward school, recreation, and the future (Newcomb & Bagwell, 1995). Tom, who enjoys school, likes to read, and plans to go to Harvard, will probably not befriend Barry, who thinks that school is stupid, listens to his disc player constantly, and plans to quit high school to become a rock star (Haselager et al., 1998). As time passes, friends become more similar in their attitudes and values (Kandel, 1978).

Although children's friendships are overwhelmingly with members of their own sex, a few children have friendships with opposite-sex children. Who are these children and why do they have opposite-sex friendships? Boys and girls are equally likely to have opposite-sex friendships. The important factor in understanding these children is whether they have same- *and* opposite-sex friends or *only* opposite-sex friends. Children with same- and opposite-sex friendships tend to be very well adjusted whereas children with only opposite-sex friendships tend to be unpopular, less competent academically and socially, and have lower self-esteem. Apparently, children with both same- and opposite-sex friends are so socially skilled and popular that both boys and girls are eager to be their friends. In contrast, children with only opposite-sex friendships are socially unskilled, unpopular youngsters who are rejected by their same-sex peers and form friendships with opposite-sex children as a last resort (Kovacs, Parker, & Hoffman, 1996).

Quality and Consequences of Friendship. If you think back to your childhood friendships, you probably remember some that were long-lasting and satisfying as well as others that rapidly wore thin and soon dissolved. What accounts for these differences in the quality and longevity of friendships? Sometimes friendships are brief because children have the skills to create friendships—they know funny stories, they kid around, they know good gossip—but lack the skills to sustain them—they can't keep secrets, or they're too bossy (Jiao, 1999; Parker & Seal, 1996). Sometimes friendships end because,

when conflicts arise, children are more concerned about their own interests and are unwilling to compromise or negotiate (Fonzi et al., 1997; Rose & Asher, 1999). And, sometimes friendships end when children discover that their needs and interests aren't as similar as they thought initially (Gavin & Furman, 1996).

Considering that friendships disintegrate for many reasons, you're probably reminded that truly good friends are to be treasured. In fact, researchers consistently find that children benefit from having good friends. Compared to children who lack friends, children with good friends have higher self-esteem, are less likely to be lonely and depressed, and more often act prosocially—sharing and cooperating with others (Hartup & Stevens, 1999; Ladd, 1998). Children with good friends, like the ones in the photo, cope better with life stresses, such as the transition from elementary-school to middle school or junior high (Berndt & Keefe, 1995) and they're less likely to be victimized by peers (Hodges et al., 1999). The benefits of friendship are also long-lasting: Children who have friends have greater self-worth as young adults (Bagwell, Newcomb, & Bukowski, 1998).

Thus, friends are not simply special playmates and companions. They are important resources. Children learn from their friends and turn to them for support in times of stress.

Popularity and Rejection

Popular and rejected children can be found in every classroom and neighborhood. In fact, studies of popularity (Newcomb, Bukowski, & Pattee, 1993) reveal that most children can be placed in one of five categories:

- *Popular children* are liked by many classmates.
- *Rejected children* are disliked by many classmates.
- *Controversial children* are both liked and disliked by classmates.
- *Average children* are liked and disliked by some classmates but without the intensity found for popular, rejected, or controversial children.
- *Neglected children* are ignored by classmates.

What determines who's hot and who's not? Why is a child popular, rejected, controversial, average, or neglected? Smarter and physically attractive children are more often popular (Johnstone, Frame, & Bouman, 1992). However, the most important ingredient in popularity is social skill. Popular children are better at initiating social interactions with other children. They are more skillful at communicating and better at integrating themselves into an ongoing conversation or play session.

Popular children also seem relatively gifted in assessing and monitoring their own social impact in various situations and in tailoring their responses to the requirements of new social situations (Ladd, 1998; Wentzel & Asher, 1995). In one study, popular youngsters were more likely than unpopular children to share, cooperate, and help and less likely to start fights and break rules (Wentzel & Erdley, 1993). In another study, popular children were more likely to take turns and less likely to interrupt others (Black & Logan, 1995).

Why do some children fail in their efforts to be popular and end up in one of the other categories—rejected, controversial, average, or neglected? We know the most about rejected children. Rejected children tend to be socially unskilled (Stormshak et al., 1999). Many rejected children are aggressive, attacking their peers without provocation (Dodge, Bates, & Pettit, 1990). Other rejected youngsters have poor self-control and are often disruptive in school (French, 1988, 1990). When conflicts arise, rejected children often become angry and retaliate (Bryant, 1992).

Being well liked seems straightforward: Be pleasant and friendly, not obnoxious. Share, cooperate, and help instead of being disruptive. Are these rules specific to American children or do they apply more generally? The Cultural Influences feature has the answer.

CULTURAL INFLUENCES

Keys to Popularity

In America, popular children seem to know how to get along with others. These results don't apply just to American children; they hold for children in many cultures around the world, including Canada, European countries, Israel, and China (e.g., Casiglia, Coco, & Zappulla, 1998). Sometimes, however, popular children have other characteristics that are unique to their cultural setting. In Israel, for example, popular children are more likely to be direct and assertive than in other countries (Krispin, Sternberg, & Lamb, 1992). In China, popular children are more likely to be shy than in other countries (Chen, Rubin, & Li, 1995). Evidently, good social skills are at the core of popularity in most countries, but other features may also be important, reflecting culturally specific values. ■

Consequences of Rejection. No one enjoys being rejected. In fact, repeated peer rejection in childhood can have serious long-term consequences (DeRosier, Kupersmidt, & Patterson, 1995; Downey et al., 1998; Ladd, 1998). Rejected youngsters are more likely than youngsters in the other categories to drop out of school, commit juvenile offenses, and suffer from psychopathology. The Looking Ahead feature describes one study that showed some of the long-term effects of popularity and rejection.

LOOKING AHEAD

Long-Term Consequences of Popularity and Rejection

When children are popular in elementary-school, what happens to them as adolescents? And what happens to unpopular elementary-school children? Patricia Morison and Ann Masten (1991) set out to answer these questions in a longitudinal study. First, they asked children in grades 3 to 6 to nominate classmates for roles in an imaginary class play. Popular children were defined as those who were frequently nominated for roles like "a good leader," "everyone likes to be with," and "has many friends." Rejected children were those frequently nominated for roles like "picks on other kids," "too bossy," and "teases other children too much." Seven years later, when the children were now in high school, they and their parents completed questionnaires measuring academic achievement, social skill, and self-worth.

> When children are rejected, they do less well in school, have lower self-esteem, and are more likely to have behavioral problems.

The table shows the correlations between popularity and rejection in grades 3 to 6 and academic achievement, social skill, and self-worth measured 7 years later. Children who were popular in grades 3 to 6 were doing well in school, were socially skilled, and had high self-esteem. In contrast, children who were rejected in grades 3 to 6 were not doing well in school and had low self-esteem.

Correlations Between Children's Popularity and Rejection in Grades 3 to 6 and Academic Achievement, Social Skill, and Self-Worth		
Outcome	**Popularity in grades 3 to 6**	**Rejection in grades 3 to 6**
Academic achievement	.27	-.25
Social skill	.24	.03
Self-worth	.24	-.22

TABLE 13–1

Apparently, popular children fit in with groups instead of trying to make groups adjust to them. When conflicts arise with peers, popular children try to understand the problem and provide useful solutions. Over time, popular children's prosocial skill pays long-term dividends; unfortunately, rejected children's lack of prosocial skill has a price as well. ■

Causes of Rejection. Peer rejection can be traced, at least in part, to parental influence (Ladd, 1998). Children see how their parents respond to different social situations and often imitate these responses later. Parents who are friendly and cooperative with others demonstrate effective social skills. Parents who are belligerent and combative demonstrate much less effective social skills. In particular, when parents typically respond to inter-personal conflict like the couple in the photo—with intimidation or aggression—their children may imitate them, hampering their development of social skills and making them less popular in the long run (Keane, Brown, & Crenshaw, 1990).

Parents' disciplinary practices also affect their children's social skill and popularity. Inconsistent discipline—punishing a child for misbehaving one day and ignoring the same behavior the next—is associated with antisocial and aggressive behavior, paving the way to rejection (Dishion, 1990). Consistent punishment that is tied to parental love and affection is more likely to promote social skill and, in the process, popularity (Dekovic & Janssens, 1992).

In sum, parenting can lead to an aggressive interpersonal style in a child, which in turn leads to peer rejection. The implication, then, is that by teaching youngsters (and their parents) more effective ways of interacting with others, we can make rejection less likely. With improved social skills, rejected children would not need to resort to antisocial behaviors. Rejected children (and other types of unpopular children) can be taught how to initiate interaction, communicate clearly, and be friendly. They can also be discouraged from behaviors that peers dislike, such as whining and fighting. Training of this sort does work. Rejected children can learn skills that lead to peer acceptance and thereby avoid the long-term harm associated with being rejected (LaGreca, 1993; Mize & Ladd, 1990).

Prejudice

By the preschool years, most children can distinguish males from females and can identify people from different ethnic groups (Aboud, 1993). Once children learn their membership in a specific group—"I'm a Vietnamese American boy"—their view of children from other groups becomes more negative. ***Prejudice* is a negative view of others based on their membership in a specific group.**

Kindergarten children more often attribute positive traits (being friendly and smart) to their own group and negative traits (being mean and fighting a lot) to other groups (Bigler, Jones, & Lobliner, 1997; Black-Gutman & Hickson, 1996). During the elementary-school years, prejudice usually declines somewhat (Powlishta et al., 1994). Cognitive development explains the decline. Preschool and kindergarten children usually view people in social groups as much more homogeneous than they really are. People from other groups are seen as all alike and, typically, not as good as people from the child's own group. Older children understand that people in social groups are heterogeneous—they know that individual European Americans, girls, and obese children, for example, are not all alike. And they have learned that people from different groups may be more alike than people from the same group. Gary, an African American whose passion is computers, finds that he enjoys being with Vic, an Italian American who shares his love of computers, but not Curtis, another African American whose passion is music. As children realize that social groups consist of all kinds of different people, prejudice lessens.

Prejudice may be less pronounced in older children, but it does not vanish. Older children (and adolescents) remain biased positively toward their own group and negatively toward others (Powlishta et al., 1994). Of course, many adults have these same biases, and children and adolescents simply reflect the attitudes of those around them.

> ## Prejudice is reduced with friendly and constructive contacts between children from different groups.

What can parents, teachers, and other adults do to rid children of prejudice? One way is to encourage friendly and constructive contacts between children from different groups (Ramsey, 1995). Adults can create situations in which children from different groups work together toward common goals. In class, this might be a class project. In sports, it might be mastering a new skill. By working together, Gary starts to realize that Vic acts, thinks, and feels as he does simply because he's Vic, not because he's an Italian American.

Interactions between children of different racial backgrounds was one of the consequences of the U.S. Supreme Court's decision in Brown vs. Board of Education, a case that shows how child-development research influenced social policy.

CHILD DEVELOPMENT AND FAMILY POLICY

Ending Segregated Schools

In 1950, African American children in most states attended separate schools. Segregated schooling had been the law of the land for more than 100 years, bolstered by several famous Supreme Court decisions. In the fall of 1950, the chapter of the National Association for the Advancement of Colored People (NAACP) in Topeka, Kansas, decided to test the constitutionality of the law. Thirteen African American parents, including Oliver Brown, attempted to enroll their children in white-only schools; when they were turned away, the NAACP sued the Topeka Board of Education.

A key element in the NAACP's case was that separate schools were inherently harmful to African American children because such schools apparently legitimized the second-class status of African American children. To support this claim, the NAACP legal team relied upon testimony from Dr. Kenneth B. Clark. In previous work, Clark (1945, Clark & Clark, 1940) had shown that African American children typically thought that white dolls were nice but that brown dolls were bad. He found the same results in African American children attending segregated Topeka schools, leading him to testify that,

> *these children ..., like other human beings who are subjected to an obviously inferior status in the society in which they live, have been definitely harmed in the development of their personalities; that the signs of instability in their personalities are clear, and I think that every psychologist would accept and interpret these signs as such. ...[i]s the kind of injury which would be as enduring or lasting as the situation endured ...*

In May 1954, the Supreme Court rendered the landmark decision that segregated schools were unconstitutional. The impact of Clark's research and testimony was evident in the decision in Brown vs. The Board of Education, delivered by Chief Justice Earl Warren:

Segregation of white and colored children in public schools has a detrimental effect upon the colored children. The impact is greater when it has the sanction of the law, for the policy of separating the races is usually interpreted as denoting the inferiority of the negro group. A sense of inferiority affects the motivation of a child to learn. Segregation with the sanction of law, therefore, has a tendency to [retard] the educational and mental development of negro children and to deprive them of ... benefits they would receive in a racial[ly] integrated school system.

After the Brown decision, Clark continued his work on civil rights and worked on behalf of African American youth. For his lifelong effort to inform public policy on African American children and their families, in 1987 he received the Gold Medal for Life Achievement in Psychology in the Public Interest from the American Psychological Foundation. ▪

Check Your Learning

1. Friends are usually alike in age, sex, race, and _____.

2. Children who have same- and opposite-sex friends tend to be _____.

3. Children with good friends have higher self-esteem, are less likely to be _____, and most often act prosocially.

4. _____ are both liked and disliked by classmates.

5. Compared to unpopular children, popular children are usually _____.

6. Some rejected children are aggressive; others have _____ and are often disruptive in school.

7. Prejudice declines somewhat as children get older because _____.

8. One way to reduce prejudice is to _____.

■ ▪ **Continuity** What do the long-term consequences of being rejected tell us about continuity of development?

Answers: (1) interests, (2) very well adjusted, (3) lonely and depressed, (4) Controversial children, (5) more skilled socially, (6) poor self-control, (7) with cognitive development, children realize that social groups are not homogeneous, (8) to encourage friendly and constructive contacts between people from different groups

Helping Others

13.3

Helping Others

- Skills Underlying Prosocial Behavior
- Situational Influences
- Socializing Prosocial Behavior

Learning Objectives

- What skills do children need to behave prosocially?

- What situations influence children's prosocial behavior?

- How can parents foster prosocial behavior in their children?

Ten-year-old Juan got his finger trapped in the VCR when he tried to remove a tape. While he cried and cried, his 6-year-old brother, Antonio, watched but did not help. Later, when their mother had soothed Juan and decided that his finger was not injured, she worried about her younger son's reactions. In the face of his brother's obvious distress, why had Antonio done nothing?

Most parents, most teachers, and most religions try to teach children to act in cooperative, helping, giving ways—at least most of the time and in most situations. **Actions that benefit others are known as *prosocial behavior*.** Of course, cooperation often "works" because individuals gain more than they would by not cooperating. ***Altruism* is a particular kind of prosocial behavior; it is behavior that helps another with no direct benefit to the individual.** Altruism is driven by feelings of responsibility for other people. Two youngsters pooling their funds to buy a candy bar to share demonstrates cooperative behavior. One youngster giving half her lunch to a friend who forgot his demonstrates altruism.

As a general rule, intentions to act prosocially increase with age, as do children's strategies for helping. Of course, as the story of Juan and Antonio demonstrates, children do not always respond to the needs of others. Some children attach greater priority to looking out for their own interests. What makes some children more likely than others to help? Why did Antonio not help? In this module, you'll learn some of the factors that promote children's prosocial behavior.

Skills Underlying Prosocial Behavior

Think back to an occasion when you helped someone. How did you know that the person needed help? Why did you decide to help? Although you didn't realize it at the time, your decision to help was probably based on some important skills:

- *Perspective-taking.* In Module 13.2, you learned about Selman's description of age-related improvements in perspective-taking. By the elementary-school years, children understand that people have different views and they are able to see themselves as others do. In general, the better children understand the thoughts and feelings of other people, the more willing they are to share and help others (Eisenberg, 1988). For example, seeing an elderly adult trying to carry many packages, elementary-school children may offer to help because they can envision that carrying many bulky things is a burden.

- *Empathy.* **The ability to experience another person's emotions is *empathy*.** Children who deeply feel another person's fear, disappointment, sorrow, or loneliness are more inclined to help that person than children who do not feel these emotions (Kochanska, Padavich, & Koenig, 1996; Roberts & Strayer, 1996). In other words, youngsters like the one in the photo, who is obviously distressed by what she is seeing, are most likely to help others.

In sum, children who help others tend to be better able to take another's view and to feel another's emotions. For example, a 10-year-old who spontaneously loans his favorite video game to a friend sees that the friend would like to play the game and feels the friend's disappointment at not owning the game.

Of course, perspective-taking and empathy do not guarantee that children always act altruistically. Even though children have the skills needed to act altruistically, they may not because of the particular situation, as we'll see in the next section.

Situational Influences

Kind children occasionally disappoint us by being cruel, and children who are usually stingy sometimes surprise us by their generosity. Why? The setting helps determine whether children act altruistically or not.

- *Feelings of responsibility.* Children act altruistically when they feel responsible to the person in need. They are more likely to help siblings and friends than strangers, simply because they feel a direct responsibility to people that they know well (Costin & Jones, 1992).

- *Feelings of competence.* Children act altruistically when they feel that they have the skills necessary to help the person in need. Suppose, for example, that a child is growing more and more upset because she can't figure out how to work a computer game. A classmate who knows little about computer games is not likely to help because he doesn't know what to do to help. By helping, he could end up looking foolish (Peterson, 1983).

- *Mood.* Children act altruistically when they are happy or feeling successful but not when they are sad or feeling as if they have failed. In other words, a child who has just scored three goals in a soccer game is more inclined to share treats with siblings than a child who was tripped in the game and badly scraped her knee (Moore, Underwood, & Rosenhan, 1973).

- *Cost of altruism.* Children act altruistically when it entails few or modest sacrifices. A child who has received a snack that she doesn't particularly like is more inclined to share it than one who has received her very favorite snack (Eisenberg & Shell, 1986).

> Children typically help when they feel responsible, have the needed skills, are happy, and believe that they will lose little by helping.

When, then, are children most likely to help? When they feel responsible to the person in need, have the skills that are needed, are happy, and do not think they have to give up a lot by helping. When are children least likely to help? When they feel neither responsible nor capable of helping, are in a bad mood, and believe that helping will entail a large personal sacrifice.

Using these guidelines, how do you explain why Antonio, the boy in the vignette, watched idly as his older brother cried? Hint: the last two factors, mood and cost, are not likely to be involved. However, the first two factors may explain Antonio's failure to help his older brother. My explanation appears on page 406, just before Check Your Learning.

So far, we've seen that altruistic behavior is determined by children's skills (such as perspective-taking) and by characteristics of situations (such as whether children feel competent to help in a particular situation). Whether children are altruistic is also determined by socialization, the topic of the next section.

Socializing Prosocial Behavior

Dr. Martin Luther King Jr. said that his pursuit of civil rights for African Americans was particularly influenced by three people: Henry David Thoreau (a nineteenth-century American philosopher), Mohandas Gandhi (the leader of the Indian movement for independence from England), and his father, Dr. Martin Luther King Sr. As is true of many humanitarians, Dr. King's prosocial behavior started in childhood, at home. But how do parents foster altruism in their children? The key factors are reasoning, modeling, and praise.

Parents whose favored disciplinary strategy is reasoning tend to have children who behave prosocially (Hoffman, 1988, 1994). The Real Children feature shows this approach in action.

REAL CHILDREN

Using Reasoning to Promote Prosocial Behavior

Jim's 6-year-old daughter, Annie, was playing with a friend, Maurice. Annie asked Maurice if she could borrow his crayons. When Maurice refused, Annie pushed him aside and grabbed the crayons, which caused Maurice to cry. At this point, Jim returned the crayons to Maurice and had the following conversation with Annie:

JIM:	Why did you take the crayons away from Maurice?
ANNIE:	Because I wanted them.
JIM:	How do you think he felt? Happy or sad?
ANNIE:	I dunno.
JIM:	I think that you know.
ANNIE:	Okay. He was sad.
JIM:	Would you like it if I took the crayons away from you? How would you feel?
ANNIE:	I'd be mad. And sad, too.
JIM:	Well, that's how Maurice felt, and that's why you shouldn't just grab things away from people. It makes them angry and unhappy. Ask first, and if they say "no," then you mustn't take them.

Jim's approach to discipline is to reason with Annie to help her see how her actions affect others. He emphasizes the rights and needs of others as well as the impact of one child's misbehavior on others. Repeated exposure to reasoning during discipline seems to promote children's ability to take the perspective of others (Hoffman, 1988). ∎

> Parents can foster altruism by using reasoning to discipline their children, by behaving altruistically themselves, and by praising children's altruism.

Reasoning is one way that parents can influence prosocial behavior; modeling is another. Children imitate others' behavior, including prosocial behavior. In laboratory studies, children imitate their peers' altruism (Wilson, Piazza, & Nagle, 1990). For example, children are more likely to donate toys to hospitalized children or help older adults with household chores when they see other children doing so.

Of course, parents are the models to whom children are most continuously exposed, so they exert a powerful influence. For example, parents who report frequent feelings of warmth and concern for others tend to have children who experience stronger feelings of empathy (Eisenberg et al., 1991). When a mother is helpful and responsive, her children often imitate her by being cooperative, helpful, sharing, and less critical of others (Bryant & Crockenberg, 1980).

Perhaps the most obvious way to foster sharing and other altruistic behavior in children is to reward them directly for acts of generosity. Many parents reward prosocial acts with praise. **Particularly effective is *dispositional praise*, linking the child's altruistic behavior to an underlying altruistic disposition.** In other words, a parent might say, "Thanks for helping me make breakfast; I knew I could count on you because you are such a helpful person." When children, like the one in the photo, repeatedly hear remarks like this, their self-concept apparently changes to include these characteristics. Children begin to believe that they really are helpful (or nice or friendly). Consequently, when they encounter a situation in which prosocial behavior is appropriate, their self-concept prompts them to act prosocially (Mills & Grusec, 1989).

Thus a host of factors, summarized in the table, contribute to children's prosocial behavior.

■■■■ SUMMARY TABLE

Factors Contributing to Children's Prosocial Behavior

General Category	Types of Influence	Children are more likely to help when...
Skills	Perspective-taking	they can take another person's point of view
	Empathy	they feel another person's emotions
Situational Influences	Feelings of responsibility	they feel responsible to the person in need
	Feelings of competence	they feel competent to help
	Mood	they're in a good mood
	Cost of altruism	the cost of prosocial behavior is smaller
Parents' Influence	Disciplinary strategy	parents use reasoning as their primary form of discipline
	Modeling	parents behave prosocially themselves
	Reward	parents reward prosocial behavior

TABLE 13-2

Combining all these ingredients, we can describe the development of children's altruistic behavior this way: As children get older, their perspective-taking and empathic skills develop, which enables them to see and feel another's needs. Nonetheless, children are never invariably altruistic (or, fortunately, invariably non-altruistic) because properties of situations dictate altruistic behavior, too.

As parents and other adults try to encourage children's prosocial behavior, one of the biggest obstacles is aggressive behavior, which is common throughout the elementary-school years. In the next module, we'll look at some of the forces that contribute to children's aggression.

Answer to question on page 402 about why Antonio didn't help: Here are two explanations: First, Antonio may not have felt particularly responsible to help because a younger sibling is less likely to feel responsible for an older brother. Second, Antonio's mom has probably told him many times to stay away from the VCR. Consequently, he may not feel competent to help because he doesn't know how it works or what he should do to help Juan remove his finger.

Check Your Learning

1. The factors that contribute to prosocial behavior are prosocial skills, _____, and socialization.

2. The skills that help children behave prosocially include _____ and empathy.

3. Children are more likely to behave prosocially when they feel responsible, competent, happy, and when _____.

4. Parents can encourage prosocial behavior by using reasoning when they discipline their children, _____, and praising them for behaving prosocially.

5. In _____, parents link a child's altruistic behavior to an underlying altruistic disposition.

Active Children: Most parents want their children to be helpful to others and parents can influence the extent to which their children are helpful. But altruism also depends on characteristics of children themselves. Describe some of these characteristics.

Answers: (1) situational influences, (2) perspective-taking, (3) the costs of prosocial behavior are minimal, (4) modeling prosocial behavior, (5) dispositional praise

Aggression

13.4

Aggression
- The Nature of Children's Aggressive Behavior
- Roots of Aggressive Behavior
- Victims of Aggression

Learning Objectives

■ **What forms of aggressive behavior are common during the elementary-school years?**

■ **How do families, television, and the child's own thoughts contribute to aggression?**

■ **Why are some children victims of aggression?**

Every day, 7-year-old Roberto follows the same routine when he gets home from school: He watches one action-adventure cartoon on TV after another until it's time for dinner. Roberto's mother is disturbed by her son's constant TV viewing, particularly because of the amount of violence in the shows that he likes. Her husband tells her to stop worrying: "Let him watch what he wants to. It won't hurt him and, besides, it keeps him out of your hair."

If you think back to your years in elementary-school, you can probably remember a class "bully"—a child who was always teasing classmates and picking fights. **Such acts typify *aggression*, behavior meant to harm others.** Aggressiveness is not the same as assertiveness, even though lay people often use these words interchangeably. You've probably heard praise for an "aggressive businessperson" or a ballplayer who was "aggressive at running the bases." Psychologists and other behavioral scientists, however, would call these behaviors assertive. Assertive behaviors are goal-directed actions to further the legitimate interests of individuals or the groups they represent, while respecting the rights of other persons. In contrast, aggressive behavior, which may be physical or verbal, is intended to harm, damage, or injure and is carried out without regard for the rights of others.

In this module, we will examine aggressive behavior in children and, in the process, learn more about the impact of Roberto's TV watching on his behavior.

The Nature of Children's Aggressive Behavior

In Module 10.3, we saw that preschool children often use aggression to resolve their conflicts and that bullying (unprovoked aggression) emerges during the preschool years. Two other forms of aggression are also seen in elementary-school children. **In *instrumental aggression*, a child uses aggression to achieve an explicit goal.** Instrumental aggression would include shoving a child to get at the head of a lunch line or grabbing a toy away from another child. **In *reactive aggression*, one child's behavior leads to another child's aggression.** Reactive aggressive would include a child who loses a game and then punches the child who won. Reactive aggressive is also shown by the child who, when he was not chosen for the starring role in a play, kicked the child who was.

Bullying and instrumental and reactive aggression are most likely to be expressed physically in younger children. As children get older, they more often use language to express their aggression. **A particularly common form of verbal aggression is *relational aggression*, in which children try to hurt others by undermining their social relationships.** In relational aggression, which is more typical of girls than boys, children try to hurt others by telling friends to avoid a particular classmate, by spreading malicious gossip, or by making remarks meant to hurt others, such as "You're the dumbest, ugliest kid in third grade and everyone hates you!" (Crick & Werner, 1998; Galen & Underwood, 1997).

Verbal aggression definitely occurs more often as children grow, but physical aggression still occurs during the elementary-school years, particularly among boys. In one study, fourth- and seventh-grade boys reported that nearly 50 percent of their conflicts with other boys involved physical aggression (Cairns et al., 1989).

Although forms of aggression change with development, individual children's tendencies to behave aggressively are moderately stable, especially among boys. Kupersmidt and Coie (1990) measured aggressiveness in a group of 11-year-olds by having children list the names of classmates who frequently started fights. Seven years later, more than half the aggressive children had police records, compared to less than 10 percent of the nonaggressive children.

In another study, conducted in Sweden by Stattin and Magnusson (1989), teachers rated the aggressive behavior of more than one thousand 10-year-olds. Their results, shown in the graph, indicate that teachers' ratings accurately predicted subsequent criminal activity. Boys in the least aggressive group committed relatively few criminal offenses of any sort, while two-thirds of the most aggressive boys had committed offenses, and nearly half had committed major offenses such as assault, theft, or robbery. Overall, girls committed far fewer offenses, but teachers' ratings of aggressive behavior still predicted which girls were more likely to have criminal records.

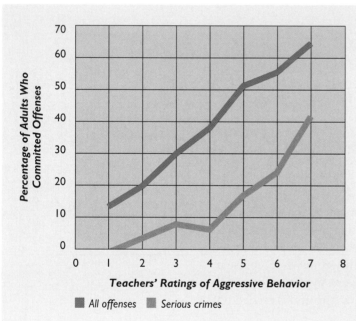
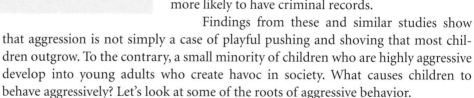

FIG 13-4

Findings from these and similar studies show that aggression is not simply a case of playful pushing and shoving that most children outgrow. To the contrary, a small minority of children who are highly aggressive develop into young adults who create havoc in society. What causes children to behave aggressively? Let's look at some of the roots of aggressive behavior.

Roots of Aggressive Behavior

For many years, psychologists believed that aggression was caused by frustration. The idea was that when children or adults were blocked from achieving a goal, they became frustrated and aggressed, often against the interfering person or object. Although frustration can lead to aggression (Berkowitz, 1989), researchers no longer believe that it's the sole cause of aggression, and therefore investigators have looked to other causes, including the family, television, and the child's own thoughts.

Impact of the Family. Early family experiences are a prime training ground for learning patterns of aggression. The pioneering work in this area was conducted by

Gerald Patterson (1984), whose findings were based almost entirely on careful, systematic observation of aggressive children in their home environments. One fact that comes through clearly in Patterson's work is that parents and siblings play an enormous role in cultivating aggressive behavior in children, and in ways that are subtle as well as obvious. Many parents and older siblings, for example, use physical punishment or threats to stop aggressive behavior. Although the immediate effect may be to suppress aggression, physical punishment also serves as a model, vividly demonstrating that physical force "works" as a means of controlling others. A parent like the one in the photo is saying, in effect, "You were right. The best way to get people to do what you want, or to stop them from doing what you don't want, is to hit them hard enough."

Not surprisingly, parents' use of harsh physical punishment is associated with aggressive behavior in children. Dodge, Bates, and Pettit (1990) studied children who were so harshly punished physically that they were bruised or needed medical treatment. These children were rated twice as aggressive by both teachers and peers as children who had not experienced such harsh punishment. But strong or aggressive parental responses are not essential in making a child aggressive. When parents are coercive, unresponsive, and emotionally uninvested, their children are more likely to be aggressive (Hart et al., 1998; Rubin et al., 1998).

In many families with aggressive children, a vicious circle seems to develop. Compared to families with nonaggressive children, both aggressive children and their parents are more likely to respond to neutral behavior with aggression. Furthermore, once an aggressive exchange has begun, both parents and children are likely to escalate the exchange, rather than break it off. And once a child has been labeled aggressive by parents and others, that child is more likely to be accused of aggression and to be singled out for punishment, even when the child has been behaving entirely appropriately on the occasion in question (Patterson, 1984). The "aggressive child" will be accused of all things that go wrong from missing cookies to broken appliances and other children's misbehaviors will be ignored.

Patterson's work emphasizes the point that hitting a child for aggression does not usually inhibit aggression for very long. What is the best response to a child's aggression? Discourage it either by ignoring it or punishing it while encouraging and rewarding other forms of nonaggressive social behavior. An older brother who simply grabs the remote control from a younger sister should be punished ("No TV for 3 days!"), and then shown a better way to resolve the conflict ("Wait until your sister finishes her program, then ask if you can change the channel. If she says, 'no,' come see me."). Later, the child should be praised for cooperating rather than aggressing ("Thanks for asking your sister instead of just grabbing the remote control.").

Parents are not the only family members who influence children's aggression—siblings matter, too. Among aggressive children, those who have good relationships with their siblings tend to be less aggressive and better adjusted than aggressive children who have conflicted relationships with their siblings (Stormshak et al., 1996). Good sibling relationships may provide aggressive children with opportunities to improve their social skills, or they may provide emotional support for aggressive youngsters.

> In families with aggressive children, a vicious circle often develops in which parents and children respond to neutral behavior aggressively and escalate aggressive exchanges.

Finally, it's important to remember that children may elicit some of the very parental behaviors that foster their aggression. That is, Module 3.3 described evocative gene-environment interactions, in which children inherit characteristics that make some experiences more likely than others. In the case of aggression, adoption and twin studies point to hereditary components in aggression (Deater-Deckard & Plomin, 1999; Rowe, Almeida, & Jacobson, 1999). Some children inherit a tendency to be impulsive, to have an angry temperament, or to regulate their own behavior poorly. These characteristics often lead parents to discipline these children more harshly, which then makes them more aggressive (Ge et al., 1998). Thus, parents and child can both contribute to a vicious circle of escalating aggression.

Impact of Television. Most children today watch television regularly by the time they're 3 years old, and by the time they turn 15, they have spent more time watching television than going to school. In fact, throughout childhood they will have spent more time watching television than in any other activity except sleep (Liebert & Sprafkin, 1988).

> Both experimental and correlational studies link children's viewing of TV violence to aggression.

What do children see when they watch all this television? The answer varies somewhat from child to child, but most American children spend considerable time watching action-adventure programs that contain a heavy dose of modeled aggression. Heroes and "good guys" on these shows almost invariably end up in a fight with the "bad guys." The good guys always win, of course, and are typically rewarded with praise, admiration, and sometimes more tangible rewards (such as a vacation in the sun).

What are the effects of watching all these rewarded aggressive models for so long? This question first attracted attention in the mid-1950s. At that time, only about half the households in the United States had television sets, yet the public was already aware of the frequent portrayal of violence in TV programs and worried about its effects on viewers, especially young ones. Anecdotal evidence suggested a link. One 6-year-old fan of Hopalong Cassidy (a TV cowboy of the 1950s) asked his father for real bullets for his toy gun because his toy bullets didn't kill people the way Hopalong's did (Schramm, Lyle, & Parker, 1961).

More than 40 years later, we are still concerned about violence on TV with good reason. Children's cartoons like the one shown in the photo typically show one violent act every 3 minutes ("violence" meaning use of physical force against another person). And the average American youngster will see several thousand murders on TV before reaching adolescence (Waters, 1993). (If you find these numbers hard to believe, try the activities described in See for Yourself at the end of the chapter.)

What does research tell us about this steady diet of televised mayhem and violence? According to Bandura's (1986) social cognitive theory, children learn by observing others; so if they watch violent behavior (either real or televised), they will act violently. In fact, laboratory studies conducted in the 1960s by Bandura, Ross, and Ross (1963) made just this point. Children watched specially created TV programs showing an adult kicking and hitting a plastic "Bobo" doll. When children were given the opportunity to play with the doll, those who had seen the TV program were much more likely to behave aggressively toward the doll than children who had not seen the program.

Critics thought the laboratory setting of this and other early studies affected the results, and they doubted that viewing TV violence in more realistic settings would have such pronounced effects on children (Klapper, 1968).

Today, however, we know that viewing TV violence "hardens" children, making them more accepting of interpersonal violence. Suppose, for example, a teen is baby-sitting two youngsters who begin to argue and then fight. Baby-sitters who are frequent viewers of TV violence are more inclined to let them "slug it out" because they see this as a normal, acceptable way of resolving conflicts (Drabman & Thomas, 1976).

Is this increased tolerance for aggression reflected in children's behavior? Will Roberto, the avid cartoon watcher in the vignette at the beginning of the module, become more aggressive? Or, as his father believes, is his TV watching simply "fun" without consequence? The answer from research is clear: Roberto's father is wrong. Frequent exposure to TV violence makes children more aggressive.

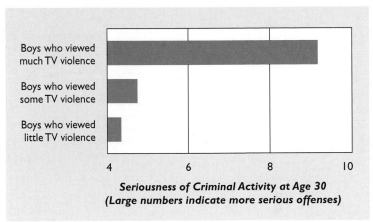

FIG 13-5

One of the most compelling studies examined the impact of children's TV viewing at age 8 on criminal activity at age 30 (Huesmann, 1986). The graph shows that 8-year-old boys who watched large doses of TV violence had the most extensive criminal records as 30-year-olds. This was true for both males and females, even though females' overall level of criminal activity was much lower.

These findings are correlational, which complicates conclusions about cause and effect. But experimental studies demonstrate that viewing televised violence breeds aggression, so it is reasonable to conclude that children who regularly view TV violence resort to aggression in interacting with others. For some, their aggression eventually puts them behind bars. Of course, TV violence is not the sole cause of aggression in children. But it is an important factor in a highly complex process to which parents and peers also contribute.

Cognitive Processes. The perceptual and cognitive skills described in Chapters 9 and 10 also play a role in aggression. Dodge, Bates, and Pettit (1990) were the first to explore the cognitive aspects of aggression. They discovered that aggressive boys often respond aggressively because they are not skilled at interpreting other people's intentions and, without a clear interpretation in mind, they respond aggressively by default. That is, aggressive boys far too often think, "I don't know what you're up to, and, when in doubt, attack."

From findings like these, Crick and Dodge (1994; Dodge & Crick, 1990) formulated the information-processing model of children's thinking shown in the diagram on page 412. According to the model, responding to a social stimulus involves several steps. First, children selectively attend to certain features of the social stimulus but not others, in the manner described in Module 9.1. Second, children try to interpret the features that they have processed; that is, they try to give meaning to the social stimulus. Third, children evaluate their goals for the situation. Fourth, children retrieve from memory a behavioral response that is associated with the interpretation and goals of the situation. Fifth, children evaluate this response to determine if it is appropriate. Finally, the child proceeds with the behavior.

Several investigators have shown that aggressive children's processing is biased and restricted in many of these steps, and that this flawed information processing is associated with increased aggression (Crick & Werner, 1998; Egan, Monson, & Perry, 1998). Aggressive children are less likely to attend to features that would signal nonhos-

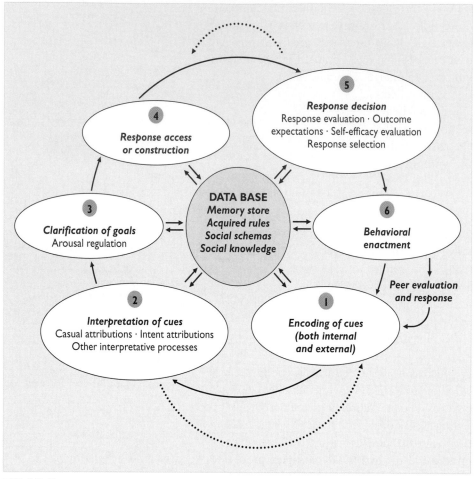

FIG 13–6

Source: Crick & Dodge, 1994.

tile motives (Crick & Dodge, 1994). For example, suppose a child accidentally tears another child's homework. The first child probably appears surprised and chagrined, cues that the child did not tear the homework on purpose. Nevertheless, aggressive children often do not process those cues and assume that the child's intent was hostile. And, based on a personal history of being rejected and ridiculed by peers, many aggressive children believe that unfamiliar peers are unfriendly and uncaring (Burks et al., 1999; MacKinnon-Lewis, Rabiner, & Starnes, 1999).

If aggressive children are unskilled at interpreting and responding to others' actions, would training in these skills improve their social behavior? The answer seems to be "yes" (Dodge & Crick, 1990). One approach is to teach aggressive children that aggression is painful and does not solve problems, that intentions can be understood by attending to relevant cues, and that there are more effective, prosocial ways to solve interpersonal disputes. This sort of training in social skills can reduce aggressive behavior and increase positive interactions with peers.

To sum up, the vicious cycle of aggression usually begins early. Once youngsters are labeled aggressive, environmental factors may lead them quite unwittingly along an aggressive path. The punishments that parents and teachers dole out may increase the child's hostility and serve as evidence that aggression "works." The child may then choose aggressive companions who further encourage aggressive behavior.

Of course, families are not the sole causes of aggression and violence. Poverty, unemployment, racism, and terrorism create a culture of aggression and violence (Coie & Dodge, 1998). But individual parents can be careful to not set the cycle of aggression in motion. Parents can respond to misbehavior with reasoning instead of physical punishment. And, children prone to aggression can be taught equally effective but more prosocial ways to deal with conflict.

Victims of Aggression

Every aggressive act is directed at someone. Most school children are the targets of an occasional aggressive act—a shove or kick to gain a desired toy, or a stinging insult by someone trying to save face. However, a small percentage of children are chronic targets of bullying. In both Europe and the United States, about 10 percent of elementary-school children and adolescents are chronic victims of aggression (Kochenderfer & Ladd, 1996; Olweus, 1994). Dorothy Allison provides a frightening glimpse of this victimization in her novel *Bastard Out of Carolina*. As Shannon got on the school bus, she

> *walked past a dozen hooting boys and another dozen flushed and whispering girls. As she made her way up the aisle, I watched each boy slide to the end of his seat to block her sitting with him and every girl flinch away as if whatever Shannon had might be catching. In the seat ahead of us Danny Yarboro leaned far over into the aisle and began making retching noises. "Cootie train! Cootie train," somebody yelled as the bus lurched into motion and Shannon still hadn't found a seat.* (pp. 153-154)

In this episode, Shannon is the victim of verbal bullying. But victimization by physical force also occurs frequently: Think of a child who is beat up daily on the playground.

As you can imagine, being tormented daily by their peers is hard on children. Research consistently shows that children who are chronic victims of aggression are often lonely, anxious, and depressed; they dislike school; and they have low self-esteem (Graham & Juvonen, 1998; Ladd & Ladd, 1998).

Why do some children suffer the sad fate of being victims? A first step in answering this question is to look at victimized children more carefully. A small percentage of victims are actually aggressive themselves (Olweus, 1978; Schwartz et al., 1997). These youngsters often overreact, are restless, and easily irritated. Their aggressive peers soon learn that these children are easily baited. A group of children will, for example, insult or ridicule them, knowing that they will probably start a fight even though outnumbered.

The vast majority of children victimized by aggression are not overreactive, restless, or irritable. Instead, these victims tend to be withdrawn and submissive. They are unwilling or unable to defend themselves from their peers' aggression, and so they are usually referred to as passive victims (Ladd & Ladd, 1998; Olweus, 1978). When attacked, like the child in the photo, they show obvious signs of distress and usually give in to their attackers, thereby rewarding their aggressive behavior.

How do children end up as victims? Family history and parenting help decide. To understand these forces, we need to distinguish victims who overreact from those who respond passively, and within the latter group, distinguish boys from girls. Victims who overreact often come from hostile, punitive, or even abusive family environments (Schwartz et al., 1997). Among passive victims, boys tend to have mothers who are overprotective or emotionally overinvolved with them; in contrast, girls who are passive victims tend to have mothers who are controlling and unresponsive (Ladd & Ladd, 1998).

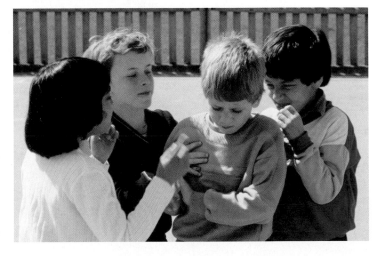

Some children who are chronic victims of aggression overreact when provoked; others withdraw and submit to aggression.

Victimization is always pathetic and sometimes tragic but these children can be helped. They can be taught ways of dealing with aggression that are more effective than either overreacting or withdrawing passively (e.g., don't lash out when you're insulted; don't show that you're afraid when you're threatened). In addition, increasing their self-esteem can help. When attacked, children with low self-esteem may think, "I'm a loser and have to put up with this because I have no choice." Increasing children's self-esteem makes them less tolerant of personal attacks (Egan & Perry, 1998). Finally, one of the easiest ways to help victims is to foster their friendships with peers. When children have friends, they're not as likely to be victimized (Hodges, Malone, & Perry, 1997).

Check Your Learning

1. During the elementary-school years, physical aggression becomes less common but _____ becomes more common, especially among girls.

2. After the preschool years, bullying is the most common form of aggression, but instrumental and _____ aggression also occur often.

3. As adults, highly aggressive children are more likely to _____.

4. Aggressive behavior in children is linked to parents' use of _____ punishment.

5. Family influences on children's aggression includes parental behavior (including punishment), _____, and inherited tendencies that may evoke harsh parenting.

6. Children who regularly watch televised violence are more likely to behave aggressively, and they also _____.

7. Aggressive children often interpret neutral stimuli in _____ terms.

8. Some chronic victims of aggression tend to overreact when provoked whereas other chronic victims tend to _____.

Connections Crick and Dodge's model of decision making draws upon the information-processing approach to cognitive development introduced in Chapters 1 and 6. Use that approach to suggest other possible causes of and remedies for children's aggressive behavior.

Answers: (1) verbal aggression, (2) reactive, (3) engage in criminal activity, (4) harsh physical, (5) the quality of children's relationships with siblings, (6) become hardened to violence, (7) hostile or aggressive, (8) withdraw or submit

Families at the Turn of the Century

Learning Objectives

▪ **How well can children care for themselves after school?**

▪ **What are some of the effects of divorce and remarriage on children?**

Jack has lived with his dad for the 4 years since his parents' divorce; he visits his mother every other weekend. Although Jack was confused and depressed when his parents divorced, he has come to terms with the new situation. He's excelling in school, where he is well liked by peers and teachers. One of Jack's friends is Troy. Troy's parents are married but bicker constantly since his dad lost his job. His parents are unable to agree on anything; the pettiest event or remark triggers an argument. Troy's grades have fallen, and while he was once a leader among the boys in his class, now he prefers to be alone.

American families face many new challenges in the twenty-first century. More families than ever before rely on two incomes for an adequate standard of living. When both parents work outside the home, no one can watch the children after school. Formal after-school care is often not available, so many children are left to care for themselves. We'll see how children fare in self-care in the first part of the module.

Another challenge is divorce. Roughly one in three American children will, before age 18, see his or her family broken apart by divorce. We'll examine the effect of divorce on children in detail in the second half of this module; as we do, we'll discover whether the effects of divorce are long-lasting or, as seems to be true for Jack, at least some are temporary.

After-School Care

When children enter elementary-school, child care becomes easier for working parents. However, many children still need care before or after school. Formal programs for before- and after-school care have been studied much less than day care for infants and toddlers (Lamb, 1999). Nevertheless, the limited research that has been done suggests that many of the same variables associated with high-quality day care for infants and toddlers are associated with high-quality before- and after-school care. Children benefit from well-trained, encouraging teachers; from low child-to-teacher ratios; and from a flexible, age-appropriate curriculum (Rosenthal & Vandell, 1996).

Many school-age children—approximately 10 percent of all 5- to 13-year-olds in the United States—receive no formal care after school; they are left alone to care for themselves (Galambos & Maggs, 1991). **Children who care for themselves are sometimes called *latchkey children*, a term that originated more than 200 years ago to describe children who raised a door latch to enter their own homes.** Some latchkey children, like the child in photo, stay at home alone (sometimes with parental

Children who care for themselves after school fare well unless they spend the time with peers, unsupervised.

supervision in absentia via the telephone). Others may stay at friends' homes where adults are sometimes present, or they may be unsupervised in public places such as shopping malls or public libraries.

The popular perception is that latchkey children are a frightened, endangered lot. But research provides little support for this view. To the contrary, most older children who care for themselves at home after school fare as well as children in the care of parents or other adults (Lamb, 1999). In one study, third, fourth, and fifth graders who cared for themselves at home were no more anxious, headstrong, or dependent than children cared for by their mothers (Vandell & Ramanan, 1991).

Research does reveal one group that is at-risk—children who spend much after-school time with peers (Galamabos & Maggs, 1991). These individuals are more prone to aggressive and delinquent behavior, particularly when other risk factors are present, as we'll see in the Focus on Research feature.

FOCUS ON RESEARCH

When Are Children in Self-Care at Risk?

Who were the investigators and what was the aim of the study? Children who spend time after school simply hanging out with peers often have behavioral problems. They may become overly aggressive or become involved in antisocial activities. Gregory Pettit and his colleagues—John Bates, Kenneth Dodge, and Darrell Meece—speculated that extensive after-school peer contact alone is probably not harmful to children; instead, that contact may combine with other factors (e.g., the extent to which parents monitor their children's after-school activities, the safety of their neighborhood) to put some children at risk. Pettit and his colleagues (1999) decided to study the impact of after-school peer contact, parental monitoring, and neighborhood safety on children's aggressive and antisocial behavior.

How did the investigators measure the topic of interest? The investigators measured four variables: after-school peer contact, parental monitoring, neighborhood safety, and children's aggressive and antisocial behaviors.

- *Peer contact* was assessed by asking children to describe what they had done for the 3 hours after school for the previous 2 days; the researchers then determined how much of this time was spent in unsupervised self-care with peers. (In addition, they asked mothers to verify their children's reports.)

- *Parental monitoring* was assessed by asking mothers about their knowledge of their child's whereabouts, the child's companions, and the degree of supervision when children were at friends' homes.

- *Neighborhood safety* was measured by asking mothers about their feelings of safety in their neighborhood and in their own home and whether they thought it was safe for children to play in the neighborhood.

- *Children's aggressive and antisocial behaviors* were measured by having children's teachers complete the Child Behavior Checklist, in which teachers indicate whether various aggressive and antisocial behaviors are typical of the child.

Who were the children in the study? This study was part of the Child Development Project, a longitudinal study of children's social development being conducted in three cities. For this study, the participants included 342 sixth graders and their mothers.

What was the design of the study? This study was correlational because Pettit and his colleagues were interested in the relation that existed naturally between various risk factors (amount of peer contact, parental monitoring, neighborhood safety) and children's aggressive and antisocial behaviors. The overall project is longitudinal (testing began in first grade and continues) and the data reported here are longitudinal because peer contact, parental monitoring, and neighborhood safety were measured in sixth grade but children's behavior was measured in seventh grade.

Were there ethical concerns with the study? No. The investigators obtained written permission from parents beforehand; children gave verbal consent prior to their interviews.

What were the results? Pettit and his colleagues discovered that all factors contributed to children's aggressive and antisocial behaviors. When children lived in safe neighborhoods, aggressive and antisocial behaviors were uncommon and unrelated to parental supervision or amount of time spent with peers. When children lived in unsafe neighborhoods, the pattern differed. As shown in the graph, aggressive and antisocial behaviors were uncommon when children living in unsafe neighborhoods spent relatively less time unsupervised with peers and their parents monitored their activities. (In fact, in this case, aggressive and antisocial behaviors are about as common as for children living in safe neighborhoods.) However, when parents do relatively little monitoring *or* children spend much time unsupervised with peers, aggressive and antisocial behaviors are more common. When parents do relatively little monitoring *and* children spend much time unsupervised with peers, aggressive and antisocial behaviors are even more common.

What did the investigators conclude? When considered alone, amount of time spent with peers, parental monitoring, and neighborhood safety do not have much influence on children's aggressive and antisocial behaviors. However, when risk factors start to multiply, children are much more prone to develop aggressive and antisocial behaviors. As Pettit and his colleagues phrase it, "Our results suggest that unsupervised self-care with peers, in the context of lack of monitoring and unsafe neighborhoods, does in fact forecast the development of [behavioral] problems." (pp. 776-777)

What converging evidence would strengthen these conclusions? Pettit and his colleagues could strengthen their conclusion with three additional kinds of evidence. First, children in the current sample were sixth graders; Pettit and his colleagues could test older children to determine whether risk factors remain the same as children grow. Second, the researchers might repeat the study with children living in rural areas to determine whether different factors place these children at risk. Third, they might supplement their teacher ratings of children's aggressive and antisocial behavior with actual observations of these behaviors in children's schools and homes. ■

This generally rosy picture does not mean that parents should begin self-care without careful planning. Robinson, Rowland, and Coleman (1986) suggest that

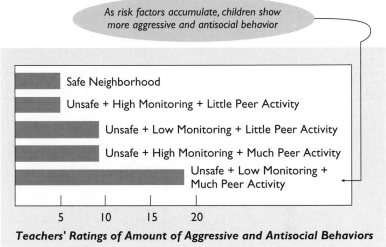

As risk factors accumulate, children show more aggressive and antisocial behavior

Safe Neighborhood

Unsafe + High Monitoring + Little Peer Activity

Unsafe + Low Monitoring + Little Peer Activity

Unsafe + High Monitoring + Much Peer Activity

Unsafe + Low Monitoring + Much Peer Activity

5   10   15   20

Teachers' Ratings of Amount of Aggressive and Antisocial Behaviors

FIG 13-7

parents contemplating self-care for their children should ask themselves several basic questions:

- Is the child old enough and emotionally mature enough, regardless of age, to assume the responsibility of self-care? For example, does the child stay home for short time periods?
- Does the child live in a safe neighborhood where crime is low and community cohesion is high and where neighbors and community facilities can be depended upon as support systems?
- Does the child's self-care arrangement provide for some type of adult supervision, such as a telephone or pager?

If each of these questions can be answered "yes," then self-care will probably work. The next step is to prepare the child for self-care. Children need to know after-school routines (e.g., acceptable ways of getting home from school and how to check in with a parent), rules for their own behavior after school (e.g., acceptable and unacceptable activities), and how to handle emergencies (Peterson, 1989). Posting procedures and emergency phone numbers in a conspicuous location is often enough reassurance for children. With adequate preparation, children can care for themselves after school.

Divorce

Like Jack, the boy in the vignette, many American youngsters' parents divorce. In fact, the following statistics show divorce has become a common part of childhood in America (Burns & Scott, 1994; Goodman, Emery, & Haugaard, 1998; Hernandez, 1997; Stevenson & Black, 1995):

- The divorce rate in the United States tripled between 1960 and 1980 but has remained fairly stable since 1980.
- The United States has, by far, the highest divorce rate in the entire world.
- Annually, approximately 1 million American children have parents who divorce.

According to all theories of child development, divorce is distressing for children because it involves conflict between parents and, usually, separation from one of them. But what aspects of children's development are most affected by divorce? To begin to understand divorce, let's start with a profile of life after divorce.

Family Life After Divorce. After divorce, children usually live with their mothers, though fathers are more likely to get custody today than in previous generations. About 15 percent of children live with their fathers after divorce (Meyer & Garasky, 1993). Not much is known about family life in homes headed by single fathers, so the description on the next few pages is based entirely on research done on children living with their mothers.

When children living with their divorced mothers enter adolescence, mothers are often close to their daughters but often fight with their sons.

The best portrait of family life after divorce comes from the Virginia Longitudinal Study of Divorce and Remarriage conducted by Mavis Hetherington (1988, 1989, 1999; Hetherington, Cox, & Cox, 1982). The Virginia Study traced the lives of families for several years after divorce along with a comparison sample of families with parents who did not divorce.

In the first few months after divorce, many mothers were less affectionate toward their children. They also accepted less mature behavior from their children than they would have before the divorce and had a harder time controlling their children. The overall picture shows both mothers and children suffering the distress of a major change in life circumstances: Children regressed to less mature forms of behavior, and mothers were less able to parent effectively. Fathers, too, were less able to control their children, but this was probably because most were extremely indulgent.

Two years after the divorce, mother-child relationships had improved, particularly for daughters. Mothers were more affectionate. They were more likely to expect age-appropriate behavior from their children and discipline their children effectively. Fathers also demanded more mature behavior of their children, but many had become relatively uninvolved with their children.

Six years after divorce, the children in the study were entering adolescence. Family life continued to improve for mothers with daughters; like the mother and daughter in the photo, many grew extremely close over the years following divorce. Unfortunately, family life was problematic for mothers with sons. These mothers often complained about their sons, who resisted discipline. Many mothers fell into the negative reinforcement trap described in Module 10.2. Mothers and sons were frequently in conflict, and overall, neither was very happy with the other or with the general quality of family life.

Results like these from the Virginia Study underscore that divorce changes family life for parents and children alike. In the next section, we'll look at the effects of these changes on children's development.

Impact of Divorce on Children. Do the disruptions, conflict, and stress associated with divorce affect children? Of course, they do. Having answered this easy question, however, a host of more difficult questions remain: Are all aspects of children's lives affected equally by divorce? Are there factors that make divorce more stressful for some children than others? Finally, *how* does divorce influence development? Some of the most convincing answers to these questions came from research by Amato and Keith (1991), who integrated the results of almost 100 studies involving more than 13,000 preschool- through college-age children. In all areas they reviewed, including school achievement, conduct, adjustment, self-concept, and parent-child relations, children whose parents had divorced fared poorly compared to children from intact families. However, the effects of divorce were greater in the 1960s and 1970s than in later years when divorce became more frequent (and thus more familiar). School achievement, conduct, adjustment, and the like are still affected by divorce but not as much as before the 1980s.

When children of divorced parents become adults, the effects of divorce persist. As adults, children of divorce are more likely to become teenage parents and to become divorced themselves. Also, they report less satisfaction with life and are more likely to become depressed (Furstenberg & Teitler, 1994; Kiernan, 1992). For example, in one study (Chase-Lansdale, Cherlin, & Kiernan, 1995), 11 percent of children of divorce had serious emotional problems as adults compared to 8 percent of children from intact families. The difference is small—11 percent versus 8 percent—but divorce does increase the risk of emotional disorders in adulthood.

Some children are more affected by divorce than others. Amato and Keith's (1991) analysis, for example, showed that although the overall impact of divorce is the same for boys and girls, divorce is more harmful when it occurs during childhood and adolescence than during the preschool or college years. Also, children who are temperamentally more emotional tend to be more affected by divorce (Lengua et al., 1999).

Some children suffer more from divorce because of their tendency to interpret events negatively. We know, from Module 13.4, that two children often have differing interpretations of exactly the same social event. Suppose, for example, that a father forgets to take a child on a promised outing. One child might believe that an emergency prevented the father from taking the child. A second child might believe that the father hadn't really wanted to spend time with the child in the first place and will never make similar plans again. Children who—like the second child—tend to interpret life events negatively are more likely to have behavioral problems following divorce (Mazur et al., 1999).

How exactly does divorce influence development? Researchers have identified several aspects of a child's life that change (Amato & Keith, 1991). First, the absence of one parent means that children lose a role model, a source of parental help and emotional support, and a supervisor. For instance, a single parent may have to choose between helping one child complete an important paper or watching another child perform in a school play. She can't do both and one child will miss out.

> Divorce harms children by making one parent less accessible and by exposing children to economic hardship and to parental conflict.

Second, single-parent families experience economic hardship, which creates stress and often means that activities once taken for granted are no longer available (Goodman et al., 1998). A family may no longer be able to afford books for pleasure reading, music lessons, or other activities that promote child development. Moreover, when a single parent worries about having enough money for food and rent, she has less energy and effort to devote to parenting.

Third, conflict between parents is extremely distressing to children and adolescents (Fincham, 1998), particularly for children who are emotionally insecure (Davies & Cummings, 1998). In fact, many of the problems that are ascribed to divorce are really caused by marital conflict occurring before the divorce (Erel & Burman, 1995; Shaw, Winslow, & Flanagan, 1999). Children like Troy, the boy in the opening vignette whose parents are married but fight constantly, often show many of the same effects associated with divorce.

The impact of divorce on children is summarized in the table.

■■■■ **SUMMARY TABLE**

Impact of Divorce on Children

Aspect of Divorce	Impact
What is affected?	children's school achievement, their conduct, psychological adjustment, self-concept, and relationships with their parents
Who is most affected?	school-age children and adolescents children who are temperamentally emotional children prone to interpret events negatively
Why is divorce harmful?	one parent is less accessible as a role model single-parent families experience economic hardship conflict between parents is distressing

TABLE 13-3

Adjusting to Divorce. Life for children after divorce is *not* all gloom and doom. Children adjust to their new circumstances (Chase-Lansdale & Hetherington, 1990). However, certain factors can ease the transition. Children adjust to divorce more readily if their divorced parents cooperate with each other, especially on disciplinary matters (Hetherington, 1989). **In *joint custody,* both parents retain legal custody of the children.** Children benefit from joint custody, if their parents get along (Maccoby et al., 1993).

Of course, many parents do not get along after a divorce, which eliminates joint custody as an option. Traditionally, mothers have been awarded custody; but in recent years fathers more often have been given custody, especially of sons. This practice coincides with findings that children like Jack, the other boy in the opening vignette, often adjust better when they live with same-sex parents: Boys often fare better with fathers and girls fare better with mothers (Goodman et al., 1998). One reason boys are often better off with their fathers is that boys are likely to become involved in negative reinforcement traps (described in Module 10.2) with their mothers. Another explanation is that both boys and girls may forge stronger emotional relationships with same-sex parents than with other-sex parents (Zimiles & Lee, 1991).

Parents can reduce divorce-related stress and help children adjust to their new life circumstances. Parents should explain together to children why they are divorcing and what their children can expect to happen to them. They should reassure children that they will always love them and always be their parents; parents must back up these words with actions by remaining involved in their children's lives, despite the increased difficulty of doing so. Finally, parents must expect that their children will sometimes be angry or sad about the divorce, and they should encourage children to discuss these feelings with them.

To help children deal with divorce, parents should *not* compete with each other for their children's love and attention; children adjust to divorce best when they maintain good relationships with both parents. Parents should neither take out their anger with each other on their children nor criticize their ex-spouse in front of the children. Finally, parents should not ask children to mediate disputes; parents should work out problems without putting the children in the middle.

Following all these rules all the time is not easy. After all, divorce is stressful and painful for adults, too. But parents owe it to their children to try to follow most of these rules most of the time in order to minimize the disruptive effects of their divorce on their children's development.

Blended Families. Following divorce, most children live in a single-parent household for about 5 years. However, like the adults in the photo, more than two-thirds of men and women eventually remarry (Glick, 1989; Glick & Lin, 1986). **The resulting unit, consisting of a biological parent, stepparent, and children is known as a *blended family.*** Because mothers are more often granted custody of children, the most common form of blended family is a mother, her children, and a stepfather. School-age boys typically benefit from the presence of a stepfather, particularly when he is warm and involved. School-age girls, however, do not adjust readily to their mother's remarriage, apparently because it disrupts the intimate relationship they have established with her. Nevertheless, as boys and girls leave the elementary-school years and enter adolescence, both benefit from the presence of a caring stepfather (Hetherington, 1993).

The best strategy for stepfathers is to be interested in their new stepchildren but avoid encroaching on established relationships. Newly remarried mothers must be careful that their enthusiasm for their new spouse does not come at the expense of time and affection for their children. And both parents and children need to have realistic expectations. The blended family can be successful but it takes effort because of the complicated relationships, conflicting loyalties, and jealousies that usually exist (Anderson et al., 1999).

Much less is known about blended families consisting of a father, his children, and a stepmother, though several factors make a father's remarriage difficult for his children (Brand, Clingempeel, & Bowen-Woodward, 1988). First, fathers are often awarded custody when judges believe that children are unruly and will profit from a father's "firm hand." Consequently, many children living with their fathers do not adjust well to many of life's challenges, which certainly includes a father's remarriage. Second, fathers are sometimes granted custody because they have a particularly close relationship with their children, especially their sons. When this is the case, children sometimes fear that their father's remarriage will disturb their relationship. Finally, noncustodial mothers are more likely than noncustodial fathers to maintain close and frequent contact with their children (Maccoby et al., 1993). The constant presence of the noncustodial mother may interfere with a stepmother's efforts to establish close relationships with her stepchildren, particularly with her stepdaughters.

> Children in blended families often fear that remarriage will disrupt the close relationship they have with their biological parent.

Over time, children adjust to the blended family. If the marriage is happy, most children profit from the presence of two caring adults. Unfortunately, second marriages are slightly more likely than first marriages to end in divorce, so many children relive the trauma. As you can imagine, another divorce—and possibly another remarriage—severely disrupts children's development, accentuating the problems that followed the initial divorce (Capaldi & Patterson, 1991).

Check Your Learning

1. High-quality after-school care has well-trained teachers, a low child-to-teacher ratio, and _____.

2. Self-care is risky when children spend their time _____.

3. In the first few months after divorce, mothers do not parent effectively and children often _____.

4. As children approach adolescence, mother- _____ relationships after a divorce remain positive.

5. The impact of divorce on children became _____ in the 1980s.

6. Divorce affects children's development by depriving them of a role model and source of help, _____, and because the conflict associated with divorce is very distressing for children.

7. Fathers are often awarded custody when _____ or when they have a particularly close relationship with their children.

8. One difficulty for custodial fathers and stepmothers is that the children's biological mother _____.

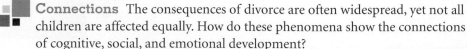 **Connections** The consequences of divorce are often widespread, yet not all children are affected equally. How do these phenomena show the connections of cognitive, social, and emotional development?

Answers: (1) a flexible, age-appropriate curriculum, (2) away from home, unsupervised, (3) revert to immature forms of behavior, (4) daughter, (5) smaller, (6) exposing them to economic hardship, (7) their children are unruly and need a father's firm hand, (8) may remain very close to the children, making it hard for stepmothers to establish relationships with her stepchildren

Chapter Critical Review

1. When gifted children are put in special classes, their intellectual development can be accelerated but sometimes at the expense of their self-esteem. Do you believe the intellectual gain is worth the potential drop in self-esteem? Why or why not?

2. Imagine that you and your child have just moved to a new town. What advice would you give your child about how to make new friends?

3. Suppose first graders want to raise money for a gift for one of their classmates who is in the hospital. Based on what you know about the factors that influence children to be altruistic, how would you help the first graders plan their fund-raising?

4. Relate the description of the development of prosocial behavior in Module 13.3 to cognitive development, as described in Module 12.1.

5. You have been asked to prepare a brochure for mothers who have recently divorced and will have custody of their children. What advice would you give them about what to expect as a single parent?

For more review material, log on to www.prenhall.com/kail

See For Yourself

This assignment may seem like a dream come true—you are being required to watch TV. Pick an evening when you can watch network television programming from 8 P.M. until 10 P.M. (prime time). Your job is to count each instance of (a) physical force by one person against another and (b) threats of harm to compel another to act against his or her will. Select one network randomly and watch the program for 10 minutes. Then turn to another network and watch that program for 10 minutes. Continue changing the channels every 10 minutes until the 2 hours are over. Of course, it won't be easy to follow the plots of all these programs, but you will end up with a wider sample of programming this way. Repeat this procedure on a Saturday morning when you can watch 2 hours of children's cartoons. (Not *South Park!*)

Now simply divide the total number of aggressive acts by 4 to estimate the amount of aggression per hour. Then multiply this figure by 11,688 to estimate the number of aggressive acts seen by an average adolescent by age 19. (Why 11,688? Two hours of daily TV viewing—a very conservative number—multiplied by 365 days and 16 years.) Then ponder the possible results of that very large number. If your parents told you, nearly 12,000 times, that stealing was okay, would you be more likely to steal? Probably. Then what are the consequences of massive exposure to the televised message, "Solve conflicts with aggression?" See for yourself!

For More Information About . . .

ways to help children deal with divorce, try Neil Kalter's *Growing Up with Divorce* (Free Press, 1990), which describes practical ways for parents to help their children deal with the stresses of divorce.

 the impact of media violence on children, visit the Web site of the University of Oregon's Media Literacy On-Line Project:
http://interact.uoregon.edu/MediaLit/HomePage

Key Terms

aggression 407	**friendship** 395	**prosocial behavior** 402
altruism 402	**instrumental aggression** 407	**reactive aggression** 407
blended family 421	**joint custody** 421	**relational aggression** 408
dispositional praise 405	**latchkey children** 415	
empathy 402	**prejudice** 399	

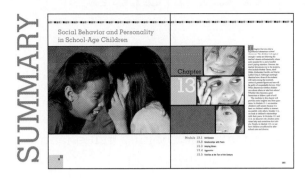

SUMMARY

13.1 Self-Esteem

Measuring Self-Esteem
One of the most common measures of self-esteem is Harter's *Self-Perception Profile for Children* (SPPC), which assesses overall self-worth and self-esteem in five areas: scholastic competence, athletic competence, social acceptance, behavioral conduct, and physical appearance.

Developmental Change in Self-Esteem
During the elementary-school years, self-esteem usually declines somewhat. Self-esteem usually becomes more differentiated as children evaluate themselves on more aspects of self-esteem, including different types of academic skills.

Sources of Self-Esteem
Children's self-esteem is greater when parents are affectionate and involved with them and when parents set rules and discuss disciplinary action. Self-esteem also depends on peer comparisons. Self-esteem is usually greater when children know that others view them positively.

Consequences of Low Self-Esteem
Children with low self-esteem are more likely to have poor peer relations, suffer psychological disorders, act antisocially, and do poorly in school. Therapy can enhance children's self-esteem.

13.2 Relationships with Peers

An Overview of Peer Interactions in School-Age Children
Peer relations improve during the elementary-school years and emphasizing talking, being together, and rough-and-tumble play.

Friendship
Friendships are based on common interests and getting along well. Friends are usually similar in age, sex, race, and attitudes. Children with friends are usually more skilled socially and better adjusted.

Popularity and Rejection
Popular children are socially skilled. They generally share, cooperate, and help others. Some children are rejected by their peers because they are too aggressive. They are often unsuccessful in school and have behavioral problems. Their aggressive style of interacting can often be traced to parents who are belligerent or inconsistent in their discipline.

Prejudice
Prejudice emerges in the preschool years, but declines during the elementary-school years as children's cognitive growth helps them understand that social groups are heterogeneous, not homogeneous. However, older children and adolescents still show prejudice, which

is best reduced by additional constructive exposure to individuals from other social groups.

13.3 Helping Others

Skills Underlying Prosocial Behavior
Children are more likely to behave prosocially when they are able to take others' perspectives and are empathic.

Situational Influences
Children's prosocial behavior is often influenced by situational characteristics. Children more often behave prosocially when they feel that they should and can help, when they are in a good mood, and when they believe that they have little to lose by helping.

Socializing Prosocial Behavior
Parenting approaches that promote prosocial behavior include using reasoning in discipline, modeling prosocial behavior, and praising children for prosocial behavior.

13.4 Aggression

The Nature of Children's Aggressive Behavior
As children grow, physical aggression decreases but verbal aggression increases. Typical forms of aggression include bullying and instrumental and reactive aggression. Overall levels of aggression are fairly stable: Very aggressive children often become involved in criminal activities as adolescents and adults.

Roots of Aggressive Behavior
Children's aggressive behavior has been linked to their parents' use of harsh physical punishment. Other factors that contribute to children's aggression are excessive viewing of televised violence and lack of skill at interpreting others' actions and intentions.

Victims of Aggression
Children who are chronic targets of aggression are often lonely and anxious. Some victims of aggression tend to overreact when provoked; others tend to withdraw and submit. Victimization can be overcome by increasing children's social skills, their self-esteem, and their number of friends.

13.5 Families at the Turn of the Century

After-School Care
Children can care for themselves after school if they are mature enough, live in a safe neighborhood, and are supervised by an adult.

Divorce
Directly after a divorce, a mother's parenting is less effective and her children behave immaturely. Family life typically improves, except for mother-son relationships, which are often filled with conflict.

Divorce harms children in many ways, ranging from school achievement to adjustment. The impact of divorce stems from less supervision of children, economic hardship, and conflict between parents. Children often benefit when parents have joint custody or when they live with the same-sex parent.

When parents remarry, children sometimes have difficulty adjusting because stepparents may disturb existing parent-child relationships.

Development in School-Age Children
IN PERSPECTIVE

■ Continuity
Early development is related to later development but not perfectly

Chapter 13 provides two interesting examples of this theme. First, look at the correlations shown in Table 13.1 on page 398. The correlations between popularity in grades 3–6 and academic achievement, social skill, and self-worth are positive—more popular children tend to have better achievement, social skill, and self-worth. But the correlations are far from a perfect 1. Not all popular children become socially skilled adolescents and not all rejected children become academic failures as adolescents.

As another example, consider the results in the graph on page 408. Among children who were rated by their teachers as the most aggressive, about 40 percent had committed serious crimes by age 30, yet 60 percent had not. Among the children who were rated least aggressive, more than 90 percent were crime-free as adults, but 5 percent had committed serious crimes. Behaving aggressively in childhood definitely increases the odds of criminal activity as an adult, but it does not guarantee it.

■ Nature and Nurture
Development is always jointly influenced by heredity and environment

Chapter 11 focused on physical development and one might naturally expect to see the nature side of the equation being prominent. Yet, it's easy to find example after example in that chapter of the interaction of heredity and environment. First, physical growth—size plainly reflects both heredity and adequate nutrition. Second, obesity—genes clearly make some children more susceptible to obesity but lifestyle factors are important as well. Third, mental retardation—some forms of mental retardation reflect hereditary factors, yet the quality of the person's life definitely hinges on the type of environment. It's easy to fall into the either-or trap in which you conclude that X is due almost entirely to environment or that Y is due largely to heredity. Avoid this trap because there are few aspects of children's elements that can easily replace the X or the Y!

■ Active Child

Children help determine their own development

Cultural differences in school achievement, described in Chapter 12, illustrate this theme. Japanese and Chinese elementary-school children typically like studying (an attitude fostered by their parents), and this makes them quite willing to do homework for 2 or 3 hours nightly. This, in turn, contributes to their high levels of scholastic achievement. American schoolchildren usually abhor homework and do as little of it as possible, which contributes to their relatively lower level of scholastic achievement. Thus, children's attitudes help to determine how they behave, which determines how much they will achieve over the course of childhood and adolescence.

Research on aggressive children, described in Chapter 13, makes the same point. When children are frequently aggressive, their peers dislike them and adults tend to punish them more harshly. This contributes to the aggressive child's view that the world is hostile and that they need to respond aggressively, perpetuating the cycle.

■ Connections

Development in different domains is connected

Let's look first at the impact of social development on cognitive development. We saw in Chapter 12 that egocentrism, a hallmark of preoperational thinking, wanes during the elementary-school years as children have more experience with their peers and begin to realize that others sometimes have different points of view. In addition, as children experience familiar routines, such as baking cookies or eating at fast-food restaurants, they create simple scripts that help them to remember those experiences.

The impact of children's cognitive development on their social development is evident in their peer relationships. As children grow, they get along better with peers. Conflicts are less frequent and when they arise, they're less disruptive. Why? Children's growing cognitive skills allow them to take another child's perspective. This helps them to avoid some conflicts and resolve others, in both cases by considering another child's needs or concerns.

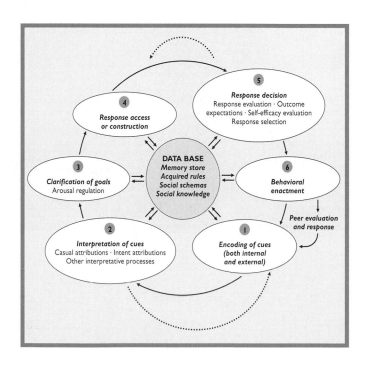

Physical Growth in Adolescents

Chapter

14

At age 11, Dominique Dawes finished 17th in the junior division of the U.S. gymnastics championships; at age 15, she earned a bronze medal in the 1992 Olympics in Barcelona; and, at age 19, she earned a gold medal in the 1996 Olympics in Atlanta.* Dominique's steady march to the top of her sport over her adolescent years is a remarkable feat. Yet, in a less dramatic and less public way, these years are times of profound physical changes for *all* adolescents. In this chapter, we'll examine physical development in adolescence. We begin, in Module 14.1, by describing the important features of physical growth in the teenage years. In Module 14.2, we look at an important byproduct of physical growth in this period—adolescent sexual behavior. Finally, in Module 14.3, we consider some of the necessary ingredients for healthy growth in adolescence.

Module **14.1** Pubertal Changes

14.2 Sexuality

14.3 Health

*And, at age 22, she was a student in my child-development class at the University of Maryland. But I doubt that this was as memorable for her as the Olympic gold medal.

Pubertal Changes

14.1

Pubertal Changes

├ Signs of Physical Maturation

├ Mechanisms of Maturation

└ Psychological Impact
of Puberty

■ **What physical changes occur in adolescence that mark the transition to a mature young adult?**

■ **What factors cause the physical changes associated with puberty?**

■ **How do physical changes affect adolescents' psychological development?**

Pete just celebrated his fifteenth birthday, but, as far as he is concerned, there is no reason to celebrate. Although most of his friends have grown about 6 inches in the past year or so, have a much larger penis and larger testicles, and have mounds of pubic hair, Pete looks just as he did when he was 10 years old. He is embarrassed by his appearance, particularly in the locker room, where he looks like a little boy among men. Won't I ever change? he wonders.

The appearance of body hair, the emergence of breasts, and the enlargement of the penis and testicles are all signs that the child is gone and the adolescent is here. Many adolescents take great satisfaction in these signs of maturity. Others, like Pete, worry through their teenage years as they wait for the physical signs of adolescence.

In this module, we'll begin by describing the normal pattern of physical changes that take place in adolescence and look at the mechanisms responsible for them. Then we'll discover the impact of these physical changes on adolescents' psychological functioning. As we do, we'll learn about the possible effects of Pete's maturing later than this peers.

Signs of Physical Maturation

Puberty **denotes two general types of physical changes that mark the transition from childhood to young adulthood.** The first are bodily changes including a dramatic increase in height and weight, as well as changes in the body's fat and muscle contents. The second concern sexual maturation, including change in the reproductive organs and the appearance of secondary sexual charactersistics, such as facial and body hair and the growth of the breasts.

Physical Growth. When it comes to physical growth, the elementary-school years represent the calm before the adolescent storm. As the graphs on page 431 show, in an average year, a typical 6- to 10-year-old girl or boy gains about 5 to 7 pounds and grows 2 to 3 inches. In contrast, during the peak of the adolescent growth spurt, a girl may gain as much as 20 pounds in a year and a boy, 25 pounds (Tanner, 1970).

The figure also shows that girls typically begin their growth spurt about 2 years before boys do. That is, girls typically start the growth spurt at about age 11, reach their peak rate of growth at about 12, and achieve their mature stature at about age 15. In contrast, boys start the growth spurt at 13, hit peak growth at 14, and reach mature stature at 17. This two-year difference in the growth spurt can lead to awkard social interactions between 11- and 12-year-old boys and girls because, as the photo on page 431 shows, girls are often taller and much more mature-looking than boys.

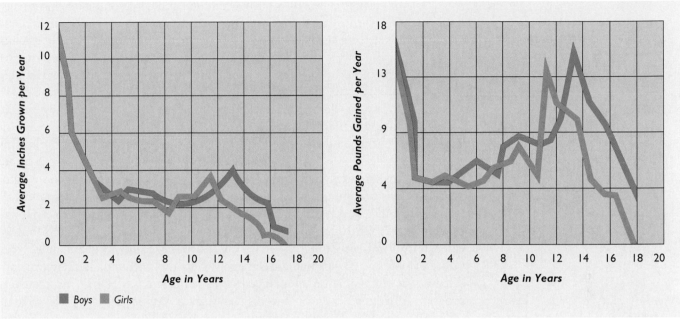

FIG 14-1

Body parts don't all mature at the same rate. Instead, the head, hands, and feet usually begin to grow first, followed by growth in the arms and legs. The trunk and shoulders are the last to grow (Tanner, 1990). The result of these differing growth rates is that an adolescent's body sometimes seems to be out of proportion—teens have a head and hands that are too big for the rest of their body. Fortunately, these imbalances don't last long as the later developing parts catch up.

During the growth spurt, bones become longer (which, of course, is why adolescents grow taller) and become more dense. Bone growth is accompanied by several other changes that differ for boys and girls. Muscle fibers become thicker and denser during adolescence, producing substantial increases in strength. However, muscle growth is much more pronounced in boys than in girls (Smoll & Schutz, 1990). Body fat also increases during adolescence, but much more rapidly in girls than boys. Finally, heart and lung capacity increase more in adolescent boys than in adolescent girls. Together, these changes help to explain why the typical adolescent boy is stronger, quicker, and has greater endurance than the typical adolescent girl.

In the Child Development and Family Policy feature, you'll see how healthy bone growth in adolescence is also an essential defense against a disease that strikes during middle age.

CHILD DEVELOPMENT AND FAMILY POLICY

Preventing Osteoporosis

Osteoporosis **is a disease in which a person's bones become thin and brittle, and, as a consequence, sometimes break.** Although osteoporosis can strike at any age, people over 50 are at greatest risk because bone tissue starts to break down more rapidly than new bone can be formed. About 10 million Americans have osteoporosis. Approximately 80 percent are women because after menopause the ovaries no longer produce estrogen, which guards against bone deterioration.

The best defense against osteoporosis is for adolescents to develop healthy bones, which requires calcium and exercise.

Osteoporosis often has its roots in childhood and adolescence, for this is when bones acquire nearly all of their mass. For bones to develop properly, children and adolescents need to consume approximately 1,300 milligrams of calcium daily. This is the equivalent of about 3 cups of milk, half an ounce of cheese, and a cup of spinach. In addition, children and adolescents should engage in weight-bearing exercise for 30 minutes daily, for at least 5 days a week. Weight-bearing exercises cause bones to carry the body weight, strengthening them. Walking, running, tennis, climbing stairs, aerobic dancing, and cross-country skiing are all good forms of weight-bearing exercise. Swimming, cycling, and rowing (machine or otherwise) do not require the bones to support body weight, so they are not good weight-bearing exercises (although, of course, they do benefit the heart, lungs, and muscles).

Unfortunately, research makes it clear that most adolescents do not get enough calcium or exercise for healthy bone growth. Consequently, the U.S. Centers for Disease Control and Prevention, the U.S. Department of Health and Human Services' Office of Women's Health, and the National Osteoporosis Foundation have collaborated to create the National Bone Health Campaign (NBHC). This multiyear program is designed to encourage 9- to 12-year-olds (girls, especially) to consume more calcium and to exercise more often. Launched in 2001, the NBHC uses several media to communicate with adolescents. Ads appearing in magazines and newspapers and on radio and TV emphasize the importance of healthy bone growth. A Web site includes information about bone health along with games that allow adolescents to learn more about how diet and exercise contribute to healthy growth. Working with partners in the public and private sectors, the NBHC establishes links with local communities, such as providing lesson plans on bone health for science and health teachers.

The NBHC is too new for us to know its effectiveness. (After all, the real test won't come for another 35 to 40 years when the children and young adolescents in the target audience reach the age when they'll be at risk for osteoporosis.) However, by communicating effectively with adolescents and their parents (emphasizing that healthy bones are an essential part of overall healthy, positive growth), the aim is to make sure that adolescents get more calcium and become more active physically, thereby forging the strong bones that are the best defense against osteoporosis. ∎

Sexual Maturation. Not only do adolescents become taller and heavier, they also become mature sexually. **Sexual maturation includes change in *primary sex characteristics*, which refer to organs that are directly involved in reproduction.** These include the ovaries, uterus, and vagina in girls and the scrotum, testes, and penis in boys. **Sexual maturation also includes change in *secondary sex characteristics*, which are physical signs of maturity that are not linked directly to the reproductive organs.** These include the growth of breasts and the widening of the pelvis in girls, the appearance of facial hair and the broadening of shoulders in boys, and the appearance of body hair and changes in voice and skin in both boys and girls.

Changes in primary and secondary sexual characteristics occur in a predictable sequence for boys and for girls. The chart on page 433 shows these changes and the ages when they typically occur for boys and girls. For girls, puberty begins with growth of the breasts and the growth spurt, followed by the appearance of pubic hair. **Menarche, the onset of menstruation, typically occurs at about age 13.** Early menstrual cycles are usually irregular and without ovulation.

For boys, puberty usually commences with the growth of the testes and scrotum, followed by the appearance of pubic hair, the start of the growth spurt, and growth of the penis. **At about age 13, most boys reach *spermarche*, the first spontaneous ejaculation of sperm-laden fluid.** Initial ejaculations often contain relatively few sperm; only months or sometimes years later are there sufficient sperm to fertilize an egg (Chilman, 1983).

Mechanisms of Maturation

What causes the many physical changes that occur during puberty? The pituitary gland is the key player. As I mentioned in Module 5.1, the pituitary helps to regulate physical development by releasing growth hormone. In addition, the pituitary regulates pubertal changes by signaling other glands to secrete hormones. During the early elementary-school years— long before there are any outward signs of puberty—the pituitary signals the adrenal glands to release androgens, initiating the biochemical changes that will produce body hair. A few years later, in girls the pituitary signals the ovaries to release estrogen, which causes the breasts to enlarge, the female genitals to mature, and fat to accumulate. In boys the pituitary signals the testes to release the androgen testosterone, which causes the male genitals to mature and muscle mass to increase.

Although estrogen is often described as a female hormone and androgen as a male hormone, estrogen and androgen are present in both boys and girls. As we've seen, in girls the adrenal glands secrete androgens. The amount is very small compared to that secreted by boys' testes but is enough to influence the emergence of body hair. In boys, the testes secrete very small amounts of estrogen, which explains why some boys' breasts enlarge, temporarily, early in adolescence.

The timing of pubertal events is regulated, in part, by genetics. For example, a mother's age at menarche is related to her daughter's age at menarche (Graber, Brooks-Gunn, & Warren, 1995). However, these genetic forces are strongly influenced by the environment, particularly an adolescent's nutrition and health. In general, puberty occurs earlier in adolescents who are well nourished and healthy than in adolescents who are not. For example, puberty occurs earlier in girls who are heavier and taller but later in girls who are afflicted with chronic illnesses or who receive inadequate nutrition (St. George et al., 1994).

Two other findings underscore the importance of nutrition and health in the onset of puberty. Cross-cultural comparisons reveal that menarche occurs earlier in areas of the world where nutrition and health care are adequate. For example, menarche occurs an average of 2 to 3 years earlier in Western European and North American countries than in African countries. And, within regions, socioeconomic status matters: Girls from affluent homes are more likely to receive adequate nutrition and health care and, consequently, they reach menarche earlier (Steinberg, 1999).

Historical data point to the same conclusion concerning the importance of nutrition and health care. In many industrialized countries around the world, the average age of menarche has declined steadily over the past 150 years. For example, in Europe the average age of menarche was 17 in 1840, compared to about 13 today.

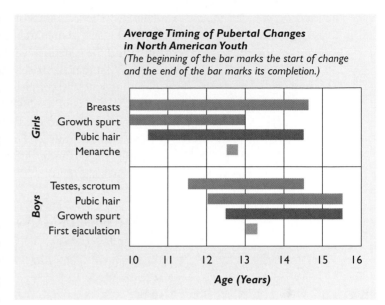

Source: Tanner, 1978.

FIG 14-2

This drop reflects improvements and better health care over this period. In these countries, age of menarche is no longer dropping, which suggests that with adequate nutrition the genetic lower limit for menarche is, on average, about 13 years.

What may surprise you is that the social environment also influences the onset of puberty, at least for girls. Menarche occurs at younger ages in girls who experience much family conflict (Belsky, Steinberg, & Draper, 1991; Moffit et al., 1992). Furthermore, girls who are depressed begin to menstruate at a younger age than girls who are not depressed (Graber et al., 1995). Family conflict and depression may lead to early menarche by affecting the levels of hormones that trigger menstruation (Graber et al., 1995).

Psychological Impact of Puberty

Of course, teenagers are well aware of the changes taking places in their bodies. Not surprisingly, some of these changes affect adolescents' psychological development.

Body Image. Compared to children and adults, adolescents are much more concerned about their overall appearance. Like the girl in the photo, many teenagers look in the mirror regularly, checking for signs of additional physical change. Generally, girls worry more about appearance and are more likely to be dissatisfied with their appearance (Brooks-Gunn & Paikoff, 1993; Unger & Crawford, 1996). In contrast, boys are concerned about their appearance in early adolescence but become more pleased over the course of adolescence as pubertal change takes place (Gross, 1984).

Response to Menarche and Spermarche. Perhaps you remember the scene from the movie *Carrie* in which the title character has her first menstrual period in the shower at school and, not knowing what is happening, is terrified. Fortunately, most adolescent girls today know about menstruation beforehand—usually from discussions with their mothers. Being prepared, their responses are usually fairly mild. Most girls are moderately pleased at this new sign of maturity but moderately irritated by the inconvenience and messiness of menstruation (Brooks-Gunn & Ruble, 1982). Girls usually tell their moms about menarche right away and, after 2 or 3 menstrual periods, tell their friends, too (Brooks-Gunn & Ruble, 1982).

The Cultural Influences feature shows how one Native American culture celebrates menarche.

CULTURAL INFLUENCES

How the Apache Celebrate Menarche

Many cultures have rituals, *rites of passage*, that mark the transition into adulthood. Rites of passage usually follow a script that changes little from year to year. During the ceremony, initiates often wear apparel reserved for the occasion that denotes their special position. For example, generations of high school students have attended a graduation ceremony in which, wearing the traditional gap and gown, they march toward a stage (often accompanied by Edward Elgar's "Pomp and Circumstance") to receive their diplomas.

The Western Apache, who live in the southwest portion of the United States, traditionally have a spectacular ceremony to celebrate a girl's menarche (Basso, 1970). After a girl's first period, a group of older adults decide when the ceremony will be held and select a sponsor—a woman of good character and wealth (she helps to pay for the ceremony) who is unrelated to the initiate. On the day before the ceremony, the sponsor serves a large feast for the girl and her family; at the end of the ceremony, the family reciprocates, symbolizing that the sponsor is now a member of their family.

The ceremony itself begins at sunrise and lasts a few hours. As shown in the photo, the initiate dresses in ceremonial attire. The ceremony includes eight distinct phases in which the initiate dances or chants, sometimes accompanied by her sponsor or a medicine man. The intent of these actions is to transform the girl into Changing Woman, a heroic figure in Apache myth. With this transformation comes longevity and perpetual strength.

The ceremony is a signal to all in the community that the initiate is now an adult. And it tells the initiate herself that her community now expects adultlike behavior from her. ■

Less is known about boys' reaction to spermarche. Most boys know about spontaneous ejactions beforehand and they get their information by reading, not by asking parents (Gaddis & Brooks-Gunn, 1985). When boys are prepared for spermarche, they feel more positive about it. Nevertheless, boys rarely tell parents or friends about this new development (Stein & Reiser, 1994).

Moodiness. Adolescents are often thought to be extraordinarily moody—moving from joy to sadness to irritation to anger over the course of a morning or afternoon. And the source of teenage moodiness is often presumed to be the influx of hormones associated with puberty—hormones running wild. In fact, the evidence indicates that adolescents are moodier than children and adults but not primarily due to hormones (Steinberg, 1999). Scientists often find that rapid increases in hormone levels are associated with greater irritability and greater impulsivity, but the relations tend to be small and are found primarily in early adolescence (Buchanan, Eccles, & Becker, 1992).

If hormones are not responsible, what causes teenage moodiness? Some insights come from an elaborate study in which teenagers carried electronic pagers for a week (Csikszentmihalyi & Larson, 1984). When paged by researchers, the adolescents briefly described what they were doing and how they felt. The record of a typical adolescent is shown on page 436. His mood shifts frequently from positive to negative, sometimes several times in a single day. For this boy, like most of the adolescents in the study, mood shifts were associated with changes in activities and social settings. Teens are more likely to report being in a good mood when with friends or during recreation; they tend to report being in a bad mood when in adult-regulated settings such as school classrooms or at a part-time job. Because adolescents often change activities and social settings many times in a single day, they appear to be moodier than adults.

Rate of Maturation. Although puberty begins at age 10 in the average girl and age 12 in the average boy, for many children puberty begins months or even years before or after these norms. An early-maturing boy might begin puberty at age 11, whereas a late-maturing boy might start at 15 or 16. An early-maturing girl might start puberty at 9, a late-maturing girl, at 14 or 15. For example, the girls shown in the photo are the same age, but only one has reached puberty.

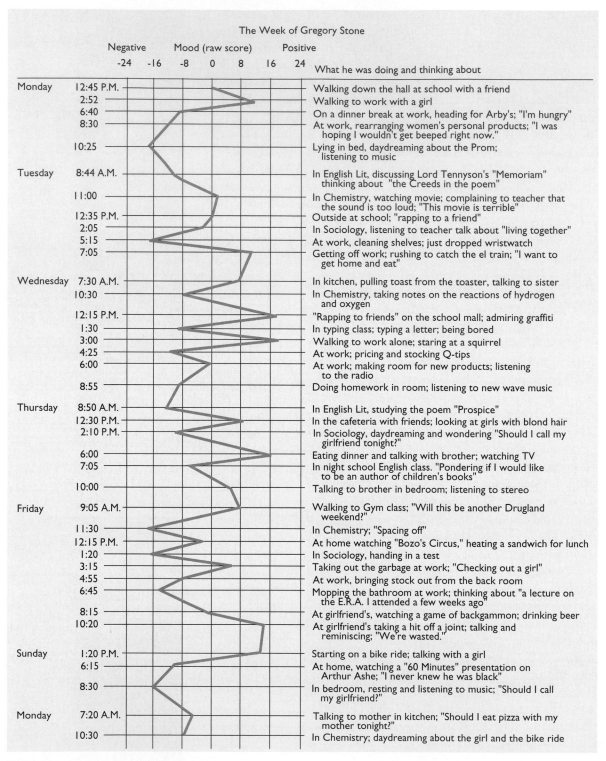

The Week of Gregory Stone

		Negative		Mood (raw score)		Positive		
		-24	-16	-8	0	8	16	24

What he was doing and thinking about

Monday	12:45 P.M.	Walking down the hall at school with a friend
	2:52	Walking to work with a girl
	6:40	On a dinner break at work, heading for Arby's; "I'm hungry"
	8:30	At work, rearranging women's personal products; "I was hoping I wouldn't get beeped right now."
	10:25	Lying in bed, daydreaming about the Prom; listening to music
Tuesday	8:44 A.M.	In English Lit, discussing Lord Tennyson's "Memoriam" thinking about "the Creeds in the poem"
	11:00	In Chemistry, watching movie; complaining to teacher that the sound is too loud; "This movie is terrible"
	12:35 P.M.	Outside at school; "rapping to a friend"
	2:05	In Sociology, listening to teacher talk about "living together"
	5:15	At work, cleaning shelves; just dropped wristwatch
	7:05	Getting off work; rushing to catch the el train; "I want to get home and eat"
Wednesday	7:30 A.M.	In kitchen, pulling toast from the toaster, talking to sister
	10:30	In Chemistry, taking notes on the reactions of hydrogen and oxygen
	12:15 P.M.	"Rapping to friends" on the school mall; admiring graffiti
	1:30	In typing class; typing a letter; being bored
	3:00	Walking to work alone; staring at a squirrel
	4:25	At work; pricing and stocking Q-tips
	6:00	At work; making room for new products; listening to the radio
	8:55	Doing homework in room; listening to new wave music
Thursday	8:50 A.M.	In English Lit, studying the poem "Prospice"
	12:30 P.M.	In the cafeteria with friends; looking at girls with blond hair
	2:10 P.M.	In Sociology, daydreaming and wondering "Should I call my girlfriend tonight?"
	6:00	Eating dinner and talking with brother; watching TV
	7:05	In night school English class. "Pondering if I would like to be an author of children's books"
	10:00	Talking to brother in bedroom; listening to stereo
Friday	9:05 A.M.	Walking to Gym class; "Will this be another Drugland weekend?"
	11:30	In Chemistry; "Spacing off"
	12:15 P.M.	At home watching "Bozo's Circus," heating a sandwich for lunch
	1:20	In Sociology, handing in a test
	3:15	Taking out the garbage at work; "Checking out a girl"
	4:55	At work, bringing stock out from the back room
	6:45	Mopping the bathroom at work; thinking about "a lecture on the E.R.A. I attended a few weeks ago"
	8:15	At girlfriend's, watching a game of backgammon; drinking beer
	10:20	At girlfriend's taking a hit off a joint; talking and reminiscing; "We're wasted."
Sunday	1:20 P.M.	Starting on a bike ride; talking with a girl
	6:15	At home, watching a "60 Minutes" presentation on Arthur Ashe; "I never knew he was black"
	8:30	In bedroom, resting and listening to music; "Should I call my girlfriend?"
Monday	7:20 A.M.	Talking to mother in kitchen; "Should I eat pizza with my mother tonight?"
	10:30	In Chemistry; daydreaming about the girl and the bike ride

FIG 14-3

Maturing early or late has psychological consequences that differ for boys and girls. Several longitudinal studies show that early maturation benefits boys but, most often, not girls. Boys who mature early tend to be more independent and self-confident. They're also more popular with peers. In contrast, girls who mature early often lack self-confidence, are less popular, and are more likely to be depressed and have behavior problems (Ge, Conger, & Elder, 1996; Simmons & Blyth, 1987; Swarr & Richards, 1996).

Early maturation usually benefits boys but not girls.

The differing consequences of early maturation on boys and girls is shown in the results of an extensive longitudinal study of adolescents growing up in Milwaukee during the 1970s (Simmons & Blyth, 1987). The early-maturing boys in this study dated more often and had more positive feelings about their physical development and athletic abilities. The early-maturing girls had more negative feelings about their physical development, received poorer grades, and were more often in trouble in school.

Why does rate of maturation have these consequences? Early maturation may benefit boys like the one in the photo because others perceive them as more mature and may be more willing to give them adultlike responsibilities. Late-maturing boys, like Pete in the vignette at the beginning of this module, are often frustrated because others treat them like little boys instead of like young men. Early maturation may hamper girls' development by leading them to associate with older adolescents who apparently encourage them to engage in age-inappropriate activities, such as drinking, smoking, and sex, for which they are ill-prepared (Ge et al., 1996).

By young adulthood, many of the effects associated with rate of maturation vanish. When Pete, for example, finally matures, others will treat him like an adult and the few extra years of being treated like a child will not be harmful. But for some adolescents, particularly early-maturing girls, rate of maturation can have long-lasting effects. A girl who matures early, is pressured into sex and becomes pregnant, ends up with a different life course than a girl who matures later and is better prepared to resist pressures for sex. Thus, sometimes rate of maturation can lead to events that pick the path that development follows through the rest of life.

Check Your Learning

1. Puberty refers to change in height and weight, to change in the body's fat and muscle contents, and to _____.

2. Girls tend to have their growth spurts about _____ earlier than boys.

3. During adolescent physical growth, boys have greater muscle growth than girls, acquire less _____, and have greater increases in heart and lung capacity.

4. Primary sex characteristics are organs directly related to reproduction whereas secondary sex characteristics are _____.

5. During puberty, the ovaries secrete estrogen, which causes the breasts to enlarge, the genitals to mature, and _____.

6. We know that nutrition and health determine the timing of puberty because puberty is earlier in girls who are taller and heavier, in regions of the world where nutrition and health care are adequate, and _____.

7. Adolescents are moodier than children and adults, primarily because
   _____.

8. Early maturation tends to benefit boys because _____.

 **Nature and Nurture** At first blush, the onset of puberty would seem to be due entirely to biology. In fact, the child's environment influences the onset of puberty. Summarize the ways in which biology and experience interact to trigger the onset of puberty.

more willing to give them adultlike responsibilities.
frequently and their moods track these changes, (8) others treat them as more mature and are
(6) in families that have a high socio-economic status, (7) they change activities and social settings
linked directly to reproductive organs, such as the appearance of body hair, (5) fat to accumulate,
not are that maturity of signs physical (4) fat, (3) years, 2 (2) maturation, sexual (1) **Answers:**

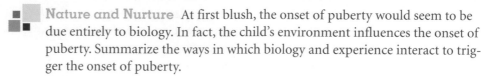

Sexuality

14.2

Sexuality
├ Sexual Behavior
├ Sexual Orientation
├ Sexual Coercion
└ A Final Remark

Learning Objectives

■ Why are some adolescents sexually active? Why do so few use contraceptives?

■ What determines an adolescent's sexual orientation?

■ What circumstances make date rape especially likely?

For 6 months, 15-year-old Rebecca has been dating Michael, a 17-year-old. She thinks she is truly in love for the first time and she often imagines being married to Michael. They have had sex a few times, each time without contraception. It sometimes crosses Rebecca's mind that if she gets pregnant, she could move into her own apartment and begin a family.

Physical changes in adolescence make sexuality a central issue for teenagers. Teens are also preoccupied with sex because it is emphasized on television and in movies and because it is seen as a way to establish adult status. In this module we'll explore the emergence of sexual behavior during adolescence and, as we do, we'll understand why Rebecca, like many teenagers, has sex without contraception.

Sexual Behavior

Many adolescents first experience sexuality in *masturbation,* **self-stimulation of the genitals.** Teenage boys are more likely than girls to masturbate and to begin masturbating at a younger age (Oliver & Hyde, 1993). From masturbation, sex progresses to kissing, to petting above the waist, to petting below the waist, to intercourse. By the end of adolescence, most American boys and girls have had intercourse at least once (Jakobsen, 1997; Miller et al., 1997; Rodgers & Rowe, 1993).

The fact that most American teenagers are sexually experienced by age 19 needs to be put in proper perspective. First, sexually "experienced" is a bit of a misnomer: Most teenagers have had intercourse with only one partner. Second, as recently as the 1960s, most American high school students did *not* have premarital intercourse; adolescent premarital sex became much more common in the 1970s, particularly among girls. Third, there are gender, regional, and ethnic differences in the prevalence of adolescent sexual activity. About 25 percent more boys have had sex than girls, African American adolescents begin sexual activity at a younger age than other groups, and teenagers living in rural areas and inner cities are more likely to be sexually active than teens living in the suburbs (Steinberg, 1999).

Although most boys and girls have sex at some point during adolescence, sexual activity has very different meanings for boys and girls (Brooks-Gunn & Paikoff, 1993). Girls tend to describe their first sexual partner as "someone they love" but boys describe their first partner as a casual date. Girls report stronger feelings of love for their first sexual partner than for a later partner, but boys don't. Girls have mixed feelings after their first sexual experience—fear and guilt mixed with happiness and excitement whereas boys' feelings are more uniformly positive. Finally, when describing their sexual experiences to peers, girls' peers typically express some disapproval but boys' peers typically do not. In short, for boys sexual behavior is viewed as recreational and self-oriented; for girls, sexual behavior is viewed as romantic and is interpreted through their capacity to form intimate interpersonal relationships (Steinberg, 1999).

> Adolescent boys view sex as recreational but adolescent girls view it as romantic.

Why are some adolescents sexually active whereas others are not? A number of factors are involved (Capaldi, Crosby, & Stoolmiller, 1996; Windle & Windle, 1996). Parents' and peers' attitudes toward sex play a key role. In one study of high school students (Treboux & Busch-Rossnagel, 1990), positive attitudes toward sex by parents and friends were associated with students' positive attitudes, which, in turn, were associated with more frequent and more intense sexual behavior. In another study of junior high and high school students (DiBlasio & Benda, 1990), sexually active adolescents believed that their friends were also sexually active. They also thought the rewards of sex (e.g., emotional and physical closeness) outweighed the costs (e.g., guilt and fear of pregnancy or disease). Thus, sexual activity reflects the influence of parents and peers as well as an individual's beliefs and values.

The Focus on Research feature describes a study in which the investigators looked carefully at the nature of parents' influence on adolescent children's sexual behavior.

FOCUS ON RESEARCH

How Parents Influence Adolescents' Sexual Behavior

Who were the investigators and what was the aim of the study? Some adolescents are more active sexually than others. Why? Kim Miller, Rex Forehand, and Beth Kotchick (1999) believed that parents influence their teenage children's sexual behavior through several different mechanisms: the degree to which they monitor their children's behavior, the degree to which they communicate openly with their children, and their own attitudes about sexual behavior. Miller and colleagues examined the role of these factors in accounting for sexual behavior in African American and Hispanic American teenagers.

How did the investigators measure the topic of interest? The researchers used a number of questionnaires to measure the variables of primary interest:

- *Monitoring:* Adolescents were asked the extent to which their mothers know where they are and what they're doing and how well their mothers know their friends.
- *General communication:* Adolescents were asked how easily they can talk to their mothers about anything and about whether their mothers know how to talk to them.
- *Sexual communication:* Adolescents were asked about the extent to which their mothers had talked with them about various sex-related topics, such as AIDS/HIV or different forms of contraception.
- *Attitudes toward sex:* Mothers were asked several questions concerning the extent to which they approved of their children having sex.

In addition, adolescents were asked how frequently they had sexual intercourse and with how many different partners.

Who were the children in the study? The study involved 907 14- to 16-year-old high school students (390 boys and 517 girls). All were either African American or Hispanic American.

What was the design of the study? This study was correlational because Miller and colleagues were interested in the relation that existed naturally between various parental behaviors and adolescent sexual behavior. The study included only one age group (middle adolescents, 14- to 16-year-olds) tested once, so it was neither cross-sectional nor longitudinal.

Were there ethical concerns with the study? No. Before testing began, an experimenter explained the entire project to mothers and to the adolescents. Both then signed forms indicating that they agreed to participate.

What were the results? The investigators looked at how accurately different parental variables predicted adolescents' sexual behavior. The findings were similar for boys and girls, for African Americans and Hispanic Americans, and for predicting frequency of intercourse and number of partners. Specifically, adolescent sexual behavior was related to monitoring, general communication, and parents' attitudes toward sex, but not to sexual communication. Adolescents tended to be less active sexually (less frequent sex and fewer partners) when parents monitored their children's behavior carefully, communicated with them effectively, and did not endorse adolescent sex. Talking about sex-related issues per se was unrelated to adolescents' sexual behavior.

What did the investigators conclude? Parents definitely influence their adolescent children's sexual behavior, a result that seems obvious enough. What's surprising, however, is the number of distinct ways in which parents influence their children's sexual behavior. To reduce teenage sex, parents should actively discourage it, know what adolescents do in their free time (and with whom), and have open, relaxed, and secure lines of communication with their children. Teen sex is most likely when parents approve of it, don't pay much attention to what their kids are doing, and rarely talk with them.

What converging evidence would strengthen these conclusions? To follow up on Miller and colleagues' findings concerning parental influence, researchers could pursue two paths. First, Miller and colleagues tested African American and Hispanic American teens. It would be useful to know whether the results would be similar for other groups such as Asian Americans and European Americans. Second, most of the information about mothers was provided by their children (e.g., degree of monitoring, extent of communication on sex-related topics). It would be useful to have these reports corroborated by (a) reports from mothers themselves, (b) reports from fathers, and (c) for some variables such as monitoring, observational data. ■

Sexually Transmitted Diseases. Adolescent sexual activity is worrisome because a number of diseases are transmitted from one person to another through sexual intercourse. For example, herpes and genital warts are two common viral infections. Other diseases, like chlamydia, syphilis, and gonorrhea are caused by bacteria. Although these diseases can have serious complications if left untreated, they are usually cured readily with penicillin. In contrast, the prognosis is bleak for individuals who contract the human immunodeficiency virus (HIV), which typically leads to acquired immunodeficiency syndrome (AIDS). In persons with AIDS, the immune system is no longer able to protect the body from infections and they often die from one of these infections.

> Adolescents rarely use contraceptives during sex, which explains why so many teens contract sexually-transmitted diseases and become pregnant.

Young adults—those in their 20s—account for roughly 15 percent of all AIDS cases in the United States (National Center for Health Statistics, 1997). Most of these people contracted the disease during adolescence. Many factors make adolescents especially susceptible to AIDS. Teenagers and young adults are more likely than older adults to engage in unprotected sex and to use intravenous drugs—common pathways for the transmission of AIDS.

Teenage Pregnancy and Contraception. Adolescents' sexual behavior is a cause for concern because approximately 1 in 10 American adolescent girls becomes pregnant. About 60 percent of pregnant teenagers give birth; the remaining 40 percent abort the pregnancy (Henshaw, 1993). The result is that roughly 500,000 babies are born to American teenagers annually. As you can see in the graph, African American and Hispanic American adolescents are the most likely to become teenage moms; Asian American adolescents are the least likely (Ventura et al., 1997).

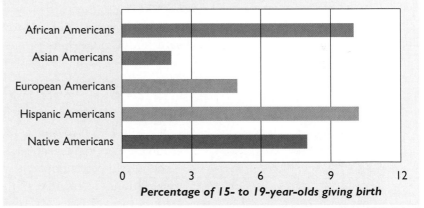

Percentage of 15- to 19-year-olds giving birth

FIG 14-4

As I described in Module 4.2, teenage mothers and their children usually face bleak futures. If this is the case, why do so many teens become pregnant? The answer is simple: Few sexually active teenagers use birth control. Those who do, often use ineffective methods, such as withdrawal, or practice contraception inconsistently (Besharov & Gardiner, 1997; National Research Council, 1987).

Adolescents' infrequent use of contraceptives can be traced to several factors (Adler, 1994; Gordon, 1996):

- *Ignorance:* Many adolescents are seriously misinformed about the facts of conception. For example, many do not know when conception is most likely to occur during the menstrual cycle.

- *Illusion of invulnerability:* Too many adolescents deny reality. They believe they are invincible—"It couldn't happen to me"—and that only others become pregnant.

- *Lack of motivation:* For some adolescent girls, becoming pregnant is appealing. Like Rebecca in the vignette, they think having a child is a way to break away from parents, gain status as an independent-living adult, and have "someone to love them."

- *Lack of access:* Some teenagers do not know where to obtain contraceptives and others are embarrassed to buy them. Still others don't know how to use contraceptives.

One attack on teen pregnancy involves making contraceptives more readily available. In many middle schools and high schools throughout the United States, students can obtain contraceptives, usually by visiting a health clinic located in the school. Many programs require parents' permission for students to obtain contraceptives, but some do not.

Providing contraceptives in schools is not the only solution to teenage pregnancy. Broader educational programs that present the truth about sex, teenage pregnancy, AIDS, and contraception can be effective for adolescents, who too often rely on peers for information about health and sexuality (Boyer & Hein, 1991). Such programs not only teach the relevant biology but also include a focus on responsible sexual behavior or abstention from premarital sex altogether (Dryfoos, 1990).

One effective program is called Postponing Sexual Involvement (Howard & McCabe, 1990). Under the direction of trained, older adolescents, students discuss the pressures to become involved sexually, common "lines" that teens use to induce others to have sex, and strategies for responding to those lines. Accompanying the discussions are opportunities for students to practice the strategies in role-playing sessions. Students who participate in these programs are less likely to have intercourse; when they do have intercourse, they are more likely to use contraceptives (Howard & McCabe, 1990).

Sexual Orientation

For most adolescents, dating and romance involve members of the opposite sex. However, as part of the search to establish an identity, many adolescents wonder, at least in passing, if they are homosexual. In fact, roughly 15 percent of adolescent boys and girls report emotional and sexual attractions to a member of their own sex (D'Augelli, 1996). For most adolescents, these experiences are simply a part of the larger process of role experimentation common to adolescence. However, like the teens in the photo, the adolescent search for self-definition leads to roughly 5 percent of teenage boys and girls identifying themselves as gay in their sexual orientation. This identification usually occurs in mid-adolescence, but not until young adulthood do most gay individuals express their sexual orientation publicly (D'Augelli, 1996).

Why do gay adolescents wait so long—3 to 5 years—before declaring their sexual orientation? Many believe, correctly, that their peers are not likely to support them (Newman & Muzzonigro, 1993). For example, in one national survey, only 40 percent of 15- to 19-year-old boys agreed that they could befriend a gay person (Marsiglio, 1993). Adolescents who said that they could not befriend a gay peer were most often younger, identified themselves as religious fundamentalists, and had parents who were less educated.

The roots of sexual orientation are poorly understood. Scientists have, however, discredited several theories of sexual orientation. Research (Bell, Weinberg, & Hammersmith, 1981; Golombok & Tasker, 1996; Patterson, 1992) shows that each of the following is *false*:

> ## Biology plays an important role in determining sexual orientation.

- Sons become gay when raised by a domineering mother and a weak father.
- Girls become lesbians when their father is their primary role model.
- Children raised by gay or lesbian parents usually adopt their parents' sexual orientation.
- Gay and lesbian adults were, as children, seduced by an older person of their sex.

If all these ideas are false, what determines a person's sexual orientation? The exact factors probably differ from one person to the next, but many scientists today believe that biology plays an important role. Some evidence suggests that heredity and hormones influence sexual orientation (Hamer et al., 1993; Meyer-Bahlburg et al., 1995). One intriguing idea (Bem, 1996) is that genes and hormones don't produce sexual orientation per se but lead to temperaments that affect children's preference for same- and opposite-sex activities. Children who do not enjoy gender-typical activities come to see themselves as different, ultimately leading to a different gender identity.

Though the origins of sexual orientation may not be obvious, it is clear that gay and lesbian individuals face many special challenges. Their family and peer relationships are often disrupted. They are often attacked, both verbally and physically. Given these problems, it's not surprising that gay and lesbian youth often experience mental health problems such as anxiety and depression (D'Augelli, 1996; Hershberger & D'Augelli, 1995; Rotheram-Borus et al., 1995).

In recent years, social changes have helped gay and lesbian youth respond more effectively to these unique challenges. The official stigma associated with being gay or lesbian was removed in 1973 when the American Psychological Association and the American Psychiatric Association declared that homosexuality was not a psychological disorder. Other helpful changes include more (and more visible) gay role models, like the couple in the photo on page 442, and more numerous centers in cities for gay and lesbian youth. These resources are making it easier for gay and lesbian youth to understand their sex orientation and to cope with the many other demands of adolescence.

Sexual Coercion

Cindy reported that her date "lifted up my skirt and took off my panties when I was drunk. Then he laid down on top of me and went to work." **Like Cindy, many adolescent and young women are forced to have sexual intercourse by males they know, a situation known as *date rape* or *acquaintance rape* (Ogletree, 1993).** Traditional sex-role socialization helps to set the stage for sexual coercion. Males learn that an intense sexual drive is a sign of masculinity. Females learn that being sexually attractive is one way to gain a male's attention. However, "good girls" are expected to be uninterested in sex and to resist attempts for sex. Both males and females learn these expectations; consequently, males often assume that a female says no because she is supposed to say no, not because she really means it (Muehlenhard, 1988). Unless, and sometimes even if, a woman's communications are crystal clear—

STOP!! I *don't* want to do this!—an adolescent or young adult male will often assume, incorrectly and egocentrically, that her interest in sex matches his own (Kowalski, 1992).

A number of circumstances increase the possibility that adolescent and young adult males will misinterpret or ignore a female's verbal or nonverbal communications regarding sexual intent. For example, heavy drinking usually impairs a female's ability to send a clear message and makes males less able and less inclined to interpret such messages (Abbey, 1991). Similarly, when a female dresses provocatively, males assume that she is interested in sex and may ignore what she says (Cassidy & Hurrell, 1995). Yet another factor is a couple's sexual history. If a couple has had sex previously, the male may tend to dismiss his partner's protests, interpreting them as fleeting feelings that can be overcome easily (Shotland & Goodstein, 1992).

> Date rape is more likely when a couple has been drinking or has had sex previously.

The Making Children's Lives Better feature describes several ways to prevent date rape.

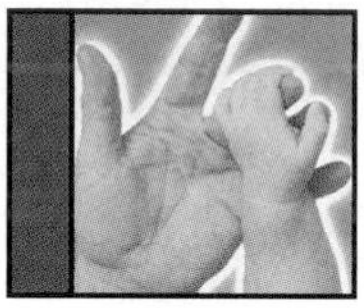

MAKING CHILDREN'S LIVES BETTER

Preventing Date Rape

Most approaches to date rape emphasize the importance of communication. The ad is part of one approach to encourage males and females to communicate about sex. Date-rape workshops represent another approach (Feltey, Ainslie, & Geib, 1991). Most emphasize the need for females to be clear and consistent in expressing their intent. Before engaging in sex, males need to understand a female's intentions, not simply assume that they know. Here are some guidelines that are often presented at such workshops; you may find them useful (Allgeier & Allgeier, 1995):

1. Know your own sexual policies. Decide when sexual intimacy is acceptable for *you*.

2. Communicate these policies openly and clearly.

3. Avoid being alone with a person until you have communicated these policies and believe that you can trust the person.

4. Avoid using alcohol or other drugs when you are with a person with whom you do not wish to become sexually intimate.

5. If someone tries to force you to have sex, make your objections known: Talk first, but struggle and scream if necessary. ∎

A Final Remark

In concluding this module, it's important to recognize that sexual behavior and sexuality are enormously complicated and emotionally charged issues, even for adults. Adults who deal with adolescents need to recognize this complexity and help provide teenagers with skills for dealing with the issues involved in their emerging sexuality.

RPEP
Rape Prevention Education Program

Women don't cause acquaintance rape. Rapists do.

But there are things you can do to reduce the risks of being raped by someone you know.

1 STAY away from men who: put you down a lot, talk negatively about women, think that "girls who get drunk should know what to expect," drink or use drugs heavily, are physically violent, don't respect you or your decisions.

2 SET sexual limits and intentions. Communicate them early and firmly.

3 DON'T pretend you don't want to have sex if you really do.

4 STAY sober.

5 DON'T make men guess what you want. Tell them.

6 REMAIN in control. Pay your own way. Make some of the decisons.

7 LISTEN to your feelings.

8 FORGET about being a "nice girl" as soon as you feel threatened.

9 LEARN self-defense. Know how to yell. Take assertiveness training.

10 TAKE care of yourself. Don't assume others will.

For more information, please phone 893-3778
A service of the Women's Center and Police Department, University of California, Santa Barbara

FIG 14-5

Check Your Learning

1. Most adolescents first experience sexuality through _____.

2. Boys more often view sexual behavior as _____ but girls view sex as romantic.

3. When parents approve of sex, their adolescent children are _____.

4. Adolescents and young adults are at particular risk for contracting AIDS because they _____ and use intravenous drugs.

5. Adolescents often fail to use contraception, due to ignorance, the illusion of invulnerability, lack of motivation, and _____.

6. Not until _____ do most gay individuals express their sexual orientation publicly.

7. _____ apparently plays a key role in determining sexual orientation.

8. Date rape is more likely if either partner has been drinking and if the couple _____.

■ **Connections** Sexually-active teenagers typically do not use contraceptives. How do the reasons for this failure show connections between cognitive, social, and emotional development?

Answers: (1) masturbation, (2) recreational, (3) more likely to be active sexually, (4) engage in unprotected sex, (5) lack of access to contraceptives, (6) young adulthood, (7) Biology, (8) has had sex previously.

Health

14.3
Health
├ Nutrition
├ Physical Fitness
└ Threats to Adolescent Well-Being

Learning Objectives

■ **What are the elements of a healthy diet for adolescents? Why do some adolescents suffer from eating disorders?**

■ **Do adolescents get enough exercise? What are the pros and cons of participating in sports in high school?**

■ **What are common obstacles to healthy growth in adolescence?**

Dana had just started the seventh grade and was overjoyed that he could try out for the junior high football team. He'd always excelled in sports and was usually the star when he played football on the playground or in gym class. But this was Dana's first opportunity to play on an actual team—with a real helmet, jersey, pads, and everything—and he was jazzed! Dana's dad played football in high school and thought Dana could benefit from the experience. His mom wasn't so sure—she was afraid that he'd be hurt and have to deal with the injury for the rest of his life.

Adolescence is a time of transition when it comes to health. On the one hand, teens are much less affected by the minor illnesses that would have kept them at home, in bed, as children. On the other hand, teens are at much greater risk for harm because of their own unhealthy and risky behaviors. In this module, we'll look at some of the factors essential to adolescent health and see whether Dana's mother should be worried about sports-related injuries. We'll start with nutrition.

Nutrition

The physical growth associated with puberty means that the body has special nutritional needs. A typical teenage girl should consume about 2,200 calories per day; a typical boy should consume about 2,700 calories. (The exact levels depend upon a number of factors, including body composition, growth rate, and activity level.) Teenagers also need calcium for growth and iron to make extra hemoglobin, the matter in red blood cells that carries oxygen. Boys need additional hemoglobin because of their increased muscle mass; girls need hemoglobin to replace that lost during menstruation.

Unfortunately, although many U.S. teenagers consume enough calories each day, too much of their intake consists of fast food rather than well-balanced meals. The result of too many meals like the one shown in the photo—burgers, french fries, and a shake—is that teens may get inadequate iron or calcium and far too much sodium and fat. With inadequate iron, teens are often listless and moody; with inadequate calcium, bones may not develop fully, placing the person at risk later in life for osteoporosis.

Fast food is not the only risky diet common among adolescents. Many teenage girls worry about their weight and are attracted to the "lose 10 pounds in 2 weeks!" diets advertised on TV and in teen magazines. Many of these diets are flatly unhealthy—they deprive youth of the many substances necessary for growth. Similarly, for philosophical or health reasons, many adolescents decide to eliminate meat from their diets. Vegetarian diets can be healthy for teens, but only when adolescents do more than eliminate meat. That is, vegetarians needs to adjust the rest of their diet to ensure that they have adequate sources of protein, calcium, and iron.

Other food-related problems common in adolescence are two similar eating disorders, anorexia and bulimia.

Anorexia and Bulimia. Tracey Gold, an actress on the TV program *Growing Pains,* had to leave the show in the early 1990s. She had begun dieting compulsively, had withered away to a mere 90 pounds, and had to be hospitalized (Sporkin, Wagner, & Tomashoff, 1992). Tracey suffered from an eating disorder. **Anorexia nervosa is a disorder marked by a persistent refusal to eat and an irrational fear of being overweight.** Individuals with anorexia nervosa have a grossly distorted image of their own body. Like the girl in the photo, they claim to be overweight despite being painfully thin (Wilson, Hefferman, & Black, 1996).

Anorexia is a very serious disorder, often leading to heart damage. Without treatment, as many as 15 percent of adolescents with anorexia die (Wicks-Nelson & Israel, 1991). The Real Children feature describes a teenage girl with anorexia.

REAL CHILDREN

Layla's Battle with Anorexia

Layla had always been a pleasant and obedient child. She was an above-average student in school, though she could never quite make the honor roll as her older brothers always did. At 15, Layla was 5 feet, $4\frac{1}{2}$ inches tall and weighed 120 pounds. Her weight was perfectly normal for her height, but she decided she was fat and began to diet. Over the next year, Layla lost 35 pounds. She looked pale, tired, and wasted, and she no longer menstruated. Layla insisted she looked fine and that nothing was wrong with her, but her parents and family doctor were so concerned they insisted she be hospitalized. Forced to eat regular meals in the hospital, Layla gained some weight and was sent home. But this cycle was repeated several times over the next 2 years: Layla would diet to the point that she looked like a skeleton draped in skin, and then she would be hospitalized. In her generally weakened condition, Layla developed mononucleosis and hepatitis; ultimately her liver and kidneys failed. Three days before her 18th birthday, Layla had a heart attack and died. ■

A related eating disorder is bulimia nervosa. **Individuals with *bulimia nervosa* alternate between binge eating—periods when they eat uncontrollably—and purging through self-induced vomiting or with laxatives.** The frequency of binge eating varies remarkably among people with bulimia nervosa, from a few times a week to more than 30 times. What's common to all is the feeling that they cannot stop eating (Mizes, 1995).

Anorexia and bulimia are alike in many respects. Both disorders primarily affect females. Girls are 10 times more likely than boys to be affected (Wilson et al., 1996). Also, both disorders emerge in adolescence and typically in girls who are well behaved, conscientious, good students (Attie, Brooks-Gunn, & Petersen, 1990).

Why do girls like Layla develop anorexia or bulimia? It probably won't surprise you that nature and nurture both play a role. Let's start with nurture and cultural ideals of the female body. In many industrialized cultures—and certainly in the United States—the ideal female body is tall and slender. As girls enter adolescence, these cultural norms become particularly influential. Also during adolescence, girls experience a "fat spurt," gaining about 25 pounds, most of it fat. Though this pattern of growth is normal, some girls unfortunately perceive themselves as overweight and begin to diet (Halpern et al., 1999). This is especially the case when the girl's mother is preoccupied with her own weight (Attie et al., 1990). Faced with a cultural value of being thin and a change in their bodies, adolescent girls believe they are fat and try to lose weight.

Family dynamics also contribute to anorexia. Adolescent girls are more prone to anorexia if their parents are autocratic, leaving their adolescent daughters with little sense of self-control. Dieting allows the girls to assert their autonomy and achieve an individual identity (Graber et al., 1994; Swarr & Richards, 1996). Layla, for example, who was entering mid-adolescence and seeking greater personal autonomy, enjoyed the sense of control over her weight that dieting gave her.

Cultural emphasis on thinness, combined with a regimented home life, can explain many cases of anorexia. Of course, most teenage girls growing up in regimented homes in the United States do *not* become anorexic, which raises the question of biological factors. Twin and family studies point to an inherited predisposition for anorexia and bulimia, perhaps in the form of personality that

> Anorexia and bulimia, eating disorders that affect teenage girls, can be linked to family dynamics and to cultural ideals concerning the female body.

tends to be rigid and anxious (Strober, 1995). Thus, anorexia is most likely to develop in girls who inherit the predisposition, who internalize cultural ideals of thinness, and whose parents grant them little independence.

Physical Fitness

Being physically active promotes mental and physical health, both during adolescence and throughout adulthood. Individuals who regularly engage in physical activity reduce their risk for obesity, cancer, heart disease, diabetes, and psychological disorders including depression and anxiety. Regular activity typically means exercising for 30 minutes, at least 3 times a week, at a pace that keeps an adolescent's heart rate at about 140 beats per minute. Running, vigorous walking, swimming, aerobic dancing, biking, and cross-country skiing are all examples of activities that can provide this level of intensity.

Unfortunately, all the evidence indicates that most adolescents rarely get enough exercise. For example, in one study the researchers (Kann et al., 1995) asked high school students whether they had exercised at least 3 times for 20 minutes during the past week, at a level that made them sweat and breathe hard. In ninth grade, about 75 percent of boys and 65 percent of girls said they had; by twelfth grade, these figures had dropped to 65 percent for boys and 40 percent for girls. Part of the problem here is that, for many high school students, physical-education classes provide the only regular opportunity for exercise, yet a minority of high school students are enrolled in physical education and most who are enrolled do not attend daily.

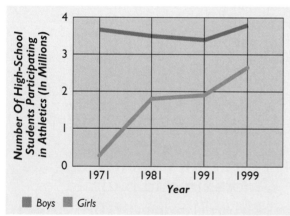

FIG 14–6

Many teenagers get exercise by participating in organized sports. Today, approximately 3.9 million boys and 2.7 million girls participate in sports. Although about 1.2 million more boys than girls participate, the graph shows that the difference is smaller than it once was. In 1971, 3.7 million boys participated, compared to only about 300,000 girls. However, in 1972 the U.S. government required that schools receiving public funds provide equal educational and athletic opportunities for boys and girls. Since that time, girls' participation in sports has grown steadily (National Federation of State High School Associations, 2000).

The most popular sport for boys is football; more than a million boys play high school football. The next most popular sports are basketball, track and field, and baseball. For girls, the most popular sport is basketball; approximately a half million girls, like those in the photo, play high school basketball. The next most popular sports are track and field, volleyball, and fast-pitch softball.

Participating in sports has many benefits for youth. In addition to improved physical fitness, sports can enhance participants' self-esteem and can help them to learn initiative (Larson, 2000; Whitehead & Corbin, 1997). Athletes can also learn about teamwork and competitiveness. At the same time, there are some potential costs. About 15 percent of high school athletes will be injured and require some medical treatment. Boys are most likely to be injured while playing football or wrestling; girls are injured while participating in cross-country or soccer (Rice, 1993). Fortunately, most of these injuries are not serious ones but are more likely to involve bruises or

strained muscles (Nelson, 1996). Dana's mom can rest easy; the odds are that he won't be injured and if he is, it won't be serious.

A more serious problem is the use of illegal drugs to improve performance (American Academy of Pediatrics, 1997). Some athletes use anabolic steroids, drugs that are chemically similar to the male hormone testosterone, to increase muscle size and strength and to promote more rapid recovery from injury. Approximately 5 to 10 percent of high school boys and 1 to $2\frac{1}{2}$ percent of high school girls report having used anabolic steroids. This is disturbing because steroid use can damage the liver, reproductive system, skeleton, and cardiovascular system (increasing blood pressure and cholesterol levels); in addition, use of anabolic steroids is associated with mood swings, aggression, and depression. Parents, coaches, and health professionals need to be sure that high school athletes are aware of the dangers of steroids and should encourage youth to meet their athletic goals through alternative methods that do not involve drug use (American Academy of Pediatrics, 1997).

Threats to Adolescent Well-Being

Every year, approximately 1 U.S. adolescent out of 1,000 dies. Relatively few die from disease; instead, they are killed in accidents, typically involving automobiles or firearms. The pie charts on page 450 show that the pattern of adolescent death depends, to a very large extent, on gender and ethnicity. Among boys, most deaths are due to accidents involving motor vehicles or firearms. For European American and Hispanic American boys, motor vehicles are more deadly than firearms, but the reverse is true for African American boys. Among girls, most deaths are due to natural causes or accidents involving motor vehicles. For European American girls, motor vehicle accidents account for nearly half of all deaths; for African American girls, natural causes account for nearly half of all deaths; and for Hispanic American girls, natural causes and motor vehicles account for about the same number of deaths and together account for about two-thirds of all deaths (Federal Interagency Forum on Child and Family Statistics, 2000).

Sadly, many of these deaths are completely preventable. Deaths in automobile accidents are often linked to driving too fast, drinking alcohol, and not wearing seat belts (U.S. Department of Health and Human Services, 1997). And deaths due to firearms are often linked to all-to-easy access to firearms in the home (Rivara & Grossman, 1996).

Adolescent deaths from accidents represent another instance of a theme that we've seen earlier in this chapter and will see again in Chapter 15: Many adolescents take risks that adults often find unacceptable. Teens, like the boy in the photo, take unnecessary risks while riding skateboards, scooters, or bicycles. They drive cars recklessly, engage in unprotected sex, and sometimes use illegal and dangerous drugs. Although it is tempting to call such behavior stupid or irrational, research suggests that adolescents and adults often make decisions similarly, even though the outcome of that decision-making process sometimes differs for adolescents and adults (Fischhoff & Quadrel, 1995). Specifically, adolescents and adults typically determine:

- the alternative courses of action available
- the consequences of each action
- the desirability and likelihood of these consequences

Then they integrate this information to make a decision.

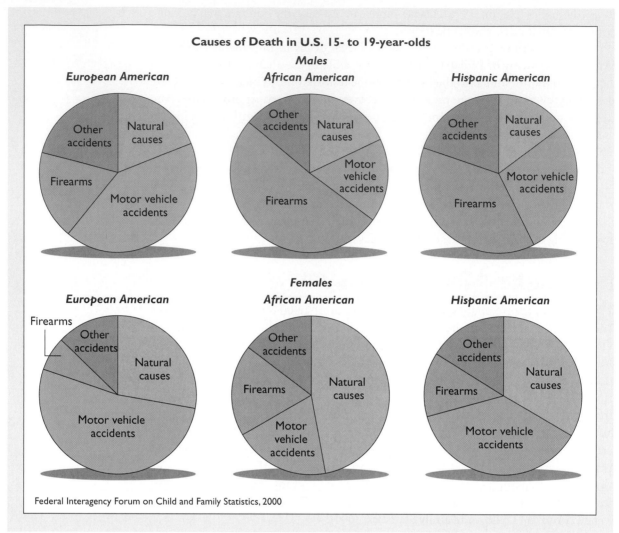

Causes of Death in U.S. 15- to 19-year-olds

Males

European American · African American · Hispanic American

Females

European American · African American · Hispanic American

Federal Interagency Forum on Child and Family Statistics, 2000

FIG 14–7

To see this decision making in action, consider a teen deciding whether to drive home from a party with friends who have been drinking alcohol. She decides that she has two alternatives: (1) try to find a ride with people who haven't been drinking but that she doesn't know well, or (2) ask her parents to come get her. Her analysis might run something like this:

> **Adolescents' decision-making is similar to adults' decision-making, but adolescents place greater emphasis on the social consequences of actions.**

If I go home with my friends, I won't upset them (+) but I might be in an accident (−). If I go home with other people, I'll definitely make my friends mad (−) but will probably make it home safely (+). If I call my parents, I'll definitely upset my friends (−), probably annoy other people at the party (−) but I'll get home safely (+).

This basic analysis is sound and not much different from what an adult might do. The difference comes in the adolescent's weighting of the desirability of different consequences. Adolescents are likely to place greater emphasis on the social consequences of their decisions, such as upsetting their friends and less emphasis on the health consequences, such as getting home safely (Steinberg, 1999). As we'll see in Module 16.2, they're particularly likely to consider these social consequences when the standards for appropriate behavior are not clear, as they often are when it comes to drinking and to having sex.

Check Your Learning

1. An adolescent's diet should contain adequate calories, _____, and iron.

2. A vegetarian diet can be healthy for teens, but only when adolescents _____.

3. Individuals with _____ alternate between binge eating and purging.

4. Teenage girls are more prone to anorexia when their parents _____.

5. Regular physical activity helps to promote _____ and physical health.

6. Girls' participation in sports has grown steadily since 1972 when _____.

7. Some teenage athletes use anabolic steroids to increase muscular strength and to _____.

8. More teenage girls die from _____ than any other single cause.

9. Because they place greater emphasis on the _____ consequences of their actions, adolescents make what adults think are risky decisions.

Active Children How does adolescent risk-taking illustrate the theme that children help to shape their own development?

Answers: (1) calcium, (2) adjust the rest of their diet so they consume adequate protein, calcium, and iron, (3) bulimia nervosa, (4) are autocratic and leave them little sense of self-control, (5) mental health, (6) the U. S. government required that schools receiving public funds provide equal athletic opportunities for boys and girls, (7) promote more rapid recovery from an injury, (8) automobile accidents, (9) social.

Chapter Critical Review

1. In what respects is the psychological impact of puberty the same for boys and girls? In what respects does it differ?

2. Describe a rite of passage that you passed through during puberty. It may be one that is unique to your ethnic group, or one that is common in North American society. What aspect of adulthood did it mark? How did it affect your self-concept?

3. How can Bem's theory of the development of sexual identity (Module 14.2) be explained in terms of the themes developed in this book?

4. Imagine that you are an "expert" who has been asked to talk to a class of sixth graders about sexual behavior. Decide what you would tell the class and how you would do it.

5. Many teenagers do not eat well-balanced meals and many do not get enough exercise. What would you do to improve teenagers' dietary and exercise habits?

For more review material, log on to www.prenhall.com/kail

See For Yourself

In recent years, colleges and universities in the United States have taken a more visible and vigorous stance against sexual assault and date rape. Many now offer a range of programs and services designed to prevent sexual assault and to assist those who are victims of it. Most universities have an office—usually associated with student services—dealing with women's issues. These offices offer educational programs as well as counseling and confidential advice to women with problems. Some campuses sponsor sexual-assault awareness days that include workshops, films, and plays planned to promote greater understanding of the issues associated with sexual assault. On some cam-

puses, female self-defense programs are offered. In these programs, which are often run by campus police, women are taught ways to reduce the risk of sexual assault and ways to defend themselves if they are attacked.

Find out which of these programs and services are available to women on your campus. If it's difficult to learn how your college deals with issues related to sexual assault and date rape, think about how you could make this information more available. And, if some of these services and activities are not available, think about how you could urge your college to provide them. See for yourself!

For More Information About . . .

how to promote good health in adolescents, read *Teenage Health Care* (Pocket Books, 1994) by Gail B. Slap and Martha M. Jablow. The authors provide excellent general information about puberty, exercise, and nutrition, but also discuss a variety of specific topics including headaches, cancer, drug abuse, and mental health.

 the causes of osteoporosis and how it can be prevented, visit the Web site of the National Osteoporosis Foundation: **http://www.nof.org**

Key Terms

anorexia 446
bulimia nervosa 447
date or acquaintance rape 443
masturbation 438

menarche 432
osteoporosis 431
primary sex characteristics 432
puberty 430

rites of passage 434
secondary sex characteristics 432
spermarche 433

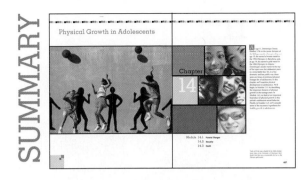

SUMMARY

Physical Growth in Adolescents

Chapter

14

Module 14.1 Pubertal Changes
14.2 Sexuality
14.3 Health

14.1 Pubertal Changes

Signs of Physical Maturation

Puberty includes bodily changes in height and weight as well as sexual maturation. Girls typically begin the growth spurt earlier than boys, who acquire more muscle, less fat, and greater heart and lung capacity. Sexual maturation, which includes primary and secondary sex characteristics, occurs in predictable sequences for boys and girls.

Mechanisms of Maturation

Pubertal changes take place when the pituitary gland signals the adrenal gland, ovaries, and testes to secrete hormones that initiate physical changes. The timing of puberty is influenced strongly by health and nutrition. In addition, the timing of puberty is influenced by the social environment, coming earlier when girls experience family conflict or depression.

Psychological Impact of Puberty

Pubertal changes affect adolescents' psychological functioning. Teens, particularly girls, become particularly concerned about their appearance. When forewarned, adolescents respond positively to menarche and spermarche. Adolescents are moodier than children and adults, primarily because their moods shift in response to frequent changes in activities and social setting. Early maturation tends to be harmful to girls but beneficial to boys.

14.2 Sexuality

Sexual Behavior

By the end of adolescence, most American boys and girls have had sexual intercourse, which boys view as recreational but girls see as romantic. Adolescents are more likely to be sexually active if they believe that their parents and peers approve of sex. Sexually transmitted diseases and pregnancy are two common consequences of adolescent sexual behavior because sexually active adolescents use contraceptives infrequently.

Sexual Orientation

A small percentage of adolescents are attracted to members of their own sex. Sexual orientation probably has its roots in biology. Gay and lesbian youth face many special challenges and consequently often suffer from mental-health problems.

Sexual Coercion

Adolescent and young adult females are sometimes forced into sex against their will, typically because males misinterpret or disregard females' intentions. Sexual coercion is particularly likely when either partner has been drinking alcohol or when the couple has had sex previously. Date-rape workshops strive to improve communication between males and females.

14.3 Health

Nutrition

For proper growth, teenagers need to consume adequate calories, calcium, and iron. Unfortunately, many teenagers do not eat properly and do not receive adequate nutrition.

Anorexia and bulimia are eating disorders that typically affect adolescent girls who have an irrational fear of being overweight. Several factors contribute to these disorders, including cultural standards of thinness, a need for independence within an autocratic family, and heredity.

Physical Fitness

Individuals who work out at least 3 times weekly often have improved physical and mental health. Unfortunately, many high school students do not get enough exercise.

Millions of American boys and girls participate in sports. Football and basketball are the most popular sports for boys and girls, respectively. The benefits of participating in sports include improved physical fitness, enhanced self-esteem, and understanding about teamwork. The potential costs include injury and abuse of performance-enhancing drugs.

Threats to Adolescent Well-Being

Accidents involving automobiles or firearms are the most common cause of death in American teenagers. Many of these deaths could be prevented if, for example, adolescents did not drive recklessly (e.g., too fast and without wearing seat belts). Adolescents and adults often make decisions similarly, considering the alternatives available, the consequences of each alternative, and the desirability and likelihood of these consequences. The outcomes of decision making sometimes differ because adolescents are more likely to emphasize the social consequences of actions.

Cognitive Processes in Adolescents

Chapter

15

One spring many years ago, the Indianapolis *Star* held a contest for all its newspaper carriers. The person who created the most words from the letters contained in the words SAFE RACE would win two tickets to the Indianapolis 500 auto race. The winning entry had 126 words. The winner had created thousands of possible words—beginning with each of the letters individually, then all possible combinations of two letters (e.g., AS, EF) and continuing through all possible combinations of all eight letters (e.g., SCAREEFA, SCAREEAF)—then looked up all these possible words in a dictionary. I know because I was the winner.

My systematic approach to problem solving is typical of adolescent cognition, which is the focus of Chapter 15. We begin, in Module 15.1, by describing some of the basic properties of adolescents' thinking. Next, in Module 15.2, we look at adolescents' reasoning about moral issues. Finally, in Module 15.3, we examine adolescents' ideas about work and careers.

Cognition

15.1

Cognition

Learning Objectives

▪ **What are the distinguishing characteristics of formal operational thought?**

▪ **How does information processing become more efficient during adolescence?**

Chris, a 14-year-old boy, was an enigma to his mother, Terri. On the one hand, Chris's growing reasoning skills impressed and sometimes even surprised her. He not only readily grasped technical discussions of her medical work, but he was becoming adept at finding loopholes in her explanations of why he wasn't allowed to do some things with his friends. On the other hand, sometimes Chris was a real teenage "space cadet." Simple problem solving stumped him, or he made silly mistakes and got the wrong answer. Chris didn't correspond to Terri's image of the formal operational thinker that she remembered from her college child-development class.

Adolescents are on the threshold of young adulthood and this is particularly evident in their cognitive skill. In Jean Piaget's theory, which we'll consider in the first half of this module, adolescence marks the beginning of the fourth and final stage of intellectual development. In information processing, which we'll consider in the second half, the transition to adultlike thinking occurs gradually throughout early and middle adolescence. As we examine these perspectives, you'll also see why adolescents like Terri's son don't always think in the sophisticated manner predicted by theories of cognitive development.

Piaget's Stage of Formal Operational Reasoning

The concrete operational skills of the elementary-school children are powerful but, as we saw in Module 12.1, linked to the real, to the here and now. **In Piaget's *formal operational stage*, which extends from roughly age 11 into adulthood, children and adolescents apply mental operations to abstract entities, allowing them to think hypothetically and reason deductively.** Freed from the concrete and the real, adolescents explore the possible—what might be and what could be.

Unlike reality-oriented concrete operational children, formal operational thinkers understand that reality is not the only possibility. They can envision alternative realities and examine their consequences. For example, ask a concrete operational child, "What would happen if gravity meant that objects floated up?" or "What would happen if men gave birth?" and you're likely to get a confused or even irritated look and comment like, "It doesn't—they fall" or "They don't—women have babies." Reality is the foundation of concrete operational thinking. In contrast, formal operational adolescents use hypothetical reasoning to probe the implications of fundamental change in physical or biological laws.

Formal operations also allow adolescents to take a different, more sophisticated approach to problem solving than concrete operational children. Formal operational thinkers can solve problems by creating hypotheses (sets of possibilities) and testing them. Piaget (Inhelder & Piaget, 1958) showed this aspect of adolescent thinking by presenting children and adolescents with several flasks, each containing what appeared to be the same clear liquid. They were told that one combination of the clear liquids would produce a blue liquid and were asked to determine the necessary combination.

A typical concrete operational youngster, like the ones in the photograph, plunges right in, mixing liquids from different flasks in a haphazard way. But formal operational adolescents understand that setting up the problem in abstract, hypothetical terms is the key. The problem is not really about pouring liquids but about forming hypotheses about different combinations of liquids and testing them systematically.

A teenager might mix liquid from the first flask with liquids from each of the other flasks. If none of those combinations produces a blue liquid, the adolescent would conclude that the liquid in the first flask is not an essential part of the mixture. Next, he or she would mix the liquid in the second flask with each of the remaining liquids. A formal operational thinker would continue in this manner until he or she finds the critical pair that produces the blue liquid. For adolescents, the problem is not one of concrete acts of pouring and mixing; rather, they understand that the problem consists of identifying possible hypotheses (in this case, combinations of liquids) and then evaluating each one.

Because adolescents' thinking is not concerned solely with reality, they are also better able to reason logically from premises and draw appropriate conclusions. **The ability to draw appropriate conclusions from facts is known as *deductive reasoning*.** Suppose we tell a person the following two facts:

1. If you hit a glass with a hammer, the glass will break.
2. Don hit a glass with a hammer.

The correct conclusion, of course, is that "the glass broke," a conclusion that formal operational adolescents will reach. Concrete operational youngsters, too, will sometimes reach this conclusion, but based on their experience and not because the conclusion is logically necessary. To see the difference, imagine that the two facts are now:

1. If you hit a glass with a feather, the glass will break.
2. Don hit a glass with a feather.

The conclusion "the glass broke" follows from these two statements just as logically as it did from the first pair. In this instance, however, the conclusion is counterfactual—it goes against what experience tells us is really true. Concrete operational 10-year-olds resist reaching conclusions that are counter to known facts; they reach conclusions based on their knowledge of the world. In contrast, formal operational 14-year-olds often reach counterfactual conclusions (Markovits & Vachon, 1989). They understand that these problems are about abstract entities that need not correspond to real-world relations.

Hypothetical and deductive reasoning are powerful tools for formal operational thinkers. In fact, we can characterize this power by paraphrasing the quotation about concrete operational thinking that appears on page 345: "Formal operational youth take an abstract, hypothetical approach to problem solving; they are not constrained by the reality that is staring them in the face but are open to different possibilities and alternatives." The ability to ponder different alternatives makes possible the experimentation with lifestyles and values that occur in adolescence.

> Formal-operational adolescents can think hypothetically and reason deductively.

With the achievement of formal operations, cognitive development is over in Piaget's theory. Of course, adolescents and adults acquire more knowledge as they grow older, but their fundamental way of thinking remains unchanged, in Piaget's view. The defining characteristics of formal operational thinking are summarized in the table.

■■■▢ SUMMARY TABLE

Characteristic Features of Formal Operational Reasoning

Feature	Defined
Abstract	Adolescents' reasoning is no longer limited to the real and concrete but readily extends to ideas and concepts that are often quite removed from reality.
Hypothetical	Adolescents solve problems by constructing hypotheses and creating tests for these hypotheses.
Deductive	Adolescents are better able to reason logically from premises, even when those premises contradict everyday experience.

TABLE 15-1

Theory of Actual Thinking or Possible Thinking? Simply because children and adolescents attain a particular level of reasoning in Piaget's theory does not mean that they always reason at that level. Adolescents who are in the formal operational period often revert to concrete operational thinking. Adolescents often fail to reason logically, even when they are capable and when it would be beneficial. For example, adolescents typically show more sophisticated reasoning when the problems are relevant to them personally than when they are not (Ward & Overton, 1990).

Also, when the product of reasoning is consistent with adolescents' own beliefs, they are less likely to find flaws in the reasoning (Klaczynski & Narasimham, 1998): You can see this aspect of adolescents' reasoning in the Focus on Research feature.

FOCUS ON RESEARCH

Beliefs Can Interfere with Effective Reasoning

Who were the investigators and what was the aim of the study? People's beliefs sometimes interfere with their ability to think clearly. When evidence is inconsistent with their beliefs, people may dismiss the evidence as being irrelevant or try to reinterpret the evidence to make it consistent with their beliefs. Paul Klaczynski and Gayathri Narasimham (1998) wanted to determine whether children and adolescents would show such biases in their scientific reasoning.

How did the investigators measure the topic of interest? The experiment was conducted in two sessions. In one session, participants completed a number of questionnaires, including one in which they indicated their religious preference. In a second session, participants read brief descriptions of hypothetical research studies that involved members of different religious groups. The studies were tailored so that each participant read about some studies that presented results depicting the participant's religion positively, some that presented results depicting the participant's religion negatively, and some that did not involve the participant's own religion. For example, if the participant was Lutheran, one study might conclude that Lutherans make better parents (favorable outcome), a second might conclude that Lutherans are less creative than Catholics (unfavorable outcome), and a third might conclude that Baptists handle stress more effectively than

> Adolescents use reasoning skills selectively, raising standards to dismiss findings that threaten their beliefs and lowering them for findings compatible with their beliefs.

Mormons (neutral outcome). After reading about each hypothetical study, participants rated how well the study was conducted on a 9-point scale ranging from 1, extremely poorly conducted, to 9, extremely well conducted. (In fact, each hypothetical study had a serious flaw, so there was reason to be critical of the results.)

Who were the children in the study? Klaczynski and Narasimham tested 41 10-year-olds, 42 13-year-olds, and 41 16-year-olds. The sample included approximately the same number of boys and girls at each age.

What was the design of the study? This study was experimental because Klaczynski and Narasimham included two independent variables: the age of the participant and the nature of the outcome in the results of the hypothetical study (favorable, unfavorable, neutral). The dependent variable was the participant's rating of the validity of the results (i.e., how well the study had been conducted). The study was cross-sectional because 10-, 13-, and 16-year-olds were all tested at approximately the same time.

Were there ethical concerns with the study? No. As soon as the participants had completed the second session, they were told that the studies they had read were completely hypothetical.

What were the results? The results are shown in the graph, which shows the average ratings for the three types of studies, separately for the three age groups. The same pattern is evident at each age. Relative to studies that had neutral outcomes, children and adolescents believed that studies with favorable outcomes were conducted better and studies with unfavorable outcomes were conducted worse. In other words, participants were quick to find flaws in studies when the results were inconsistent with their beliefs but overlooked similar flaws when the results were consistent with their beliefs. This pattern is particularly strong for the 10-year-olds, but was also found for the 13- and 16-year-olds.

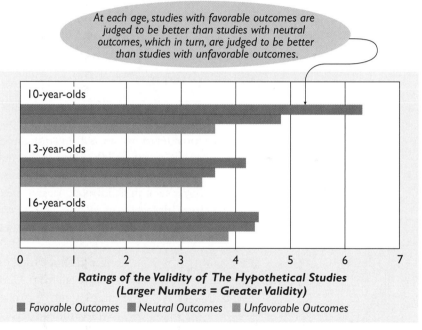

FIG 15–1

What did the investigators conclude? Klaczynski and Narasimham believe that adolescents use their scientific reasoning skills selectively, raising their standards to dismiss findings that threaten their beliefs and lowering them to admit findings compatible with their beliefs. Such biased reasoning can be traced to two factors. One concerns self-esteem: When outcomes favor groups to which a person belongs, self-esteem is enhanced; consequently, people overlook flaws in studies that produce results favorable to their groups. That is, children and adolescents may have ignored flaws in studies that were critical about their own religious group because accepting the evidence would have reduced their own self-esteem. A second factor concerns people's naive theories of the world (like those described in Modules 6.1 and 9.1). Such theories are often created over long periods of time and individuals come to believe them to be self-evident and true. Consequently, a person's naive theories are protected by adjusting standards depending on the fit of the results with the person's theory. That is, children and adolescents may have ignored flaws in studies that were critical about their own religious group because accepting the flaws would force them to revise a well-developed and well-believed naive theory about their religious group.

What converging evidence would strengthen these conclusions? An obvious way to bolster these results would be to show that they are not specific to religious beliefs but, instead, extend to other types of beliefs. For example, they might study political beliefs (although this would be difficult with the younger participants in the study). The prediction is that adolescents who, for example, identified themselves with the Democratic party would be less likely to detect flaws in studies that portrayed Democrats positively. ■

The Focus on Research feature tell us that Terri, the mother in the opening vignette, should not be so perplexed by her son's seemingly erratic thinking: Adolescents (and adults, for that matter) do not always use the most powerful levels of thinking that they possess. Piaget's account of intellectual development is really a description of how children and adolescents *can* think, not how they always or even usually think.

In the next section, we'll see how information-processing theorists describe adolescents' thinking.

Information Processing During Adolescence

For information-processing theorists, adolescence does not represent a distinct, qualitatively different stage of cognitive development. Instead, adolescence is considered to be a transitional period between the rapidly changing cognitive processes of childhood and the mature cognitive processes of young adulthood. Cognitive changes do take place in adolescence, but they are small compared to those seen in childhood. Adolescence is a time when cognitive processes are tweaked to adult levels.

These changes take place in several different elements of information processing.

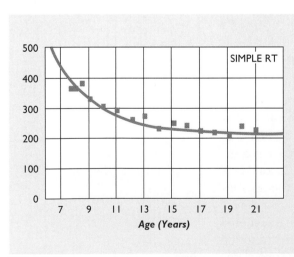

FIG 15-2

Basic Processes of Working Memory and Processing Speed. You recall from Module 6.2 that working memory is the site of ongoing cognitive processing and processing speed is the speed with which individuals complete basic cognitive processes. Both achieve adultlike levels during adolescence. Adolescents' working memory has about the same capacity as adults' working memory, which means teenagers are better able to store information needed for ongoing cognitive processes. In addition, the graph illustrates change in processing speed, exemplified in this case by performance on a simple response-time task in which individuals press a button as rapidly as possible in response to a visual stimulus. Simple response time declines steadily during childhood—from about one-third of a second at age 8 to one-quarter of a second at age 12—but changes little thereafter. This pattern of change is not specific to simple response time but is, instead, found for a wide range of cognitive tasks: Adolescents generally process information just about as quickly as young adults (Kail, 1991). Change in working memory and processing speed means that, compared to children, adolescents process information very efficiently.

Content Knowledge. As children move into adolescence, they acquire adultlike levels of knowledge and understanding in many domains. Children, for example, may enjoy baseball or computers, but as adolescents they acquire true expertise. For example, like the parent and child in the photo, many parents turn to their teens for help learning how to navigate the Internet. This increased knowledge is useful for its own sake, but it also has the indirect effect of allowing adolescents to learn, understand, and remember more of new experiences (Schneider & Bjorklund, 1998; Schneider & Pressley, 1997). Imagine two junior high students—one a baseball expert, the other not—watching a baseball game. Compared to the novice, the adolescent expert would understand many of the nuances of the game and, later, remember many more features of the game.

Strategies and Metacognitive Skill. Adolescents become much better skilled at identifying strategies appropriate for a specific task, then monitoring the chosen strategy to verify that it is working (Schneider & Pressley, 1997). For example, like the teen in the bottom photo, adolescents are more likely to outline and highlight information in a text. They are more likely to make lists of material they don't know well and should study more. And they more often embed these activities in a master study plan (e.g., a list of assignments, quizzes, and tests for a 2-week period). All these activities help adolescents learn more effectively and remember more accurately (Schneider & Pressley, 1997; Thomas et al., 1993).

These changing features of information processing are summarized in the table.

■■■■ SUMMARY TABLE

Information Processing during Adolescence

Feature	State in Adolescence
Working memory and processing speed	Adolescents have adultlike working memory capacity and processing speed, allowing them to process information efficiently.
Content knowledge	Adolescents' greater knowledge of the world facilitates understanding and memory of new experiences.
Strategies and metacognition	Adolescents are better able to identify task-appropriate strategies and to monitor the effectiveness of those strategies.

TABLE 15–2

Change in each of these elements of information processing occurs gradually. When combined, they contribute to the steady progress to mature thinking that is the destination of adolescent cognitive development.

Check Your Learning

1. The main difference between concrete and formal operational thought is that formal operational adolescents are able to reason _____.

2. The formal operational period marks the onset of _____ reasoning and deductive reasoning.

3. Compared to what would be expected from Piaget's theory, adolescents' thinking is often _____.

4. When evidence is inconsistent with their beliefs, adolescents often

   _____.

5. According to information-processing theorists, adolescence is a time of important changes in working memory, processing speed, _____, strategies, and metacognition.

6. In contrast to Piaget's view, information-processing theorists view adolescence as a time of _____.

Nature and Nurture The information-processing account of cognitive change in adolescence emphasizes working memory, knowledge, and strategies. How might each of these factors be influenced by nature? By nurture?

Answers: (1) abstractly, (2) hypothetical, (3) less sophisticated, (4) ignore or dismiss the evidence, (5) content knowledge (6) gradual cognitive change

Reasoning About Moral Issues

15.2

Reasoning About Moral Issues

├─ Kohlberg's Theory

├─ Beyond Kohlberg's Theory: Gilligan's Ethic of Caring

└─ Promoting Moral Reasoning

Learning Objectives

■ How do adolescents reason about moral issues?

■ How do concern for justice and caring for other people contribute to moral reasoning?

■ What factors help promote more sophisticated reasoning about moral issues?

> *Howard, the least popular boy in the entire eighth grade, had been wrongly accused of stealing a sixth grader's CD player. Min-shen, another eighth grader, knew that Howard was innocent but said nothing to the school prinicpal for fear of what his friends would say about siding with Howard. A few days later, when Min-shen's father heard about the incident, he was upset that his son apparently had so little "moral fiber." Why hadn't Min-shen acted in the face of an injustice?*

On one of the days when I was writing this module, my local paper had two articles about youths from the area. One article was about a 15-year-girl who was badly burned while saving her younger brothers from a fire in their apartment. Her mother said she wasn't surprised by her daughter's actions because she had always been an extraordinarily caring person. The other article was about two 17-year-old boys who had beaten an elderly man to death. They had only planned to steal his wallet, but when he insulted them and tried to punch them, they became enraged.

Reading articles like these, you can't help but question why some teenagers (and adults, as well) act in ways that earn our deepest respect and admiration, whereas others earn our utter contempt as well as our pity. And, at a more mundane level, we wonder why Min-shen didn't tell the truth about the stolen CD player to the principal. In this module, we'll start our exploration of moral reasoning with an influential theory proposed by Lawrence Kohlberg.

Kohlberg's Theory

To begin, I'd like to tell you a story about Heidi, a star player on a soccer team that I coached. Heidi was terribly upset because our team was undefeated and scheduled to play in a weekend tournament to determine the league champion. But on Sunday of this same weekend, a Habitat for Humanity house was to be dedicated to her grandfather, who had died a few months previously. If Heidi skipped the tournament game, her friends on the team would be upset; if she skipped the dedication, her family would be disappointed. Heidi couldn't do both and didn't know what to do.

Kohlberg created stories like this one to study how people reason about moral dilemmas. He made it very difficult to reach a decision in his stories because every alternative involved some undesirable consequences. In fact, there is no "correct" answer—that's why the stories are referred to as moral "dilemmas." For Heidi, pleasing her friends means disappointing her family; pleasing her family means letting down her teammates. Kohlberg was more interested in the reasoning used to justify a decision—Why should Heidi go to the tournament? Why should she go to the dedication?—not the decision itself. *

Kohlberg's best-known moral dilemma is about Heinz, whose wife is dying:

> In Europe, a woman was near death from cancer. One drug might save her, a form of radium that a druggist in the same town had recently discovered. The druggist was charging $2,000, ten times what the drug cost him to make. The sick woman's husband, Heinz, went to everyone he knew to borrow the money, but he could only get together about half of what it cost. He told the druggist that his wife was dying and asked him to sell it cheaper or let him pay later. But the druggist said, "No." The husband got desperate and broke into the man's store to steal the drug for his wife. (Kohlberg, 1969, p. 379)

Although more hangs in the balance for Heinz than for Heidi, both are moral dilemmas in that the alternative courses of action have desirable and undesirable features.

Kohlberg analyzed children's, adolescents', and adults' responses to a large number of dilemmas and identified three levels of moral reasoning, each divided into 2 stages. Across the 6 stages, the basis for moral reasoning shifts. In the earliest stages, moral reasoning is based on external forces, such as the promise of reward or the threat of punishment. At the most advanced levels, moral reasoning is based on a personal, internal moral code and is unaffected by others' views or society's expectations. You can clearly see this gradual shift in the three levels:

> In Kolberg's theory, moral reasoning is first based on obedience to authority but ultimately is based on a personal moral code.

- *Preconventional level:* **For most children, many adolescents, and some adults, moral reasoning is controlled almost solely by obedience to authority and by rewards and punishments.**

  Stage 1: Obedience orientation. People believe that adults know what is right and wrong. Consequently, a person should do what adults say is right to avoid being punished. A person at this stage would argue that Heinz should not steal the drug because it is against the law (which was set by adults).

  Stage 2: Instrumental orientation. People look out for their own needs. They often are nice to others because they expect the favor to be returned in the future. A person at this stage would say it was all right for Heinz to steal the drug because his wife might do something nice for him in return (i.e., she will reward him).

---

*As is turned out, Heidi didn't have to wrestle with the moral dilemma. We lost our game on Saturday, so she went to the dedication on Sunday.

• *Conventional level:* **For most adolescents and most adults, moral decision making is based on social norms—what is expected by others.**

Stage 3: Interpersonal norms. Adolescents and adults believe that they should act according to others' expectations. The aim is to win the approval of others by behaving like "good boys" and "good girls." An adolescent or adult at this stage would argue that Heinz should not steal the drug because then others would see him as a honest citizen who obeys the law, and the teenager in the photo helps the elderly woman because she wants others to think she is a nice person.

Stage 4: Social system morality. Adolescents and adults believe that social roles, expectations, and laws exist to maintain order within society and promote the good of all people. An adolescent or adult in this stage would reason that Heinz should steal the drug because a husband is obligated to do all that he possibly can to save his wife's life. Or a person in this stage would reason that Heinz should not steal the drug because stealing is against the law and society must prohibit theft.

• *Postconventional level:* **For some adults, typically those older than 25, moral decisions are based on personal, moral principles.**

Stage 5: Social contract orientation. Adults agree that members of cultural groups adhere to a "social contract" because a common set of expectations and laws benefits all group members. However, if these expectations and laws no longer promote the welfare of individuals, they become invalid. Consequently, an adult in this stage would reason that Heinz should steal the drug because social rules about property rights are no longer benefiting individuals' welfare.

Stage 6: Universal ethical principles. Abstract principles like justice, compassion, and equality form the basis of a personal moral code that may sometimes conflict with society's expectations and laws. An adult at this stage would argue that Heinz should steal the drug because life is paramount and preserving life takes precedence over all other rights.

Putting all of the stages together, this is what Kohlberg's theory looks like:

Stages in Kohlberg's Theory
Preconventional Level: Punishment and Reward
Stage 1: obedience to authority
Stage 2: nice behavior in exchange for future favors
Conventional Level: Social Norms
Stage 3: live up to others' expectations
Stage 4: follow rules to maintain social order
Postconventional Level: Moral Codes
Stage 5: adhere to a social contract when it is valid
Stage 6: personal morality based on abstract principles

TABLE 15–3

Support for Kohlberg's Theory. Kohlberg proposed that his stages form an invariant sequence. That is, individuals move through the 6 stages in the order listed and in only that order. If his stage theory is right, then level of moral reasoning should be strongly associated with age and level of cognitive development: Older and more advanced thinkers should, on the average, be more advanced in their moral development, and indeed, they usually are (Stewart & Pascual-Leone, 1992).

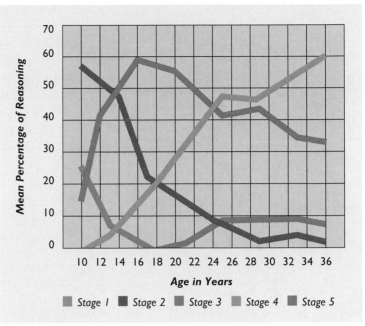

FIG 15–3

For example, the graph shows developmental change in the percentage of individuals who reason at Kohlberg's different stages. Stages 1 and 2 are common among children and young adolescents but not older adolescents and adults. Stages 3 and 4 are common among older adolescents and adults. The graph also shows that most individuals do not progress to the final stages. Most adults' moral reasoning is at Stages 3 and 4.

Support for Kohlberg's invariant sequence of stages also comes from longitudinal studies measuring individuals' level of reasoning over several years. Individuals do progress through each stage in sequence, and virtually no individuals skip any stages (Colby et al., 1983). Longitudinal studies also show that, over time, individuals become more advanced in their level of moral reasoning or remain at the same level. They do not regress to a lower level (Walker & Taylor, 1991).

Additional support for Kohlberg's theory comes from research on the link between moral reasoning and moral behavior. In general, level of moral reasoning should be linked to moral behavior. Remember that less advanced moral reasoning reflects the influence of external forces such as rewards and social norms, whereas more advanced reasoning is based on a personal moral code. Therefore, individuals at the preconventional and conventional levels would act morally when external forces demand, but otherwise they may not. In contrast, individuals at the postconventional level, where reasoning is based on personal principles, should be compelled to moral action even when external forces may not favor it.

Let's return to the example in the vignette. Suppose that you knew that one of the least popular students has been wrongly accused of stealing a CD player; you know that some friends in your group are actually responsible. What would you do? Speaking out on behalf of the unpopular student is unlikely to lead to reward. Furthermore, there are strong social norms against "squealing" on friends. So if you are in the preconventional or conventional level of moral reasoning like Min-shen, the boy in the vignette, you would probably let the unpopular student be punished unfairly. But if you are at the postconventional level and see the situation in terms of principles of justice and fairness, you would be more likely to identify the real perpetrators, despite the price to be paid in rejection by the group.

> When reasoning is based on a personal moral code, individuals are more likely to take moral action.

Many researchers report findings that support the hypothesized link between moral reasoning and moral action. In one study (Gibbs et al., 1986), high school teachers were asked to judge whether their students would defend their principles in difficult situations, or if they would act morally only when it was fashionable or handy. High school students who were judged by their teachers to have greater moral courage tended to be more advanced in Kohlberg's stages than students who were

judged less courageous. That is, students like those in the photo who protest social conditions tend to have higher moral reasoning scores. The converse is also true: Delinquent adolescents, whose actions are more likely to be morally offensive, tend to have lower moral reasoning scores than nondelinquent adolescents (Chandler & Moran, 1990). That is, delinquent adolescents are more likely to emphasize punishment and reward in their moral reasoning, not social norms and personal moral codes.

On another point of Kohlberg's theory, support is mixed. Kohlberg claimed his sequence of stages is universal: All people in all cultures progress through the 6-stage sequence. Some research shows that children and adolescents in cultures worldwide reason about moral dilemmas at Stages 2 or 3, just like North American children and adolescents. But as we'll see in the Cultural Influences feature, beyond the earliest stages, moral reasoning in other cultures is often not described well by Kohlberg's theory (Snarey, 1985).

CULTURAL INFLUENCES

Moral Reasoning in India

Many critics note that Kohlberg's emphasis on individual rights and justice reflects traditional American culture and Judeo-Christian theology. Not all cultures and religions share this emphasis; consequently, moral reasoning might be based on different values in other cultures (Carlo et al., 1996; Keller et al., 1998).

The Hindu religion, for example, emphasizes duty and responsibility to others, not individual rights and justice (Simpson, 1974). Accordingly, children and adults reared with traditional Hindu beliefs might emphasize caring for others in their moral reasoning more than individuals brought up in the Judeo-Christian tradition.

Miller and Bersoff (1992) tested the hypothesis that cultural differences affect moral reasoning by constructing dilemmas with both justice- and care-based solutions. For example:

> **Moral reasoning can be based on a concern for individual rights and justice as well as on a concern for caring for others.**

Ben planned to travel to San Francisco in order to attend the wedding of his best friend. He needed to catch the very next train if he was to be on time for the ceremony, as he had to deliver the wedding rings. However, Ben's wallet was stolen in the train station. He lost all of his money as well as his ticket to San Francisco.

Ben approached several officials as well as passengers . . . and asked them to loan him money to buy a new ticket. But, because he was a stranger, no one was willing to lend him the money he needed.

While Ben . . . was trying to decide what to do next, a well-dressed man sitting next to him walked away. . . . Ben noticed that the man had left his coat unattended. Sticking out of the man's coat pocket was a train ticket to San Francisco. . . . He also saw that the man had more than enough money in his coat pocket to buy another train ticket (p. 545).

One solution emphasized individual rights and justice:

Ben should not take the ticket from the man's coat pocket even though it means not getting to San Francisco in time to deliver the wedding rings to his best friend (p. 545).

The other solution placed a priority on caring for others:

Ben should go to San Francisco to deliver the wedding rings to his best friend even if it means taking the train ticket from the other man's coat pocket (p. 545).

When children and adults living in the United States responded to dilemmas like this one about Ben, a slight majority selected the justice-based alternative. In contrast, when Hindu children and adults living in India, like the mother and son in the photo, responded to the same dilemmas, the overwhelming majority selected the care-based alternative.

Clearly, moral reasoning reflects the culture in which a person is reared. Consistent with Kohlberg's theory, judgments by American children and adults reflect their culture's emphasis on individual rights and justice. But judgments by Indian children and adults reflect their culture's emphasis on caring for other people. The bases of moral reasoning are not universal as Kohlberg claimed; instead, they reflect cultural values. ■

Beyond Kohlberg's Theory: Gilligan's Ethic of Caring

Kohlberg's theory obviously is not the final word on moral development. Much about his theory seems valid, but findings like those described in the Cultural Influences feature indicate that Kohlberg's theory applies primarily to cultures with Western philosophical and religious traditions. However, researcher Carol Gilligan (1982; Gilligan & Attanucci, 1988) questions how applicable Kohlberg's theory is even within the Western tradition. Gilligan argues that Kohlberg's emphasis on justice applies more to men than to women, whose reasoning about moral issues is often rooted in concern for others. Gilligan writes, "The moral imperative that emerges repeatedly in interviews with women is an injunction to care, a responsibility to discern and alleviate the real and recognizable trouble of this world." (1982, p. 100)

Gilligan proposes a developmental progression in which individuals gain greater understanding of caring and responsibility. In the first stage, children are preoccupied with their own needs. In the second stage, people care for others, particularly those who are less able to care for themselves, like infants and the aged. The third stage unites caring for others and for oneself by emphasizing caring in all human relationships and by denouncing exploitation and violence between people. For example, consider the teen in the photo, who is helping at a homeless shelter. She does so not because she believes the homeless are needy but because she believes, first, that all humans should care for each other, and, second, that many people are in the shelter because they've been exploited.

Like Kohlberg, Gilligan also believes that moral reasoning becomes qualitatively more sophisticated as individuals develop, progressing through a number of distinct stages. However, Gilligan emphasizes care (helping people in need) instead of justice (treating people fairly).

What does research tell us about the importance of justice and care in moral reasoning? Gilligan's claim that females and males differ in the bases of their moral reasoning is not supported. Girls and boys as well as men and women reason about moral issues similarly (Walker, 1995). Both females and males often think about moral issues in terms of care and interpersonal relationships. Justice and care both serve as the basis for moral reasoning. It is the nature of the moral problem that largely determines whether justice, care, or both will be the basis for moral reasoning (Smetana, Killen, & Turiel, 1991).

Promoting Moral Reasoning

Whether it is based on justice or care, most cultures and most parents want to encourage adolescents to think carefully about moral issues. What can be done to help adolescents develop more mature forms of moral reasoning? Sometimes simply being exposed to more advanced moral reasoning is sufficient to promote developmental change (Walker, 1980). Adolescents may notice, for example, that older friends do not wait to be rewarded to help others. Or a teenager may notice that respected peers take courageous positions regardless of the social consequences. Such experiences apparently cause adolescents to re-evaluate their reasoning on moral issues and propel them toward more sophisticated thinking. The Child Development and Family Policy feature shows another way to foster moral thinking.

CHILD DEVELOPMENT AND FAMILY POLICY

Promoting More Advanced Moral Reasoning

Kohlberg wasn't content to simply chart how moral reasoning changed with age. He also wanted to devise ways to foster sophisticated moral reasoning. Kohlberg discovered that discussion can be particularly effective in revealing shortcomings in moral reasoning. When people, like the adolescents in the photo, reason about moral issues with others whose reasoning is at a higher level, the usual result is that individuals' reasoning at lower levels improve (Berkowitz & Gibbs, 1985). Imagine, for example, two 13-year-olds discussing the Heinz dilemma. Suppose one takes the position that Heinz should not steal the drug because he might get caught—reasoning at the preconventional level. The other argues that Heinz should steal the drug because a husband should do anything to save his wife's life—reasoning at the conventional level. During conversations of this sort, individuals at the preconventional level usually adopt the logic of the adolescents arguing at the higher conventional level.

Adolescents' moral reasoning becomes more sophisticated when they are exposed to more advanced moral reasoning and when they discuss moral issues with others.

To foster discussion and expose students to more advanced moral thinking, Kohlberg and his colleagues set up Just Communities, special groups of students and teachers within public high schools (Higgins, 1991; Power, Higgins, & Kohlberg, 1989). Teachers and students met weekly to plan school activities and discuss school policies. Decisions were reached democratically, with teachers and students alike each having one vote. However, during discussions, teachers acted as facilitators, encouraging students to consider the moral consequences of different courses of action. Students who participated in Just Communities tended to be more advanced in their moral thinking (Higgins, 1991; Power, Higgins, & Kohlberg, 1989).

Research findings such as these send an important message to parents: Discussion is probably the best way for parents to help their children think about moral issues in more mature terms (Walker & Taylor, 1991). Research consistently shows that mature moral reasoning comes about when adolescents are free to express their opinions on moral issues to their parents, who are, in turn, expressing their own opinions and, consequently, exposing their adolescent children to more mature moral reasoning (Hoffman, 1988, 1994). ∎

Check Your Learning

1. Kohlberg's theory includes the preconventional, conventional, and _____ levels.

2. For children and adolescents in the preconventional level, moral reasoning is strongly influenced by _____.

3. Supporting Kohlberg's theory are findings that level of moral reasoning is associated with age, that people progress through the stages in the predicted sequence, and that _____.

4. Gilligan's view of morality emphasizes _____ instead of justice.

5. When boys' and girls' moral reasoning is compared, the typical result is that _____.

6. In Just Communities, teachers encourage students to _____.

7. If parents wish to foster their children's moral development, they should _____ with them.

■ ■ **Connections** How similar is Piaget's stage of formal operational thought to
■ ■ Kohlberg's stage of conventional moral reasoning?

Answers: (1) postconventional, (2) reward or punishment, (3) more advanced moral reasoning is associated with moral action, (4) caring for others, (5) they do not differ, (6) consider the moral consequences of their decisions, (7) discuss moral issues

---

The World of Work

15.3
The World of Work
├ Career Development
└ Part-Time Employment

Learning Objectives

■ How do adolescents select an occupation?

■ What is the impact of part-time employment on adolescents?

> *When 15-year-old Aaron announced that he wanted an after-school job at the local supermarket, his mother was delighted, believing that he would learn much from the experience. Five months later, she has her doubts. Aaron has lost interest in school and they argue constantly about how he spends his money.*

What do you want to be when you grow up? Children are often asked this question in fun. Beginning in adolescence, however, it takes on special significance because work is such an important of element of the adult life that is looming on the horizon. A job—be it as a bricklayer, reporter, or child-care worker—helps define who we are. In this module, we'll see how adolescents begin to think about possible occupations. We'll also look at adolescents' first exposure to the world of work, which usually comes about with part-time jobs after school or on weekends. As we do, we'll see if Aaron's changed behavior is typical of teens who work part-time.

"Your son has made a career choice, Mildred. He's going to win the lottery and travel a lot."

By permission of Bunny Hoest, Wm. Hoest Enterprises, Inc.

Career Development

Faced with the challenge of selecting a career, many adolescents may be attracted by the approach taken by the teenage boy in the cartoon. Choosing a career is difficult, in part because it involves determining the kinds of jobs that will be available in the future. Predicting the future is risky, but the U.S. Bureau of Labor Statistics projects that by the year 2006, about 75 percent of all jobs will be in service industries, such as education, health care, and banking. The remaining 25 percent of jobs will be associated with the production of goods. In the future, there will be fewer jobs in agriculture, forestry, and manufacturing (Franklin, 1997).

Knowing the types of jobs that experts predict will be plentiful, how do adolescents begin the long process of selecting an occupation that will bring fame and fortune? Theories of vocational choice describe this process. According to a theory proposed by Donald Super (1976, 1980), identity is a primary force in an adolescent's choice of a career. **At about age 13 or 14, adolescents use their emerging identities as a source of ideas about careers, a process called** *crystallization.* Teenagers use their ideas about their own talents and interests to limit potential career prospects. A teenager who is extroverted and sociable may decide that working with people would be the career for him. Another who excels in math and science may decide she'd like to teach math. Decisions are provisional, and adolescents experiment with hypothetical careers, trying to envision what each might be like.

At about age 18, adolescents extend the activities associated with crystallization and enter a new phase. **During** *specification,* **individuals further limit their career possibilities by learning more about specific lines of work and starting to obtain the training required for a specific job.** Our extroverted teenager who wants to work with people may decide that a career in sales would be a good match for his abilities and interests. The teen who likes math may have learned more about careers and decided she'd like to be an accountant. Some teens, like the young man in the photo, may begin an apprenticeship as a way to learn a trade.

The end of the teenage years or the early 20s marks the beginning of the third phase. **During** *implementation,* **individuals enter the work force and learn firsthand about jobs.** This is a time of learning about responsibility and productivity, of learning to get along with coworkers, and of altering one's lifestyle to accommodate work. This period is often unstable; individuals may change jobs frequently as they adjust to the reality of life in the workplace.

In the Real Children feature, you can see these three phases in one young woman's career development.

REAL CHILDREN

The Life of Lynne, A Drama in Three Acts

Act 1: Crystallization. Throughout high school, Lynne was active in a number of organizations. She enjoyed being busy and liked the constant contact with people. Lynne was often nominated for office, and more often than not, she asked to be treasurer. Not that she was greedy or had her hand in the till; she simply found it satisfying to keep the financial records in order. By the end of her junior year, Lynne decided that she wanted to study business in college, a decision that fit with her good grades in English and math.

Act 2: Specification. Lynne was accepted into the business school of a large state university. She decided that accounting fit her skills and temperament, so this became her major. During the summers, she worked as a cashier at Target. This helped to pay for college and gave her experience in the world of retail sales.

Act 3: Implementation. A few months after graduation, Lynne was offered a junior accounting position with Wal-Mart. Her job required that she work Tuesday through Friday, auditing Wal-Mart stores in several nearby cities. Lynne liked the pay, the company car, the pay, the feeling of independence, and the pay. However, having to hit the road every morning by 7:30 A.M. was a jolt to someone used to rising casually at 10 A.M. Also, Lynne often found it awkward to deal with store managers, many of whom were twice her age and very intimidating. She was coming to the conclusion that there was much more to a successful career as an accountant than simply having the numbers add up correctly. ■

> According to Super, the early phases of career development involve crystallization, specification, and implementation.

The Life of Lynne illustrates the progressive refinement that takes place in a person's career development. An initial interest in math and finance led to a degree in business, which led to a job as an accountant. However, one other aspect of Lynne's life sheds more light on Super's theory. After 18 months on the job, Lynne's accounting group was merged with another; this would have required Lynne to move to another state, so she quit. After 6 months looking for another accounting job, Lynne gave up and began to study to become a real estate agent. The moral? Economic conditions and opportunities also shape career development. Changing times can force individuals to take new, often unexpected career paths.

Personality-Type Theory. Super's (1976, 1980) work helps to explain how self-concept and career aspirations develop hand in hand, but it does not explain why particular individuals are attracted to one line of work rather than another. Explaining the match between people and occupations has been the aim of a theory devised by John Holland (1985, 1987, 1996). **According to Holland's *personality-type theory*, people find work fulfilling when the important features of a job or profession fit the worker's personality.** Holland identified six prototypic personalities that are relevant to the world of work. Each one is best suited to a specific set of occupations, as indicated in the right-hand column of the table on page 472. Remember, these are merely prototypes. Most people do not match any one personality type exactly. Instead, their work-related personalities are a blend of the six.

This model is useful in describing the career preferences of African, Asian, European, Native, and Mexican American adolescents; it is also useful for both males and females (Day, Rounds & Swaney, 1998). And, research shows that when people have jobs that match their personality type, in the short run they are more productive employees, and in the long run they have more stable career paths (Holland, 1996). For example, an enterprising youth, like the one in the photo, is likely to be successful in business because he will enjoy positions of power in which he can use his verbal skills.

Combining Holland's work-related personality types with Super's theory of career development gives us a very comprehensive picture of vocational growth. On the one hand, Super's theory explains the developmental progression by which individuals translate general interests into a specific career; on the other hand, Holland's theory explains what makes a good match between specific interests and specific careers.

Personality Types in Holland's Theory		
Personality Type	**Description**	**Careers**
Realistic	Individuals enjoy physical labor and working with their hands, and they like to solve concrete problems.	mechanic, truck driver, construction worker
Investigative	Individuals are task-oriented and enjoy thinking about abstract relations.	scientist, technical writer
Social	Individuals are skilled verbally and interpersonally, and they enjoy solving problems using these skills.	teacher, counselor, social worker
Conventional	Individuals have verbal and quantitative skills that they like to apply to structured, well-defined tasks assigned to them by others.	bank teller, payroll clerk, traffic manager
Enterprising	Individuals enjoy using verbal skills in positions of power, status, and leadership.	business executive, television producer, real estate agent
Artistic	Individuals enjoy expressing themselves through unstructured tasks.	poet, musician, actor

TABLE 15–4

Of course, trying to match interests to occupations can be difficult. Fortunately, several tests can be used to describe a person's work-related personality and the jobs for which he or she is best suited. In the Strong Interest Inventory® (SII®), for example, people express their liking for different occupations, school subjects, activities, and types of people (e.g., very old people, people who live dangerously). These answers are compared to the responses obtained from a normative sample of individuals from different occupations. The result is a profile, a portion of which is shown on page 473.

You can see that each of Holland's types, called general occupational themes on the SII®, is listed. Under each heading are brown and shaded bars that show typical responses of women and men. The dot shows where the person's responses fall compared to other people of the person's own gender. Looking in the left column, you can see that this woman has less interest than the average female on the realistic, investigative, and artistic themes. In the right column, this woman has average interest on the social theme, but average or high interest on the conventional theme. Of the six general occupational themes, this person's interests seem to correspond best with the conventional personality in Holland's theory.

Holland's theory explains what makes a good match between a person's interests and specific careers.

By looking at the basic interest scales that are listed under the conventional occupational theme, we can get an even more precise idea of this woman's interests. Compared to the average female, this woman shows high interest in data management, computer activities, and office services. Evidently, her ideal job would be working in computer and office systems management.

Looking at the remaining occupational themes will serve as a reminder that the match between interests and occupations is often far from perfect. Although this woman's interest in the social occupational theme is only average overall, she has slightly higher than average interest in social services.

If you are still undecided about a career, I encourage you to visit your college's counseling center and arrange to take a test like the SII®. The results will help you to focus on careers that would match your interests and help you to choose a college major that would lead to those careers.

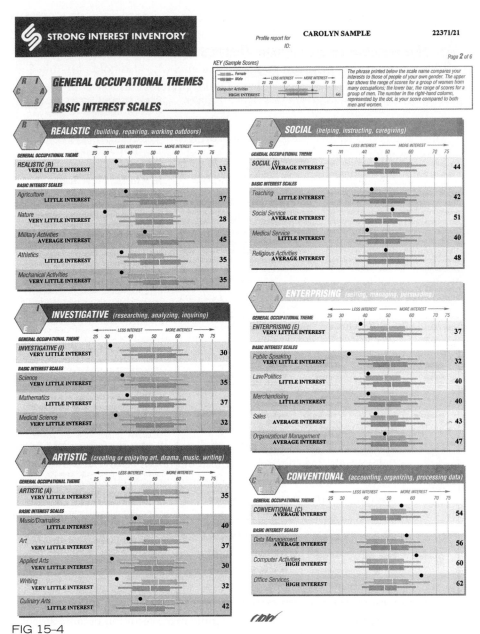

FIG 15–4

Strong Interest Inventory® (Strong Interest Inventory is a registered trademark of Stanford University Press.)

Even if you are fairly certain of your vocational plans, you might take one of these tests anyway. As we saw with Lynne, career development does not end with the first job. People continuously refine their career aspirations over the life span, and these test results might be useful later in your life.

Part-Time Employment

Today, a substantial majority of high school seniors work part-time. Out of every five adolescent part-time workers, one works at a fast-food restaurant like McDonald's or Burger King, and another works in a retail store as a cashier or salesperson. Boys are more likely to be manual laborers, busboys, or newspaper carriers. Girls are more often baby sitters, housekeepers, or restaurant workers, and they are usually paid less than boys (Call, 1996; Mortimer, 1991).

Part-time work is a new aspect of adolescence. In the 1970s, only 25 percent of high school students worked part-time compared to 75 percent in the 1980s and 1990s. This development is unique to the United States. In other industrialized countries in Western Europe and Asia, high school students who also hold part-time jobs are a clear minority. But compared to high school students in these countries, U.S. students have a shorter school day and much less homework, which means they have time to work (Reubens, Harrison, & Kupp, 1981).

Most adults believe that early exposure to the workplace teaches adolescents self-discipline, self-confidence, and important job skills (Snedeker, 1992). For most adolescents, however, part-time work can actually be harmful, for several reasons:

1. *School performance suffers.* When students work more than approximately 15 hours per week, they devote less time to homework and are more apt to cut classes. Not surprisingly, their grades are lower than those of their peers who work less or not at all (Steinberg, Fegley, & Dornbusch, 1993). Why should 15 hours of work be so detrimental to school performance? A 15-hour work schedule usually means four 3-hour shifts after school and another 3-hour shift on the weekend. This would seem to leave ample opportunity to study, but only if students use their time effectively. In fact, many high school students apparently do not have the foresight and discipline necessary to consistently meet the combined demands of work and school. Like the boy in the photo, many teens have great difficulty balancing work, study, and sleep.

2. *Mental health and behavioral problems.* Adolescents who work long hours—more than 15 or 20 hours a week—are more likely to experience anxiety and depression, and their self-esteem often suffers. Many adolescents find themselves in jobs that are repetitive and boring but stressful, and such conditions undermine self-esteem and breed anxiety. Extensive part-time work frequently leads to substance abuse, including cigarettes, alcohol, marijuana, and cocaine (Mortimer et al., 1996; Valois et al., 1999). Extensive work is also associated with more frequent problem behavior, including violence toward others, trouble with police, and arguments with parents (Bachman & Schulenberg, 1993). Why employment is associated with all of these problems is not clear. Perhaps employed adolescents turn to drugs to help them cope with the anxiety and depression brought on by work. Arguments with parents may become more common because anxious, depressed adolescents are more prone to argue or because wage-earning adolescents may believe that their freedom should match their income. Whatever the exact mechanism, extensive part-time work is clearly detrimental to the mental health of most adolescents.

3. *Misleading affluence.* Adults sometimes argue that work teaches teenagers the value of a dollar. Yet, the typical teenage pattern is to earn and spend. Working adolescents spend most of their earnings on themselves to buy clothing, snack food, or cosmetics, and to pay for entertainment. Few working teens set aside much of their income for future goals, such as a college education, or use it to contribute to their family's expenses (Shanahan et al., 1996a). Because parents customarily pay for rent, utilities, and groceries, for example, working adolescents often have a vastly higher percentage of their income available for discretionary spending than working adults. Thus, for many teens, the part-time work experience provides unrealistic expectations about how income can be allocated (Bachman, 1983).

The message that emerges repeatedly from research on part-time employment is hardly encouraging. Like Aaron, the teenage boy in the vignette, adolescents who work long hours at part-time jobs do not benefit from the experience. To the contrary, they do worse in school, are more likely to have behavioral problems, and learn how to spend money rather than how to manage it. These effects are similar for adolescents from different ethnic groups (Steinberg & Dornbusch, 1991) and are comparable for boys and girls (Bachman & Schulenberg, 1993).

Does this mean that teenagers who are still in school should never work part-time? Not necessarily. Part-time employment can be a good experience, depending on the circumstances. One key is the number of hours of work. Most students could easily work 5 hours weekly without harm, and many could work 10 hours weekly. Another key is the type of job (Barling, Rogers, & Kelloway, 1995). When adolescents have jobs that allow them to use their skills (e.g., bookkeeping, computing, or typing) and acquire new ones, self-esteem is enhanced, and they learn from their work experience. Yet another factor is how teens spend their earnings. When they save their money or use it to pay for clothes and school expenses, their parent-child relationships often improve (Shanahan et al., 1996b).

> When adolescents work many hours in part-time jobs, they do worse in school, often have behavioral problems, and experience misleading affluence.

By these criteria, who is likely to show the harmful effects of part-time work? A teen who spends 30 hours a week bagging groceries and spends most of it on CDs or videos. And who is likely to benefit from part-time work? A teen who likes to tinker with cars and spends Saturdays working in a repair shop and who sets aside some of his earnings for college.

Finally, summer jobs typically do not involve conflict between work and school. Consequently, many of the harmful effects associated with part-time employment during the school year do not hold for summer employment. In fact, such employment sometimes enhances adolescents' self-esteem, especially when they save part of their income for future plans (Marsh, 1991).

Check Your Learning

1. During the _____ phase of vocational choice, adolescents learn more about specific lines of work and begin training.

2. Individuals with a(n) _____ personality type are best suited for a career as a teacher or counselor.

3. Adolescents who work extensively at part-time jobs during the school year often get lower grades, have behavior problems, and _____.

4. Part-time employment during the school year can be beneficial if adolescents limit the number of hours that they work and _____.

■ **Continuity** Based on the description of Lynne's career, how would you describe continuity of vocational development during adolescence and young adulthood?

Answers: (1) specification, (2) social, (3) experience misleading affluence, (4) hold jobs that allow them to use and develop skills

Chapter Critical Review

1. Adolescents typically are introduced to the study of complex topics such as psychology, philosophy, and experimental science just when they are reaching Piaget's formal operational stage (described in Module 15.1). Explain how the ability to use formal operations contributes to the study of these and other subject areas.

2. What does is mean to state that a cognitive theory (Module 15.1) or moral-development theory (Module 15.2) describes how individuals can think, not how they do think?

3. How do culture, ethnicity, and gender affect moral development (Module 15.2)? Give at least two specific examples from your own experiences.

4. How do the different personality types in Holland's theory relate to the different types of intelligence proposed by Howard Gardner (described in Module 12.2)?

For more review material, log on to www.prenhall.com/kail

See For Yourself

Make Super's stages of vocational choice come alive by interviewing people in their 20s who have been in the work force for a few years. Ask them when they had their first ideas about a career (crystallization). Find out when they began learning about specific careers and the training that was required (specification). Ask about the experience of entering the work force for the first time (implementation). How well do the ages they report for each of the stages match those that Super provides? Are the steps similar for men and women? Do some people report missteps along the way and career changes? See for yourself!

For More Information About . . .

 people who have devoted their lives to helping others, read Anne Colby and William Damon's *Some Who Do Care: Contemporary Lives of Moral Commitment* (The Free Press, 1992). The authors, developmental psychologists interested in moral development, use biographies of humanitarians to identify the forces that make some people commit their lives to helping others.

 careers, including advice about first jobs and internships, tips on interviewing and resumes, and other helpful job-related information, visit the Career Advice–Career Stages portion of the Washington *Post*'s Web site:
http://www.washingtonpost.com/wl/Content.shtml?Content'/Career_Advice/

Key Terms

conventional level 464	**formal operational stage** 456	**postconventional level** 464
crystallization 470	**implementation** 470	**preconventional level** 463
deductive reasoning 457	**personality-type theory** 471	**specification** 470

SUMMARY

15.1 Cognition

Piaget's Stage of Formal Operational Reasoning

With the onset of the formal operational stage, adolescents can think hypothetically and reason abstractly. In deductive reasoning, they understand that conclusions are based on logic, not necessarily on experience. Adolescents' reasoning is not always as sophisticated as expected by Piaget's theory. For example, adolescents' beliefs sometimes interfere with their reasoning.

Information Processing During Adolescence

According to information-processing theorists, adolescence is a time of gradual cognitive change. Working memory and processing speed achieve adultlike levels; content knowledge increases, to expert-like levels in some domains; and strategies and metacognitive skills become much more sophisticated.

15.2 Reasoning About Moral Issues

Kohlberg's Theory

Kohlberg proposed that moral reasoning includes preconventional, conventional, and postconventional levels. Moral reasoning is first based on rewards and punishments and, much later, on personal moral codes. As predicted by Kohlberg's theory, people progress through the stages in sequence and do not regress, and morally advanced reasoning is associated with more frequent moral behavior. However, few people attain the most advanced levels, and cultures differ in the bases of moral reasoning.

Beyond Kohlberg's Theory: Gilligan's Ethic of Caring

Gilligan proposed that females' moral reasoning is based on caring and responsibility for others, not justice. Research does not support consistent sex differences in moral reasoning, but has found that males and females both consider caring as well as justice in their moral judgments, depending on the situation.

Promoting Moral Reasoning

Many factors can promote more sophisticated moral reasoning, including (a) observing others reason at more advanced levels, and (b) discussing moral issues with peers, teachers, and parents.

15.3 The World of Work

Career Development

In his theory of vocational choice, Super proposes three phases of vocational development during adolescence and young adulthood: crystallization, in which basic interests are identified; specification, in which jobs associated with interests are identified; and, implementation, which marks entry into the work force.

Holland proposes six different work-related personalities: realistic, investigative, social, conventional, enterprising, and artistic. Each is uniquely suited to certain jobs. People are happier when their personality fits their job and less happy when it does not.

Part-Time Employment

Most adolescents in the United States have part-time jobs. Adolescents who are employed more than 15 hours per week during the school year typically do poorly in school, often have lowered self-esteem and increased anxiety, and have problems interacting with others. Employed adolescents save relatively little of their income. Instead, they spend it on clothing, food, and their entertainment, which can give misleading expectations about how to allocate income.

Part-time employment can be beneficial if adolescents work relatively few hours, if the work allows them to use existing skills or acquire new ones, and if teens save some of their earnings. Summer employment, which does not conflict with the demands of school, can also be beneficial.

Social and Personality Development in Adolescents

Chapter

16

Brooke Pacy, an English teacher in Baltimore, once wrote that adolescents "...need time and space to stretch in weird directions. They need to survive disasters of their own making or they will never know anything about themselves" (1993, p. 38). Stretching in weird directions (and the occasional disaster that results!) makes adolescence a challenging time for parents and their offspring (who now resent being called "children"). In this chapter, we'll examine adolescent stretching, beginning in Module 16.1, by looking at the adolescent search for identity. In Module 16.2, we'll see how relationships with parents and peers change during adolescence. Finally, in Module 16.3, we'll consider problems that affect some adolescents and what we can do to help youth afflicted with these problems.

Identity and Self-Esteem

16.1

Identity and Self-Esteem

├─ The Search for Identity

├─ Ethnic Identity

└─ Self-Esteem in Adolescence

Learning Objectives

■ **How do adolescents achieve an identity?**

■ **What is an ethnic identity? What are the stages in acquiring an ethnic identity?**

■ **How does self-esteem change in adolescence?**

Dea was born in Seoul of Korean parents but was adopted by a Dutch couple in Michigan when she was 3 months old. Growing up, she considered herself a red-blooded American. In high school, however, Dea realized that others saw her as an Asian American, an identity about which she had never given much thought. She began to wonder, Who am I really? American? Dutch American? Asian American?

Like Dea, do you sometimes wonder who you are? We learned in Module 7.3 that self-concept refers to the attitudes, behaviors, and values that make a person unique. In adolescence, self-concept takes on special significance as adolescents struggle to achieve an identity that will allow them to participate in the adult world. Through self-reflection, youth search for an identity to integrate the many different and sometimes conflicting elements of the self. In this module we'll learn more about the adolescent search for an identity. Along the way, we'll learn more about Dea's struggle to learn who she is.

The Search for Identity

Erik Erikson's (1968) account of identity formation has been particularly influential in our understanding of adolescence. Erikson argued that adolescents face a crisis between identity and role confusion. This crisis involves balancing the desire to try out many possible selves and the need to select a single self. Adolescents who achieve a sense of identity are well prepared to face the next developmental challenge—establishing intimate, sharing relationships with others. However, Erikson believed that teenagers who are confused about their identity can never experience intimacy in any human relationship. Instead, throughout their lives, they remain isolated and respond to others stereotypically.

How do adolescents achieve an identity? They use the hypothetical reasoning skills of the formal operational stage to experiment with different selves to learn more about possible identities (Nurmi, Poole, & Kalakoski, 1996). Adolescents' advanced cognitive skills allow them to imagine themselves in different roles.

Much of the testing and experimentation is career oriented. Some adolescents, like the ones shown in the photo, may envision themselves as rock stars; others may imagine being a professional athlete, a Peace Corps worker, or a best-selling novelist. Other testing is romantically oriented. Teens may fall in love and imagine living with the loved one. Still other exploration involves religious and political beliefs (King, Elder, & Whitbeck, 1997; Yates

& Youniss, 1996). Teens give different identities a trial run just as you might test drive different cars before selecting one. By fantasizing about their future, adolescents begin to discover who they will be.

As adolescents strive to achieve an identity, they often progress through different phases or statuses listed in the summary table (Marcia, 1980, 1991).

■■■ SUMMARY TABLE

Four Different Identity Statuses

Status	Definition	Example
Diffusion	The person is overwhelmed by the task of achieving an identity and does little to accomplish the task.	Larry hates the idea of deciding what to do with his future, so he spends most of his free time playing video games.
Foreclosure	The person has a status determined by adults rather than from personal exploration.	For as long as she can remember, Sakura's parents have told her that she should be an attorney and join the family law firm. She plans to study prelaw in college, though she's never given the matter much thought.
Moratorium	The person is examining different alternatives but has yet to find one that's satisfactory.	Brad enjoys almost all his high school classes. Some days he thinks it would be fun to be a chemist, some days he wants to be a novelist, and some days he'd like to be an elementary-school teacher. He thinks it's a little weird to change his mind so often, but he also enjoys thinking about different jobs.
Achievement	The person has explored alternatives and has deliberately chosen a specific identity.	Throughout middle school, Efrat wanted to play in the WNBA. During 9th and 10th grade, she thought it would be cool to be a physician. In 11th grade, she took a computing course and everything finally clicked—she'd found her niche. She knew that she wanted to study computer science in college.

TABLE 16-1

Unlike Piaget's stages, these four phases do not necessarily occur in sequence. Most young adolescents are in a state of diffusion or foreclosure. The common element in these phases is that teens are not exploring alternative identities. They are avoiding the crisis altogether or have resolved it by taking on an identity suggested by parents or other adults. However, as individuals move beyond adolescence and into young adulthood, they have more opportunity to explore alternative identities, and so diffusion and foreclosure become less common, and as the pie charts at the top of page 482 show, achievement and moratorium become more common (Meilman, 1979).

Typically, young people do not reach the achievement status for all aspects of identity at the same time (Dellas & Jernigan, 1990; Kroger & Green, 1996). Some ado-

> In achieving identity, most adolescents begin in a state of diffusion or foreclosure and end in states of moratorium or achievement.

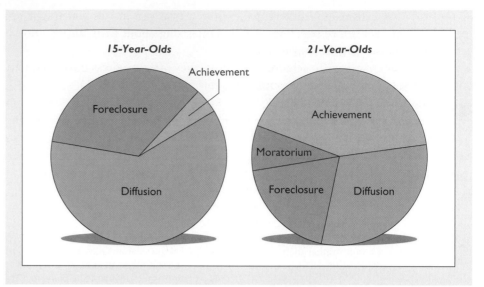

FIG 16–1

lescents may reach the achievement status for occupations before achieving it for religion and politics. Others reach the achievement status for religion before other domains. Evidently, few youth achieve a sense of identity all at once; instead, the crisis of identity is first resolved in some areas and then in others.

When the achievement status is attained, the period of active experimentation ends and individuals have a well-defined sense of self. However, during adulthood, an individual's identity is sometimes reworked in response to new life challenges and circumstances. Consequently, individuals may return to the moratorium status for a period, only to reemerge later with a changed identity. In fact, adults may go through these changes several times, creating MAMA cycles in which they alternate between the moratorium and achievement statuses as they explore new alternatives in response to personal and family crises (Marcia, 1991). For example, a man, like the one in the photo, who has placed career above all else but finds himself unemployed, may reorganize his life around family and become the primary caregiver of his children.

During the search for identity, adolescents often reveal a number of characteristic ways of thinking. They are often very self-oriented. **The self-absorption that marks the teenage search for identity is referred to as *adolescent egocentrism*** (Elkind, 1978). Unlike preschoolers, adolescents know that others have different perspectives on the world. Adolescents are simply *much* more interested in their own feelings and experiences than in anyone else's experiences. In addition, as they search for an identity, many adolescents wrongly believe that they are the focus of others' thinking. A teen, like the one in the photo who has spilled her drink on herself, may imagine that all her friends are thinking only about the stain on her blouse and how sloppy she is. **Many adolescents feel that they are, in effect, actors whose performance is watched constantly by their peers, a phenomenon known as the *imaginary audience.***

Adolescent self-absorption is also demonstrated by the *personal fable*, teenagers' tendency to believe that their

experiences and feelings are unique, that no one has ever felt or thought as they do. Whether the excitement of first love, the despair of a broken relationship, or the confusion of planning for the future, adolescents often believe that they are the first to experience these feelings and that no one else could possibly understand the power of their emotions (Elkind & Bowen, 1979). **Adolescents' belief in their uniqueness also contributes to an *illusion of invulnerability*—the belief that misfortune only happens to others.** They think they can have sex without becoming pregnant, and they can drive recklessly without being in an auto accident. Those misfortunes only happen to other people.

These characteristics of adolescents' thinking is summarized in the table.

■■■ SUMMARY TABLE

Characteristics of Adolescents' Thinking

Feature	Definition	Example
Adolescent egocentrism	Adolescents are overly concerned with their own thoughts and feelings.	When Levi's grandmother died unexpectedly, Levi was preoccupied with how the funeral would affect his weekend plans and ignored how upset his mother was by her own mother's death.
Imaginary audience	Adolescents believe that others are watching them constantly.	Tom had to ride his bike to football practice because his dad wouldn't let him have the car; he was sure that all his car-driving friends would see and make fun of him.
Personal fable	Adolescents believe that their experiences and feelings are unique.	When Rosa's boyfriend decided to date another girl, Rosa cried and cried. She couldn't believe how sad she was and she was sure her mom had never felt this way.
Illusion of invulnerability	Adolescents think that misfortune only happens to others.	Kumares and his girlfriend had been having sex for about 6 months. Although she thought it would be a good idea to use birth control, he thought it was unnecessary: There was no way his girlfriend would get pregnant.

TABLE 16–2

As adolescents make progress toward achieving an identity, adolescent egocentrism, imaginary audiences, personal fables, and the illusion of invulnerability become less common. What circumstances help adolescents achieve identity? Parents are influential (Marcia, 1980). When parents encourage discussion and recognize children's autonomy, their children are more likely to reach the achievement status. Apparently these youth feel encouraged to undertake the personal experimentation that leads to identity. In contrast, when parents set rules with little justification and enforce them without explanation, children are more likely to remain in the foreclosure status. These teens are discouraged from experimenting personally; instead, their parents simply tell them what identity to adopt. Overall, adolescents are most likely to establish a well-defined identity in a family atmosphere where parents encourage children to explore alternatives on their own but do not pressure or provide explicit direction (Harter, 1990, 1999).

> Adolescents best achieve an identity when parents encourage discussion and recognize their children's autonomy.

Ethnic Identity

For many adolescents growing up in North America today, achieving an identity is even more challenging because they are members of ethnic minority groups. The Cultural Influences feature describes one example.

CULTURAL INFLUENCES

Dea's Ethnic Identity

Dea, the adolescent in the opening vignette, belongs to the one-third of adolescents and young adults living in the United States who are members of ethnic minority groups. They include African Americans, Asian Americans, Hispanic Americans, and Native Americans. **These individuals typically develop an *ethnic identity*: They feel a part of their ethnic group and learn the special customs and traditions of their group's culture and heritage (Phinney, 1996).**

Achieving an ethnic identity seems to occur in three phases. Initially, adolescents have not examined their ethnic roots. A teenage African American girl in this

phase remarked, "Why do I need to learn about who was the first Black woman to do this or that? I'm just not too interested" (Phinney, 1989, p. 44). For this girl, ethnic identity is not yet an important personal issue.

In the second phase, adolescents begin to explore the personal impact of their ethnic heritage. The curiosity and questioning that is characteristic of this stage is captured in the comments of a teenage Mexican American girl who said, "I want to know what we do and how our culture is different from others. Going to festivals and cultural events helps me to learn more about my own culture and about myself" (Phinney, 1989, p. 44). Part of this phase involves learning cultural traditions; for example, like the girl in the photo, many adolescents learn to prepare ethnic food.

In the third phase, individuals achieve a distinct ethnic self-concept. One Asian American adolescent explained his ethnic identification like this: "I have been born Filipino and am born to be Filipino. . . . I'm here in America, and people of many different cultures are here, too. So I don't consider myself only Filipino, but also American" (Phinney, 1989, p. 44).

To see if you understand the differences between these stages of ethnic identity, reread the vignette on page 480 about Dea and decide which stage applies to her. The answer appears on page 487, just before Check Your Learning. ■

Older adolescents are more likely than younger ones to have achieved an ethnic identity, because they are more likely to have had opportunities to explore their cultural heritage (Phinney & Chavira, 1992). Also, as is the case with overall identity, adolescents are most likely to achieve an ethnic self-concept when their parents encourage them to explore alternatives instead of pressuring them to adopt a particular ethnic identity (Rosenthal & Feldman, 1992).

Do adolescents benefit from a strong ethnic identity? Yes. Adolescents who have achieved an ethnic identity tend to have higher self-esteem and find their interactions with family and friends more satisfying (Phinney, Cantu, & Kurtz, 1997). In addition, many investigators have found that adolescents with a strong ethnic identity do better in school than adolescents whose ethnic identities are weaker (Stalikas & Gavaki, 1995; Taylor et al., 1994).

Some individuals achieve a well-defined ethnic self-concept and, at the same time, identify strongly with the mainstream culture. In the United States, for example, many Chinese Americans embrace both Chinese and American culture; in England, many Indians identify with both Indian and British cultures. For other individuals, the cost of strong ethnic identification is a weakened tie to mainstream culture. Some investigators report that for Hispanic Americans, strong identification with American culture is associated with a weaker ethnic self-concept (Phinney, 1990).

> Adolescents who have achieved an ethnic identity have higher self-esteem, get more satisfaction from interactions with others, and do better in school.

We shouldn't be too surprised that identifying with mainstream culture weakens ethnic identity in some groups but not others (Berry, 1993). Racial and ethnic groups living in the United States are diverse. African American, Asian American, Hispanic American, and Native American cultures and heritages differ, and so we should expect that the nature and consequences of a strong ethnic self-concept will differ across these and other ethnic groups.

Even within any particular group, the nature and consequences of ethnic identity may change over successive generations (Cuellar et al., 1997). As successive generations become more acculturated to mainstream culture, they may identify less strongly with ethnic culture. Thus, parents may maintain strong feelings of ethnic identity that their children don't share.

Ethnic identity is a particularly salient issue for children like Dea, who are members of minority groups and are adopted by European American parents. The Focus on Research feature shows how identity develops in these children.

FOCUS ON RESEARCH

Identity in Children of Transracial Adoptions

Who were the investigators and what was the aim of the study? For many years, the policy of many adoption agencies was that children could be adopted only by adults of their own race. However, in the 1960s, transracial adoption became more common. Why was this? Children from minority groups needing adoption far outnumbered the adults from minority groups who wanted to adopt, yet many European American adults were eager to adopt these children. When African American children are reared by European American parents, what racial identity do the children acquire? How does this identity affect their development? Kimberly DeBerry, Sandra Scarr, and Richard Weinberg (1996) wanted to answer these questions.

How did the investigators measure the topic of interest? The investigators created a structured interview that included 83 different items. Some items measured the children's orientation towards African Americans, including the number of African American friends they had, their knowledge of people of African descent, and whether they referred to themselves as African American. Other, comparable items measured children's orientation toward European Americans. Finally, general psychological adjustment was measured with questions addressing behavioral, emotional, interpersonal, and academic problems. Children and parents were interviewed separately.

Who were the children in the study? Scarr and Weinberg began the Minnesota Transracial Adoption Project in the 1970s. Their original sample included 131 families with 176 adopted children and 145 biological children. DeBerry and her colleagues focused on a subsample that included 88 African American children, 29 boys and 59 girls.

What was the design of the study? This study was correlational because DeBerry and her colleagues were interested in the relations that existed naturally between children's identity as African or European Americans and their adjustment. The study was longitudinal because testing took place when the children were approximately 4, 7, and 17 years old. However, I am describing only the results that were obtained when the children were 17.

Were there ethical concerns with the study? No. The investigators obtained permission from the parents for the children to participate.

What were the results? Parents' and children's responses to the interview were similar, so I'll just describe children's responses. Two results are key. First, most of the children in this sample identified more strongly as European American than as African American. Second, having a strong cultural identity was associated with better psychological adjustment. The correlation with adjustment was 0.45 for identifying with African Americans and 0.50 for identifying with European Americans. In other words, adolescents who identified strongly with *either* African or European Americans tended to be better adjusted than adolescents who identified with neither African nor European Americans.

What did the investigators conclude? The investigators caution that their results, which are based on African American children reared by European Americans in Minnesota, may not apply to all transracial adoptions. Nevertheless, the results underscore the importance of being able to identify with a cultural group. Being able to think of oneself as a member of some larger, recognized cultural group is an important part of being psychologically healthy. Adolescents who do not feel a part of any group are at risk for psychological problems.

What converging evidence would strengthen these conclusions? As I just mentioned, the authors caution that their results may be specific to African American youth adopted by European Americans living in Minnesota. A useful next step would be to determine whether similar results are obtained in other instances of transracial adoption. For example, like Dea in the opening vignette, many children from Asian countries such as Korea and China have been adopted by European American adults. Studying identity in a sample of adopted Asian American adolescents would provide an informative test of the generality of the present findings. If the results are general, Asian American adolescents should be better adjusted psychologically if they identify with either Asian or European Americans. ■

Self-Esteem in Adolescence

We've seen in earlier modules that self-esteem is usually very high in preschool children but declines gradually during the early elementary-school years as children compare themselves to others. By the later elementary-school years, self-esteem has usually stabilized—it neither increases nor decreases in these years (Harter, Whitesell, & Kowalski, 1992). Evidently, children learn their place in the "pecking order" of different domains and adjust their self-esteem accordingly.

Some studies indicate that self-esteem changes when children move from elementary school to middle school or junior high (Seidman et al., 1994). Apparently, when students from different elementary schools enter the same middle school or junior high, they know where they stand compared to their old elementary-school classmates but not

Self-esteem often declines as young adolescents enter middle school or junior high school because adolescents don't know where they stand compared to their new classmates.

to students from other elementary schools. Thus, peer comparisons begin anew, and self-esteem often suffers.

The drop in self-esteem associated with the transition to middle school or junior high is usually temporary. As children enter middle and late adolescence, self-esteem frequently increases (Savin-Williams & Demo, 1984). New schools become familiar and students gradually adjust to the new pecking order. In addition, adolescents begin to compare themselves to adults. They see themselves acquiring more and more adult skills, such having a job or driving a car. Also, they see themselves acquiring many of the signs of adult status, such as greater independence and greater responsibility for their decisions. These changes apparently foster self-esteem.

Response to question on page 484 about Dea's ethnic identity: Dea, the Dutch Asian American college student, doesn't know how to integrate the Korean heritage of her biological parents with the Dutch American culture in which she was reared. This would put her in the second phase of acquiring an ethnic identity. On the one hand, she is examining her ethnic roots, which means she's progressed beyond the initial stages. On the other hand, she has not yet integrated her Asian and European roots, and so has not reached the third and final phase.

Check Your Learning

1. According to Erikson, adolescents face a crisis between identity and _____ .

2. The _____ status would describe an adolescent who has attained an identity based almost entirely on her parents' advice and urging.

3. A person who has simply put off searching for an identity because it seems too confusing and too overwhelming is in the _____ status.

4. _____ refers to the fact that adolescents sometimes believe that their lives are a performance, with their peers watching them constantly.

5. Adolescents are most likely to achieve an identity when parents encourage them _____ .

6. In the second phase of achieving an ethnic identity, adolescents _____ .

7. When individuals have a strong ethnic identity, their identification with mainstream culture _____ .

8. Self-esteem often drops when students enter middle school or junior high school because young adolescents _____ .

Connections Although Piaget's theory of cognitive development was not concerned with identity formation, how might his theory explain why identity is a central issue in adolescence?

Answers: (1) role confusion, (2) foreclosure, (3) diffusion, (4) Imaginary audience, (5) to explore alternative identities but do not pressure them or provide direction, (6) start to explore the personal impact of their ethnic roots, (7) is sometimes strong and sometimes weak, depending on specific circumstances, (8) no longer know where they stand among their peers, so they must establish a new pecking order.

Relationships with Parents and Peers

16.2

Relationships with Parents and Peers

├─ Parent-Child Relationships in Adolescence

└─ Relationships with Peers

■ How do parent-child relationships change in adolescence?

■ What are the important features of groups in adolescence? How do groups influence adolescents?

■ What are the important features of adolescents' friendships?

Only 36 hours had passed since campers arrived at Silver Lake Camp. Nevertheless, campers had already formed strong allegiances with their cabins. Campers in Eagles' Nest cabin had created their own chant and those in Lions' Den had made matching necklaces. In other cabins, campers were involved in similar projects that proclaimed their identity with their cabin. The counselors encouraged these activities but also knew that it had a downside: Invariably some campers took them too seriously and started hassling campers from other cabins. The counselors wished they knew a way to prevent strong cabin identities from causing problems.

As adolescents move away from childhood and approach adulthood, their relationships with other people change. Their greater physical and cognitive maturity makes teenagers less dependent on parents and more invested in relationships with peers. We'll trace these changes in this module and, as we do, we'll learn more about group identities like those that form so rapidly every year at Silver Lake Camp.

Parent-Child Relationships in Adolescence

Despite adolescents' drive toward independence, many features of parent-child relationships are unchanged from childhood. The authoritative parenting that is best for children's development works best for adolescents, too: Teenagers flourish when parents are warm and caring while still establishing reasonable rules and enforcing them consistently. Like parents of children, parents of adolescents sometimes fall into the negative reinforcement trap that I described on page 295. That is, they inadvertently reinforce the very behaviors they want to eliminate. Mothers of adolescent sons seem particularly vulnerable to this problem. For example, when a mother expected her son to walk the dog before going to school, he complained bitterly, often refused to eat breakfast, and was sometimes late to school. The mother ultimately gave up—walking the dog herself—because she wanted to eliminate this early-morning hassle. Finally, like elementary-school children, adolescents often endure the stress associated with their parents' divorce—their schoolwork and adjustment suffers. Or, teenagers face the challenge of adjusting to a new stepparent, one who may be encroaching on intimate parent-child relationships.

> *Parent-child relationships become more egalitarian during adolescence, but most adolescents still admire, love, and rely upon their parents.*

Of course, parent-child relations *do* change during adolescence. As teens become more independent, their relationships with their parents become more egalitarian. Parents must adjust to their children's growing sense of autonomy by treating them more like equals (Laursen & Collins, 1994). This growing independence means that teens spend less time with their parents, are less affectionate toward them, and argue more often with them about matters of style, taste, and freedom. Teenagers are also more moody and more likely to enjoy spending some time alone (Larson, 1997; Wolfson & Carskadon, 1998).

According to American novelists and filmmakers, adolescence is often a time of storm and stress—a period in which parent-child relationships deteriorate in the face of a combative, argumentative youth. Although this view may make for best-selling novels and hit movies, in reality, the rebellious teen is largely a myth. Think about the following conclusions derived from research findings (Steinberg, 1990). Most adolescents

- admire and love their parents
- rely upon their parents for advice
- embrace many of their parents' values
- feel loved by their parents

Not exactly the image of the rebel, is it? Cross-cultural research provides further evidence that adolescence is not necessarily a time of turmoil and conflict. Offer and his colleagues (1988) interviewed adolescents from 10 different countries: the United States, Australia, Germany, Italy, Israel, Hungary, Turkey, Japan, Taiwan, and Bangladesh. These investigators found most adolescents moving confidently and happily toward adulthood. As the graphs show, most adolescents around the world reported that they were usually happy, and few avoided their homes.

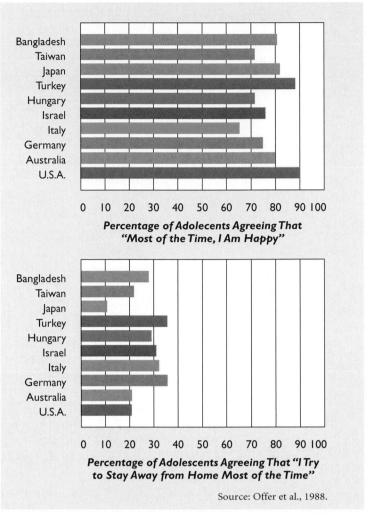

Source: Offer et al., 1988.

FIG 16-2

Thus, adolescence is definitely an interesting and challenging time for youth and their parents, as both parties deal with challenges brought on by an evolving parent-child relationship, in which the child is nearly a fully independent young adult (Steinberg, 1990). However, it is not inherently tempestuous as the myth of "storm and stress" would lead us to believe.

Relationships with Peers

Many of the major developmental theorists—including Freud, Erikson, Piaget, and Vygotsky—believed that adolescents' development is strongly shaped by their social interactions with peers. Whether at a summer camp, in school, on a sports team, or in a small circle of close friends, an individual adolescent's interactions with agemates are important developmental events. In the remainder of this module, we'll look at groups like those that form at summer camps and then examine adolescents' friendships.

Groups. As was the case at the summer camp in the opening vignette, whenever strangers are brought together, they form groups. Psychologist Muzafer Sherif and his colleagues (1961) used this phenomenon to conduct a landmark study of groups at The Robbers Cave State Park in Oklahoma. The boys in this study did not know one another before coming to camp. They were put in two groups that were comparable in the boys' size, their athletic ability, and previous camping experience. For the first week, the two groups were kept apart and spent their time in traditional camp activities that required considerable cooperation, such as transporting camping equipment and organizing hikes.

After just a few days, leaders emerged within each group. Boys acquired nicknames and the groups themselves acquired names, Rattlers and Eagles. Each group established norms to regulate behavior within the group. For example, boys who complained about minor injuries or being homesick were teased for not being "tough."

At the end of the first week, it was arranged that the groups discover each other. Each immediately insisted that the other had intruded on its "turf," which helped solidify the emerging feelings of group membership. Each group challenged the other in baseball, so a game was planned, along with other competitions (such as tent pitching and cleaning the cabins). Prizes were announced for the winners.

Preparing for these events further solidified group loyalties, and activities that had once been avoided—cleaning the cabins, for example—were now pursued vigorously because they contributed to the goal of establishing the group's superiority. In this phase, boys became antagonistic to members of the other group. During the competitions, boys heckled and cursed the other group. After losing to the Rattlers in the first baseball game, the Eagles burned the Rattlers' flag and hung the remnants for the Rattlers to find. One Eagle said, "You can tell those guys *I* did it if they say anything. I'll fight 'em!"

Relations deteriorated so rapidly between the groups that in just a few days the boys abandoned displays of good sportsmanship and refused to eat together in the same mess hall. And stereotypes formed. Rattlers were convinced that Eagles were unfriendly and sneaky. Of course, Eagles felt the same way about Rattlers.

After two weeks, the final phase of the study began: Now the aim was to reduce hostility between the groups. First, researchers arranged for the two groups to participate in enjoyable, noncompetitive events, such as watching a movie or shooting firecrackers together. This approach failed completely, and the antagonism continued.

The second approach involved creating common goals for the two groups that required cooperation. When the boys wanted to see a popular movie, the staff said that the camp could not afford the rental. After some debate, the two groups agreed to contribute equally to the cost of the movie. A few days later, a truck that was to pick up supplies would not start. A Rattler suggested they use a rope to pull the truck to start it. As the photo shows, all group members joined in and, after a few tries, started the truck (which was in working condition all along). The boys congratulated one another, and the groups intermingled.

These and other situations involving common goals eliminated the hostility between groups just as rapidly as the competition had elicited it. By the end of the week, Rattlers and Eagles were sitting together in the mess hall. When camp was over, the Rattlers and Eagles asked to travel home on the same bus.

The Robbers Cave study tells us a great deal about group formation and group functioning. Three conclusions are particularly worth remembering. First, when groups of children and adolescents are brought together, a structure emerges rapidly with individuals having specific roles, for example, as a leader. Second, when groups compete for scarce resources (e.g., prizes), individuals identify with and support their own group more strongly. At the same time, they develop negative stereotypes of members of other groups and feel antagonistic toward them. Third, when common goals require that groups cooperate, group boundaries become less pronounced and hostility between groups ceases. Counselors at Silver Lake Camp could create camp-wide projects to ensure that campers' allegiance with their cabin did not lead to antagonism toward other cabins.

Though it's been nearly 50 years since the Sherif study at Robbers Cave, the findings are still important to understanding the social landscape of late childhood and adolescence. Two types of groups are particularly common as children enter adolescence. **A *clique* consists of 4 to 6 individuals who are good friends and, consequently, tend to be similar in age, sex, race, and interests.** Members of a clique spend time together and often dress, talk, and act alike. Cliques are often part of a larger group, too. **A *crowd* is a larger group of older children or adolescents who have similar values and attitudes and are known by a common label.** Maybe you remember some of the different crowds from your own youth. "Jocks," "preppies," "burnouts," "nerds," and "brains"—adolescents use these or similar terms to refer to crowds of older children or adolescents (Brown et al., 1993; Cairns et al., 1995). Looking at the photos on the right, it's easy to know which crowd is which!

Some crowds have more status than others. For example, students in many junior and senior high schools claim that the "jocks" are the most prestigious crowd whereas the "burnouts" are among the least prestigious. Self-esteem in older children and adolescents often reflects the status of their crowd. During the school years, youth from high-status crowds tend to have greater self-esteem than those from low-status crowds (Brown & Lohr, 1987).

Why do some students become nerds while others join the burnouts? Parenting style is part of the answer. A study by Brown and his colleagues (1993) examined the impact of three parental practices on students' membership in particular crowds. The investigators measured the extent to which parents emphasized academic achievement, monitored their children's out-of-school activities, and involved their children in joint decision making. When parents emphasized achievement, their children were more likely to be in the popular, jock, and normal crowds and less likely to be in the druggie crowd. When parents monitored out-of-school behavior, their children were more likely to be in the brain crowd and less likely to be in the druggie crowd. Finally, when parents included their children in joint decision making, their children were more likely to be in the brain and normal crowds and less likely to be in the druggie crowd. These findings were true for African

American, Asian American, European American, and Hispanic American children and their parents.

What seems to happen is that when parents practice authoritative parenting—they are warm but controlling—their children become involved with crowds that endorse adult standards of behavior (e.g., normals, jocks, brains). But, when parents' style is neglecting or permissive, their children are less likely to identify with adult standards of behavior and, instead, join crowds like druggies that disavow adult standards.

> Groups have a dominance hierarchy in which group members defer to a leader, who usually has skills important to the group's function.

Group Structure. Groups—whether in school, at a summer camp, or anyplace else—typically have a well-defined structure. **Most groups have a *dominance hierarchy* consisting of a leader to whom all other members of the group defer.** Other members know their position in the hierarchy. They yield to members who are above them in the hierarchy and assert themselves over members who are below them. A dominance hierarchy is useful in reducing conflict within groups because every member knows his or her place.

What determines where members stand in the hierarchy? With children, especially boys, physical power is often the basis for the dominance hierarchy. The leader is usually the most physically intimidating child (Pettit et al., 1990). Among girls and older boys, hierarchies are often based on individual traits that relate to the group's main function. At Silver Lake Camp, for example, the leaders most often are the children with the greatest camping experience. Among Girl Scouts, girls chosen to be patrol leaders tend to be bright, goal oriented, and have new ideas (Edwards, 1994). These characteristics are appropriate because the primary function of patrols is to help plan activities for the entire troop of Girl Scouts. Thus, leadership based on key skills is effective because it gives the greatest influence to those with the skills most important to group functioning (Hartup, 1983).

Peer Pressure. Groups establish norms—standards of behavior that apply to all group members—and groups may pressure members to conform to these norms. Such "peer pressure" is often characterized as an irresistible, harmful force. The stereotype is that teenagers exert enormous pressure on each other to behave antisocially. In reality, peer pressure is neither all powerful nor always evil. For example, most junior and senior high students resist peer pressure to behave in ways that are clearly antisocial, such as stealing (Brown, Lohr, & McClenahan, 1986). Peer pressure can be positive, too; peers often urge one another to participate in school activities, such as trying out for a play or working on the yearbook, or become involved in community-action projects, such as Habitat for Humanity.

Peer pressure is most powerful when the standards for appropriate behavior are not clear-cut. Taste in music and clothing, for example, is completely subjective, so youth conform to peer group guidelines, as you can see in the all too familiar sight shown in the photo—girls all wearing "in" clothing.

Similarly, standards on smoking, drinking, and using drugs are often fuzzy. Drinking is a good case in point. Parents and groups like SADD (Students Against Driving Drunk) may discourage teens from drinking, yet American culture is filled with youthful models who drink, seem to enjoy it, and suffer no apparent ill effects. To the contrary, they seem to enjoy life even more. With such contradictory messages, it is not surprising that youth look to their peers for answers (Urberg, Değirmencioğlu, & Pilgrim, 1997). Consequently, some youth drink (or smoke, use drugs, or have sex) to conform to their group's norms, while others abstain, again, reflecting their group's norms.

Friendship. As was true in childhood, adolescent friendships are based on common interests and mutual liking. And, adolescents tend to befriend peers who are like themselves in age, gender, and race. However, friendships during adolescence take on new and special significance: Adolescents believe that loyalty, trust, and intimacy are the essential ingredients of friendship. Also, adolescents, much more so than children, believe that friends should defend one another. They also strongly believe that friends should not deceive or abandon one another (Newcomb & Bagwell, 1995).

You can see these key features of adolescent friendships in the Real Children feature.

REAL CHILDREN

Heather's Best Friend

I interviewed Heather, a 13-year-old, about Anna, her best friend since third grade.

RK:	Why is Anna your best friend?
HEATHER:	We have fun together. We both play basketball and we like the same music.
RK:	What else tells you that Anna's your best friend?
HEATHER:	She helps me. And we think alike. My mom says we're like twins!
RK:	I know that Katie is one of your friends, too. But she's not your best friend. How is being friends with Anna different than being friends with Katie?
HEATHER:	Because I can tell Anna stuff—special stuff, like secrets—and I know that she won't tell anybody else.
RK:	What else?
HEATHER:	Well, once some girls at school were picking on me because my mom said I couldn't go to a movie with them. Anna helped me. She told the girls that she thought the movie was stupid and nobody who had any brains would want to go see it.
RK:	Do you and Anna ever fight?
HEATHER:	Sure. But later we always make up. And we tell each other that we're sorry.

For Heather, best friends have common interests and like each other. But her friendship with Anna goes further: She and Anna share secrets and defend each other. And, although they do argue, they both agree that their friendship is too important to be spoiled by petty disagreements, so they always make up. ■

Loyalty, intimacy, and trust are the key elements of adolescents' friendships.

Loyalty is more important in adolescents' friendships than in children's friendships. The emphasis on loyalty apparently goes hand in hand with the emphasis on intimacy: If a friend is disloyal, adolescents are afraid that they may be humiliated because their intimate thoughts and feelings will become known to a much broader circle of people (Berndt & Perry, 1990).

Intimacy is more common in friendships among girls, who are more likely than boys to have one exclusive "best friend." Because intimacy is at the core of their friendships, girls are also more likely to be concerned about the faithfulness of their friends and worry about being rejected (Buhrmester & Furman, 1987). And when one friend makes another mad, girls' anger tends to be more intense and last longer (Whitesell & Harter, 1996).

The emergence of intimacy in adolescent friendships means that friends also come to be seen as sources of social and emotional support. Levitt, Guacci-Franco, and Levitt (1993) asked African American, European American, and Hispanic American 7-, 10-, and 14-year-olds to whom they would turn if they needed help or were bothered by something. For all ethnic groups, 7- and 10-year-olds relied upon close family members—parents, siblings, and grandparents—as primary sources of support, but not friends. However, 14-year-olds relied upon close family members less often and said they would turn to friends instead. Because adolescent friends share intimate thoughts and feelings, they can provide support during emotional or stressful periods. And, as you'll see in the Looking Ahead feature, the benefits of friendship can last a lifetime.

LOOKING AHEAD

Adolescent Friendships Predict Quality of Relationships in the Mid-30s

Friendships can have long-lasting impact on adolescents' development. When adolescents have friends with conventional, prosocietal attitudes, they grow up to be adults who find life satisfying. These long-term consequences are demonstrated in a 20-year-longitudinal study conducted by Stein and Newcomb (1999). These investigators questioned junior high students about the nature of their friendships, including whether they discussed homework with their friends, whether their friends get good grades and plan to go to college, and whether their parents approve of their friends. When the junior high students were in their 30s, Stein and Newcomb asked them about their romantic relationships, about their relationships with parents, families, and peers, as well as about their overall life satisfaction. Having conventional, prosocietal friendships during adolescence was positively related to all these variables. That is, when junior high students with conventional friends were in their 30s, they tended to be happy with life in general and with most of their social relationships in particular. Stein and Newcomb believe that identifying with prosocietal friends apparently leads adolescents to forge a prosocial identity and a positive sense of self, features that later pave the way for positive interactions with others and a positive sense of self in adulthood. ■

Romantic Relationships. American boys and girls typically begin to date at about age 15 (Miller et al., 1997). The first experiences with dating often occur when same-sex groups go places knowing that a mixed-sex crowd will be attending. Examples would include going to a school dance or, as shown in the photo, going to a mall with friends. A somewhat more advanced form of dating involves several boys and several girls going out together as a group. Ultimately, dates involve well-defined couples. By the high school years, most students will have had at least one steady girlfriend or boyfriend.

As you might suspect, cultural factors strongly influence dating patterns. For example, European American parents tend to encourage independence in their teenagers more than traditional Hispanic American and Asian American parents, who emphasize family ties and loyalty to parents. Dating is a sign of independence and usually results in less time spent with family, which explains why Hispanic American and Asian American adolescents often begin to date at an older age and date less frequently (Xiaohe & Whyte, 1990).

Originally, the primary function of dating was to select a mate, but today dating serves a variety of functions for adolescents (Padgham & Blyth, 1991; Sanderson & Cantor, 1995). Dating

- is a pleasant form of recreation and entertainment
- helps to teach adult standards of interpersonal behavior
- is a means to establish status among peers
- provides an outlet for sexual experimentation
- provides companionship like that experienced between best friends
- leads to intimacy, in which teens share innermost feelings with their partners

The functions of dating change during adolescence. As adolescents mature, companionship and intimacy become more important while recreation and status seeking become less important (Roscoe, Diana, & Brooks, 1987; Sanderson & Cantor, 1995).

Check Your Learning

1. As is true for children, adolescents benefit most from a(n) _____ style.

2. Children's relations with their parents change in adolescence, reflecting adolescents' growing independence and a _____ parent-child relationship.

3. In most high schools, the jocks are the most prestigious crowd and the _____ are the least prestigious.

4. As groups form, a _____ typically emerges, with the leader at the top.

5. Peer pressure is most powerful when _____.

6. Compared to children's friendships, adolescents' friendships place greater emphasis on loyalty and _____.

7. When teenagers need help or are bothered by something, they are most likely to turn to _____.

8. Compared to European American teenagers, Hispanic American and _____ teens usually begin to date at an older age and date less frequently.

9. As adolescents mature, _____ and intimacy become the most important functions of dating.

■■ **Continuity** How is the quality of adolescents' friendships related to their relationships during adulthood? What does this say about the continuity of relationships across adolescence and adulthood?

Answers: (1) authoritative, (2) more egalitarian, (3) burnouts, (4) dominance hierarchy, (5) standards for appropriate behavior are not clear-cut, (6) intimacy, (7) friends, (8) Asian American, (9) companionship

The Dark Side

16.3

The Dark Side

├ Drug Use

├ Depression

└ Delinquency

◼ **Why do teenagers drink?**

◼ **What leads some adolescents to become depressed? How can depression be treated?**

◼ **What are the causes of juvenile delinquency?**

Rod was an excellent student and a starter on his high school basketball team. He was looking forward to going to the senior prom with Peggy, his longtime girlfriend, and then going to the state college with her in the fall. Then, without a hint that anything was wrong in their relationship, Peggy dropped Rod and moved in with the drummer of a local rock band. Rod was stunned and miserable. Without Peggy, life meant so little. Basketball and college seemed pointless. Some days Rod wondered if he should just kill himself to make the pain go away.

Some young people do not adapt well to the new demands and responsibilities of adolescence and respond in ways that are unhealthy. In this last section of Chapter 16, we look at three problems, often interrelated, that create the three D's of adolescent development: drugs, depression, and delinquency. As we look at these problems, you'll understand why Rod feels so miserable without Peggy.

Drug Use

Throughout history, people have used substances that alter their behavior, thoughts, or emotions. Today, drugs used commonly in America include alcohol, marijuana, hallucinogens (like LSD), heroin, cocaine, barbiturates, and amphetamines. The graph provides a picture of the use of these drugs by U.S. adolescents (Johnston, O'Malley, & Bachman, 2000). In fact, most adolescents avoid drugs, with one glaring exception—alcohol. A majority of high school seniors have drunk alcohol within the past month (Johnston, O'Malley, & Bachman, 2000).

Teenage Drinking. Why do so many adolescents drink alcohol? There are a number of reasons (Fields, 1992):

• *Experimentation.* Something new to try

• *Relaxation.* A means to reduce tension

• *Escape.* To avoid a harsh or unpleasant real world

• *Feelings of exhilaration.* To increase one's self-confidence, usually by reducing one's inhibitions

Of course, these reasons don't apply to all teenagers. Some never drink. Others experiment briefly with

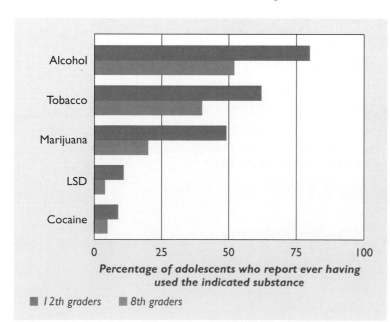

Percentage of adolescents who report ever having used the indicated substance

◼ *12th graders* ◼ *8th graders*

FIG 16–3

drinking, then decide it is not for them. Still others, however, drink heavily: Nearly one-third of high school seniors report having had five or more drinks within the previous two weeks (Johnston et al., 1993).

What determines whether an adolescent joins the majority who drink? Many factors contribute (Petraitis, Flay, & Miller, 1995). Parents are instrumental in determining adolescents' drinking. When drinking is an important part of parents' social lives—for example, stopping at a bar after work or inviting friends over for a drink—adolescents apparently learn that drinking is a pleasant activity and are more likely themselves to drink. In contrast, when parents don't drink at all or limit their drinking to small quantities of alcohol to complement meals, their adolescent children are less likely to drink (Andrews, Hops, & Duncan, 1997; Kline, Canter, & Robin, 1987).

Not surprisingly, peers are influential. As the photo shows, many adolescents drink because their peers do so and exert pressure on them to join the group (Dielman et al., 1992).

Finally, like adults, many adolescents drink to cope with stress. Teens who report frequent life stresses—problems with parents, with interpersonal relationships, or at school—are more likely to drink and to drink more often (Rhodes & Jason, 1990; Windle & Windle, 1996).

Because teenage drinking has so many causes, no single approach is likely to eliminate alcohol abuse. Adolescents who drink to reduce their tension can profit from therapy designed to teach them more effective means of coping with stress. School-based programs that are interactive—featuring student-led discussion—can be effective in teaching the facts about drinking and strategies for resisting peer pressure to drink (Baker, 1988; Tobler & Stratton, 1997).

Depression

Sometime in your life, you have probably had the blues, days when you had little energy or enthusiasm for activities that you usually enjoy. You wanted to be alone, and you may have doubted your abilities. These feelings are perfectly normal, can usually be explained as reactions to specific events, and vanish in a matter of hours or days. For example, after an exciting vacation with family and friends, you may be depressed at the thought of returning to school to start new and difficult courses. Yet your mood improves as you renew friendships and become involved in activities on campus.

Now imagine experiencing these same symptoms continuously for weeks or months. Also suppose that you lost your appetite, slept poorly, and were unable to concentrate. **Pervasive feelings of sadness, irritability, and low self-esteem characterize an individual with *depression.*** About 3 to 10 percent of adolescents are depressed; adolescent girls are more often affected than boys (Nolen-Hoeksema & Girgus, 1994).

Research reveals that unhappiness, anger, and irritation often dominate the lives of depressed adolescents. They believe that family members, friends, and classmates are not friendly to them (Cole & Jordan, 1995). Depressed adolescents wish to be left alone much more often than do nondepressed adolescents (Larson et al., 1990). Rather than being satisfying and rewarding, life is empty and joyless for depressed adolescents.

For some adolescents, depression is triggered by a life event that results in fewer positive reinforcements. The loss of a friend, for example, would deprive a

teenager of many rewarding experiences and interactions, making the teen feel sad. Feeling lethargic and melancholy, like the girl in the photo, the adolescent withdraws from social interaction and thereby misses further opportunities for rewarding experiences. This situation can degenerate rapidly into a vicious circle in which the depressed adolescent becomes progressively more depressed and more likely to avoid interactions that might be rewarding (Lewinsohn & Gotlib, 1995).

Depression often begins with a situation in which an adolescent feels helpless to control the outcome. Think back to Rod, the adolescent in the vignette at the beginning of this module. His girlfriend had been the center of his life. When she left him unexpectedly, he felt helpless to control his own destiny. Similarly, an athlete may play poorly in the championship game because of illness; or, a high school senior may get a lower score on the SAT exam due to a family crisis the night before taking the test. In each case, the adolescent could do nothing to avoid an undesirable result. Most teens recognize that such feelings of helplessness are specific to the particular situation. **In *learned helplessness*, however, adolescents and adults generalize these feelings of helplessness and believe that they are always at the mercy of external events, with no ability to control their own destinies.** Such feelings of learned helplessness often give rise to depression (Peterson, Maier, & Seligman, 1993).

Experiences like these do not lead all adolescents to become depressed. Some adolescents seem more vulnerable to depression than others, which has led scientists to look for biological factors. Studies of twins and adopted children indicate that heredity definitely has a part in depression. The exact biochemical mechanism seems to involve neurotransmitters (Sevy, Mendlewicz, & Mendelbaum, 1995). **Some depressed adolescents have reduced levels of *norepinephrine* and *serotonin*, neurotransmitters that help regulate brain centers that allow people to experience pleasure.** Some adolescents may feel depressed because lower levels of neurotransmitters make it difficult for them to experience happiness, joy, and other pleasurable emotions (Peterson, 1996).

> Depression can be treated with drugs and by teaching adolescents social skills and how to interpret life events.

Treating Depression. It is essential to treat depression; otherwise, depressed adolescents are prone to more serious problems (including suicide, which is examined in the Making Children's Lives Better feature). Two general approaches are commonly used in treating depression (Kazdin, 1990). One is to administer antidepressant drugs designed to correct the imbalance in neurotransmitters. The well-known drug Prozac, for example, is designed to reduce depression by increasing levels of serotonin (Peterson, 1996). The other approach is psychotherapy. Many different forms are available (Lewinsohn & Gotlib, 1995; Sacco & Beck, 1995), but the most effective teach social skills—so that adolescents can have rewarding social interactions—and ways to restructure their interpretation of events—so that teens can recognize situations where they can exert control over their lives.

MAKING CHILDREN'S LIVES BETTER
Preventing Teen Suicides

Suicide is the third most frequent cause of death (after accidents and homicide) among U.S. adolescents. Roughly 10 adolescents in 100 report having attempted suicide at least once, but only 1 in 10,000 actually commits suicide. The figure shows three important characteristics of suicide in adolescence and young adulthood (National Center for Health Statistics, 2000). Suicide is, first, more common among boys than girls, second, more common among older adolescents and young adults than among young adolescents and older children, and, third, more common among European American adolescents than among African American adolescents. Although it's not shown in the figure, Native American adolescents have the highest rate of suicide of any ethnic group in the United States (Garland & Zigler, 1993).

Depression is one frequent precursor of suicide; substance abuse is another (Rich, Sherman, & Fowler, 1990; Summerville, Kaslow, & Doepke, 1996). Few suicides are truly spontaneous; in most cases, there are warning signals (Atwater, 1992). Here are some common signs:

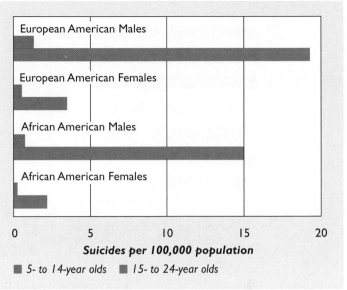

FIG 16–4

- Threats of suicide
- Preoccupation with death
- Change in eating or sleeping habits
- Loss of interest in activities that were once important
- Marked changes in personality
- Persistent feelings of gloom and helplessness
- Giving away valued possessions

If someone you know shows these signs, *don't ignore them*, hoping that they aren't for real. Instead, ask the person if he or she is planning on hurting himself or herself. Be calm and supportive and, if the person appears to have made preparations to commit suicide, don't leave him or her alone. Stay with the person until other friends or relatives can come. More important: *Insist* that the adolescent seek professional help. Therapy is essential to treat the feelings of depression and hopelessness that give rise to thoughts of suicide (Garland & Zigler, 1993). ■

Delinquency

Skipping school. Shoplifting. Selling cocaine. Murder. **When adolescents commit acts like these, which are illegal as well as destructive toward themselves or others, this represents *juvenile delinquency.*** Because delinquency applies to such a broad range of activities, it is useful to identify different forms of delinquent behavior. ***Status offenses* are acts that are not crimes if committed by an adult, such as truancy, sexual promiscuity, and running away from home.** (An adult is someone older than 16, 17, 18, or 19, depending on the state.) ***Index offenses* are acts such as robbery, rape, and arson, which are crimes regardless of the age of the perpetrator.**

Adolescents are responsible for many of the index offenses committed in the United States. The graph on page 500, based on information presented in the FBI's *Uniform Crime Reports* (1996), shows the percentage of cases of motor vehicle theft, burglary, robbery, murder, arson, rape, and assault that were committed by 15- to 20-year-olds. Adolescents are responsible for nearly half of the cars stolen in the United States and for more than one-fourth of the murders.

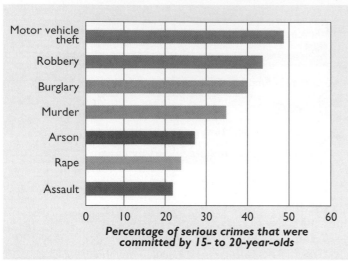

FIG 16–5

Causes of Delinquency. Why is delinquent behavior so common among adolescents? To answer this question, Moffitt (1993) has shown it's important to distinguish two kinds of delinquent behavior. *Life-course persistent antisocial behavior* **refers to antisocial behavior that emerges at an early age and continues throughout life.** These individuals may start with hitting at 3 years, then progress to shoplifting at age 12, and then to car theft at 16. Perhaps only 5 percent of youth fit this pattern of antisocial behavior, but they account for most of the criminal activity shown in the graph.

A second form of delinquent behavior described by Moffitt (1993) is far more common. *Adolescent-limited antisocial behavior* **refers to youth who engage in relatively minor criminal acts yet aren't consistently antisocial.** These youth may become involved in petty crimes, such as shoplifting or using drugs, but may be careful to follow all school rules. And, as the name implies, their antisocial behavior is short-lived, usually vanishing in late adolescence or early adulthood.

Why do so many teens have this brief bout of delinquent activity? Remember, part of the struggle of adolescence is to acquire adult status. Youth with life-course persistent antisocial behavior are often high-status models. These youth often seem to be relatively independent (free of parental influence), they often have desirable possessions like cars and expensive clothes, and they're often sexually experienced. These are attractive features, so many youth apparently imitate the criminal activity that supports this adultlike lifestyle. However, as adolescence ends, the same desirable outcomes can be reached through more prosocial means and the potential costs of antisocial behavior increase, so most youth rapidly abandon this antisocial behavior. Thus, adolescence-limited antisocial behavior can be understood as one way for adolescents to achieve adultlike status and privileges (Moffitt, 1993).

Explaining life-course persistent antisocial behavior is more complex. Researchers have identified several forces that contribute to this type of delinquent behavior.

> Life-course persistent antisocial behavior can be linked to social class, family processes, lack of self-control, and biological forces.

1. *Social class.* Adolescent crime occurs in all social strata but is more frequent among adolescents from lower social classes. This relationship may reflect a number of factors. First, crime is more common in lower-class neighborhoods, so adult criminal models are readily available to children. Second, lower-class adolescents often experience little success in school and usually have little invested in the outcome of their academic efforts; criminal activity is an arena in which they can excel and gain the recognition of their peers. According to Katie Buckland, a prosecutor in Los Angeles, youth who join gangs are "the ambitious kids...trying to climb up their own corporate ladder. And the only corporate ladder they see has to do with gangs and drugs" (Kantrowitz, 1993, p. 44). Third, the constant stress of life on the brink of economic disaster can reduce the effectiveness of parenting in lower-class homes (Patterson, DeVaryshe, & Ramsey, 1989).

2. *Family processes.* Delinquent behavior is often related to inadequate parental supervision. Adolescents who are unsupervised (because, for example, their

parents are at work) are much more likely to become involved in delinquent acts. Parents may also contribute to delinquent behavior if their discipline is inconsistent and if their marital relationship is marked by constant conflict (Patterson, 1995). When family life is riddled with stress, arguments, and threats, a gang, like the one shown in the photo, represents an appealing makeshift family for some adolescents.

3. *Self-control.* As most children develop, they become more capable of regulating their own behavior. They become better able to inhibit impulsive tendencies, to delay gratification, and to consider the impact of their behavior on others (Rotenberg & Mayer, 1990). That is, they learn to rise above the immediate pressures of a situation, to avoid giving in to impulses, and to think about the consequences of their actions. Delinquent youth do not follow the usual developmental pattern. Instead, they are much more inclined to act impulsively, and they often are unable or unwilling to postpone pleasure (Patterson, 1995). Seeing a fancy new CD player or a car, delinquent youth are tempted to steal it, simply so that they can have it *right now.* When others inadvertently get in their way, delinquent adolescents often respond without regard to the nature of the other person's acts or intentions.

4. *Biological forces.* The aggressive and impulsive behavior that is a common part of antisocial behavior has biological roots. Some antisocial youth apparently inherit a predisposition to behave aggressively and impulsively (Carey, 1996). This is *not* an "antisocial gene." Instead, individuals who are genetically predisposed to aggression and impulsivity will be more sensitive to experiences that foster antisocial behavior than will individuals who are not genetically predisposed in this way.

Treatment and Prevention. Given the wide-ranging causes of delinquency, it would be naive to expect a single or simple cure. Instead, delinquency must be attacked along several fronts simultaneously:

- Delinquent adolescents can be taught effective techniques for self-control.
- Parents of delinquent youth can be taught the importance of supervising and monitoring their children's behavior and the necessity for consistent discipline.
- Families of delinquents can learn to function more effectively as a unit, with special emphasis on better means of resolving conflict.
- Schools can develop programs that motivate delinquent youth to become invested in their school performance.
- Communities can improve economic conditions in neighborhoods where delinquency reigns.

Programs that include many of these strategies have met with success; adolescents who participate are less likely to be arrested again. The programs thereby address a major problem affecting not only adolescent development but all of North American society (Alexander et al., 1989; Dryfoos, 1990).

I end this chapter (and the book) with a Child Development and Family Policy feature that describes an effective program for preventing violent behavior and delinquency.

CHILD DEVELOPMENT AND FAMILY POLICY
Preventing Violence

The research on life-course persistent antisocial behavior, as well as research on aggressive behavior described in Module 13.4 warns us of two important factors that must be considered in preventing delinquent behavior. First, it is early in childhood that some youth head down the trail of aggression, violence, and crime. Second, no single force turns a child down this trail; instead, many forces contribute.

Recognizing these factors, in 1990 John Reid and his associates at the Oregon Social Learning Center used a grant from the National Institute of Mental Health to create a model program called Linking the Interests of Families and Teachers (LIFT). The aim of the LIFT program is to nip aggressive behavior in the bud during the elementary-school years. LIFT includes a 10-week intervention that attacks aggressive behavior on many fronts. Parents receive training on discipline, resolving disputes with their children, and monitoring their children's schoolwork. Children receive training designed to improve their social skills, with a particular emphasis on effective problem solving and nonaggressive play. At school, teachers are taught effective ways of dealing with off-task and disruptive behavior while playground and cafeteria monitors are trained to reward children for positive social interactions and to prevent children from bullying peers. Finally, each classroom has a dedicated phone line with an answering machine so that teachers can record daily homework assignments and parents can leave messages for teachers.

In the short run, LIFT is effective in reducing aggression at school (particularly among those children who were most aggressive initially) and in improving children's behavior in the classroom (Reid et al., 1999; Stoolmiller, Eddy, & Reid, 2000). In addition, family interactions were smoother, with fewer disputes over discipline. Three years later, children who had participated in LIFT remained better behaved in the classroom and were less likely to begin drinking alcohol. Obviously, the ultimate proof of LIFT's success will be the demonstration that, as adolescents and young adults, LIFT participants are less likely to be involved in criminal activity. In the interim, the evidence clearly indicates that fewer youngsters are taking the first steps down the path to criminal activity. And LIFT serves as a wonderful example of a model program that draws upon child-development research to create an effective approach to solving a pressing social problem. ■

Check Your Learning

1. The reasons that teenagers drink include relaxation, escape, a desire for feelings of exhilaration, and _____.

2. Teens are less likely to drink when their parents drink _____.

3. Depression has been linked to life events that produce fewer positive reinforcements, situations in which teenagers feel helpless, and _____.

4. Treatments for depression include drugs that correct imbalances in neurotransmitters and therapy that emphasizes _____.

5. Acts like truancy and running away from home, which are not crimes when committed by adults, are known as _____.

6. The factors that contribute to juvenile delinquency include social class, _____, and inadequate self-control.

Nature and Nurture Describe potential biological and environmental contributions to delinquency.

Answers: (1) experimentation, (2) in small amounts to complement meals, (3) an imbalance in neurotransmitters, (4) the development of social skills, (5) status offenses, (6) disrupted family processes

Chapter Critical Review

1. Your local newspaper has just printed a feature describing all the "storm and stress" that typifies adolescence. Write a letter to the editor in which you set the record straight.

2. Discuss the stages of identity formation (Module 16.1) in terms of the formal operation stage of cognitive development (Module 15.1). How is identity formation related to cognitive development?

3. What factors might reduce the drop in self-esteem (Module 16.1) that's associated with the transition from elementary school to middle school?

4. Given what you know about cognitive development in adolescence (Chapter 15), what types of anti-drug, anti-alcohol, or anti-pregnancy messages would be most effective with young adolescents? with older adolescents?

For more review material, log on to www.prenhall.com/kail

See For Yourself

Most junior high and high school students know the different crowds in their school and the status of each. The number of crowds varies, as do their names, but the existence of crowds seems to be a basic fact of social life in adolescence. To learn more about crowds, try to talk individually to four or five students from the same junior high or high school. You could begin by describing one of the crowds from your own high school days. Then ask each student to name the different crowds in his or her school. Ask each student to describe the defining characteristics of people in each crowd. Finally, ask each student which crowd has the highest status in school and which has the lowest.

When you've interviewed all the students, compare their answers. Do the students agree about the number and types of crowds in their school? Do they agree on the status of each? Next, compare your results with those of other students in your class. Are the results similar in the different schools? Can you find any relation between the types of crowds and characteristics of the schools (e.g., rural versus urban)? See for yourself!

For More Information About . . .

 ways to deal with adolescents and guidelines for recognizing when a teenager has a problem that may require professional help, read *You and Your Adolescent : A Parent's Guide for Ages 10 to 20,* by Laurence D. Steinberg and Ann Levine (Harper Perennial, 1997).

 factors that contribute to violent and aggressive behaviors, as well as ways to discourage such behaviors, visit the Web site of the Oregon Social Learning Center:
http://www.oslc.org/

Key Terms

achievement 481
adolescent egocentrism 482
adolescent-limited antisocial
  behavior 500
clique 491
crowd 491
depression 497
diffusion 481

dominance hierarchy 492
ethnic identity 484
foreclosure 481
illusion of invulnerability 483
imaginary audience 482
index offense 499
juvenile delinquency 499
learned helplessness 498

life-course persistent antisocial
  behavior 500
moratorium 481
norepinephrine 498
personal fable 482
serotonin 498
status offense 499

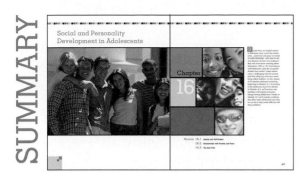

SUMMARY

Social and Personality
Development in Adolescents

16.1 Identity and Self-Esteem

The Search for Identity
The task for adolescents is to find an identity. This search typically involves four statuses. Diffusion and foreclosure are more common in early adolescence; moratorium and achievement are more common in late adolescence and young adulthood. As they seek identity, adolescents often believe that others are always watching them and that no one else has felt as they do.

Adolescents are more likely to achieve an identity when parents encourage discussion and recognize their autonomy; they are least likely to achieve an identity when parents set rules and enforce them without explanation.

Ethnic Identity
Adolescents from ethnic groups often progress through three phases in acquiring an ethnic identity: initial disinterest, exploration, and identity achievement. Achieving an ethnic identity usually results in higher self-esteem but is not consistently related to the strength of one's identification with mainstream culture.

Self-Esteem in Adolescence
Social comparisons begin anew when children move from elementary school to middle or junior high school, and, consequently, self-esteem usually declines somewhat during this transition. However, self-esteem begins to rise in middle and late adolescence as teenagers see themselves acquiring more adult skills and responsibilities.

16.2 Relationships

Parent-Child Relationships in Adolescence
As was true for parent-child relationships in childhood, adolescents benefit from authoritative parenting and often face the challenges of their parents' divorce or remarriage. The parent-child relationship becomes more egalitarian during the adolescent years, reflecting adolescents' growing independence. Contrary to myth, adolescence is not usually a period of storm and stress. Most adolescents love their parents, feel loved by them, rely on them for advice, and adopt their values.

Relationships with Peers
Adolescents often form cliques—small groups of like-minded individuals that become part of a crowd. Some crowds have a higher status than others, and members of higher-status crowds often have higher self-esteem than members of lower-status crowds. Most groups have a dominance hierarchy, a well-defined structure with a leader at the top. Physical power often determines the dominance hierarchy in children and boys. With older children and adolescents, dominance hierarchies are more often based on the skills important to group functioning. Peer pressure is greatest when standards for behavior are unclear, such as for taste in music or clothing, or concerning drinking, using drugs, and sex.

Compared to friendships in childhood, adolescent friendships emphasize loyalty and intimacy. Intimacy is more common in girls' friendships than boys, which makes girls more concerned about friends being faithful. When they need help, teenagers turn to friends more often than to parents.

Boys and girls begin to date in mid-adolescence. Dating often begins with the meeting of same-sex groups and progresses to well-defined couples. For younger adolescents, dating is for both recreation and status; for older adolescents, it is a source of intimacy and companionship.

16.3 The Dark Side

Drug Use
Today many adolescents drink alcohol regularly. Adolescents are attracted to alcohol and other drugs by their need for experimentation, for relaxation, for escape, and for feelings of exhilaration. The primary factors that influence whether adolescents drink are encouragements from others (parents and peers) and stress.

Depression
Depressed adolescents have little enthusiasm for life, believe that others are unfriendly, and wish to be left alone. Depression can be triggered by an event that deprives them of rewarding experiences, by an event in which they feel unable to control their own destiny, or by an imbalance in neurotransmitters. Treating depression relies on medications that correct the levels of neurotransmitters and on therapy designed to improve social skills and restructure adolescents' interpretation of life events.

Delinquency
Many young people engage in antisocial behavior briefly during adolescence. In contrast, the small percentage of adolescents who engage in life-course persistent antisocial behavior are involved in one-fourth to one-half of the serious crimes committed in the United States. Life-course persistent antisocial behavior has been linked to social class, family processes, lack of self-control, and heredity. Efforts to reduce adolescent criminal activity must address all of these variables.

Development in Adolescents
IN PERSPECTIVE

■ Continuity

Early development is related to later development but not perfectly

These last chapters provide an interesting contrast of continuity and lack of continuity in development. In Chapter 16, we learned that when adolescents have conventional, prosocietal friendships, they tend to be more satisfied with life when they're in their 30s. Such adolescents more often have a generally positive view of life and report satisfying relationships with spouses, peers, and parents, apparently because the adolescent friendships helped to forge a positive sense of self. This pattern can be contrasted with the long-term impact of rate of maturation, discussed in Chapter 14. Maturing early tends to benefit adolescent boys and to harm adolescent girls. However, these effects apparently vanish during young adulthood, indicating a discontinuity of development: Rate of maturation has a short-term effect but, unlike the quality of adolescent friendships, not one that persists into adulthood.

■ Nature and Nurture

Development is always jointly influenced by heredity and environment

Chapter 14 included several examples of this theme. One is onset of puberty, which is definitely influenced by heredity—mothers who matured early tend to have early maturing daughters. But the environment also contributes—girls mature early when depressed or living in stress. A second example is osteoporosis. Menopause is a genetically-triggered event that places women over 50 at risk for osteoporosis. Yet an adolescent's experiences—in the form of how much calcium she eats and how often she exercises—can protect her from the disease. The dark side of adolescence, described in Chapter 16, also illustrates the theme. Delinquent behavior shows the joint influence of nature and nurture. Environmental influences on delinquency are many, including poverty and disrupted family processes. But heredity is also factor, making some adolescents impulsive and aggressive. In osteoporosis, onset of puberty, delinquent behavior, and countless other instances in this and other chapters, nature and nurture are the Board of Directors of Development, working together to orchestrate growth and change in childhood and adolescence.

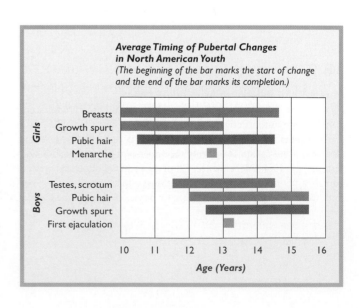

Average Timing of Pubertal Changes in North American Youth
(The beginning of the bar marks the start of change and the end of the bar marks its completion.)

■ Active Child
Children help determine
their own development

Adolescents become increasingly independent, so it's
no surprise that the last three chapters are filled with
examples of adolescents shaping their own destinies. For
example, girls with anorexia and bulimia, described in
Chapter 14, have extraordinarily distorted body images,
which cause them to diet (when they should be eating).
And adolescents see themselves as impervious to risk, so
they expose themselves to all sorts of dangerous activities.
In Chapter 15, adolescents' extensive belief systems make
them resist new experiences. For example, they reject
arguments that are inconsistent with those beliefs. Finally,
in Chapter 16, we traced the phases involved in achieving
an ethnic identity. Adolescents in the second phase of this
process deliberately seek information and experiences that
will help them forge an ethnic identity. In each of these
cases, adolescents use their growing self-understanding
(even if it's incorrect, as in the case of girls with anorexia
and bulimia) to guide their own development, looking for
developmental paths that fit their sense of self.

■ Connections
Development in different
domains is connected

Chapter 15 shows links between different domains of
development. Take moral reasoning as an example.
On the one hand, the bases of moral reasoning often
depend on one's culture: Concern for others is paramount
in India but concern for justice is a key factor in the United States. On the other hand, as cognitive skills increase in
childhood and adolescence, understanding of these root
moral ideas becomes much more sophisticated and prin-
cipled. Career choice also shows the connectedness of
development. Lynne's decision to be an accounted reflected a good match between her skill in math (cognitive)
with a desire to be with others (social). Lynne shows that
cognitive and social factors combine to shape adolescent
development.

Glossary

A

accommodation According to Piaget, the process by which schemes are modified based on new experiences.

achievement According to Marcia, phase of identity formation in which individuals have examined alternatives and chosen an identity.

acquaintance rape See date rape.

active gene-environment interaction Phenomenon in which individuals actively seek an environment conducive to their heredity.

active-passive child issue The issue of whether development is at the mercy of the environment, or whether children actively influence the environment and their own development.

activity Dimension of temperament defined by tempo and vigor of a person's activities.

adolescent egocentrism Self-absorption that typically marks a teen-ager's search for identity.

adolescent-limited antisocial behavior the behavior of youth who engage in relatively minor criminal acts yet aren't consistently antisocial

age of viability Period from 22 to 28 weeks after conception when the fetus becomes able to survive outside the uterus.

aggression Behavior meant to harm others.

allele A variation of a specific gene.

altruism Prosocial behavior that does not benefit the individual who undertakes it.

amniocentesis Medical procedure in which a sample of amniotic fluid is obtained and analyzed.

amnion Fluid-filled sac that envelops the developing embryo.

amniotic fluid Fluid within the amnion that protects the embryo and maintains a constant temperature.

animism Tendency seen in preoperational children to endow inanimate objects with lifelike properties.

anorexia nervosa Condition marked by persistent refusal to eat and irrational fear of being overweight.

anoxia Lack of oxygen to the fetus during delivery.

Apgar score Measure used to evaluate a newborn's condition.

assimilation According to Piaget, the process by which new experiences are readily incorporated into existing schemes.

attachment Enduring social-emotional relationship.

attention Process by which people select information for further cognitive processing.

attention deficit hyperactivity disorder (ADHD) Condition in which a child exhibits overactivity, inattention, and/or impulsivity.

auditory threshold The quietest sound a person's ear can detect.

authoritarian parenting Parenting style that combines high control with little warmth.

authoritative parenting Parenting style that combines moderate control with warmth and responsiveness.

autobiographical memory Memories of the significant events and experiences of one's own life.

autonomous adults Adults who describe childhood experiences objectively, including both positive and negative aspects.

autosomes The 22 pairs of human chromosomes excluding the sex chromosomes.

avoidant attachment A relationship in which infants turn away from their mothers when they are reunited after a brief separation.

axon Part of a neuron that sends information to other cells.

B

babbling Production of speechlike but meaningless sounds, such as "dah-bah-dah."

basal metabolic rate The speed with which the body consumes calories.

basic cry Cry that starts softly and gradually intensifies; associated with hunger or fatigue.

behavioral genetics The branch of genetics that studies the inheritance of behavioral and psychological traits.

blended family Family consisting of a biological parent, stepparent, and children.

breech presentation A birth in which the feet or buttocks are delivered first.

bulimia nervosa Condition marked by binge-purge cycles of overeating and self-induced vomiting or laxative use.

bullying Unprovoked aggression aimed at intimidating, harassing, or humiliating another child.

C

cardinality principle Basic principle of counting that states that the last number name in a counting sequence denotes the number of objects.

cell body Center of a neuron; contains the biological machinery of the cell.

centration According to Piaget, narrowly focused type of thought characteristic of preoperational children.

cephalocaudal principle Law of development that states that structures nearest the head develop first.

cerebral hemispheres Two halves of the cerebral cortex.

cerebral cortex Wrinkled outer surface of the brain that regulates important human functions.

cesarean section (C-section) Surgical delivery of a baby through an incision in the mother's abdomen.

chorionic villus sampling (CVS) Procedure in which a sample of tissue from the chorion is obtained and analyzed.

chromosomes Threadlike structures in the nuclei of cells that contain genetic material

classical conditioning A form of learning that involves pairing a neutral stimulus and a response originally produced by another stimulus.

clique Small group of close friends.

cohort effects In cross-sectional research designs, results caused by environmental effects resulting from differences among age groups, rather than by developmental processes.

component According to Sternberg, any basic cognitive process.

componential subtheory According to Sternberg, the part of intelligence that consists of basic cognitive processes, or components.

comprehension Ability to extract meaning from a sequence of words.

concrete operational stage   According to Piaget, the third stage of cognitive development, from age 7 to 11.

cones   Specialized neurons in the retina that detect color.

constricting   Interaction style in which one person tries to emerge as the victor by threatening, contradicting, or exaggerating; typical of boys.

contextual subtheory   According to Sternberg, the component of intelligence that includes skillful adaptation to the environment.

continuity-discontinuity issue   The issue of whether development follows a smooth progression or a series of abrupt shifts.

conventional level   According to Kohlberg, the second stage of moral development, in which decision making is based on social norms.

cooing   Production of vowel-like sounds, such as "oooooo" and "ahhhhh."

cooperative play   Social play in which children organize their activities around a theme and take on special roles based on the theme.

corpus callosum   Thick bundle of tissue that connects the two cerebral hemispheres.

correlation coefficient *(r)*   A measure of the direction and strength of the relation between two variables.

correlational study   A research design in which investigators study relations between variables as they exist naturally.

counterimitation   Type of observational learning in which a child learns what should not be done.

critical period   A time in development when a specific type of learning can take place.

cross-sectional study   A research design in which investigators study children of different ages at one point in their development.

crowd   Large group of individuals who share values and attitudes.

crowning   Appearance of the top of the baby's head at the opening of the birth canal during labor.

crystallization   Adolescent's use of emerging knowledge about his or her identity as a source of ideas about careers.

culture   The knowledge, attitudes, and behaviors associated with a group of people.

culture-fair intelligence test   Test that includes items based on experiences common to many cultures.

D

date rape   Forced sexual intercourse between partners who know one another socially.

deductive reasoning   Ability to draw appropriate conclusions from facts.

dendrite   Part of a neuron that receives information from other cells.

deoxyribonucleic acid (DNA)   The molecule that is the basis of heredity.

dependent variable   In an experiment, the variable that the investigator does not manipulate; the behavior that is measured.

depression   Condition characterized by pervasive feelings of sadness, irritability, and low self-esteem.

design stage   Stage in development of drawing skills in which children combine basic shapes to create complex patterns; occurs around age 3 or 4.

differentiation   In motor skill development, the process of distinguishing and mastering individual motions.

diffusion   According to Marcia, phase of identity formation in which individuals are overwhelmed by the task.

direct instruction   Parental behavior in which adults tell children what to do, when, and why.

disinhibition   Type of observational learning in which all behaviors like those observed increase after observation.

dismissive adults   Adults who describe childhood experiences in general terms and may idealize their parents.

disorganized (disoriented) attachment   A relationship in which babies seem to be confused when they are reunited with their mothers after a brief separation.

dispensing-family-wisdom grandparents   Grandparents who provide information and advice to parents and child.

dispositional praise   Praise that links a child's behavior to his or her underlying disposition.

distant grandparents   Grandparents who have little contact with grandchildren except on formal occasions.

dizygotic twins   Fraternal twins; twins that result from two eggs fertilized by two sperm.

dominance hierarchy   Ordering of individuals within a group in which members with lower status defer to those of higher status.

dominant   The form of an allele whose chemical instructions are followed.

Down syndrome   Genetic disorder caused by an extra 21st chromosome characterized by mental retardation and physical defects.

dynamic testing   Intelligence testing in which a subject learns something in the presence of the examiner.

dynamic systems theory   A theory that views motor development as involving many distinct skills that are organized and reorganized over time to meet specific needs.

E

ectoderm   Outer layer of the embryo; develops into hair, outer layer of skin, and nervous system.

edge   Line that marks the boundaries of an object.

ego   According to Freud, the practical, rational component of personality that emerges during the first year of life.

egocentric frame of reference   According to Piaget, the infants' inability to think of objects except in relation to the self.

egocentrism   Inability to view the world from another's point of view; typical of the preoperational stage.

electroencephalogram (EEG)   Pattern of brain wave activity recorded from electrodes placed on the scalp.

embryo   A zygote that is completely embedded in the uterine wall.

emotionality   Dimension of temperament defined by strength of emotional response, ease with which a response is triggered, and the ease with which the person returns to a nonemotional state.

empathy   The ability to experience another person's emotions.

enabling   Interaction style characterized by actions and remarks that tend to support others and sustain the interaction; typical of girls.

endoderm   Inner layer of embryo; develops into digestive system and lungs.

epiphyses   Ends of cartilage structures, the first part to turn to bone.

equilibration   According to Piaget, the process by which children reorganize their schemes to return to a state of equilibrium and thereby reach the next developmental level.

ethnic identity   Feeling of belonging to a specific ethnic group.

ethological theory   A theory that views development from an evolutionary perspective; behaviors are investigated for their survival value.

evocative gene-environment interaction   Phenomenon in which different genotypes provoke different reactions from the environment.

exosystem   According to Bronfenbrenner, the social systems that influence one's development indirectly.

experiential subtheory   According to Sternberg, the component of intelligence that includes the ability to adapt to unfamiliar tasks.

experiment   A research design in which an investigator manipulates variables thought to cause a particular behavior.

expressive traits   Psychological constructs that describe a person who is focused on emotion and interpersonal relationships.

expressive style   Learning style of children whose vocabulary consists mainly of social phrases used as single words.

F

family policy   Laws and regulations that directly or indirectly affect families with children.

fast mapping   Children's ability to connect new words to references so rapidly that they cannot consider all possible meanings for the words.

fetal medicine   Medical specialty that treats prenatal problems before birth.

fetal alcohol syndrome (FAS)   Disorder affecting babies whose mothers consume large quantities of alcohol during pregnancy.

field experiment   An experiment carried out in a natural setting, such as a classroom or playground.

fine motor skills   Motor skills associated with grasping, holding, and manipulating objects.

foreclosure   According to Marcia, phase of identity formation in which identity is largely determined by adults.

formal operational stage   According to Piaget, the fourth and final stage of cognitive development, beginning around age 11.

formal grandparents   Grandparents who express strong interest in a child but are uninvolved with child-rearing.

friendship   Voluntary relationship between two people based on mutual liking.

frontal cortex   Areas at the front of the cerebral cortex responsible for personality and intentionality.

fun-seeking grandparents   Grandparents who have fun with their grandchildren but avoid serious interactions.

functional magnetic resonance imaging (F-MRI)   Method of studying brain activity by using magnetic fields to track blood flow in the brain.

G

gender stereotypes   Cultural beliefs about how males and females differ in personality traits, interests, and behaviors.

gender roles   Social roles that are culturally prescribed and considered appropriate for males and females.

gender identity   Permanent perception of oneself as either male of female.

gender stability   Stage of gender identity formation in which children understand that gender is stable throughout life.

gender consistency   Stage of gender identity formation in which children understand that gender is unrelated to situation or personal wishes; occurs between ages 4 and 7.

gender constancy   Stage of gender identity formation in which children understand gender labeling, stability, and consistency.

gender labeling   Stage of gender identity formation in which children understand that they are either boys or girls; occurs at age 2 or 3.

gender-scheme theory   Theory that children learn gender roles by first deciding if something is female or male and use this information to decide if they should learn more about it.

gene   A sequence of nucleotide bases that provides genetic instructions for a specific protein.

genotype   The complete set of genes that makes up a person's genetic instructions.

germ disk   Cluster of cells near the center of the zygote that develops into the baby.

grammatical morphemes   words or word endings (e.g., -ing, -ed) that make a sentence grammatical.

H

habituation   Diminished response to a stimulus as it becomes more familiar.

heterozygous   The condition of having two different alleles for a given trait.

homozygous   The condition of having two identical alleles for a given trait.

hormones   Chemicals released in endocrine glands that travel through the bloodstream to affect other body parts.

Huntingdon's disease   Dominant genetic disease characterized by degeneration of the nervous system.

I

id   According to Freud, the element of personality that is present at birth and that seeks immediate gratification of physical wants.

illusion of invulnerability   Adolescents' belief that misfortunes cannot happen to them.

imaginary audience   Adolescents' feeling that their behavior is continually being watched by their peers.

implantation   Process by which the zygote burrows into the uterine wall and forms connections to the mother's blood vessels.

implementation   Stage of career development in which adolescents obtain firsthand knowledge of jobs.

imprinting   Rapid, innate learning that occurs within a critical period of time and that involves attachment to the first moving object the infant sees.

in vitro fertilization   Technique of mixing eggs and sperm in a laboratory dish and placing fertilized eggs in the uterus.

incomplete dominance   The condition in which one allele does not dominate the other completely.

independent variable   In an experiment, the variable that the investigator manipulates.

index offenses   Offenses that are crimes regardless of the perpetrator's age.

indifferent-uninvolved parenting   Parenting style that provides neither warmth nor control.

indulgent-permissive parenting   Parenting style that offers warmth and caring but little control.

infant mortality rate   Number of infants per 1,000 births who die before the first birthday.

infant-directed speech   Form of speech adults use to talk to infants; includes exaggerated changes in pitch and loudness as well as slow rate.

infantile amnesia Inability to remember events that occurred in infancy.

information processing theory The view that cognition results from the interaction between mental hardware (cognitive structures) and software (cognitive processes).

inhibition Type of observational learning in which all behaviors like those observed decrease after observation.

inner speech Vygotsky's term for thought.

instrumental traits Psychological constructs that describe a person who acts on and influences the world.

instrumental aggression Aggression used to achieve a goal.

integration In motor skills development, the process of combining individual motions in proper sequence in a coherent whole.

intelligence quotient (IQ) According to Ternan, the ratio of mental age to chronological age, multiplied by 100.

internal working model Set of expectation about relationships, based on past experience.

interposition Depth cue based on the fact that nearby objects partially obscure distant objects.

intonation Patterns of rising and falling pitch in speech.

irregular sleep See rapid-eye-movement sleep.

J

joint custody Situation in which both parents retain legal custody of their children after divorce.

juvenile delinquency Adolescent behavior that is illegal and destructive toward the self and others.

K

knowledge-telling strategy Writing strategy that involves writing down information as it is retrieved from memory.

knowledge-transforming strategy Writing strategy that involves deciding what information to include and how best to organize it.

L

latchkey children Children who care for themselves after school.

learned helplessness An individual's belief that he or she is always at the mercy of external events.

learning disability Condition in which a child with normal intelligence has difficulty mastering a school subject.

life-course persistent antisocial behavior antisocial behavior that emerges at an early age and continues throughout life

locomotion The ability to move around in the world.

long-term memory Limitless, permanent storehouse of information.

longitudinal study A research design in which investigators observe the same people repeatedly at different points in development.

M

macrosystem According to Bronfenbrenner, the subcultures and cultures in which the microsystem, mesosystem, and exosystem are embedded.

mad cry Intense version of a basic cry.

mainstreaming Placement of children with disabilities in regular classrooms.

malnourished Refers to a child who is small for his or her chronological age because of inadequate nutrition.

malocclusion Condition in which the upper and lower teeth do not meet properly.

masturbation Self-stimulation of the genitals.

maturational theory The view that child development reflects a specific, prearranged physical plan.

memory strategies Activities and rules that improve remembering.

menarche Onset of menstruation.

mental operations Strategies and rules that make thinking more systematic and powerful.

mental rotation Ability to imagine how an object will look after it is moved in space.

mental retardation Condition in which substantially below-normal intelligence and problems adapting to the environment emerge before age 18.

mental age According to early intelligence researchers, the difficulty of problems a child could solve correctly.

mesoderm Middle layer of embryo; develops into muscles, bones, and circulatory system.

mesosystem According to Bronfenbrenner, the interactions among different microsystems.

microgenetic study A type of longitudinal research design in which investigators observe the same people repeatedly over a well-defined, relatively brief period.

microsystem According to Bronfenbrenner, the people, and objects that make up one's immediate environment.

monozygotic twins Identical twins; twins that result from a single fertilized egg.

moratorium According to Marcia, phase of identity formation in which individuals are examining different alternatives.

motor skills Coordinated movement of the muscles and limbs.

myelin Fatty material that protects the axon and allows it to transmit information rapidly.

myopia Condition in which the lens projects images in front of the retina instead of on it; causes fuzzy vision.

N

naming explosion Rapid learning of new words that occurs around the age of 18 months.

naturalistic observation A method of observation in which investigators watch children and record their behavior in a real-life situation.

nature-nurture issue An issue that concerns the relative influence of heredity and environment on development.

negative reinforcement trap Situation in which parents unwittingly reinforce the behaviors they want to suppress.

neural plate A group of cells that forms approximately 3 weeks after conception; forms the neural tube and ultimately, the brain and spinal cord.

neuron Nerve cell; cell that is specialized for receiving and sending information.

neuroplasticity Extent to which brain organization is flexible.

neurotransmitter Chemical that carries information to nearby neurons.

niche picking Process of actively seeking an environment conducive to one's heredity.

night terror State of partial consciousness associated with panic, rapid breathing, and heavy perspiration; may result from waking rapidly from a deep sleep.

nightmare Vivid, frightening dream that occurs toward morning and wakes the child.

nonREM sleep Sleep in which breathing, heart rate, and brain activity are steady and the sleeper lies quietly.

nonshared environmental influences Forces within a family that make siblings different from one another.

nonsocial play Play in which children play alone or watch others without playing themselves.

norepinephrine Neutotransmitter that helps regulate brain centers that aid in experiencing pleasure.

O

object permanence Understanding that objects exist independently of oneself and one's actions; according to Piaget, a milestone of cognitive development during infancy.

objective frame of reference According to Piaget, the understanding that an object's location can be defined in terms of its relations to other objects.

observational learning (imitation) Learning that results from observing others' behavior.

one-to-one principle Basic principle of counting that states that there is one and only one number name for each object.

operant conditioning A view of learning, proposed by Skinner, that focuses on the consequences of behavior.

organic mental retardation Mental retardation that can be traced to a biological or physical problem.

orienting response Response to an unfamiliar stimulus; consists of startling, fixing the eyes on the stimulus, and changes in heart rate and brain wave activity.

osteoporosis Condition in which the bones become thin and brittle.

overextension Defining a word too broadly.

overregularization Application of grammatical rules to words that are exceptions to the rule (e.g., "bringed").

P

pain cry Cry that begins with a sudden, long burst , followed by a pause, and then gasping.

parallel play Social play in which children play alone but show interest in activities of other children.

passive gene-environment relation Phenomenon in which parents pass on both genes and an environment that supports the expression of those genes.

period of the fetus Development from the ninth week after conception until birth.

personal fable Adolescents' tendency to believe that their experiences and feelings are unique.

personality-type theory Theory that work is most fulfilling when the job fits the worker's personality.

phenotype A person's physical, behavioral, and psychological features; the outward expression of the genotype.

phonemes Unique sounds that can be joined to create words.

phonological awareness Ability to recognize the distinct sounds associated with letters.

pictorial stage Stage in development of drawing skills in which children depict recognizable shapes; occurs around age 4 or 5.

placenta Structure through which nutrients and wastes are exchanged between the mother and the developing child.

placental abruption Emergency condition in which the placenta becomes detached from the uterine wall.

polygenic inheritance A phenotype that results from the actions of many more than one pair of genes.

population The entire group of individuals who are the focus of research in a particular study.

positron emission tomography (PET scan) Method of studying brain activity by tracking glucose use.

postconventional level According to Kohlberg, the level of development in which moral decisions are based on personal principles.

postpartum depression Condition in which irritability continues for months, accompanied by feelings of low self-worth, disturbed sleep, poor appetite, and apathy.

preconventional level According to Kohlberg, the first stage of moral reasoning, marked by obedience to authority.

premature infant Infant born less than 38 weeks after conception.

prenatal development The changes that transform a fertilized egg into a newborn.

preoccupied adults Adults who describe childhood experiences emotionally and often express anger or confusion.

preoperational stage According to Piaget, the second stage of cognitive development, from age 2 to age 7.

primary sex characteristics Physical signs of maturity directly linked to the reproductive organs.

primary circular reaction According to Piaget, a reaction that occurs when an infant accidentally produces a pleasing event and then tries to recreate it.

private speech Spoken comments intended to help young children regulate their own behavior.

proposition An idea; a person derives meaning from text or speech by combining propositions.

prosocial behaviors Actions that benefit others.

proximodistal principle Law of development that states that structures nearest the center of the body develop first.

psychodynamic theory The view, originated by Sigmund Freud, that development is largely determined by how well individuals resolve conflicts they face at different ages.

psychometricians Psychologists who specialize in measuring characteristics such as intelligence and personality.

psychosocial theory Erikson's view that personality development results from resolution of a series of challenges that are based on the interaction of maturational and societal demands.

puberty Physical transition from childhood to adulthood, including rapid growth and sexual maturation.

punishment A consequence that decreases the likelihood that a behavior will be repeated.

purpose In Erikson's theory, a state achieved in the preschool years by balancing initiative with a willingness to cooperate with others.

Q

quasi-experimental design A research design in which people are assigned to groups using nonrandom methods.

R

rapid-eye-movement (REM) sleep Sleep in which the eyes dart rapidly beneath the eyelids, while the body is active.

reaction range The phenomenon that causes a particular genotype to be manifested as a range of phenotypes, depending on the environment.

reactive aggression Aggression used in reaction to another child's behavior.

recessive The form of an allele whose chemical instructions are ignored.

referential style Learning style of a child whose vocabulary consists mainly of names for things, people, and actions.

reflex Unlearned response that is triggered by a specific form of stimulation.

regular sleep See nonREM sleep.

reinforcement A consequence that increases the likelihood that a behavior will be repeated.

relational aggression Aggression used to hurt others by undermining their social relationships.

relative size Depth cue based on the fact that nearby objects appear larger than distant ones.

reliability The degree to which the results obtained from a measure are consistent over time.

resistant attachment A relationship in which, after a brief separation from their mothers, infants want to be held but are difficult to console.

retinal disparity Depth cue based on the fact that the left and right eyes see slightly different versions of the same scene.

rite of passage Cultural ritual that marks the transition to adulthood.

S

sample A subset of a population chosen to represent the entire population in research.

savant Individual with mental retardation who is extremely talented in one domain, such as drawing or music.

scaffolding A teaching style that matches the amount of assistance given to the learner's needs.

schemes According to Piaget, psychological structures used to organize experiences.

schizophrenia Condition characterized by hallucinations, confused language and thought, and bizarre behavior.

script A list of events that describes the sequence in which events occur.

secondary circular reaction According to Piaget, a novel action that involves an object in addition to the infant's body.

secondary sex characteristics Physical signs of maturity not directly linked to reproductive organs.

secular trends Changes in development from one generation to the next.

secure attachment A relationship in which infants have come to trust and depend on their mothers.

self-efficacy The belief that one is capable of performing a certain task.

self reports Children's answers to questions about an investigator's topic of interest.

self-concept Attitudes, values, and behaviors that a person believes make him or her unique.

self-control Ability to rise above immediate pressures and not give in to impulse.

self-esteem A person's judgments about his or her own worth.

semantic bootstrapping hypothesis Theory that children use their knowledge of word meanings to discover grammatical rules.

sensorimotor stage According to Piaget, the first stage of cognitive development, from birth to age 2.

sensory memory Type of memory that holds information in raw, unanalyzed form for no more than a few seconds.

serotonin Neutotransmitter that helps regulate brain centers that aid in experiencing pleasure.

sex chromosomes The pair of human chromosomes that determine a person's sex.

shape stage Stage in development of drawing skills in which children draw six basic shapes; occurs around age 3.

sickle cell trait A disorder that occurs in people who are heterozygous for the sickle cell gene; causes mild anemia only when the person is deprived of oxygen.

simple social play Play in which children engage in similar activities, talk or smile at each other, and offer each other toys.

size constancy Realization that an object's size remains the same despite changes in the size of its retinal image.

small-for-date infant Infant that is born smaller than expected, based on the estimated date of conception.

sociability Dimension of temperament defined by degree of preference for being with other people.

social smile Smile elicited by the sight of another human face.

social conventions Arbitrary standards of behavior agreed to by a cultural group to facilitate interactions within the group.

social cognitive theory Bandura's theory, which proposes that children use reward, punishment, and imitation to make sense of the world.

social referencing Phenomenon in which an infant in an unfamiliar situation looks at a parent for cues about how to react.

social role Set of cultural guidelines for how a person should behave.

social-cognitive flexibility A person's skill in solving social problems using relevant social knowledge.

specification Process during which adolescents limit their career possibilities by learning more and training for specific jobs.

spermache First spontaneous ejaculation of sperm.

spina bifida Disorder in which the embryo's neural tube does not close properly.

stable-order principle Basic principle of counting that states that number names must always be counted in the same order.

status offenses Offenses that are crimes if committed by a juvenile, but not if committed by an adult.

stranger wariness Fear of strangers that typically develops at about 6 months of age.

stress Physical and psychological responses to threatening or challenging conditions.

structured observation A method of observation in which investigators watch children and record their behavior in a situation likely to elicit the behavior of interest.

sudden infant death syndrome (SIDS) Disorder in which a healthy baby dies suddenly and without apparent cause.

superego According to Freud, the moral component of the personality that emerges during the preschool years and incorporates adult standards of right and wrong.

surrogate-parent grandparents Grandparents who assume the normal responsibilities of a parent.

synapse   Gap between one neuron and the next.

synaptic pruning   Gradual reduction in the number of synapses, beginning in infancy and continuing until early adolescence.

systematic observation   A method of observation in which investigators watch children and record what they do or say.

T

telegraphic speech   Speech consisting only of words directly related to meaning; characteristic of two-word stage of language development.

temperament   Consistent mood and style of behavior.

teratogen   Agent that causes abnormal prenatal development.

terminal button   Structure at the ends of axons that releases neurotransmitters.

tertiary circular reaction   According to Piaget, repetition of an old scheme with a novel objects.

texture gradient   Depth cue based on the fact that nearby objects appear to have a coarser but more distinct texture than distant objects.

theory of mind   A person's ideas about interconnections among thoughts, beliefs, and behavior.

theory   An organized set of ideas that is designed to explain and make predictions.

thyroxine   Hormone produced by the thyroid gland; essential for development of nerve cells.

time-out   Form of punishment is which a child must briefly sit alone in an unstimulating location.

triarchic theory   Sternberg's theory that intelligence consists of contextual, experiential, and componental parts.

U

ultrasound   Medical procedure that uses sound waves to produce a picture of the fetus.

umbilical cord   Structure that connects the embryo to the placenta.

underextension   Defining a word to narrowly.

V

validity   The extent to which a test measures what it is supposed to measure.

variable   A characteristic that can take on different values in different individuals.

vernix   Substance that protects the fetus's skin during development.

visual cliff   A glass-covered platform that appears to have a shallow side and a deep side; used to study infants' depth perception.

visual acuity   The smallest pattern a person's eye can reliably distinguish.

W

word recognition   Ability to recognize a pattern of letters as unique and meaningful.

working memory   The site of ongoing cognitive processes as well as the information they require.

Z

zone of proximal development   According to Vygotsky, the difference between what one can do with help and what one can do alone.

zygote   A fertilized egg.

References

Abbey, A. (1991). Acquaintance rape and alcohol consumption on college campuses: How are they linked? *Journal of American College Health, 39,* 165-169.

Ablow, J. C., & Measelle, J. R. (1993). *Berkeley Puppet Interview: Administration and Scoring System Manuals.* Berkeley: University of California.

Aboud, F. E. (1993). The developmental psychology of racial prejudice. *Transcultural Psychiatric Research Review, 30,* 229-242.

Ackerman, B. P. (1993). Children's understanding of the speaker's meaning in referential communication. *Journal of Experimental Child Psychology, 55,* 56-86.

Acredolo, L. P. (1978). Development of spatial orientation in infancy. *Developmental Psychology, 14,* 224-234.

Acredolo, L. P. (1979). Laboratory versus home: The effect of environment on the 9-month-old infant's choice of spatial reference system. *Developmental Psychology, 15,* 666-667.

Adair, R. H., & Bauchner, H. (1993, April). Sleep problems in childhood. *Current Problems in Pediatrics,* 147-170.

Adams, M. J., Treiman, R., & Pressley, M. (1998). Reading, writing, and literacy. In W. Damon (Ed.) *Handbook of child psychology,* Vol 4. New York: Wiley.

Adams, R. J., & Courage, M. L. (1995). Development of chromatic discrimination in early infancy. *Behavioural Brain Research, 67,* 99-101.

Adler, N. (1994). Adolescent sexual behavior looks irrational—But looks are deceiving. Washington, DC: *Federation of Behavioral, Psychological, and Cognitive Sciences.*

Adolph, K. E. (1997). Learning in the development of infant locomotion. *Monographs of the Society for Research in Child Development, 62,* 1-140.

Adolph, K. E., Eppler, M. A., & Gibson, E. J. (1993). Crawling versus walking infants' perception of affordances for locomotion over sloping surfaces. *Child Development, 64,* 1158-1174.

Adolph, K. E., Vereijken, B., & Denny, M. A. (1998). Learning to crawl. *Child Development, 69,* 1299-1312.

Ainsworth, M. D. S. (1978). The development of infant-mother attachment. In B. M. Caldwell, & H. N. Ricciuti (Eds.), *Review of child development research* (Vol. 3). Chicago: The University of Chicago Press.

Ainsworth, M. S. (1993). Attachment as related to mother-infant interaction. *Advances in Infancy Research, 8,* 1-50.

Ales, K. L., Druzin, M. L., & Santini, D. L. (1990). Impact of maternal age on the outcome of pregnancy. *Surgery, Gynecology & Obstetrics, 171,* 209-216.

Alexander, J. F., Waldron, H. B., Barton, C., & Mas, C. H. (1989). The minimizing of blaming attributes and behaviors in delinquent families. *Journal of Consulting and Clinical Psychology, 57,* 19-24.

Allgeier, A. R., & Allgeier, E. R. (1995). *Sexual interactions* (4th ed.). Lexington, MA: Heath.

Allison, D. (1993). *Bastard out of Carolina.* New York: Plume.

Aman, C. J., Roberts, R J., & Pennington, B. F. (1998). A neuropsychological examination of the underlying deficit in attention deficit hyperactivity disorder: Frontal lobe versus right parietal lobe theories. *Developmental Psychology, 34,* 956-969

Amato, P. R., & Keith, B. (1991). Parental divorce and the well-being of children: A meta-analysis. *Psychological Bulletin, 110,* 26-46.

American Academy of Pediatrics (AAP). (1992, Spring). Bedtime doesn't have to be a struggle. *Healthy Kids,* pp. 4-10.

American Academy of Pediatrics. (1997). Adolescents and anabolic steroids: A subject review (RE9720). *Pediatrics, 99.*

American Academy of Pediatrics (AAP) Committee on Drugs and Committee on Bioethics. (1997). Considerations related to the use of recombinant human growth hormone in children. *Pediatrics, 99,* 122-128.

American Academy of Pediatrics (AAP) Committee on Sports Medicine and Committee on School Health. (1989). Organized athletics for preadolescent children. *Pediatrics, 84,* 583-584.

American Psychiatric Association. (1987). *Diagnostic and statistical manual of mental disorders* (3rd ed., revised). Washington, DC: Author.

American Psychiatric Association. (1994). *Diagnostic and statistical manual of mental disorders* (4th ed.). Washington, DC: American Psychiatric Association.

Anand, K. J., & Hickey, P. R. (1987). Pain and its effect in the human neonate and fetus. *New England Journal of Medicine, 31,* 1321-1329.

Anastasi, A. (1988). *Psychological testing* (6th ed.) New York: Macmillan.

Anastopoulos, A. D., Shelton, T. L., DuPaul, G. J., & Guevremont, D. C. (1993). Parent training for attention-deficit hyperactivity disorder: Its impact on parent functioning. *Journal of Abnormal Child Psychology, 21,* 581-596.

Anderson, E. R., Greene, S. M., Hetherington, E. M., & Clingempeel, W. G. (1999). The dynamics of parental remarriage: Adolescent, parent, and sibling. In E. M. Hetherington (Ed). *Coping with divorce, single parenting, and remarriage: A risk and resiliency perspective.* Mahwah, NJ: Erlbaum.

Andrews, J. A., Hops, H., & Duncan, S. C. (1997). Adolescent modeling of parent substance abuse: The moderating effect of the relationship with the parent. *Journal of Family Psychology, 11,* 259-270.

Anisfeld, M. (1991). Neonatal imitation. *Developmental Review, 11,* 60-97.

Anisfeld, M. (1996). Only tongue protrusion modeling is matched by neonates. *Developmental Review, 16,* 149-161.

Antonarakis, S. E., & the Down Syndrome Collaborative Group. (1991). Parental origin of the extra chromosome in trisomy 21 as indicated by analysis of DNA polymorphisms. *New England Journal of Medicine, 324,* 872-876.

Apgar, V. (1953). A proposal for a new method of evaluation of the newborn infant. *Current Researches in Anesthesia and Analgesia, 32,* 260-267.

Arcus, D., & Kagan, J. (1995). Temperament and craniofacial variation in the first two years. *Child Development, 66,* 1529-1540.

Arterberry, M., Yonas, A., & Bensen, A. S. (1989). Self-produced locomotion and the development of responsiveness to linear perspective and texture gradients. *Developmental Psychology, 25,* 976-982.

Ashcraft, M. H. (1982). The development of mental arithmetic: A chronometric approach. *Developmental Review, 2,* 212-236.

Aslin, R. N. (1987). Visual and auditory discrimination in infancy. In J. D. Osofsky (Ed.), *Handbook of infant development* (2nd ed.). New York: Wiley.

Aslin, R. N., Jusczyk, P. W., & Pisoni, D. B. (1998). Speech and auditory processing during infancy: Constraints on and precursors to language. In W. Damon (Ed.), *Handbook of child psychology,* Volume 2. New York: Wiley.

Aslin, R. N., Saffran, J. R., & Newport, W. L. (1998). Computation of conditional probability statistics by 8-month-old infants. *Psychological Science, 9,* 321-324.

Attie, J., Brooks-Gunn, J., & Petersen, A. C. (1990). A developmental perspective on eating disorders and eating problems. In M. Lewis and S. M. Miller (Eds.), *Handbook of developmental psychopathology.* New York: Plenum.

Atwater, E. (1992). *Adolescence*. Englewood Cliffs, NJ: Prentice Hall.

Au, T. K. (1994). Developing an intuitive understanding of substance kinds. *Cognitive Psychology, 27,* 71-111.

Au, T. K., & Glusman, M. (1990). The principle of mutual exclusivity in word learning: To honor or not to honor? *Child Development, 61,* 1474-1490.

Aviezer, O., Sagi, A., Joels, T., & Ziv, Y. (1999). Emotional availability and attachment representations in kibbutz infants and their mothers. *Developmental Psychology, 35,* 811-821.

Bachman, J. (1983, Summer). Premature affluence: Do high school students earn too much? *Economic Outlook USA,* 64-67.

Bachman, J. G., & Schulenberg, J. (1993). How part-time work intensity relates to drug use, problem behavior, time use, and satisfaction among high school seniors: Are these consequences or merely correlates? *Developmental Psychology, 29,* 229-230.

Backscheider, A. G., Shatz, M., & Gelman, S. A. (1993). Preschoolers' ability to distinguish living kinds as a function of regrowth. *Child Development, 64,* 1242-1257.

Baddeley, A. (1996). Exploring the central executive. *Quarterly Journal of Experimental Psychology: Human Experimental Psychlogy, 49,* 5-28.

Baenninger, M., & Newcombe, N. (1995). Environmental input to the development of sex-related differences in spatial and mathematical ability. *Learning & Individual Differences, 7,* 363-379.

Baer, D. M., & Wolf, M. M. (1968). The reinforcement contingency in preschool and remedial education. In R. D. Hess and R. M Baer (Eds.), *Early education.* Chicago: Aldine.

Bagwell, C. L., Newcomb, A. F., & Bukowski, W. M. (1998). Preadolescent friendship and peer rejection as predictors of adult adjustment. *Child Development, 69,* 140-153.

Bahrick, L. E. (1992). Infants' perceptual differentiation of amodal and modality-specific audio-visual relations. *Journal of Experimental Child Psychology, 53,* 180-199.

Bahrick, L. E., Netto, D., & Hernandez-Reif, M. (1998). Intermodal perception of adult and child faces and voices by infants. *Child Development, 69,* 1263-1275.

Bailey, D. A., & Rasmussen, R. L. (1996). Sport and the child: Physiological and skeletal issues. In F. L. Smoll & R. E. Smith (Eds.), *Children and youth in sport: A biopsychological perspective* (pp. 187-199). Dubuque, IA: Brown & Benchmark.

Baillargeon R. (1987). Object permanence in 3- and 4-month-old infants. *Developmental Psychology, 23,* 655-664.

Baillargeon R. (1994). How do infants learn about the physical world? *Current Directions in Psychological Science, 3,* 133-140.

Baillaargeon, R. (1998). Infants' understanding of the physical world. *Advances in Psychological Science, 2,* 503-529.

Baker, C. (1993). *Foundations of bilingual education and bilingualism.* Clevedon, England: Multilingual Matters.

Baker, L. (1994). Fostering metacognitive development. In H. W. Reese (Ed.), *Advances in child development and behavior,* Vol. 25. San Diego: Academic Press.

Baker, L., & Brown, A. L. (1984). Metacognitive skills and reading. In P. D. Pearson (Ed.), *Handbook of Reading Research, Part 2.* New York: Longman.

Baker, T. B. (1988). Models of addiction. *Journal of Abnormal Psychology, 97,* 115-117.

Baldwin, D. A., Markman, E. M, Bill, B., Desjardins, R. N., & Irwin, J. M. (1996). Infants' reliance on a social criterion for establishing word-object relations. *Child Development, 67,* 3135-3153.

Bancroft, J., Axworthy, D., & Ratcliffe, S. (1982). The personality and psycho-sexual development of boys with 47-XXY chromosome constitution. *Journal of Child Psychology and Psychiatry, 23,* 169-180.

Bandura, A. (1977). *Social learning theory.* Englewood Cliffs, N. J.: Prentice Hall.

Bandura, A. (1986). *Social foundations of thought and action: A social cognitive theory.* Englewood Cliffs, NJ: Prentice Hall.

Bandura, A., & Mischel, W. (1965). Modification of self-imposed delay of reward through exposure to live and symbolic models. *Journal of Personality and Social Psychology, 2,* 698-705.

Bandura, A., Ross, D., & Ross, S. A. (1963). Imitation of film-mediated aggressive models. *Journal of Abnormal and Social Psychology, 66,* 3-11.

Barinaga, M. (1997). Researchers find signals that guide young brain neurons. *Science, 278,* 385-386.

Barkley, R. A. (1990). Attention deficit disorders: History, definition, and diagnosis. In M. Lewis and S. M. Miller, (Eds.), *Handbook of developmental psychopathology.* New York: Plenum.

Barkley, R. A. (1994). Impaired delayed responding: A unified theory of attention-deficit hyperactivity disorder. In R. A. Barkley (Ed.), *Disruptive behavior disorders in childhood.* New York: Plenum.

Barkley, R. A. (1996). Attention-deficit hyperactivity disorder. In E. J. Mash & R. A. Barkley (Eds.), *Child psychopathology.* New York: Guilford.

Barling, J., Rogers, K., & Kelloway, E. K. (1995). Some effects of teenagers' part-time employment: The quantity and quality of work make the difference. *Journal of Organizational Behavior, 16,* 143-154.

Barr, R., & Hayne, H. (1999). Developmental changes in imitation from television during infancy. *Child Development, 70,* 1067-1081.

Barton, M. E., & Tomasello, M. (1991). Joint attention and conversation in mother-infant-sibling triads. *Child Development, 62,* 517-529.

Bartsch, K., & Wellman, H. M. (1995). *Children talk about the mind.* New York: Oxford University Press.

Baskett, L. M. (1985). Sibling status effects: Adult expectations. *Developmental Psychology, 21,* 441-445.

Basso, K. H. (1970). *The Cibecue Apache.* New York: Holt, Rinehart, and Winston.

Bates, E., Benigni, L., Bretherton, I., Camaioni, L., & Volterra, V. (1979). *The emergence of symbols: Cognition and communication in infancy.* New York: Academic Press.

Bates, E., Bretherton, I., & Snyder, L. (1988). *From first words to grammar: Individual differences and dissociable mechanisms.* New York: Cambridge University Press.

Bates, J. E., Pettit, G. S., Dodge, K. A., & Ridge, B. (1998). Interaction of temperamental resistance to control and restrictive parenting in the development of externalizing behavior. *Developmental Psychology, 34,* 982-995.

Bates, E., & MacWhinney, B. (1987). Competition, variation, and language learning. In B. MacWhinney (Ed.), *Mechanisms of language acquisition* (pp. 157-193). Hillsdale, NJ: Erlbaum.

Baumeister, A. A., & Baumeister, A. A. (1995). Mental retardation. In M. Hersen & R. T. Ammerman (Eds.), *Advanced abnormal child psychology.* Hillsdale NJ: Erlbaum.

Baumrind, D. (1975). *Early socialization and the discipline controversy.* Morristown, NJ: General Learning Press.

Baumrind, D. (1991). Parenting styles and adolescent development. In R. M. Lerner, A. C. Petersen, and J. Brooks-Gunn (Eds.), *Encyclopedia of adolescence.* New York: Garland.

Bayley, N. (1970). Development of mental abilities. In P. H. Mussen, (Ed.), *Carmichael's manual of child psychology.* New York: John Wiley.

Bayley, N. (1993). *Bayley scales of infant development: Birth to two years* (2nd ed.). San Antonio TX: Psychological Corporation.

Beal, C. R. (1996). The role of comprehension monitoring in children's revision. *Educational Psychology Review, 8,* 219-238.

Beal, C. R., & Belgrad, S. L. (1990). The development of message evaluation skills in young children. *Child Development, 61,* 705-712.

Beautrais, A. L., Fergusson, D. M., & Shannon, F. T. (1982). Life events and childhood morbidity: A prospective study. *Pediatrics, 70,* 935-940.

Beck, M. (1994). How far should we push Mother Nature? *Newsweek* (January 16), 54-57.

Beckwith, L., Cohen, S. E., & Hamilton, C. E. (1999). Maternal sensitivity during infancy and subsequent life events relate to attachment representation at early adulthood. *Developmental Psychology, 35,* 693-700.

Behnke, M., & Eyler, F. D. (1993). The consequences of prenatal substance use for the developing fetus, newborn, and young child. *International Journal of the Addictions, 28,* 1341-1391.

Bell, A. P., Weinberg, M. S., & Hammersmith, S. K. (1981). *Sexual preference: Its development in men and women.* New York: Simon & Schuster.

Beller, M., & Gafni, N. (1996). The 1991 international assessment of educational progress in mathematics and sciences: The gender differences perspective. *Journal of Educational Psychology, 88,* 365-377.

Bellinger, D., Leviton, A., Waternaux, C., Needleman, H., & Rabinowitz, M. (1987). Longitudinal analyses of prenatal and postnatal lead exposure and early cognitive development. *New England Journal of Medicine, 316,* 1037-1043.

Belsky, J. (1993). Etiology of child maltreatment: A developmental-ecological analysis. *Psychological Bulletin, 114,* 413-434.

Belsky, J., Fish, M., & Isabella, R. A. (1991). Continuity and discontinuity in infant negative and positive emotionality: Family antecedents and attachment consequences. *Developmental Psychology, 27,* 421-431.

Belsky, J., Steinberg, L., & Draper, P. (1991). Childhood experience, interpersonal development, and reproductive strategy: An evolutionary theory of socialization. *Child Development, 62,* 647-670.

Belsky, J., Woodworth, S., & Crnic, K. (1996). Trouble in the second year: Three questions about family interaction. *Child Development, 67,* 556-578.

Bem, D. J. (1996). Exotic becomes erotic: A developmental theory of sexual orientation. *Psychological Review, 103,* 320-335.

Benton, S. L., Corkill, A. J., Sharp, J. M., Downey, R. G., et al. (1995). Knowledge, interest, and narrative writing. *Journal of Educational Psychology, 87,* 66-79.

Bereiter, C., & Scardamalia, M. (1987). *The psychology of written composition.* Hillsdale, NJ: Erlbaum.

Berenbaum, S. A., & Snyder, E. (1995). Early hormonal influences on childhood sex-typed activity and playmate preferences: Implications for the development of sexual orientation. *Developmental Psychology, 31,* 31-42.

Berk, L. E. (1992). Children's private speech: An overview of theory and the status of research. In R. M. Diaz & L. E. Berk (Eds.), *Private speech: From social interaction to self-regulation.* Hillsdale, NJ: Erlbaum.

Berk, L. E. (1994). Vygotsky's theory: The importance of make believe play. *Young Children, 50,* 30-38.

Berko, J. (1958). The child's learning of English morphology. *Word, 14,* 150-177.

Berkowitz, L. (1989). Frustration-aggression hypothesis: Examination and reformulation. *Psychological Bulletin, 106,* 59-73.

Berkowitz, M. W., & Gibbs, J. C. (1985). The process of moral conflict resolution and moral development. In M. W. Berkowitz (Ed.), *Peer conflict and psychological growth* (pp. 71-84). San Francisco: Jossey-Bass.

Berndt, T. J., & Keefe, K. (1995). Friends' influence on adolescents' adjustment to school. *Child Development, 66,* 1312-1329.

Berndt, T. J., & Perry, T. B. (1990). Distinctive features and effects of adolescent friendships. In R. Montemeyer, G. R. Adams, & T. P. Gullotta, (Eds.), *From childhood to adolescence: A transition period?* London: Sage.

Bernier, J. C., & Siegel, D. H. (1994). Attention-deficit hyperactivity disorder: A family ecological systems perspective. *Families in Society, 75,* 142-150.

Berry, J. W. (1993). Ethnic identities in plural societies. In M. E. Bernal & G. P. Knight (Eds.), *Ethnic identity: Formation and transmission among Hispanics and other minorities.* New York: State University of New York Press.

Bertenthal, B. H., & Clifton, R. K. (1998). Perception and action. In W. Damon (Ed.), *Handbook of child psychology,* Volume 2. New York: Wiley.

Berthier, N. E. (1996). Learning to reach: A mathematical model. *Developmental Psychology, 32,* 811-823.

Besharov, D. J., & Gardiner, K. N. (1997). Trends in teen sexual behavior. *Children and Youth Services Review, 19,* 341-367.

Best, C. T. (1995). Learning to perceive the sound pattern of English. In C. Rovee-Collier (Ed.), *Advances in infancy research.* Norwood NJ: Ablex.

Best, D. L., Williams, J. E., Cloud, J. M., Davis, S. W., Robertson, L. S., Edwards, J. R., Giles, H., & Fowles, J. (1977). Development of sex-trait stereotypes among young children in the United States, England, and Ireland. *Child Development, 48,* 1375-1384.

Bialystok, E. (1988). Levels of bilingualism and levels of linguistic awareness. *Developmental Psychology, 24,* 560-567.

Bialystok, E. (1997). Effects of bilingualism and biliteracy on children's emerging concepts of print. *Developmental Psychology, 33,* 429-440.

Bigler, R. S., Jones, L. C., & Lobliner, D. B. (1997). Social categorization and the formation of intergroup attitudes in children. *Child Development, 68,* 530-543.

Bigner, J. J., & Jacobsen, R. B. (1989). Parenting behavior of homosexual and heterosexual fathers. *Journal of Homosexuality, 18,* 173-186.

Birch, L. L. (1991). Obesity and eating disorders: A developmental perspective. *Bulletin of the Psychonomic Society, 29,* 265-272.

Birch, L. L., & Fisher, J. A. (1995). Appetite and eating behavior in children. *Pediatric Clinics of North America, 42,* 931-953.

Birnholz, J. C., & Benacerraf, B. R. (1983). The development of human fetal hearing. *Science, 222,* 516-518.

Bisanz, G. L., Das, J. P., Varnhagen, C. K., & Henderson, H. R. (1992). Structural components of reading time and recall for sentences in narratives: Exploring changes with age and reading ability. *Journal of Educational Psychology, 84,* 103-114.

Black, B., & Logan, A. (1995). Links between communication patterns in mother-child, father-child, and child-peer interactions and children's social status. *Child Development, 66,* 255-271.

Black-Gutman, D., & Hickson, F. (1996). The relationship between racial attitudes and social-cognitive development in children: An Australian study. *Developmental Psychology, 32,* 448-456.

Bloom, L., Margulis, C., Tinker, E., & Fujita, N. (1996). Early conversations and word learning: Contributions from child and adult. *Child Development, 67,* 3154-3175.

Bloom, L., Rocissano, L., & Hood, L. (1976). Adult-child discourse: Developmental interaction between information processing and linguistic knowledge. *Cognitive Psychology, 8,* 521-552.

Bogatz, G. A., & Ball, S. (1972). *The second year of "Sesame Street": A continuing evaluation.* Princeton, NJ: Educational Testing Service.

Bohannon, J. N., Padgett, R. J., Nelson, K. E., & Mark, M. (1996). Useful evidence on negative evidence. *Developmental Psychology, 32,* 551-555.

Bohannon, J. N., MacWhinney, B., & Snow, C. (1990). No negative evidence revisited: Beyond learnability or who has to prove what to whom. *Developmental Psychology, 26,* 221-226.

Boivin, M., Vitaro, F., & Gagnon, C. (1992). A reassessment of the self-perception profile for children: Factor structure, reliability, and convergent validity of a French version among second through sixth grade children. *International Journal of Behavioral Development, 15*, 275-290.

Bolger, K. E., Patterson, C. J., & Kupersmidt, J. B. (1998). Peer relationships and self-esteem among children who have been maltreated. *Child Development, 69*, 1171-1197.

Booth, J. R., Perfetti, C. A., MacWhinney, B. (1999). Quick, automatic, and general activation of orthographic and phonological representations in young readers. *Developmental Psychology, 35*, 3-19.

Bork, A. (1985). *Personal computers for education.* New York: Harper & Row.

Bornstein, M. H. (1981). Psychological studies of color perception in human infants: Habituation, discrimination and categorization, recognition, and conceptualization. *Advances in Infancy Research, 1*, 1-40.

Bornstein, M. H. (1997). Stability in mental development from early life: Methods, measures, models, meanings, and myths. In G. E. Butterworth & F. Simion (Eds.), *The development of sensory, motor, and cognitive capacities in early infancy: From sensation to perception.* Hove, England: Psychology Press.

Bornstein, M. H., Haynes, O. M., O'Reilly, A. W., & Painter, K. M. (1996). Solitary and collaborative pretense play in early childhood: Sources of individual variation in the development of representational competence. *Child Development, 67*, 2910-2929.

Bornstein, M. H., Haynes, O. M., Pascual, L., Painter, K. M., & Galperin, C. (1999). Play in two societies: Pervasiveness of process, specificity of structure. *Child Development, 70*, 317-331.

Bower, B. (1985). The left hand of math and verbal talent. *Science News, 144*, 40-42.

Bowlby, J. (1969). *Attachment and loss* (Vol. 1). New York: Basic Books.

Bowlby, J. (1991). Ethological light on psychoanalytical problems. In P. Bateson et al. (Eds.), *The development and integration of behaviour: Essays in honour of Robert Hinde.* Cambridge, England: Cambridge University Press.

Boyer, C. B., & Hein, K. (1991). AIDS and HIV infection in adolescents: The role of education and antibody testing. In R. M. Lerner, A. C. Petersen, & J. Brooks-Gunn (Eds.), *Encyclopedia of adolescence* (Vol. 1). New York: Garland.

Bradley, R. H., Caldwell, B. M., & Rock, S. L. (1988). Home environment and school performance: A ten-year follow-up and examination of three models of environmental action. *Child Development, 59*, 852-867.

Bradley, R. H., Caldwell, B. M., Rock, S. L., Casey, P. M., & Nelson, J. (1987). The early development of low-birthweight infants: Relationship to health, family status, family context, family processes, and parenting. *International Journal of Behavioral Development, 10*, 301-318.

Bradley, R. H., Caldwell, B. M., Rock, S. L., Ramey, C. T., Barnard, K. E., Gray, C., Hammond, M. A., Mitchell, S., Gottfried, A. W., Siegel, L., & Johnson, D. L. (1989). Home environment and cognitive development in the first 3 years of life: A collaborative study involving six sites and three ethnic groups in North America. *Developmental Psychology, 25*, 217-235.

Braet, C., Mervielde, I., & Vandereycken, W. (1997). Psychological aspects of childhood obesity: A controlled study in a clinical and nonclinical sample. *Journal of Pediatric Psychology, 22*, 59-71.

Braine, M. D. S. (1992). What sort of innate structure is needed to "bootstrap" into syntax? *Cognition, 45*, 77-100.

Brand, E., Clingempeel, W. G., & Bowen-Woodward, D. (1988). Family relationships and children's psychological adjustment in stepmother and stepfather families. In E. M. Hetherington & J. D. Arasten (Eds.), *Impact of divorce, single parenting and step parenting on children* (pp. 299-324). Hillsdale, NJ: Erlbaum.

Braungart, J. M., Plomin, R., DeFries, J. C., & Fulker, D. W. (1992). Genetic influence on tester-rated infant temperament as assessed by Bayley's Infant Behavior Record: Nonadoptive and adoptive siblings and twins. *Developmental Psychology, 28*, 40-47.

Brazelton, T. B. (1984). *Brazelton Behavior Assessment Scale* (rev. ed.). Philadelphia: Lippincott.

Brazelton, T. B., Nugent, J. K., & Lester, B. M. (1987). Neonatal behavioral assessment scale. In J. D. Osofsky (Ed.), *Handbook of infant development* (2nd ed). New York: Wiley.

Bretherton, I. (1992). The origins of attachment theory: John Bowlby and Mary Ainsworth. *Developmental Psychology, 28*, 759-775.

Brigham, J. C., & Spier, S. A. (1992). Opinions held by professionals who work with child witnesses. In H. Dent & R. Flin (Eds.), *Children as witnesses.* New York: J. Wiley & Sons.

Brockington, I. (1996). *Motherhood and mental health.* Oxford, England: Oxford University Press.

Brody, G. H. (1998). Sibling relationship quality: Its causes and consequences. *Annual Review of Psychology, 49*, 1-24.

Brody, G. H., & Flor, D. L. (1998). Maternal resources, parenting practices, and child competence in rural, single-parent African American families. *Child Development, 69*, 803-816.

Brody, G. H., Stoneman, A., & McCoy, J. K. (1994). Forecasting sibling relationships in early adolescence from child temperaments and family processes in middle childhood. *Child Development, 65*, 771-784.

Brody, N. (1992). *Intelligence* (2nd ed.). San Diego: Academic Press.

Bronfenbrenner, U. (1979). *The ecology of human development.* Cambridge: Harvard University Press.

Bronfenbrenner, U. (1989). Ecological systems theory. In R. Vasta (Ed.), *Annals of child development,* Vol. 6. Greenwich, CT: JAI Press.

Bronfenbrenner, U. (1995). Developmental ecology through space and time: A future perspective. In P. Moen, G. H. Elder, Jr., & K. Luscher (Eds.), *Examining lives in context: Perspectives on the ecology of human development.* Washington, D.C: American Psychological Associaton.

Bronfenbrenner, U. (1999). Environments in developmental perspective: Theoretical and operational models. In S. L. Friedman & T. D. Wachs (Eds.), *Measuring environments across the life span: Emerging methods and concepts.* Washington, DC: American Psychological Association.

Brooks-Gunn, J. (1988). The impact of puberty and sexual activity upon the health and education of adolescent girls and boys. *Peabody Journal of Education, 64*, 88-113.

Brooks-Gunn, J., Klebanov, P. K., & Duncan, G. J. (1996). Ethnic differences in children's intelligence test scores: Role of economic deprivation, home environment, and maternal characteristics. *Child Development, 67*, 396-408.

Brooks-Gunn, J., & Paikoff, R. (1993). "Sex is a gamble, kissing is a game": Adolescent sexuality, contraception, and sexuality. In S. P. Millstein, A. C. Petersen, & E. O. Nightingale, (Eds.), *Promoting the health behavior of adolescents.* New York: Oxford University Press.

Brooks-Gunn, J., & Ruble, D. N. (1982). The development of menstrual-related beliefs and behaviors during early adolescence. *Child Development, 53*, 1567-1577.

Brown, B. B., & Lohr, M. J. (1987). Peer-group affiliation and adolescent self-esteem: An integration of ego-identity and symbolic-interaction theories. *Journal of Personality and Social Psychology, 52*, 47-55.

Brown, B. B., Lohr, M. J., & McClenahan, E. L. (1986). Early adolescents' perceptions of peer pressure. *Journal of Early Adolescence, 6*, 139-154.

Brown, B. B., Mounts, N., Lamborn, S. D., & Steinberg, L. (1993). Parenting practices and peer group affiliation in adolescence. *Developmental Psychology, 64*, 467-482.

Brown, J. R., & Dunn, J. (1992). Talk with your

mother or your sibling? Developmental changes in early family conversations about feelings. *Child Development, 63,* 336-349.

Brown, L. J., Kaste, L. M., Selwitz, R. H., & Furman, L. J. (1996). Dental caries and sealant usage in the U.S. children, 1988-1991. *Journal of the American Dental Association, 127,* 335-343.

Brown, R. (1973). *A first language: The early stages.* Cambridge, MA: Harvard University Press.

Brown, R., Pressley, M., Van Meter, P., & Schuder, T. (1996). A quasi-experimental validation of transactional strategies instruction with low-achieving second-grade readers. *Journal of Educational Psychology, 88,* 18-37.

Bryant, B. K., (1992). Conflict resolution strategies in relation to children's peer relations. *Journal of Applied Developmental Psychology, 13,* 35-50.

Bryant, B. K., & Crockenberg, S. B. (1980). Correlates and dimensions of prosocial behavior: A study of female siblings with their mothers. *Child Development, 51,* 529-554.

Buchanan, C. M., Eccles, J. S., & Becker, J. B. (1992). Are adolescents the victims of raging hormones? Evidence for activational effects of hormones on moods and behavior at adolescence. *Psychological Bulletin, 111,* 62-107.

Buchholz, M., Karl, H. W., Pomietto, M., & Lynn, A. (1998). Pain scores in infants: A modified infant pain scale versus visual analogue. *Journal of Pain & Symptom Management, 15,* 117-124.

Buhrmester, D., & Furman, W. (1987). The development of companionship and intimacy, *Child Development, 58,* 1101-1113.

Buhrmester, D., & Furman, W. (1990). Perceptions of sibling relationships during middle childhood and adolescence. *Child Development, 61,* 1387-1398.

Bullock, M., & Lutkenhaus, P. (1990). Who am I? The development of self-understanding in toddlers. *Merrill-Palmer Quarterly, 36,* 217-238.

Burchinal, M. R., Roberts, J. E., Riggins, R., Zeisel, S. A., Neebe, E., & Bryant, D. (2000). Relating quality of center-based child care to early cognitive and language development longitudinally. *Child Development, 71,* 338-357.

Burks, V. S., Dodge, K. A., Price, J. M., & Laird, R. D. (1999). Internal representational models of peers: Implications for the development of problematic behavior. *Developmental Psychology, 35,* 802-810.

Burns, A., & Scott, C. (1994). *Mother-headed families and why they have increased.* Hillsdale, NJ: Erlbaum.

Buss, A. H., & Plomin, R. (1975). *A temperamental theory of personality development.* New York: Wiley-Interscience.

Buss, A. H., & Plomin, R. (1984). *Temperament: Early developing personality traits.* Hillsdale, NJ: Lawrence Erlbaum.

Buss, K. A., & Goldsmith, H. H. (1998). Fear and anger regulation in infancy: Effects on the temporal dynamics of affective expression. *Child Development, 69,* 359-374.

Butler, R. (1992). What young people want to know when: The effects of mastery and ability on social information seeking. *Journal of Personality and Social Psychology, 62,* 934-943.

Button, E. J., Sonuga-Burke, E. J. S., Davis, J., & Thompson, M. (1996). A prospective study of self-esteem in the prediction of eating problems in schoolgirls: Questionnaire findings. *British Journal of Clinical Psychology, 35,* 193-203.

Byrne, B. M., & Gavin, D. W. (1996). The Shavelson model revisited: Testing for the structure of academic self-concept across pre-, early, and late adolescents. *Journal of Educational Psychology, 88,* 215-228.

Cairns, R. B., Cairns, B. D., Neckerman, H. J., Ferguson, L. L., & Gariépy, J-L. (1989). Growth and aggression: 1. Childhood to early adolescence. *Developmental Psychology, 25,* 320-330.

Cairns, R. B., Leung, M. C., Buchannan, L., & Cairns, B. D. (1995). Friendships and social networks in childhood and adolescence: Fluidity, reliability, and interrelations. *Child Development, 66,* 1330-1345.

Caldwell, B. M., & Bradley, R. H. (1994). Environmental issues in developmental follow-up research. In S. L. Friedman & H. C. Haywood (Eds.), *Developmental follow-up.* San Diego: Academic Press.

Calkins, S. D., Fox, N. A., & Marshall, T. R. (1996). Behavioral and physiological antecedents of inhibited and uninhibited behavior. *Child Development, 67,* 523-540.

Call, K. T. (1996). Adolescent work as an "arena of comfort" under conditions of family discomfort. In J. T. Mortimer & M. D. Finch (Eds.), *Adolescents, work, and family: An intergenerational developmental analysis.* Thousand Oaks CA: Sage.

Campbell, F. A., & Ramey, C. T. (1994). Effects of early intervention on intellectual and academic achievement: A follow-up study of children from low-income families. *Child Development, 65,* 684-698.

Campbell, R., & Sais, E. (1995). Accelerated metalinguistic (phonological) awareness in bilingual children. *British Journal of Developmental Psychology, 13,* 61-68.

Campbell, S. B., Cohn, J. F., Flanagan, C., Popper, S., & Meyers, T. (1992). Course and correlates of postpartum depression during the transition to parenthood. *Development and Psychopathology, 4,* 29-47.

Campos, J. J., Hiatt, S., Ramsay, D., Henderson, C., & Svejda, M. (1978). The emergence of fear on the visual cliff. In M. Lewis & L. Rosenblum (Eds.), *The origins of affect.* New York: Plenum.

Camras, L. A., Oster, H., Campos, J., Campos, R., Ujiie, T., Miyake, K., Wang, L., & Meng, Z. (1998). Production of emotional facial expressions in European, American, Japanese, and Chinese infants. *Developmental Psychology, 34,* 616-628.

Canfield, R. L., & Smith, E. G. (1996). Number-based expectations and sequential enumeration by 5-month-old infants. *Developmental Psychology, 32,* 269-279.

Capaldi, D. M., Crosby, L., & Stoolmiller, M. (1996). Predicting the timing of first sexual intercourse for at-risk adolescent males. *Child Development, 67,* 344-359.

Capaldi, D. M., & Patterson, G. R. (1991). Relation of parental transitions to boys' adjustment problems: I. A linear hypothesis. II. Mothers at risk for transitions and unskilled parenting. *Developmental Psychology, 27,* 489-504.

Carey, G. (1996). Family and genetic epidemiology of aggressive and antisocial behavior. In D. M. Stoff & R. B. Cairns (Eds.), *Aggression and violence: Genetic, neurobiological, and biosocial perspectives.* Mahwah, NJ: Erlbaum.

Carey, S. (1978). The child as a word learner. In M. Halle, J. Bresnan, and G. Miller (Eds.), *Linguistic theory and psychological reality.* Cambridge, MA: MIT Press.

Carey, S. (1992). Becoming a face expert. In V. Bruce, A. Cowey, A. W. Ellis, and D. I. Perrett (Eds.), *Processing the facial image.* Oxford: Clarendon Press.

Carlo, G., Koller, S. H., Eisenberg, N., Da Silva, M. S., & Frohlich, C. B. (1996). A cross-national study on the relations among prosocial moral reasoning, gender role orientations, and prosocial behaviors. *Developmental Psychology, 32,* 231-240.

Carlson, C. L, Pelham, W. E., Milich, R., & Dixon, J. (1992). Single and combined effects of methylphenidate and behavior therapy on the classroom performance of children with attention-deficit hyperactivity disorder. *Journal of Abnormal Child Psychology, 20,* 213-232.

Carlson, E. A. (1998). A prospective longitudinal study of attachment disorganization/disorientation. *Child Development, 69,* 1107-1128.

Carpenter, P. A., & Daneman, M. (1981). Lexical retrieval and error recovery in reading: A model based on eye fixations. *Journal of Verbal Learning and Verbal Behavior, 20,* 137-160.

Carrere, S. & Gottman, J. M. (1999). Predicting the future of marriages. In E. M. Hetherington (Ed.) *Coping with divorce, single parenting, and remarriage: A risk and resiliency perspective.* Mahwah, NJ: Erlbaum.

Carroll, J. B. (1993). *Human cognitive abilities: A survey of factor-analytic studies.* New York: Cambridge University Press.

Carroll, J. L., & Loughlin, G. M. (1994). Sudden infant death syndrome. In F. A. Oski, C. D. DeAngelis, R. D. Feigin, J. A. McMillan, & J. B. Warshaw (Eds.), *Principals and practice of pediatrics.* Philadelphia: Lippincott.

Casaer, P. (1993). Old and new facts about perinatal brain development. *Journal of Child Psychology and Psychiatry, 34,* 101-109.

Casey, M. B., Nuttall, R. L., & Pezaris, E. (1997). Mediators of gender differences in mathematics college entrance test scores: A comparison of spatial skills with internalized beliefs and anxieties. *Developmental Psychology, 33,* 669-680.

Casey, M. B., Nuttall, R. L., & Pezaris, E. (1999). Evidence in support of a model that predicts how biological and environmental factors interact to influence spatial skills. *Developmental Psychology, 35,* 1237-1247.

Casiglia, A. C., Coco, A. L., & Zappulla, C. (1998). Aspects of social reputation and peer relationships in Italian children: A cross-cultural perspective. *Developmental Psychology, 34,* 723-730.

Cassidy, J. (1994). Emotion regulation: Influences of attachment relationships. *Monographs of the Society for Research in Child Development, 59,* 228-283.

Cassidy, L., & Hurrell, R. M. (1995). The influence of victim's attire on adolescents' judgments of date rape. *Adolescence, 30,* 319-323.

Cattell, R. B. (1965). *The scientific analysis of personality.* Baltimore: Penguin.

Ceci, S. J., & Bruck, M. (1995). *Jeopardy in the courtroom: A scientific analysis of children's testimony.* Washington, DC: American Psychological Association.

Ceci, S. J., & Bruck, M. (1998). Children's testimony: Applied and basic issues. In W. Damon (Ed.), *Handbook of child psychology,* Volume 4. New York: Wiley.

Center for Disease Control and Prevention. (2000). *Childhood injury fact sheet.* http://www.cdc.gov/ncipc/factsheets/childh.htm

Chan, R. W., Raboy, B., & Patterson, C. J. (1998). Psychosocial adjustment among children conceived via donor insemination by lesbian and heterosexual mothers. *Child Development, 69,* 443-457.

Chandler, M., & Moran, T. (1990). Psychopathy and moral development: A comparative study of delinquent and nondelinquent youth. *Development and Psychopathology, 2,* 227-246.

Chao, R. K. (1994). Beyond parental control and authoritarian parenting style: Understanding Chinese parenting through the cultural notion of training. *Child Development, 65,* 1111-1119.

Chapman, P. D. (1988). *Schools as sorters: Lewis M. Terman, applied psychology, and the intelligence testing movement, 1890-1930.* New York: New York University Press.

Chase-Lansdale, P. L., Brooks-Gunn, J., & Zamsky, E. S. (1994). Young African-American multigenerational families in poverty: Quality of mothering and grandmothering. *Child Development, 65,* 373-393.

Chase-Lansdale, P. L., Cherlin, A. J., & Kiernan, K. E. (1995). The long-term effects of parental divorce on the mental health of young adults: A developmental perspective. *Child Development, 66,* 1614-1634.

Chase-Lansdale, P. L., & Hetherington, E. M. (1990). The impact of divorce on life-span development: Short and long term effects. In P. B. Baltes, B. L. Featherman, and R. M. Lerner, (Eds.), *Life-span development and behavior* (Vol. 10). Hillsdale, NJ: Lawrence Erlbaum.

Chehab, F. F., Mounzih, K., Lu, R., & Lim, M. E. (1997, January 3). Early onset of reproductive function in normal female mice treated with leptin. *Science, 275,* 88-90.

Chen, X., Rubin, K. H., & Li, Z. (1995). Social functioning and adjustment in Chinese children. *Developmental Psychology, 31,* 531-539.

Chess, S., & Thomas, A. (1986). *Temperament in clinical practice.* New York: Guilford.

Chi, M. T. H. (1978). Knowledge structures and memory development. In R. Siegler (Ed.), *Children's thinking: What develops?* Hillsdale, NJ: Erlbaum.

Children's Defense Fund. (1996). *The state of America's children yearbook, 1996.* Washington, DC: author.

Chilman, C. S. (1983). *Adolescent sexuality in a changing American society* (2nd ed.). New York: Wiley.

Chisholm, J. S. (1983). *Navajo infancy: An ethological study of child development.* New York: Aldine.

Chomitz, V. R., Cheung, L. W. Y., & Lieberman, E. (1995). The role of lifestyle in preventing low birth weight. *The Future of Children, 5,* 121-138.

Chomsky, N. (1957). *Syntactic structures.* The Hague: Mouton.

Chomsky, N. (1995). *The minimalist program.* Cambridge: MIT Press.

Christensen, A., & Heavey, C. L. (1999). Intervention for couples. *Annual Review of Psychology, 50,* 165-190.

Chugani, H. T., & Phelps, M. E. (1986). Maturational changes in cerebral function in infants determined by 18FDG positron emission tomography. *Science, 231,* 840-843.

Cipani, E. (1991). Educational classification and placement. In J. L. Matson and J. A. Mulick (Eds.), *Handbook of mental retardation* (2nd ed.). New York: Pergamon Press.

Clark, K. B. (1945). A brown girl in a speckled world. *The Journal of Social Issues, 1,* 10-15.

Clark, K. B., & Clark, M. K. (1940). Skin color as a factor in racial identification of Negro preschool children. *The Journal of Social Psychology, 11,* 159-169.

Clifton, R., Perris, E., & Bullinger, A. (1991). Infants' perception of auditory space. *Developmental Psychology, 27,* 187-197.

Cohen, S., & Williamson, G. M. (1991). Stress and infectious disease in humans. *Psychological Bulletin, 109,* 5-24.

Coie, J. D., & Dodge, K. A. (1998). Aggression and antisocial behavior. In W. Damon (Ed.), *Handbook of child psychology,* Vol. 3. New York: Wiley.

Colby, A., Kohlberg, L., Gibbs, J., & Lieberman, M. (1983). A longitudinal study of moral judgment. *Monographs of the Society for Research in Child Development, 48* (Serial #200).

Cole, D. A. (1991). Preliminary support for a competency-based model of depression in children. *Journal of Abnormal Psychology, 100,* 181-190.

Cole, D. A., & Jordan, A. E. (1995). Competence and memory: Integrating psychosocial and cognitive correlates of child depression. *Child Development, 66,* 459-473.

Collaer, M. L., & Hines, M. (1995). Human behavioral sex differences: A role for gonadal hormones during early development? *Psychological Bulletin, 118,* 55-107.

Coltheart, M., Curtis, B., Atkins, P., & Haller, M. (1993). Models of reading aloud: Dual-route and parallel-distributed-processing approaches. *Psychological Review, 100,* 589-608.

Committee on Genetics. (1996). Newborn screening fact sheet. *Pediatrics, 98,* 473-501.

Conger, R. D., Patterson, G. R., & Ge, X. (1995). It takes two to replicate: A mediational model for the impact of parents' stress on adolescent adjustment. *Child Development, 66,* 80-97.

Coopersmith, S. (1967). *The antecedents of self-esteem.* San Francisco: W. H. Freeman.

Coplan, R. J., Rubin, K. H., Fox, N. A., Calkins, S. D. et al. (1994). Being alone, playing alone, and acting alone: Distinguishing among reticence and passive and active solitude in young children. *Child Development, 65,* 129-137.

Copper, R. L., Goldenberg, R. L., Das, A., Elder, N., Swain, M., Norman, G., Ramsey, R., Cotroneo, P., Collins, B. A., Johnson F., Jones P., & Meier, A. M. (1996). The preterm prediction study: Maternal stress is associated with spontaneous preterm birth at less than thirty-five weeks' gestation. National Institute of Child Health and Human Development Maternal-Fetal Medicine Units Network. *American Journal of Obstetrics & Gynecology, 175,* 1286-1292.

Corballis, M. C. (1997). The genetics and evolution of handedness. *Psychological Review, 104,* 714-727.

Corbin, C. B., & Pangrazi, R. P. (1992). Are American children and youth fit? *Research Quarterly for Exercise and Sport, 63,* 96-106.

Coren, S. (1992). *The left-hander syndrome: The causes and consequences of left-handedness.* New York: Free Press.

Coren, S., & Halpern, D. F. (1991). Lefthandedness: A marker for decreased survival fitness. *Psychological Bulletin, 109,* 90-106.

Cornelius, M., Taylor, P., Geva, D., & Day, N. (1995). Prenatal tobacco exposure and marijuana use among adolescents: Effects on offspring gestational age, growth, and morphology. *Pediatrics, 95,* 738-743.

Cornwell, K. S., Harris, L. J., & Fitzgerald, H. E. (1991). Task effects in the development of hand preference in 9-, 13-, and 20-month-old infant girls. *Developmental Neuropsychology, 7,* 19-34.

Costin, S. E., & Jones, D. C. (1992). Friendship as a facilitator of emotional responsiveness and prosocial interventions among young children. *Developmental Psychology, 28,* 941-947.

Coulton, C. J., Korbin, J. E., Su, M., & Chow, J. (1995). Community level factors and child maltreatment rates. *Child Development, 66,* 1262-1276.

Cox, M. J., Owen, M. T., Henderson, V. K., & Margand, N. A. (1992). Prediction of infant-father and infant-mother attachment. *Developmental Psychology, 28,* 474-483.

Craft, M. J., Montgomery, L. A., & Peters, J. (1992, October). *Comparative study of responses in preschool children to the birth of an ill sibling.* Nursing seminar series presentation, University of Iowa College of Nursing, Iowa City, IA.

Craig, K. D., Whitfield, M. F., Grunau, R. V. E., Linton, J., & Hadjistavropoulos, H. D. (1993). Pain in the preterm neonate: Behavioural and physiological indices. *Pain, 52,* 238-299.

Cratty, B. (1979). *Perceptual and motor development in infants and children* (2nd ed.). Englewood Cliffs, NJ: Prentice Hall.

Crawford, M., Chaffin, R., & Fitton, L. (1995). Cognition in social context. *Learning & Individual Differences, 7,* 341-362.

Crick, N. R., Casas, J. F., Ku, H. (1999). Relational and physical forms of peer victimization in preschool. *Developmental Psychology, 35,* 376-385.

Crick, N. R., & Dodge, K. A. (1994). A review and reformulation of social information-processing mechanisms in children's social adjustment. *Psychological Bulletin, 115,* 74-101.

Crick, N. R., & Werner, N. E. (1998). Response decision processes in relational and overt aggression. *Child Development, 69,* 1630-1639.

Crowder, R. G., & Wagner, R. K. (1992). *The psychology of reading : an introduction* (2nd ed.). New York: Oxford University Press, 1992.

Csikszentmihalyi, M., & Larson, R. (1984). Being adolescent: conflict and growth in the teenage years. New York: Basic Books.

Cuellar, I., Nyberg, B., Maldonado, R. E., & Roberts, R. E. (1997). Ethnic identity and acculturation in a young adult Mexican-origin population. *Journal of Community Psychology, 25,* 535-549.

Cunningham, F. G., MacDonald, P. C., & Gant, N. F. (1989). *Williams obstetrics* (18th ed.) London: Appleton & Lange.

Curtiss, S. (1989). The independence and task-specificity of language. In M. H. Bornstein & J. S. Bruner (Eds.,), *Interaction in human development* (pp. 105-137). Hillsdale, NJ: Erlbaum.

D'Augelli, A. R. (1996). Lesbian, gay, and bisexual development during adolescence and young adulthood. In R. P. Cabaj & T. S. Stein (Eds.), *Textbook of homosexuality and mental health.* Washington DC: American Psychiatric Press.

Daly, M., & Wilson, M. (1996). Violence against stepchildren. *Current Directions in Psychological Science, 5,* 77-81.

Damon, W., & Hart, D. (1988). *Self-understanding in childhood and adolescence.* New York: Cambridge University Press.

Dannemiller, J. L. (1998). Color constancy and color vision during infancy: Methodological and empirical issues. In V. Walsh & J. Kulikowski (Eds.), *Perceptual constancy: Why things look as they do.* New York: Cambridge University Press.

Dannemiller, J. L., & Stephens, B. R. (1988). A critical test of infant pattern preference models. *Child Development, 59,* 210-216.

Davidson, K. M., Richards, D. S., Schatz, D. A., & Fisher, D. A. (1991). Successful in utero treatment of fetal goiter and hypothyroidism. *New England Journal of Medicine, 324,* 543-546.

Davies, P. T., & Cummings, E. M. (1998). Exploring children's emotional security as a mediator of the link between marital relations and child adjustment. *Child Development, 69,* 124-139.

Day, J. D., Engelhardt, S. E., Maxwell, S. E., & Bolig, E. E. (1997). Comparison of static and dynamic assessment procedures and their relation to independent performance. *Journal of Educational Psychology, 89,* 358-368.

Day, N. L., Richardson, G. A., Goldschmidt, L., & Cornelius, M. D. (2000). Effects of prenatal tobacco exposure on preschoolers' behavior. *Journal of Developmental & Behavioral Pediatrics, 21,* 180-188.

Day, S. X., Rounds, J., & Swaney, K. (1998). The structure of vocational interests for diverse racial-ethnic groups. *Psychological Science, 9,* 40-44.

Deak, G. O. (2000). Hunting the fox of word learning: Why "constraints" fail to capture it. *Developmental Review, 20,* 29-80.

Deater-Deckard, K. (2000). Parenting and child behavioral adjustment in early childhood: A quantitative approach to studying family processes. *Child Development, 71,* 468-484.

Deater-Deckard, K., & Plomin, R. (1999). An adoption study of the etiology of teacher and parent reports of externalizing behavior problems in middle childhood. *Child Development, 70,* 144-154.

DeBerry, K. M., Scarr, S. & Weinberg, R. (1996). Family racial socialization and ecological competence: Longitudinal assessments of African-American transracial adoptees. *Child Development, 67,* 2375-2399.

DeCasper, A. J., & Spence M. J. (1986). Prenatal maternal speech influences newborn's perception of speech sounds. *Infant Behavior and Development, 9,* 133-150.

Dekovic, M., & Janssens, J. M. (1992). Parents' child-rearing style and child's sociometric status. *Developmental Psychology, 28,* 925-932.

Dellas, M., & Jernigan, L. P. (1990). Affective personality characteristics associated with undergraduate ego identity formation. *Journal of Adolescent Research, 5,* 306-324.

DeLoache, J. S. (1984). Oh where, oh where: Memory-based searching by very young children. In C. Sophian (Ed.), *Origins of cognitive skills.* Hillsdale, NJ: Erlbaum.

DeLoache, J. S. (1995). Early understanding and use of models: The model model. *Current Directions in Psychological Science, 4,* 109-113.

DeLoache, J. S., Miller, K. F., & Rosengren, K. S. (1997). The credible shrinking room: Very young children's performance with symbolic and nonsymbolic relations. *Psychological Science, 8,* 308-313.

Dennis, W., & Dennis, M. G. (1940). The effects of cradling practices upon the onset of walking in Hopi children. *Journal of Genetic Psychology, 56,* 77-86.

DeRosier, M. E., Kupersmidt, J. B., & Patterson, C. J. (1995). Children's academic and behavioral adjustment as a function of the chronicity and proximity of peer rejection. *Child Development, 65,* 1799-1813.

deVilliers, J. G., & deVilliers, P. A. (1985). The acquisition of English. In D. I. Slobin (Ed.), *The cross-linguistic study of language acquisition.* Hillsdale, NJ: Erlbaum.

DeWolff, M. S., & van IJzendoorn, M. H. (1997). Sensitivity and attachment: A meta-analysis on parental antecedents of infant attachment. *Child Development, 68,* 571-591.

Diamond, A., Prevor, M. B., Callender, G., & Druin, D. P. (1997). Prefontal cortex deficits in children treated early and continuously for PKU. *Monographs of the Society for Research in Child Development, 62* (4, Serial No. 252).

Diamond, M., Johnson, R., Young, D., & Singh, S. (1983). Age-related morphologic differences in the rat cerebral cortex and hippocampus: Male-female; right-left. *Experimental Neurology, 81,* 1-13.

DiBlasio, F. A., & Benda, B. B. (1990). Adolescent sexual behavior: Multivariate analysis of a social learning model. *Journal of Adolescent Research, 5,* 449-466.

Dielman, T., Schulenberg, J., Leech, S., & Shope, J. T. (1992, March). Reduction of susceptibility to peer pressure and alcohol use/misuse through a school-based prevention program. Paper presented at the meeting of the Society for Research on Adolescence, Washington, DC.

Dietrich, K. N. (2000). Environmental neurotoxicants and psychological development. In K. O. Yeates and M. D. Ris (Eds.), *Pediatric neuropsychology: Research, theory, and practice. The science and practice of neuropsychology: A Guilford series* (pp. 206-234). New York: The Guilford Press.

DiPietro, J. A., Hodgson, D. M., Costigan, K. A., & Hilton, S. C. (1996). Fetal neurobehavioral development. *Child Development, 67,* 2553-2567.

DiPietro, J. A., Hodgson, D. M., Costigan, K. A., & Johnson, T. R. B. (1996). Fetal antecedents of infant temperament. *Child Development, 67,* 2568-2583.

Dishion, T. J. (1990). The family ecology of boys' peer relations in middle childhood. *Child Development, 61,* 874-892.

Dockrell, J., & McShane, J. (1993). *Children's learning difficulties: A cognitive approach.* Cambridge: Blackwell Publishers.

Dodge, K. A., Bates, J. E., & Pettit, G. S. (1990). Mechanisms in the cycle of violence. *Science, 250,* 1678-1683.

Dodge, K. A., & Crick, N. R. (1990). Social information-processing bases of aggressive behavior in children. *Personality and Social Psychology Bulletin, 16,* 8-22.

Downey, G., Lebolt, A., Rincon, C., & Freitas, A. L. (1998). Rejection sensitivity and children's interpersonal difficulties. *Child Development, 69,* 1074-1091.

Downey, J., Elkin, E. J., Ehrhardt, A. A., Meyer-Bahlburg, H. F. L., Bell, J. J., & Morishima, A. (1991). Cognitive ability and everyday functioning in women with Turner syndrome. *Journal of Learning Disabilities, 24,* 32-39.

Drabman, R. S., & Thomas, M. H. (1976). Does watching violence on television cause apathy? *Pediatrics, 52,* 329-331.

Dryfoos, J. G. (1990). *Adolescents at risk: Prevalence and prevention.* New York: Oxford University Press.

DuBois, D. L., & Hirsch, B. J. (1990). School and neighborhood friendship patterns of black and whites in early adolescence. *Child Development, 61,* 524-536.

Dubow, E. F., Edwards, S., & Ippolito, M. F. (1997). Life stressors, neighborhood disadvantage, and resources: A focus on inner-city children's adjustment. *Journal of Clinical Child Psychology, 26,* 130-144.

Dumas, J. E., LaFreniere, P. J., & Serketich, W. J. (1995). "Balance of power": A transactional analysis of control in mother-child dyads involving socially competent, aggressive, and anxious children. *Journal of Abnormal Psychology, 104,* 104-113.

Dunham, P. J., Dunham, F., & Curwin, A. (1993). Joint-attentional states and lexical acquisition at 18 months. *Developmental Psychology, 29,* 827-831.

Dunn, J., & Kendrick, C. (1981). Social behavior of young siblings in the family context: Differences between same-sex and different-sex dyads. *Child Development, 52,* 1265-1273.

Dunn, J., & Plomin, R. (1990). *Separate lives: Why siblings are so different.* New York, NY: Basicbooks.

Dunn, J., Slomkowski, C., & Beardsall, L. (1994). Sibling relationships from the preschool period through middle childhood and early adolescence. *Developmental Psychology, 30,* 315-324.

Dunne, R. G., Asher, K. N., & Rivara, F. P. (1992). Behavior and parental expectations of child pedestrians. *Pediatrics, 89,* 486-490.

Durik, A., Hyde, J. S., & Clark, R. (2000). Sequelae of cesarean and vaginal deliveries: Psychosocial outcomes for mothers and infants. *Developmental Psychology, 36,* 251-260.

Eacott, M. J. (1999). Memory for the events of early childhood. *Current Directions in Psychological Science, 8,* 46-49.

Eaton, W. O., Chipperfield, J. G., & Singbeil, C. E. (1989). Birth order and activity level in children. *Developmental Psychology, 25,* 668-672.

Eaton, W. O., & Yu, A. P. (1986). Are sex differences in child motor activity level a function of sex differences in maturational status? *Child Development, 60,* 1005-1011.

Eccles, J. S., & Harold, R. D. (1991). Gender differences in sport involvement: Applying the Eccles' expectancy-value model. *Journal of Applied Sports Psychology, 3,* 7-35.

Eccles, J. S., Jacobs, J. E., & Harold, R. D. (1990). Gender role stereotypes, expectancy effects, and parents' socialization of gender differences. *Journal of Social Issues, 46,* 183-201.

Edwards, C. A. (1994). Leadership in groups of school-age girls. *Developmental Psychology, 30,* 920-927.

Edelbrock, C., Rende, R., Plomin, R., & Thompson, L. A. (1995). A twin study of competence and problem behavior in childhood and early adolescence. *Journal of Child Psychology and Psychiatry, 36,* 775-785.

Egan, S. K., Monson, T. C., & Perry, D. G. (1998). Social-cognitive influences on change in aggression over time. *Developmental Psychology, 34,* 996-1006.

Egan, S. K. & Perry, D. G. (1998). Does low self-regard invite victimization? *Developmental Psychology, 34,* 299-309.

Eisenberg, N. (1988). The development of prosocial and aggressive behavior. In M. H. Bornstein and M. E. Lamb (Eds.), *Developmental psychology: An advanced textbook* (2nd ed.). Hillsdale, NJ: Erlbaum.

Eisenberg, N., Fabes, R. A., Schaller, M., Carlo, G., & Miller, P. A. (1991). The relations of parental characteristics and practices to children's vicarious emotional responding. *Child Development, 62,* 1393-1408.

Eisenberg, N., Fabes, R. A., Shepard, S. A., Murphy, B. C., Guthrie, I. K., Jones, S., Friedman, J., Poulin, R., & Maszk, P. (1997). Contemporaneous and longitudinal prediction of children's social functioning from regulation emotionality. *Child Development, 68,* 642-664.

Eisenberg, N., Guthrie, I. K., Fabes, R. A., Reiser, M., Murphy, B. C., Hogren, R., Maszk, P., & Losoya, S. (1997). The relations of regulation and emotionality to resiliency and competent social functioning in elementary school children. *Child Development, 68,* 295-311.

Eisenberg, N., & Shell, R. (1986). Prosocial moral judgment and behavior in children: The mediating role of cost. *Personality and Social Psychology Bulletin, 12,* 426-433.

Eisenberg, N., Shepard, S. A., Fabes, R. A., Murphy, B. C., & Guthrie, I. K. (1998). Shyness and children's emotionality, regulation, and coping: Contemporaneous, longitudinal, and across-context relations. *Child Development, 69,* 767-790.

Eizenman, D. R., & Bertenthal, B. I. (1998). Infants' perception of object unity in translating and rotating displays. *Developmental Psychology, 34,* 426-434.

Elicker, J., Englund, M., & Sroufe, L. A. (1992). Predicting peer competence and peer relationships in childhood from early parent-child relationships. In R. D. Parke & G. W. Ladd (Eds.), *Family-peer relationships: Modes of linkage.* Hillsdale, NJ: Erlbaum.

Elkind, D. (1978). *The child's reality: Three developmental themes.* Hillsdale, NJ: Erlbaum.

Elkind, D., & Bowen, R. (1979). Imaginary audience behavior in children and adolescents. *Developmental Psychology, 15,* 38-44.

Ellis, W. K., & Rusch, F. R. (1991). Supported employment: Current practices and future directions. In J. L. Matson and J. A. Mulick (Eds.), *Handbook of mental retardation* (2nd ed.). New York: Pergamon Press.

Elmer-DeWitt, P. (1994). The genetic revolution. *Time* (January 17), 46-53.

Enns, J. T. (1990). Relations between components of visual attention. In J. T. Enns (Ed.), *The development of attention*. Amsterdam: North Holland.

Epstein, L. H., & Cluss, P. A. (1986). Behavioral genetics of childhood obesity. *Behavior Therapy, 17,* 324-334.

Epstein, L. H., Valoski, A. M., Vara, L. S., McCurley, J. et al. (1995). Effects of decreasing sedentary behavior and increasing activity on weight change in obese children. *Health Psychology, 14,* 109-108.

Erel, O., & Burman, B. (1995). Interrelatedness of marital relations and parent-child relations: A meta-analytic review. *Psychological Bulletin, 118,* 108-132.

Erel, O., Margolin, G., & John, R. S. (1998). Observed sibling interaction: Links with the marital and the mother-child relationship. *Developmental Psychology, 34,* 288-298.

Erikson, E. H. (1968). *Identity: Youth and crisis.* New York: Norton.

Fagot, B. I. (1985). Changes in thinking about early sex role development. *Developmental Review, 5,* 83-98.

Falbo, T., & Polit, E. F. (1986). Quantitative review of the only child literature: Research evidence and theory development, *Psychological Bulletin, 100,* 176-186.

Farver, J. M., & Branstetter, W. H. (1994). Preschoolers' prosocial responses to their peers' distress. *Developmental Psychology, 30,* 334-341.

Farver, J. M., & Shin, Y. L. (1997). Social pretend play in Korean- and Anglo-American preschoolers. *Child Development, 68,* 544-556.

Federal Interagency Forum on Child and Family Statistics (2000). *America's Children: Key National Indicators of Well-Being, 2000.* Federal Interagency Forum on Child and Family Statistics, Washington, DC: U.S. Government Printing Office.

Feingold, A. (1993). Cognitive gender differences: A developmental perspective. *Sex Roles, 29,* 91-112.

Feldman, S. S., & Wentzel, K. R. (1990). The relationship between parental styles, sons' self-restraint, and peer relations in early adolescence. *Journal of Early Adolescence, 10,* 439-454.

Feltey, K. M., Ainslie, J. J., & Geib, A. (1991). Sexual coercion attitudes among high school students: The influence of gender and rape education. *Youth and Society, 23,* 229-250.

Fenson, L., Dale, P. S., Reznick, J. S. Bates, E. et al. (1994). Variability in early communicative development. *Monographs of the Society for Research in Child Development, 59,* Whole No. 173.

Fergusson, D. M., Horwood, L. J., & Shannon, F. T. (1987). Breastfeeding and subsequent social adjustment in six- to eight-year-old children. *Journal of Child Psychology and Psychiatry and Allied Disciplines, 28,* 379-386.

Field, T. M. (1990). *Infancy.* Cambridge, MA: Harvard University Press.

Field, T. M., & Widmayer, S. M. (1982). Motherhood. In B. J. Wolman (Ed.), *Handbook of developmental psychology.* Englewood Cliffs, NJ: Prentice Hall.

Fields, R. (1992). *Drugs and alcohol in perspective.* Dubuque, IA: William C. Brown.

Fincham, F. (1998). Child development and marital relations. *Child Development, 69,* 543-574.

Finn-Stevenson, M., Desimone, L., & Chung. A. (1998). Linking child care and support services with the school: Pilot evaluation of the School of the 21st Century. *Children and Youth Services Review, 20,* 177-205.

Fisch, S., & McCann, S. K. (1993). Making broadcast television participative: Eliciting mathematical behavior through *Square One TV. Educational Technology Research and Development, 41,* 103-109.

Fischer, M., Barkley, R. A., Fletcher, K. E., & Smallish, L. (1993). The adolescent outcome of hyperactive children: Predictors of psychiatric, academic, social, and emotional adjustment. *Journal of the American Academy of Child and Adolescent Psychiatry, 32,* 324-332.

Fischhoff, B., & Quadrel, M. J. (1995). Adolescent alcohol decisions. In G. M. Boyd, J. Howard, & R. A. Zucker (Eds.), *Alcohol problems among adolescents: Current directions in prevention research.* Hillsdale, NJ: Lawrence Erlbaum Associates.

Fisher, C. (1996). Structural limits on verb mapping: The role of analogy in children's interpretations of sentences. *Cognitive Psychology, 31,* 41-81.

Fitzgerald, H. E., & Brackbill, Y. (1976). Classical conditioning in infancy: Development and constraints. *Psychological Bulletin, 83,* 353-375.

Fitzgerald, J. (1987). Research on revision in writing. *Review of Educational Research, 57,* 481-506.

Flavell, J. H. (1985). *Cognitive development* (2nd ed.). Englewood Cliffs, NJ: Prentice Hall.

Fonzi, A., Schneider, B. H., Tani, F., & Tomada, G. (1997). Predicting children's friendship status from their dynamic interaction in structured situations of potential conflict. *Child Development, 68,* 496-506.

Foreyt, J. P., & Goodrick, G. K. (1995). Obesity. In R. T. Ammerman & M. Hersen (Eds.), *Handbook of child behavior therapy in the psychiatric setting.* New York: Wiley.

Foster, S. H. (1986). Learning discourse topic management in the preschool years. *Journal of Child Language, 13,* 231-250.

Fox, N. A. (1991). If it's not left, it's right. *American Psychologist, 46,* 863-872.

Fox, N. A., Kimmerly, N. L., & Schafer, W. D. (1991). Attachment to mother/attachment to father: A meta-analysis. *Child Development, 62,* 210-225.

Franklin, J. C. (1997, November). Industry output and employment projections to 2006. *Monthly Labor Review.*

French, D. C. (1988). Heterogeneity of peer-rejected boys: Aggressive and nonaggressive subtypes. *Child Development, 53,* 976-985.

French, D. C. (1990). Heterogeneity of peer-rejected girls. *Child Development, 61,* 2028-2031.

Fried, P. A., O'Connell, C. M., & Watkinson, B. (1992). 60- and 72-month follow-up of children prenatally exposed to marijuana, cigarettes, and alcohol: Cognitive and language assessment. *Journal of Developmental & Behavioral Pediatrics, 13,* 383-391.

Friedman, J. M., & Polifka, J. E. (1996). *The effects of drugs on the fetus and nursing infant:A handbook for health care professionals.* Baltimore: Johns Hopkins University Press, 1996.

Friend, M., & Davis, T. L. (1993). Appearance-reality distinction: Children's understanding of the physical and affective domains. *Developmental Psychology, 29,* 907-914.

Frye, D. (1993). Causes and precursors of children's theories of mind. In D. F. Hay & A. Angold (Eds.), *Precursors and causes in development and psychopathology.* Chichester, England: Wiley.

Furstenberg, F. F. (1993). How families manage risk and opportunity in dangerous neighborhoods. In W. J. Wilson (Ed.), *Sociology and the public agenda.* Newbury Park CA: Sage.

Furstenburg, F. F., Brooks-Gunn, J., & Morgan, S. P. (1987). *Adolescent mothers and their children in later life.* Cambridge: Cambridge University Press.

Furstenburg, F. F., & Teitler, J. O. (1994). Reconsidering the effects of marital disruption: What happens to children of divorce in early adulthood? *Journal of Family Issues, 15,* 173-190.

Gable, S., & Isabella, R. A. (1992). Maternal contributions to infant regulation of arousal. *Infant Behavior and Development, 15,* 95-107.

Gaddis, A., & Brooks-Gunn, J. (1985). The male experience of pubertal change. *Journal of Youth and Adolescence, 14,* 61-69.

Galambos, N. L., & Maggs, J. L. (1991). Out-of-school care of young adolescents and self-reported behavior. *Developmental Psychology, 27,* 644-655.

Galen, B. R. & Underwood, M. K. (1997). A developmental investigation of social aggression among children. *Developmental Psychology, 33,* 589-600.

Galler, J. R., & Ramsey, F. (1989). A follow-up study of the influence of early malnutrition on development: Behavior at home and at school. *Journal of the American Academy of Child and Adolescent Psychiatry, 28,* 254-261.

Galler, J. R., Ramsey, F., & Forde, V. (1986). A follow-up study of the influence of early malnutrition on subsequent development: IV. Intellectual performance during adolescence. *Nutrition and Behavior, 3,* 211-222.

Garai, J. E., & Scheinfeld, A. (1968). Sex differences in mental and behavioral traits. *Genetic Psychology Monographs, 77,* 169-299.

Garbarino, J., & Kostelny, K. (1992). Child maltreatment as a community problem. *Child Abuse and Neglect, 16,* 455-464.

Garber, J., Robinson, N. S., & Valentiner, D. (1997). The relation between parenting and adolescent depression: Self-worth as a mediator. *Journal of Adolescent Research, 12,* 12-33.

Gardner, H. (1983). *Frames of mind: The theory of multiple intelligences.* New York: Basic Books.

Gardner, H. (1993). *Multiple intelligences: The theory in practice.* New York: Basic Books.

Gardner, H. (1995). Reflections on multiple intelligences: Myths and messages. *Phi Delta Kappan, 77,* 200-203, 206-209.

Garfinkel, I., Hochschild, J. L., & McLanahan, S. S. (1996) Introduction. In I. Garfinkel, J. L. Hochschild, & S. S. McLanahan (Eds.), *Social policies for children.* Washington, D. C.: The Brookings Institution.

Garland, A. F., & Zigler, E. (1993). Adolescent suicide prevention: Current research and social policy implications. *American Psychologist, 48,* 169-182.

Garner, P. W., Jones, D. C., & Palmer, D. J. (1994). Social cognitive correlates of preschool children's sibling caregiving behavior. *Developmental Psychology, 30,* 905-911.

Garvey, C., & Berninger, G. (1981). Timing and turn taking in children's conversations. *Discourse Processes, 4,* 27-59.

Gavin, L. A., & Furman, W. (1996). Adolescent girls' relationships with mothers and best friends. *Child Development, 67,* 375-386.

Ge, X., Conger, R. D., Cadoret, R. J., Neiderhiser, J. M., et al. (1996). The developmental interface between nature and nurture: A mutual influence model of child antisocial behavior and parent behaviors. *Developmental Psychology, 32,* 574-589.

Ge, X., Conger, R. D., & Elder, G. H. (1996). Coming of age too early: Pubertal influences on girls' vulnerability to psychological distress. *Child Development, 67,* 3386-3400.

Geisel, T. (1960). *Green eggs and ham, by Dr. Seuss.* New York: Beginner.

Gelman, R., & Meck, E. (1986). The notion of principle: The case of counting. In J. Hiebert (Ed.), *Conceptual and procedural knowledge: The case of mathematics.* Hillside, NJ: Lawrence Erlbaum.

Gelman, S. A., & Gottfried, G. M. (1996). Children's casual explanations of animate and inanimate motion. *Child Development, 67,* 1970-1987.

Gelman, S. A., & Markman, E. M. (1985). Implicit contrast in adjectives vs. nouns: Implications for word-learning in preschoolers. *Journal of Child Language, 12,* 125-143.

George, C., Kaplan, N., & Main, M. (1985). *The Adult Attachment Interview.* Unpublished manuscript, University of California, Department of Psychology, Berkeley.

Ghim, H. (1990). Evidence for perceptual organization in infants: Perception of subjective contours by young infants. *Infant Behavior and Development, 13,* 221-248.

Gibbs, J. C., Clark, P. M., Joseph, J. A., Green, J. L., Goodrick, T. S., & Makowski, D. (1986). Relations between moral judgment, moral courage, and field independence. *Child Development, 57,* 185-193.

Giberson, P. K., & Weinberg, J. (1992). Fetal alcohol syndrome and functioning of the immune system. *Alcohol Health and Research World, 16,* 29-38.

Gibson, E. J., Riccio, G., Schmuckler, M. A., Stoffregen, T. A., Rosenberg, D., & Taormina, J. (1987). Detection of the traversability of surfaces by crawling and walking infants. *Journal of Experimental Psychology: Human Perception & Performance, 13,* 533-544.

Gibson, E. J., & Walk, R. D. (1960). The "visual cliff." *Scientific American, 202,* 64-71.

Gibson, E. J., & Walker, A. S. (1984). Development of knowledge of visual-tactual affordances of substance. *Child Development, 55,* 453-460.

Gilliam, F. D., & Bales, S. N. (2001). Strategic frame analysis: Reframing America's youth. *Social Policy Report,* volume XV, no. 3. Ann Arbor, MI: Society for Research in Child Development.

Gilligan, C. (1982). *In a different voice: Psychological theory and women's development.* Cambridge, MA: Harvard University Press.

Gilligan, C., & Attanucci, J. (1988). Two moral orientations: Gender differences and similarities. *Merrill-Palmer Quarterly, 34,* 223-237.

Gleason, P. M. (1995). Participation in the National School Lunch Program and School Breakfast Program. *American Journal of Clinical Nutrition, 61,* 213S-220S.

Glick, P. C. (1989). The family life cycle and social change. *Family Relations, 38,* 123-129.

Glick, P. C., & Lin, S. (1986). Recent changes in divorce and remarriage. *Journal of Marriage and the Family, 48,* 737-747.

Goldenberg, R. L., & Klerman, L. V. (1995). Adolescent pregnancy—another look. *New England Journal of Medicine, 332,* 1161-1162.

Goldman, S. R. (1989). Strategy instruction in mathematics. *Learning Disability Quarterly, 12,* 43-55.

Goldsmith, H. H., Buss, K. A., & Lemery, K. S. (1997). Toddler and childhood temperament: Expanded content, stronger genetic evidence, new evidence for the importance of environment. *Developmental Psychology, 33,* 891-905.

Goldsmith, H. H., & Harman, C. (1994). Temperament and attachment: Individuals and relationships. *Current Directions in Psychological Science, 3,* 53-57.

Goldsmith, H. H., Lemery, K. S., Buss, K. A., & Campos, J. J. (1999). Genetic analyses of focal aspects of infant temperament. *Developmental Psychology, 35,* 972-985.

Golinkoff, R. M. (1993). When is communication a "meeting of minds"? *Journal of Child Language, 20,* 199-207.

Golombok, S., & Fivush, R. (1994). *Gender development.* Cambridge, England: Cambridge University Press.

Golombok, S., & Tasker, F. (1996). Do parents influence the sexual orientation of their children? Findings from a longitudinal study of lesbian families. *Developmental Psychology, 32,* 3-11.

Good, T. L., & Brophy, J. E. (1994). *Looking in classrooms* (6th ed.). New York: HarperCollins.

Goodman, G. S., Emery, R. E., & Haugaard, J. J. (1998). Developmental psychology and law: Divorce, child maltreatment, foster care, and adoption. In W. Damon (Ed.), *Handbook of child psychology,* Volume 4. New York: Wiley.

Goodnow, J. J. (1992). *Parental belief systems: The psychological consequences for children.* Hillsdale, NJ: Erlbaum.

Goodwyn, S. W., & Acredolo, L. P. (1993). Symbolic gesture versus word: Is there a modality advantage for onset of symbol use? *Child Development, 64,* 688-701.

Gordon, C. P. (1996). Adolescent decision making: A broadly based theory and its application to the prevention of early pregnancy. *Adolescence, 31,* 561-584.

Goswami, U., & Bryant, P. (1990). *Phonological skills and learning to read.* London: Erlbaum.

Gottesman, I. I. (1993). Origins of schizophrenia: Past as prologue. In R. Plomin & G. E. McClearn (Eds.), *Nature, nurture, and psychology.* Washington, DC: American Psychological Association.

Gottfredson, L. S. (1997). Why *g* matters: The complexity of everyday life. *Intelligence, 24,* 79-132.

Gottlieb, L. N., & Mendelson, M. J. (1990). Parental support and firstborn girls' adaptation to the birth of a sibling. *Journal of Applied Developmental Psychology, 11,* 29-48.

Gottman, J. M. (1986). The world of coordinated play: Same- and cross-sex friendships in children. In J. M. Gottman and Jeffrey G. Parker (Eds.), *Conversations of friends.* New York: Cambridge University Press.

Gottman, J. M., Katz, L. F., & Hooven, C. (1996). Parental meta-emotion philosophy and the emotional life of families: Theoretical models and preliminary data. *Journal of Family Psychology, 10,* 243-268.

Graber, J. A., Brooks-Gunn, J., Paikoff, R. L., & Warren, M. P. (1994). Prediction of eating problems: An 8-year study of adolescent girls. *Developmental Psychology, 30,* 823-834.

Graber, J. A., Brooks-Gunn, J., & Warren, W. P. (1995). The antecedents of menarcheal age: Heredity, family environment, and stressful life events. *Child Development, 66,* 346-359.

Graesser, A. C., Singer, M., & Trabasso, T. (1994). Constructing inferences during narrative text comprehension. *Psychological Review, 101,* 371-395.

Graham, S., Berninger, V. W., Abbott, R. D., Abbott, S. P., & Whitaker, D. (1997). Role of mechanics in composing of elementary school students: A new methodological approach. *Journal of Educational Psychology, 89,* 170-182.

Graham, S., & Juvonen, J. (1998). Self-blame and peer victimization in middle school: An attributional analysis. *Developmental Psychology, 34,* 587-599.

Granrud, C. E. (1986). Binocular vision and spatial perception in 4- and 5-month-old infants. *Journal of Experimental Psychology: Human Perception and Performance, 12,* 36-49.

Gray, S. W., & Klaus, R. A. (1965). An experimental preschool program for culturally deprived children. *Child Development, 36,* 887-898.

Greenberg, M. T., & Crnic, K. A. (1988). Longitudinal predictors of developmental status and social interaction in premature and full-term infants at age two. *Child Development, 59,* 554-570.

Greer, T., & Lockman, J. J. (1998). Using writing instruments: Invariances in young children and adults. *Child Development, 69,* 888-902.

Grigorenko, E. L., & Sternberg, R. J. (1998). Dynamic testing. *Psychological Bulletin, 124,* 75-111.

Groen, G. J., & Resnick, L. B. (1977). Can preschool children invent addition algorithms? *Journal of Educational Psychology, 69,* 645-652.

Gross, R. T. (1984). Patterns of maturation: Their effects on behavior and development. In M. D. Levine & P. Satz (Eds.), *Middle childhood: Development and dysfunction.* Baltimore: University Park Press.

Grovak, M. (1999, February 4). Baby born after spina bifidia surgery seems fine. *Journal and Courier,* p. A1.

Guillemin, J. (1993). Cesarean birth: Social and political aspects. In B. K. Rothman (Ed.), *Encyclopedia of childbearing.* Phoenix AZ: Oryx Press.

Guttmacher, A. F., & Kaiser, I. H. (1986). *Pregnancy, birth, and family planning.* New York: New American Library.

Hahn, W. (1987). Cerebral lateralization of function: From infancy through childhood. *Psychological Bulletin, 101,* 376-392.

Hall, D. G., & Graham. S. A. (1999). Lexical form class information guides word-to-object mapping in preschoolers. *Child Development, 70,* 78-91.

Hall, D. G., Waxman, S. R., & Hurwitz, W. R. (1993). How two- and four-year-old children interpret adjectives and count nouns. *Child Development, 64,* 1651-1664.

Hallinan, M. T., & Teixeira, R. A. (1987). Opportunities and constraints: Black-white differences in the formation of interracial friendships. *Child Development, 58,* 1358-1371.

Halpern, C. T., Udry, J. R., Campbell, B., & Suchindran, C. (1999). Effects of body fat on weight concerns, dating, and sexual activity: A longitudinal analysis of black and white adolescent girls. *Developmental Psychology, 35,* 721-736.

Halpern, D. F. (1986). *Sex differences in cognitive abilities.* Hillsdale, NJ: Lawrence Erlbaum.

Halpern L. F., MacLean, W. E., & Baumeister, A. A. (1995). Infant sleep-wake characteristics: Relation to neurological status and the prediction of developmental outcome. *Developmental Review, 15,* 255-291.

Hamer, D. H., Hu, S., Magnuson, V. L., & Hu, N. (1993). A linkage between DNA markers on the X chromosome and male sexual orientation. *Science, 261,* 321-327.

Hammill, D. D. (1990). On defining learning disabilities: An emerging consensus. *Journal of Learning Disabilities, 23,* 74-84.

Harley, K. & Reese, E. (1999). Origins of autobiographical memory. *Developmental Psychology, 35,* 1338-1348.

Harris, B., Lovett, L., Newcombe, R. G., Read, G. F., Walker, R., & Riad-Fahmy, D. (1994). Maternity blues and major endocrine changes: Cardiff puerperal mood and hormone study II. *British Medical Journal, 308,* 949-953.

Harris, L. J. (1983). Laterality of function in the infant: Historical and contemporary trends in theory and research. In G. Young, S. J. Segalowitz, C. M. Corter, and S. E. Trehub (Eds.), *Manual specialization and the developing brain.* New York: Academic Press.

Harris, P. L., Brown, E., Marriot, C., Whithall, S., & Harmer, S. (1991). Monsters, ghosts, and witches: Testing the limits of the fantasy-reality distinction in young children. *British Journal of Developmental Psychology, 9,* 105-123.

Harris, P. L., & Kavanaugh, R. D. (1993). Young children's understanding of pretense. *Monographs of the Society for Research in Child Development, 58,* Serial No. 231.

Harrist, A. W., Zaia, A. F., Bates, J. E., Dodge, K. A., & Pettit, G. S. (1997). Subtypes of social withdrawal in early childhood: Sociometric status and social-cognitive differences across four years. *Child Development, 68,* 278-294.

Hart, C. H., Charlesworth, R., Burts, D. C., & DeWolf,M. (1993, March). The relationship of attendance in developmentally appropriate or inappropriate kindergarten classrooms to first-grade behavior. Paper presented at the biennial meeting of the Society for Research in Child Development, New Orleans.

Hart, C. H., Nelson, D. A., Robinson, C. C., Olsen, S. F., & McNeilly-Choque, M. K. (1998). Overt and relational aggression in Russian nursery-school-age children: Parenting style and marital linkages. *Developmental Psychology, 34,* 687-697.

Harter, S. (1985). *Manual for the self-perception profile for children.* Denver, CO: University of Denver.

Harter, S. (1988). Developmental processes in the construction of the self. In T. D. Yawkey & J. E. Johnson (Eds.), *Integrative processes and socialization: Early to middle childhood.* Hillsdale, NJ: Erlbaum.

Harter, S. (1990). Self and identity development. In S. S. Feldman & G. R. Elliott (Eds.), *At the threshold: The developing adolescent.* Cambridge, MA: Harvard University Press.

Harter, S. (1999). *The construction of the self: a developmental perspective.* New York: Guilford Press.

Harter, S., & Pike, R. (1984). The pictorial scale of perceived competence and social acceptance for young children. *Child Development, 55,* 1969-1982.

Harter, S., Whitesell, N. R., & Kowalski, P. S. (1992). Individual differences in the effects of educational transitions on young adolescents' perceptions of competence and motivational orientation. *American Educational Research Journal, 29,* 777-807.

Hartup, W. W. (1992b). Friendships and their developmental significance. In H. McGurk (Ed.), *Contemporary issues in childhood social development.* London: Routledge.

Hartup, W. W. (1983). Peer relations. In R. H. Mussen (Ed.), *Handbook of child psychology* (Vol. 4). New York: Wiley.

Hartup, W. W. (1992a). Peer relations in early and middle childhood. In V. B. Van Hasselt and M. Hersen (Eds.), *Handbook of social development: A lifespan perspective.* New York: Plenum.

Hartup, W. W., & Stevens, N. (1999). Friendships and adaptation across the life span. *Current Directions in Psychological Science, 8,* 76-79.

Haselager, G. J. T., Hartup, W. W., van Lieshout, C. F. M., & Riksen-Walraven, J. M. A. (1998). Similarities between friends and nonfriends in middle childhood. *Child Development, 69,* 1198-1208.

Hastings, P. D., & Rubin, K. H. (1999). Predicting mothers' beliefs about preschool-aged children's social behavior: Evidence for maternal attitudes moderating child effects. *Child Development, 70,* 722-741.

Hatcher, P. J., & Hulme, C. (1999). Phonemes, rhymes, and intelligence as predictors of children's responsiveness to remedial reading instruction: Evidence from a longitudinal study. *Journal of Experimental Child Psychology, 72,* 130-153.

Haviland, J. M., & Lelwica, M. (1987). The induced affect response: 10-week-old infants' responses to three emotion expressions. *Developmental Psychology, 23,* 97-104.

Hay, D. F., Castle, J., & Davies, L. (2000). Toddlers' use of force against familiar peers: A precursor of serious aggression? *Child Development, 71,* 457-467.

Hearold, S. (1986). A synthesis of 1,043 effects of television on social behavior. In G. Comstock (Ed.), *Public communications and behavior* (Vol. 1, pp. 65-133). New York: Academic Press.

Hedges, L. V., & Nowell, A. (1995). Sex differences in mental test scores, variability, and numbers of high-scoring individuals. *Science, 269,* 41-45.

Hellige, J. B. (1994). *Hemispheric asymmetry: What's right and what's left.* Cambridge, MA: Harvard University Press.

Henshaw, S. K. (1993). Teenage abortion, birth and pregnancy statistics by state, 1988. *Family Planning Perspectives, 25,* 122-126.

Hernandez, D. J. (1997). Child development and the social demography of childhood. *Child Development, 68,* 149-169.

Herrnstein, R. J., & Murray, C. (1994). *The bell curve: Intelligence and class structure in American life.* New York: Free Press.

Hershberger, S. L., & D'Augelli, A. R. (1995). The impact of victimization on the mental health and suicidality of lesbian, gay, and bisexual youths. *Developmental Psychology, 31,* 65-74.

Hetherington, E. M. (1988). Family relations six years after divorce. In K. Pasley & M. Ihinger-Tallman (Eds.), *Remarriage and stepparenting: Current research and theory.* New York: Guilford Press.

Hetherington, E. M. (1989). Coping with family transitions: Winners, losers and survivors. *Child Development, 60,* 1-14.

Hetherington, E. M. (1993). An overview of the Virginia Longitudinal Study of Divorce and Remarriage with a focus on early adolescence. *Journal of Family Psychology, 7,* 39-56.

Hetherington, E. M. (1999). Social capital and the development of youth from nondivorced, divorced, and remarried families. In W. A. Collins & B. Laursen (Eds.) *Minnesota Symposia on Child Psychology.* Mahwah, NJ: Erlbaum.

Hetherington, E. M., Cox, M., & Cox, R. (1982). Effects of divorce on parents and children. In M. E. Lamb (Ed.), *Nontraditional families.* Hillsdale, NJ: Erlbaum.

Hetherington, S. E. (1990). A controlled study of the effect of prepared childbirth classes on obstetric outcomes. *Birth, 17,* 86-90.

Higgins, A. (1991). The Just Community approach to moral education: Evolution of the idea and recent findings. In W. M. Kurtines & J. L. Gewirtz (Eds.), *Handbook of moral behavior and development:* Vol. 3. Hillsdale, NJ: Erlbaum.

Hirshberg, L. M., & Svejda, M. (1990). When infants look to their parents: I. Infants' social referencing of mothers compared to fathers. *Child Development, 61,* 1175-1186.

Hiscock, M., & Kinsbourne, M. (1987). Specialization of the cerebral hemispheres: Implications for learning. *Journal of Learning Disabilities, 20,* 130-143.

Ho, C. S., & Bryant, P. (1997). Phonological skills are important in learning to read Chinese. *Developmental Psychology, 33,* 946-951.

Hodges, E. V. E., Malone, M. J., & Perry, D. G. (1997). Individual risk and social risk as interacting determinants of victimization in the peer group. *Developmental Psychology, 33,* 1032-1039.

Hoff-Ginnsberg, E. (1990). Maternal speech and the child's development of syntax: A further look. *Journal of Child Language, 17,* 85-99.

Hoffman, M. L. (1988). Moral development. In M. H. Bornstein and M. E. Lamb (Eds.), *Developmental psychology : An advanced textbook* (2nd ed.). Hillsdale, NJ: Lawrence Erlbaum.

Hoffman, M. L. (1994). Discipline and internalization. *Developmental Psychology, 30,* 26-28.

Hoge, D. D., Smit, E. K., & Hanson, S. L. (1990). School experiences predicting changes in self-esteem of sixth- and seventh-grade students. *Journal of Educational Psychology, 82,* 117-127.

Hogge, W. A. (1990). Teratology. In I. R. Merkatz & J. E. Thompson (Eds.), *New perspectives on prenatal care.* New York: Elsevier.

Holden, G. W., & Miller, P. C. (1999). Enduring and different: A meta-analysis of the similarity in parents' child rearing. *Psychological Bulletin, 125,* 223-254.

Holland, J. L. (1985). *Making vocational choices: A theory of vocational personalities and work environments* (2nd ed.). Englewood Cliffs, NJ: Prentice-Hall.

Holland, J. L. (1987). Current status of Holland's theory of careers: Another perspective. *Career Development Quarterly, 36,* 24-30.

Holland, J. L. (1996). Exploring careers with a typology: What we have learned and some new directions. *American Psychologist, 51,* 397-406.

Howard, M., & McCabe, J. B. (1990). Helping teenagers postpone sexual involvement. *Family Planning Perspectives, 22,* 21-26.

Howe, M. L., & Courage, M. L. (1997). The emergence and early development of autobiographical memory. *Psychological Review, 104,* 499-523.

Howe, N., Petrakos, H., & Rinaldi, C. M. (1998). "All the sheeps are dead. He murdered them": Sibling pretense, negotiation, internal state language, and relationship quality. *Child Development, 69,* 182-191.

Howe, N., & Ross, H. S. (1990). Socialization perspective taking and the sibling relationship. *Developmental Psychology, 26,* 160-165.

Howes, C., & Matheson, C. C. (1992). Sequences in the development of competent play with peers: Social and social pretend play. *Developmental Psychology, 28,* 961-974.

Howes, C., Unger, O., & Seidner, L. B. (1990). Social pretend play in toddlers: Parallels with social play and with solitary pretend. *Child Development, 60,* 77-84.

Hudson, J. (1988).Children's memory for atypical actions in script-based stories Evidence for a disruption effect. *Journal of Experimental Child Psychology, 46,* 159-173.

Huesmann, L. R. (1986). Psychological processes promoting the relation between exposure to media violence and aggressive behavior by the viewer. *Journal of Social Issues, 42,* 125-139.

Huston, A. C. (1983). Sex typing. In P. H. Mussen (Ed.), *Handbook of child psychology,* Vol. 4. New York: John Wiley.

Huston, A. C., Donnerstein, E., Fairchild, H., Feshbach, N. D., Katz, P. A., Murray, J. P., Rubinstein, E. A., Wilcox, B. L., & Zuckerman, D. (1992). *Big world, small screen: The role of television in American society.* Lincoln, NE: University of Nebraska Press.

Huston, A. C., & Wright, J. C. (1998). Mass media and children's development. In W. Damon (Ed.), *Handbook of child psychology,* Vol. 4. New York: Wiley.

Hutchins, E. (1983). Understanding Micronesian navigation. In D. A. Gentner and A. Stevens (Eds.), *Mental models.* Hillsdale, NJ: Erlbaum.

Hyde, J. S., Fennema, E., & Lamon, S. J. (1990). Gender differences in mathematics performance: A meta-analysis. *Psychological Bulletin, 107,* 139-155.

Hyde, J. S., & Linn, M. C. (1988). Gender differences in verbal ability. *Psychological Bulletin, 104,* 53-69.

Hymel, S., Rubin, K. H., Rowden, L., & LeMare, L. (1990). Children's peer relationships: Longitudinal prediction of internalizing and externalizing problems from middle to late childhood. *Child Development, 61,* 2004-2021.

Inhelder, B., & Piaget, J. (1958). *The growth of logical thinking from childhood to adolescence.* New York: Basic Books.

Institute of Medicine. (1990). *Nutrition during pregnancy.* Washington, DC: National Academy Press.

Isley, S. L., O'Neil, R., Clatfelter, D., & Parke, R. D. (1999). Parent and child expressed affect and children's social competence: Modeling direct and indirect pathways. *Developmental Psychology, 35,* 547-560.

Israel, A. C., Guile, C. A., Baker, J. E., & Silverman, W. K. (1994). An evaluation of enhanced self-regulation training in the treatment of childhood obesity. *Journal of Pediatric Psychology, 19,* 737-749.

Izard, C. E. (1991). *The psychology of emotions.* New York: Plenum Press.

Izard, C. E., Fantauzzo, C. A., Castle, J. M., Haynes, O. M., Rayias, M. F., & Putnam, P. H. (1995). The ontogeny and significance of infants' facial expressions in the first 9 months of life. *Developmental Psychology, 31,* 997-1013.

Jacobson, J. L., Jacobson, S. W., & Humphrey, H. E. B. (1990). Effects of in utero exposure to polychlorinated biphenyls and related contaminants on cognitive functioning in young children. *The Journal of Pediatrics, 116,* 38-45.

Jakobsen, R. (1997). Stages of progression in non-coital sexual interactions among young adolescents: An application of the Mokken scale analysis. *International Journal of Behavioral Development, 21,* 537-553.

Jensen, M. D., Benson, R. C., & Bobak, I. M. (1981). *Maternity care.* St. Louis, MO: C. V. Mosby.

Jiao, S., Ji, G., & Jing, Q. (1996). Cognitive development of Chinese urban only children and children with siblings. *Child Development, 67,* 387-395.

Jiao, Z. (1999, April). Which students keep old friends and which become new friends across school transition? Paper presented at the 1999 meeting of the Society for Research in Child Development, Albuquerque, New Mexico.

Johanson, R. B., Rice, C., Coyle, M., Arthur, J., Anyanwu, L., Ibrahim, J., Warwick, A., Redman, C. W. E., & O'Brien, P. M. S. (1993). A randomized prospective study comparing the new vacuum extractor policy with forceps delivery. *British Journal of Obstetrics and Gynecology, 100,* 524-530.

Johnson, M. H. (1998). The neural basis of cognitive development. In W. Damon (Ed.), *Handbook of child psychology,* Volume 2. New York: Wiley.

Johnson, S. P., & Aslin, R. N. (1995). Perception of object unity in 2-month-old infants. *Developmental Psychology, 31,* 739-745.

Johnston, L. D., O'Malley, P. M., & Bachman, J. G. (1993). National survey results on drug use from Monitoring the Future Study, 1975-1992 (Vol. 1). Rockville, MD: National Institute on Drug Abuse.

Johnston, L. D., O'Malley, P. M., & Bachman, J. G. (2000). *"Ecstasy" use rises sharply among teens in 2000; use of many other drugs steady, but significant declines are reported for some.* University of Michigan News and Information Services: Ann Arbor, MI. [On-line]. Available: www.monitoringthefuture.org.

Johnstone, B., Frame, C. L., & Bouman, D. (1992). Physical attractiveness and athletic and academic ability in controversial-aggressive and rejected-aggressive children. *Journal of Social and Clinical Psychology, 11,* 71-79.

Jones, D., & Christensen, C. A. (1999). Relationship between automaticity in handwriting and students' ability to generate written text. *Journal of Educational Psychology, 91,* 44-49.

Jones, K., & Day, J. D. (1997). Discrimination of two aspects of cognitive-social intelligence from academic intelligence. *Journal of Educational Psychology, 89,* 486-497.

Joseph, R. (2000). Fetal brain behavior and cognitive development. *Developmental Review, 20,* 81-98.

Jusczyk, P. W. (1995). Language acquisition: Speech sounds and phonological development. In J. L. Miller & P. D. Eimas (Eds.), *Handbook of perception and cognition: Vol. 11. Speech, language, and communication.* Orlando, FL: Academic Press.

Jusczyk, P. W., & Aslin, R. N. (1995). Infants' detection of the sound patterns of words in fluent speech. *Cognitive Psychology, 29,* 1-23.

Kagan, J. (1989). Temperamental contributions to social behavior. *American Psychologist, 44,* 668-674.

Kagan, J., Arcus, D., Snidman, N., Feng, W. Y., Hendler, J., & Greene, S. (1994). Reactivity in infants: A cross-national comparison. *Developmental Psychology, 30,* 342-345.

Kagan, J., & Moss, H. A. (1962). *Birth to maturity: A study in psychological development.* New York, NY: John Wiley.

Kagan, J., Snidman, N., & Arcus, D. (1998). Childhood derivatives of high and low reactivity in infancy. *Child Development, 69,* 1483-1493.

Kaijura, H., Cowart B., J., & Beauchamp, G. K. (1992). Early developmental change in bitter taste responses in human infants. *Developmental Psychobiology, 25,* 375-386.

Kail, R. (1990). *The development of memory in children* (3rd ed.). New York: W. H. Freeman.

Kail, R. (1991). Processing time declines exponentially during childhood and adolescence. *Developmental Psychology, 27,* 259-266.

Kail, R., & Bisanz, J. (1992). The information-processing perspective on cognitive development in childhood and adolescence. In R. J. Sternberg, and C. A. Berg (Eds.), *Intellectual development.* New York: Cambridge University Press.

Kamerman, S. B. (1993). International perspectives on child care policies and programs. *Pediatrics, 91,* 248-252.

Kandel, D. B. (1978). Homophily, selection, and socialization in adolescent friendships. *American Journal of Sociology, 84,* 427-436.

Kann L., Collins, J. L., Pateman, B. C., Small, M. L., Ross, J. G., & Kolbe, L. J. (1995). The School Health Policies and Programs Study (SHPPS): Rationale for a nationwide status report on school health programs. *Journal of School Health. 65*(8):291-294.

Kantrowitz, B. (1993, August 2). Murder and mayhem, guns and gangs: A teenage generation grows up dangerous and scared. *Newsweek,* pp. 40-46.

Kaplan, P. S., Goldstein, M. H., Huckeby, E. R., & Cooper, R. P. (1995). Habituation, sensitization, and infants' responses to motherese speech. *Developmental Psychobiology, 28,* 45-57.

Karniol, R. (1989). The role of manual manipulative states in the infant's acquisition of perceived control over objects. *Developmental Review, 9,* 205-233.

Kazak, A. E., Barakat, L. P., Meeske, K., Christakis, D., Meadows, D., Casey, R., Penati, B., & Stuber, M. (1997). Posttraumatic stress, family functioning, and social support in survivors of childhood leukemia and their mothers and fathers. *Journal of Consulting and Clinical Psychology, 65,* 120-129.

Kazdin, A. E. (1990). Childhood depression. *Journal of Child Psychology and Psychiatry and Allied Disciplines, 31,* 121-160.

Keane, S. P., Brown, K. P., & Crenshaw, T. M. (1990). Children's intention-cue detection as a function of maternal social behavior: Pathways to social rejection. *Developmental Psychology, 26,* 1004-1009.

Keller, M., Edelstein, W., Schmid, S., Fang, F., & Fang, G. (1998). Reasoning about responsibilities and obligations in close relationships: a comparison across two cultures. *Developmental Psychology, 34,* 731-741.

Kelley, M. L., Power, T. G., & Wimbush, D. D. (1992). Determinants of disciplinary practices in low-income Black mothers. *Child Development, 63,* 573-582.

Kellman, P. J., & Banks, M. S. (1998). Infant visual perception. In W. Damon (Ed.), *Handbook of child psychology,* Volume 2. New York: Wiley.

Kellogg, R. (1970). Understanding children's art. In P. Cramer (Ed.), *Readings in developmental psychology today.* Celmar, CA: CRM.

Kerr, M., Lambert, W. W., & Bem, D. J. (1996). Life course sequelae of childhood shyness in Sweden: Comparison with the United States. *Developmental Psychology, 32,* 1100-1105.

Kiernan, K. E. (1992). The impact of family disruption in childhood on transitions made in young adult life. *Population Studies, 46,* 213-234.

Kim, Y. H., & Goetz, E. T. (1994). Context effects on word recognition and reading comprehension of good and poor readers: A test of the interactive compensatory hypothesis. *Reading Research Quarterly, 29,* 178-188.

Kimball, M. M. (1986). Television and sex-role attitudes. In T. M. Williams (Ed.), *The impact of television* (pp. 265-301). New York: Academic Press.

Kimball, M. M. (1989). A new perspective on women's math achievement. *Psychological Bulletin, 105,* 198-214.

King, V., Elder, G. H., & Whitbeck, L. B. (1997). Religious involvement among rural youth: An ecological and life-course perspective. *Journal of Research on Adolescence, 7,* 431-456.

Kisilevsky, B. S., & Low, J. A. (1998). Human fetal behavior: 100 years of study. *Developmental Review, 18,* 1-29.

Klaczynski, P. A., & Narasimham, G. (1998). Development of scientific reasoning biases: Cognitive versus ego-protective explanations. *Developmental Psychology, 34,* 175-187.

Klahr, D., & MacWhinney, B. (1998). Information processing. In W. Damon (Ed.), *Handbook of child psychology,* Volume 2. New York: Wiley.

Klapper, J. T. (1968). The impact of viewing "aggression": Studies and problems of extrapolation. In O. N. Larsen (Ed.), *Violence and the mass media.* New York: Harper & Row.

Klatzky, R. L. (1980). *Human memory (2nd ed.).* San Francisco: Freeman.

Kline, R. B., Canter, W. A., & Robin, A. (1987). Parameters of teenage alcohol use: A path analytic conceptual model. *Journal of Consulting and Clinical Psychology, 55,* 521-528.

Kochanska, G. (1991). Socialization and temperament in the development of guilt and conscience. *Child Development, 62,* 1379-1392.

Kochanska, G. (1993). Toward a synthesis of parental socialization and child temperament in early development of conscience. *Child Development, 64,* 325-347.

Kochanska, G. (1995). Children's temperament, mothers' discipline, and security of attachment: Multiple pathways to emerging internalization. *Child Development, 66,* 597-615.

Kochanska, G. (1997). Mutually responsive orientation between mothers and their young children: Implications for early socialization. *Child Development, 68,* 94-112.

Kochanska, G. (1997). Multiple pathways to conscience for children with different temperaments: From toddlerhood to age 5. *Developmental Psychology, 33,* 228-240.

Kochanska, G., Casey, R. J., & Fukumoto, A. (1995). Toddlers' sensitivity to standard violations. *Child Development, 66,* 643-656.

Kochanska, G., DeVet, K., Goldman, M., Murray, K. et al. (1994). Maternal reports of conscience development and temperament in young children. *Child Development, 65,* 852-868.

Kochanska, G., Padavich, D. L., & Koenig, A. L. (1996). Children's narratives about hypothetical moral dilemmas and objective measures of their conscience: Mutual relations and socialization antecedents. *Child Development, 67,* 1420-1436.

Kochanska, G., & Radke-Yarrow, M. (1992). Inhibition in toddlerhood and the dynamics of the child's interaction with an unfamiliar peer at age five. *Child Development, 63,* 325-335.

Kochenderfer, B. J., & Ladd, G. W. (1996). Peer victimization: Cause or consequence of school maladjustment? *Child Development, 67,* 1305-1317

Kohlberg, L. (1969). Stage and sequence: The cognitive-developmental approach to socialization. In D. Goslin (Ed.), *Handbook of socialization theory and research* (pp. 347-480). Chicago: Rand McNally.

Kohlberg, L., & Ullian, D. Z. (1974). Stages in the development of psychosexual concepts and attitudes. In R. C. Friedman, R. M. Richart, & R. L. Van Wiele (Eds.), *Sex differences in behavior.* New York: John Wiley.

Kolb, B. (1989). Brain development, plasticity, and behavior. *American Psychologist, 44,* 1203-1212.

Kolb, B. & Whishaw, I. Q. (1998). Brain plasticity and behavior. *Annual Review of Psychology, 49,* 43-64.

Kopp, C. B. (1982). The antecedents of self-regulation. *Developmental Psychology, 18,* 199-214.

Kopp, C. B. (1987). The growth of self-regulation: Caregivers and children. In N. Eisenberg (Ed.), *Contemporary topics in developmental psychology.* New York: Wiley.

Kopp, C. B., & McCall, R. B. (1982). Predicting later mental performance for normal, at-risk, and handicapped infants. In P. B. Baltes & O. G. Brim (Eds.), *Life-span development and behavior,* Vol. 4. New York: Academic Press.

Korbin, J. E. (1987). Child abuse and neglect: The cultural context. In R. E. Helfer & R. S. Kempe (Eds.), *The battered child* (4th ed., pp. 23-41). Chicago: The University of Chicago Press.

Kotovsky, L., & Baillargeon, R. (1998). The development of calibration-based reasoning about collision events in young infants. *Cognition, 67,* 311-351.

Kovacs, D. M., Parker, J. G., & Hoffman, L. W. (1996). Behavioral, affective, and social correlates of involvement in cross-sex friendship in elementary school. *Child Development, 67,* 2269-2286.

Kowal, A., & Kramer, L. (1997). Children's understanding of parental differential treatment. *Child Development, 68,* 113-126.

Kowalski, R. M. (1992). Nonverbal behaviors and perceptions of sexual intentions: Effects of sexual connotativeness, verbal response, and rape outcome. *Basic and Applied Social Psychology, 13,* 427-445.

Kramer, L., Perozynski, L. A., & Chung, T. (1999). Parental responses to sibling conflict: The effects of development and parent gender. *Child Development, 70,* 1401-1414.

Krispin, O., Sternberg, K. J., & Lamb, M. E. (1992). The dimensions of peer evaluation in Israel: A cross-cultural perspective. *International Journal of Behavioral Development, 15,* 299-314.

Kroger, J., & Green, K. E. (1996). Events associated with identity status change. *Journal of Adolescence, 19,* 477-490.

Kuhl, P. K. (1993). Early linguistic experience and phonetic perception: Implications for theories of developmental speech perception. *Journal of Phonetics, 21,* 125-139.

Kunzig, R. (1998). Climbing through the brain. *Discover, 19,* 60-69.

Kupersmidt, J. B., & Coie, J. D. (1990). Preadolescent peer status, aggression, and school adjustment as predictors of externalizing problems in adolescence. *Child Development, 61,* 1350-1362.

Ladd, G. W. (1998). Peer relationships and social competence during early and middle childhood. *Annual Review of Psychology, 50,* 333-359.

Ladd, G. W., & Ladd, B. K. (1998). Parenting behaviors and parent-child relationships: Correlates of peer victimization in kindergarten? *Developmental Psychology, 34,* 1450-1458.

Ladd, G. W., & Le Sieur, K. D. (1995). Parents and children's peer relationships. In M. H. Bornstein (Ed.), *Handbook of parenting. Vol. 4. Applied and practical parenting* (pp. 377-410). Mahwah, NJ: Erlbaum.

LaFreniere, P., Strayer, F. F., & Gauthier, R. (1984). The emergence of same-sex affiliative preferences among preschool peers: A developmental/ethnological perspective. *Child Development, 55,* 1958-1965.

LaGreca, A. M. (1993). Social skills training with children: Where do we go from here? *Journal of Clinical Child Psychology, 22,* 288-298.

Lamb, M. E. (1999). Nonparental child care: context, quality, correlated, and consequences. In M. E. Lamb (Ed.), *Parenting and child development in "nontraditional" families.* Mahwah, NJ: Erlbaum.

Lampinen, J. M., & Smith, V. L. (1995). The incredible (and sometimes incredulous) child witness: Child eyewitnesses' sensitivity to source credibility cues. *Journal of Applied Psychology, 80,* 621-627.

Langlois, J. H., & Downs, A. C. (1980). Mothers, fathers, and peers as socialization agents of sex-typed play behaviors in young children. *Child Development, 51,* 1237-1247.

Lanza, E. (1992). Can bilingual two-year-olds code-switch? *Journal of Child Language, 19,* 633-658.

Larson, R. W. (1997). The emergence of solitude as a constructive domain of experience in early adolescence. *Child Development, 68,* 80-93.

Larson, R. W. (2000). Toward a psychology of positive youth development. *American Psychologist, 55,* 170-183.

Larson, R. W., Raffaelli, M., Richards, M. H., Ham, M., & Jewell, L. (1990). Ecology of depression in late childhood and early adolescence: A profile of daily states and activities. *Journal of Abnormal Psychology, 99,* 92-102.

Laursen, B., & Collins, W. A. (1994). Interpersonal conflict during adolescence. *Psychological Bulletin, 115,* 197-209.

Lazar, I., & Darlington, R. (1982). Lasting effects of early education: A report from the Consortium for Longitudinal Studies. *Monographs of the Society for Research in Child Development, 47,* (2-3, Serial No. 195).

Leach, P. (1991). *Your baby and child: From birth to age five* (2nd ed.). New York: Knopf.

Leichtman, M. D., & Ceci, S. L. (1995). The effects of stereotypes and suggestions on preschoolers' reports. *Developmental Psychology, 31,* 568-578.

LeMare, L. J., & Rubin, K. H. (1987). Perspective taking and peer interaction: Structural and developmental analyses. *Child Development, 58,* 306-315.

Lemery, K. S., Goldsmith, H. H., Klinnert, M. D., & Mrazek, D. A. (1999). Developmental models of infant and childhood temperament. *Developmental Psychology, 35,* 189-204.

Lengua, L. J., Sandler, I. N., West, S. G., Wolchik, S. A., & Curran, P. J. (1999). Emotionality and self-regulation, threat appraisal, and coping in children of divorce. *Development & Psychopathology, 11,* 15-37.

Lepper, M. R., & Gurtner, J. (1989). Children and computers. *American Psychologist, 44,* 170-178.

Levine, L. E. (1983). *Mine:* Self-definition in 2-year-old boys. *Developmental Psychology, 19,* 544-549.

Levitt, A. G., & Utman, J. A. (1992). From babbling towards the sound systems of English and French: A longitudinal two-case study. *Journal of Child Language, 19,* 19-49.

Levitt, M. J., Guacci-Franco, N., & Levitt, J. L. (1993). Convoys of social support in childhood and early adolescence: Structure and function. *Developmental Psychology, 29,* 811-818.

Levy, G. D., & Boston, M. B. (1994). Preschoolers' recall of own-sex and other-sex gender scripts. *Journal of Genetic Psychology, 155,* 367-371.

Levy, G. D., Taylor, M. G., & Gelman, S. A. (1995). Traditional and evaluative aspects of flexibility in gender roles, social conventions, moral rules, and physical laws. *Child Development, 66,* 515-531.

Levy, J. (1976). A review of evidence for a genetic component in the determination of handedness. *Behavior Genetics, 6,* 429-453.

Lewinsohn, P. M., & Gotlib, I. H. (1995). Behavioral therapy and treatment of depression. In E. E. Beckham & W. R. Leber (Eds.), *Handbook of depression* (2nd ed.). New York: Guilford Press.

Lewis, M. (1987). Social development in infancy and early childhood. In J. D. Osofsky (Ed.), *Handbook of infant development.* New York: Wiley.

Lewis, M. (1992). *Shame: The exposed self.* New York: Free Press.

Lewis, M., Alessandri, S. M., & Sullivan, M. W. (1992). Differences in shame and pride as a function of children's gender and task difficulty. *Child Development, 63,* 630-638.

Lewis, M., & Brooks-Gunn, J. (1979). *Social cognition and the acquisition of self.* New York: Plenum.

Lewis, M., Ramsay, D. S., & Kawakami, K. (1993). Differences between Japanese infants and Caucasian American infants in behavioral and cortisol response to inoculation. *Child Development, 64,* 1722-1731.

Lewis, M. D., Koroshegyi, C., Douglas, L., & Kampe, K. (1997). Age-specific associations between emotional responses to separation and cognitive performance in infancy. *Developmental Psychology, 33,* 32-42.

Liben, L. S., & Signorella, M. L. (1993). Gender schematic processing in children: The role of initial interpretations of stimuli. *Developmental Psychology, 29,* 141-149.

Lie, S. O. (1990). Children in the Norwegian health care system. *Pediatrics, 86,* 1048-1052.

Lieberman, M., Doyle, A., & Markiewicz, D. (1999). Developmental patterns in security of attachment to mother and father in late childhood and early adolescence: Associations with peer relations. *Child Development, 70,* 202-213.

Liebert, R. M., & Sprafkin, J. (1988). *The early window: Effects of television on children and youth.* New York: Pergamon.

Lillard, A. (1999). Developing a cultural theory of mind: The CIAO approach. *Current Directions in Psychological Science, 8,* 57-61.

Lin, C. C., & Fu, V. R. (1990). A comparison of childrearing practices among Chinese, immigrant Chinese, and Caucasian-American parents. *Child Development, 61,* 429-433.

Linden, M. G., Bender, B. G., Harmon, R. J., Mrazek, D. A., & Robinson, A. (1988). 47,XXX: What is the prognosis? *Pediatrics, 82,* 619-630.

Lipsitt, L. P. (1990). Learning and memory in infants. *Merrill-Palmer Quarterly, 36,* 53-66.

Looney, M. A., & Plowman, S. A. (1990). Passing rates of American children and youth on the FITNESSGRAM criterion-referenced physical fitness standards. *Research Quarterly of Exercise and Sport, 61,* 215-223.

Lord, S. E., Eccles, J. S., & McCarthy, K. A. (1994). Surviving the junior high transition: Family processes and self-perception as protective and risk factors. *Journal of Early Adolescence, 14,* 162-199.

Loveland, K. A. (1987a). Behavior of young children with Down syndrome before the mirror: Exploration. *Child Development, 58,* 768-778.

Loveland, K. A. (1987b). Behavior of young children with Down syndrome before the mirror: Finding things reflected. *Child Development, 58,* 928-936.

Lovett, S. B., & Pillow, B. H. (1996). Development of the ability to distinguish between comprehension and memory: Evidence from goal-state evaluation tasks. *Journal of Educational Psychology, 88,* 546-562.

Lozoff, B., Wolf, A. W., & Davis, N. S. (1985). Sleep problems seen in pediatric practice. *Pediatrics, 75,* 477-483.

Ludemann, P. M. (1991). Generalized discrimination of positive facial expressions by seven- and ten-month-old infants. *Child Development, 62,* 55-67.

Ludemann, P. M., & Nelson, C. A. (1988). Categorical representation of facial expressions by 7-month-old infants. *Developmental Psychology, 24,* 492-501.

Luecke-Aleksa, D., Anderson, D. R., Collins, P. A., & Schmitt, K. L. (1995). Gender constancy and television viewing. *Developmental Psychology. 31,* 773-780.

Lutz, S. E., & Ruble, D. N. (1995). Children and gender prejudice: Context, motivation, and the development of gender conceptions. In R. Vasta (Ed.), *Annals of child development: A research annual,* Vol. 10. London, England: Jessica Kingsley Publishers.

Lynsky, M. T., & Fergusson, D. M. (1997). Factors protecting against the development of adjustment difficulties in young adults exposed to childhood sexual abuse. *Child Abuse and Neglect, 21,* 1177-1190.

Lyon, G. R. (1996). Learning disabilities. In E. J. Mash & R. A. Barkley (Eds.), *Child psychopathology.* New York: Guilford.

Lytton, H. (2000). Toward a model of family-environmental and child-biological influences on development. *Developmental Review, 20,* 150-179.

Lytton, H., & Romney, D. M. (1991). Parents' differential socialization of boys and girls: A meta-analysis. *Psychological Bulletin, 109,* 267-296.

Maccoby, E. E. (1984). Socialization and developmental change. *Child Development, 55,* 317-328.

Maccoby, E. E. (1988). Gender as a social category. *Developmental Psychology, 24,* 755-765.

Maccoby, E. E. (1990). Gender and relationships: A developmental account. *American Psychologist, 45,* 513-520.

Maccoby, E. E., Buchanon, C. M., Mnookin, R. H., & Dornbusch, S. M. (1993). Postdivorce roles of mothers and fathers in the lives of their children. *Journal of Family Psychology, 7,* 24-38.

Maccoby, E. E., & Martin, J. A. (1983). Socialization in the context of the family: Parent-child interaction. In P. H. Mussen (Ed.), *Handbook of child psychology,* Vol. 4. New York: Wiley.

MacKinnon-Lewis, C., Rabiner, D., & Starnes, R. (1999). Predicting boys' social acceptance and aggression: The role of mother-child interactions and boys' beliefs about peers. *Developmental Psychology, 35,* 632-639.

MacWhinney, B. (1998). Models of the emergence of language. *Annual Review of Psychology, 49,* 199-227.

Main, M., & Cassidy, J. (1988). Categories of response to reunion with the parent at age 6: Predictable from infant attachment classifications and stable over a 1-month-period. *Developmental Psychology, 24,* 415-426.

Malinosky-Rummell, R., & Hansen, D. J. (1993). Long-term consequences of childhood physical abuse. *Psychological Bulletin, 114,* 68-79.

Mandel, D. R., Jusczyk, P. W., & Pisoni, D. B. (1995). Infants' recognition of the sound patterns of their own names. *Psychological Science, 6,* 314-317.

Mandler, J. M., & McDonough, L. (1998). Studies in inductive inference in infancy. *Cognitive Psychology. 37,* 60-96.

Mangelsdorf, S., Gunnar, M., Kestenbaum, R., Lang, S., & Andreas, D. (1990). Infant proneness-distress temperament, maternal personality, and mother-infant attachment: Associations and goodness of fit. *Child Development, 61,* 820-831.

Mangelsdorf, S. C. (1992). Developmental changes in infant-stranger interaction. *Infant Behavior and Development, 15,* 191-208.

Mangelsdorf, S. C., Shapiro, J. R., & Marzolf, D. (1995). Developmental and temperamental differences in emotional regulation in infancy. *Child Development, 66,* 1817-1828.

Mannino, D. M., Homa, D. M., Pertowski, C. A., Ashizawa, A., Nixon, L. L., Johnson, C. A., Ball, L. B., Jack, E., & Kang, D. S. (1998). Surveillance for asthma—United States, 1960-1995. Centers for Disease Control Morbidity and Mortality *Weekly Report.* Washington, DC: U.S. Government Printing Office.

Maratsos, M. (1998). The acquisition of grammar. In W. Damon (Ed.), *Handbook of child psychology,* Volume 2. New York: Wiley.

Marcia, J. E. (1980). Identity in adolescence. In J. Adelson (Ed.), *Handbook of adolescent psychology.* New York: Wiley.

Marcia, J. E. (1991). Identity and self-development. In R. M. Lerner, A. C. Petersen, and J. Brooks-Gunn (Eds.), *Encyclopedia of adolescence* (Vol. 1). New York: Garland.

Marcovitch, S., & Zelazo, P. D. (1999). The A-not-B error: Results from a logistic meta-analysis. *Child Development, 70,* 1297-1313.

Marcus, G. F., Pinker, S., Ullman, M., Hollander, M., Rosen, T. J., & Xu, F. (1992). Overregularization in language acquisition. *Monographs of the Society for Research in Child Development, 58* (4, Serial No. 228).

Markovits, H., & Vachon, R. (1989). Reasoning with contrary-to-fact propositions. *Journal of Experimental Child Psychology, 47,* 398-412.

Marsh, H. W. (1991). Employment during high school: Character building or a subversion of academic goals? *Sociology of Education, 64,* 172-189.

Marsh, H. W., Chessor, D., Craven, R., & Roche, L. (1995). The effects of gifted and talented programs on academic self-concept: The big fish strikes again. *American Educational Research Journal, 32,* 285-319.

Marsh, H. W., & Yeung, A. S. (1997). Causal effects of academic self-concept on academic achievement: Structural equation models of longitudinal data. *Journal of Educational Psychology, 89,* 41-54.

Marshall, E. (1995). Gene therapy's growing pains. *Science, 269,* 1050-1052.

Marsiglio, W. (1993). Attitudes toward homosexual activity and gays as friends: A national survey of heterosexual 15- to 19-year-old males. *Journal of Sex Research, 30,* 12-17.

Martin, C. L. (1989). Children's use of gender-related information in making social judgments. *Developmental Psychology, 25,* 80-88.

Martin, C. L., Eisenbud, L., & Rose, H. (1995). Children's gender-based reasoning about toys. *Child Development, 66,* 1453-1471.

Martin, C. L., & Halverson, C. F. (1987). The roles of cognition in sex roles and sex typing. In D. B. Carter (Ed.), *Current conceptions of sex roles and sex typing: Theory and research.* New York: Praeger.

Martin, C. L., & Little, J. K. (1990). The relation of gender understandings to children's sex-typed preferences and gender stereotypes. *Child Development, 61,* 1427-1439.

Martin, R. P., Olejnik, S., & Gaddis, L. (1994). Is temperament an important contributor to schooling outcomes in elementary school? Modeling effects of temperament and scholastic ability on academic achievement. In W. B. Casey & S. C. McDevitt (Eds.), *Prevention and early intervention.* New York: Brunner/Mazel.

Masur, E. F. (1995). Infants' early verbal imitation and their later lexical development. *Merrill-Palmer Quarterly, 41,* 286-306.

Mattys, S. L., Jusczyk, P. W., Luce, P. A., & Morgan, J. L. (1999). Phonotactic and prosodic effects on word segmentation in infants. *Cognitive Psychology, 38,* 465-494.

Mazur, E., Wolchik, S. A., Virdin, L., Sandler, I. N., & West, S. G. (1999). Cognitive moderators of children's adjustment to stressful divorce events: The role of negative cognitive errors and positive illusions. *Child Development, 70,* 231-245.

McCall, R. B. (1979). *Infants.* Cambridge, MA: Harvard University Press.

McCall, R. B. (1989). Commentary. *Human Development, 32,* 177-186.

McCarty, M. E., & Ashmead, D. H. (1999). Visual control of reaching and grasping in infants. *Developmental Psychology, 35,* 620-631.

McClure, E. B. (2000). A meta-analytic review of sex differences in facial expression processing and their development in infants, children, and adolescents. *Psychological Bulletin, 126,* 424-453.

McCutchen, D., Covill, A., Hoyne, S. H., & Mildes, K. (1994). Individual differences in writing: Implications of translating fluency. *Journal of Educational Psychology. 86,* 256-266.

McCutchen, D., Francis, M., & Kerr, S. (1997). Revising for meaning: Effects of knowledge and strategy. *Journal of Educational Psychology. 89,* 667-676.

McGee, R., Stanton, W. R., & Sears, M. R. (1993). Allergic disorders and attention deficit disorder in children. *Journal of Abnormal Child Psychology, 21,* 79-88.

McGee, R., Williams, S., & Feehan, M. (1992). Attention deficit disorder and age of onset of problem behaviors. *Journal of Abnormal Child Psychology, 20,* 487-502.

McGraw, M. B. (1935). *Growth: A study of Johnny and Jimmy.* East Norwalk, CT: Appleton-Century-Crofts.

McKusick, V. A. (1995). *Mendelian inheritance in man: Catalogs of autosomal dominant, autosomal recessive, and X-linked phenotypes* (10th ed.). Baltimore: Johns Hopkins University Press.

McManus, I. C., Sik, G., Cole, D. R., Kloss, J., Mellon, A. F., & Wong, J. (1988). The development of handedness in children. *British Journal of Developmental Psychology, 6,* 257-273.

McNaughton, S., & Leyland, J. (1990). The shifting focus of maternal tutoring across different difficulty levels on a problem solving task. *British Journal of Developmental Psychology, 8,* 147-155.

Measelle, J. R., Ablow, J. C., Cowan, P. A., & Cowan, C. P. (1998). Assessing young children's views of their academic, social, and emotional lives: An evaluation of the self-perception scales of the Berkeley puppet interview. *Child Development, 69,* 1556-1576.

Meilman, P. W. (1979). Cross-sectional age changes in ego identity status during adolescence. *Developmental Psychology, 15,* 230-231.

Meltzoff, A. N., & Moore, M. K. (1989). Imitation in newborn infants: Exploring the range of gestures imitated and the underlying mechanisms. *Developmental Psychology, 25,* 954-962.

Meltzoff, A. N., & Moore, M. K. (1994). Imitation, memory, and the representation of persons. *Infant Behavior and Development, 17,* 83-99.

Mennella, J. A., & Beauchamp, G. K. (1996). The human infant's response to vanilla flavors in mother's milk and formula. *Infant Behavior and Development, 19,* 13-19.

Mennella, J., & Beauchamp, G. K. (1997). The ontogeny of human flavor perception. In G. K. Beauchamp & L. Bartoshuk (Eds.), *Tasting and smelling. Handbook of perception and cognition.* San Diego, CA: Academic Press.

Meyer, D. R., & Garasky, S. (1993). Custodial fathers: Myths, realities, and child support policy. *Journal of Marriage and the Family, 55,* 73-79.

Meyer-Bahlburg, H. F. L., Ehrhardt, A. A., Rosen, L. R., Gruen, R. S. et al (1995). Prenatal estrogens and the development of homosexual orientation. *Developmental Psychology, 31,* 12-21.

Meyers, A. F., Sampson, A. E., Weitzman, M., Rogers, B. L., & Kayne, H. (1989). School breakfast program and school performance. *American Journal of Diseases of Children, 143,* 1234-1239.

Miller, B. C., Norton, M. C., Curtis, T., Hill, E. J., Schvaneveldt, P., & Young, M. H. (1997). The timing of sexual intercourse among adolescents: Family, peer, and other antecedents. *Youth and Society, 29,* 54-83.

Miller, J. G., & Bersoff, D. M. (1992). Culture and moral judgment: How are conflicts between justice and interpersonal responsibilities resolved? *Journal of Personality and Social Psychology, 62,* 541-554.

Miller, K. F., Smith, C. M., Zhu, J., & Zhang, H. (1995). Preschool origins of cross-national differences in mathematical competence: The role of number-naming systems. *Psychological Science, 6,* 56-60.

Miller, K. S., Forehand, R., & Kotchik, B. A. (1999). Adolescent sexual behavior in two ethnic minority samples: The role of family variables. *Journal of Marriage and the Family, 61,* 85-98.

Miller, L. K. (1999). The Savant Syndrome: Intellectual impairment and exceptional skill. *Psychological Bulletin, 125,* 31-46.

Mills, R. S. L., & Grusec, J. E. (1989). Cognitive, affective, and behavioral consequences of praising altruism. *Merrill-Palmer Quarterly, 35,* 299-326.

Mindell, J. A., & Cashman, L. (1995). Sleep disorders. In A. R. Eisen, C. A. Kearney, & C. E. Schaefer (Eds.), *Clinical handbook of anxiety disorders in children and adolescents.* Northvale, NJ: Aronson.

Miringoff, M., & Miringoff, M. L. (1999). *The social health of the nation: How America is really doing.* New York: Oxford University Press.

Miringoff, M. L., Miringoff, M., & Opdycke, S. (1996). Monitoring the nation's social performance: The Index of Social Health. In E. F. Zigler, S. L. Kagan, & N. W. Hall (Eds.), *Children, families, and government: Preparing for the twenty-first century.* New York: Cambridge University Press.

Mischel, W. (1970). Sex-typing and socialization. In P. H. Mussen, (Ed.) *Carmichaels' manual of child psychology,* Vol. 2. New York: Wiley.

Mischel, W., & Ebbesen, E. (1970). Attention in delay of gratification. *Journal of Personality and Social Psychology, 16,* 329-337.

Mischel, W., Shoda, Y., & Rodriguez, M. L. (1989). Delay of gratification in children. *Science, 244,* 933-938.

Mitchell, J. E., Baker, L. A., & Jacklin, C. N. (1989). Masculinity and femininity in twin children: Genetic and environmental factors. *Child Development, 60,* 1475-1485.

Miura, I. T., Kim, C. C., Chang, C. M., & Okamoto, Y. (1988). Effects of language characteristics on children's cognitive representation of number: Cross-national comparisons. *Child Development, 59,* 1445-1450.

Mize, J., & Ladd, G. W. (1990). A cognitive social-learning approach to social skill training with low-status preschool children. *Developmental Psychology, 26,* 388-397.

Mize, J. & Pettit, G. S. (1997). Mothers' social coaching, mother-child relationship style, and children's peer competence: Is the medium the message? *Child Development, 68,* 312-332.

Mize, J., Pettit, G. S., & Brown, E. G. (1995). Mothers' supervision of their children's peer play: Relations with beliefs, perceptions, and knowledge. *Developmental Psychology, 31,* 311-321.

Mizes, J. S. (1995). Eating disorders. In M. Hersen, R. T. Ammerman, et al (Eds.), *Advanced abnormal child psychology* (pp. 375-391). Hillsdale, NJ: Erlbaum.

Moats, L. C., & Lyon, G. R. (1993). Learning disabilities in the United States: Advocacy, science, and the future of the field. *Journal of Learning Disabilities, 26,* 282-294.

Moffitt, T. E. (1993). Adolescence-limited and life-course-persistent antisocial behavior: A developmental taxonomy. *Psychological Review, 100,* 674-701.

Moffitt, T. E., Caspi, A., Belsky, J., & Silva, P. A. (1992). Childhood experience and the onset of menarche: A test of a sociobiological model. *Child Development, 63,* 47-58.

Molfese, D. L., & Burger-Judisch, L. M. (1991). Dynamic temporal-spatial allocation of resources in the human brain: An alternative to the static view of hemisphere differences. In F. L. Ketterle (Ed.), *Cerebral laterality: Theory and research. The Toledo symposium.* Hillsdale, NJ: Lawrence Erlbaum.

Monk, C., Fifer, W. P., Myers, M. M., Sloan, R. P., Trien, L. & Hurtado, A. (2000). Maternal stress responses and anxiety during pregnancy: Effects on fetal heart rate. *Developmental Psychobiology, 36,* 67-77.

Moore, B. S., Underwood, B., & Rosenhan, D. L. (1973). Affect and altruism. *Developmental Psychology, 8,* 99-104.

Moore, C., Angelopoulos, M., & Bennet, P. (1999). Word learning in the context of referential and salience cues. *Developmental Psychology, 35,* 60-68.

Moore, K. L., & Persaud, T. V. N. (1993). *Before we are born* (4th ed.). Philadelphia: W. B. Saunders Co.

Morgan, B., & Gibson, K. R. (1991). Nutritional and environmental interactions in brain development. In K. R. Gibson and A. C. Peterson (Eds.), *Brain maturation and cognitive development: Comparative and crosscultural perspectives.* New York: Aldine De Gruyter.

Morgane, P. J., Austin-LaFrance, R., Bronzino, J. D., Tonkiss, J., Diaz-Cintra, S., Cintra, L., Kemper, T., & Galler, J. R. (1993). Prenatal malnutrition and development of the brain. *Neuroscience and Biobehavioral Reviews, 17,* 91-128.

Morison, P., & Masten, A. S. (1991). Peer reputation in middle childhood as a predictor of adaptation in adolescence: A seven-year follow-up. *Child Development, 62,* 991-1007.

Mortimer, J. T. (1991). Employment. In R. M. Lerner, A. C. Petersen, & J. Brooks-Gunn (Eds.), *Encyclopedia of adolescence,* Vol. 1. New York: Garland.

Mortimer, J. T., Finch, M. D., Rye, S., Shanahan, M. J., & Call, K. T. (1996). The effects of work intensity on adolescent mental health, achievement, and behavioral adjustment: New evidence from a prospective study. *Child Development, 67,* 1243-1261.

Morton, J., & Johnson, M. H. (1991). CONSPEC and CONLERN: A two-process theory of infant face recognition. *Psychological Review, 98,* 164-181.

Muehlenhard, C. L. (1988). "Nice women" don't say yes and "real men" don't say no: How miscommunication and the double standard can cause sexual problems. *Women & Therapy, 7*(2-3), 95-108.

Mumme, D. L., Fernald, A., & Herrera, C. (1996). Infants' responses to facial and vocal emotional signals in a social referencing paradigm. *Child Development, 67,* 3219-3237.

Murray, L., Fiori-Cowley, A., Hooper, R., & Cooper, P. (1996). The impact of postnatal depression and associated adversity on early mother-infant interactions and later infant outcomes. *Child Development, 67,* 2512-2526.

NAEYC (1997). Developmentally appropriate practice in early childhood programs serving children from birth through age 8. http://www.naeyc.org/resources/position_statements/daptoc.html

Naigles, L. G., & Gelman, S. A. (1995). Overextensions in comprehension and production revisited: Preferential-looking in a study of dog, cat, and cow. *Journal of Child Language, 22,* 19-46.

Nation, K., Adams, J. W., Bowyer-Crane, C. A., & Snowling, M. J. (1999). Working memory deficits in poor comprehenders reflect underlying language impairments. *Journal of Experimental Child Psychology, 73,* 139-158.

National Center for Education Statistics. (1997). *Pursuing excellence: A study of U.S. fourth-grade mathematics and science achievement in an international context.* Washington, DC: U.S. Government Printing Office.

National Center for Health Statistics (1997). Report of final mortality statistics, 1995. Washington, DC: Public National Center for Health Statistics. (2000). *National Vital Statistics Reports, 48.* Author. Health Services. (Also available through the Web site http://www.cdc.gov/nchswww/releases)

National Center on Child Abuse and Neglect. (1979). *Child maltreatment 1995: Reports from the states to the National Center on Child Abuse and Neglect.* Washington, DC: Department of Health, Education, and Welfare. (OHDS 78-30137).

National Federation of State High School Associations. *(2000). NFHS participation survey,* 1999-2000.

National High Blood Pressure Education Program Working Group on Hypertension Control in Children and Adolescents. (1996). Update on the 1987 task force report on high blood pressure in children and adolescents: A working group report from the National High Blood Pressure Education Program. *Pediatrics, 98,* 649-658.

National Institutes of Health. (1997). *Controlling your asthma.* NIH Publication No. 97-2339.

National Institutes of Health. (2000). *To reduce SIDS risk, doctor's advice most important in choice of placing infants to sleep on their backs.* Washington, DC: Author.

National Research Council (1987). *Risking the future: Adolescent sexuality, pregnancy, and childbearing.* Washington, DC: National Academy Press.

National Research Council (1989). *Recommended dietary allowances (10th edition).* Washington, D. C.: National Academy Press.

Neiderhiser, J. M., Reiss, D., Hetherington, E. M., & Plomin, R. (1999). Relationships between parenting and adolescent adjustment over time: Genetic and environmental contributions. *Developmental Psychology, 35,* 680-692.

Neisser, U., Boodoo, G., Bouchard, T. J., Boykin, A. W., Brody, N., Ceci, S. J., Halpern, D. F., Loehlin, J. C., Perloff, R., Sternberg, R. J., & Urbina, S. (1996). Intelligence: Knowns and unknowns. *American Psychologist, 51,* 77-101.

Nelson, C. A. (1999). Neural plasticity and human development. *Current Directions in Psychological Science, 8,* 42-45.

Nelson, K. (1973). Structure and strategy in learning to talk. *Monographs of the Society for Research in Child Development, 38,* No. 149.

Nelson, K. (1993). Explaining the emergence of autobiographical memory in early childhood. A. F. Collins & S. E. Gathercole (Eds). *Theories of memory.* Hove, England UK: Erlbaum.

Nelson, M. A. (1996). Protective equipment. In O. Bar-Or (Ed.), *The child and adolescent athlete.* Oxford: Blackwell.

Neugarten, B. L., & Weinstein, K. K. (1964). The changing American Grandparent. *Journal of Marriage and the Family, 26,* 299-304.

Newcomb, A. F., & Bagwell, C. L. (1995). Children's friendship relations: A meta-analytic review. *Psychological Bulletin, 117,* 306-347.

Newcomb, A. F., Bukowski, W. M., & Pattee, L. (1993). Children's peer relations: A meta-analytic review of popular, rejected, neglected, controversial, and average sociometric status. *Psychological Bulletin, 113,* 99-123.

Newman, B. S., & Muzzonigro, P. G. (1993). The effects of traditional family values on the coming out process of gay male adolescents. *Adolescence, 28,* 213-226.

Newman, L. S., Cooper, J., & Ruble, D. N. (1995). Gender and computers: II. Interactive effects of knowledge and constancy on gender-stereotyped attitudes. *Sex Roles, 33,* 325-351.

Newport, E. L., (1991). Contrasting conceptions of the critical period for language. In S. Carey & R. Gelman (Eds.), *The epigenesis of mind: Essays on biology and cognition* (pp. 111-130). Hillsdale, NJ: Erlbaum.

NICHD Early Child Care Research Network. (1997). The effects of infant child care on infant-mother attachment security: Results of the NICHD Study of Early Child Care. *Child Development, 68,* 860-879.

Niebyl, J. R. (1991). Drugs in pregnancy and lactation. In S. G. Gabbe, J. R. Niebyl, & J. L. Simpson (Eds.), *Obstetrics: Normal and problem pregnancies* (2nd ed.). New York: Churchill Livingstone.

Nolen-Hoeksema, S., & Girgus, J. S. (1994). The emergence of gender differences in depression during adolescence. *Psychological Bulletin, 115,* 424-443.

Nucci, L. & Weber, E. K. (1995). Social interactions in the home and the development of young children's conceptions of the personal. *Child Development, 66,* 1438-1452.

Nurmi, J., Poole, M. E., & Kalakoski, V. (1996). Age differences in adolescent identity exploration and commitment in urban and rural environments. *Journal of Adolescence, 19,* 443-452.

Offer, D., Ostrov, E., Howard, K. I., & Atkinson, R. (1988). *The teenage world: Adolescents' self-image in ten countries.* New York: Plenum.

Ogletree, R. J. (1993). Sexual coercion experience and help-seeking behavior of college women. *Journal of American College Health, 41,* 149-153.

Ohlendorf-Moffat, P. (1991). Surgery before birth. *Discover* (February), 59-65.

Okagaki, L., & Frensch, P. A. (1994). Effects of video game playing on measures of spatial performance: Gender effects in late adolescence. *Journal of Applied Developmental Psychology, 15,* 33-58.

Okagaki, L., & Sternberg, R. J. (1993). Parental beliefs and children's school performance. *Child Development, 64,* 36-56.

Oller, D. K., & Eilers, R. E. (1988). The role of audition in infant babbling. *Child Development, 59,* 441-449.

Oller, D. K., & Lynch, M. P. (1992). Infant vocalizations and innovations in infraphonology: Toward a broader theory of development and disorders. In C. A. Ferguson, L. Menn, & C. Stoel-Gammon (Eds.), *Phonological development: Models, research, and implications* (pp. 509-538). Timonium, MD: York Press.

Oliver, M. B., & Hyde, J. S. (1993). Gender differences in sexuality: A meta-analysis. *Psychological Bulletin, 114,* 29-51.

Olweus, D. (1978). *Aggression in the schools: Bullies and whipping boys.* Washington, DC: Hemisphere.

Olweus, D. (1994). Bullying at school: Basic facts and effects of school based intervention program. *Journal of Child Psychology and Psychiatry, 35,* 1171-1190.

O'Neill, D. K. (1996). Two-year-old children's sensitivity to a parent's knowledge state when making requests. *Child Development, 67,* 659-677.

Paarlberg, K. M., Vingerhoets, A. J. J. M., Passchier, J., Dekker, G. A. et al. (1995). Psychosocial factors and pregnancy outcome: A review with emphasis on methodological issues. *Journal of Psychosomatic Research, 39,* 563-595.

Pacifici, C., & Bearison, D. J. (1991). Development of children's self-regulations in idealized and mother-child interactions. *Cognitive Development, 6,* 261-277.

Pacy, B. (1993, Spring) Plunged into flux. *Notre Dame Magazine, 22,* 34-38.

Padgham, J. J., & Blyth, D. A. (1991). Dating during adolescence. In R. M. Lerner, A. C. Petersen, & J. Brooks-Gunn (Eds.), *Encyclopedia of adolescence* (Vol. 1). New York: Garland.

Padilla, A. M., Lindholm, K. J., Chen, A., Duran, R., Hakuta, K., Lambert, W., & Tucker, G. R. (1991). The English-only movement. Myths, reality, and implications for psychology. *American Psychologist, 46,* 120-130.

Palca, J. (1991). Fetal brain signals time for birth. *Science, 253,* 1360.

Panksepp, J. (1998). Attention deficit hyperactivity disorders, psychostimulants, and intolerance of childhood playfulness: A tragedy in the making? *Current Directions in Psychological Science, 7,* 99-103.

Parazzini, F., Luchini, L., La Vecchia, C., & Crosignani, P. G. (1993). Video display terminal use during pregnancy and reproductive outcome—a meta-analysis. *Journal of Epidemiology and Community Health, 47,* 265-268.

Parcel, G. S., Simons-Morton, B. G., O'Hara, N. M., Baranowski, T., Kolbe, L. J., & Bee, D. E. (1989). School promotion of healthful diet and exercise behavior: An integration of organizational change and social learning theory interventions. *Journal of School Health, 57,* 150-156.

Parke, R. D. (1977). Punishment in children: Effects, side effects and alternative strategies. In H. L. Hom, Jr., & A. Robinson (Eds.), *Psychological processes in early education.* New York: Academic.

Parke, R. D. (1990). In search of fathers: A narrative of an empirical journey. In I. Sigel & G. Brody (Eds.), *Methods of family research.* Hillsdale, NJ: Erlbaum.

Parke, R. D., & Bhavnagri, N. P. (1989). Parents as managers of children's peer relationships. In D. Belle (Ed.), *Children's social networks and social supports.* New York: Wiley.

Parke, R. D., & Buriel, R. (1998). Socialization in the family: Ethnic and ecological perspectives. In W. Damon (Ed.), *Handbook of child psychology, Vol. 3.* New York: Wiley.

Parker, J. G., & Seal, J. (1996). Forming, losing, renewing, and replacing friendships: Applying temporal parameters to the assessment of children's friendship experiences. *Child Development, 67,* 2248-2268.

Parker, J. G., & Herrera, C. (1996). Interpersonal processes in friendship: A comparison of abused and nonabused children's experiences. *Developmental Psychology, 32,* 1025-1038.

Parmalee, A. H. (1986). Children's illnesses: Their beneficial effects on behavioral development. *Child Development, 57,* 1-10.

Parritz, R. H. (1996). A descriptive analysis of toddler coping in challenging circumstances. *Infant Behavior and Development, 19,* 171-180.

Parten, M. (1932). Social participation among preschool children. *Journal of Abnormal and Social Psychology, 27,* 243-269.

Patterson, C. J. (1992). Children of lesbian and gay parents. *Child Development, 63,* 1025-1042.

Patterson, G. R. (1980). Mothers: The unacknowledged victims. *Monographs of the Society for Research in Child Development, 45* (5, Serial No. 186).

Patterson, G. R. (1984). Microsocial process: A view from the boundary. In J. C. Masters and K. Yarkin-Levin (Eds.), *Boundary areas in social and developmental psychology.* New York: Academic Press.

Patterson, G. R. (1995). Coercion as a basis for early age of onset for arrest. In J. McCord (Ed.), *Coercion and punishment in long-term perspectives.* New York: Cambridge University Press.

Patterson, G. R., DeVaryshe, B. D., & Ramsey, E. (1989). A developmental perspective on antisocial behavior. *American Psychologist, 44,* 329-335.

Pearlman, M., & Ross, H. S. (1997). The benefits of parent intervention in children's disputes: An examination of concurrent changes in children's fighting styles. *Child Development, 68,* 690-700.

Pearson, J. L., Hunter, A. G., Ensminger, M. E., & Kellam, S. G. (1990). Black grandmothers in multigenerational households: Diversity in family structure and parenting involvement in the Woodlawn community. *Child Development, 61,* 434-442.

Pederson, D. R., Gleason, K. E., Moran, G., & Bento, S. (1998). Maternal attachment representations, maternal sensitivity, and the infant-mother attachment relationship. *Developmental Psychology, 34,* 925-933.

Pellegrini, A. D., & Smith, P. K. (1998). Physical activity play: The nature and function of a neglected aspect of play. *Child Development, 69,* 577-598.

Pennington, B. F., Groisser, D., & Welsh, M. C. (1993). Contrasting cognitive deficits in attention deficit hyperactivity disorder versus reading disability. *Developmental Psychology, 29,* 511-523.

Perfetti, C. A., & Curtis, M. E. (1986). Reading. In R. F. Dillon & R. J. Sternberg (Eds.), *Cognition and instruction.* Orlando, FL: Academic Press.

Perlman, M., & Ross, H. S. (1997). The benefits of parent intervention in children's disputes: An examination of concurrent changes in children's fighting styles. *Child Development, 68,* 690-700.

Peterson, C. (1996). *The psychology of abnormality.* Fort Worth, TX: Harcourt Brace.

Peterson, C., Maier, S. F., & Seligman, M. E. P. (1993). *Learned helplessness: A theory for the age of personal control.* New York: Oxford University Press.

Peterson, C. & Rideout, R. (1998). Memory for medical emergencies experienced by 1- and 2-year-olds. *Developmental Psychology, 34,* 1059-1072.

Peterson, L. (1983). Role of donor competence, donor age, and peer presence on helping in an emergency. *Developmental Psychology, 19,* 873-880.

Peterson, L. (1989). Latchkey children's preparation for self-care: Overestimated, under rehearsed and unsafe. *Journal of Child Clinical Psychology, 18,* 36-43.

Peterson, L., & Oliver, K. K. (1995). Prevention of injuries and disease. In M. C. Roberts (Ed.), *Handbook of pediatric psychology* (2nd ed., pp. 185-199). New York: Guilford.

Petraitis, J., Flay, B. R., & Miller, T. Q. (1995). Reviewing theories of adolescent substance use: Organizing pieces in the puzzle. *Psychological Bulletin, 117,* 67-86.

Petrie, R. H. (1991). Intrapartum fetal evaluation. In S. G. Gabbe, J. R. Niebyl, & J. L. Simpson (Eds.), *Obstetrics: Normal & problem pregnancies* (2nd ed.). New York: Churchill Livingstone.

Pettit, G. S., Bakshi, A., Dodge, K. A., & Coie, J. D. (1990). The emergence of social dominance in young boys' play groups: Developmental differences and behavioral correlates. *Developmental Psychology, 26,* 1017-1025.

Pettit, G. S., Bates, J. E., & Dodge, K. A. (1997). Supportive parenting, ecological context, and children's adjustment: A seven-year longitudinal study. *Child Development, 68,* 908-923.

Pettit, G. S., Bates, J. E., & Dodge, K. A., & Meece, D. W. (1999). The impact of after-school peer contact on early adolescent externalizing problems is moderated by parental monitoring, perceived neighborhood safety, and prior adjustment. *Child Development, 70,* 768-7778.

Pettito, L. A., & Marentette, P. F. (1991). Babbling in the manual mode: Evidence for the ontogeny of language. *Science, 251,* 1493-1496.

Phinney, J. (1989). Stage of ethnic identity in minority group adolescents. *Journal of Early Adolescence, 9,* 34-49.

Phinney, J. (1990). Ethnic identity in adolescents and adults. *Psychological Bulletin, 108,* 499-514.

Phinney, J. S. (1996). When we talk about American ethnic groups, what do we mean? *American Psychologist, 51,* 918-927.

Phinney, J. S., & Chavira, V. (1992). Ethnic identity and self-esteem: An exploratory longitudinal study. *Journal of Adolescence, 15,* 271-281.

Phinney, J. S., Cantu, C. L., & Kurtz, D. A. (1997). Ethnic and American identity as predictors of self-esteem among African American, Latino, and White adolescents. *Journal of Youth and Adolescence, 26,* 165-185.

Piaget, J. (1929). *The child's conception of the world.* New York: Harcourt, Brace.

Piaget, J., & Inhelder, B. (1956). *The child's conception of space.* Boston: Routledge & Kegan Paul.

Piaget, J., & Inhelder, B. (1967). *The child's conception of space.* New York: W. W. Norton.

Plomin, R. (1990). *Nature and nurture.* Pacific Grove CA: Brooks/Cole.

Plomin, R., Fulker, D. W., Corley, R., & DeFries, J. C. (1997). Nature, nurture, and cognitive development from 1 to 16 years: A parent-offspring adoption study. *Psychological Science, 8,* 442-447.

Plomin, R., Nitz, K., & Rowe, D. C. (1990). Behavioral genetics and aggressive behavior in childhood. In M. Lewis & S. M. Miller (Eds.), *Handbook of developmental psychopathology: Perspectives in developmental psychology.* (pp. 119-133). New York: Plenum Press.

Plomin, R & Petrill, S. A. (1997). Genetics and intelligence: What's new? *Intelligence, 24,* 53-77.

Plomin, R., & Rowe, D. C. (1979). Genetic and environmental etiology of social behavior in infancy. *Developmental Psychology, 15,* 62-72.

Plomin, R. & Rutter, M. (1998). Child development, molecular genetics, and what to do with genes once they are found. *Child Development, 69,* 1223-1242.

Plumert, J. M., & Nichols-Whitehead, P. (1996). Parental scaffolding of young children's spatial communication. *Developmental Psychology, 32,* 523-532.

Pollitt, E. (1994). Poverty and child development: Relevance of research in developing countries to the United States. *Child Development, 65,* 283-295.

Pollitt, E. (1995). Does breakfast make a difference in school? *Journal of the American Dietetic Association, 95,* 1134-1139.

Porter, R. H., Makin, J. W., Davis, L. B., & Christensen, K. M. (1991). An assessment of the salient olfactory environment of formula-fed infants. *Physiology and Behavior, 50,* 907-911.

Poulin-Dubois, D., Serbin, L. A., Kenyon, B., & Derbyshire, A. (1994). Infants' intermodal knowledge about gender. *Developmental Psychology, 30,* 436-442.

Poulson, C. L., Kymissis, E., Reeve, K. F., Andreatos, M., & Reeve, L. (1991). Generalized vocal imitation in infants. *Journal of Experimental Child Psychology, 51,* 267-279.

Povinelli, D. J., & Simon, B. B. (1998). Young children's understanding of briefly versus extremely delayed images of the self: Emergence of the autobiographical stance. *Developmental Psychology, 34,* 188-194.

Power, F. C., Higgins, A., & Kohlberg, L. (1989). *Lawrence Kohlberg's approach to moral education.* New York, NY: Columbia University Press.

Powers, S. W., & Roberts, M. W. (1995). Simulation training with parents of oppositional children: Preliminary findings. *Journal of Clinical Child Psychology, 24,* 89-97.

Powlishta, K., Serbin, L. A., Doyle, A., & White, D. R. (1994). Gender, ethnic, and body type biases: The generality of prejudice in childhood. *Developmental Psychology, 30,* 526-536.

Pozzi, S., Healy, L., & Hoyles, C. (1993). Learning and interaction in groups with computers: When do ability and gender matter? *Social Development, 2,* 222-241.

Priel, B., & deSchonen, S. (1986). Self-recognition: A study of a population without mirrors. *Journal of Experimental Child Psychology, 41,* 237-250.

Quas, J. A., Goodman, G. S., Bidrose, S., Pipe, M., Craw, S., & Ablin, D. S. (1999). Emotion and memory: Children's long-term remembering, forgetting, and suggestibility. *Journal of Experimental Child Psychology, 72,* 235-270.

Rakic, P. (1995). Corticogenesis in human and nonhuman primates. In M. S. Gazzaniga (Ed). *The cognitive neurosciences.* Cambridge, MA: MIT Press.

Ramey, C. T., & Campbell, F. A. (1991). Poverty, early childhood education, and academic competence: The Abecedarian experiment. In A. Huston (Ed.), *Children reared in poverty.* New York: Cambridge University Press.

Ramey, C. T., & Ramey, S. L. (1990). Intensive educational intervention for children of poverty. *Intelligence, 14,* 1-9.

Ramsey, P. G. (1995). Growing up with the contradictions of race and class. *Young Children, 50,* 18-22.

Rappaport, L. (1993). The treatment of nocturnal enuresis—where are we now? *Pediatrics, 92,* 465-466.

Rapport, M. D. (1995). Attention-deficit hyperactivity disorder. In M. Hersen & R. T. Ammerman (Eds.), *Advanced abnormal child psychology.* Hillsdale NJ: Erlbaum.

Rasmussen, P., & Gillberg, C. (2000). Natural outcome of ADHD with developmental coordination disorder at age 22 years: A controlled, longitudinal, community-based study. *Journal of the American Academy of Child and Adolescent Psychiatry, 39,* 1424-1431.

Reese, E., & Cox, A. (1999). Quality of adult book reading affects children's emergent literacy. *Developmental Psychology, 35,* 20-28.

Reich, P. A. (1986). *Language development.* Englewood Cliffs, NJ: Prentice-Hall.

Reid, D. H., Wilson, P. G., & Faw, G. D. (1991). Teaching self-help skills. In J. L. Matson & J. A. Mulick (Eds.), *Handbook of mental retardation* (2nd ed.). New York: Pergamon.

Reid, J. B., Eddy, J. M., Fetrow, R. A., & Stoolmiller, M. (1999). Description and immediate impacts of a preventive intervention for conduct problems. *American Journal of Community Psychology, 27,* 483-517.

Repacholi, B. M. (1998). Infants' use of attentional cues to identify the referent of another person's emotional expression. *Developmental Psychology, 34,* 1017-1025.

Reubens, B., Harrison, J., & Kupp, K. (1981). *The youth labor force, 1945-1995: A cross-national analysis.* Totowa, NJ: Allanheld, Osmun.

Reynolds, A. J., & Temple, J. A. (1998). Extended early childhood intervention and school achievement: Age thirteen findings from the Chicago longitudinal study. *Child Development, 69,* 231-246.

Rhodes, J. E., & Jason, L. A. (1990). A social stress model of substance abuse. *Journal of Consulting and Clinical Psychology, 58,* 395-401.

Ricciuti, H. N. (1993). Nutrition and mental development. *Current Directions in Psychological Science, 2,* 43-46.

Rice, M. L., Huston, A. C., Truglio, R., & Wright, J. (1990). Words from "Sesame Street": Learning vocabulary while viewing. *Developmental Psychology, 26,* 421-428.

Rice, S. G. (1993). [Injury rates among high school athletes 1979-1992]. Unpublished raw data.

Rich, C. L., Sherman, M., & Fowler, R. C. (1990, Winter). San Diego suicide study: The adolescents. *Adolescence,* pp. 855-865.

Richardson, G. A. (1998). Prenatal cocaine exposure. A longitudinal study of development. *Annals of the New York Academy of Sciences, 846,* 144-152.

Ritchie, K. L. (1999). Maternal behaviors and cognitions during discipline episodes: A comparison of power bouts and single acts of noncompliance. *Developmental Psychology, 35,* 580-589.

Rivara, F. P., & Grossman, D. C. (1996). Prevention of traumatic deaths to children in the United States: How far have we come and where do we need to go? *Pediatrics, 97,* 791-798.

Roberts, J. E., Burchinal, M., & Durham, M. (1999). Parents' report of vocabulary and grammatical development of African American preschoolers: Child and environmental associations. *Child Development, 70,* 92-106.

Roberts, W., & Strayer, J. (1996). Empathy, emotional expressiveness, and prosocial behavior. *Child Development, 67,* 449-470.

Robinson, B. E., Rowland, B. H., & Coleman, M. (1986). *Latchkey kids: Unlocking doors for children and their families.* Lexington MA: Lexington Books, Heath.

Robinson, E. J., Champion, H., & Mitchell, P. (1999). Children's ability to infer utterance veracity from speaker informedness. *Developmental Psychology, 35,* 535-546.

Rodgers, J. L., & Rowe, D. C. (1993). Social contagion and adolescent sexual behavior: A developmental EMOSA model. *Psychological Review, 100,* 479-510.

Roffwarg, H. P., Muzio, J. N., & Dement, W. C. (1966). Ontogenetic development of the human sleep-dream cycle. *Science, 152,* 604-619.

Rooks, J. P., Weatherby, N. L., Ernst, E. K. M., Stapleton, S., Rosen, D., & Rosenfield, A. (1989). Outcomes of care in birth centers: The national birth center study. *New England Journal of Medicine, 321,* 1804-1811.

Roopnarine, J. (1992). Father-child play in India. In K. MacDonald (Ed.), *Parent-child play.* Albany: State University of New York Press.

Roscoe, B., Diana, M. S., & Brooks, R. H. (1987). Early, middle, and late adolescents' views on dating and factors influencing partner selection. *Adolescence, 22,* 59-68.

Rose, A. J., & Asher, S. R. (1999). Children's goals and strategies in response to conflicts within a friendship. *Developmental Psychology, 35,* 69-79.

Rose, S. A., Feldman, J. F., Futterweit, L. R., & Jankowski, J. J. (1997). Continuity in visual recognition memory: Infancy to 11 years. *Intelligence, 24,* 381-392.

Rosen, K. S., & Burke, P. B. (1999). Multiple attachment relationships within families: Mothers and fathers with two young children. *Developmental Psychology, 35,* 436-444.

Rosengren, K. S., Gelman, S. A., Kalish, C., & McCormick, M. (1991) As time goes by: Children's early understanding of growth in animals. *Child Development, 62,* 1302-1320.

Rosenthal, D. A., & Feldman, S. S. (1992). The relationship between parenting behaviour and ethnic identity in Chinese-American and Chinese-Australian adolescents. *International Journal of Psychology, 27,* 19-31.

Rosenthal, R., & Vandell, D. L. (1996). Quality of care at school-aged child-care programs: Regulatable features, observed experiences, child perspectives, and parent perspectives. *Child Development, 67,* 2434-2445.

Rostenstein, D., & Oster, H. (1997). Differential facial responses to four basic tastes in newborns. In P. Ekman & E. L. Rosenberg (Eds.), *What the face reveals: Basic and applied studies of spontaneous expression using the Facial Action Coding System (FACS). Series in affective science.* New York, NY: Oxford University Press.

Rotenberg, K. J., & Mayer, E. V. (1990). Delay of gratification in native and white children: A cross-cultural comparison. *International Journal of Behavioral Development, 13,* 23-30.

Rothbaum, F., & Weisz, J. R. (1994). Parental caregiving and child externalizing behavior in nonclinical samples: A meta-analysis. *Psychological Bulletin, 116,* 55-74.

Rotheram-Borus, M. J., Rosario, M., Van Rossem, R., & Reid, H. (1995). Prevalence, course, and predictors of multiple problem behaviors among gay and bisexual male adolescents. *Developmental Psychology, 31,* 75-85.

Rotto, P. C., & Kratochwill, T. R. (1994). Behavioral consultation with parents: Using competency-based training to modify child noncompliance. *School Psychology Review, 23,* 669-693.

Rovee-Collier, C. (1987). Learning and memory in infancy. In J. D. Osofsky (Ed.), *Handbook of infant development* (2nd ed.). New York: Wiley.

Rovee-Collier, C. (1997). Dissociations in infant memory: Rethinking the development of implicit and explicit memory. *Psychological Review, 104,* 467-498.

Rovee-Collier, C. (1999). The development of infant memory. *Current Directions in Psychological Science, 8,* 80-85.

Rowe, D. C. (1994). No more than skin deep. *American Psychologist, 49,* 215-216.

Rowe, D. C., Almeida, D. M., & Jacobson, K. C. (1999). School context and genetic influences on aggression in adolescence. *Psychological Science, 10,* 277-280.

Rubin, K. H., Bukowski, W., & Parker, J. G. (1998). Peer interactions, relationships, and groups. In W. Damon (Ed.), *Handbook of child psychology, Vol. 3.* New York: Wiley.

Ruble, D. N., Boggiano, A. K., Feldman, N. S., & Loebl, N. H. (1980). Developmental analysis of the role of social comparison in self-evaluation. *Developmental Psychology, 16,* 105-115.

Ruble, T. L. (1983). Sex stereotypes: Issues of changes in the 1970s. *Sex Roles, 9,* 397-402.

Ruff, H. A., Capozzoli, M., & Weissberg, R. (1998). Age, individuality, and context as factors in sustained visual attention during the preschool years. *Developmental Psychology, 34,* 454-464.

Rymer, R. (1993). *Genie.* New York: HarperCollins.

Sacco, W. P., & Beck, A. T. (1995). Cognitive theory and therapy. In E. E. Beckham & W. R. Leber (Eds.), *Handbook of depression* (2nd ed.). New York: Guilford Press.

Saffran, J. R., Aslin, R. N., & Newport, E. L. (1996). Statistical learning by 8-month-old infants. *Science, 274,* 1926-1928.

Sagi, A., van IJzendoorn, M. H., Aviezer, O., Donnell, F., & Mayseless, O. (1994). Sleeping out of home in a kibbutz communal arrangement: It makes a difference for infant-mother attachment. *Child Development, 65,* 992-1004.

Sandberg, D. E., Brook, A. E., & Campos, S. P. (1994). Short stature: A psychosocial burden requiring growth hormone therapy? *Pediatrics, 94,* 832-840.

Sanderson, C. A., & Cantor, N. (1995). Social dating goals in late adolesence: Implications for safer sexual activity. *Journal of Personality and Social Psychology, 68,* 1121-1134.

Savage-Rumbaugh, E. S., Murphy, J., Sevcik, R. A., Brakke, K. E., Williams, S. L., & Rumbaugh, D. M. (1993). Language comprehension in ape and child. *Monographs of the Society for Research in Child Development, 58* (3-4, Serial No. 233).

Savin-Williams, R. C., & Demo, D. H. (1984). Developmental change and stability in adolescent self-concept. *Developmental Psychology, 20,* 1100-1110.

Saxe, G. B. (1988). Candy selling and math learning. *Educational Researcher, 17,* 14-21.

Scarr, S. (1992). Developmental theories for the 1990s: Development and individual differences. *Child Development, 63,* 1-19.

Scarr, S. (1993). Genes, experience, and development. In D. Magnusson & P. J. M. Casaer (Eds.), *Longitudinal research on individual development: Present status and future perspectives. European network on longitudinal studies on individual development, 8.* (pp. 26-50). Cambridge, England: Cambridge University Press.

Scarr, S., & McCartney, K. (1983). How people make their own environments: A theory of genotype environment effects. *Child Development, 54,* 424-435.

Schaal, B., Marlier, L., & Soussignan, R. (1998). Olfactory function in the human fetus: Evidence from selective neonatal responsiveness to the odor of amniotic fluid. *Behavioral Neuroscience, 112,* 1438-1449.

Schmidt, F. L. & Hunter, J. E. (1998). The validity and utility of selection methods in personnel psychology: Practical and theoretical implications of 85 years of research findings. *Psychological Bulletin, 124,* 262-274.

Schneider, M. L. (1992). The effect of mild stress during pregnancy on birthweight and neuromotor maturation in rhesus monkey infants (Macaca mulatta). *Infant Behavior and Development, 15,* 389-403.

Schneider, M. L., Roughton, E. C., Koehler, A. J., & Lubach, G. R. (1999). Growth and development following prenatal stress exposure in primates: An examination of ontogenetic vulnerability. *Child Development, 70,* 253-274.

Schneider, W. & Bjorklund, D. F. (1998). Memory. In W. Damon (Ed.), *Handbook of child psychology, Volume 2.* New York: Wiley.

Schneider, W., & Pressley, M. (1997). *Memory development between 2 and 20* (2nd ed.). Mahwah, NJ: Erlbaum.

Schnorr, T. M., Grajewski, B. A., Hornung, R. W., Thun, M. J., Egeland, G. M., Murray, W. E., Conover, D. L., & Halperin, W. E. (1991). Video display terminals and the risk of spontaneous abortion. *The New England Journal of Medicine, 324,* 727-733.

Schramm, W., Lyle, J., & Parker, E. B. (1961). *Television in the lives of our children.* Stanford, CA: Stanford University Press.

Schwartz, D., Dodge, K. A., Pettit, G. S., & Bates, J. E. (1997). The early socialization of aggressive victims of bullying. *Child Development, 68,* 665-675.

Schwebel, D. C., & Plumert, J. M. (1999). Longitudinal and concurrent relations among temperament, ability estimation, and injury proneness. *Child Development, 70,* 700-712.

Scott, W. A., Scott, R., & McCabe, M. (1991). Family relationships and children's personality: A cross-cultural, cross-source comparison. *British Journal of Social Psychology, 30,* 1-20.

Sears, R. R. (1975). Your ancients revisited: A history of child development. In E. M. Hetherington (Ed.), *Review of child development research, Vol. 5.* Chicago: University of Chicago Press.

Secada, W. G., Fennema, E., & Adajian, L. B. (Eds). (1995). *New directions for equity in mathematics education.* New York, NY: Cambridge University Press.

Seidenberg, M. S., & McClelland, J. L. (1989). A distributed, developmental model of word recognition and naming. *Psychological Review, 96,* 523-568.

Seidman, E., Allen, L., Aber, J. L., Mitchell, C., & Feinman, J. (1994). The impact of school transitions in early adolescence on the self-system and perceived social context of poor urban youth. *Child Development, 65,* 507-522.

Seifer, R., Schiller, M., Sameroff, A. J., Resnick, S., & Riordan, K. (1996). Attachment, maternal sensitivity, and infant temperament during the first year of life. *Developmental Psychology, 32,* 12-25.

Selman, R. L. (1980). *The growth of interpersonal understanding: Developmental and clinical analyses.* New York: Academic Press.

Selman, R. L. (1981). The child as a friendship philosopher: A case study in the growth of interpersonal understanding. In S. R. Asher & J. M. Gottman (Eds.), *The development of children's friendships.* Cambridge, England: Cambridge University Press.

Sénéchal, M., Thomas, E., & Monker, J. (1995). Individual differences in 4-year-old children's acquisition of vocabulary during storybook reading. *Journal of Educational Psychology, 87,* 218-229.

Serdula, M. K., Ivery, D., Coates, R. J., Freedman, D. S., Williamson, D. F., & Byers, T. (1993). Do obese children become obese adults? A review of the literature. *Preventive Medicine, 22,* 167-177.

Sevy, S., Mendlewicz, J., & Mendelbaum, K. (1995). Genetic research in bipolar illness. In E. E. Beckham & W. R. Leber (Eds.), *Handbook of depression* (2nd ed.). New York: Guilford Press.

Seyfarth, R., & Cheney, D. (1996). Inside the mind of a monkey. In M. Bekoff & D. Jamieson (Eds), *Readings in animal cognition.* Cambridge, MA: MIT Press.

Shanahan, M. J., Elder, G. H., Burchinal, M., & Conger, R. D. (1996a). Adolescent paid labor and relationships with parents: Early work-family linkages. *Child Development, 67,* 2183-2200.

Shanahan, M. J., Elder, G. H., Burchinal, M., & Conger, R. D. (1996b). Adolescent earnings and relationships with parents: The work-family nexus in urban and rural ecologies. In J. T. Mortimer & M. D. Finch (Eds.), *Adolescents, work, and family: An intergenerational developmental analysis.* Thousand Oaks CA: Sage.

Sharpe, R. M., & Skakkebaek, N. E. (1993). Are oestrogens involved in falling sperm counts and disorders of the male reproductive tract? *Lancet, 341,* 1392-1395.

Shatz, M. (1983). Communication. In P. H. Mussen (Ed.), *Handbook of child psychology, Vol. 3.* New York: Wiley.

Shatz, M., & Gelman, R. (1973). The development of communication skills: Modifications in the speech of young children as a function of listener. *Monographs of the Society for Research in Child Development, 38* (5, Serial No. 152).

Shaw, D. S., Winslow, E. B., & Flanagan, C. (1999). A prospective study of the effects of marital status and family relations on young children's adjustment among African American and European American families. *Child Development, 70,* 742-755.

Shaw, G. M., Schaffer, D., Velie, E. M., Morland, K., & Harris, J. A. (1995). Periconceptional vitamin use, dietary folate, and the occurrence of neural tube defects. *Epidemiology, 6,* 219-226.

Shelov, S. P. (1993). *Caring for your baby and young child: Birth to age 5.* New York: Bantam.

Sherif, M., Harvey, O. J., White, B. J., Hood, W. R., & Sherif, C. W. (1961). *Intergroup conflict and cooperation.* Norman, OK: The University Book Exchange.

Sherrod, K. B., O'Connor, S., Vietze, P. M., & Altemeier, W. A. II (1984). Child health and maltreatment. *Child Development, 55,* 1174-1183.

Shiner, R. L. (1998). How shall we speak of children's personalities in middle childhood? A preliminary taxonomy. *Psychological Bulletin, 124,* 308-332.

Shiwach, R. (1994). Psychopathology in Huntington's disease patients. *Acta Psychiatrica Scandinavica, 90,* 241-246.

Shoda, Y., Mischel, W., & Peake, P. K. (1990). Predicting adolescent cognitive and self-regulatory competencies from preschool delay of gratification: Identifying diagnostic conditions. *Developmental Psychology, 26,* 978-986.

Shotland, R. L., & Goodstein, L. (1992). Sexual precedence reduces the perceived legitimacy of sexual refusal: An examination of attribution concerning date rape and consensual sex. *Personality and Social Psychology Bulletin, 18,* 756-764.

Shuter-Dyson, R. (1982). Musical ability. In D. Deutsch (Ed.), *The psychology of music.* New York: Academic Press.

Shwe, H. I., & Markman, E. M. (1997). Young children's appreciation of the mental impact of their communicative signals. *Developmental Psychology, 33,* 630-636.

Siddiqui, A. (1995). Object size as a determinant of grasping in infancy. *Journal of Genetic Psychology, 156,* 345-358.

Siegal, M. & Peterson, C. C. (1998). Preschoolers' understanding of lies and innocent and negligent mistakes. *Developmental Psychology, 34,* 332-341.

Siegel, L. S. (1994). Working memory and reading: A life-span perspective. *International Journal of Behavioral Development, 17,* 109-124.

Siegler, R. S. (1986). Unities in strategy choices across domains. In M. Perlmutter (Ed.), *Minnesota symposia on child development, Vol. 19.* Hillsdale, NJ: Erlbaum.

Siegler, R. S. (1988). Strategy choice procedures and the development of multiplication skill. *Journal of Experimental Psychology: General, 117,* 258-278.

Siegler, R. S. (1998). *Children's thinking* (3rd ed). Upper Saddle River NJ: Prentice-Hall.

Siegler, R. S., & Jenkins, E. (1989). *How children discover new strategies.* Hillsdale, NJ: Erlbaum.

Siegler, R. S., & Robinson, M. (1982). The development of numerical understandings. In H. W. Reese and L. P. Lipsitt (Eds.), *Advances in child development and behavior (Vol. 16).* New York: Academic Press.

Siegler, R. S., & Shrager, J. (1984). Strategy choices in addition and subtraction: How do children know what to do? In C. Sophian (Ed.), *Origins of cognitive skills.* Hillsdale, NJ: Erlbaum.

Signorella, M. L., Bigler, R. S., & Liben, L. S. (1993). Developmental differences in children's gender schemata about others: A meta-analytic review. Early gender-role development. *Developmental Review, 13,* 147-183.

Signorielli, N., & Lears, M. (1992). Children, television, and conceptions about chores: Attitudes and behaviors. *Sex Roles, 27,* 157-170.

Silverman, I. W., & Ragusa, D. M. (1990). Child and maternal correlates of impulse control in 24-month-old children. *Genetic, Social, and General Psychology Monographs, 116,* 435-473.

Simmons, R., & Blyth, D. (1987). *Moving into adolescence.* New York: Aldine de Gruyter.

Simons, D. J., & Keil, F. C. (1995). An abstract to concrete shift in the development of biological thought: The inside story. *Cognition, 56,* 129-163.

Simons, R. L., Whitbeck, L. B., Conger, R. D., & Chyi-In, W. (1991). Intergenerational transmission of harsh parenting. *Developmental Psychology, 27,* 159-171.

Simons-Morton, B. G., McKenzie, T. J., Stone, E., Mitchell, P., Osganian, V., Strikmiller, P. K., Ehlinger, S., Cribb, P., & Nader, P. R. (1997). Physical activity in the multiethnic population of third graders in four states. *American Journal of Public Health, 87,* 45-50.

Simpson, E. L. (1974). Moral development research: A case study of scientific cultural bias. *Human Development, 17,* 81-106.

Singer, J. D., Fuller, B., Keiley, M. K., & Wolf, A. (1998). Early child-care selection: Variation by geographic location, maternal characteristics, and family structure. *Developmental Psychology, 34,* 1129-1144.

Skinner, B. F. (1957). *Verbal behavior.* New York: Appleton-Century-Crofts.

Slate, J. R., Jones, C. H., & Dawson, P. (1993). Academic skills of high school students as a function of grade, gender, and academic track. *High School Journal, 76,* 245-251.

Slobin, D. I. (1985). Crosslinguistic evidence for the language-making capacity. In D. I. Slobin (Ed.), *The crosslinguistic study of language acquisition: Vol. 2: Theoretical issues.* Hillsdale, NJ: Erlbaum.

Smetana, J. G., & Braeges, J. L. (1990). The development of toddlers' moral and conventional judgments. *Merrill-Palmer Quarterly, 36,* 329-346.

Smetana, J. G., Killen, M., & Turiel, E. (1991). Children's reasoning about interpersonal and moral conflicts. *Child Development, 62,* 629-644.

Smith, L. B., Thelen, E., Titzer, R., & McLin, D. (1999). Knowing in the context of acting: The task dynamics of the A-not-B error. *Psychological Review, 106,* 235-260.

Smith, R. E., & Smoll, F. L. (1990). Self-esteem and children's reactions to youth sport coaching behaviors: A field study of self-enhancement processes. *Developmental Psychology, 26,* 987-993.

Smith, R. E., & Smoll, F. L. (1996). The coach as the focus of research and intervention in youth sports. In F. L. Smoll & R. E. Smith (Eds.), *Children and youth in sport: A biopsychological perspective* (pp. 125-141). Dubuque, IA: Brown & Benchmark.

Smith, R. E., & Smoll, F. L. (1997). Coaching the coaches: Youth sports as a scientific and applied behavioral setting. *Current Directions in Psychological Science, 6* (1), 16-21.

Smoll, F. L., & Schutz, R. W. (1990). Quantifying gender differences in physical performance: A developmental perspective. *Developmental Psychology, 26,* 360-369.

Smoll, F. L., Smith, R. E., Barnett, N. P., & Everett, J. J. (1993). Enhancement of children's self-esteem through social support training for youth sport coaches. *Journal of Applied Psychology, 78* (4), 602-610.

Snarey, J. R. (1985). Cross-cultural universality of social-moral development: A critical review of Kohlbergian research. *Psychological Bulletin, 97,* 202-232.

Snedeker, B. (1992). *Hard knocks: Preparing youth for work.* Baltimore, MD: Johns Hopkins University Press.

Snow, C. W. (1998). *Infant development* (2nd ed.). Upper Saddle River, NJ: Prentice Hall.

Snow, M. E., Jacklin, C. N., & Maccoby, E. E. (1983). Sex-of-child differences in father-child interaction at one year of age. *Child Development, 54,* 227-232.

Soken, N. H., & Pick, A. D. (1999). Infants' perception of dynamic affective expressions: Do infants distinguish specific expressions? *Child Development, 70,* 1275-1282.

Sokolov, J. L. (1993). A local contingency analysis of the fine-tuning hypothesis. *Developmental Psychology, 29,* 1008-1023.

Solomon, G. E. A., Johnson, S. C., Zaitchik, D., & Carey, S. (1996). Like father, like son: Young children's understanding of how and why offspring resemble their parents. *Child Development, 67,* 151-171.

Spelke, E. S. (1994). Initial knowledge: Six suggestions. *Cognition, 50,* 431-445.

Spence, J. T. (1985). Achievement American style: The rewards and costs of individualism. *American Psychologist, 40,* 1285-1295.

Sperduto, R. D., Seigel, D., Roberts, J., & Rowland, M. (1983). Prevalence of myopia in the United States. *Archives of Opthamology, 101,* 405-407.

Springer, K., & Keil, F. C. (1991). Early differentiation of causal mechanisms appropriate to biological and nonbiological kinds. *Child Development, 62,* 767-781.

Springer, S. P., & Deutsch, G. (1998). *Left brain, right brain: Perspectives from cognitive neuroscience* (5th ed.). New York, NY: Freeman.

Sporkin, E., Wagner, J., & Tomashoff, C. (1992, February). A terrible hunger. *People,* 92-98.

Sroufe, L. A., & Fleeson, J. (1986). Attachment and the construction of relationships. In W. W. Hartup and Z. Rubin (Eds.), *Relationships and development.* Hillsdale, NJ: Erlbaum.

Sroufe, L. A., & Waters, E. (1976). The ontogenesis of smiling and laughter: A perspective on the organization of development in infancy. *Psychological Review, 83,* 173-189.

Sroufe, L. A., & Wunsch, J. P. (1972). The development of laughter in the first year of life. *Child Development, 43,* 1324-1344.

St. George, I. M., Williams, S., & Silva, P. A. (1994). Body size and the menarche: The Dunedin study. *Journal of Adolescent Health, 15,* 573-576.

St. James-Roberts, I. & Plewis, I. (1996). Individual differences, daily fluctuations, and developmental changes in amounts of infant waking, fussing, crying, feeding, and sleeping. *Child Development, 67,* 2527-2450.

Stalikas, A., & Gavaki, E. (1995). The importance of ethnic identity: Self-esteem and academic achievement of second-generation Greeks in secondary school. *Canadian Journal of School Psychology, 11,* 1-9.

Stanovich, K. E. (1993). Dysrationalia: A new specific learning disability. *Journal of Learning Disabilities, 26,* 501-515.

Stattin, H., & Magnusson, D. (1989). The role of early aggressive behavior in the frequency, seriousness, and types of later crime. *Journal of Consulting and Clinical Psychology, 57,* 710-718.

Steelman, J. D. (1994). Revision strategies employed by middle level students using computers. *Journal of Educational Computing Research, 11,* 141-152.

Stein, J. A., & Newcomb, M. D. (1999). Adult outcomes of adolescent conventional and agentic orientations: A 20-year longitudinal study. *Journal of Early Adolescence, 19,* 39-65.

Stein, J. H., & Reiser, L. W. (1994). A study of white middle-class adolescent boys' responses to "semenarche" (the first ejaculation). *Journal of Youth and Adolescence, 23,* 373-384.

Steinberg, L. (1990). Autonomy, conflict, and harmony in the family relationship. In S. S. Feldman & G. R. Elliott (Eds.), *At the threshold: The developing adolescent.* Cambridge, MA: Harvard University Press.

Steinberg, L., & Dornbusch, S. M. (1991). Negative correlates of part-time employment during adolescence: Replication and elaboration. *Developmental Psychology, 27,* 304-313.

Steinberg, L., Fegley, S., & Dornbusch, S. M. (1993). Negative impact of part-time work on adolescent adjustment: Evidence from a longitudinal study. *Developmental Psychology, 29,* 171-180.

Steinberg, L., Lamborn, S. D., Dornbusch, S. M., & Darling, N. (1992). Impact of parenting practices on adolescent achievement: Authoritative parenting, school involvement, and encouragement to succeed. *Child Development, 63,* 1266-1281.

Steinberg, L. D. (1999). *Adolescence* (5th ed.). Boston, MA: McGraw-Hill.

Stern, M., & Karraker, K. H. (1989). Sex stereotyping of infants: A review of gender labeling studies. *Sex Roles, 20,* 501-522.

Sternberg, C. R., & Campos, J. (1990). The development of anger expressions in infancy. In N. Stein, B. Leventhal, & T. Trabasso (Eds.), *Psychological and biological approaches to emotion.* Hillsdale NJ: Erlbaum.

Sternberg, R. J. (1977). *Intelligence, information processing, and analogical reasoning.* Hillsdale, NJ: Erlbaum

Sternberg, R. J. (1985). *Beyond IQ: A triarchic theory of human intelligence.* Cambridge: Cambridge University Press.

Sternberg, R. J., & Kaufman, J. C., (1998). Human abilities. *Annual Review of Psychology, 49,* 479-502.

Stevenson, H. W., & Lee, S. (1990). Contexts of achievement. *Monographs of the Society for Research in Child Development, 55,* Serial No. 221.

Stevenson, H. W., Parker, T., Wilkinson, A., Hegion, A., & Fish, E. (1976). Longitudinal study of individual differences in cognitive development and scholastic achievement. *Journal of Educational Psychology, 68,* 377-400.

Stevenson, H. W., & Stigler, J. W. (1992). *The learning gap.* New York: Summit Books.

Stevenson, M. R., & Black, K. N. (1995). *How divorce affects offspring: A research approach.* Madison, WI: Brown & Benchmark.

Stewart, L., & Pascual-Leone, J. (1992). Mental capacity constraints and the development of moral reasoning. *Journal of Experimental Child Psychology, 54,* 251-287.

Stewart R. B., Mobley, L. A., Van Tuyl, S. S., & Salvador, W. A. (1987). The firstborns' adjustment to the birth of a sibling: A longitudinal assessment. *Child Development, 58,* 341-355.

St George, I. M., Williams, S., & Silva, P. A. (1994). Body size and the menarche: The Dunedin study. *International Journal of Adolescent Health, 15,* 573-576.

Stice, E., & Barrera, M., Jr. (1995). A longitudinal examination of the reciprocal relations between perceived parenting and adolescents' substance use and externalizing behaviors. *Developmental Psychology, 31,* 322-334.

Stifter, C. A., & Fox, N. A. (1990). Infant reactivity: Physiological correlates of newborn and 5-month temperament. *Developmental Psychology, 26,* 582-588.

Stifter, C. A., Spinrad, T. L., & Braungart-Rieker, J. M. (1999). Toward a developmental model of child compliance: The role of emotion regulation in infancy. *Child Development, 70,* 21-32.

Stiles, J. (1998). The effects of early focal brain injury on lateralization of cognitive function. *Current Directions in Psychological Science, 7,* 21-26.

Stiles, J. (2000). Spatial cognitive development following prenatal or perinatal focal brain injury. In H. S. Harvey & J. Grafman (Eds.), *Cerebral reorganization of function after brain damage* (pp 201-217). New York: Oxford University Press.

Stiles, J., Bates, E. A., Thal, D., Trauner, D., & Reilly, J. (1999). Linguistic, cognitive, and affective development in children with pre- and perinatal focal brain injury: A ten-year overview from the San Diego Longitudinal Project. In C. Rovee-Collier (Ed.), *Advances in infancy research.* Norwood, NJ: Ablex.

Stoolmiller, M., Eddy, J. M., & Reid, J. B. (2000). Detecting and describing preventive intervention effects in a universal school-based randomized trial targeting delinquent and violent behavior. *Journal of Consulting and Clinical Psychology, 68,* 296-306.

Stormshak, E. A., Bellanti, C. J., Bierman, K. L., & Conduct Problems Prevention Research Group (1996). The quality of sibling relationships and the development of social competence and behavioral control in aggressive children. *Developmental Psychology, 32,* 79-89.

Strauss, M. S., & Curtis, L. E. (1984). Development of numerical concepts in infancy. In C. Sophian (Ed.), *Origins of cognitive skills.* Hillsdale, NJ: Erlbaum.

Strayer, J., & Schroeder, M. (1989). Children's helping strategies: Influences of emotion, empathy, and age. In N. Eisenberg (Ed.), *New directions for child development: Empathy and related emotional responses,* Vol. 44. San Francisco: Jossey-Bass.

Streissguth, A. P., Barr, H. M., Sampson, P. D., & Bookstein, F. L. (1994). Prenatal alcohol and offspring development: The first fourteen years. *Drugs & Alcohol Dependence, 36,* 89-99.

Strober, M. (1995). Family-genetic perspectives on anorexia nervosa and bulimia nervosa. In K. Brownell & C. G. Fairburn (Eds.), *Eating disorders and obesity: A comprehensive handbook.* New York: Guilford Press.

Stunkard, A. J., Sorensen, T. I. A., Hanis, C., Teasdale, T. W., Chakraborty, R., Schull, W. J., & Schulsinger, F. (1986). An adoption study of human obesity. *New England Journal of Medicine, 314,* 193-198.

Sullivan, L. W. (1987). The risks of the sickle-cell trait: Caution and common sense. *New England Journal of Medicine, 317,* 830-831.

Sullivan, S. A., & Birch, L. L. (1990). Pass the sugar, pass the salt: Experience dictates preference. *Developmental Psychology, 26,* 546-551.

Summerville, M. B., Kaslow, N. J., & Doepke, K. J. (1996). Psychopathology and cognitive and family functioning in suicidal African-American adolescents. *Current Directions in Psychological Science, 5,* 7-11.

Super, C. M. (1981). Cross-cultural research on infancy. In H. C. Triandis and A. Heron (Eds.), *Handbook of cross-cultural psychology,* Vol. 4: Developmental psychology. Boston: Allyn and Bacon.

Super, C. M., Herrera, M. G., & Mora, J. O. (1990). Long-term effects of food supplementation and psychosocial intervention on the physical growth of Colombian infants at risk of malnutrition. *Child Development, 61,* 29-49.

Super, D. E. (1976). *Career education and the meanings of work.* Washington, DC: U. S. Offices of Education.

Super, D. E. (1980). A life span, life space approach to career development. *Journal of Vocational Behavior, 16,* 282-298.

Swarr, A. E., & Richards, M. H. (1996). Longitudinal effects of adolescent girls' pubertal development, perceptions of pubertal timing, and parental relations in eating problems. *Developmental Psychology, 32,* 636-646.

Szkrybalo, J., & Ruble, D. N. (1999). "God made me a girl": Sex-category constancy judgments and explanations revisited. *Developmental Psychology, 35,* 392-402.

Tager-Flusberg, H. (1993). Putting words together: Morphology and syntax in the preschool years. In J. Berko Gleason (Ed.), *The development of language* (3rd ed.). New York: Macmillan.

Tamis-LeMonda, C. S., & Bornstein, M. H. (1996). Variation in children's exploratory, nonsymbolic, and symbolic play: An explanatory multidimensional framework. In C. Rovee-Collier & L. P. Lipsitt (Eds.), *Advances in infancy research,* Vol. 10. Norwood, NJ: Ablex Publishing Corp.

Tanner, J. M. (1970). Physical growth. In P. H. Mussen (Ed.), *Carmichael's manual of child psychology* (3rd ed.). New York: Wiley.

Tanner, J. M. (1990). *Foetus into man* (2nd ed.). Cambridge, MA: Harvard University Press.

Taylor, M., Cartwright, B. S., & Carlson, S. M. (1993). A developmental investigation of children's imaginary companions. *Developmental Review, 29,* 276-285.

Taylor, M. G. (1996). The development of children's beliefs about social and biological aspects of gender differences. *Child Development, 67,* 1555-1571.

Taylor, R., Casten, R., Flickinger, S. M., Roberts, D., & Fulmore, C. D. (1994). Explaining the school performance of African-American adolescents. *Journal of Research on Adolescence, 4,* 21-44.

Taylor, R. D., & Roberts, D. (1995). Kinship support and maternal and adolescent well-being in economically disadvantaged African-American families. *Child Development, 66,* 1585-1597.

Teller, D. Y., & Bornstein, M. H. (1987). Infant color vision and color perception. In P. Salapatek and

L. Cohen (Eds.), *Handbook of infant perception* (Vol. 1.) Orlando, Fla.: Academic Press.

Thelen, E. & Smith, L. B. (1998). Dynamic systems theories. In W. Damon (Ed.), *Handbook of Child Psychology,* Vol. 1. New York, NY: Wiley.

Thelen, E., & Ulrich, B. D. (1991). Hidden skills. *Monographs of the Society for Research in Child Development, 56,* Serial No. 223.

Thelen, E., Ulrich, B. D., & Jensen, J. L. (1989). The developmental origins of locomotion. In M. H. Woollacott and A. Shumway-Cook (Eds.), *Development of posture and gait across the life span.* Columbia, SC: University of South Carolina Press.

Thomas, A., Chess, S., & Birch, H. G. (1968). *Temperament and behavior disorders in children.* New York: New York University Press.

Thomas, H., & Kail, R. (1991). Sex differences in the speed of mental rotation and the X-linked genetic hypothesis. *Intelligence, 15,* 17-32.

Thomas, J. R., & French, K. E. (1985). Gender differences across age in motor performance: A meta-analysis. *Psychological Bulletin, 98,* 260-282.

Thomas, J. W., Bol, L., Warkentin, R. W., Wilson, M., Strage, A., & Rohwer, W. D. (1993). Interrelationships among students' study activities, self-concept of academic ability, and achievement as a function of characteristics of high-school biology courses. *Applied Cognitive Psychology, 7,* 499-532.

Thompson, G. G. (1952). *Child psychology.* Boston: Houghton Mifflin.

Thompson, R. A., & Limber, S. (1991). "Social anxiety" in infancy: Stranger wariness and separation distress. In H. Leitenberg (Ed.), *Handbook of social and evaluation anxiety.* New York: Plenum.

Thurstone, L. L., & Thurstone, T. G. (1941). Factorial studies of intelligence. *Psychometric Monograph,* No. 2.

Tincoff, R., & Jusczyk, P. W. (1999). Some beginnings of word comprehension in 6-month-olds. *Psychological Science, 10,* 172-175.

Tizard, B., & Hodges, J. (1978). The effect of early institutional rearing on the development of eight-year-old children. *Journal of Child Psychology and Psychiatry and Allied Disciplines, 19,* 99-118.

Tobin, J. J., Wu, D. Y. H., & Davidson, D. H. (1989). *Preschools in three cultures: Japan, China, and the United States.* New Haven: Yale University Press.

Tobler, N. S., & Stratton, H. H. (1997). Effectiveness of school-based drug prevention programs: A meta-analysis of the research. *Journal of Primary Prevention, 18,* 71-128.

Toda, S., & Fogel, A. (1993). Infant response to the still-face situation at 3 and 6 months. *Developmental Psychology, 29,* 532-538.

Todd, R. D., Swarzenski, B., Rossi, P. G., & Viscon-

ti, P. (1995). Structural and functional development of the human brain. In D. Cicchetti & D. J. Cohen (Eds.), *Developmental psychopathology. Vol. 1, Theory and Methods* (pp. 161-194). New York: Wiley.

Treboux, D., & Busch-Rossnagel, N. A. (1995). Age differences in parent and peer influences on female sexual behavior. *Journal of Research on Adolescence, 5,* 469-487.

Trickett, P. K., Aber, J. L., Carlson, V., & Cicchetti, D. (1991). Relationship of socioeconomic status to the etiology and developmental sequelae of physical child abuse. *Developmental Psychology, 27,* 148-158.

Trickett, P. K., & Kuczinski, L. (1986). Children's misbehaviors and parental discipline strategies in abusive and nonabusive families. *Developmental Psychology, 22,* 115-123.

Trickett, P. K., & McBride-Chang, C. (1995). The developmental impact of different forms of child abuse and neglect. *Developmental Review, 15,* 311-337.

Tuchfarber, B. S., Zins, J. E., & Jason, L. A. (1997). Prevention and control of injuries. In R. Weissberg, T. P. Gullotta, R. L. Hampton, B. A. Ryan, & G. R. Adams (Eds.), *Enhancing children's wellness* (pp. 250-277). Thousand Oaks, CA: Sage.

U. S. Bureau of the Census. (1994). *Marital status and living arrangements: March 1993.* Washington, DC: U. S. Government Printing Office.

U. S. Bureau of the Census. (1995a). *Statistical abstract of the United States* (115th ed.). Washington, D. C.: U. S. Government Printing Office.

U.S. Bureau of the Census (1995b). *Population Profile of the United States: 1995.* Washington, DC: U.S. Government Printing Office.

U. S. Department of Health and Human Services. (1995). *Vital statistics of the United States, 1992.* Washington, DC: U. S. Government Printing Office.

U.S. Department of Health and Human Services. (1997). *Vital statistics of the United States, 1994.* Washington, DC: U.S. Government Printing Office.

U.S. Department of Health and Human Services. (1997). Youth risk behavior surveillance—U.S., 1995. *MMWR, 45,* (No. SS-4).

Unger, R., & Crawford, M. (1996). *Women and gender: A feminist psychology* (2nd ed.). New York: McGraw-Hill.

Uniform Crime Reports for the United States (1996). Washington, DC: U.S. Government Printing Office.

Urberg, K. A., Değirmencioğlu, S. M., & Pilgrim, C. (1997). Close friend and group influence on adolescent cigarette smoking and alcohol use. *Developmental Psychology, 33,* 834-844.

USDA (2000). Dietary guidelines for Americans, 2000 (5th ed.). Home and garden bulletin, No. 32.

Valenzuela, M. (1997). Maternal sensitivity in a developing society: The context of urban poverty and infant chronic undernutrition. *Developmental Psychology, 33,* 845-855.

Valkenburg, P. M., & van der Voort, T. H. A. (1994). Influence of TV on daydreaming and creative imagination: A review of research. *Psychological Bulletin, 116,* 316-339.

Valkenburg, P. M., & van der Voort, T. H. A. (1995). The influence of television on children's daydreaming styles: A 1-year-panel study. *Communication Research, 22,* 267-287.

Valois, R. F., Dunham, A. C. A., Jackson, K. L., & Waller, J. (1999). Association between employment and substance abuse behaviors among public high school adolescents. *Journal of Adolescent Health, 25,* 256-263.

van den Boom, D. C. (1994). The influence of temperament and mothering on attachment and exploration: An experimental manipulation of sensitive responsiveness among lower-class mothers with irritable infants. *Child Development, 65,* 1457-1477.

van den Boom, D. C. (1995). Do first-year intervention effects endure? Follow-up during toddlerhood of a sample of Dutch irritable infants. *Child Development, 66,* 1798-1816.

van IJzendoorn, M. H., & Kroonenberg, P. M. (1988). Cross-cultural patterns of attachment: A meta-analysis of the Strange Situation. *Child Development, 59,* 147-156.

Vandell, D. L., & Ramanan, J. (1991). Children of the National Longitudinal Survey of Youth: Choices in after-school care and child development. *Developmental Psychology, 27,* 637-643.

Vaughn, B. E., Kopp, C. D., & Krakow, J. B. (1984). The emergence and consolidation of self-control from eighteen to thirty months of age: Normative trends and individual differences. *Child Development, 55,* 990-1004.

Vederhus, L. & Krekling, S. (1996). Sex differences in visual spatial ability in 9-year-old children. *Intelligence, 23,* 33-43.

Ventura, S. J., Martin, J. A., Curtin, S. C., & Mathews, T. J. (1997). *Report of final natality statistics, 1995.* Monthly Vital Statistics Report, 45, June 1997.

Verbrugge, H. P. (1990). The national immunization program of the Netherlands. *Pediatrics, 86,* 1060-1063.

Verma, I. M. (1990). Gene therapy. *Scientific American, 263,* 68-84.

Volling, B. L., & Belsky, J. (1992). The contribution of mother-child and father-child relationships to the quality of sibling interaction: A longitudinal study. *Child Development, 63,* 1209-1222.

von Hofsten, C., Vishton, P., Spelke, E. S., Feng, Q., & Rosander, K. (1998). Predictive action in infancy: Tracking and reaching for moving objects. *Cognition, 67,* 255-285.

Vorhees, C. V., & Mollnow, E. (1987). Behavior teratogenesis: Long-term influences on behavior. In J. D. Osofsky (Ed.). *Handbook of infant development* (2nd ed.). New York: Wiley.

Voyer, D., Voyer, S., & Bryden, M. P. (1995). Magnitude of sex differences in spatial abilities: A meta-analysis and consideration of critical variables. *Psychological Bulletin, 117,* 250-270.

Vurpillot, E. (1968). The development of scanning strategies and their relation to visual differentiation. *Journal of Experimental Child Psychology, 6,* 632-650.

Vygotsky, L. S. (1934/1986). *Thought and language* (A. Kozulin, Trans.). Cambridge, MA: MIT Press. (Original work published in 1934)

Vygotsky, L. S. (1978). *Mind in society: The development of higher psychological processes* (M. Cole, V. John-Steiner, S. Scribner, & E. Soubermen, Eds.). Cambridge, MA: Harvard University Press.

Waber, D. P. (1977). Sex differences in mental abilities, hemispheric lateralization, and rate of physical growth at adolescence. *Developmental Psychology, 13,* 29-38.

Wachs, T. D. (1983). The use and abuse of environment in behavior-genetic research. *Child Development, 54,* 396-407.

Wagner, N. E., Schubert, H. J. P., & Schubert, D. S. P. (1985). Family size effects: A revision. *Journal of Genetic Psychology, 146,* 65-78.

Wagner, R. K., Torgesen, J. K., & Rashotte, C. A. (1997). Development of reading-related phonological processing abilities: New evidence of bidirectional causality from a latent variable longitudinal study. *Developmental Psychology, 30,* 73-87.

Wagner, R. K., Torgesen, J. K., Rashotte, C. A., Hecht, S. A., Barker, T. A., Burgess, S. R., Donahue, J., & Garon, T. (1997). Changing relations between phonological processing abilities and word-level reading as children develop from beginning to skilled readers: A 5-year longitudinal study. *Developmental Psychology, 33,* 468-479.

Wakschlag, L. S., & Hans, S. L. (1999). Relation of maternal responsiveness during infancy to the development of behavior problems in high-risk youths. *Developmental Psychology, 35,* 569-579.

Walberg, H. J. (1995). General practices. In G. Cawelti (Ed.), *Handbook of research on improving student achievement.* Arlington VA: Educational Research Service.

Walker, L. J. (1980). Cognitive and perspective-taking prerequisites for moral development. *Child Development, 51,* 131-139.

Walker, L. J. (1995). Sexism in Kohlberg's moral psychology? In W. M. Kurtines & J. L. Gewirtz (Ed.), *Moral development: An introduction.* Boston: Allyn and Bacon.

Walker, L. J., & Taylor, J. H. (1991). Family inter-

actions and the development of moral reasoning. *Child Development, 62,* 264-283.

Ward, S. L. & Overton, W. F. (1990). Semantic familiarity, relevance, and the development of deductive reasoning. *Developmental Psychology, 26,* 288-493.

Waters, H. F. (1993, July 12). Networks under the gun. *Newsweek,* 64-66.

Waters, H. S. (1980). "Class news": A single-subject longitudinal study of prose production and schema formation during childhood. *Journal of Verbal Learning and Verbal Behavior, 19,* 152-167.

Watson, J. B. (1925). *Behaviorism.* New York: Norton.

Waxman, S. R., & Markow, D. B. (1995). Words as invitations to form categories: Evidence from 12- to 13-month-old infants. *Cognitive Psychology, 29,* 257-303.

Webber, L. S., Wattigney, W. A., Srinivasan, S. R., & Berenson, G. S. (1995). Obesity studies in Bogalusa. *American Journal of Medical Science, 310,* S53-S61.

Wechsler, D. (1991). *Manual for the Wechsler Intelligence Test for Children - III.* New York: The Psychological Corporation.

Wegman, M. E. (1994). Annual summary of vital statistics—1993. *Pediatrics, 95,* 792-803.

Weinberg, M. K., & Tronick, E. Z. (1994). Beyond the face: An empirical study of infant affective configurations of facial, vocal, gestural, and regulatory behaviors. *Child Development, 65,* 1503-1515.

Weissman, M. D. & Kalish, C. W. (1999). The inheritance of desired characteristics: Children's view of the role of intention in parent-offspring resemblance. *Journal of Experimental Child Psychology, 73,* 245-265.

Wellman, H. M. (1991). From desire to belief: Acquisition of a theory of mind. In A. Whiten (Ed.), *Natural theories of mind: Evolution, development, and simulation of everyday mindreading* (pp. 19-38). Oxford: Basil Blackwell, Inc.

Wellman, H. M. (1992). *The child's theory of mind.* Cambridge MA: MIT Press.

Wellman, H. M., Cross, D., & Bartsch, K. (1986). Infant search and object permanence: A meta-analysis of the A not B error. *Monographs of the Society for Research in Child Development, 51,* Serial No. 214.

Wellman, H. M. & Gelman, S. A. (1998). Knowledge acquisition in foundational domains. In W. Damon (eds.), *Handbook of Child Psychology,* Volume 2. New York, NY: John Wiley & Sons, Inc.

Welsh, M. C., Pennington, B. F., & Groisser, D. B. (1991). A normative-developmental study of executive function: A window on prefrontal function in children. *Developmental Neuropsychology, 7,* 131-149.

Wendland-Carro, J., Piccinini, C. A., & Millar, W. S. (1999). The role of an early intervention on enhancing the quality of mother-infant interaction. *Child Development, 70,* 713-721.

Wentzel, K. R., & Asher, S. R. (1995). The academic lives of neglected, rejected, popular, and controversial children. *Child Development, 66,* 754-763.

Wentzel, K. R., & Erdley, C. A. (1993). Strategies for making friends: Relations to social behavior and peer acceptance. *Developmental Psychology, 29,* 819-826.

Werker, J. F., & Lalonde, C. E. (1988). Cross-language speech perception: Initial capabilities and developmental change. *Developmental Psychology, 24,* 672-683.

Werner, E. E. (1995). Resilience in development. *Current Directions in Psychological Science, 4,* 81-85.

Werner, H. (1948). *Comparative psychology of mental development.* Chicago: Follet.

Wertsch, J. V., & Tulviste, P. (1992). L. S. Vygotsky and contemporary developmental psychology. *Developmental Psychology, 28,* 548-557.

West, S. G., Biesanz, J. C., & Pitts, S. C. (2000). Causal inference and generalization in field settings: Experimental and quasi-experimental designs. In H. T. Reis & C. M. Judd (Eds.), *Handbook of research methods in social and personality psychology* (pp. 40-84). New York: Cambridge University Press.

Whaley, L. F., & Wong, D. F. (1991). *Nursing care of infants and children.* St. Louis, MO: Mosby-Year Book.

Whitaker, R. C., Wright, J. A., Pepe, M. S., Seidel, K. D., & Dietz, W. H. (1997). Predicting obesity in young adulthood from childhood and parental obesity. *New England Journal of Medicine, 337,* 869-873.

White, S. A., Duda, J. L., & Keller, M. R. (1998). The relationship between goal orientation and perceived purposes of sport among youth sport participants. *Journal of Sport Behavior, 21* (4), 474-483.

White, S. H. (1996). The relationships of developmental psychology to social policy. Health. In E. F. Zigler, S. L. Kagan, & N. W. Hall (Eds.), *Children, families, and government: Preparing for the twenty-first century.* New York: Cambridge University Press.

Whitehead, J. R., & Corbin, C. B. (1997). Self-esteem in children and youth: The role of sport and physical education. In K. R. Fox, et al (Eds.), *The physical self: From motivation to well-being.* Champaign, IL: Human Kinetics.

Whitehurst, G. J., & Vasta, R. (1975). Is language acquired through imitation? *Journal of Psycholinguistic Research, 4,* 37-59.

Whitehurst, G. J., & Vasta, R. (1977). *Child behavior.* Boston: Houghton Mifflin.

Whitesell, N. R., & Harter, S. (1996). The interpersonal context of emotion: Anger with close friends and classmates. *Child Development, 67,* 1345-1359.

Whiting, J. W. M., & Child, I. L. (1953). *Child training and personality: A cross-cultural study.* New Haven: Yale University Press.

Whitney, E. N., Cataldo, C. B., & Rolfes, S. R. (1987). *Understanding normal and clinical nutrition* (2nd ed.). St. Paul, Minn: West Publishing.

Whitney, E. N., & Hamilton, E. M. N. (1987). *Understanding nutrition (4th ed).* St. Paul: West.

Wicks-Nelson, R., & Israel, A. C. (1991). *Behavior disorders of childhood* (2nd ed.). Englewood Cliffs, NJ: Prentice Hall.

Wigfield, A., Eccles, J. S., Mac Iver, D. Reuman, D. A., & Midgley, C. (1991). Transitions during early adolescence: Changes in children's domain-specific self-perceptions and general self-esteem across the transition to junior high school. *Developmental Psychology, 27,* 552-564.

Wille, S. (1994). Primary nocturnal enuresis in children. *Scandinavian Journal of Urology and Nephrology,* 156 (Supplement 156), 6-23.

Williams, J. E., & Best, D. L. (1990). *Measuring sex stereotypes: A thirty-nation study (rev. ed.).* Newbury Park: Sage Publications.

Williams, J. M. (1997). *Style: Ten lessons in clarity and grace* (5th ed.). New York: Longman.

Willinger, M. (1995). Sleep position and sudden infant death syndrome. *Journal of the American Medical Association, 273,* 818-819.

Wilson, C. C., Piazza, C. C., & Nagle, R. (1990). Investigation of the effect of consistent and inconsistent behavioral example upon children's donation behavior. *Journal of Genetic Psychology, 151,* 361-376.

Wilson, G. T., Hefferman, K., & Black, C. M. D. (1996). Eating disorders. In E. J. Mash & R. A. Barkley (Eds.), *Child psychopathology.* New York: Guilford.

Wilson, M. (1989). Child development in the context of the black extended family. *American Psychologist, 44,* 380-383.

Wilson, R. S. (1983). The Louisville Twin Study: Developmental synchronies in behavior. *Child Development, 54,* 298-316.

Wilson, R. S. (1986). Growth and development of human twins. In F. Falkner and J. M. Tanner (Eds.), *Human growth: A comprehensive treatise,* Vol. 3. New York: Plenum.

Windle, M., & Windle, R. C. (1996). Coping strategies, drinking motives, and stressful life events among middle adolescents: Associations with emotional and behavioral problems and with academic functioning. *Journal of Abnormal Psychology, 105,* 551-560.

Winner, E. (1989). Development in the visual arts. In W. Damon (Ed.), *Child Development Today and Tomorrow.* San Francisco: Jossey Bass.

Wise, B. W., Ring, J., & Olson, R. K. (1999). Training phonological awareness with and without explicit attention to articulation. *Journal of Experimental Child Psychology, 72,* 271-304.

Wishart, J. G., & Bower, T. G. R. (1982). The development of spatial understanding in infancy. *Journal of Experimental Psychology, 33,* 363-385.

Witelson, S. F. (1987). Neurobiological aspects of language in children. *Child Development, 58,* 653-688.

Witelson, S. F., & Kigar, D. L. (1988). Anatomical development of the corpus callosum in humans: A review with reference to sex and cognition. In D. L. Molfese & S. J. Segalowitz (Eds.), *Brain lateralization in children* (pp. 35-57). New York: Guilford Press.

Wolfe, D. A. (1985). Child-abusive parents: An empirical review and analysis. *Psychological Bulletin, 97,* 462-482.

Wolff, P. H. (1987). *The development of behavioral states and the expression of emotions in early infancy.* Chicago: University of Chicago Press.

Wolfson, A. R., & Carskadon, M. A. (1998). Sleep schedules and daytime functioning in adolescents. *Child Development, 69,* 875-887.

Wolraich, M. L., Lindgren, S. D., Stumbo, P. J., Stegink, L. D., Appelbaum, M. I., & Kiritsy, M. C. (1994). Effects of diets high in sucrose or aspartame on the behavior and cognitive performance of children. *New England Journal of Medicine, 330,* 301-307.

Wong-Fillmore, L., Ammon, P., McLaughlin, B., & Ammon, M. S. (1985). *Learning English through bilingual instruction.* Rosslyn, VA: National Clearinghouse for Bilingual Education.

Woodward, A. L., & Markman, E. M. (1998). Early word learning. In W. Damon (Ed.), *Handbook of child psychology,* Volume 2. New York: Wiley.

Woollacott, M. H., Shumway-Cook, A., & Williams, H. (1989). The development of balance and locomotion in children. In M. H. Woollacott, & A. Shumway-Cook (Eds.), *Development of posture and gait across the life span.* Columbia, SC: University of South Carolina Press.

World Health Organization. (1995). *First annual report on global health.* Geneva, Switzerland: Author.

World Health Organization. (1997). Integrated Management of Childhood Illness: A WHO/UNICEF Initiative *Bulletin of the World Health Organization, 75,* Supplement 1.

World Health Organization. (1999). *Removing obstacles to healthy development.* World Health Organization.

Wynbrandt, J. (1998). *The excruciating history of dentistry: Toothsome tales and oral oddities from Babylon to braces.* New York: St. Martin's Press.

Wynn, K. (1996). Infants' individuation and enumeration of actions. *Psychological Science, 7,* 164-169.

Xiaohe, X., & Whyte, M. K. (1990). Love matches and arranged marriages: A Chinese replication. *Journal of Marriage and the Family, 52,* 709-722.

Yang, B., Ollendick, T. H., Dong, Q., Xia, Y., & Lin, L. (1995). Only children and children with siblings in the People's Republic of China: Levels of fear, anxiety, and depression. *Child Development, 66,* 1301-1311.

Yates, M., & Youniss, J. (1996). Community service and political-moral identity in adolescents. *Journal of Research on Adolescence, 6,* 271-284.

Yonas, A., & Owsley, C. (1987). Development of visual space perception. In P. Salapatek and L. Cohen (Eds.), *Handbook of infant perception* (Vol. 2). Orlando, Fla.: Academic Press.

Young, S. K., Fox, N. A., & Zahn-Waxler, C. (1999). The relations between temperament and empathy in 2-year-olds. *Developmental Psychology, 35,* 1189-1197.

Youngblade, L. M., & Dunn, J. (1995). Individual differences in young children's pretend play with mother and sibling: Links to relationships and understanding of other people's feelings and beliefs. *Child Development, 66,* 1472-1492.

Zahn-Waxler, C., Friedman, R. J., Cole, P. M., Mizuta, I., & Hiruma, N. (1996). Japanese and United States preschool children's responses to conflict and distress. *Child Development, 67,* 2462-2477.

Zahn-Waxler, C., Radke-Yarrow, M., Wagner, E. & Chapman, M. (1992). Development of concern for others. *Developmental Psychology, 28,* 126-136.

Zarbatany, L., Hartmann, D. P., & Rankin, D. B. (1990). The psychological functions of preadolescent peer activities. *Child Development, 61,* 1067-1080.

Zelazo, N. A., Zelazo, P. R., Cohen, K. M., & Zelazo, P. D. (1993). Specificity of practice effects on elementary neuromotor patterns. *Developmental Psychology, 29,* 686-691.

Zelazo, P. R. (1983). The development of walking: New findings and old assumptions. *Journal of Motor Behavior, 15,* 99-137.

Zelazo, P. R., Weiss, M. J., Papageorgiou, A. N., & Laplante, D. P. (1989). Recovery and dishabituation of sound localization among normal-, moderate-, and high-risk newborns: Discriminant validity. *Infant Behavior and Development, 12,* 321-340.

Zeman, J., & Garber, J. (1996). Display rules for anger, sadness, and pain: It depends on who is watching. *Child Development, 67,* 957-973.

Zeman, J., & Shipman, K. (1997). Social-contextual influences on expectancies for managing anger and sadness: The transition from middle childhood to adolescence. *Developmental Psychology, 33,* 917-924.

Zigler, E. (1992). *Head Start: The inside story of America's most successful educational experiment.* New York: Basic Books.

Zigler, E. (1998). A place of value for applied and policy studies. *Child Development, 69,* 532-542.

Zigler, E., & Finn-Stevenson, M. (1992). Applied developmental psychology. In M. H. Bornstein & M. E. Lamb (Eds.), *Developmental psychology: An advanced textbook.* Hillsdale NJ: Erlbaum.

Zigler, E., & Hall, N. W. (1989). Physical child abuse in America: Past, present, and future. In D. Cicchetti & V. Carlson (Eds.), *Child maltreatment: Theory and research on the causes and consequences of child abuse and neglect.* New York: Cambridge University Press.

Zigler, E., & Styfco, S. J. (1994). Head start: Criticisms in a constructive context. *American Psychologist, 49,* 127-132.

Zigler, E. F., & Gilman, E. (1996). Not just any care: Shaping a coherent child care policy. In E. F. Zigler, S. L. Kagan, & N. W. Hall (Eds.), *Children, families, and government: Preparing for the twenty-first century.* New York: Cambridge University Press.

Zimiles, H., & Lee, V. E. (1991). Adolescent family structure and educational progress. *Developmental Psychology, 27,* 314-320.

Zins, J. E., Garcia, V. F., Tuchfarber, B. S., Clark, K. M., & Laurence, S. C. (1994). Preventing injury in children and adolescents. In R. J. Simeonsson et al (Ed.), *Risk, resilience, and prevention: Promoting the well-being of all children* (pp. 183-202). Baltimore: Paul H. Brookes.

Zubrick, S. R., Kurinczuk, J. J., McDermott, B. M. C., McKelvey, R. S., Silburn, S. R., & Davies, L. C. (2000). Fetal growth and subsequent mental health problems in children aged 4 to 13 years. *Developmental Medicine & Child Neurology, 42,* 14-20.

Acknowledgments

Photographs

About the Author Page xxiii, Courtesy of Prof. Robert Kail

Chapter 1 Page 11 (top) AP/Wide World Photos; (bottom) Nina Leen, TimePix; p. 12 CORBIS; p. 13 Jon Erikson, Library of Congress; p. 14 (top) B.F. Skinner Foundation; (bottom) Bob Daemmrich, The Image Works; p. 15 (top) Albert Bandura; (bottom) Corbis; p. 16 Laura Dwight, PhotoEdit; p. 18 (top) Lawrence Migdale, Stock Boston; (middle) Dr. Michael Cole, A.R. Luria; (bottom) AP/Wide World Photos; p. 24 David Young-Wolff, PhotoEdit

Chapter 2 Page 33 (top) Tony Freeman, PhotoEdit; (bottom) Pamela Johnson Meyer, Photo Researchers, Inc.; p. 37 Ogust, The Image Works; p. 39 Will and Deni McIntyre/Science Source, Photo Researchers, Inc.; p. 43 Jonathan Nourok, PhotoEdit; p. 45 (top) Hoby Finn, Getty Images, Inc./PhotoDisc, Inc.

Chapter 3 Page 52 (left) Dr. Gopal Murti/Science Photo Library, Custom Medical Stock Photo, Inc.; (right) Francis Leroy/Biocosmos/Science Photo Library, Photo Researchers, Inc.; p. 53 (top) David Phillips, Photo Researchers, Inc.; (middle) Alexander Tsiaras/Science Source, Photo Researchers, Inc.; (bottom) Biophoto Associates, Photo Researchers, Inc.; p. 58 CORBIS; p. 64 Laura Dwight, Peter Arnold, Inc.; p. 70 Catherine Karnow, Woodfin Camp & Associates

Chapter 4 Page 77 Lennart Nilsson, Albert Bonniers Forlag AB; p. 78 (left) Lennart Nilsson, Albert Bonniers Forlag AB; (right) Petit Format/Nestle/Science Source, Photo Researchers, Inc.; p. 80 Lennart Nilsson, Albert Bonniers Forlag AB; p. 84 Amy Etra, PhotoEdit; p. 85 David Young-Wolff, PhotoEdit; p. 87 University of Washington FAS; p. 92 Brownie Harris, Corbis/Stock Market; p. 98 (top) Lawrence Migdale, Photo Researchers, Inc.; (bottom) Margaret Miller, Photo Researchers, Inc.; p. 100 Tom Stewart, Corbis/Stock Market; p. 101 Prof. Robert Kail; p.102 Jennie Woodcock; Reflections Photolibrary, CORBIS; p. 103 Stephen R. Swinburne, Stock Boston; p. 104 Prof. Robert Kail

Chapter 5 Page 113 Tony Freeman, PhotoEdit; p. 116 Stock Boston; p. 117 David Woo, Stock Boston; p. 118 Nazima Kowall, CORBIS; p. 119 Rhoda Sidney, Stock Boston; p. 121 (left), (middle), (right) Ed Reschke; p. 122 Alexander Tsiaras, Stock Boston; p. 123 Dr. Michael E. Phelps, U.C.L.A. School of Medicine; p.124 Peter Menzel, Stock Boston; p. 127 (left), Kevin Morris, CORBIS; (right) Greg Flume, CORBIS; p. 130 Dexter Gormley; p. 131 Alan Carey, The Image Works; p. 132 (top) Felicia Martinez, PhotoEdit; (bottom) Erika Stone, Photo Researchers, Inc.; p. 133 (top) Mary Kate Denny, PhotoEdit; (bottom) Rick Browne, Stock Boston; p. 134 Mitch Reardon, Photo Researchers, Inc.; p. 137 Michael Tamborrino, Medichrome/The Stock Shop, Inc.; p. 140 Innervisions; p. 141 (top) Tadao Kimura, Getty Images Inc.; (bottom) Bob Daemmrich, Stock Boston; p. 142 (top) John William Banagan, Getty Images Inc.; (bottom) Michael Agliolo Productions, International Stock Photography Ltd.

Chapter 6 Page 153 Laura Dwight, Laura Dwight Photography; p. 155 Laura Dwight, Laura Dwight Photography; p. 156 Gary Goodman, Index Stock Imagery, Inc.; p. 164 Laima Druskis, Pearson Education/Ph College; p. 165 John Eastcott, The Image Works; p. 166 (bottom) Carolyn Rovee-Collier; p. 167 Prof. Robert Kail; p. 172 Hermine Dreyfuss; p. 173 Peter Southwick, Stock Boston; p. 175 Laura Dwight, Laura Dwight Photography; p. 176 David Young-Wolff, PhotoEdit; p. 177 Jeff Persons, Stock Boston

Chapter 7 Page 185 (left) Laura Dwight, Laura Dwight Photography; (middle) Michael Newman, PhotoEdit; (right) Comstock Images; (bottom) Elizabeth Hathon, Corbis/Stock Market; p. 186 Prof. Robert Kail; p. 187 Myrleen Ferguson Cate, PhotoEdit; p. 190 (top) Michael Newman, PhotoEdit; (bottom) Mark Richards, PhotoEdit; p. 192 Laura Dwight, Laura Dwight Photography; p. 193 Frank Clarkson, Getty Images, Inc.; p. 196 Boulton-Wilson, Jeroboam, Inc.; p. 197 David M. Grossman; p. 198 PT Santana, Getty Images, Inc.; p. 200 Comstock Images; p. 202 Prof. Robert Kail; p. 203 Myrleen Ferguson Cate, PhotoEdit; p. 204 Steve Starr, Stock Boston

Chapter 8 Page 217 Bob Daemmrich, Stock Boston; p. 220 The Photo Works, Photo Researchers, Inc.; p. 225 Ellen B. Senisi, Photo Researchers, Inc.; p. 226 Bob Daemmrich, The Image Works; p. 228 Francis Dean, The Image Works; p. 229 (top) Eric Fowke, PhotoEdit; p. 230 Junebug Clark, Photo Researchers, Inc.; p. 231 Steve Grand/Science Photo Library, Photo Researchers, Inc.; p. 235 (top) Stephen Agricola, The Image Works; (bottom) Alan S. Weiner, Getty Images, Inc.

Chapter 9 Page 243 Tony Freeman, PhotoEdit; p. 245 Tony Freeman, PhotoEdit; p. 246 Prof. Robert Kail; p. 252 Tony Freeman, PhotoEdit; p. 253 Alan Oddie, PhotoEdit; p. 254 (top) D. Young-Wolff, PhotoEdit; (bottom) Tom Prettyman, PhotoEdit; p. 257 Tom Prettyman, PhotoEdit; p. 258 Elena Rooraid, Photo Edit; p. 262 Susan Kuklin/Science Source, Photo Researchers, Inc.; p. 266 (top) Tony Freeman, PhotoEdit; (bottom) Beaura Katherine Ringrose; p. 270 (left) Ellen Sinisi, The Image Works; (right) E. Crews, The Image Works; p. 273 R. Termine/CTW, Everett Collection, Inc.

Chapter 10 Page 282 D. Young-Wolff, PhotoEdit; p. 283 (middle) CORBIS; (bottom) George Goodwin; p. 287 Elizabeth Crews, Elizabeth Crews Photography; p. 292 Jean Hangarter, Index Stock Imagery, Inc.; p. 293 Phyllis Picardi, Stock Boston; p. 295 Michael Newman, PhotoEdit; p. 296 (top) Laura Dwight, CORBIS; (bottom) Charles Thatcher, Getty Images, Inc.; p. 298 Pam Francis, Getty Images, Inc.; p. 301 (top) Bachmann, PhotoEdit; (bottom) A. Ramey, Woodfin Camp & Associates; p. 302 Owen Franken, CORBIS; p. 303 Cathlyn Melloan, Getty Images, Inc.; p. 304 (top) Laura Dwight, Laura Dwight Photography; (bottom) Lawrence Migdale, Lawrence Migdale/Pix; p. 305 Laura Dwight, Laura Dwight Photography; p. 306 Rob Crandall, Stock Boston; p. 309 Elizabeth Hathon, Corbis/Stock Market

Chapter 11 Page 323 Bob Daemmrich, Stock Boston; p. 324 (top) Bob Daemmrich, The Image Works; (bottom) M. Douglas, The Image Works; p. 325 David Young-Wolff, PhotoEdit; p. 326 Lonnie Duka, Index Stock Imagery, Inc.; p. 280 Mark Richards, PhotoEdit; p. 281 Myrleen Ferguson, PhotoEdit; p. 286 Laura Dwight; p. 287 Bob Daemmrich: p. 290 D. & I. MacDonald, Picture Cube, Inc.; p. 295 David Young-Wolff, PhotoEdit; p. 296 Bob Daemmrich, Stock

Boston; p. 298 Bruno Maso, Photo Researchers, Inc.; p. 333 Lawrence Migdale, Stock Boston; p. 335 SuperStock Inc.; p. 336 Coco McCoy, Rainbow

Chapter 12 Page 348 Gale Zucker, Stock Boston; p. 353 Paul L. Merideth; p. 354 (middle) Macduff Everton; (bottom) Anna E. Zuckerman, PhotoEdit; p. 358 Laura Dwight, Laura Dwight Photography; p. 367 Kirk Anderson, International Stock Photography Ltd.; p. 368 Bob Daemmrich, Stock Boston; p. 372 (top) Laura Dwight, CORBIS; (bottom) Laura Dwight, Laura Dwight Photography; p. 376 Jennie Woodcock; Reflections Photolibrary, CORBIS; p. 377 Elizabeth Zuckerman, PhotoEdit; p. 378 Audrey Gottlieb; p. 381 (top) Jose L. Pelaez, Corbis/ Stock Market; (bottom) Blair Seitz, Photo Researchers, Inc.

Chapter 13 Page 390 Bob Daemmrich, Stock Boston; p. 391 D&I MacDonald, Index Stock Imagery, Inc.; p. 395 D. Young-Wolff, PhotoEdit; p. 396 Bob Daemmrich, Stock Boston; p. 399 Bob Daemmrich, Stock Boston; p. 400 Robert Maass, CORBIS; p. 405 Amy Etra, PhotoEdit; p. 409 Mark M. Walker, Index Stock Imagery, Inc.; p. 410 Owen Franken, Stock Boston; p. 413 Yale; p. 415 Jeff Dunn/Stock Boston, PictureQuest Vienna; p. 421 Laura Dwight, PhotoEdit

Chapter 14 Page 431 Michael Newman, PhotoEdit; p. 434 Myrleen Ferguson Cate, PhotoEdit; p. 435 (top) Bill Gillette, Stock Boston; (bottom) Pete Byron, Photo Researchers, Inc.; p. 442 Barbara Penoya, Getty Images, Inc./PhotoDisc, Inc.; p. 446 (top) Richard Hutchings, PhotoEdit; (bottom) David Young-Wolff, PhotoEdit; p. 448 Michael Newman, PhotoEdit

Chapter 15 Page 457 Richard Hutchings, Photo Researchers, Inc.; p. 461 (top) Bob Daemmrich, Stock Boston; (middle) Sybil Shackman; p. 464 Michael Newman, PhotoEdit; p. 466 John Boykin, Index Stock Imagery, Inc.; p. 467 (top) David R. Frazier, David R. Frazier Photolibrary, Inc.; (bottom) Steve Skjold, PhotoEdit; p. 468 Bob Daemmrich, Stock Boston.; p. 470 Stock Boston; p. 471 Michael Newman, PhotoEdit; p. 473 David Young-Wolff, PhotoEdit; p. 474 Billy E. Barnes, Stock Boston

Chapter 16 Page 480 Richard Hutchings, PhotoEdit; p. 482 (middle) Spencer Grant, PhotoEdit; p. 484 Myrleen Ferguson, PhotoEdit; p. 490 Prof. Robert Kail; p. 491 (top) Michael Newman, PhotoEdit; p. 492 Richard Hutchings, Photo Researchers, Inc.; p. 497 Richard Hutchings, PhotoEdit; p. 498 Dennis McDonald, PhotoEdit; p. 501 A. Ramey, Stock Boston

Cartoons, Figures and Tables

Chapter 1 Page 23 Hi and Lois © 1993. Reprinted with special permission of King Features Syndicate

Chapter 2 Fig. 2-6 Fordham Institute for Innovation in Social Policy

Chapter 3 Fig. 3-5 From I. Gottesman (1963). Genetic aspects of intellectual behavior. In N.R. Ellis (Ed.), *Handbook of mental deficiency*. New York: McGraw-Hill. Reprinted courtesy of Norman R. Ellis

Chapter 4 Figs. 4-4 and 4-6 From Moore and Persaud (1993). *Before we are born*, Philadelphia: W.B. Saunders. Reprinted with permission

Chapter 5 Table 5-1 From *Understanding Normal Clinical Nutrition*, 2nd ed., by E. Whiney, C.B. Cataldo, S.R.F. © 1987. Reprinted

with permission of Wadsworth, an imprint of the Wadsworth Group, a division of Thomson Learning; Fig. 5-11 From H. Ghim, Evidence for perceptual organization in infants. *Infant Behavior and Development, 13*, 221-248. Copyright © 1990 by Ablex Publishing Corporation. Reprinted by permission; Fig. 5-14 From J. Morton & M.H. Johnson (1991). CONSPEC and CONLERN: A two-process theory of infant face recognition. *Psychological Review, 98*, 164-181. Copyright © 1991 by the American Psychological Association. Reprinted with permission

Chapter 6 Page 175 Reprinted by permission of Johnny Hart and Creators Syndicate

Chapter 8 Fig. 8-5 From Martini, Anatomy & Physiology 3rd ed., Prentice Hall.

Chapter 9 Fig. 9-4 From U. Frith (1989). Autism: Explaining the enigma. Oxford, UK: Blackwell Publishers. Copyright © Axel Scheffler, Illustrator. Reprinted with permission.

Chapter 10 Fig. 10-4 Adapted from S. Harter & R. Pike (1984). The pictorial scale of perceived competence and social acceptance for young children. *Child Development, 55*, 1973. Copyright © Society for Research in Child Development, Inc. Reprinted with permission; Page 300 Peanuts © 1993. Reprinted with permission of United Feature Syndicate; Page 309 Calvin and Hobbes © 1993 Watterson. Distributed by Universal Press Syndicate. Reprinted with permission. All rights reserved; Table 10-2 From Y. Shoda, W. Mischel, & P.K. Peake (1994). Predicting adolescent cognitive and self-regulatory competencies from preschool delay of gratification: Identifying diagnostic conditions. *Developmental Psychology, 26*, 978-986. Copyright © by the American Psychological Association. Reprinted with permission

Chapter 11 Page 276 Copyright by Axel Scheffler. Reprinted with permission of Axel Scheffler and Blackwell Publishers; p. 280 Reprinted by permission of Bunny Hoest, Wm. Hoest Enterprises, Inc.; p. 286 Adapted from S. Harter & R. Pike (1984). The pictorial scale of perceived competence and social acceptance for young children. *Child Development, 55*, 1973. Copyright © Society for Research in Child Development, Inc. Reprinted with permission

Chapter 12 Fig. 12-3 From *The development of memory in children*, 3rd ed. by R. Kail. © 1990 by W.H. Freeman and Co. Used with permission; Fig. 12-4 from J. B. Carroll (1993). *Human cognitive abilities: A survey of factor-analytic studies.* New York: Cambridge University Press. Copyright Cambridge University Press. Reprinted with permission of Cambridge University Press; Fig. 12-6 Simulated items similar to those in the Wechsler Intelligence Scales for Adult and Children. Copyright 1949, 1955, 1974, 1981, and 1990 by the Psychological Corporation. Reproduced by permission. All rights reserved; Fig. 12-8 From R. Plomin, D.W. Fulker, R. Corlev, & J.C. Defries (1997) . Nature, nurture, and cognitive development from 1 to 16 years. *Psychological Science 8*, 442-447. Reprinted with permission; Fig. 12-13 From J.W. Pellegrino & R. Kail (1982), Process analyses of spatial aptitude. In R. Sternberg, (ed.) *Advances in the psychology of human intelligence*, Vol. 1. Hillsdale, NJ: Lawrence Erlbaum Associates. Copyright by Lawrence Erlbaum Associates. Reprinted with permission

Chapter 13 Table 13-1 Adapted from R. Morison & A.S. Masten (1991). Peer reputation in middle childhood as a predictor of adaptation in adolescence: A seven-year follow-up. *Child Development, 62*, 1001. Copyright © Society for Research in Child Development,

Inc. Reprinted with permission; Fig. 13-6 From N.R. Crick & K.A. Dodge (1994). A review and reformulation of social information processing mechanisms in children's social adjustment. *Psychological Bulletin, 115,* 74-101. Copyright © 1994 by the American Psychological Association. Reprinted with permission; Fig. 13-7 Adapted from C.L. Martin & C.F. Halvorsen, Jr. (1981). A schematic processing model of sex typing and stereotyping in children. *Child Development, 52.* 1121. Copyright © Society for Research in Child Development, Inc. Reprinted with permission

Chapter 14 Fig. 14-2 From J.M. Tanner (1989). *Fetus into man.* Cambridge, MA: Harvard University Press. Reprinted with permission of the publishers. Copyright © 1978, 1989 by J.M. Tanner; Fig. 14-3 From Csikszentmihalyi & Larson; Fig. 14-5 Rape Treatment Center Santa Monica Hospital; Fig. 14-7 Federal Interagency Forum on Child and Family Statistics, 2000

Chapter 15 Page 470 Reprinted by permission of Bunny Hoest, Wm. Hoest Enterprises, Inc.; Fig. 15-4 Modified and reproduced by special permission of the Publisher, Consulting Psychologists Press, Inc., Palo Alto, CA 94303 from **Strong Interest Inventory® Occupational Themes Profile for Carloyn Sample** of the Strong Vocational Interest Blanks® Form T317. Copyright © 1933, 1938, 1945, 1946, 1966, 1968, 1974, 1981, 1985, 1994, by the Board of Trustees of the Leland Stanford Junior University. All rights reserved. Printed and scored under license from Stanford University Press, Stanford, CA 94305. Strong Interest Inventory, and Strong Vocational Interest Blanks are registered trademarks of Stanford University Press. All rights reserved. Further reproduction is prohibited without the Publisher's written consent.

Chapter 16 Fig. 16-3 From Monitoring the Future Study, 2000; Fig. 16-4 From National Center for Health Statistics, 2000; Fig. 16-5 FBI crime data

Name Index

Subject Index

Turner's syndrome, 65
Twins
    fraternal versus identical, 57–58
    heredity and, 114
    used in studies, 57–58, 60–61

U
Ultrasound, 92
Umbilical cord, 78
Underextension, 178
United States
    adolescents in, happiness of, 489
    attachments in infants, 192
    day care in, 195–96
    gender stereotypes in, 282
    handedness in, 133
    health care in, 231
    infant mortality rates in, 100
    mathematical competence in, 377–79
    physical punishment in, 235
    puberty in, average timing of, 433

V
Validity
    of intelligence tests, 360
    of measures, 33
Variable, 31
Venezuela, gender stereotypes in, 282
Verbal ability, gender differences in, 366
Virginia Longitudinal Study of Divorce and
    Remarriage, 418–19
Visual acuity, 138
Visual cliff, 140
Vygotsky, Lev, 18, 253–55, 360

W
Watson, John, 14
Wechsler Intelligence Scale for
    Children–Revised, 169
White. *See* European American
WISC-III intelligence test, 359–60
Withdrawal reflex, 128
Word recognition, 370, 372–73, 374
Working memory, 163, 373, 460, 461
Writing, 374–76

X
XXX syndrome, 65
XYY complement, 65

Z
Zone of proximal development, 253–4, 255
Zygote, period of the, 76 77